Slovakia

the Bradt Travel Guide

Lucy Mallows

edition

www.bradtguides.com

Bradt Travel Guides Ltd, UK
The Globe Pequot Press Inc, USA

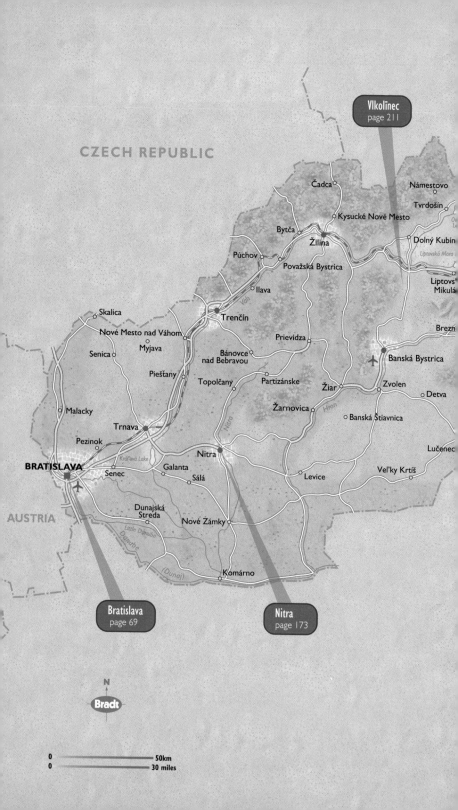

CZECH REPUBLIC

AUSTRIA

Vlkolínec
page 211

Bratislava
page 69

Nitra
page 173

Čadca
Námestovo
Tvrdošín
Kysucké Nové Mesto
Bytča
Žilina
Dolný Kubín
Púchov
Považská Bystrica
Liptovská Mara
Ilava
Liptovs'
Mikulá
Trenčín
Skalica
Nové Mesto nad Váhom
Prievidza
Brezň
Myjava
Bánovce
nad Bebravou
Banská Bystrica
Senica
Piešťany
Topoľčany
Partizánske
Žiar
Zvolen
Malacky
Žarnovica
Hron
Detva
Trnava
Banská Štiavnica
Pezinok
Kráľová Lake
Nitra
Lučenec
BRATISLAVA
Senec
Galanta
Levice
Veľky Krtíš
Sáľá
Dunajská
Streda
Little Danube
Nové Žámky
Danube
(Dunaj)
Komárno

N

Bradt

0 ———— 50km
0 ———— 30 miles

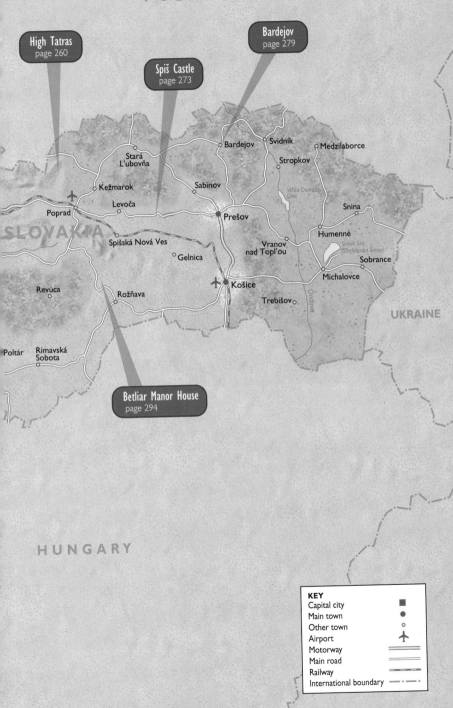

POLAND

High Tatras
page 260

Spiš Castle
page 273

Bardejov
page 279

Stará
Ľubovňa

Kežmarok

Sabinov

Bardejov Svidník Medzilaborce

Stropkov

Poprad

Levoča

Prešov

SLOVAKIA

Spišská Nová Ves

Gelnica

Snina

Vranov
nad Topľou

Humenné

Slovak Sea
(Zemplínska Šírava)

Veľká Domaša
Lake

Sobrance

Michalovce

Košice

Revúca

Rožňava

Trebišov

UKRAINE

Poltár Rimavská
Sobota

Betliar Manor House
page 294

HUNGARY

KEY
Capital city
Main town
Other town
Airport
Motorway
Main road
Railway
International boundary

Slovakia
Don't
miss...

**Bratislava: the
vibrant capital**
St Michael's Tower at dusk,
Bratislava
(EN/Alamy) page 108

Hillside villages
Vlkolínec UNESCO-listed world
heritage site
(LM) page 211

World-class hiking
Kežmarská dolina valley, High Tatras
(TL) page 260

Period architecture
The medieval square at Bardejov
(LM) page 277

Castles and fortresses
Spiš castle looms above the small town of Spišské podhradie
(LM) page 273

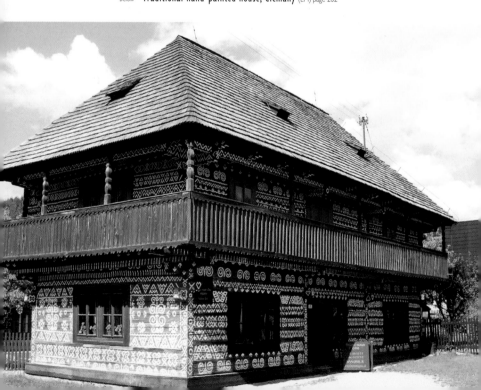

AUTHOR

Born and educated in the UK, Lucy Mallows spent 12 years in Budapest working as a writer and editor. Recently she moved to Brussels where she works as a freelance travel writer and translator. She contributes regularly to many international dailies and magazines and has written for all the top travel publishers on countries from Estonia to Portugal. She is an expert on central Europe, particularly the culture, history and politics of the region, and speaks six foreign languages including Russian, Hungarian and a fair attempt at Slovak.

AUTHOR STORY

Bradt is the only travel guide publisher to devote an entire guide book to this underappreciated country and it is typical of their attitude that they are the first to recognise how much Slovakia has to offer.

I discovered a fascination for Slavic history, culture and language at school where I was at the time the only person in Somerset taking Russian 'A' level – they used to joke that I must be an embryonic spy. As part of my Russian degree, I had the choice of Czech or Bulgarian as a second language and, choosing Czech, I spent a term at Brno University. In 1982, we had plenty of time and opportunity to explore the then-Czechoslovak countryside and we headed first for the High Tatras.

Even then, we spotted that Slovakia had something really special and secret up in the hills. Slovakia has some of the most gorgeous and unspoilt countryside in Europe and it's a mystery to me why people don't take more notice of the country.

I wanted to write the first travel guide to Slovakia, because I don't think any travel guide has done Slovakia justice. It's always shoved into a few chapters at the end of the Czech Republic guides and these few pages miss out so much.

There's still a great sense of space and freedom, driving along through the Rusyn region in the 'Far East' and feeling like you're the first person in the world to find a dinky wooden church. Slovakia is extremely good value for money and it's only a few hours away.

To write this guide, I spent the best part of a year travelling throughout the beautiful countryside, exploring all the hidden villages by the Polish and Ukrainian borders as well as lively, cosmopolitan cities such as Trnava, Nitra, Banská Bystrica and Prešov.

Bradt's unique brief gave me the chance to express personal feelings about the country and Slovakia is a country that, once visited, really tugs at the heart. The people are so welcoming and hospitable. Last summer in Handlová, in a typical Slovak restaurant, complete with friendly waitress in folk costume, they switched channels for us to watch an England World Cup football match even though the entire population of the venue was already absorbed in a Slovak game show.

I just heard a politician on Radio 4 talk about Czechoslovakia! Even now, 14 years after independence and three years after joining the EU, Slovakia still isn't getting the attention it deserves. I hope this guidebook goes some way to redressing the balance.

PUBLISHER'S FOREWORD   *Hilary Bradt*

The first Bradt travel guide was written in 1974 by George and Hilary Bradt on a river barge floating down a tributary of the Amazon. In the 1980s and '90s the focus shifted away from hiking to broader-based guides covering new destinations – usually the first to be published about these places. In the 21st century Bradt continues to publish such ground-breaking guides, as well as others to established holiday destinations, incorporating in-depth information on culture and natural history with the nuts and bolts of where to stay and what to see.

Bradt authors support responsible travel, and provide advice not only on minimum impact but also on how to give something back through local charities. In this way a true synergy is achieved between the traveller and local communities.

* * *

Back in 1987 I published the first ever guide to Czechoslovakia, a Communist country which saw only a handful of intrepid travellers willing to brave the red tape and travel restrictions. Even then I was struck by the descriptions of the High Tatras mountains with their well-marked hiking trails, by the traditional small villages, the wooden churches and the castles. Despite the appeal of Prague, it was Slovakia that I wanted to go to. Lucy Mallows already has the successful city guide to Bratislava under her belt, so 20 years after I first published Czechoslovakia it is a pleasure to welcome this enticing guide to the now independent Slovakia.

First published April 2007
Bradt Travel Guides Ltd, 23 High Street, Chalfont St Peter, Bucks SL9 9QE, England.
www.bradtguides.com
Published in the USA by The Globe Pequot Press Inc, 246 Goose Lane,
PO Box 480, Guilford, Connecticut 06475-0480

Text copyright © 2007 Lucy Mallows
Maps copyright © 2007 Bradt Travel Guides Ltd
Illustrations © 2007 Individual photographers and artists (see below)
Editorial Project Manager: Emma Thomson

British Library Cataloguing in Publication Data
A catalogue record for this book is available from the British Library
ISBN-10: 1 84162 188 9   ISBN-13: 978 1 84162 188 3

Photographers Lucy Mallows (LM), Eric Nathan (EN/Alamy), Walter Bibikow (WB/Alamy), Slovakia Tourist Board (STB), Karolek (K/Alamy), Isifa Image Service/Alamy (IIS/Alamy), LookGaleria/Alamy (LG/Alamy), The Travel Library (TL), EJ Baumeister Jr/ Alamy (EJB/Alamy), Paul Thompson Images/Alamy (PTI/Alamy), Stephen L Saks/ Pictures Colour Library (SlS/PCL), Pegaz/Alamy (P/Alamy) *Front cover* Bojnice Castle (P/Alamy)   *Back cover* Strbské pleso lake and Vysoké Tatry mountains (TL) *Title page* Bratislava Hviezdoslavovo námestie Atlas guarding doorway (LM), St Katarina's Church in Handlová (LM), Façade on Winterová ulica, Piešťany's pedestrian street (LM)
Illustrations Carole Vincer   **Maps** Steve Munns, Alan Whitaker, Terence Crump

Typeset from the author's disc by Wakewing
Printed and bound in Italy by Legoprint SpA

ACKNOWLEDGEMENTS

There's not enough space on the page to mention all the kind people who offered help, suggestions, advice and tips. However, some cannot be omitted. A big thank you to all at Bradt, especially Hilary Bradt, Tricia Hayne and, as always, Adrian Phillips. In Bratislava, a gigantic *ďakujem* to Saša Bučkova and her BKIS team, also in the capital many thanks to Milan Vajda and Peter Barecz for insight, Lucia Arbetova, Eva Boskovičová and Ľubomír Kapitančik for support. In Poprad, Jan Telenský, Silvia Nawratovitzová, Michaela Bartková, Iveta Brejčáková, Alena Dzinová, Katerina Smžová and Eric Wiltsher all gave vital assistance. Many thanks also to Mike Wallace and Jana Obertová for support and good humour in Piešťany. In Banská Bystrica, Lívia Lukačová at SACR and Adela Hegedus both gave invaluable advice. Jana Poprendová helped with insider views also. I would have been lost without Anna Lališova and her cartographer team at Mapa Slovakia. Paul and Maeve Carr were lifesavers just when I needed it most. Thanks also to all the readers who offered feedback on *Bratislava: The Bradt City Guide* and some great tips. Thank you also to the contributors whose work added so much to the flavour of this guide: Andreea Anca for photographic creativity and good company, Eszter Balázs for her Slovak skiing experience, Leigh Banks for numerous boxes and wit, Peterjon Cresswell for football, Petra Gájdošíkova for some great hints on property investment, Gerard Gorman for his wildlife knowledge and Ágnes Szarka for a fresh, unbiased take on the complicated history. Thanks mum, for morale-boosting phone calls late at night and finally, I hope it doesn't sound trite, but I'd really like to say *ďakujem veľmi pekne* to the people of Slovakia.

☞ POZOR!

POZOR! (attention! watch out! beware!) Visitors to Slovakia will frequently hear or come across a sign with the word *pozor!* It can mean beware of the dog, watch for an oncoming train, mind the step and more. It generally has a negative meaning, but I have used it in the guide when readers should look out for something – good or bad.

FEEDBACK REQUEST

Slovakia is constantly evolving, changing and improving. I've tottered from one end of the country to the other, from Bratislava to Medzilaborce and back, scribbling notes about every possible castle, cave, church and café that I came across, but I know that even as I write things will be changing, Slovakia can't keep still! Please help me keep up with the constant barrage of information and I'll endeavour to squeeze everything into the next edition. I look forward to reading your tips, ideas, personal reflections, criticism (constructive hopefully!) by email at slovakiaguide@yahoo.co.uk or by snail mail c/o Bradt Travel Guides, 23 High Street, Chalfont St Peter, Bucks SL9 9QE.
Na zdravie! (Cheers!) Lucy.

Contents

LIST OF MAPS

Introduction

If one more person asks me how it was in Ljubljana I think I'll scream. I can really sympathise with the Slovaks; not only are their great sports stars always called Czech and their history dominated by Hungarian and Habsburg overlords but they also have to face linguistically challenged foreigners confusing their gorgeous 'little big country' with Slovenia.

I am sometimes amazed that I don't meet more foreign travellers in the depths of Slovakia as it seems to be the perfect destination. It really has everything. With more than 300 castles, 12 caves open to the public, nine national parks, five UNESCO-listed sites, 210 ski slopes, 23 spa towns and a dozen *skanzen* (open-air folk museum), it's difficult to know where to begin.

My love affair with Slovakia goes back to 1982, when it was the forgotten little sister of the glorious Czechoslovak state. I spent several weeks exploring the country between Bratislava and Poprad and can remember, through a haze of courage-inducing beer, some terrifying rides up the Tatra Mountains in cable cars that seemed to be constructed entirely from creaking, rotting wood. I hardly recognise the Tatra resorts these days. Sadly, the devastating storm of November 2004 has altered the landscape, but the facilities and attitudes have also changed, and for the better.

My relationship with Slovakia has sometimes been stormy but I have an underlying affection and enthusiasm for what the country has to offer. Why don't people notice Slovakia more? It's a constant source of mystery for me.

For a start there's some of the most beautiful countryside in Europe, the magnificent Tatras, the gorgeous Fatras, mountain lakes, clean reservoirs, seemingly endless rivers, national parks and nature reserves. If it had a sea coast, I would venture to call it paradise.

Then there's the history: more Gothic churches than you can shake a stick at, fantastic medieval towns like Bardejov, Kežmarok, Levoča, Kremnica, the shimmering jewel, Banská Štiavnica and my personal favourite, Špania Dolina. There are places where the waitresses appear in full folk costume even though it's not a Berni Inn. I've clambered around almost all the castles, chateaux, palaces, manor houses and ruins and got a glimpse into Slovakia's complicated history in stunning settings like Spiš, Bojnice, Budmerice and Beckov.

I've admired the stunning wooden churches in the Ruthenian (Rusyn) region of the far east and wallowed in fabulous spas, sitting in a thermal pool – outdoors – in the depths of winter, enjoying a cocktail and gazing in awe at the beauty of the Tatras while snow settled on my nose. Don't forget the drink: Slovakia produces some of the best beer in the world yet not many people know that the wine is also highly drinkable. There are lethal spirits made from fresh fruit and hearty peasant dishes that really warm the cockles after a long mountain hike. There are some caves to explore offering sights that I haven't found anywhere else. Slovakia seems to me like the ideal holiday destination. It's extremely good value for money and it's only a few hours away.

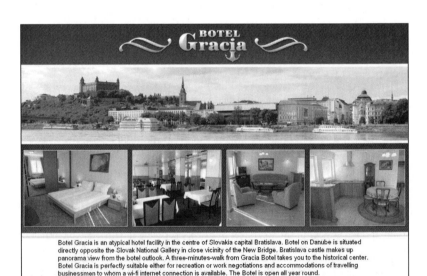

Part One

GENERAL INFORMATION

Country name Slovak Republic (Slovenská republika – SR) or Slovakia (Slovensko)

Location Slovakia is situated in central Europe, south of Poland and the Czech Republic, north of Hungary, east of Austria and west of the Ukraine

Size/area (km²) 48,845km² (land 48,800km², water 45km²)

Population 5,423,567 (July 2004): Slovak 85.8%, Hungarian 9.7%, Roma 1.7%, Czech 0.8%, Ruthenian 0.4%, Ukrainian 0.2%, German 0.1%, Polish 0.1%, other 1.2%

President Ivan Gašparovič (elected June 2004)

Prime Minister Robert Fico (elected July 2006)

Capital Bratislava, population 5,401,000

Languages Slovak (official), Hungarian, Romany, Rusyn, Czech

Nationalities Slovak 85.8%, Hungarian 9.7%, Roma 1.7%, Czech 0.8%, Ruthenian 0.4%, Ukrainian 0.2%, other 1.4%

Religion Roman Catholic 68.9%, Evangelical Church of Augsburg Confession 6.9%, Greek-Catholic 4.1%, Reformed Christian 2%, Orthodox 0.9%, Jehovah Witness 0.4%, Evangelic Methodist 0.1%, Brethren Baptist Union 0.1%, without religious affiliation 16.6%

Currency Slovak koruna (Slovenská koruna) (Sk) 1 Slovak koruna (Sk) = 100 halier (h), banknotes with a value of 20, 50, 100, 200, 500, 1,000, 5,000Sk, coins with a value of 1, 2, 5, 10Sk, 1 coin with a value of 50h

Exchange rate £1 = 50Sk, US$1 = 25Sk, €1 = 34Sk (March 2007)

International telephone code Slovakia +421, Bratislava +421 (0) 2

Time CET (GMT + 1)

Electrical voltage 220V/50Hz; two-pin plugs

Flag Three equal horizontal bands of white, blue and red, descending. Hoist side, the national emblem, the double cross in white in a red Gothic shield mounted on the central peak of a group of three blue hills.

National anthem The score for *Tatrou sa blyska* (Lightning over the Tatras) was written in 1844 during a trip by students of Bratislava's Evangelical school to Levoča in support of Ľudovít Štúr. The lyricist, Janko Matúška, set his words to the Slovak folk song *Kopala studienku* (She was digging a well).

Tourist board website www.sacr.sk

Public holidays and feast days 1 January New Year's Day and Anniversary of the Establishment of the Slovak Republic in 1993, 6 January Epiphany, Three Magi, Orthodox Christmas, Good Friday, Easter Monday, 1 May Labour Day, 8 May Victory against Fascism Day – end of World War II, 5 July Sts Cyril and Methodius Day, 29 August Anniversary of the Slovak National Uprising, 1 September Slovak Republic Constitution Day, 15 September Holy Mary, Our Lady of Sorrows, Patron Saint of Slovakia, 1 November All Saints' Day, 17 November Day of Struggle against Totalitarianism/Fight for Democracy (the start of the Velvet Revolution in 1989), Christmas Eve, Christmas Day, 26 December St Stephen's Day

Background Information

East of Vienna, the Orient begins (*Östlich von Wien fängt der Orient an*)

Austrian statesman Prince Klemens Von Metternich

The Republic of Slovakia occupies a territory of 48,845km^2, is landlocked and surrounded by five countries: Austria, the Czech Republic, Poland, Ukraine and Hungary. The border of 1,524km divides up as Austria 91km, Czech Republic 215km, Poland 444km Ukraine 97km and Hungary 677km. Despite the distance from the sea, Slovakia has many lakes, streams and rivers and 45km^2 of its total territory is covered by water. Slovakia is situated at 16° 50'–22° 34' longitude east and 47° 42'–49° 37' latitude north. More than 80% of the country sits at over 750m above sea level The mountain peak of Krahule (1,062m), near Banská Bystrica in central Slovakia is considered the geographical centre of Europe.

Bratislava is Slovakia's capital and is situated at the western tip of the country, in a highly strategic position on the mighty Danube River at the meeting point of three countries: Slovakia, Austria and Hungary. Bratislava is only 60km from Vienna; the two cities are the closest capitals in the world. The state border with Austria is just over the Danube River from Bratislava, within walking distance of the town centre. The state border with Hungary is just 16km away, just beyond Bratislava city limits. The Danube flows through Bratislava dividing the historic Old Town centre from the modern housing district of Petržalka.

The Carpathian Mountains, the eastern wing of the great European Central Mountain System, begin north of Bratislava with the Small Carpathian range, known for its wine route. They then make a mighty swoop south, scooping up all of the Hungarian plain and Transylvania in a giant semicircle before heading north through the western end of Ukraine, winding up on the border of Slovakia and Poland in an impressive climax. The highest peak in the entire Carpathians is Gerlachovský štít (2,655m) in the High Tatras. The lowest point is at Bodrog River (94m). The Váh (Waag in German, Vág in Hungarian), a tributary of the Danube River, is the longest river in Slovakia with a length of 403km. The Danube (Dunaj) connects Slovakia with the harbours of the Black Sea and European harbours through the Rhine–Main–Danube waterway. The Danube also separates the Carpathians from the Alps. In the past, two significant trade routes led through Slovakia; the Amber (Jantarová) and Czech routes, along which goods (gold, amber and fur) flowed.

Slovakia is essentially a rugged, mountainous country criss-crossed by many rivers and dotted with mountain lakes. The land is rich in brown coal and lignite and small amounts of iron, copper and manganese ore. The central region around Banská Štiavnica produced 40% of Europe's gold in the 14th and 15th centuries. Silver and copper mines were also highly successful before the discovery of the New World (see the box on pages 248–9).

3

CLIMATE

Slovakia's climate is temperate with warm, wet summers and cold, hard winters, and is located in a mild climatic zone of continental nature, characterised by wide differences between temperatures in summer and winter, as well as by four distinct seasons of the year. Average temperatures in Bratislava for winter are - 1–4°C (34–40°F), spring and autumn 9–21°C (49–69°F) and summer 24–26°C (75–79°F), although in recent years, spring and autumn have merged into the more dramatic seasons. Snow cover on the High and Low Tatras, Greater and Lesser Fatras in the north is consistent although less than it has been in the past. The lowest annual temperature (-3.7°C) is in the mountains at Lomnický Štít (peak) The warmest zone (30.2°C) is the Podunajská rovina (plain) by the Danube River. For more information before you set off, ie: on whether to pack an extra jumper, look at www.meteo.sk.

NATURAL HISTORY AND CONSERVATION

Gerard Gorman (e gerard@probirder.com; www.probirder.com)
Slovakia is essentially a mountainous country, though there are stretches of lowland along the Danube in the south and in the far southeast of the country. Altitudes range from a low of 94m by the Bodrog River in the far southeast, to 2,655m at Gerlachovský štít in the High Tatras. Most mountain ranges are blanketed in vast, dense forests of both broad-leaved and coniferous trees – indeed some 45% of Slovakia is forested. Generally, oaks grow below 350m, beech between 550m and 600m, mixed fir-beech up to 700m, spruce-beech between 700m and 1,050m, and above this spruce and then mountain pine at the highest elevations. Besides forests there are other, diverse landscapes such as rugged limestone crags and gorges, rocky scree slopes, barren boulder terrain with isolated tarns, lush alpine pastures, water-meadows, riverine woodlands and stream valleys with white-water rapids and picturesque waterfalls. There are nine National Parks in Slovakia (Tatra National Park, Low Tatras, Malá Fatra, Veľká Fatra, Pieniny, Muránska Planina, Slovenský Raj, Slovenský kras and Poloniny), all of them uplands. Though these areas include some wild and rugged terrain they can be explored by following colour-coded walking and hiking trails which are marked on detailed local maps. The highest alpine-like areas would be virtually inaccessible were it not for the ski-lift and cable car network. These can be used to get one right up onto the highest peaks to look for alpine fauna and flora without having to do hours of tiring trekking.

Most **birdwatchers** visit Slovakia to look for upland and forest species. There are ten species of woodpecker in Europe and all of them occur in Slovakia. The largest, the black woodpecker, is widespread, whilst the rarest, the white-backed woodpecker, is found in areas with old-growth deciduous forests. Owls such as Ural, pygmy, eagle and Tengmalm's are actually fairly common but not easy to find without local knowledge. Birds of prey include red kite, saker falcon and lesser spotted, golden and eastern imperial eagles. The higher alpine-like peaks are the home of alpine accentor and wallcreeper, the latter one of Europe's most sought-after birds. Another bird which is rare in western Europe but relatively common in Slovakia's forests is hazel grouse.

One of the best non-mountain birdwatching areas in Slovakia is Záhorie. This is the flood plain of the river Morava along the Austrian border and is a complex of water-meadows, marshes, bogs, ponds, pools, reed beds, pine, oak and poplar forest and damp willow and alder woodland. In spring and summer, white storks, red and black kites, marsh harriers, kingfishers, river and marsh warblers, collared flycatchers, penduline tits and red-backed shrikes are fairly common here. Though rarer, corncrakes, short-eared owls and white-tailed eagles might also be seen with a little luck and patience. The area north of Malacky is drier and typified by pine-forested sand dunes where there are nightjars, hoopoe and woodlark. Záhorie is also conveniently close to Bratislava beginning just to the north by the E65 motorway and stretching to the Czech border.

Slovakia is home to internationally important populations of three of Europe's rarest large **mammals**: lynx, wolf and brown bear. Between 400 and 500 lynx, around 450 wolves and between 600 and 800 brown bears are estimated to reside in the country. Though these magnificent animals inhabit most mountain forests in the centre and northeast of Slovakia, this does not mean that you can expect to encounter them on the first, or even the tenth, trip you make, wolf and lynx in particular being highly mobile and shy creatures that have learned to avoid people. Bears are not as wary or shy but are nevertheless difficult to find. Some tour companies offer bear-watching trips but these invariably involve sitting in hides for long periods. The bears are attracted to these hides by food being regularly placed out and though the chances of seeing bears are greatly increased by participating in such tours the rather artificial environment may not be to everyone's taste. The wisdom of feeding wild bears in this way is also questionable. Bears which become accustomed to being fed can become dependent upon such food sources and seek out places with people and it is then that problems may arise with the bear becoming more aggressive. When this happens the problem is always solved by the poor bear being shot. Somewhat easier to find and observe are two mammals that live at the highest elevations in the Low and High Tatras: alpine marmot (a large ground squirrel) and chamois (a mountain goat, the skin of which is used for 'chammy' leather).

In Slovak, the chamois is called *Kamzík vrchovský* (*Rupicapra rupicapra*) and the hilly area north of Bratislava also bears the name Kamzík. Once up in the alpine meadows and boulder country above the tree line, listen out for shrill whistles which are the calls of the marmots and which often betray their presence. The chamois found in Slovakia belong to an endangered sub-species known as Tatra chamois and are usually seen perched on precarious crags. From June to August Slovakia is also rich in **butterflies** with some spectacular species such as great banded grayling, dryad, scarce and common swallowtails and camberwell beauty, as well as numerous fritillaries, ringlets, heaths, skippers, coppers, blues and whites being locally common. The limestone plateaux and gorges of the Slovenský kras (Slovak Karst) and Muránska planina (Muran Plateau) national parks are two of the best areas for lepidopterists to visit.

When planning a visit to Slovakia's mountains to look for wildlife local weather must always be taken into consideration and at all times the right clothing should be worn and a compass or GPS handset taken along. Many ranges are covered in deep snow well into April and wetlands frozen solid. Late spring is ultimately the best season for birdwatching, particularly if grouse, owls and woodpeckers are the targets. Lowlands and wetlands are also worth visiting in April for wildfowl, waders and warblers. The manmade fish farms which dot Slovakia 's lowlands are often worth a look, too. In summer more reliable weather means that walking in the mountains is easier and safer, but there is a trade-off as forest birds are quieter in this season. On the other hand butterflies are more numerous. Autumn is a fairly quiet season for birds as they have finished breeding and are thus less active and hence more difficult to find. There is however some wildfowl and wader migration in September at the wetlands. Winter is a picturesque season but not the best for watching wildlife as, for example, many birds have migrated south to warmer climes. Winter is however arguably the best time of year to track large mammals as their presence is revealed by their prints left in snow. All in all, wildlife-watching holidays to Slovakia should concentrate on mountain and forest habitats and species.

NINE NATIONAL PARKS There are nine national parks in Slovakia and also many other natural protection areas and reserves. The most famous national park is the Tatras National Park (TANAP) although the Low Tatras (NAPANT) is also very popular with hikers and skiers. The Greater and Lesser Fatra mountain ranges both have national parks with their own unique attributes and attractions. The Pieniny National Park straddles the border with Poland and includes the spectacular Dunajec River, navigable on white-water rafts through a canyon. The Slovenský kras (Slovak karst) National Park is located in the south on the border with Hungary and includes several UNESCO-listed caves. The Slovak Paradise (Slovenský Raj) has many specially created trails for hikers and the famous Dobšinská ice cave. The Muránska planina (Muran Plateau) National Park also contains karst caves and the Poloniny National Park on the Ukrainian border is dotted with Ruthenian wooden churches. See the relevant chapters for more on these parks.

A DOZEN CAVES Slovakia is riddled with caves, pot-holes, ice caves and aragonite caves. There are 12 caves open to the public, some being quite spectacular. The Demänovská ice cave has magnificent ornamentation, while the caves in the Košice region have been listed as natural heritage by UNESCO. The Ochtinská aragonite cave is quite unique, embellished with a variety of tufts, branches and shrub-like formations of milky-white aragonite. Some caves are used for the treatment of children with asthma and allergies. See the relevant chapters for more on these caves.

HISTORY

THE EARLY YEARS Archaeological finds have shown the existence of man in the area now known as Slovakia from the Middle Palaeolithic Era (200,000–35,000BC). The region where Bratislava now stands was colonised in the 5th millennium BC and Slovakia was a significant centre for bronze production. The Celtic tribes settled here in the 5th century BC and four centuries later, the Celts built fortified settlements on the Danube banks at Bratislava and Devín nearby. The strategic advantages were developed in AD400 when Gerulata became a Roman staging post. Remnants of this can still be seen at Rusovce, 5km downriver from central Bratislava. Slavic tribes arrived in the region during the 5th century and the empire of Samo, a Frankish warrior merchant, was established two centuries later.

GREAT MORAVIAN EMPIRE Christianity came with the establishment of the Great Moravian Empire in AD833. This empire encompassed the lands of modern Slovakia and Moravia as well as parts of Hungary, Austria, Bohemia and the southern part of Poland. In AD828, during the reign of Prince Pribina, the first Christian church in central Europe was built in Nitra, the ancient home of the Slovak princes.

In AD863, at the invitation of Great Moravian Prince Rastislav, the brothers and missionaries Cyril and Methodius came from Thessaloniki to Great Moravia and created the Old Church Slavonic alphabet, the origins of today's Cyrillic alphabet. They also translated liturgical books into Old Church Slavonic, which they codified.

THE MIDDLE AGES AND THE MAGYARS In AD907, after much political intrigue, the Great Moravian Empire collapsed and the region was invaded by the Magyars whose King St István (Stephen) founded the Christian Hungarian state in the Carpathian Basin in AD1000. By the end of the 11th century, Slovakia had become an integral and the most developed part of old Hungary, a relationship which was to last for almost 1,000 years, despite rude interruptions by the Tatars in 1241, the Turks in 1526 and the Habsburgs for more than 300 years. The territory now known as the Slovak Republic was then called Felvidék ('Upper Countryside' in Hungarian) and remained so until the end of the World War I.

Between the 11th and 15th centuries, the region experienced a period of great economic growth and cultural advancement. In 1291, King András III granted Bratislava the privileges of a Free Royal Town and in 1436, King Zsigmond of Luxembourg granted the city a coat of arms featuring a castle. During the Renaissance, and particularly the enlightened rule of King Mátyás Corvinus, cultural life blossomed in Bratislava. The Academia Istropolina, the first university in what is now Slovakia, was founded in Bratislava in 1465 and you can still see the building, now hosting the Music and Drama Academy, on Ventúrska.

OTTOMANS AND HABSBURGS Life in the entire region was to change dramatically in 1526 at the Battle of Mohács (in southern Hungary), where the Ottoman forces wiped out the Hungarian army on one tragic day. The Habsburgs assumed the Hungarian crown and ten years later, after the fall of Buda, when the Turks had taken the city, the capital of Hungary was moved to Bratislava (Pozsony in Hungarian, Pressburg in German). Many of the subsequent conflicts, of Hungarian nobles siding with Turks in continuous efforts to dislodge the Habsburgs, were played out in Slovakia.

In 1536, Pressburg became not only the capital of Hungary, but also the centre of all administrative offices and the seat of the Hungarian archbishop. The Hungarian crown jewels were moved to Pressburg in 1552 and between 1563 and 1830 a total of 19 Hungarian kings and queens were crowned in St Martin's Cathedral. In 1683, with the help of the Polish king, Ján Sobieski, the Habsburgs defeated the Turks who had almost reached the gates of Vienna. The Turks were driven out of central Europe for good.

At the beginning of the 18th century, Hungarian nobles such as Ferenc Rákóczi II, then *župan* (head) of Šariš county and a Transylvanian prince (*fejedelem*), rose up against the Habsburgs, challenging their authority in battles carried out mostly on Slovak territory. Many castles were ruined during these uprisings. Rákóczi's band of anti-Habsburg rebels were called Kuruc while the pro-Habsburg were known as Labanc.

Maria Theresa was crowned in St Martin's Cathedral in 1741 and, towards the end of the 18th century, her reforms and those of her son Joseph II formed the basis of a modern state administration, tax and transportation system, army and schools and made life a little easier for Slovaks. Bratislava's time of prominence came to an end in 1783 when the capital returned to Buda, however coronations were held in the city until 1830 and the Magyar presence still affected all aspects of life.

THE SLOVAK NATIONAL AWAKENING (NÁRODNÉ OBRODENIE) By the late 18th century, the Slovaks were attempting to assert their national and cultural identity and rise up against Hungarian domination, similar to their neighbouring Czechs' reaction against German overlords. In 1792, the linguist Anton Bernolák founded the Slovak Learned Society (*Slovenské učené tovarišstvo*) in Modra, near Bratislava. He was joined by many Slovak intellectuals who recognised the opportunity of subverting the Austro-Hungarian monarchy. The lower classes were not inspired until 1843, when Ľudovít Štúr, the son of a Lutheran pastor, codified the Slovak literary language. Previously all literature was written in Czech. This made the Slovak nationalist movement more accessible to ordinary Slovaks.

By 1848, revolutions were widespread in Europe. The Hungarian uprising against the Habsburgs was inspired by the poet Sándor Petőfi, born in Kiskőrös, Hungary, but with Slovak roots (his name registered at his first school in Aszód, Hungary, was Alexander Petrovič). Slovakia was desperate for change and volunteer groups formed in many parts of the country to battle against the Habsburgs.

The Slovak National Council (*Slovenská národná strana*) developed as the first representative Slovak political organ of modern history. In 1849, its members endeavoured, through co-operation with Vienna, to effect the separation of Slovakia from Hungary and its incorporation as an autonomous entity within the system of the federal Habsburg monarchy. In 1861, the Martin Memorandum issued in the town of Martin in central Slovakia, urged the establishment of a Slovak district and language within Greater Hungary and two years later, saw the foundation of a cultural and educational foundation, Matica Slovenská. In 1867, the Austro-Hungarian Empire, after suffering humiliating defeats against Prussia and Italy, was forced to sign a Compromise (*Ausgleich* or *Kiegyezés*) with Hungary and create a dual monarchy. For the Slovaks this was nothing short of disaster. Slovakia was still *Felvidék* (Upper Countryside) and the Slovaks were subjected to an even more ruthless programme of 'Hungarisation'. This policy made Hungarian the only language in schools and large swathes of land were confiscated for use by Hungarian settlers, causing poverty and famine throughout the country. By the outbreak of World War I, almost 20% of Slovaks had emigrated, mostly to the USA.

WORLD WAR I When war broke out, the Slovaks and Czechs decided that they would be better off together, uniting with their Slavic brothers, the Serbs and Russians and large numbers defected from the Austro-Hungarian armies to fight against them on the Eastern Front.

In 1915, representatives of the Slovak and Czech ethnic organisations went to the USA to sign the Cleveland Agreement, brokered by President Woodrow Wilson, which established a common federal state. Under the Pittsburgh Agreement, the autonomous position of Slovakia within a democratic Czechoslovak Republic was proclaimed.

By the end of World War I, the notion of establishing an independent Czecho-Slovakia was fully supported by the United States, England, France and Italy. On 28 October 1918 the Czecho-Slovak National Committee in Prague proclaimed the existence of Czecho-Slovakia. Two days later, in the Martin Declaration, the Slovak National Council declared its desire for Slovakia to join with the Czech lands in one common state.

On 1 January 1919, Pressburg (in German, Pozsony in Hungarian) was occupied by Czechoslovak legions and annexed to the new Czechoslovak republic. The city's name was changed to Bratislava, which had a more Slavic sound and suggested the glory (*slava*) of Slavic brother (*brat*) hood. The skilful politician Tomáš Masaryk became president of the new republic and during his tenure from 1918–35, did much to defend democracy.

On 5 June 1920, at Versailles, the Treaty of Trianon returned the territory of Slovakia to the Slovaks and confirmed the controversial new border with

Hungary along the Danube River. However, this carving up of central Europe left some 750,000 Hungarians stranded on Slovak soil.

WORLD WAR II The new republic of Czechoslovakia inherited 80% of the Austro-Hungarian industry in the region but also a diverse and tricky blend of peoples in its population.

In the 1930s, as the world plunged into depression, Czechoslovakia began to crumble under the internal tensions. The 1935 elections saw victory for the Hlinka Party, the Agrarian Party and the Hungarian Agrarian Party.

Masaryk resigned from power in 1935 due to bad health and died two years later in 1937, leaving the less capable Socialist deputy, Edvard Beneš in charge of the Czech lands. Hitler had annexed the mainly German-speaking Sudetenland region of the Czech lands. He summoned the Slovak People's Party leader, Jozef Tiso, a Catholic priest and staunch nationalist, to Munich and gave him an ultimatum: either declare independence as a Nazi puppet state or we will carve up Slovakia between Germany, Hungary and Poland. On 14 March 1939, the Slovak parliament voted unanimously for independence. Beneš resigned on 5 October 1939 and German troops took the Sudetenland and the rest of the Czech region.

Wartime Slovakia's 'independence' lasted from 1939 to 1945, during which time Tiso banned all opposition parties, instituted censorship along Nazi lines and deported Jews to the extermination camps of Sobibor, Majdanka, Treblinka and Auschwitz-Birkenau. Deportation began in March 1942 and in seven months, 74,000 had been taken away. Tiso was very anti-Semitic and he terrorised the people with the fascist Hlinka Guard, named after the controversial patriot priest (see page 199), whose symbol was a sinister double cross. Recently, it was revealed that Tiso struck a deal with the Nazis and paid them 500 Reich Marks for each Jew taken away. The Nazis promised 'they will never come back'. Tiso fled the country in 1945 and was captured, tried and executed. To this day, Tiso remains a highly controversial figure in Slovak history. A play which showed recently at Bratislava's Aréna Theatre examined the character, and also, more worryingly, on the anniversary of the 14 March 1939 declaration of Slovak independence, skinheads make a habit of gathering at Tiso's grave in Martinský Cemetery. However, not all Slovaks supported the puppet Nazi state and in August 1944, the Slovak National Uprising (Slovenské národné povstanie, or SNP) took place. It was quashed within two months by German troops, at Tiso's request, but the SNP is still remembered in street, bridge and square names throughout the country. (See the box on page 235.)

POST-WAR AND COMMUNISM In April 1945, Czechoslovkia was 'liberated' by the Red Army. At this time, the Slovak state collapsed and Czecho-Slovakia was once again united, this time as a centralised state based in Prague.

In 1948, an ailing President Beneš resigned and died shortly afterwards. His place was taken by former Communist Party leader Klement Gottwald. A programme of Stalinisation began with five-year plans, arrests, class war and gulags.

THE PRAGUE SPRING On 5 January 1968, the Stalinist First Secretary Antonín Novotný was replaced by a young Slovak reformist, Alexander Dubček. He encouraged civil society and freedom of expression in what was called 'socialism with a human face'. Dubček implemented the 1960 constitution granting Czechs and Slovaks equal rights as separate yet federal states and the optimistic period of 1968 became known as the Prague Spring.

On 21 August 1968, Soviet tanks, supported by Warsaw Pact troops, rolled into Prague, Bratislava and other towns and wiped out all of Dubček's reforms. The Czech and Slovak republics remained separate in name, but the real power stayed in Prague.

VELVET REVOLUTION In November 1989, the fall of the Iron Curtain enabled the establishment of a democratic government, the restoration of civil freedom and human rights. On 24 November, Dubček appeared on a balcony above Wenceslas Square in Prague alongside former playwright turned Charter 77 spokesperson, Vaclav Havel. On 27 November, a general strike was held throughout the country and the people of Bratislava also demonstrated in the streets supporting student movements, the Public against Violence and Civic Forum initiatives. The bloodless demonstrations were later dubbed the Velvet Revolution.

After the Velvet Revolution, Slovaks were keen for autonomy and in February 1992, rejected a treaty that would have continued with a federal Czechoslovakia.

VELVET DIVORCE AND INDEPENDENCE In June 1992, the left-leaning government of HZDS (Hnutie za Demokratické Slovensko or Movement for a Democratic Slovakia) was elected, headed by the populist leader Vladimír Mečiar, a staunch supporter of Slovak independence. Pushed on by Mečiar, the Slovak parliament proclaimed the sovereignty of the Slovak Republic in July 1992 and the Slovak Constitution was signed on 3 September 1992.

On 1 January 1993, Slovakia celebrated the Velvet Divorce, when the newly independent and sovereign Slovak Republic came into being, followed six weeks later by the election of the first democratic Slovak president, Michal Kováč, once an HZDS ally of Mečiar, but now less of a friend.

Slovakia gained independence in 1993 and in the early years it lurked in the shadow of the populist authoritarian rule of Vladimír Mečiar, a former boxer and inflammatory public speaker. Slovakia became a member of the UN, OSCE (the Organisation for Security and Co-operation in Europe), IMF, etc but the internal politics and economy got into a severe crisis. Compared with 1989, in 1993 the GDP dropped to 74%, and previously unknown mass unemployment appeared. Slovak industry, producing until then mainly for the Soviet market, collapsed. Foreign investors also hesitated because of the uncertain political climate. Mečiar carried out a relentless campaign to remove Kováč from office, and rumours abound that he was behind the bizarre kidnapping in August 1995 of Kováč's son Michal, who was blindfolded, forced to drink a bottle of whisky and then abandoned in a car boot in Vienna.

GOVERNMENT AND POLITICS

In May 1997, a referendum was held on NATO membership and also the method of choosing the president. Voting papers were tampered with and Mečiar's boorish replies to reporters resulted in Slovakia being removed from the first group of east European countries lining up to join the EU or NATO.

Many Slovaks blamed the Mečiar government for not doing more to join the EU, by far Slovakia's largest trading partner after the Czech Republic. Slovaks were less upset by the rebuff from NATO; only 46% had voted to join the organisation in the 1997 referendum. Immediately following the EU announcement, President Kováč called for Mečiar's resignation and demanded early elections. Mečiar however managed to hang on until the elections of September 1998.

At the 1998 elections, Mečiar's HZDS won the largest percentage of the vote but were unable to form a government and so lost out to the right-wing coalition of the SDKU (Slovak Democratic and Christian Union), led by Prime Minister Mikuláš Dzurinda.

On 16 October 2002, the SDKU coalition won a second term in office, when President Rudolf Schuster appointed a new Slovak government, again headed by Prime Minister Dzurinda. The coalition comprised three centre-right parties; the SDKU, the SMK (Hungarian Coalition Party), the KDH (Christian Democratic Movement) and the liberal party ANO (New Citizens' Alliance). The three right-wing parties followed a liberal, EU-friendly and conservative economic policy, worked out by Ivan Miklós and his team at the Finance Ministry in Bratislava. The opposition was made up of the HZDS, SMER (Direction) and other political parties include the Free Forum, the HZD (Movement for Democracy), the HZDS-LS (Mečiar's branching-off Movement for a Democratic Slovakia-People's Party), the LU (People's Union), the SNS (Slovak National Party) and the KSS (Communist Party of Slovakia).

The New Citizen Alliance (ANO – Aliancia Nového Občana) is a liberal party ('ano' means 'yes'), led by Pavol Rusko, founder and former owner of Slovakia's largest TV channel, Markíza. In the June 2006 elections, ANO won only 1.42% of the vote and lost parliamentary representation. The Hungarian Coalition Party (SMK – Strana maďarskej koalície), led by Béla Bugár has 20 seats in parliament making it the largest Hungarian party in Slovakia.

On 15 June 2004, Ivan Gašparovič replaced Schuster as President of the Republic of Slovakia. This produced some nervous reactions, as while Rudolf Schuster was a former communist official 15 years ago, Ivan Gašparovič was the right-hand man of Vladimír Mečiar until just a few years previously.

The president of the republic is elected directly by the citizens and remains in office for five years. The 150 members of the Slovak parliament and the government are elected for a four-year term.

Dzurinda's sensible, west-looking government put the country back on track with the rest of Europe and the country was let back into the exclusive EU/NATO wannabes club. On 3 March 2004, Slovakia joined NATO along with Slovenia, Bulgaria and Romania, and on 1 May 2004, Slovakia joined the European Union along with nine other states in the largest expansion in EU history. Slovak economists hope the country will join the euro mechanism in 2006–07 and introduce the euro in 2008–09. Joining the Schengen Agreement in October 2007 will remove the need for passports within the signed-up EU countries (see *Chapter 2, Red Tape*, page 25).

In June 2006, after serving two terms, the Dzurinda government was kicked out by SMER. Robert Fico's left-wing SMER-Sociálna demokracia (Direction-Social Democracy) party won the elections in June 2006 and entered into an apparently bizarre coalition with the far-right Slovak National Party (SNS) led by Ján Slota and Vladimír Mečiar's HZDS-LS. Both parties were part of coalition government ruling in Slovakia between 1994 and 1998 and were criticised for their extreme policies. Slota was Mayor of Žilina for a record four terms from 1990 to December 2006 (see *Chapter 8, Žilina*, pages 197–8). In the 1990s, Mečiar's government led Slovakia into international isolation.

The new government came under attack immediately by European politicians and the economic elites. First, the left-wing SMER made an alliance with the extreme-right SNS. This is without precedent in European politics. At a meeting in Brussels in October 2006, the PES (Party of European Socialists) suspended SMER temporarily from its ranks because of this alliance.

The SNS is well known for its extreme politics and harsh rhetoric, targeting minorities such as Hungarians, Roma and homosexuals. According to Ján Slota, 'Hungarians are the cancer of the Slovak nation', 'Slovaks should jump into their tanks and flatten Budapest' and 'the best policy for Gypsies is a long whip in a small yard'.

In 2003, Slota stirred up controversy when he suggested that Roma men should be offered money in exchange for undergoing sterilisation. As a part of the coalition agreement, neither Slota nor Mečiar obtained a government position. However, they both exercise considerable power behind the scenes and, together with Fico, they form the Slovak Coalition Council.

The European economic elites are also critical of the new government, fearing a setback to Slovakia's reform agenda. Investors are worried that the Fico's government will reject the neo-liberal stance of the former Dzurinda government.

It remains to be seen how the new government will proceed with the economic reforms, keeping in mind that Slovakia aims to adopt the euro in 2008–09.

NEW FRIENDS, OLD ENEMIES Mečiar's brutish populist stance had not helped relations with the neighbours. A law passed in 1995 recognised Slovak as the only official language, meaning that officially the large Hungarian minority could not use their mother tongue in public places. A separate law was passed in 1995 to protect the Slovak Republic, which allowed for the arrest of anyone criticising the government.

On the other side of the fence, the 1998–2002 right-wing Fidesz-led government in Hungary did little to endear themselves to the Slovaks, especially with the Status Law, promoted by the then Hungarian Prime Minister Viktor Orbán, which promised dual nationality and extra benefits for all Hungarians living beyond Hungary's borders. In a 2004 referendum, Hungarians voted against offering dual citizenship to ethnic Hungarians outside Hungary.

Since the Fico government entered office in 2006, relations between Slovakia and Hungary have been steadily deteriorating. The numerous attacks, both verbal and physical, on the Hungarian minority fuelled ethnic tension. Some analysts claim that the SNS's participation in the government encouraged the anti-Hungarian mood in Slovakia. Others point out that the supporters of Slota are simply afraid of the increasing Hungarian influence in politics and the idea of 'Greater Hungary', supported by some Hungarians; before 1918, Slovakia was a part of Hungary. However, the new Slovak government promised to clamp down on political extremism and punish all attacks on ethnic minorities. Both Slovakia and Hungary are members of the EU and NATO, so one would hope that sober, forward-looking politics will prevail.

The Slovaks and Czechs continue to argue over the repercussions following the Velvet Divorce, in which Slovakia feels it came off worse. Slovaks always felt like the neglected little sister in the federal Czechoslovakia, but now they are overtaking the Czech Republic in economic reforms and progress.

ADMINISTRATIVE REGIONS In 1996, Slovakia was divided up into eight administrative regions, each named after the main town of the region. The eight *samosprávny kraj* (self-governing or autonomous region) are usually just known as *kraj*. These are: Bratislava, Trnava, Trenčín, Nitra, Žilina, Banská Bystrica, Prešov and Košice.

The chapters of this guide correspond to these eight regions with a ninth chapter devoted to Bratislava, Slovakia's capital.

However, before 1918 and the creation of Czechoslovakia, there were 20 (and before that 21) counties of the 900-year Kingdom of Hungary that were situated completely or partially in present-day Slovakia. These provinces were known in Hungarian as *Vármegye* (castle county) because they were usually named after the main castle in the region, and often belonged to noble families who participated in the national assembly and elected members of parliament. Visitors to Slovakia will frequently come across the names of some of these regions, particularly Gemer, Hont, Orava and Spiš.

INTERNATIONAL DISPUTES Consultations continue between Slovakia and Hungary over the Gabčíkovo-Nagymaros hydro-electric dam project along the Danube. As a member state that forms part of the EU's external border, Slovakia must implement the strict Schengen border rules by October 2007. Hungary amended its status law extending special social and cultural benefits to ethnic Hungarians in Slovakia.

ENVIRONMENTAL ISSUES There are nuclear power stations at Republic and Mochovce (southeast of Nitra) and Jaslovské Bohunice (north of Trnava). Mochovce was built in 1983 and consists of four Soviet-designed water reactors. Environmental groups feared that the reactor was a serious threat to the local environment, such as degradation or even a catastrophe like Chernobyl. Under a deal with the EU, Slovakia has shut down one V1 reactor and will close a second by the end of 2008. However, the Slovak government wants to build a total of five reactors at Mochovce. Construction of the plant at Jaslovské Bohunice began in 1973 and causes even more worry for environmentalists.

ECONOMY

THE TATRA TIGER In recent years, Slovakia's booming economy has become the envy of the region. Dubbed the 'Tatra Tiger' after the mountains in the north and spiritual symbol of the country, Slovakia's economy was a slow starter after the Velvet Divorce from the Czech Republic on 1 January 1993, but has now taken off.

The Dzurinda government, spearheaded by Finance Minister Ivan Miklós made excellent progress during 2001–04 in macroeconomic stabilisation and structural reform. Major privatisations are nearly complete, the banking sector is almost completely in foreign hands, and the government has helped facilitate a foreign investment boom with business-friendly policies, such as the labour market liberalisation.

However, the most attractive measure was on 1 January 2004, when the government replaced the income, corporate and sales tax with a 19% flat tax rate, dramatically changing the economic landscape of the entire region and luring many international companies away from neighbouring countries. Slovakia now has one of the best investment environments in Europe. Taking into account the total tax burden, Slovakia has the lowest taxes of all of the EU and OECD countries. In the summer of 2006, the new social-democrat Fico government was formed. Many analysts expressed concern that the new government will not carry on the pro-market reforms introduced by the Dzurinda government. Fico's election programme included the scrapping of key pieces of economic reforms, introduced by the former government such as the 19% flat tax rate. Fico also promised to stop privatisation and restore welfare benefits. According to Fico, high economic growth had not benefited most Slovaks and he wanted to soften the economic reforms, creating an efficient welfare state. However, some analysts say that the post-election agenda might be a watered-down version of the election programme with only minor policy changes. For example, the tax policy changes might be limited to introducing a second (lower) VAT rate. It remains to be seen how the reforms will carry on. The continuity of the main policies seems likely, specially that the 2009 adoption of the euro is the new government's priority.

Despite the general slowdown throughout Europe, Slovakia's economic growth exceeded expectations in 2001–04. Unemployment in August 2004 was an unacceptable 17.8% (the second highest in the EU, after Poland); while the GDP (€28.8 billion) is on the up, inflation is a steady 4.1%. Slovakia's real GDP growth was 5.1% in 2005. In the second quarter of 2006, Slovakia's GDP growth was a record 6.6%, the second-highest figure in the EU after Lithuania. (In the same period, the average GDP growth in the EU was 2.6 %.)

Foreign investment was expected to total about 2.2 billion euro in 2005, twice the amount in the previous year. Foreign companies are attracted by the highly skilled, stable and relatively young labour force and the low labour costs.

In recent years, multi-nationals such as IBM, Johnson Controls, Fujitsu, Samsung, Coca-Cola, Whirlpool, Henkel, Siemens, Dell, Heineken and South Africa Breweries have launched operations in Slovakia, however the biggest investments in the country have been in car plants.

The Sony electronics firm is to build a 1.8 billion-koruna factory for making TV sets in Nitra, about 40km from its existing plant in Trnava in western Slovakia. The factory will employ approximately 3,800 people making LCD sets and will gradually include the manufacture of video equipment. The Samsung company is also looking at nearby Galanta as the location of a further 15 billion-koruna investment in building a factory for LCD panels. The firm already makes LCD and plasma TV sets at its existing Galanta plant.

A huge car-manufacturing plant for Peugeot-Citroën has sprung up in less than a year, just 50km from Bratislava. Volkswagen is already present, but soon it will be joined by Kia Motors, Ford Motors and Hyundai and in less than two years, Slovakia is expected to produce more cars per head than any other country in the world.

The only part of Slovakia not benefiting from this boom is the far east of the country, which still suffers from poor infrastructure and unemployment reaching 20%. It takes more than five hours to get to the isolated east by bus, whereas Vienna is less than an hour by car and Budapest just under two hours. Slovakia hopes to use EU funds to develop the far east regions. However, driving around the eastern, more isolated regions of Slovakia, visitors may be surprised to find remarkably prosperous-looking villages, with large houses and spacious gardens. Visitors will come across pockets of impoverished, entirely Roma settlements, to the east of Košice and south of Rimavská Sobota on the border with Hungary, however it can be quite an eye-opener to discover palatial mansions and farmsteads up near the border with the Ukraine. One wonders where the owners commute to for work.

PEOPLE

The strangest figures we saw were the Slovaks, who are more barbarian than the rest, with their big cowboy hats, great baggy dirty-white trousers, white linen shirts, and enormous heavy leather belts, nearly a foot wide, all studded over with brass nails...They are very picturesque, but do not look prepossessing. On the stage they would be set down at once as some old Oriental band of brigands. They are, however, I am told, very harmless and rather wanting in natural self-assertion.

From Jonathan Harker's Journal in *Dracula* by Bram Stoker.

Slovaks embody the stereotype of Slavic hospitality, tempered by a generous portion of dour realism. However, they are neither gloomy like their Hungarian neighbours nor uptight like the Austrians over the river. Slovaks welcome visitors with open arms, and usually an open bottle. Then there's the legendary razor-cheekboned beauty of Slovak females, deriving from a fascinatingly exotic gene pool. Many top models are from Slovakia.

It's impossible to generalise, but many Slovaks share an intense love for nature and the family. They like nothing better than to go out trekking through the woods, finishing up with a huge meal of hearty cuisine washed down with fantastic beer, fiery spirits or quality Slovak wine.

Slovaks have chips on their shoulders about the Czechs, and with reason. Only recently has the dynamic Slovak economy allowed them to hold their heads high in the region after years of being treated like a problematic little sister. It still rankles that most people think the greatest stars of Czechoslovak ice hockey, football and Olympic teams of the past were all Czech, as many were Slovak. If that weren't enough, many people still confuse Slovakia with Slovenia and this irritates people from both countries. They don't even share a common border.

Bratislava locals are a brainy lot. Imagine living in a town where often old Pressburg families have three first languages, and not the easy ones either: Slovak, Hungarian and German are widely spoken.

There is quite a lot of jealousy from other parts of the country that Bratislava gets the best of everything. Bratislava is closer to Vienna than to many other Slovak cities, in terms of both geography and attitude. Towns in the 'far east' feel neglected and there is a problem of demographics as almost all students leave to study in Bratislava then decide to stay there, causing a brain drain in towns further east and a desperate housing shortage in the capital.

More than 9% of the population is ethnic Hungarian. Around 600,000 Magyars live in Slovakia, mostly in the south and east of the country around Komárno and Dunajská Streda. The Slovak Constitution of 1992 guaranteed the rights of minorities and most Hungarian children receive education in their mother tongue. Politically, Slovakia and Hungary are always arguing; in private Slovaks and Hungarians get along fine. However in 1996, the Mečiar government did not help relations by making Slovak the only official language, revenge perhaps for ruthless Magyarisation in the past.

The new Fico government (June 2006) helped fan the flames of Slovak–Magyar friction by letting Mečiar and the nationalist mayor of Žilina, Ján Slota, back into the government coalition. In 2005, Slota said, 'If the Slovak nationalist party is extremist, then Hungarians are radioactively extremists, they radiate more than Chernobyl. The best solution would be to entomb them with cement'. Ironically, there are few Hungarians living in the Žilina region in the north of Slovakia where Slota bangs on about what he perceives as 'the Hungarian threat' (see *Politics*, pages 11–12).

The Roma are the second-largest minority group and it is estimated that as many as half a million live mostly in the neglected eastern regions with few amenities, high unemployment and almost no schooling. Under communism, everybody had to have a job, but now potential employers can openly display their prejudices and reject Roma workers. Roma children are tested in Slovak instead of their own language then dumped in 'special schools'. On the Roma side, integration into Slovak society is difficult because of the complicated caste system and community rules and ties.

In World War II, 80,000 Slovak Roma escaped extermination because the Germans only occupied Slovakia after the Slovak National Uprising (SNP) in 1942. The communists provided homes and jobs for the Roma, but in the process destroyed their nomadic lifestyle.

The remaining Jewish population (less than 4,000) of Slovakia live mostly in Bratislava and Košice. They are the smallest Holocaust-surviving community in Europe and are mostly elderly. However, many younger people have rediscovered their Jewish roots and the Union of Jewish Youth is fairly active.

The Ruthene (Rusyn) minority live in the Slovakian far east on the border with Ukraine. They have a distinct yet dying culture as many young people leave to find work elsewhere. In Slovakia, Rusyns are best known for the wooden Greek Catholic and Orthodox churches found in the region beyond Prešov, which can all be visited. They are also known for their beautiful icons and Easter egg designs which you can see in the museum in Bardejov, as well as folk dancing and singing.

The ethnic make-up of Slovakia is 85.8% Slovak, 9.7% Hungarian, 1.7% Roma (although the Roma community is continually under-reported, and estimated at more than 500,000), 0.8% Czech, 0.4% Ruthene, 0.2% Ukrainian, 0.1% German, 0.1% Polish, 1.2% other.

RELIGION

Some 69% of Slovaks say they are Roman Catholic, although in practice they are not as fervent as their northern neighbours, the Poles, and rather more enthusiastic than the Magyars to the south. Young Slovaks are also more devout than their Czech peers. Many young Slovaks pop into church to pray during their lunch hour; it's not just the terrain of the elderly. The Roman Catholic Church is the largest in Slovakia followed by the Evangelical Church of the Augsburg Confession and the Greek-Catholic Church. The first Christian church in Slovakia was founded in AD833 in the city of Nitra.

Orthodox and Greek-Catholic believers are found in the north and east of the country, where the Orthodox icons resemble those of Russia. The beautiful wooden churches of Ruthenia in eastern Slovakia hold Greek-Catholic and Orthodox treasures.

The late Pope John Paul II visited Bratislava in 1990, 1995 and 2002, and the city is one of the few in the world which His Holiness visited three times. His last visit to Bratislava in 2002 drew vast crowds to the Sad Janka Kráľa (park) on the southern side of the Danube.

John Paul II remains very popular in Slovakia. There are statues of the late pope in Trnava and Banská Bystrica, draped in rosaries and much visited. In 2006, Bratislava residents voted overwhelmingly to name the new fifth bridge, which opened in 2006, after John Paul II. However, the City Council eventually chose the name Apollo after a nearby refinery. The EU is worried by an attempt by the Vatican to reduce the number of abortions in Slovakia. A draft treaty between Slovakia and the Holy See would allow hospital staff to refuse to do abortions or fertility treatment on religious grounds.

There is a huge statue of Andrej Hlinka, the controversial priest politician and 'father of the nation' (*otec národa*) in Žilina's main square (see *History*, page 9).

Until World War II, the Jews played a significant role in Bratislava's multi-national, multi-cultural population. According to the Jewish Museum, there is evidence that Jewish merchants operated in the Roman province of Kvadia, now Slovakia. After the anti-Jewish riots in western Europe in the 11th century, many Jews found refuge in Bratislava and during the Middle Ages the Jewish community had established itself, with certain privileges and rights.

In 1750, some 15,000 Jews lived in Bratislava, in a ghetto between the town walls and Castle Hill. Židovska ulica (Jewish Street) still recalls part of this district.

Bratislava was a centre of Jewish Orthodox education, led by Rabbi Mose Schreiber (Chatam Sofer, whose mausoleum can be visited, see page 97) and a yeshiva founded in 1806 was the only university in the city.

When Slovakia allied itself to Hitler's Germany, around 74,000 Slovak Jews were deported, the survivors emigrated and today fewer than 4,000 remain in the entire country, 800 in Bratislava. At one time there were 29 synagogues in Bratislava.

Like most post-communist countries in the region, Slovakia has its fair share of 'new' religions, moving into the supposed spiritual vacuum: Jehovah's Witnesses, Mormons, Baha'is, Hari Krishnas and Scientologists are all active in Slovakia. Religious affiliations in Slovakia are: Roman Catholic 68.9%, Evangelical Church of Augsburg Confession 6.9%, Greek-Catholic 4.1%, Reformed Christian 2%, Orthodox 0.9%, Jehovah Witness 0.4%, Evangelic Methodist 0.1%, Brethren Baptist Union 0.1%, without religious affiliation 16.6%.

EDUCATION

Slovakia has a high standard of education, a legacy of the communist system. Slovak children face nine years of compulsory education at almost entirely state-run schools, however since 1990 some private and church-owned schools opened. Primary education lasts from the age of six to ten, followed by secondary school until the age of 15. Students can continue their studies at a gymnázium or high school where they prepare for higher education. The most prestigious high schools are found in Bratislava and Košice. Slovakia's largest university, Univerzita Komenského (Comenius) is located in the capital. Other fine universities are found in Trnava, Nitra, Banská Bystrica, Zvolen, Žilina and Košice.

CULTURE

Much as it pains them to admit it, Slovak history, culture, including literature, is bound up inextricably with that of Hungary. From the 10th century until 1918, the country was known as Upper Country (*Felvidék* in Hungarian) and during the Middle Ages Czech was used alongside Hungarian, German and Latin. Surviving texts from the region are all in Latin, the earliest known being the 11th-century *Legends of Saints Svorak and Benedict*. The earliest specimens of Czech vernacular are 15th-century town documents and devotional texts, such as the *Špis Prayers* from 1480. Magyar culture thrived during the enlightened rule of Hungarian King Mátyás Corvinus, who founded the Academia Istropolitana in 1465.

ART For visual arts, a trip to the Slovak National Gallery reveals the wealth of early religious painting from the region. Pavol of Levoča was the most outstanding Gothic sculptor. Baroque art by painters such as Ján Kracker and Jakub Bogdan are found in churches across the country. The 19th-century Slovak National Revival threw up a crop of Slovak painters. The solitary, strange painter Ladislav Medňanský, was born in Beckov in what is now Slovakia in 1850. He depicted the vivid Slovak landscapes and lives of tramps and poor people with great authority. Many of his powerful paintings can be seen at the Slovak National Gallery. Under communism, statues were chunky Soviet constructivist. Július Bártfay created numerous World War II monuments, including the Slavín monument. His son, Tibor, sculpted the peace fountain in front of Bratislava's Presidential Palace and has recently created the new statue of Hans Christian Andersen on Hviezdoslavovo námestie in the capital. Nowadays, Bratislava is bulging with private galleries, many of which have artwork for sale. Check out the list on pages 99–102 for places to spot a new Slovak master, or mistress.

CINEMA Slovak cinema is not as well known abroad as Czech. Few films were made in Slovakia before World War II. After the war, the light-hearted *Cathy* (1949) by Ján Kádar was a big hit. In 1953, the first film studio, Koliba, opened in Bratislava, creating a backbone for Slovak cinema to this day. The 1960s saw a 'new wave' of Slovak cinema as Kádar joined with Elmar Klos to create *Obchod na korze* (The Shop on Main Street) in 1965 which won an Oscar. In the 1970s, Duáan Dušek and Dušan Hanák made powerful, gritty documentaries, and often their films were banned by the communist authorities. The best-loved director is Juraj Jakubisko whose films reflect and comment on life in Slovakia. *Tisicročna včela* (Millennial Bee – 1983) and *Sedím na konári a je mi dobre* (I'm sitting on a branch and I'm fine – 1989) are classics. Slovak cinema has struggled in recent years; however Slovakia's stunning scenery, the high-quality Koliba and L+S studios and the favourable economic climate make the country a top location destination for film companies. Many Hollywood films use the natural beauty as a bargain-priced backdrop. (See the box on page 40.) Orava Castle, Dolný Kubín and the Vrátna Valley were used as settings for *Nosferatu* back in 1922, and recently *Dragonheart* (1996), *The Peacemaker* (1997), *Uprising* (2001) and *Behind Enemy Lines* (2001) were all filmed in Slovakia.

LITERATURE In 1787, Catholic priest and linguist Anton Bernolák published his *Grammatica Slavica* and in 1790 he created a massive six-volume dictionary of Slovak–Czech–Latin–German–Hungarian, published in 1827 after his death. Two years later, Bernolák helped found the Slovak Learned Society and stirred a national cultural awakening in the country. The first writer to use Bernolák's Slovak was Juraj Fándly, although more successful was another Catholic priest Ján Holly (1785–1849) who translated Virgil's *Aeneid* and wrote on emotive Slovak-Slav themes such as the *Svatopluk* (1833) about the Moravian prince. Holly is considered the founding father of Slovak poetry and there's a statue of him seated in a courtyard just behind St Martin's Cathedral. There was much traditional folksong and balladry in the 17th and 18th centuries. A popular tale told of a real-life Robin Hood figure, Juraj Jánošík (1688–1713), who led a group of bandits around Terchová in northern Slovakia. In 1843, Ľudovít Štúr codified the Slovak literary language. He started a Slovak-language daily paper in 1845 and in literature stressed the importance of local and original writers. Three poets, Janko Kráľ, Ján Botto and Andrej Sládkovič, personified the folk romanticism of the Štúr generation. Kráľ was a strange, solitary figure who battled against the Hungarians. Sládkovič is best known for the long poem *Marína*, inspired by an unhappy love affair. To learn more about life in the Slovak countryside, we can also turn to the eccentric Hungarian author Kálmán Mikszáth (1847–1910) who described life in Felvidék with a gentle ironic humour. His novel *The Siege of Beszterce* (*Beszterce ostroma* in Hungarian) appears surprisingly relevant in theme. Amongst contemporary authors, Klára Jarunková, born 1922, is one of the few female writers to be translated from Slovak. Her teenage novels have a psychological sensitivity and fresh charm. A book to look out for is by Martin Šimečka, the son of the well-known Bratislava-based Czech dissident writer Milan Šimečka. His autobiographical novel *Džin* was translated as *Year of the Frog*.

POETRY Oppressed in literature by the Hungarian and Czech languages, Slovak writers found more success in poetry. The lawyer Pavol Országh Hviezdoslav (1849–1921) was the most creative of his generation. His long narrative poem *Hájnikova žena* (The Gamekeeper's Wife) celebrates the freedom of the countryside opposed to the moral corruption of some of the aristocracy. In the years preceding World War I, a group known as the 'Slovak Literary Moderna' appeared with Ivan Krasko at the forefront, describing atmospheric, melancholic moods. After World War II, Stalinism restricted creativity with its emphasis on dreary Socialist Realism. Poet and dramatist Ladislav Mňačko became the leading Slovak literary dissident describing the life of a corrupt communist politician in *Ako chutí moc* (Who tastes Power) in 1967.

CLASSICAL MUSIC Bratislava was visited by musical megastars: Mozart, Haydn, Barťok, Liszt and Beethoven, many of whom studied within the Old Town walls and gave concerts.

Home-grown music star, Johann Nepomuk Hummel (1778–1837), was a disciple of Mozart and Haydn and a friend to Beethoven and Paganini. The piano virtuoso, composer and world-famous music teacher created music in many styles and the house where he was born can be visited, at Klobúčnicka 2. In the 18th century, Slovaks wanted to redefine their folk music heritage and composers used folk motifs in classical compositions. Mikulaš Schneider-Trnavský and Ján Levoslav Bela were the most well known.

JAZZ MUSIC Communism stifled modern music in the second half of the 20th century, although there was a significant jazz movement, led in the 1960s by bands such as Combo 4, the Bratislava Jazz Quartet, the Medik Quintet and Traditional Club Bratislava. Jazz clubs are popular in Bratislava today and there are many places to hear live music. Peter Lipa, 64, head of the Slovak Jazz Association, and chief organiser of the country's largest jazz festival, is an iconic figure in the Slovak jazz world. He has made 18 albums and his latest, *Beatles in Blue(s)*, sees him covering songs by his teenage idols. A good introduction to the Slovak jazz world can be found on his website (*www.peterlipa.com*).

POPULAR MUSIC Rock and pop artists are popular with singers such as Paľo Habera and his former band, Team. Reggae (*www.reggae.sk*) is also thriving in the Slovak capital alongside ambient music, death metal and the inevitable techno.

DOBRO GUITARS - GOOD IN ANY LANGUAGE

The word *dobro* not only means 'good' in Slovak but it's the name of a musical instrument, invented by a Slovak family, the Dopyeras. Ján Dopyera was born in 1893 in Stráže and in his youth demonstrated great skill as a craftsman. Guided by his father, Ján made his first fiddle as a child in Dolná Krupá. After the family emigrated to Los Angeles in 1908, he made and repaired musical instruments at his music shops in the 1920s. He was fascinated by the problem of how to make acoustic instruments louder. After numerous attempts, in 1926 he succeeded with a steel bodied guitar fitted with three aluminium resonators amplifying the sound of the instrument mechanically. He patented the new guitar and, joined by his brothers Rudy and Emil and some other investors, founded the National String Instrument Corporation. Even though the guitar, known as the Tri Plate National, met with enormous success, it was not long before the brothers founded their own company, Dopyera Brothers. They began making their latest patented instrument, the new resonator guitar, the Dobro, which took its name from the first letters of the 'Dopyera' and 'Brothers' and incorporated the Slovak word, *dobro* meaning 'good'. To promote the new guitar, they used the slogan 'Dobro means good in any language!'. The resophonic Dobro's inventor died in 1988 in Grants Pass, Oregon. John (Ján) Dopyera's musical achievements are remembered at an annual 'Dobrofest' festival near Trnava. See page 127.

The most popular programme on Slovak television recently was *Superstar*, a singing talent contest along the lines of *Pop Idol*.

DJS AND RAVES Many top DJs go to Bratislava. Music festivals are held in Trenčín, Trnava, Poprad and other towns throughout the summer.

FOLK MUSIC Because of the range of influences in Slovakia: Celtic, Roma, Hungarian, Slavic, German and others, Slovakia has a remarkably varied folk song and dance heritage. The *fujara* is an instrument unique to Slovakia that looks like a didgeridoo but is played like a flute. The Slovak State Folk Ensemble, known as Sluk (*www.sluk.sk*) perform often and other bands such as Šarišan (*www.sarisan.sk*) from Prešov give highly rated performances of music and dance. Try also to catch a show by Lúčnica, (*www.lucnica.sk*) another superb folk dance ensemble. Ghymes (*www.ghymes.hu*), a folk group formed in 1984 by Hungarian students at Nitra's College of Education play music rooted in the central European tradition. They are based in Galanta but hardly played on Slovak radio; they're much more successful in Hungary (see *Chapter 7, Jelenec village*, page 181).

ROMA MUSIC TRADITIONS The earliest mention of Roma musicians in Slovakia dates from 1489. In the 18th and 19th centuries, music was a good way of making a living as Roma music played an essential role in weddings and feasts. Roma musicians also played at the Hungarian aristocratic courts. The female violinist Panna Cinková (1711–72) and her band were legendary for their concerts. Music still plays a vital role in everyday life and is played at all important events. The sometimes joyous, sometimes mournful music uses clarinet, violins, double bass and dulcimers. Romathan, based in Košice, are the only state-funded Roma theatre group in Europe and use music and dance to fight racism.

ARCHITECTURE Slovakia has some spectacular architecture found all over the country in both towns and villages. The former Free Royal Towns such as Levoča, Bardejov, Nitra and Trnava offer a wide variety of architectural styles and influences. There are many fascinating and unique villages and examples of folk architecture in the decorative Čičmany, the UNESCO-listed Vlkolínec and Ždiar in the Prešov region. Here you can also find the incredible Rusyn wooden churches. Many of Slovakia's striking castles are connected with Hungary and Hungarian architects. The nobility commissioned castles and manors such as Betliar, Červeny Kamen, Bojnice and Smolenice or restored them in their own style and it was the Hungarian uprising against the Habsburgs, led by Transylvanian prince Ferenc Rákóczi II that ruined many of them. The names of four Magyar dynasties: Pálffy, Balassa, Thurzó and Andrássy turn up again and again in association with castles. See page 52 for the *skanzens* (open-air folk museum), of which there are a dozen or so in Slovakia.

SLOVAKIA'S UNESCO WORLD HERITAGE SITES

Slovakia has five sites on UNESCO's World Heritage list and a further 16 on the proposed list. There are four cultural and one natural. The cultural are the historic town of Banská Štiavnica and the technical monuments in the vicinity (1993), Bardejov town conservation reserve (2000), Spiš Castle and associated cultural monuments (1993) and Vlkolínec (1993). The caves of Aggtelek karst and Slovak karst are the one natural site (1995).

2

Practical Information

WHEN TO VISIT

Bratislava gets a lot of visitors all year round. It takes only two hours to fly there from London, while on the ground Bratislava is an hour from Vienna, two from Budapest and three from Prague. The 'little big city' is a strategic hot-spot with a leisure industry to match. Outside of Christmas and Easter, the hotel rates will be significantly cheaper and business hotels offer alluring rates at weekends.

Slovakia's climate is continental with hot summers and chilly winters. Every season in Slovakia has its own merits. In the height of summer it can get scorching, but there are numerous rivers and lakes where you can cool off. The Tatra Mountains get the majority of visitors in winter for the ski season, however hiking is better in spring and autumn. Winter is a great time to visit Bratislava for the Christmas market and attractive snow-covered streets. Stay warm with a spine-tingling hot toddy and some sturdy Slovak cuisine. Spring is a lovely time to tour the country, when the flowers bloom and the fruit trees lining the roads are pink and white with blossom. Autumn is a great time to visit and make the most of the many wine festivals in forest locations, enjoying the seasonal colours. Personally, I got badly sunburnt in April as the sun is deceptively strong, although the weather is as unpredictable as anywhere in Europe in the 21st century. Pack an anorak for occasional downpours, or secret trainspotting. Bear in mind that some museums and castles are either closed during the winter or have a limited opening time.

SEASONAL IDEAS

Spring Hiking in the national parks, exploring the 'far east' and the Rusyn wooden churches

Summer Enjoying the many pools and spas, cool mountain air and caves

Autumn Wine festivals, beautiful countryside, castles and chateaux

Winter Skiing in the High Tatras and Lesser Fatras; the 'affordable Alps' with superb facilities and imaginative après-ski ideas

ITINERARIES

A LONG WEEKEND In Bratislava spend a leisurely morning exploring the castle and the Old Town with regular coffee and cake (or beer) stops. After a sustaining lunch make for the hills at Kamzík just a trolleybus ride away. There you can go on a bobsleigh or take a chairlift down to a beautiful meadow. Don't forget to try out the Veža (tower) café with a fantastic view. In the evening take in an opera performance before some fine dining; maybe you'll even get in at the Ufo café's swanky nightclub. The following day, check out the Blue Church before heading off up the Small Carpathian wine trail taking in Červený Kameň's fantastic castle. Alternatively, fly direct to Poprad in the Tatra Mountains and spend the weekend exploring the High Tatra resorts, Poprad, the historic towns of Kežmarok and Levoča, not forgetting the magnificent Spiš Castle.

ONE WEEK Explore the towns and castles of western Slovakia, taking in the trio of Trnava, Trenčín and Nitra before finishing off with a pampering at Piešťany spa resort, located on an island.

TWO WEEKS Fly to Poprad and take in the mountains. Then head east to explore the wooden churches beyond Prešov and the bizarre Warhol Museum, taking in the historic cities of Prešov, Košice, Levoča and Kežmarok. Try white-water rafting on a wooden plť raft on the Dunajec River and visit Červený Kláštor Monastery nearby. Climb the hill of the medieval Spiš Castle and admire the beautiful surroundings. There'll be lots more castles, chateaux and manor houses *en route*. Hike around the Slovak Paradise and visit a spectacular cave or two. From Poprad, you'll still have time to visit the historic mining towns of Banská Bystrica, Banská Štiavnica and the hidden jewel of Špania Dolina.

 TOURIST OFFICES

ABROAD The Slovak tourist board, SACR, has offices abroad:

Germany Slowakische Zentrale für Tourismus; Vertretung Deutschland, Zimmerstrasse 27, 10969 Berlin; ☏ +49 30 2594 2640; e sacr-berlin@ botschaft-slowakei.de (part of the Slovak consulate, no website)
The Netherlands Slowaaks Verkeersbureau; WTC Amsterdam, Strawinskylaan 623, 1077 XX Amsterdam; ☏ +31 20 5752 181; e info@slowaaks-verkeersbureau.nl; www.slowaaks-verkeersbureau.nl
UK & USA Slovakia is the only Visegrád 4 country (Poland, Hungary, Slovakia and the Czech Republic)

with no national tourist office in either the UK or USA. In London, seek advice from the Slovak Embassy UK, 25 Kensington Palace Gdns, London W8 4QY, ☏ +44 (0)20 7313 6470. Consular & visa information: e consular@slovakembassy.co.uk; embassy: e mail@slovakembassy.co.uk; www.slovakembassy.co.uk. Slovak Embassy in the USA 3523 International Court, NW, Washington DC 20008; ☏ +1 202 237 1054; e info@slovakembassy-us.org; www.slovakembassy-us.org

IN SLOVAKIA The National Tourist Office, SACR, has its head office in Banská Bystrica but their website (www.sacr.sk) is very helpful and inspiring. More useful to the traveller are the AICES offices which are most often – but not always – the local information office found in towns and some villages all over Slovakia. Sometimes they will operate under a different name such as TIK (Turisticko-informačná kancelária) but the services and organisation are the same. The website has details of AICES offices throughout Slovakia according to region but not much else. However, if you visit personally, each office can advise on accommodation, sights and trips. They are usually incredibly helpful and enthusiastic. SATUR is more of a tourist agency for Slovaks going abroad, however they can help visitors to Slovakia by organising guided tours, trips or dinners in a traditional restaurant.

SACR (Slovenská agentúra pre cestovný ruch) Head office is in Banská Bystrica Námestie Ľ. Štúra 1, PO Box 35, Banská Bystrica;

☏ 048 4136 146; f 048 4136 149; e sacr@sacr.sk; www.sacr.sk

AICES (Asociácia Informačných Centier Slovenska) Headquarters are in Liptovský Mikuláš at Námestie mieru I; ☎ 044 5514 541; f 044 5514 448; e info@infoslovak.sk; www.infoslovak.sk

SATUR (Slovak National Tourist Board) Miletičova I; ☎ 02 5542 2828; f 02 5556 1426; e info@ acr.satur.sk; www.satur.sk

TOUR OPERATORS

City breaks, tailor-made tours, package holidays and flights to Slovakia are appearing almost weekly, especially by tour operators in the UK, US and Australia who specialise in eastern Europe. In addition to those below, see also *Chapter 3, Local tours,* page 78 and *Local travel agents,* page 78, some of which can arrange accommodation etc.

UK

Czech Travel Unit 9k, Brookfield Park, 1210 Lincoln Road, Peterborough, PE4 6LA; ☎ 01733 327 766; e info@czechtravelonline.com; www.czechtravelonline.com. Trips to Slovakia, especially AquaCity, Poprad (page 172).
Glajd UK History in Harmony, PO Box 1829, Shrewton, Salisbury, Wilts SP3 4PN; ☎ 0870 011 3994; (no email, use form on website); www.historyinharmony.com. Offers a museum tour of Slovakia.
Great Rail Journeys Saviour Hse, 9 St Saviourgate, York YO1 8NL; ☎ 01904 521936; e grj@greatrail.com; www.greatrail.co.uk. Offers a Danube cruise through Germany, Austria, Slovakia & Hungary.
Interhome Ltd Richmond Rd, Twickenham TW1 2EF; ☎ 020 8891 1294; e info@interhome.co.uk; www.interhome.co.uk. Accommodation in apartments, private houses or villas.
Martin Randall Travel Voysey Hse, Barley Mow Passage, London W4 4GF; ☎ 020 8742 3355; e info@martinrandall.co.uk; www.martinrandall.com. Tours entitled Habsburg Empire, The Austro-Hungarian Music Festival & the Iron Curtain.
Railway Touring Company 14A Tuesday Market Pl, King's Lynn PE30 1JN; ☎ 01553 661500; e enquiries@railwaytouring.co.uk; www.railwaytouring.co.uk.

Week-long trips by steam train through the Tatra Mountains.
Regent Holidays 15 John St, Bristol BS1 2HR; ☎ 0117 921 1711; e regent@regent-holidays.co.uk; www.regent-holidays.co.uk. Independent operator specialising in eastern European destinations. Offering luxury chateau breaks at Šalgovce, city breaks in Bratislava, Slovakia fly-drives & tailor-made itineraries. An 8-day fly-drive to eastern Slovakia is an excellent way to discover the off-the-beaten-track gems of the 'far east'. Spa breaks & Christmas & New Year programmes are offered, as well as special offers throughout the year.
Sherpa Expeditions 131a Heston Rd, Hounslow TW5 0RF; ☎ 020 8577 2717; e sales@sherpa-walking-holidays.co.uk; www.sherpa-walking-holidays.co.uk. Offers self-guided hikes in the Tatras.
Slovakian Travel Part of JD Windborne Travel Ltd, 17 Bedford St, Barrowford, Nelson, Lancd BB9 6DA; ☎ 0870 850 1694; e info@slovakiantravel.co.uk; www.slovakiantravel.co.uk. Specialist tour operator to Slovakia offers a wide variety of trips to Slovakia; city breaks, golf, fishing, walking, aqua parks and family trips.
Vamos Travel The central & east European city break specialists; ☎ 0870 762 4017; e brett.smith@ vamostravel.com; www.vamostravel.com. Opera & ballet, stag trips, activity holidays.

IRELAND

Abbey Travel (part of the Exodus group) Colette Pearson, Abbey Travel, 43–45 Middle Abbey St, Dublin I; ☎ +353 01 804 7153; e exodus@abbeytravel.ie; www.exodus.co.uk. Adventure holidays.

AUSTRALIA & NEW ZEALAND

Intrepid Travel 360 Bourke St, Melbourne, Victoria 3000; ☎ +61 03 8602 0500; e info@ intrepidtravel.com; www.intrepidtravel.com. With many trips to central Europe, Intrepid has been coming to Bratislava for four years.

Peregrine & Gecko's Adventures Level 4/380, Lonsdale St, Melbourne, Victoria 3000; ☎ +61 03 8601 4444; e websales@peregrineadventures.com; www.peregrineadventures.com. Cycling & hiking trips.

2

CANADA

GAP Traveller (part of the Exodus group) 19 Charlotte St, Toronto, Ontario M5P 2H5; ☏ +1 416 977 0043; toll free: +1 866 732 5885; e travel@ gap.ca. Adventure holidays.

Voyages Paradis with Carslon Wagonlit, 8875 Henri Bourrassa, Charlesbourge, Quebec G1G 4E4; ☏ +1 418 627 0911; www.voyagesparadis.com. Offers 'Les Grandes Capitales de l'Europe de l'Est': Budapest, Vienna, Bratislava & Prague.

US

Blue Danube Holidays ☏ +1 800 268 4155; e bluedanube@bluedanubeholidays.com. Offers escorted & independent tours, cruises & spa holidays.
Pathfinders 2225 Crestline Bd, Olympia, WA 98502; ☏/f +1 360 450 5959; e info@pathfinders.cz;

www.pathfinders.cz. Personal ancestral tours, family reunions.
Weber Travel Agency 3729 Grand Bd, Brookfield, IL 60513; ☏ +1 800 886 7012, +1 708 485 1333; e travel@webertravel.com; www.webertravel.com. Tours for individuals or groups in Slovakia.

NATURE SPECIALISTS IN THE UK

Avian Adventures Gerry Griffiths, 49 Sandy Rd, Norton, Stourbridge DY8 3AJ; ☏ 01384 372013; e aviantour@argonet.co.uk; www.avianadventures.co.uk. Mountains, plains & forests of Slovakia, 'an unspoilt paradise for botanists'. Birds & bears tour.
Birdquest Mark Beaman; Two Jays, Kemple End, Stonyhurst, Clitheroe, Lancashire BB7 9QY; ☏ 01254 826317; e birders@birdquest.co.uk; www.birdquest.co.uk. Offers a Hungary, Slovakia & Transylvania birdwatching trip in May.
Birdwatching Breaks Mark Finn, Cygnus Hse, Gordons Mill, Balblair, Ross-shire IV7 8LQ; ☏ 01381 610495; e enquiries@birdwatchingbreaks.com; www.birdwatchingbreaks.com. Hungary & Slovakia – spring migration on the plains.
Limosa Holidays Chris Kightley, Northrepps, Norfolk NR27 0LZ; ☏ 01263 578143; e enquiries@ limosaholidays.co.uk; www.limosaholidays.co.uk. Tours to Slovakia.

Naturetrek David & Maryanne Mills; Cheriton Mill, Cheriton, Nr Alresford, Hampshire SO24 0NG; ☏ 01962 733051; e info@naturetrek.co.uk; www.naturetrek.co.uk. The mountains & forests of Slovakia tour in May.
Probirder e gerard@probirder.com; www.probirder.com. Based in Budapest, wildlife/bird expert Gerard Gorman & his team take tours around Slovakia & Hungary.
Sunbird Steve Rooke, PO Box 76, Sandy, Bedfordshire; ☏ 01767 262522; e sunbird@ sunbirdtours.co.uk; www.sunbirdtours.co.uk. Trips to the Carpathian Mountains, for bird- & bear-watching. Combined Slovakia & Hungary trip.
Travelling Naturalist Jamie McMillan, PO Box 3141, Dorchester, Dorset DT1 2XD; ☏ 01305 267994; e jamie@naturalist.co.uk; www.naturalist.co.uk. Now in its 18th year of operation. Butterflies, flowers & birds tour or birds & bears tour.

STAG TOURS However much the idea horrifies of sloshed young men mooning the local grannies, stag parties are now a fact of life in central Europe. According to reports, on some weekends as many as 600 British tourists arrive on low-cost flights to enjoy the delights of cheap beer, attractive girls and themed events.

Bratislava Stags Radlinského 27; ☏ 02 52451441; e info@bratislavastags.com; www.bratislavastags.com. Based in Bratislava.
Red Seven Leisure Kensington St, Brighton BN1 4AJ; ☏ 0870 751 7377; www.redsevenleisure.co.uk.

Stag & hen weekends, in the Tatras too.
Stag Bratislava Pribinova 23; ☏ 0903 717 899; e info@stagbratislava.com; www.stagbratislava.com. Run by 3 Slovak ladies.

LOCAL TRAVEL AGENTS Local travel agents can help with trips, accommodation, excursions and car rental. They also have endless supplies of pamphlets about Slovakia.

Limba Michalská 3; ✆ 02 5441 8601; f 02 5920 6969; e limba@limba.sk; www.limba.sk. Limba has a great selection of mountain huts (*chata*) & cottages. Also family boarding houses, bungalows, hotels & spas.

Pilgrimtour Garbiarska 4, 031 01 Liptovský Mikuláš; ✆ 044 5570 834; f 044 5570 832; pilgrim@pilgrimtours.sk; www.pilgrimtours.sk. Founded in 1989, Pilgrimtour arranged the first Slovak expedition to the North Pole in 1992. For the last 8 years, Pilgrimtours has been specialising in mountain skiing tours & activities for children in the Tatras.

Slovakia Green Tours Radlinského 27; ✆ 02 5249 1641; f 02 5249 1651; e contact@ slovakiagreentours.com; www.slovakiagreentours.com. A family-run company established at the beginning of 2003 to promote Slovakia.

Top Bicycle ✆ +420 519 513 746; e info@ topbicycle.com; www.topbicycle.com. Biking in Slovakia.

Via Carpathia Ltd CSA 20 974 01 Banská Bystrica; ✆ +421 48 414 8325; f 048 4148 326, e info@viacarpathia.com; www.viacarpathia.com. All kinds of tours: winter fun, snowshoe hiking in Veľká Fatra, Slovakia by rail, Bratislava uncovered.

RED TAPE

Slovakia hopes to join the 15-member Schengen zone, abolishing border controls among participating countries, in the near future but the exact date is uncertain. The original date was set for October 2007. However, there could be delays in the technical preparations, ie: getting the computers ready for the EU's new eastern borders.

ENTRY REQUIREMENTS All visitors to Slovakia still need a valid passport for the duration of their stay in the country or if a visa is required, visitors must present a passport with more than three months left to the date of expiry.

Citizens from EU member countries and Switzerland can enter Slovakia just with a valid national identity card (where the country concerned issues such cards).

British nationals may visit Slovakia with a valid passport for a period of up to 180 days, while the other EU countries' citizens may stay in the country for up to 90 days.

Nationals from Australia, Canada, Israel, South Korea, Liechtenstein, Malaysia, New Zealand, Andorra and Chile may stay in Slovakia with a valid passport for up to 90 days.

Nationals from Iceland, Monaco, Norway and Switzerland may stay for up to three months and if this seems the same as 90 days, it is probably because most passport and visa regulations are reciprocal and highly tit-for-tat, following each detail to the last letter. Nationals from the USA along with Bulgaria, Croatia, Cuba, Romania, San Marino, South Africa and Vatican City may stay for up to 30 days, while nationals from Singapore and Hong Kong only get up to 14 days.

Nationals from all other countries require a visa and should contact the embassy of the Slovak Republic in their home country before setting off. Slovak embassies and consulates abroad are listed on page 26.

The list on the website at www.foreign.gov.sk/En/index.html (then click on 'visa requirements') gives an updated list of all mutual, unilateral and partial visa agreements.

CUSTOMS REGULATIONS Travellers over 16 can take 200 cigarettes, 400 cigarillos, 200 cigars or 3kg of smoking tobacco (or a combination of the respective amounts), 250ml of cologne and 50g of perfume in and out of Slovakia. As for alcohol, you can carry in one litre of spirits or two litres of wine; however you'll find much better prices in the Bratislava supermarkets so why bother lugging over a load of bottles. Save your energy for picking up a nice bottle of

Borovička to take home and tempt your maiden aunts. A maximum of ten litres of petrol can be carried in canisters for emergency use and presents and other items up to the value of €175 can be brought in and taken out of the country. Pets can be transported only with all the necessary pet passports and vaccination certificates. Antiques and works of art require a licence and are subject to customs duty.

If you take your own car to Slovakia, then the booze cruise amount could apply. In reality, the EU ruling is a guideline rather than a hard-and-fast law, and the key phrase in the debate is 'personal use', how much alcohol and nicotine the average person might reasonably consume. In terms of what you can fit into the back of a car, the limits are quite generous. For the record, they are: 3,200 cigarettes, 200 cigars, 3kg of tobacco, 110 litres of beer, 90 litres of wine, 10 litres of spirits and 20 litres of fortified wine.

For more information, see www.hmrc.gov.uk.

 ## SLOVAK EMBASSIES AND CONSULATES

ABROAD

Australia (Austrália) 47 Culgoa Circuit, O' Malley OBEO, Canberra ACT 2606; ✆ 2 6290 1516; e slovak@cyberone.com.au; www.slovakemb-aust.org. *Open Mon–Fri 09.00–16.00.*

Austria (Rakúsko) Armbrustergasse 24, A-1190 Vienna; ✆ 1 318 9055 200; e slovakembassy@vienna.mfa.sk; www.vienna.mfa.sk

Canada (Kanada) 50 Rideau Terrace, Ottawa, Ontario K1M 2A1; ✆ 613 749 4442; e slovakemb@sprint.ca; www.ottawa.mfa.sk

Ireland (Írsko) 20 Clyde Rd, Ballsbridge, Dublin 4: ✆ 1 6600 012; e slovak@iol.ie; www.dublin.mfa.sk

United Kingdom & Northern Ireland (Veľká Británia) 25 Kensington Palace Gdns, London W8 4QY; ✆ 0207 313 6470; e mail@slovakembassy.co.uk; www.slovakembassy.co.uk. *Open Mon & Wed 09.00–12.00, & 14.00–16.00, Tue, Thu & Fri 09.00–12.00.*

US (Spojené štáty americké) 3523 International Court, NW, Washington DC 20008; ✆ 202 237 1054; e info@slovakembassy-us.org; www.slovakembassy-us.org. *Open Mon–Fri 09.00–12.00.*

IN SLOVAKIA

Austria (Rakúske veľvyslanectvo) Venturska 10; ✆ 02 5930 1500; e pressburg-ob@bmaa.gv.at; www.embassyaustria.sk. *Open Mon–Fri 08.00–12.00.*

The Office of the Canadian Embassy in Bratislava At the Carlton Courtyard & Savoy Bldg, Mostová 2; ✆ 02 5920 4031; e brslva@

international.gc.ca. *Open Mon–Fri 08.30–12.00 & 13.30–16.30.*

Ireland Carlton Savoy Bldg, Mostová 2, ✆ 02 5930 9611; e Bratislava@iveagh.irlgov.ie; hotline: ✆ 02 5443 0690. *Open Mon–Fri 09.00–12.30 & 14.30–16.30.*

UK Panská 16; ℡ 02 5998 2000; e bebra@
internet.sk; www.britishembasssy.sk. *Open Mon–Thu*
08.30–17.00, Fri 08.30–16.00. Consulate open Mon–Fri
09.00–12.00 & 14.00–15.30 (1 Jun–31 Aug
08.30–14.00).

US Hviezdoslavovo námestie 4; ℡ 02 5443 3338;
e arc_brat@pd.state.gov; www.usembassy.sk.
Consular section open for American citizens Mon–Fri
08.00–12.00 & 14.00–15.30; closed at weekends &
public holidays.

GETTING THERE AND AWAY

There are 46 road crossings and 17 rail crossings from the surrounding five
countries (Austria, Czech Republic, Poland, Ukraine and Hungary) into Slovakia.

Four international airports: M R Štefánik Airport in Bratislava, Barca Airport
in Košice, Poprad-Tatry Airport and Sliač Airport bring visitors to Slovakia from
all parts of the globe. There is also Schwechat Airport in Vienna, only 64km from
Bratislava, giving travellers another option. Visitors can also arrive by boat or
hydrofoil along the Danube heading downstream from Vienna or upstream from
Budapest.

✈ **BY AIR** Travellers to Slovakia are lucky as they have two options of airport –
Bratislava and Vienna airports (only 64km/40 miles apart) – giving more variety
of route, cost, timing and budget flight options. Ticket prices to Bratislava/Vienna
will be higher during the peak summer season (June–August) and at Christmas
and New Year. The airports at Košice offer air links to Bratislava providing a
gateway to Slovakia's eastern regions, and Poprad-Tatry which now offers direct
flights to the UK on SkyEurope airlines.

Discount travel websites such as www.cheapflights.co.uk, www.expedia.com
and www.lastminute.co.uk can offer bargain flights.

From the UK

Austrian Airlines ℡ 02 7434 7350; www.aua.com.
Flies London Heathrow to Vienna followed by 45min
fast road or rail connection to Bratislava.
Czech Airlines Štúrova 13; ℡ 02 5296 1325; f 02
5296 1070; e bts@czechairlines.com; www.csa.cz or
www.czechairlines.com. Flies London to Bratislava
via Prague.
Lufthansa www.lufthansa.co.uk. Has some special
deals on flights to Bratislava. Comfortable Airline
which offers flights to Bratislava. Daily from London
Heathrow, Manchester, Edinburgh & Birmingham.
Ryanair www.ryanair.com. Flies London Stansted
to Bratislava twice daily; prices from £5.99
(excluding taxes).
SkyEurope ℡ 020 7365 0365; www.skyeurope.com.

The Slovak budget airline flies between London
Stansted & Bratislava, Manchester & Bratislava & also
London Stansted & Poprad-Tatry.
Wizzair Call centre (Budapest) +361 470 9499;
www.wizzair.com. One of central Europe's largest
low-cost carriers, Wizzair has made Bratislava one
of its operating bases, launching flights to 13
destinations including London & Cork from
Bratislava's M R Štefánik Airport in spring 2007.
From spring 2007, Wizzair offers flights from
Bratislava to new destinations such as Dortmund,
Eindhoven, Liverpool, Malmo & Stockholm, as well
as a number of destinations already served by other
carriers such as Athens, Barcelona, Brussels, London,
Paris & Rome.

From the Irish Republic

SkyEurope ℡ 020 7365 0365; www.skyeurope.com.
Flights from Dublin to Bratislava with very

reasonable prices.

From the US There are no direct flights from the US to Bratislava; instead fly to
Amsterdam, London or Frankfurt and then get a low-cost flight to Bratislava. Also
you could fly to Vienna then go by land (shuttle bus) to Bratislava. Eight buses a
day stop at Vienna Schwechat International Airport *en route* to Bratislava; the
journey takes just over an hour. An option for travelling to Slovakia is Prague-

Ruzyné Airport. The Czech national carrier, CSA, has a regular service to Prague from Newark and Montréal. These flights generally have direct connections from Prague to Bratislava that take about an hour.

Bratislava MR Štefánik Airport (BTS/LZIB) Bratislava's international M R Štefánik Airport (*www.letiskobratislava.sk*) is connected by daily flights to many European destinations, such as Košice, Prague, Split, Milan, Zurich, Munich, Berlin, Stuttgart, Zadar and Dubrovnik. Many of these flights are provided by SkyEurope. For more information call (24 hours a day); ❧ +421 2 4857 3353. The airport central information office telephone number is ❧ +421 2 3303 3353.

In February 2006 was sold by the Slovak government to a consortium TwoOne led by the airport in neighbouring Vienna.

Poprad-Tatry Airport (TAT) Poprad-Tatry Airport (TAT) (❧ *052 7763 875;* e *airport@pp.sknet.sk; www.airport-poprad.sk*) is situated 5km from town, and is the gateway to the Tatras, Fatras and the eastern region of Slovakia. SkyEurope (*www.skyeurope.com*) has scheduled flights between Poprad-Tatry Airport and London Stansted by Boeing 737 every Wednesday and Saturday. Ryanair is expected to start flying to Poprad-Tatry soon.

Košice Barca Airport (KSC/LZKZ) Košice Airport (❧ *055 6832 123;* e *secretariat@ airportkosice.sk; www.airportkosice.sk*) is 10km west of the city centre. Taxis take 15 minutes and buses are also available. SkyEurope (*reservation centre in Slovakia;* ❧ *02 4850 4850*) connects Košice with London Stansted, Amsterdam, Paris, Rome, Milan and more via Bratislava. Austrian Airlines also flies twice daily Vienna to Košice.

Sliač Airport (SLD) The international airport at Sliác (❧ *045 5443 323, 045 5442 592;* e *handling@airportsliac.sk; www.airportsliac.sk*), historically known as Three oaks (Tri duby) is situated in the centre of Slovakia, between Zvolen and Banská Bystrica. Czech Airlines fly Prague–Sliač six times a week with the 45-seater ATR 42.

Military aircraft use Sliač and in the summer, eight local travel agencies use charter airlines to fly holidaymakers from Sliač to Bourgas, a Bulgarian Black Sea resort. Hron Air (formerly Tatra Air) flies Prague–Sliač daily and in March 2007 launched a regular Poprad–Sliač–Prague route in a 33-seater SAAB 340 plane.

Direct flights to Vienna Schwechat International Airport (VIE) Vienna International Airport (Schwechat) is only 64km from Bratislava and can be used as a gateway for international travellers. Information (24hrs); ❧ +43 1 7007 2233; www.viennaairport.com.

Air Berlin www.airberlin.com. Offers some very good-value tickets to Vienna from London Stansted. **Austrian Airlines** ❧ 020 7434 7350; www.aua.com.

Flies from London Heathrow to Vienna 5 times a day. The Austrian Airlines Group is revitalising links from Vienna to Bratislava.

🚆 **BY TRAIN** If you don't fancy flying, or want to stop off *en route*, try the train. First cross the channel by Eurostar (*www.eurostar.com*). Slovak State Railways (ŽSR or Železnice Slovenskej Republiky) (*www.zsr.sk*) has information in English about train connections. The most convenient route to the Slovak Republic from western Europe is via Vienna or Prague. You'll arrive at Bratislava's main railway station, *hlavná stanica*, a bustling centre of life. Bratislava is connected to all the major cities in central Europe: Budapest, Vienna, Brno, Prague and Krakow.

Rail passes Interrail (*www.interrail.com*) divides Europe up into a number of zones. Passes for adults (over 26) cost from £206 (for 16 days' travel in Zone D: Slovakia, Czech Republic, Hungary, Poland, Croatia, Bosnia) to £393 for one month's journey around a possible 28 countries of Europe. Under-26 year olds can get a youth ticket costing £140–277 for the same parameters. Remember that an Interrail pass is not valid in the holder's country of residence. Passes can be bought from the Rail Europe Travel Centre (*178 Piccadilly, London W1;* ☏ *0870 830 2000;* e *reservations@raileurope.co.uk;* *www.raileurope.co.uk*). You cannot buy a London–Bratislava train ticket online because it involves more than three changes. It's really better to fly.

BY COACH Check out Eurolines (*in Bratislava;* ☏ *02 5542 4870, in London;* ☏ *0870 514 3219; www.eurolines.com or www.nationalexpress.co.uk*) although the 31-hour journey is totally exhausting and unlikely to be cheaper than a budget flight. Two companies manage Coach Line Bratislava–Vienna: SkyEurope Airlines and Eurolines.

The Slovak national bus company (Slovenská autobusová doprava) (*www.sad.sk*) is abbreviated rather mournfully as SAD. Bratislava bus station is at Mlynské nivy 21, ten minutes' walk from the city centre. More information can be found on www.dpb.sk.

BY CAR You need motorway stickers for toll payments. See www.viamichelin.co.uk for details of routes. It is about 1,500km by road from London to Bratislava and a non-stop journey would take more than 18 hours. The route, once on the continent, goes via Dunkerque, Brussels, Leuven, Aachen, Cologne, Frankfurt and Linz.

The road signs correspond to European norms. The speed limit in the cities and villages is 60km/h, outside the cities and villages 90km/h, and on highways 130km/h. Safety belts must also be used in cities. Drivers are strictly prohibited from drinking alcohol.

Car rental For international companies see pages 74–5, for local car-hire companies see page 77.

Car-rental companies like Hertz, Avis and Europcar have offices in most major cities: Bratislava, Poprad, Prešov, Košice, Nitra, Žilina, Banská Bystrica, Trenčín and Trnava.

BY HYDROFOIL Down the Danube from Vienna, upstream from Budapest (*www.lod.sk*). See page 75 for full details.

＋ HEALTH with Dr Felicity Nicholson

The standard of public health in Slovakia is very good. The tap water is potable and safe; it even has a fairly palatable taste. However, safer, cheaper and more beneficial is the mineral water (10–20Sk for a 1.5 litre bottle) available in shops, cafés, restaurants and hotel minibars.

No vaccinations are legally required but it is wise to be up to date with routine vaccinations such as **diphtheria, tetanus** and **polio. Hepatitis A** should also be considered. For those who are going to be working in hospitals or in close contact with children, a **hepatitis B** vaccination is recommended. Rabid deer and foxes roam the Slovak countryside so pre-exposure **rabies** vaccine (ideally three doses given over a minimum of 21 days) should also be considered for anyone who is going to be working with animals. More rarely typhoid vaccine may be recommended for workers in refugee camps, those staying in poorer areas and during outbreak situations. The sun is very strong in central Europe. Take a supply of suntan lotion and after-sun care, or look in the local shopping mall. The air content is relatively good as there is not so much heavy industry in Slovakia, however almost everybody smokes heavily and the concept of non-smoking areas in restaurants has been slow to catch on.

The cuisine is very heavy on the meat and fat, and locals have already joined the world trend towards obesity. A survey in 2006 revealed that Slovaks do not eat enough fruit, vegetables or dairy products. People in east and south Slovakia have the worst eating habits, while the best results were in Košice and Bratislava.

Cases of bovine spongiform encephalopathy (**mad cow disease**) have been reported in cattle in Slovakia. To avoid risk don't try the often-offered beef tartare which involves raw meat spread on toast. Alcoholism is not as widespread as in neighbouring countries, however with the availability of powerful, cheap spirits, it's sensible to watch your intake.

Cases of the H5N1 '**bird flu**' virus were found in a duck and a falcon at Bratislava and Gabčíkovo in early 2006 and protection surveillance zones were set up around the sites where the dead birds were found. The Slovak government also banned the sale of poultry in markets.

People don't swim in the Danube because of the strong current and pollution, but Slovakia is dotted throughout with lakes and reservoirs where the water is refreshing and clean (Senec, Orava, Liptovská Mara and the Slovak Sea, Zemplínska Šírava). **Mosquitoes** are irritating; the Danube in summer is plagued by the little devils. If you stay on one of the three botels (hotels on a boat), take a good supply of insect repellent and cream.

If you intend to go walking or cycling in the countryside remember that a tick bite can cause the potentially deadly disease **encephalitis**. The TBE- (tick-borne encephalitis) infected tick population is now endemic in 16 European countries including Slovakia, Austria and Hungary. Vaccination against tick-borne encephalitis may be available in the UK (on a named patient basis) and comprises a series of three injections that can be done over three to four weeks. Take advice from your doctor or a reputable travel clinic. Whether you are immunised or not you should make sure that you wear suitable clothing, such as long trousers tucked into boots and a hat and use tick repellents. Ticks should ideally be removed as soon as possible as leaving ticks on the body increases the chance of infection. They should be removed with special tick tweezers that can be bought in good travel shops. Failing that you can use your fingernails by grasping the tick as close to your body as possible and pulling steadily and firmly away at right angles to your skin. The tick will then come away complete as long as you do not jerk or twist. If possible douse the wound with alcohol (any spirit will do) or iodine. Irritants (eg: Olbas oil) or lit cigarettes are to be discouraged since they can cause the ticks to regurgitate and therefore increase the risk of disease. It is best to get a travelling companion to check you for ticks and if you are travelling with small children remember to check their heads, and particularly behind the ears. If you think you have been bitten by a tick then seek medical advice locally, as treatment following exposure may be available. Tell the doctor whether or not you have been immunised.

Tick alert (*www.masta.org/tickalert*) has more information.

THE EUROPEAN HEALTH INSURANCE CARD Slovakia has one of the cheapest and most professional health services in the world. Tourists with health insurance

will be well cared for and those from EU countries need to carry an electronic card (European Health Insurance Card – EHIC) which replaced the E111 form guaranteeing free healthcare. UK citizens should ask for this card at their local social security or sickness insurance offices. UK residents can apply for the EHIC card online at the Department of Health website (*www.ehic.org.uk*). It can also be obtained from the post office with form T7. The card is free so avoid those websites that charge for processing the application. The card is valid in 28 European countries, however the kind of treatment you can access varies from country to country, according to their healthcare policies and their arrangements with the UK. Everyone travelling to Slovakia should take out travel insurance, even for a short weekend break. The UK Foreign & Commonwealth Office has a website for its 'Know Before You Go' campaign (*www.fco.gov.uk/health*), giving advice on all aspects of travel.

TRAVEL CLINICS AND HEALTH INFORMATION A full list of current travel clinic websites worldwide is available from the International Society of Travel Medicine on www.istm.org. For other journey preparation information, consult www.tripprep.com. Information about various medications may be found on www.emedicine.com.

MEDICAL INSURANCE FOR FOREIGNERS IN THE SLOVAK REPUBLIC
Foreigners can be insured in Slovakia. As a general instruction, every doctor is obliged to provide treatment in case of need. For more detailed information about the provision of assistance in Slovakia enquire at an insurance office in your home country. More information is available at Union (*Tolstého 7, Bratislava;* ⟍ *02 5443 4225*).

PHARMACIES For minor ailments, a visit to the nearest pharmacy (*lekáreň*) may suffice. Every town in Slovakia has dozens of pharmacies, some opening until late and some offering a 24-hour emergency service.

SPAS Those central Europeans in the know are wildly enthusiastic about the curative powers of spa waters. Slovakia offers a great wealth of curative springs, thermal spas, climatic health resorts and natural mineral waters. There are 23 spa towns officially recognised by the state authorities. Check out the *Spas and thermal pools* section on page 53 for more details and also see the relevant chapters for added information on each spa.

SAFETY

Slovakia is an extremely safe country with a low rate of violent crime. However, in the capital, Bratislava, and larger cities there are incidences of petty theft. Pickpockets operate around the main tourist areas, railway stations and in large shopping malls and foreigners are easily identified and targeted. Cameras, mobile phones and small electrical items (computers, games, etc) are as attractive as cash and credit cards. Take sensible precautions against bag snatching and mugging. Do not leave valuables unattended or anything on show in a hire car.

You will see many homeless in Bratislava, sitting outside Tesco, on Námestie SNP and on Hviezdoslavovo námestie but almost none outside the capital.

Some towns and villages in eastern Slovakia are 100% Roma ghettos and wary of outsiders. Be on your guard if hitchhiking. (See the *Hostel Horror* box on page 40.) You must carry your passport with you at all times as identification. Keep it

Gordon Rattray (www.able-travel.com)

Although there is not yet enough effective legislation in Slovakia to enable complete accessibility, disability bodies are pushing for this and recent European Union entry has helped speed up the process. If you want to thoroughly explore the country, you may need to compromise somewhat, but with some effort a rewarding visit is possible for all.

ACCOMMODATION Many hotels have ground floor rooms and lifts, but only top of the range establishments can boast facilities to suit all abilities; Bratislava's Holiday Inn (see page 79) even has a lift into the swimming pool. The more adventurous your itinerary, or the smaller your budget, the more basic your lodgings will be. Tour operators and travel agents should be able to give you an idea of what to expect, and independent adventurers can discuss their needs with proprietors in advance by email.

GETTING AROUND

By air Bratislava airport has aisle chairs, trained staff, wheelchairs and accessible toilets. When booking your ticket, it is essential that you state any help you will need then and there and check your ticket is marked correctly when it arrives.

By bus and train In Bratislava there are only a few buses designed to cope with wheelchairs, and rail travel is equally inaccessible, with a five-day advance booking necessary on the only fully accessible routes (those to Prague and Vienna). Therefore, unless you are at least partially ambulant, you will need to depend on a lot of help to use these services.

By taxi and hire car The following taxi companies can provide 'barrier free' services to and from Bratislava airport, although there is no guarantee that vehicles with lifts or ramps will be available.

safe, in a zipped-up pocket or secure bag and keep a photocopy of the details separately in case you do lose it. Contact your embassy in Bratislava immediately if you do lose your passport; the embassy contact list is on pages 26–7.

Check restaurant bills: restaurants are legally required to provide a receipt from the electronic till. Taxi drivers have a reputation for ripping off foreigners, and be wary when taking a taxi from the main railway station as I have heard some depressing accounts of outrageous overcharging. Taking photographs of anything that could be perceived as a military establishment or somehow of security interest used to be a problem but everyone's much more relaxed now.

When driving, remember there is a zero tolerance of alcohol and hand-held mobile phone use is also illegal. There are on-the-spot fines for speeding or drinking.

When walking around at night, avoid the stations or deserted parts of town. Travellers with darker skin colour should be aware that there is a nasty rash of nationalist skinheads in parts of Bratislava, Žilina and other more industrial towns. They tend to be spotty nerds who focus on what they see as historical injustices but they would not be pleasant to encounter in a dark alley.

For emergency telephone numbers see page 61.

WOMEN ON THEIR OWN Slovak men are courteous, if a little old-fashioned regarding women. Feminism is still a strange, new concept and women on their own are more pitied than pestered.

Štefan Homola ⟍ 0903 462 598
Tibor Pupák ⟍ 0905 320 686
Ján Sekáč ⟍ 0905 632 807
P Pavol ⟍ 0907 767 690

I found no car hire companies providing vehicles suitable for disabled drivers. Scott Rains (quadriplegic wheelchair user) said, 'our travels required a rental car. Germany had the nearest rental agencies offering cars with hand controls so we picked up a regular rental car in Vienna and my sister did all the driving.'

PUBLIC BUILDINGS & ATTRACTIONS Many banks, post offices and libraries are accessible to a degree, although you may need to take a detour around the rear of the building to find a ground level entrance or a door that is wide enough.

Some museums and recreation facilities do have lifts, ramps and facilities for visitors with visual and hearing problems, and it is commonplace for disabled people and their assistants to enter at a reduced rate or free of charge. Scott Rains remarked, 'tourist sites are sparsely visited early in the season and I found staff more than willing to help me around their wheelchair obstacle courses.'

TOUR OPERATORS Enjoy Slovakia (⟍ *+421 33 6409026;* f *+421 33 6409029;* e *info@slovakiatravel.com; www.slovakiatravel.com*) is an operator based in Slovakia, and although they cater more to the general market, they can provide first hand information about accessibility.

FURTHER INFORMATION The National Council of People with Disabilities in Slovakia has drawn up extensive lists of accessible hotels, museums and recreation facilities, and these can be obtained from Gordon Rattray (e *gordon@able-travel.com*).

POLICE

POLICE In Slovakia, the police are badly paid and susceptible to bribes. They will often set up road checks and target cars with a foreign number plate. Foreigners are allowed to drive in Slovakia as long as they have a valid licence from their home country and have been in Slovakia for less than 30 days. If you have been speeding or have committed a traffic infraction, the police can fine you up to 500Sk on the spot, or to take you to the station and fine you up to 2,000Sk. Ask for a receipt for the fine; if nothing appears, ask for the policeman's badge number. If you intend to stay in Slovakia for more than 30 days, you must hold an international driver's licence valid for Europe.

TERRORISM There is a continuous police presence outside Bratislava's US embassy on Hviezdoslavovo námestie, next to the Radisson SAS Carlton Hotel. This has been in operation since the Bush–Putin summit (February 2005) when security was stepped up, but fortunately these are the only signs a visitor will see. You will only undergo a security check when entering certain government offices, airports and embassies.

There have been no terrorist attacks in Slovakia. Slovakia is a very small player on the international scene and there are no cities with more than 500,000 inhabitants. Nevertheless the threat of terrorism is taken seriously and all necessary preventive measures are in place. On 11 June 2005, Reuters reported that a suicide bomber blew himself up outside the Slovak embassy in Baghdad; he was reportedly targeting a meeting of agents of the US Central Intelligence

Agency at the embassy. As a member of NATO and the allied coalition, Slovakia has sent troops to Iraq and Afghanistan.

WHAT TO TAKE

Back in the bad old days, visitors to the 'wild east' had to pack a squash ball with their toiletries to plug up the gaping hole in the bathroom sink. Fortunately such brutalities are a thing of the past. The two-pin electrical plugs are still problematic, however you can find adaptors plus everything and anything else you might need in Bratislava and all other large towns.

A swimming costume is a good idea for all visitors, as the country has many spas, thermal pools and lido complexes. Many of the historic towns are best explored on foot, so pack some comfortable shoes and perhaps an anorak for the occasional, unexpected summer shower. Winters can be chilly and summers stifling so choose clothes accordingly. The mountains are significant skiing and hiking venues: take sturdy walking boots, water, a whistle and snacks. (See page 54.)

There are no restaurants in Slovakia that require a dinner jacket, but some exclusive eateries, casinos and nightclubs require a certain degree of smartness.

Take out comprehensive travel insurance before your trip to cover lost baggage, theft and medical emergencies, and bring photocopies of the documentation with you.

Although Slovakia is still a cash-based system, take back-up travellers' cheques and a secreted credit/debit card for topping up at the many ATMs (auto teller machines) that can be found all across the country (www.zbk.sk has a database of ATMs in Slovakia, although you will have to decipher the Slovak-language site).

If you lose money, your family can send extra to Western Union offices, also found throughout Slovakia. Tatrabank (*www.tatrabanka.sk*) has the facility in all its branches.

In Slovakia, you are supposed to carry your passport or identity card at all times. Take extra passport photos for extended travel passes and make extra copies of your passport, driving licence and insurance documents to leave in the hotel safe. You'll need a passport for many transactions: mobile phone SIM cards, gym/spa membership and when checking into your hotel.

Eye patches purloined from long-haul flights are helpful as many hotels have flimsy curtains and earplugs could be advisable if staying in a hotel or botel favoured by stag partyers.

Bear in mind that Slovakia, along with its big sister the Czech Republic, is famous for brewing some of the best beer in the world. The wines and spirits also merit serious investigation.

Pack a penknife with corkscrew and bottle opener, but remember not to take such an implement in hand luggage on planes but in checked-in luggage.

Slovak cuisine is hearty and rib-sticking. Bearing all these factors in mind, it might be a good idea to pack extra supplies of headache and indigestion tablets.

ELECTRICITY

Slovakia's electrical current is 220 Volts/50Hz, accessible via the European two-pin plug. Plug adaptors for use with three-pronged plugs are generally available from large supermarkets and chemists throughout Slovakia. Light bulbs are usually the screw-type.

MONEY After the split of Czechoslovakia in 1993, the National Bank of Slovakia introduced new banknotes and coins. Slovakia's basic currency unit is the crown (koruna), with smaller sums denominated in haliers (halier). Coins come in denominations of 1, 2, 5 and 10 crowns and now only 50 haliers; bills in denominations of 20, 50, 100, 200, 500, 1,000 and 5,000 crowns. One koruna equals 100 haliers (haliers are of very little value and not used much any more: the 50h piece is the only legal tender).

The Slovak Republic became a member of the European Union on 1 May 2004 and is expected to join the Schengen Visa System (due October 2007) and Euro Monetary System (due 2008–09).

However, many top restaurants and hotels accept the euro and often list their prices in euro, while referring back to the base unit of Slovak koruna. The current exchange rate (Feb 2007) is £1 = 50Sk, US$1 = 25Sk, €1 = 34Sk.

For information on banks, exchanging currency, ATMs and travellers' cheques, see pages 36–7.

BUDGETING You can still find great bargains in Slovakia, although Bratislava is more expensive than the rest of the country. However, you can also go to the other end of the scale and have a right royal blow-out. Everyone will find something to suit their taste and purse and your money will go further in shops, restaurants, hotels and on public transport than in the west. The following guide lists daily budgets for one person, based on two people sharing accommodation (and therefore paying slightly less on the room, but not the beer bill...).

Penny-pinching You can probably get by on a budget of around 900Sk (£15/US$28/€23) for a hostel dorm, eating in one of the self-service canteens (*jedaleň*), entry to a few museums and rounded off by a meal with drinks in a modest pub.

Modest You'll spend about 1,500Sk (£26/US$47/€39) a day if you want basic accommodation in a two-star hotel, cheered on by occasional treats; the cheapest opera tickets are from 380Sk/€10 although you can get last-minute tickets for as little as €2.

Comfortable A daily allowance of 3,500Sk (£60/US$111/€91) will allow a stay in a three-star hotel, some sightseeing, stops for coffee, cake and beer, a meal in a decent restaurant, late-night drinks in a club and a taxi back to base.

Luxurious On a daily stipend of 6,000Sk (£104/US$190/€156) you can stay in one of the top four-star hotels in the city centre, drink cocktails, eat like a lord, purchase some glassware or ceramics, wind down by taking a cable car up a mountain for a coffee and spectacular view, then back to town to a swish restaurant and on to a jazz club for some chill-out sounds.

A royal splurge The wallet could be as much as 10,000Sk (£174/US$317/€260) a day lighter if you're going to go berserk and Bratislava's about the only place in Slovakia that you could do this. Book into one of the top trio of hotels, take your pick from the designer shops along Michalská and Ventúrska, take a trip out to the Small Carpathian Wine Route, dine out at Le Monde and splash out on more vintage white wines, including a Slovak Tokaj. Get the best seats in the house at the opera and then gamble what's left in your pocket at one of the four classy casinos.

2

TIPPING Tipping is standard practice in restaurants, cafés, bars and pubs. It is called *prepitné* (for a drink) in Slovak. To calculate a tip it is best to round off the figure to the nearest 10Sk (koruna). However, if two beers came to 58Sk, giving 60Sk is a bit mean, when it's just over €2, so round it up to 70Sk. The standard rate is around 10–15% and say the amount you are giving when you pay, don't just leave it on the table. In taxis, round the figure up to the nearest 50Sk or 100Sk (if it's over 50Sk) or calculate 10–15% percent. Saying *d'akujem* (thank you) when you hand over any money is a good way of adding in the tip but must be done with extreme care as it means 'I don't want any change back, thank you'.

EXCHANGING CURRENCY AND TRAVELLERS' CHEQUES ATMs have sprouted up all over Slovakia and, as a result, travellers' cheques are becoming less and less convenient. Change cash and travellers' cheques at proper banks or bureaux de change as kiosks offer poor exchange rates. Thomas Cook, American Express and Visa travellers' cheques are accepted at all larger banks (VÚB, Tatra Banka, Slovenská Sporiteľňa) and exchange offices. The exchange fee is in the range of at least 1% of the face value of the cheque. If your money is lost or stolen you can arrange for friends or relatives in the UK to transfer money through Western Union to the Tatra Banka. Call Western Union in the UK (❜ *0800 833 833*) for information. International accounts can be drawn from at an ATM on a bank's exterior wall, usually marked 'Bankomat'.

VISA TRAVELMONEY Visa TravelMoney (*Travelex;* ❜ *020 7837 9580;* e *customerservices@travelex.com*) is a convenient, safe alternative to carrying piles of cash or cheques. The system is based on a pre-paid travel card that allows holders 24-hour access to their money in any local currency. You load up the card with funds before your trip and draw the cash out as you go along from an ATM. When you've used up your funds simply throw the card away.

CREDIT CARDS Major credit cards (American Express, Diners Club, Visa and MasterCard/Eurocard) and debit cards (Maestro and Visa Electron) may be used to withdraw cash from automatic dispensers of major banks (VÚB, TatraBanka, Slovenská Sporiteľňa) and for payments in larger hotels, restaurants, shops and petrol stations. Smaller shops, museums and ticket offices outside the capital may be reluctant to accept credit cards, so keep some koruna handy.

DISCOUNT CARDS The International Student Discount Card (ISIC) or International Youth Travel Card (for students under 26) will entitle you to reductions on entry to many museums, galleries and other attractions, and on journeys on some public transport networks. Concessionary rates for pensioners apply – in theory – to EU nationals. However, deep in the Slovak countryside, explanations can get lost in translation. Show a passport and try an official-melting smile.

BANKS Banking services are provided in Bratislava by both Slovak and foreign banks. Inside banks visitors can use the exchange offices during office hours which are usually Monday–Thursday 08.00–17.00, Friday 08.00–15.00, and ATMs on the outer walls or within a secure room reached with a swipe card. The most frequently accepted credit cards are MasterCard and Visa. Businesses are usually open Monday–Friday 09.00–17.00. The website www.banky.sk gives advice on Slovak banks. The website www.zbk.sk has a database of ATMs throughout Slovakia (in Slovak). Click on 'zoznam bankomatov'.

ČSOB (Československá obchodná banka). *Open Mon–Thu 08.00–17.00, Fri 08.00–16.00.*

TB (TatraBanka) www.tatrabanka.sk. Has a list of ATMs and where to find them.

GETTING AROUND

Public transport in Slovakia is reliable and cheap; most towns and villages can be accessed one way or another. Sometimes bus is better than train and vice versa. The transport network has many idiosyncrasies and the main Bratislava–Košice train line does a huge loop into the mountains. However, it's efficient although crowded. The far eastern region is best explored by car.

&. **IN A WHEELCHAIR** Slovakia is not very wheelchair-friendly. Many towns have winding, cobbled streets which can make for a bumpy, uncomfortable ride. The mountain regions and resorts in the north, whilst an ideal destination for hikers and skiers, are not designed with wheelchairs in mind and some hotels do not even have a lift to their upper floors. Having said that, almost every larger town has a restored centre with a pedestrian heart built of smooth concrete, but side/back streets are riddled with pot-holes and bumps to make getting around a tiring and tiresome procedure. Every bank and many hotels have an entrance ramp and lifts to floors, however many restaurants are situated in inaccessible cellars or up the side of a mountain. Almost all the spa hotels are designed for visitors with limited mobility and have a range of facilities and treatments. Two intrepid readers who got a wheelchair onto a Bratislava tram said it's only possible if someone strong hauls the wheelchair up the very steep steps and on board. People always come to assist, but it's hard going. On trains, wheelchairs and their users have to travel in the luggage van, after negotiating more vertiginous steps. See box on pages 33–4 for more information.

☞ *POZOR!* Pedestrians should approach busy roads with care. Car drivers are unwilling to stop at zebra crossings, so step off the pavement at your own peril and never in front of an approaching car unless you're following a nun, a heavily pregnant lady or a tiny child.

&. **HITCHHIKING** Hitchhiking in Slovakia is called *autostop*. It's not so common these days, but spotted around university towns when students go home at weekends. As in all European countries, women travellers should avoid hitching alone. Prospective hitchers hold up a piece of cardboard with their destination as an abbreviated town name, eg: BA – Bratislava, TT – Trnava, TN – Trenčín, KE – Košice, PO – Prešov, NR – Nitra, MT – Martin, ZA – Žilina, PP – Poprad, LM – Liptovský Mikuláš and BB – Banská Bystrica.

&. **BY BICYCLE** An elaborate 5,400km network of cycle routes and regions criss-crosses Slovakia. The Slovak Cyclist Association (SCK) administers a uniform system of marking the routes. A sign featuring a large capital 'C' and a figure on a bike appears and on larger signs one or two destinations are indicated. The colour coding refers to the type of route. A red 'C' denotes a long-distance route or main route (*magistrála*). The other three colours are regional routes: a blue 'C' denotes a parallel route, a green 'C' means a shorter route, one suitable for all the family, while a yellow 'C' indicates a short, connecting route.

✈ **BY AIR** It can be more convenient and pleasant to fly between Bratislava and Poprad or Košice out in the 'far east' of Slovakia. If you have already 'done' Bratislava and western Slovakia, or you specifically want a ski, hiking or spa family holiday, you can fly direct from London Stansted to Poprad with SkyEurope airlines. You can also fly from Bratislava to Košice and explore the southeast region.

BY TRAIN Slovakia has a dense network of 3,662km of railways. Most of these tracks form part of the network of international railways. An extensive railway network connects Slovakia with all neighbouring countries, especially the Czech Republic, Hungary and Austria. However, two-thirds of the Slovak railway network is single track and services can be slow. The most important line leaves Bratislava and loops up north around Žilina, through the Tatras and down to Košice. It's a lovely journey but it can be irritating that important cities that don't appear on this artery (Nitra, Banská Bystrica and Prešov) can be very tricky to reach by train. In the High Tatras, a sweet electric train (*električka*) leaves Poprad for the resorts in the mountains. It's extremely reliable, cheap and fun. There are some stunning views through the Tatras, along the Váh River near Žilina, on the Čierny Hron valley railway, Vychylovka steam railway and the line near Kremnica. The trains will get you to most parts of the country and tickets are excellent value at between 2Sk and 5Sk/km. If you're really keen on rail travel, get the *ŽSR cestovný poriadok* (Slovak Railway Timetable) booklet which comes out every May and is available from most bookshops and tobacconists. More information is available on the Railways of the Slovak Republic site (*www.zsr.sk*) and the Railway Company site (*www.slovakrail.sk*).

TIMETABLES

These appear incredibly complicated and bewildering until you learn a few key rules:

* *pr* or *prích* means arrivals
* *od* or *odch* means departures
* the platform or *nástupište* is divided into two *kolaj* (lines) on either side

Choose your route from the map and note down the serial number of the route, find it above a timetable on rollers behind glass at the back of the waiting room.

The main station in larger towns is *hlavná stanica* while minor stations have *zástavka* (stop) *or mesto* (town) after the name.

TRAIN ABBREVIATIONS

Os	*Osobný vlak* slow train
Mos	*Motorový osobný vlak* motorised slow train
Zr	*Zrýchlený vlak fast train*
ER	*EURegio International zrýchlený vlak* Euregion international fast train
R	*rýchlik* fast train
Ex	*Expresný vlak* express train
IC	*vlak intercity s osobitným príplatkom* intercity train with special supplementary charge
EC	*vlak eurocity* Eurocity (higher quality with supplementary charge)
†	running on Sundays and public holidays, *sviatok* (literally saints' days)
✹	running on working days

Two non-official websites (*www.cp.sk and www.busy.sk*) have good train and bus search engines in English.

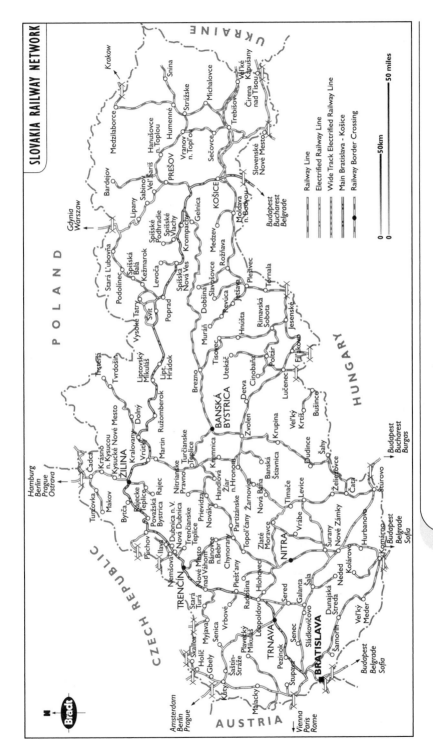

SLOVAKIA RAILWAY NETWORK

Railway Line
Electrified Railway Line
Wide Track Electrified Railway Line
Main Bratislava - Košice
Railway Border Crossing

0 50km
0 50 miles

☞ *POZOR!* When travelling on Friday evenings, public holidays, Easter and Christmas insist on a *miestenka* (seat reservation). The ticket seller will often be reluctant to sell you one and many speak only Slovak, so it can be frustrating but it is worth the fight. If possible, avoid travelling at these times altogether because the trains are so full the corridors are blocked and you may never reach your seat anyway. It's always well worth the extra 200Sk (€5) to upgrade to first class, particularly on a long journey like Bratislava to Košice. First class isn't much cleaner than second but it is less cramped. Try to avoid visiting the train toilets; they will definitely spoil your appetite and mood.

🚗 **BY CAR** Although Slovakia has an extensive rail and road network, these can be slow moving, especially local buses which run infrequently and stop at every minuscule hamlet *en route*.

Hiring a car is really the best option for exploring rural Slovakia, especially in the regions east of the towns of Prešov and Košice. The stunning countryside here is filled with wooden churches, gems of Rusyn architecture and the roads are pleasantly traffic-free, although watch out for the odd wandering cow or chicken. Driving is a pleasure in these areas, you can explore the hidden region virtually undisturbed. Hire cars are available in all large towns and the price for local car firms is significantly cheaper than for international companies. Be sure to read the small print, though. On motorways you'll need to buy a *dialnicná známka* or toll sticker (one-week sticker 174Sk, one month 347Sk) but it hardly seems worth it as there are so few motorways, and you'll probably prefer to pootle along the scenic route anyway.

When more motorways are eventually built, all the lorries and speeding drivers can go and leave the main roads to others. The big problem is that there are just not enough motorways in Slovakia. Of the total road network of 18,000km only 198km is motorway. Everyone therefore has to use the same stretch of – often narrow and winding – road: tractors, lorries, SUVs, speeding silver Mercs, psychotic white vans, ancient rusting Skodas with no powers of acceleration, and bicycles. It's totally chaotic. Slovak males view driving as an extreme sport and overtake on the brow of a hill, before a bend in a mountain road, double overtake on cliffside highways and love to tailgate.

HOSTEL HORROR

You are probably unlikely to find American teenagers hitching around Slovakia this summer. Not if they're film buffs. Most likely they will still be quivering behind the sofa after renting the DVD *Hostel*. The low-budget slasher film, directed by Eli Roth and produced by Quentin Tarantino, was a surprise hit in the US in early 2006, but Slovaks weren't so charmed by its depiction of their country as peopled with bloodthirsty sex maniacs preying on innocent young American backpackers abroad. Scenes of the youths locked in a dungeon somewhere in Slovakia, tortured with chainsaws and blowtorches and sold to sadists have annoyed the tiny nation, already exhausted by trying to lure tourists away from the beaten paths leading to Prague, Budapest and Vienna. Alžbeta Melicharová, marketing head at Slovakia's state tourist board: 'It's so sad, the events in the film are so absurd. They have nothing to do with reality. We are actually one of central Europe's safest places. It's one of our selling points.' Ironically, *Hostel* was filmed in the Czech Republic with Czech actors speaking Czech and finding their way around using signposts in Czech.

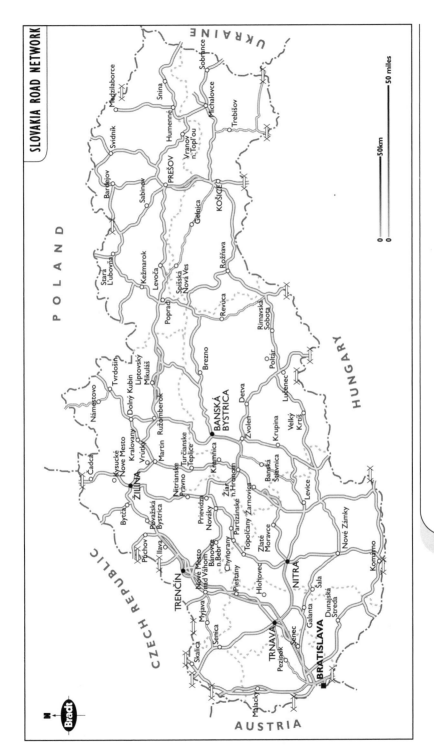

SLOVAKIA ROAD NETWORK

POLAND

UKRAINE

HUNGARY

AUSTRIA

CZECH REPUBLIC

Medzilaborce
Svidník
Bardejov
Sabinov
Snina
Humenné
PREŠOV
Vranov
n. Topľou
Sobrance
Michalovce
Trebišov
Gelnica
KOŠICE
Stará
Ľubovňa
Kežmarok
Levoča
Spišská
Nová Ves
Rožňava
Poprad
Revúca
Rimavská
Sobota
Brezno
Poltár
Tvrdošín
Námestovo
Dolný Kubín
Liptovský
Mikuláš
Ružomberok
BANSKÁ
BYSTRICA
Detva
Lučenec
Kremnica
Zvolen
Velký
Krtíš
Cadca
Kysucké
Nové Mesto
Kráľovany
Vrútky
Martin
Turčianske
Teplice
Banská
Štiavnica
Krupina
ŽILINA
Nitrianske
Pravno
Žiar
n. Hronom
Levice
Bytča
Považská
Bystrica
Prievidza
Nováky
Partizánske
Zlaté
Moravce
Nové Zámky
Púchov
Ilava
Bánovce
n. Bebr.
Topoľčany Žarnovica
NITRA
Komárno
TRENČÍN
Nové Mesto
nad Váhom
Myjava
Piešťany
Chynorany
Hlohovec
Šaľa
Skalica
Senica
Pezinok
TRNAVA
Senec
Galanta
Dunajská
Streda
Málacky
BRATISLAVA

0 ——— 50km
0 ——— 50 miles

N

Bradt

Prices

- Petrol Super plus 98 40Sk per litre
- Petrol Super Natural 95 39Sk per litre
- Petrol Special 91 38Sk per litre
- Diesel 38Sk per litre
- Intercity local train, 2nd class, average 100km journey 126Sk
- Intercity bus 100km journey 128Sk
- Parking, one hour 20–100Sk

Car rental The rates of Slovak car-rental agencies are substantially cheaper than those of western firms, ranging from 690–1,500Sk per day and the process is marked by much less red tape. Slovak companies usually charge koruna (and cheaper) while the international companies charge euro. See pages 74–5 and 77 for details of car-hire firms.

 BY BUS Comfortable Eurolines (sometimes called 'Slovaklines') coaches can be a more convenient way of reaching cities not on the main Bratislava–Košice train line: Nitra, Banská Bystrica and Skalica. Coaches depart from stands in front of the main railway station for destinations within Slovakia. Eurolines depart from the bus station for international destinations.

Bratislava main bus station Mlynské nivy 21; ↘
02 5542 2773; www.sad.sk

Eurolines/Slovaklines ↘ 02 5542 4870;
www.eurolines.sk

Prices are approx 500Sk to Košice, 400Sk to Poprad, 170Sk to Piešťany.

Some words to look out for are:

- *odchody*   departures
- *príchody*   arrivals
- *premáva...*   runs on...
- *nepremáva...*   does not run on...

 BY BOAT Slovakia has 2,372km of navigable waterways. The Danube is the main artery for transport by ship which is operated by Slovak Shipping & Ports (*www.lod.sk*). Trips can be taken along the Danube to Devín, Gabčíkovo and Komárno as well as further afield to Budapest or Vienna (see pages 75–6).

ACCOMMODATION

Since the Velvet Divorce from the Czech Republic in 1993, Slovakia has been working really hard to get its house in order. Bratislava's Old Town has had a wash and brush up and most of the hotels have also buffed up their buildings, improved amenities and gone all out to attract the anticipated flood of visitors. Many larger towns throughout Slovakia have greatly improved the quality of accommodation on offer with a superb choice of price, venue and style.

Like many in the region, the Slovak hoteliers are fixated about the star system of grading hotels, another hangover from the communist mania for point-scoring, be it ice skating or extra marks for those creepy welcome messages that spring into life on the TV screen when you enter your new bedroom.

I never met anybody who could accurately explain to me the starring system, however if you are one of those in the know, although sometimes whimsical in intent they apparently give an indication as to services, amenities and standard of interior, but sometimes it seems quite arbitrary. The Crowne Plaza in Bratislava should be a five-star hotel but it doesn't have the separate loo and bathroom and so loses a star. The AquaCity in Poprad constantly mentions how they have 'four-star amenities at three-star prices' and they do have a point, with an Olympic-sized swimming pool, a luxury wellness centre and a view to die for. The best rule is to look at the star system for price, but amenities on offer may vary incredibly. High season is generally May–October and the period over New Year. During low season rates drop by around 30%. As for paying, all the hotels listed of three-star and above accept the major credit cards; check with others first about methods of payment. The 19% VAT (DPH) is often added to the charge, but where it is extra, it is noted. Likewise, there is a city tourist tax (€0.50–1 per person per night), which some hotels add on after and some include. Advance reservations, group bookings, and stays of more than one night will bring room charges down, and with the hot competition for guests, almost all hotels above three stars offer discounted deals on weekend breaks. If travelling independently, keep an eye on websites like www.lastminute.com and www.expedia.com.

HORSKÝ HOTELS A *horský hotel* is a mountain hotel and these vary from a modest family-run chalet in a great location to a superb hunting lodge hidden in the hills. These hotels are often attached to a ski resort or situated in the middle of a superb hiking area. These are great if you have your own transport.

PENSIONS AND INNS Pensions are popular with many travellers as they are often smaller and cheaper than regular hotels and have a family atmosphere missing in a big international venue. Some are more basic, others quite luxurious. All provide clean, modern rooms with en-suite bathroom and/or shower. Some have restaurants which can hold their own against the best in town. If it calls itself a *hotel garni* it means it doesn't have its own restaurant and offers only a simple bed and breakfast

PRIVATE APARTMENTS Staying with a family is a great way to get an idea of how Slovaks live. In some scenic villages such as Terchová the possibilities line the street and there are more private apartments than you can shake a stick at.

HOSTELS These are usually only open in the summer when the students are out of town. If you're on a tight budget it's worth looking around in the student towns and finding out where the campuses are located. Major student towns are Bratislava, Nitra, Trnava, Žilina, Košice and Banská Bystrica.

CHATA *Chata* are mountain refuges where you can turn up in the evening after a hard day's hike and stay in pretty basic accommodation, but at least you're not left stranded on a deserted mountainside. In the Liptov region and environs *chata* can also refer to a smaller pension in the mountain region, also called *chalupa* (cottage). I've also seen the term *chata* used for a chalet-style bungalow on a campsite.

CAMPSITES Slovakia is covered with campsites. These are often situated right next to, or in a well-appointed thermal lido complex. Inside the *termálne kúpalisko* (thermal lido) there will usually be a variety of accommodation opportunities from little *chata* to caravan parks to campsites.

Láska ide cez žalúdok (*Love goes through the stomach*)

FOOD Slovak cuisine is a mélange of central European influences, taking a bit of everything from its neighbours: goulash from the Magyars, strudels and schnitzels from the Austrians and dumplings from the Germans. Slovak chefs are expertly trained in the meat, potato and cabbage school of cooking, and finding something a little lighter will involve hunting down a restaurant with an international menu, or at least one that does lighter versions of the sturdy traditional dishes. Fortunately, Slovak cuisine is not as stodgy and bland as that in the Czech Republic and due to the culinary influence of southern neighbours, it has a perkier, spicier tang. A hundred years ago, most Slovaks lived on and from the land and sturdy peasant cooking still dominates the national psyche. This is the land of cabbage, caraway seeds, cheese, wheat flour, potatoes, and endless variations on a theme of pork. However, after a day hiking through the High Tatras or visiting castle ruins, such hearty fare can be just the thing.

After 1,000 years under Magyar domination and 40 years of communism, Slovakia's restaurant culture remains in its infancy, although in Bratislava and larger towns such as Košice, Nitra, Žilina and Prešov they are catching on quickly. Gourmet restaurants can now be found all over the country, sometimes in the most unexpected places. Petr Říha and Dana Říhova's Nostalgie restaurant in Spišská Nová Ves constantly receives rave reviews and in distant Prešov, Ludwig restaurant and Monika Uličná's Carpe Diem set a high standard of dining. Gourmets can combine feasting with appetite-inducing exercise at the ski resort of Jasná where celebrity chef Vojtech Artz reigns in the kitchen of the Hotel Tri Studničky. Most Slovak chefs still follow the traditional methods and sturdy ingredients but be prepared for some delicious surprises.

Many restaurants place copies of the menu by the front door on the outside wall, so you can get an idea of the food and the prices before you venture in. This is not compulsory, but because of a 'good local habit' to be helpful. It also gives restaurants the chance of showing their wares in the hope of tempting visitors to enter. Big-name restaurants don't have to do it, as they rely on their considerable reputation. All restaurants in Slovakia are required by law to issue a printed receipt from the electronic cash register, so if you have any concerns over the bill, make sure you get one. Major credit cards are usually accepted in larger venues around the country but not in little towns in the eastern regions. Always check first, before launching into the champagne and chateaubriand steak for two.

Breakfast (*raňajky*) at home is bread with butter, cheese, ham, sausage, eggs, peppers and tomatoes, jam and yoghurt, washed down with tea with lemon or strong coffee.

Some new cafés in Bratislava serve pastries or local versions of croissants (*lúpačky*).

On the run, some people nibble on frankfurters (*párky*) and crescent rolls at the buffet on the way to work, followed by elevenses early at 10.00. Slovakia has excellent milk products, the yoghurts are creamy and the cheeses are also much better than most other countries in the region. The local sheep's cheese, *bryndza* is tangy and definitely worth trying, usually offered with dumplings in the traditional *bryndzové halušky* dish. *Tvaroh* is like a blend of cottage and cream cheese.

To see how Slovaks **snack**, visit the local market (*trznica*), where there'll be a variety of stalls offering pies (*buchty*), potato pancakes (*lokša*) with savoury fillings such as cabbage, poppy seed or garlic, giant deep-fried doughnuts (*langoše*) topped with sour cream or grated cheese. There are also pancakes (*palacinky*) with a choice of fillings. A Bratislava city official got into trouble for saying the national dish of Slovakia was another favourite snack: cold, shredded cod fish meat in mayonnaise. Markets are the place to see wine drinking beginning at 09.00. **Lunch** (*obed*) is the main meal of the day; a serious event of soup, followed by a substantial main course and dessert. Unless they eat out, **dinner** (*večera*) for Slovaks is a bit like breakfast, a do-it-yourself affair consisting of bread with cold meats, cheeses and pickles.

Back to the main event – *obed*. This usually begins with a soup (*polievka*). Slovak cooking is so sturdy that appetisers (*predjedlá*) are rarely required. Soups are usually thick and hearty. Cabbage soup (*kapustnica*) is one of the best-known soups, livened up with smoked pork, cream, mushrooms and sometimes plums. Garlic soup (*cesnaková polievka*) is great and often arrives in a scooped-out bread roll (*bosniak*).

☞ *POZOR!* Those with high blood pressure should be aware that every single bowl of soup I supped in Slovakia had way too much salt in it. Either the chef is in love, as the famous saying about super-saline dishes goes, or the restaurant was trying to force guests to drink more water and beer. Either way, for a soup fan it was always very disappointing that the flavour was overwhelmed by sodium chloride even in the most expensive restaurants.

Until recently, the only **vegetarian** option used to be fried cheese (*vyprážaný syr*) however that's all changed now and many places do great salads (*šalát*). Deep in the countryside they thoughtfully make a vegetarian dish (*zapekaná brokolica*), broccoli (usually deep-frozen) baked with smoked cheese. This can also have potatoes, egg or more vegetables. Look out for the *cestoviny* section, as pasta often comes without meat. The supermarkets stock an impressive range of gluten-free products and health foods. The best-known dish is *bryndzové halušky*, boiled

WHERE TO EAT AND DRINK

In Slovakia, eating and drinking venues announce themselves with words that may not be immediately recognisable. Apart from *reštaurácia* and *bufet*, the signs on establishments can leave visitors confused. Here is an explanation of some of the places to check out for food and drink:

Reštaurácia	restaurant
Jedáleň	canteen
Bufet	stand up noshing venue
Samobsluha	means 'self-service' dining
Cukráreň	patisserie (from *cukor* – sugar)
Piváreň	beer hall
Vináreň	wine tavern (literally 'wine cellar')
Kaviarieň	coffee house (from *káva* – coffee)
Koliba	a rustic country restaurant offering grilled meats (literally 'a hut')
Krčma	pub
Salaš	a basic shepherd's summer hut serving traditional fare
Herňa	a gaming house or saloon, often used in the countryside for a basic pub
Hostinec	a pub in the countryside, the centre of all life in the village

gnocchi-sized dumplings made of potato dough and served with tangy sheep's cheese and topped with bacon cubes. It's excellent for soaking up the alcohol after an evening of beer sampling, however those watching their cholesterol or waistline should not risk it more than once a week. This dish is quite often served to vegetarians, as some Slovaks don't grasp the concept of not eating meat, and anyway bacon fat isn't meat, is it?

Magyar neighbours gave Slovaks goulash (*guláš*), a hearty stew with meat (pork, beef, or both), potatoes and carrots, laced with onions, caraway seeds and paprika. *Lečo* is eaten throughout central Europe. It's a delicious concoction of tomatoes, peppers and onions, a kind of poor man's ratatouille. It can be supplemented with chopped frankfurters, a stirred-in raw egg or boiled rice.

Slovak main courses are usually based on meat (*mäso*). Pork (*bravčové*) is king here, although grilled or roast turkey (*morčacie*) and chicken (*kuracie*) are also popular. Beef (*hovädzie*) is more expensive than the other meats. Freshwater fish from local rivers such as carp (kapor) and trout (*pstruh*) can be bony but tasty. Restaurant menus give a base price for 150g then add on a charge for every 10g over. When ordering fish, tell the waiter the general size of fish you'd like. After selecting a main course, you then have to choose the side dish (*príloha*) separately: potatoes (*zemiaky*), rice (*ryža*) or a salad. Slovak restaurants charge extra for side dishes, and waiters are perturbed if you don't order one. The potatoes are always reliable and arrive baked (*zapekané zemiaky*), boiled (*varené zemiaky*), mashed (*zemiaková kaša*) or fried (*opekané zemiaky*). Chips or French fries (*hranolky*) are everywhere.

The favourite on dessert (*dezert*) menus is the pancake (*palacinky*). These have sweet fillings: chocolate (s *čokoládou*), jam (s *džemom*) or soft cheese (s *tvarohom*).

DRINK Slovak mineral water (*minerálna voda*) is delicious, cheap and contains many life-enhancing properties. Also popular are soft drinks like *kofola* (Czech cola) that's mixed with soda water and often available on draught in half-litre mugs. *Vinea* is a refreshing red or white grape juice drink sold in tall glass bottles. Local fruit juices are excellent with unusual choices like peach, pear or a lip-puckering quince variety.

For centuries under Hungarian rule, the peasant population had little access to wine (*víno*), which went to nobles, although the lower-quality stuff did serve as an everyday drink in wine-producing areas. Beer (*pivo*), the beverage of the rising burgher class, cost too much for most peasants to buy, and it was illegal to make it without a licence from the king. **Burčiak** is a young grape cider that doesn't last long, and can explode in the bottle. Try it at Pezinok and Modra festivals (see pages 121–3). Slovaks used to distil at home the produce from their orchards, creating the famous, fiery **slivovica** (plum brandy), and similar paint-stripping brews *hruškovica* (pear), *jablčkovica* (apple), *malinovica* (raspberry), *čerešňovica* (cherry), *marhuľovica* (apricot) and even *repovica* (beetroot brandy). **Borovička** is made from juniper berries and tastes a bit like gin. It's said to be the best cure for a cold. **Demänovka** is another bittersweet herbal liqueur. **Medovina** (a honey wine) used to be made in nearly every village home. This custom has dwindled although most villages still have at least one beekeeper. This mead-like drink is still served hot at Bratislava Christmas Market. There is another bizarre festive drink which the brave can try at the market. **Hriatô** is an alcoholic 'speciality' made from heated honey and goose fat, giving off a powerful aroma. It makes a good cough mixture, if you can get it down.

☞ *POZOR!* Enjoy sampling all the bizarre beverages on offer but keep in mind the Slovak proverb *Opitý sa aj starej koze klaňi* (A drunkard will bow even to an old goat) and remember there's zero tolerance for alcohol for car drivers in Slovakia.

Kde niet vína – niet lásky (Where there's no wine, there's no love)

Slovak proverb

Slovak winemaking history dates back to the 7th century BC when Celts grew vines on the hilly land northeast of Bratislava. The continental climate makes Slovakia, like Hungary, ideal for producing fruity whites (favoured by German and Austrian drinkers) and robust reds. It's still almost impossible to find *Slovenské víno* outside Slovakia but pop into local Tesco or Billa supermarkets and you'll be amazed first by the price (average 200Sk/£4 a bottle) then pleasantly stunned by the quality. The white wine is more reliable than the red and the Tokaj could be taken home as an excellent gift to sweeten up your mother-in-law. To be sure of getting something drinkable, stick to wines above 200Sk.

Words to look for on the label are *červené* (red), *biele* (white), *ružové* (rosé), *suché* (dry), *sladké* (sweet), *akostné* (quality), *výber* (choice) and *vína s prívlastkom* (wine with a special attribute).

☞**POZOR!** You can only buy *Tokaj* in Slovakia. The EU doesn't allow Slovakia to export it due to a dispute with Hungary over the name.

THE WHITES
Chardonnay This French variety is a popular grape in Slovakia.
Devín A new, spicy cross-variety developed by Slovak oenologists with hints of grapefruit and lemon balm.
Müller-Thurgau The most widely planted grape in Slovakia. Created by Dr Hermann Müller from the Swiss canton of Thurgau in 1882 by crossing Riesling and Silvaner grape varieties.
Pálava As in 'what a palaver'. Another new variety developed in the Czech Republic, it's a cross between Tramín and Müller-Thurgau.
Rizling Rýnsky German Riesling with a crisp, fruity finish.
Rizling Vlašský Welsch Riesling from the Champagne region of France.
Rulandské Biele French Pinot Blanc with good acids.
Sauvignon Blanc French variety popular with Slovak winemakers.
Tokaj Grapes are normally associated with Hungary, but after the 1920 Trianon treaty some got left in Slovakia when the borders were re-drawn. It's a sweet dessert wine like a Sauterne.
Tramín Gewürztraminer and very flowery.
Tramín červený (not red, despite the name) The grape's skin has a reddish tinge. Very flowery yet dry, a great accompaniment to Slovak cheeses or mountain river trout
Veltlínske zelené One of the most reliable: flowery, crisp and fresh.

THE REDS
Alibernet Cabernet Sauvignon hybrid.
Frankovka modrá Popular on the wine route, you can find it in Pezinok. This was Empress Maria Theresa's favourite wine and she called it the 'pregnancy wine' as she thought it helped her fertility. From 1767, Frankovka modrá was supplied regularly to her court from the wine-producing town of Rača.
Modrý Portugal Blauer Portugueser is lighter than most.
Neronet Like Alibernet, it's a Cabernet hybrid.
Rulandské modré Pinot Noir, an ingredient of Burgundy.
Svätovavrinecké French St Lawrence with good body.

Practical Information EATING AND DRINKING

2

I've only mentioned the most frequently encountered beers. Some pubs will have more varieties. Look out for *svetlé* (light, lager), *tmavé pivo* (dark beer) and *výčapné pivo* (draught/on-tap beer). The website www.pivo.sk is useful but only if your language skills are as good as your beer-drinking capacity. In touristy pubs and bars, particularly in stag-infested Bratislava, specify what brand of beer you'd like otherwise they'll just plonk down a half litre of the most expensive brew, which probably won't be Slovak and will thus render your 'research' meaningless. If the waiter is impressed with your Slovak skills he might enquire whether you'd like a *desaťka* (10° – about 4% alcohol), *jedenástka* (11° – about 5% alcohol) or *dvanástka* (12° – about 6% alcohol), as many of the beers come in different strengths.

SOME SLOVAK BEERS

Corgoň Produced by Heineken, rub the Corgoň's feet (a statue in Nitra) for luck.

Gambrinus Made by Šariš near Prešov.

Golem A microbrewery and restaurant in Košice since 2002.

Kaltencker Brewed at Rožňava since 1996.

Kelt Produced by Heineken.

Kláštorný ležiak From the Codecon microbrewery in Svätý Jur since 1995.

Martiner From the town of Martin originally, now produced by Heineken.

Popper A weak, light beer from Bytča, but also the powerful 16° dark Palatin.

Šariš (*svetlé* – light and *tmavé* – dark) Brewed in Velký Šariš near Prešov in eastern Slovakia (*www.saris.sk*).

Smädný Mních (Thirsty Monk) Made by Šariš.

Steiger Light and dark, and a beer called 'Hell' from a brewery founded in 1473 in Vyhne, near Banská Štiavnica (*www.steiger.sk*).

Stein (*svetlé* – light and *tmavé* – dark) Brewed in Bratislava.

Tatran Made at the Pilsberg Poprad since 1812, a refreshing lager, not too strong or wheaty (*www.pilsberg.com*).

Topvar (light, dark and alcohol-free) From Topoľčany (*www.topvar.sk*).

Velkopopovický Kozel Light beer from the Czech Republic (the name means 'ram').

Zlatý Bažant (Golden Pheasant) (*svetlé* – light and *tmavé* – dark) Started in 1968 in Hurbanovo, near Komárno, as a state-owned enterprise supplying beer to western Slovakia, bought by Heineken in 1995 (*www.zlatybazant.sk*).

PUBLIC HOLIDAYS AND FESTIVALS

Many of Slovakia's festivals are based around two great loves: folklore and wine. If Slovaks can combine the two, even better. Sometimes it seems like there is a festival or event of one kind or another every week. During the harvest season, the events come thick and fast and in the Bratislava region around the Small Carpathians there's all kinds of merry-making going on. Trenčianske Teplice hosts an international film festival while Bojnice Castle has an unusual and amusing festival devoted to ghosts and spirits. There's even a joke festival in Kremnica in August. The largest folklore festival takes place in Východná near Liptovský Mikuláš in July. To find out what's going on where, see the beginning of each regional chapter.

PUBLIC HOLIDAYS AND FEAST DAYS Businesses and shops close for national holidays.

1 January	New Year's Day and Anniversary of the Establishment of the Slovak Republic in 1993
6 January	Epiphany, Three Magi, Orthodox Christmas
March/April	Good Friday
March/April	Easter Monday
1 May	Labour Day
8 May	Victory against Fascism Day – end of World War II (Russia observes it on 9 May)
5 July	Sts Cyril and Methodius Day
29 August	Anniversary of the Slovak National Uprising
1 September	Slovak Republic Constitution Day
15 September	Holy Mary, Our Lady of Sorrows, Patron Saint of Slovakia
1 November	All Saints' Day
17 November	Day of Struggle against Totalitarianism/Fight for Democracy (the start of the Velvet Revolution in 1989)
24 December	Christmas Eve
25 December	Christmas Day
26 December	St Stephen's Day

Easter Easter brings some unusual customs. On Easter Monday (*Veľká noc*) the young men of the village go around the houses where single girls live and sprinkle them with water. These days it's a splash of water or eau de toilette but in the past it could have been a whole bucket of cold water or a dunk in the nearest river. It is considered very flattering to get watered as only the pretty girls are targets. In return for this compliment the young men receive a painted egg (*kraslica*) and usually a shot of *slivovica*. On the tour of the houses most suitors end up pretty giddy. It is also a custom to whip the girls' legs with a whip made from willow twigs. If you're in Bratislava at Easter time, you can still buy symbolic willow whips in the festive market. The whipping and the watering are supposed to ensure the young woman's beauty and fertility.

Christmas food The Slovak words for Christmas Eve are literally 'bountiful eve' and the bounty lies in the wide range of festive dishes. The dinner must consist of 12 dishes. To this day many Slovak families keep garlic on the Christmas table to ward off evil spirits. To this they add a wide range of foods: honey, wafers, nuts, cooked peas or French beans, dried fruit, garlic mushrooms, *kapustnica* (cabbage

NAME DAYS

In Slovakia, each day of the year corresponds to a personal name (the original list was the Roman Catholic calendar of saints). People celebrate their name day (*sviatok* or more formally *meniny*) on the date corresponding to their own given name. The list of the names assigned to the corresponding date is normally published in the calendar. Names are listed in the calendar, but there are other names which may be officially given to a child. The name day (*meniny*) is not as important as the birthday for a Slovak but still a recognised event. Traditionally, friends, family and colleagues should be presented with flowers, chocolates or a small gift and say *Všetko najlepšie k meninám* (All the best for your name day).

soup) and *opekance* which are dough balls flavoured with poppy seed and honey. Since the turn of the last century, carp has been the traditional main course served (their scales are said to bring wealth into the house) in the Catholic section of the population, while the Lutherans would add smoked meats and sausage to their cabbage soup. Christmas holidays are also very rich in Slovak pastries and baked goods that are prepared over many evenings during the month of December.

🛒 SHOPPING

While Slovakia's not the first place shopaholics think of heading for, there is still a range of interesting souvenirs from folk crafts such as wooden carvings and folk ceramics to high-quality glassware and crystal. Hand-embroidered clothing such as pretty white shirts can make gifts with a difference. If you need to stock up on jugs, mugs and decorative plates, the best place to go is Modra, near Bratislava and conveniently on the Small Carpathian Wine Route. On the way you could also pick up a few bottles of local wine.

Another wine to look out for is Tokaj. Because of a dispute with Hungary, Slovaks are not allowed to export the 'king of wines, wine of kings', so taking a few bottles of the famous dessert wine home will make you really popular at the party.

Distinctive Slovak folk art includes naïve, primitive paintings on wood or glass, painted Easter eggs, woodcut prints and woodcarvings. Traditional handicrafts include lace, embroidery, baskets, costumes and metalwork such as cowbells.

The best place to find traditional handicrafts are the ÚĽuv (*Ústredie ľudovej umeleckej výroby* or Centre for Folk Art Production) shops dotted around Slovakia and there are four in Bratislava. Check out some of the products on their website (*www.uluv.sk*) before you set off. For atmosphere and fresh fruit, check out the markets held usually on Saturday mornings in every town. These are often outdoors and full of local colour and spice. In Bratislava, there are many outdoor craft markets especially at Easter and Christmas, when there are superb gift-shopping opportunities. Shopping for food and drink is never a problem in Slovakia. There are excellent supermarkets which are really fun to explore, filled with unusual items in jars and a range of crazy spirits to take back for your wild uncles. Look for *borovička* (like gin), *slivovica* (plum brandy) and *demänovka*, a herbal liqueur that'll put hairs on anyone's chest. Shops are usually open Monday–Friday 08.00–18.00; the large department stores and shopping centres until 19.00 or 21.00 on Thursday and Friday. In general, shops are open from 09.00 to 13.00 on Saturday. Look for the Co-op supermarket which has very good opening hours, including Sunday mornings for provisions. Ubiquitous chains Tesco, Carrefour, Billa and others are open Saturday and Sunday also. Tesco is everywhere and after a while, the sight of yet another Tesco sign poking out of a beautiful forest scene will bring tears to your eyes. You have been warned.

ARTS AND ENTERTAINMENT

Slovakia has a rich musical heritage and in the past has witnessed performances by Beethoven, Mozart, Bartók, Haydn and Dohnanyi who all popped in to perform for the nobility. In the last few years, opera buffs from abroad have also cottoned on to a fantastic secret that one of the best places to see first-class **opera** performances for the price of a pint in a London pub is Bratislava. More of a bargain than Budapest, and certainly better value than Vienna, the Slovak National Theatre (*www.snd.sk*) puts on some of the best shows in town and along with the Slovak Philharmonic (*www.filharm.sk*) across the square at the beautiful Reduta offer opera, **classical music**, **theatre** and **ballet**. Slovaks love cultural events and these performances get booked up quickly, but the websites have helpful ticket booking in English and hotel receptions can help. I've also met many people in Bratislava on specialised opera tours, or, even better opera and wine tours, combining two great pleasures in life in one of the most scenic locations in which to enjoy them.

Bratislava and other cities such as Trnava, Nitra, Košice and Prešov have a year-round packed cultural programme with many performances taking place in churches, cultural houses or beautiful turn-of-the-last-century theatres. **Piano recitals** or **chamber music** concerts often take place in historic mansions and the setting makes the effect even more atmospheric and evocative. For a really bizarre experience, take in a show at the inverted pyramid building of the **Slovak Radio** which has amazing acoustics. **Theatrical performances** can be tricky, although there are many musicals on offer, which don't need language skills so much for the effect.

Bratislava is packed with **cultural centres**, both Slovak and of other nations such as France, Britain, Germany, Poland, Austria and the Czech Republic. These are good places to catch a musical performance, book presentation, theatrical show or wine tasting in a more accessible language. There's even a branch of the British Council in Banská Bystrica, helping with language learning and cultural events. At many cultural houses you can also take part in a '**dance house**' (*tanečný dom*), a combination of folk dance lesson and performance. The larger cities have massive concert halls and attract a mix of international bands, world stars and the more modest local singers. **Musicals** and big spectaculars are also popular. There's a slight Twilight Zone aspect to some of these live music gigs. Bands and singers you thought had long since given up touring for a life of slippers and cutting the lawn are still playing here. Demis Roussos and Janis Joplin's original backing band, Big Brother and the Holding Company, help to give the city a sleepy, lotus-eaters' ambience, a little stranded in the 1970s at times. In the last couple of years, however, the capital has seen an influx of hip bands: Massive Attack, Depeche Mode, Seal and some top DJs have given Bratislava a cool musical cachet. Beyond the capital's city limits, however, the musical trend is more for 1970s' style heavy rock bands, jangly 1980s' pop and a huge favourite is, bizarrely, country and western music. **Contemporary music** concerts can be heard all over the country and are extremely popular. In student towns, the capitals of each region, you'll never be short of something to do in the evening. Slovaks work and study hard but also play hard.

You can catch all the latest Hollywood blockbusters at gigantic multiplexes. There are also quite a lot of smaller art house **cinemas** but they may be showing an obscure or vintage film only in Slovak. At the multiplexes many films are in the original language with subtitles in Slovak and/or Czech. Comedies and children's movies are usually dubbed. If you want to see a film look out for ST (with Slovak subtitles), ČT (with Czech subtitles) and watch out for those films with SD (Slovak dubbing) or ČD (Czech dubbing). ČV means it's the Czech version.

Slovakia has an usually large number of **museums** and **galleries**, all beautifully put together and thought out and also often in lovely old mansions. Museums pop up unexpectedly all over the country, sometimes in the most unlikely places. A tiny village will have a house devoted to a writer who once lived there, or one who popped in for a visit. Head to the far, far east of the country, to the unprepossessing town of Medzilaborce to find an incongruously huge Warhol Museum with many works by the artist, whose parents were Rusyns and came from a village nearby. There are museums to glass works, wheels, watermills, wine, all manner of folk crafts and allegedly the only tinker museum in the world located evocatively in Žilina's Budatin Castle. Then of course there's

Two dozen fabulous castles, chateaux, palaces, manor houses and ruins:

Beckov (Trenčín) Sited on a 70m limestone cliff, ruins of 12th–13th century castle, more impressive than Čachtice nearby
Betliar Manor (Košice) An 18th-century chateau, Renaissance-Baroque
Bojnice Chateau (Trenčin) From the 12th century, rebuilt in Romantic style in the 19th century
Branč (Trnava) Ruins of a Gothic guard castle from the 13th century
Bratislava Castle (Bratislava) First mentioned in AD907, turned into a Gothic fortress in the 15th century, rebuilt in Renaissance style in the 16th century
Budatín (Žilina) A 13th-century chateau over the river from Žilina
Čachtice (Trenčín) Ruins, home to Erzsébet Báthory, the Bloody Countess
Červený Kameň (Bratislava) A fabulous fortress with immense cellars
Červený Kláštor (Prešov) A 14th-century Carthusian monastery
Fiľakovo (Banská Bystrica) A 13th-century castle ruins on a hill above town
Kežmarok (Prešov) A 15th-century Gothic castle fortress in town
Krásna Hôrka (Košice) A fortress on a hill
Lietava (Žilina) 13th-century castle ruins on a hilltop
Nitra (Nitra) Fortress overlooking the city centre
Orava (Žilina) A fortress on a high cliff (112m) above the Orava River, built in three high terraces. Founded before 1267, expanded in 1483 and again in 1540–45.
Pajštún (Bratislava) 13th-century castle ruins on a hill in the forest
Smolenice (Bratislava) Looks like a fairytale palace
Spiš (Prešov) A fantastic sight of the medieval ruins rising up from a hill
Stará Ľubovná (Prešov) Fortress on a hill
Strečno (Žlina) Ruins of a Gothic castle on a steep cliff above the left bank of the Váh River
Topoľčany (Nitra) 13th-century castle ruins, modified many times
Topoľčianky (Nitra) Late Gothic castle, rebuilt into Renaissance chateau, later modified Baroque with Classicist façade, large English park with hunting lodge, statuary and 300 foreign tree species, bison preserve
Trenčín (Trenčín) Originally the northernmost Roman military settlement in central Europe – castle founded in the 11th century
Zvolen (Banská Bystrica) Gothic chateau from the second half of the 14th century, summer residence of Hungarian kings, rebuilt in Renaissance style with Gothic fortifications

the *skanzens*, open-air folk museums of which Slovakia has an enthusiastically large quantity. These make great destinations for a walk in the fresh air, a dose of culture and a glimpse into Slovakia's rich history, all in one.

SKANZENS There are around a dozen open-air museums in Slovakia, presenting traditional folk architecture and folk activities. The first, an exhibition of Nordic culture, opened in 1891 in Stockholm: its recreational part was in the former royal gardens on the knoll named Skansen. The word 'skansen', spelled *skanzen* in Slovak, is now a synonym for the open-air museum.

Slovakia's history of *skanzens* goes back to 1927 when a timber church (*cerkev*) from Kožuchovce was moved to the Museum of Eastern Slovakia in Košice. This was followed in 1932 by the removal of a timber *cerkev* from Mikulášová

(Mikľová) to Bardejov Spa. Other timber *cerkev* from the eastern regions of Slovakia were moved to some Czech towns and cities (Hradec, Králové and Prague). World War II interrupted the architecture moving for a while and the idea was resurrected in the ICOM 1957. Whole villages are preserved as *skanzens* and the largest is in Martin at the Museum of the Slovak Village. The Museum of Orava Village at Zuberec is a personal favourite, a superbly put together and presented depiction of a folk village. There are also mining *skanzens* such as the one in Banská Štiavnica. See the relevant chapters for more on *skanzens*.

SPAS AND THERMAL POOLS

Slovakia offers a wealth of curative springs, thermal spas, climatic health resorts and natural mineral waters. There are 23 spa towns and many open-air thermal pools where you can wallow outside even in winter. There are also many modern spa hotels and thermal fun parks where children can slide down the chutes while their parents sip cocktails in the water bar. Several of these are in the mountains and it is sublime to sit in thermal water and gaze at the snow-capped peaks. Amongst the curative spas, Bardejovské Kúpele was already established as a health resort in the 13th century, once the playground of the Hungarian and Russian nobility. Its healing properties have been said to cure indigestion, disturbed metabolism and various respiratory problems. Dudince's spring is rated among the best in the area with a mineral composition suitable for the curing of internal organs, neurological and vascular diseases. The world-famous thermal health resort of Piešťany specialises in rheumatic treatment, with its opulent late 19th-century Thermia Palace Hotel. Sliač, first mentioned in 1244, is regarded as the most important spa for the treatment of cardiovascular disorders. Trencianské Teplice, established since 1488, is situated near a sulphuric spring and is suitable for the treatment of the motor neurone system; it is best reached by narrow-gauge railway. Bojnice is one of the most renowned spas for the treatment of rheumatism, while Smrdáky's waters are excellent in relieving skin complaints, such as psoriasis and eczema. Slovaks pride themselves on the curative powers of their spas. For tourists interested in exploring this aspect of Slovakia, here is a list of the major spas and the diseases they claim to treat.

Bardejov Treats diseases of the respiratory and digestive systems
Bojnice Nervous system and circulatory problems
Brusno Digestive system diseases
Číž Perthes' disease in children
Dudince Locomotor apparatus problems, nervous system diseases
Korytnica Digestive system diseases
Kováčová Nervous system and locomotor apparatus diseases
Lúčky Gynaecological problems
Nimnica Digestive system diseases

Piešťany Locomotor apparatus diseases, nervous system diseases
Rajecké Teplice Nervous system and locomotor apparatus diseases
Sklené Teplice Nervous system diseases, in a cave pool
Sliač Circulatory system diseases
Smrdáky Skin diseases
Trenčianske Teplice Locomotor apparatus and nervous system diseases
Turčianske Teplice Locomotor apparatus, kidney and urinary tract disease

SPORT

Slovakia has always had a rich sporting tradition. Among the winter sports, ice hockey and skiing are especially dominant, but figure skating also has a great tradition. The natural conditions implore the inhabitants of this country to cultivate winter sports.

Football, volleyball and tennis are popular. There is a very good network of marked trails in all mountain areas, and it is possible to plan a walking tour in advance. There is also an excellent well laid-out network of cycle routes.

GOLF Since the early 1990s, golf has become ever more accessible and popular in Slovakia. There are nine-hole golf courses at Bernolákovo, Piešťany on Spa Island, Košice, the Black Stork (*www.blackstork.sk*) golf course at Tatranská Lomnica (*www.tatrygolf.sk*) and the First Golf Club Trenčín (*www.pgc.sk*) while the first 18-hole course can be found at Gray Bear (*www.graybear.sk*) Tále, Horná Lesna, near Brezno in Banská Bystrica region. Designed by Robert Walton, it opened in 2002 with Tony Jacklin as a special guest.

HIKING Slovakia is a walker's paradise. There are endless routes, with varying degrees of difficulty and style, from the High Tatras hikes verging on mountaineering to the equally challenging yet scenically different Lesser Fatras to the ladders and bridges of the Slovak Paradise.

Safety in the mountains No matter how short or seemingly innocent the hiking trip, remember that in the mountains the weather conditions can change suddenly and without warning. Carry in your knapsack the following items: a full water bottle, a penknife, insect repellent, a torch (there are good wind-up versions on sale), a basic first aid kit with a few plasters and painkillers, and a whistle (the recognised emergency call is six blasts). Take a mobile phone and if in trouble call the mountain rescue number.

Mountain Rescue (Horská záchranná služba) (☏ 18 300; also: *www.hzs.sk; wap.hzs.sk* or *hzs@hzs.sk*). The website www.tanap.sk has lots of advice about hiking, conditions, preparation and what to do in an emergency. They also give contact details for mountain guides who can take hikers on the more challenging trips. For how to read a hiking trail see the box on page 204.

CYCLING Cycling is very popular in Slovakia and the 5,400km network of cycle routes follows all the most beautiful, scenic and interesting routes. One route follows the Danube from Bratislava to Komárno, another swerves its way up the Small Carpathian Wine Route.

For the fit, there's a route through the historic Spiš region passing castles and ruins.

Slovak Cycle Club Námestie Slobody 6, 921 01 Piešťany: ☏/f 033 7740 548; e sck@nextra.sk.

FOOTBALL After ice hockey, football is the most popular spectator sport in Slovakia. The Slovaks are pretty good too. The 2004/05 Corgoň Liga champions Artmedia Bratislava whomped Glasgow Celtic 5-0 in a Champions League preliminary in July 2005 and in October 2006, the national team beat Wales 5-1 in Cardiff. Only those who'd never seen Slovak football before called it a surprise result.

TENNIS The first Slovak tennis courts were built in Bratislava between 1880 and 1890, where the game became popular with the elite classes. The first official tennis tournament was played in 1910. The 1988 Seoul Olympic gold medal-winner Miloslav Mečir has played a big part in popularising tennis in Slovakia; now they have ten men and ten women in the world top 100 rankings. Dominik Hrbaty and Karol Kučera have been hanging around the top 20 for years. Daniela

Peterjon Cresswell

Slovak football is nothing if not surprising. While the game in Poland, Hungary and the Czech Republic tends to be dominated by one or two teams, Slovakia has seen six clubs win its modest league since its inauguration in 1993–94. The most recent were the least expected of all. In 2006, little-known Ružomberok, a factory town in the Lower Tatras with a 5,000-seater football stadium, achieved a league and cup double. The year before, Artmedia Bratislava, the capital's third and smallest outfit based over the Danube in Petržalka, not only won the Corgoň Liga for the first time, they shocked Scottish giants Celtic by beating them 5-0 in a Champions League preliminary. Artmedia thus sat beside Barcelona, AC Milan and Chelsea in football's most lucrative tournament. Although Slovak teams are never going to challenge these multi-million euro enterprises – Artmedia's primitive 8,000-capacity ground would befit a semi-professional outfit in the English regional leagues – they add a touch of individuality to the European game. Artmedia themselves, Slovakia's first professional club founded in 1892, have a convoluted history embellished with several strange, occasionally Hungarian, name changes. Slovakia's own football history is often subsumed into Czechoslovakia's, as the better-known players and clubs at international tournaments were Czech ones. An ardent international soccer fan would be hard pushed to name a Slovak player before the 1993 separation, although Slovan Bratislava and Spartak Trnava performed regularly in Europe, Slovan winning the European Cup-Winners' Cup in 1969. Slovan dominated the new Slovak league in the 1990s. Playing at the national stadium, the Tehelne Pole, wearing the Slovak national colours of blue and white, with the national emblem as the club badge and a significant right-wing core of supporters, Slovan's success reflected the dark days of corrupt nationalist politics and distasteful, even dangerous, business dealings. One infamous match with the equally nationalist Hungarian champions Ferencváros in 1992 saw masked Slovak commandos wade in viciously to quell disquiet among visiting Magyar fans. The solitary Slovan supporter who braved the return match in Budapest was given a season ticket for life. On another occasion, when Slovan's hegemony was challenged by Spartak Trnava, then Slovan president (and head of newly privatised Slovak Gas) Jan Ducky was shot dead by masked gunmen after expressing anti-Trnava comments. Inter Bratislava, whose Pasienky Stadium is dwarfed by nearby Slovan's, then assumed their neighbour's mantle. With Slovan's demise and enterprising football in the provinces, today's game has few rogue elements, either on the terraces or in the boardroom. Domestic football is cheap and often fun to watch. Matches, played before small crowds on Saturday afternoons, show a reasonable technical ability from both sides. At national level, Slovakia has few star players. The one it had, Peter Dubovsky, a member of Real Madrid's squad, died in a freak diving accident in Thailand in 2000. Current top scorer is Szilárd Németh, a successful player at Middlesbrough before moving to France. Dusan Galis, in place since 2003, coaches a motivated side who narrowly missed out on the 2006 World Cup Finals. Qualification for Euro 2008 sees Slovakia play World Cup semi-finalists Germany and, enticingly, a fading Czech Republic.

Hantuchova is one of the statuesque blonde babes of modern tennis. Few people know that former world number one and now resurgent Swiss tennis star Martina Hingis (see box on page 297) was born in Košice and originally known as

Martina Hingisová-Molitorová, named after the great Bohemian Navrátilová. Other tennis champions include Dominik Hrbatý, Karol Beck, Karina Habšudová and Henrieta Nagyová.

ICE HOCKEY Without doubt, ice hockey is the most popular spectator sport in Slovakia. The world championship trophy brought home by the Slovak national team in 2002 was celebrated with street parties of a scale previously unseen in Slovakia. Bratislava is represented in the Slovak national league by HC Slovan Bratislava (*www.hcslovan.sk*). HC Slovan Bratislava are a world-beating team and Slovakia are ranked fourth in the world after Canada, Sweden and the Czech Republic.

PETER ŠŤASTNÝ - A LEGEND IN TWO LANDS

Ice hockey player Peter Šťastný, born in Bratislava in 1956, is a Slovak sporting legend. He played in the NHL (National Hockey League of North America) from 1980 to 1995. After Wayne Gretzky, Peter Šťastný was the most prolific scorer in the NHL in the 1980s. Peter Šťastný and his brothers, Anton and Marian, were one of the most successful brother trios in the NHL. Peter Šťastný was only 19 years old when he made his Canada Cup debut for Czechoslovakia in 1976. Despite his young age, his playmaker skills were imminent. According to many, he was one of the best players of the tournament. In the summer of 1980, Peter and Anton decided to go to Canada, stirring up a lot of emotion in their home country. This was the first time that major ice hockey stars from the eastern bloc played in the NHL. The Šťastný brothers' defection from Czechoslovakia was organised by their future NHL team, the Quebec Nordiques. They fled in a style like an episode from a spy film (involving the Canadian embassy and the Austrian police) during a European Cup tournament in Austria. In the spring of 1984, Peter Šťastný became a Canadian citizen and in the same year, at the Canadian Cup he played for Canada, causing a major upset for Czechoslovakia. His inclusion in the Canadian team was labelled a 'provocation' by the state-run Czechoslovak media. Šťastný became the first ever European born and trained player to represent a Canadian national hockey team. He was extremely proud of his Canadian citizenship but admitted that he had a Slovak heart in his Canadian jersey. Šťastný eventually represented Slovakia when the country became independent. He was the flag bearer for the entire Slovak team at the 1994 Olympics in Lillehammer and finished second in the Lillehammer scoring race. He also played for Slovakia in 1995 in the International Ice Hockey Federation (IIHF) World Championships. Peter's two sons Yan and Paul inherited the Šťastný ice skills. Paul plays with the Colorado Avalanche, formerly called Quebec Nordiques, his father's and uncles' team. Yan made his NHL debut in 2006 with the Edmonton Oilers. Yan played for Team USA in the 2005 IIHF World Championships, making the Šťastnýs the first hockey family known to have represented four different countries (Czechoslovakia, Canada, Slovakia and the USA) in international play. Nowadays, Peter Šťastný is involved in politics. He was elected as member of the European Parliament in 2004 and he is the leader of the Slovak delegation of the Group of the European People's Party (Christian Democrats) and European Democrats.

In Slovak, the word *šťastný* means 'lucky' or 'happy'. The phrase *šťastný ako blcha* means 'happy as a sandboy' (literally 'happy as a flea').

SKIING In the communist days, the good skiers of the Soviet bloc had nowhere else to go but to the Tatra Mountains of Czechoslovakia. The Czechs and more significantly, the Slovaks maintained a large system of ski resorts ranging from backyard slopes for the exclusive use of a small village community to extensive track systems where Polish and Hungarian comrades shared the joys of the winter with the locals.

These snowy joys did not resemble much of what pampered westerners are used to. There was no slope maintenance whatsoever, the caterpillar trucks familiar on resorts in the Alps or the Dolomites were unknown. Therefore all slopes were what we know today as mogul slopes, and meetings with malignant rocks and stones were frequent. The injured skis were then repaired in everyone's own garage since services, like ski rentals, were virtually nonexistent.

Ski lifts were also scarce, and so the queues were painfully long, especially in areas where a single lift carried up skiers up to the resort. A ride on the lift seemed not a momentary suspension of the downhill enjoyment but a much-awaited blessing, the result of which had to be savoured at the top station. There, in turn, were no cosy mountain huts serving warm drinks: the brave skier had to face the tough ride without being equipped with any fluid courage.

Now these heroic times are history even if there are still some obscure places available for nostalgia fans. Although the height of the mountains in Slovakia remains inferior to those in alpine countries, Slovak winter sports' opportunities are developing as fast as an avalanche, and the standard of the services is slowly approaching the levels expected in the western European ski nations.

In the bigger Slovak resorts, the tracks are maintained, high-performance ski lifts are abundant, and equipment can be rented in most resorts. Nearly every resort has at least one ski-rental shop offering equipment for about € 10 per day. They also offer lessons in English. Full-day ski passes rarely go for more than € 13.

A few remnants of the pioneer times remain. Slope-side restaurants are still quite rare, and are mostly understood as glass-walled tents serving sausage and *párky* (frankfurters) at the bottom station. The mulled wine or some of the famous herb-based spirits such as *borovička* or the Czech *becherovka* are available too, served in hotel bars or out of caravan windows.

Evening entertainment is appearing in most of the resorts. Après-ski entertainment consists of a hearty meal and a lot of liquid refreshment at bargain prices. Be aware that the ski lifts may close suddenly if the weather changes or it gets dark, and it's not good to get stuck on the wrong side of the mountain as night falls. Night skiing is starting up in several resorts. The start of the ski season in Slovakia appears to have little to do with the amount of snow: despite the heaps of snow the lifts won't start before the preset date, usually around Christmas. Closing time is around the end of March.

Nevertheless, with an open mind, skiing can be highly enjoyable in Slovakia even for those with an experience of the more elegant and better-serviced resorts. The high, rising mountains are located in the northern and middle areas of the country, with only a few scattered resorts lying to the west of the Váh River. Regular snow reports as well as information about the tracks, the temperature and more useful data are available in English from www.holidayinfo.sk as well as at www.ski.sk.

WATERSPORTS There are numerous lakes and rivers amidst the glacial landscape, offering excellent fishing, canoeing, boating and swimming. Rafting on traditional wooden *plt'* is particularly good on the Dunajec River in the Pieniny National Park. Other fast-running rivers such as the Orava, Váh and Danube offer numerous opportunities for canoeing, rafting, fishing and swimming, while the many lakes and reservoirs attract windsurfers.

PRINT The Slovak press is independent (foreign and locally owned) and suffers from hangovers of the past suffocating regime combined with an excess of magazines. Thousands of trees have been pulped to produce the vast range of magazines on every subject under the sun, but particularly lifestyle and women's magazines. *Kam do Mesta* (Where to go in Town) is a handy pocket-sized free listings guide available in large towns throughout Slovakia. *Nový čas* (New Time) the best-selling Slovak daily tabloid, is published by Ringier Slovakia, a subsidiary of the Swiss Ringier company (*www.novycas.sk*).

Život (Life) a weekly, *Nový čas pre ženy* (New Time for Women), *Eurotelevízia* and *Telemagazín* and the monthlies *Eva* and *Rebecca* are also all published by Ringier Slovakia.

The Slovak daily *Pravda* (Truth) is a colour tabloid and available free if you are walking around the Old Town as there is always a teenager handing out complimentary copies, or you can buy it in the newsagents for 10Sk. One of its supplements is *Moment* (*www.moment.sk*), formerly a loss-making TV listings magazine now incorporated into *Pravda* and published every Thursday. *Pravda* is second in popularity behind *Nový čas* and has a good online edition at www.pravda.sk

Týžden (Week) is the newest weekly on the stands, with one-third owned by entrepreneur Ladislav Rehák, formerly involved with the radio station Radio Expres.

HINTS ON PHOTOGRAPHY

Nick Garbutt and John Jones

From the majestic snow-covered peaks of the High Tatras to the rolling green hills and waterfalls of the Lesser Fatras, Slovakia is jam-packed with photogenic natural attributes. There are fairytale chateaux and romantic castle ruins, picturesque wooden churches of the Rusyn minority in the 'far east' of the country, plus UNESCO-listed folk villages with locals dressed in traditional costume and gorgeous architecture in towns such as Bardejov, Trenčín, Kežmarok, Nitra and Levoča. Combined with the enchanting capital, Bratislava, these are all tempting photographic opportunities. For the best results, give some thought to the following tips.

As a general rule, if it doesn't look good through the viewfinder, it will never look good as a picture. Don't take photographs for the sake of taking them: be patient and wait until the image looks right.

Photographing people is never easy and more often than not it requires a fair share of luck. If you want to take a portrait shot of a stranger, it is always best to ask first. Focus on the eyes of your subject since they are the most powerful ingredient of any portrait, and be prepared for the unexpected.

There is no mystery about good wildlife photography. The secret is getting into the right place at the right time and then knowing what to do when you are there. Look for striking poses, aspects of behaviour and distinctive features. Try not only to take pictures of the species itself, but also to illustrate it within the context of its environment. Alternatively, focus in close on a characteristic which can be emphasised.

Photographically, the eyes are the most important part of an animal – focus on these, make sure they are sharp and try to ensure they contain a highlight.

Look at the surroundings – there is nothing worse than a distracting twig or a highlighted leaf lurking in the background. Getting this right is often the difference between a mediocre and a memorable image.

Sme (*www.sme.sk*) a daily paper and flagship of Petit Press, Alaxej Fulmek's group, is backed by the German Veragsgruppe Passau company. *Sme* used to wage war against the Mečiar government, but now it is more moderate. *Plus 7 dní* (Plus 7 days) is the greatest success of the 7 Plus group, formed by three Slovak partners. Other titles published by the 7 Plus group include *Šarm* (Charm) and *Báječna žena* (Wonderful Woman).

The Slovak news agency, *Tasr*, has an English-language page on its website (*www.tasr.sk/indeng.php*). The *Sita* press agency also has a website (*www.sita.sk*).

English-language press The *Slovak Spectator* is a weekly newspaper published on Mondays with news, features, arts and sports. The *Spectator* also publishes a large number of offshoots: *Spex* (40Sk), a monthly glossy magazine, *Spectacular Slovakia* (185Sk) an annual magazine, the annual *Book of Lists* (149Sk) and a clutch of other publications. The *Slovak Spectator* costs 40Sk although you can pick up a complimentary copy in most hotel foyers. The online edition (*www.slovakspectator.sk*) requires subscription.

Business Slovakia, published by *Bratislava Business Journal* (BBJ) and editor-in-chief Ian Brodie, is a tabloid-sized bi-monthly with only 12 shiny pages. The magazine sells for 40Sk and their offices are on a steep street leading up to the castle at Zámocké schody 4 (✆ 02 5464 1471; e businessslovakia@stonline.sk).

Just to confuse us all there is another similarly named publication in this modest-sized business community: *Business Journal Slovakia* (BJS). This monthly glossy A4-sized publication costs 59Sk and comes from another British

A powerful flashgun adds the option of punching in extra light to transform an otherwise dreary picture. Artificial light is no substitute for natural light, though, so use it judiciously.

Getting close to the subject correspondingly reduces the depth of field. At camera-to-subject distances of less than a metre, apertures between f16 and f32 are necessary to ensure adequate depth of field. This means using flash to provide enough light. If possible, use one or two small flashguns to illuminate the subject from the side.

Landscapes are forever changing, even on a daily basis. Good landscape photography is all about good light and capturing mood. Generally the first and last two hours of daylight are best, or when peculiar climatic conditions add drama or emphasise distinctive features. Never place the horizon in the centre – in your mind's eye divide the frame into thirds and either exaggerate the land or the sky.

FILM It's possible to find all major brands of film in Slovak shops. If you're using conventional film (as opposed to a digital camera), select the right film for your needs. Film speed (ISO number) indicates the sensitivity of the film to light. The lower the number, the less sensitive the film, but the better quality the final image. For general print film, ISO 100 or 200 fit the bill perfectly. If you are using transparencies for home use or for lectures, then again ISO 100 or 200 film is fine. However, if you want to get your work published, the superior quality of ISO 25 to 100 film is best.

- Try to keep your film cool. Never leave it in direct sunlight.
- Don't allow fast film (ISO 800 and above) to pass through X-ray machines.
- Under weak light conditions use a faster film (ISO 200 or 400).

Practical Information **MEDIA**

2

gentleman, James Mackintosh (✆ *02 5443 1467;* e *editor@bjs.sk; www.bjs.sk).* The full text of the BJS is also available online.

What's On Bratislava & Slovakia is a bilingual lifestyle and cultural magazine, selling for 40Sk and also from the stables of Mr Mackintosh. The print version is more helpful than that available online (*www.whatsonslovakia.com*).

TELEVISION The TV networks (*televízne siete*) you can watch in Slovakia with only an aerial are the three basic terrestrial Slovak ones: State TV channels STV1 and STV2 (*www.stv.sk*) managed to boost their ratings recently by showing *Superstar,* a talent contest for singers along the lines of *Pop Idol.* As an antidote to the dry, dull programmes of the socialist era, the commercial stations (such as Markíza and JOJ) offer fairly dumbed-down evening entertainment, with a ratings-winning selection of game shows, reality TV and soap operas. Markíza (*www.markiza.sk*) is a privately owned commercial station, the most popular station in the region at the moment. One of Markíza's most popular shows was *Mojsejovci,* a reality programme in which 15 youngsters moved into the garage of a former rock star and his much older rich wife and lived in *Big Brother*-style togetherness, with contestants voted off by the public each week. The prize money was seductive at two million koruna (approximately €50,000) JOJ (*www.joj.sk*) is a commercial Slovak station, local to Bratislava, with cheap programmes and sports in an attempt to challenge Markíza. It transmits a lot of sports live and NOVA shows news, soap operas and films. Czech station Prima shows sports, American soap operas and the *Big Brother*-style reality show *Vy Volení,* while TA3 (*www.ta3.com*) is a Slovak news channel. The Czech channels ČT1 and ČT2 relay a lot of bizarre local soap operas where characters spend the entire time checking and reciting text messages. Hungarian stations RTL Klub, Duna, MTV1 and MTV2 are all available.

Being situated right in the heart of central Europe, Slovak televisions can also pick up broadcasts from TV stations in Poland, Germany and Austria.

RADIO Radio Slovensko is broadcast by Slovenský Rozhlas (*www.slovakradio.sk*) from the wonderful inverted pyramid building on Mýtna just north of Námestie Slobody. Slovak Radio operates five national networks (Slovensko, Devín, FM, Regina and Patria) and an external service. Radio Slovakia International started broadcasting in English in March 1993. In the daily 30-minute broadcasts, they present news and extensive information on all aspects of life in Slovakia. Listeners can also tune into *Slovakia Today* worldwide on shortwave via the World Radio Network or the internet (*www.wrn.org*).

Radio Okey (*www.okey.sk*), part of the TV Markíza group and set up a few years back under the name Radio Koliba is now the most listened-to station in the Bratislava area.

Private radio stations competing for listeners in Bratislava include Radio Expres (*www.expres.sk*) doing well recently after purchase by an international communications group, Radio Regina, Fun Radio (*www.funradio.sk*) and Radio Twist (*www.twist.sk*).

In the Tatras, check out *Radio Tatra International* (*www.rti.fm*), broadcasting travel news with skiing and hiking conditions in the Tatra mountain region on 94.2FM.

C COMMUNICATIONS

TELEPHONE AND FAX Cheap local calls can be made from any phone, but for international calls use a card phone: buy a card (*telefonná karta*) from a tobacconist or post office.

Bratislava's area code is 02 (remove the zero when calling from outside Slovakia). Bratislava telephone numbers are eight digits long (after the 02). For calling mobile phones, the numbers usually begin with 0903, 0904, 0905 etc followed by a six-digit number.

For calls out of the country, dial the international access code '00', listen for the second burring tone, and proceed with the relevant country code and number.

Some country codes (including Slovakia's) are listed below:

Australia	61	Germany	49	Poland	48
Austria	43	Greece	30	Slovakia	421
Belgium	32	Hungary	36	Spain	34
Canada	1	Ireland	353	UK	44
France	33	Italy	39	USA	1

Slovak city codes When dialling the number it is necessary to use the international code 00 followed by the country code (+421 for Slovakia) plus the local code (minus the first zero) then the telephone or fax number.

Banská Bystrica	048	Bratislava	02	Košice	055
Nitra	037	Poprad	052	Prešov	051
Trenčín	032	Trnava	033	Žilina	041

Useful and emergency telephone numbers
Police   ☏ 158 (emergency contact in English 112)
Ambulance   ☏ 155 (emergency contact in English 112)
Fire brigade   ☏ 150 (emergency contact in English 112)
Autoclub helpline (ASA Slovakia)   ☏ 0123
Emergency Road Service   ☏ 0154
Assistance for motorists   ☏ 18 124
Mountain rescue (Horská záchranná služba)   ☏ 18 300 (also www.hzs.sk; wap.hzs.sk; hzs@hzs.sk)

Other useful numbers
Local directory enquiries   ☏ 0120
International directory enquiries   ☏ 0139, 0149
Recently changed numbers   ☏ 0128
Tourist information   ☏ 02 5443 3715, 02 16 186
Eurolines international bus transport   ☏ 02 5542 4870
Information on air transport   ☏ 02 4857 3353
BKIS main office   ☏ 02 5441 5801

Cellphones/mobiles GSM (global system for mobile communication) signals cover virtually all of Slovakia, and travellers must use a triband GSM mobile phone. Orange and T-Mobile shops are in every town throughout the country (*outlets on www.orange.sk and www.t-mobile.sk*). From personal experience, getting an Orange SIM card with a new Slovak number was a convenient way of making cheap calls and text messages. A no-subscription 'Prima štart' package with pre-paid credit costs 599Sk (€20) with top-up cards for 300Sk (€10). Take your passport to a local outlet and it's quick and simple.

 POST OFFICES Slovenská Pošta delivers a reliable, helpful service throughout the country. Their website (*www.slposta.sk*) has a useful English-language section. Most post offices (*pošta*) open Monday–Friday 08.00–17.00. You can also buy stamps (*známky*) from some tobacconists (*tabák*) and street kiosks. Poste restante is available in major towns: write Pošta 1 (the main office), followed by the name of the town. Bratislava's main post office is at Námestie SNP 34–35 and is open Monday–Friday 07.00–20.00, Saturday 07.00–18.00, Sunday 09.00–14.00. See *Appendix 1, Language*, page 303, for letter-sending vocabulary.

ⓔ INTERNET Internet cafés have sprouted up all over Slovakia; expect to pay 60–120Sk per hour.

Many hotels offer either WiFi connections in rooms (for a fee) or some have free WiFi zones in their cafés and lobbies. Many hotels also offer fast broadband internet although these can be much more expensive than in the local café.

MAPS

Mapa Slovakia (*www.mapa.sk*) make excellent maps of Slovakia. Their Slovensko Autoatlas 1:200 000 (189Sk) is invaluable for anybody touring the country by car. They also have an online map at www.navigate.sk (in Slovak) with zoom-in maps of Slovakia.

VKÚ (*Vojenský kartografický ústav*) military maps produce excellent hiking and cycling maps from their HQ in Harmanec, near Banská Bystrica. With a distinctive green cover and numbered according to region, they are available from bookshops and tourist offices all over Slovakia (*www.vku.sk*).

Local tourist offices (AICES) around Slovakia sell maps and the occasional guidebook.

Try asking what free maps they have available as sometimes they do good photocopied street plans with points of interest marked.

BUSINESS

Bratislava's excellent strategic location at the meeting point of Slovakia, Austria and Hungary makes it a popular destination for business travellers and international business conferences. The city is served by two airports, Bratislava and Vienna, giving more possibilities for flights. Bratislava is also accessible by motorway or even by boat or hydrofoil along the Danube.

Bratislava bulges with three- and four-star hotels, specialised 'business hotels' with superb facilities, such as WiFi in every room and state-of-the-art technical equipment.

In other parts of Slovakia, Košice is considered the breeding ground for the country's brightest business minds. Trnava is a centre of commerce and foreign car manufacturers such as Kia, Peugeot-Citroën, Volkswagen, Ford and Hyundai have all opened huge plants in Žilina, Trnava and Bratislava.

The Tatra mountain resort hotels are popular venues for international conferences with a difference. Hotels such as the Grand Hotel in Starý Smokovec and the Grand Hotel Praha in Tatranská Lomnica are booked up with business events throughout the year.

Business etiquette is similar to that of western Europe, the only difference being the central European mania for handing out business cards like confetti at a wedding.

The language of business is English, although most Slovaks are equally at home in German, some older people speak Russian although they may not be too happy about speaking it. Slovaks can also get by on a passive level in most of the other Slavic tongues and many people speak Hungarian as well. Slovaks and Czechs can easily understand each other and the linguistic differences to a foreign ear are minimal. Don't feel intimidated linguistically by their superior powers, Slovak businesspeople are charming and relaxed and will happily adapt to your needs.

To maintain effective business relations, you should have regular face-to-face meetings, and remember to dress conservatively for official meetings, use surnames and formalities such as *Pan* (Mr) and *Pani* (Mrs) until invited to use first names. Don't even think of arranging a business meeting during the holiday months of July and August and also be aware that most companies shut down between 24 December and 2 January.

The usual business hours are 09.00–17.00, although don't expect to find any government workers still in their offices after 15.00 on a Friday afternoon. Banks operate from 08.00–16.00 and shops usually open 08.00–18.00. Shops close at midday on Saturday but some malls are open all weekend.

USEFUL CONTACTS

American Chamber of Commerce Rybné námestie 1, Bratislava; ✆ 02 5464 0534; e office@amcham.sk; www.amcham.sk
British Chamber of Commerce Sedlárska 5; Bratislava; ✆ 02 5292 0371; e director@britcham.sk; www.britcham.sk

Slovak-Austrian Chamber of Commerce Kutlíková 17, PO Box 228, Bratislava; ✆ 02 6353 6787; e sohk@sohk.sk; www.sohk.sk
Slovak Chamber of Commerce and Industry Gorkého 9, Bratislava; ✆ 02 5443 3291; e sopkurad@sopk.sk; www.sopk.sk

TIME

Slovak time is on CET (Central European Time), one hour ahead of GMT (Greenwich Mean Time), six hours ahead of New York (Eastern Standard Time) and nine hours ahead of Los Angeles (Pacific Standard Time).

PUBLIC TOILETS

Slovakia is not overly blessed with public conveniences. In the country, behind a bush will often be the only (and certainly most salubrious) option. In villages, the best solution is to pop into a pub or café for a coffee and hope that their services include a toilet, although these are not always available. Petrol stations usually have clean and equipped public conveniences. Doors are marked *žena* or *ženy* (woman/women) and *muž* or *muži* (man/men). Try asking *Kdy WC?* (Where is the toilet?). Lavatory is *záchod/ WC* (pronounced 'vay-tsay').

CULTURAL ETIQUETTE

GET UP, STAND UP On trams, trolleybuses and buses, it is expected that young people and men will stand up and give their seat to an elderly traveller or pregnant woman. If they don't notice, it will be pointed out by all those in surrounding seats and severe chastisement will follow.

CZECHO-SLOVENIA Be sensitive to the fact that Slovakia has always played second fiddle to the Czech Republic (never even getting its own guidebook before Bradt!) and remember the difference between Slovakia and Slovenia. Nationals of both these countries are equally irritated by the western media's (CNN, BBC, USA Today) and President George W Bush's apparent inability to tell these two very different countries apart.

FORMALITIES Office workers and civil servants can be very formal when addressing colleagues. Older-generation workers insist on using *Pani* (Mrs) plus the surname or *Pan* (Mr) even if they've known the person for years, and the colleague is younger (but more important). *Slečna* is also used for 'Miss'. The polite *Vy* (thou) is used as well instead of the familiar *ty* (you). Foreigners attempting to speak Slovak should use the formal version to be safe, until told otherwise.

ICE, ICE BABY The older generation of Slovaks have a morbid fear of ice in drinks. Ice cubes in drinks can cause sore throats or, worse still, pneumonia. This seems somewhat illogical when you can get a lovely chilled beer or even ice cream from an outdoor stall in the bleak midwinter.

OXYGEN PHOBIA Don't open a window on the tram, even in the height of summer: fresh air is dangerous in draught form. Also, if you have a small child, make sure you take a hat and scarf to Bratislava, even in midsummer, or you risk incurring the wrath of Slovak grannies berating you for endangering your tiny tot's health.

ON THE RIGHT SIDE OF THE TRACKS When approaching other pedestrians on a narrow path remember that they want to adhere to the same rules as on the road. Stick to the right. I was scolded in Košice for straying onto the wrong side while distracted by a photo opportunity.

HOME VISITS If lucky enough to be invited to a Slovak home, take a gift. Alcohol always goes down well: a bottle of excellent local white wine, *slivovica* (plum

Slovakia an exciting property destination for second-home buyers and investors alike.

Apart from the main tourist centres in the mountains, property investors are attracted by the fast-growing market of Bratislava where good-quality apartments – particularly in the city centre – are in high demand from both buyers and tenants, offering solid rental yields and high appreciation. While classic Old Town flats offer the best rental potential, newly built properties outside the city centre are also popular with foreign investors. Prices of apartments range from £20,000 for communist-era panel-block studios up to £500,000 for very spacious properties in the prestigious first district (city centre). Investor buyers will typically spend between £50,000 and £150,000 for a one- to two-bedroom Bratislava flat.

Increasingly, the more adventurous foreign buyers are looking at secondary cities offering lower prices and good long-term potential. In particular the towns of Trnava and Žilina have been on property investors' radar for the last year, an effect of the significant automobile investments by Peugeot Citroën and Kia Hyundai respectively.

Good-quality apartments in the regional capitals of western Slovakia (Trnava, Žilina, Trenčín and Nitra) are available at £30,000–100,000 depending on location, size in square metres and type of construction: small communist-built flats start under £15,000. Properties in towns of the less prosperous central and eastern Slovakia, excluding ski resorts, come at lower prices.

In Slovakia there are properties for all tastes and budgets. Most, however, will not suit for investment or letting. Buyers looking for investment rather than personal use will generally do best with city-centre apartments in Bratislava and perhaps the regional capitals. These, typically period properties, offer the best rental potential and experience the highest appreciation. Those wishing to dip into the emerging holiday-let market should focus on the top ski resorts such as Jasná, Donovaly, Veľká Rača or Štrbské Pleso.

brandy) or the gin-like *borovička* (juniper brandy). Chocolates and flowers are welcome with the hostess, but don't take dried flowers or even-numbered bunches as these have a morbid significance. You will probably be expected to remove your shoes at the door and don grandpa's old slippers.

Slovaks are incredibly hospitable. The Slovak expression, *Host do domu, Boh do domu* means 'A guest in the home is like God in the home'.

GREETINGS It is customary to say hello and goodbye when entering/leaving a shop, lift, office or quiet café. To enter without a word is considered ill mannered. There are many ways of saying hello and goodbye in Slovakia. *Dobrý deň* is used with elderly neighbours, business associates, waiters and shop assistants.

Ruky bozkávam (I kiss your hands) is a very formal greeting which melts grannies' hearts.

Dovidenia is the polite goodbye, though the more final *zbohom* (adieu) can be used. *Dopočutia* ('until I hear you next') is used to say goodbye on the phone.

Ahoj and *čau* (pronounced 'ciao') are the most common informal greetings. These words serve both as hello and goodbye. *Ahoj* (pronounced like 'ahoy' me hearties) sounds like it came from sailors.

Servus comes from the Latin 'I serve' and is also popular in Hungary.

GAY RIGHTS Outside Bratislava, rural Slovakia is still very conservative in its attitudes. Old and young alike are quite religious and although they are tolerant by nature, it would not be advisable to stroll through town hand in hand with your same-sex partner. Bratislava has several gay clubs and there are discreet gay get-togethers in other large cities such as Košice and Nitra but don't expect Amsterdam or San Francisco attitudes and adjust accordingly.

DRINK AND DRUGS People over 18 can buy alcohol and cigarettes. The consumption of alcohol in public open spaces is forbidden, although you will see groups of homeless gathering in squares, particularly in the capital, with a bottle or two. In Bratislava, the locals are getting increasingly irritated by groups of UK stags lurching loudly around town in varying stages of inebriation. Recently, a band of revellers, fuelled by bargain beer, knocked over and damaged the statue of Schöne Náci in the Old Town. Cannabis is illegal and even small amounts for personal consumption are not tolerated. The law doesn't distinguish between hard and soft drugs when handing out sentences, so think twice before lighting up a joint in a pub.

GIVING SOMETHING BACK

Bratislava Groove at UFO Watch Taste Groove Nový most; ℸ 02 6252 0300; e info@u-f-o.sk; www.u-f-o.sk. A campaign run by the new restaurant/nightclub to help abandoned children growing up in orphanages. The cover charge for Groove (the party every Sat night) is 150Sk, 30Sk of which goes to the orphanages in a non-profit project. Supporters receive and wear a 3-coloured wristband.
Food not Bombs Charity (*Jedlo namiesto zbraní*) Local contacts in Bratislava: Mlynské Nivy 41; ℸ/f 02 5542 2176; e mail@jedlo.sk; www.jedlo.sk
International Women's Club (IWC) of Bratislava Meets in room 171, Hotel Danube, Rybné námestie 1; charity co-ordinator Karen Ochotnicka; e charity@iwc.sk; www.iwc.sk
Nádej deťom (Hope for Children) PO Box 12, 974 11 Banská Bystrica; ℸ 048 4130 698, f 048 4151 789; e jolana@oznd.sk & hfc@stonline.sk. Based in Banská Bystrica, the organisation cares for orphans & neglected Roma children. Manager: Jolana Nátherová.
Nota Bene OZ Proti prudu, Karpatská 10; ℸ/f 02 5262 5962; e protiprudu@notabene.sk; www.nota-bene.sk. A *Big Issue*-style magazine for the homeless to sell. *Nota Bene* is a member of INSP, the International Network of Street Papers, a global association of over 45 street papers in 27 countries around the world. Launched in 1994 by *The Big Issue*,

INSP now has a combined monthly sales figure of over 2 million. *Nota Bene* in Bratislava is supported by local celebrities & actors.
Red Cross (*Slovenský Cervený Kríž*); Grösslingova 24; ℸ 02 5292 5305; f 02 5292 3279; www.redcross.sk
Sloboda Zvierat (Freedom for Animals) Mlynské Nivy 37; ℸ 02 5442 4033; www.slobodazvierat.sk (also PO Box 35, 814 99 Bratislava). Founded in August 1992, it provides 2 shelters for the many stray dogs & cats. They also campaign against the long-distance transportation across Europe of live animals, against cruel farming methods, bears kept in captivity & animal experimentation. Shelters are at Polianky 8; ℸ 02 16187; m 0903 727 015 (*open daily 10.00–18.00*) & at Rožňavská cesta (*open daily 14.00–18.00*).
Usmev ako dar (Smile as a gift) Ševčenkova 21; ℸ 02 6381 5209; www.usmev.sk; bank a/c No: 4040 029 105/3100. Organisation for orphans to 'let every child have a family'. There is a strange law in Slovakia that doesn't allow a child to be adopted if the real parent visits the children's home at least once a month, preventing many adoptions. Usmev ako dar is the oldest & the biggest voluntary organisation for the support of abandoned children in Slovakia. Manager: Bruno Biscontini.

Part Two

THE GUIDE

Bratislava Castle

3

Bratislava

Area code 02

A PRACTICAL OVERVIEW

Central Bratislava is small, neat and compact and you will not find it easy to get lost. Having said that, the twisting, turning streets of the Old Town may get a bit confusing after sampling the excellent local brews. Bratislava's Old Town and the castle are separated by the main road Staromestká leading to the Nový most (New Bridge). To build this bridge and flyover section of the road in 1972, the Jewish synagogue and ghetto were demolished. The Danube runs along the side of the Old Town, flowing west to east as it passes through Bratislava. The business area of Bratislava is situated to the east of the Old Town, as well as to the north, clustered around Námestie SNP although some banks and offices are found within the Old Town too. The gruesome modern housing district of Petržalka spreads out in a vast concrete jungle on the southern side of the Danube, and the district is trapped in an enclave of Slovakia that lies between the Danube and the borders with Austria and Hungary. Five bridges cross the Danube in Bratislava, the most recognisable being the Nový sometimes called SNP Most. This bridge is also called the UFO Bridge by tourists because of the flying saucer space ship and UFO café that perches on top of the western column. The 'new bridge' title was usurped by a newer, Apollo Bridge, which opened in 2005 as an elegant white arc across the river. You can still tread warily across the wooden slats of the Old (railway) Bridge linking the Old Town with Sad Janka Kráľa Park. Trams used to run across this bridge all the way to Vienna. Bratislava's M R Štefánik Airport is located 9km northeast of the city and several top business hotels are found *en route*. Many people find flying into Vienna's Schwechat International Airport then taking a one-hour minibus transfer or taxi ride along the 64km road just as convenient. See *Appendix 1, Language*, pages 303–4, for orientation vocabulary.

BRATISLAVA HISTORY TIMELINE

Walking around Bratislava's beautiful, peaceful Old Town centre, it's hard to guess its turbulent and busy history, never mind all the different names it has been called. Here is a brief summary of the events which took place within the elegant walls and, for simplicity's sake, the city is always referred to as Bratislava. To check out the ever-changing names see the box *Identity crisis* on page 73.

5000BC	Colonisation of the Bratislava region in the late Stone Age
100BC	Celts built fortified settlements at Devín and Bratislava and establish a mint producing silver coins called 'Biatecs'
AD400	Gerulata – Roman staging post, today called Rusovce, near Bratislava
AD864	Dowina – the first written reference to Devín Castle in the *Fulda Almanacs*

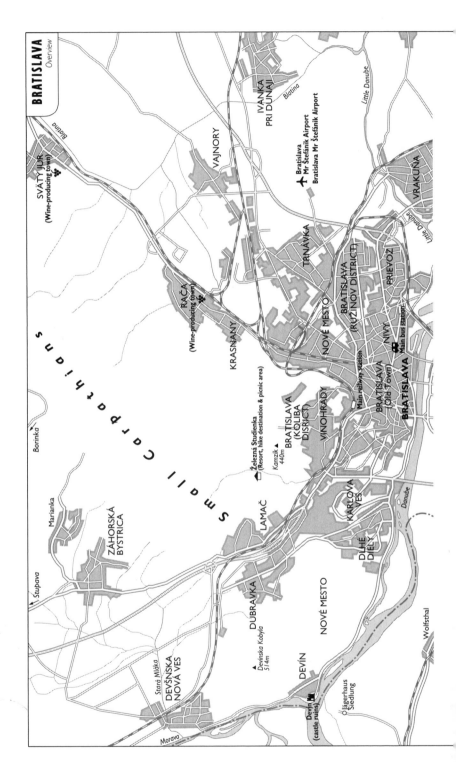

Little Danube

Blatina

IVANKA
PRI DUNAJI

✈ Bratislava
Mr Štefánik Airport
Bratislava Mr Štefánik Airport

VAJNORY

SVÄTÝ JUR
(Wine-producing town)

Blatina

VRAKUŇA

TRNÁVKA

BRATISLAVA
(RUŽINOV DISTRICT)

PRIEVOZ

RAČA
(Wine-producing town)

KRASNANY

NOVÉ MESTO

NIVY

Main bus station

Little Danube

Main railway station

BRATISLAVA
(Old Town)

BRATISLAVA

Main railway station

Small Carpathians

Borinka

Železná Studienka
(Resort, hike destination & picnic area)

Kamzík ▲
440m

BRATISLAVA
(KOLIBA
DISTRICT)

VINOHRADY

Danube

Marianka

ZÁHORSKÁ
BYSTRICA

LAMAČ

KARLOVA
VES

Stupava

DLHÉ
DIELY

Wolfsthal

Devínska Kobyla
514m

DÚBRAVKA

NOVÉ MESTO

Stará Mláka

DEVÍNSKA
NOVÁ VES

DEVÍN

Devín
(castle ruins)

Jägerhaus
Siedlung

Morava

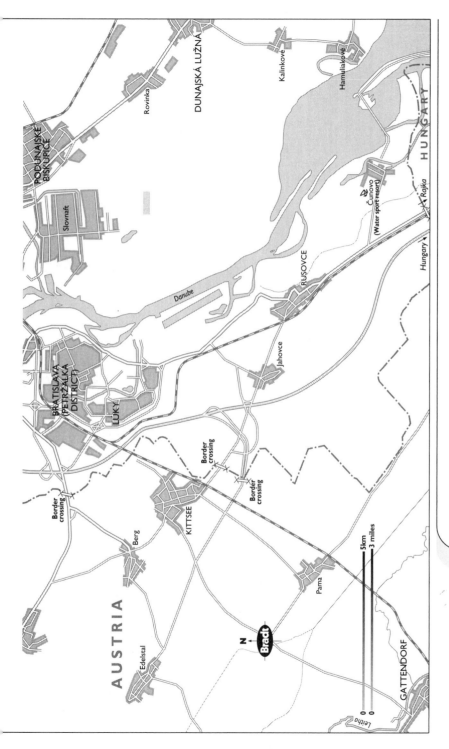

AD907	Braslavespurch – the first written reference to Bratislava in the *Salzburg Almanacs*
1291	The privilege of a Free Royal Town, granted by King András III to Bratislava
1436	King Zsigmond of Hungary grants a coat of arms to Bratislava
1465	Academia Istropolitana, the first university in what is now Slovak territory founded by Hungarian King Mátyás Corvinus
1526	Battle of Mohács (southern Hungary, Ottoman Turks invade the country) and the Habsburgs assume the Hungarian crown
1536	The Fall of Buda, the Ottomans take over Buda, the Hungarian capital moves to Bratislava First session of the Hungarian parliament in Bratislava (last session in 1848)
1536–1783	Bratislava is made capital of Hungary. It remains the capital of Hungary, the assembly town and seat of the central administrative offices until 1783 when the capital moves back to Buda.
1543	Bratislava becomes the seat of the Hungarian archbishop
1552–1783	The Hungarian Royal Crown Jewels are kept in the Bratislava Crown Tower, then moved to Vienna
1563–1830	Bratislava is the coronation town for 19 Hungarian kings and queens
1608	Parliament divided into two chambers
1683	The Habsburgs defeat the Turks almost at the gates of Vienna
1711	Plague epidemic during which 3,860 people die
1741	Coronation of Maria Theresa in St Martin's Cathedral in Bratislava
1775	Queen Maria-Theresa orders the city walls to be pulled down
1776	Establishment of the Theatre of Estates with a permanent company of actors
1780	Establishment of the first manufacturer in Bratislava.
1783	Capital of Hungary moves back to Buda
1792	Anton Bernolák founds the Slovak Learned Society in Modra, part of a national cultural awakening in Slovakia
1805	The signing of the Pressburg Peace Treaty in the Primate's Palace after battle of three emperors at Austerlitz
1809	Napoleonic troops besiege Bratislava
1811	A huge fire destroys Bratislava castle
1818	The first steamboat on the Danube River
1840	Horse-drawn railway starts running between Bratislava and Svätý Jur
1843	Ľudovít Štúr codifies the Slovak literary language
1848	King Ferdinand V signs the so-called Laws of March on abolition of serfdom in the Mirror Hall of the Primate's Palace. Last session of the Hungarian parliament in Bratislava.
1848–49	Hungarian revolution against the Habsburgs
1849	The Slovak National Council developed as the first representative Slovak political body in modern history. Its members spend 1849 co-operating with imperial Vienna to effect the separation of Slovakia from Hungary.
1861	The Martin Memorandum issued in Martin, central Slovakia, urging the establishment of a Slovak district and language within Greater Hungary
1863	Creation of Matica Slovenská (Little Mother of the Slovaks), a cultural and educational foundation

Reflecting the turbulent history and different succession of occupants and occupiers, the city's name has also varied over the centuries. In the Old Town Hall, they have collected all the names:

AD805	Wratislaburgum
AD907	Braslavespurch
1038	Breslava Civitas
1042	Brezezburg
1050	Brezalauspurch
1052	Preslawaspurch
1108	Bresburg, Bresburch
1146	Bosonium
1300s–1400s	Poson, Posonium
1465	Istropolis
1500s	Posonium, Pressburg
1848	Pozsony, Pressburg, Prešporok, Bratislava
1918	After World War I, following many centuries of Austro-Hungarian domination, Czechs and Slovaks were so grateful to American President Woodrow Wilson for supporting their independent common state, Czechoslovakia, that they renamed Bratislava 'Wilsonovo Mesto' (Wilson City) but the new name didn't last long.
1919	Bratislava
2006	Young locals sometimes abbreviate the name to Blava
2007	Visiting stag weekenders have started calling it 'Partyslava' or 'Bratislover'.

1867   Formation of a Dual Monarchy (Austro-Hungarian). Slovaks are subject to ruthless Magyarisation (Magyarosítás).

1886   The present Slovak National Theatre built on the site of the Theatre of Estates

1891   Opening of the first bridge 'Old Bridge' over the Danube

1895   The first tram runs in Bratislava

1918   Bratislava becomes the administrative centre of Slovakia in the first Czechoslovak state, proclaimed a republic on 28 October 1918. Tomáš Masaryk becomes the first president, after the Pittsburgh Agreement in May 1918
        30 October Martin Declaration. The Slovak National Council voted to federate with the Czechs (they hadn't been informed of events two days earlier in Prague!).

1919   **1 January** Occupation of the town by Czechoslovak legions and its annex to the Czechoslovak Republic. The city's name is changed from Pressburg (German) and Pozsony (Hungarian) to Bratislava

1938   **November** Czech President Edvard Beneš lets the Germans take Czech lands; Slovaksdeclare desire for autonomy

1939   **14 March** Slovakia forced to declare itself a separate state, the day before Hitler makes Bohemia and Moravia a 'German protectorate'

1941   Jozef Tiso forms quasi Nazi government, bans all opposition parties and deports 73,000 Jews to Nazi extermination camps

1944	Slovak National Uprising (SNP – Slovenské Narodné Povstanie) quashed by German army
1945	Collapse of Slovak State **4 April** Czechoslovakia liberated by Red Army
1946	Foundation of Greater Bratislava by annexing the villages of Devín, Dúbravka, Lamač, Petržalka, Prievoz, Rača and Vajnory
1948	**February** The second Czechoslovak state was to be federal, but following communist takeover, administration is centralised in Prague
1968	**5 January** Alexander Dubček replaces Novotny as Party boss (Prague Spring, granting Czechs and Slovaks equal rights) **21 August** Russian tanks roll into Prague, Bratislava and other towns, quash everything except the declaration on paper of separate but federated Czech and Slovak states. However, the power remains in Prague.
1969	**30 October** Agreement on the Czechoslovak Federation signed at Bratislava Castle. Bratislava gains official status as the capital of Slovakia.
1971	Bratislava grows as villages of Čunovo, Devínska Nová Ves, Jarovce, Podunajské Biskupice, Rusovce, Vrakuňa and Záhorská Bystrica are annexed
1989	**27 November** General strike of citizens of the town, supporting the movements Public against Violence and Civic Forum as well as student movements, later known as the Velvet Revolution
1993	**1 January** Velvet Divorce, Foundation of the Republic of Slovakia
2004	**3 March** Slovakia joined NATO finally along with Slovenia, Bulgaria and Romania **1 May** Slovakia joins the EU along with nine other new member states, mostly from central Europe
2008–09	Slovakia plans to adopt the euro

GETTING THERE

For details of international flights to and from Bratislava and Vienna as well as Košice, Poprad and Sliač, see pages 27–8. There are scheduled flights within Slovakia (Bratislava–Košice) as well as regular flights from London Stansted to Poprad. International passengers have the following options for travelling into Bratislava city centre from Bratislava Airport or Vienna Airport.

AIRPORT TRANSFERS

From Bratislava Airport into the city centre Airport transfer is operated non-stop by Hunter Slovakia (⊠ *02 4364 3033 or* m *0904 977 907 & 0908 977 907*). The website www.airportshuttle.sk is helpful with airline and hotel details, but bear in mind that the airport transfer must be booked 24 hours in advance. Alternatively, you can take bus 61 from the airport to the main railway station (*hlavá stanica*), then tram 1 into the centre. This will take 30–40 minutes and you'll need change to buy tickets (*lístky*) at the airport. Taxis take 20 minutes from the centre and cost 330–500Sk depending on your starting point.

Car rental There are five car-hire firms at Bratislava Airport arrivals:

🚗 **Avis** ⊠ 02 5341 6111; www.avis.sk. Cars available from Bratislava M R Štefánik Airport, Hotel	Danube, Crowne Plaza & Radisson SAS Carlton Hotel. Opel Corsas available from €51 per day.

Europcar M R Štefánik Airport; ⟍ 02 4926 2637; e europcar@porsche.sk; www.europcar.sk. *Office open Mon–Fri 08.00–18.00, Sat–Sun 24hrs.*
Hertz M R Štefánik Airport; ⟍ 02 4329 1482; e hertz@hertz.sk; www.hertz.sk. Opel Corsas from 1,210Sk per day, Škoda Octavias from 2,680Sk per day.

Sixt M R Štefánik Airport; ⟍ 02 4824 5178; 24hr service, ⟍ 0903 732 292; www.e-sixt.co.uk. Ford Fiestas from 9,210Sk per week.
Budget Car Rental M R Štefánik Airport; ⟍ 02 3303 6231; m 0918 800 600; e airportba@ budget.sk; www.budget.cz. *Open daily 08.00–20.00.*

Local car-hire firms are found on page 77.

Vienna airport details and transfer to Bratislava Flying to Vienna Schwechat International Airport and then taking the 64km bus/shuttle/taxi ride to Bratislava greatly increases your options on when and how to travel to and from Bratislava. There are more flights (including budget), a greater range of airlines and a great choice of when you fly (so you don't have to get up at 04.00, as with some low-cost flights). The trip fro the airport usually takes under an hour.

SkyEurope www.skyeurope.com. New bus shuttle service between Vienna's city centre & Bratislava Airport.

Slovakia Green Tours www.slovakiagreentours.com. Also offers a shuttle and limousine service from Schwechat Airport to Bratislava.

BY TRAIN International rail travellers arrive at Bratislava's main railway station, *hlavná stanica*, a bustling centre of life. From here, tram 13 takes you straight into town, or there are banks of taxis who'll do the same for around 300Sk. If worried about Bratislava cabbies' reputation for overcharging, ask about the price first, and check your destination on the map first before getting in a cab. The most convenient route to the Slovak Republic from western Europe is via Vienna, Budapest or Prague.

Slovak State Railways (ŽSR or *Železnice Slovenskej Republiky*) (*www.zsr.sk/english*) gives information about connections.

BY BUS Bratislava's main bus station (*www.sad.sk*) is at Mlynské nivy 21. It's a 15-minute walk from the bus station to the Old Town centre, but too far to walk if carrying luggage. Taxis will whisk you into town, or take trolleybus 206 or 208 to Hodžovo námestie or trolleybus 210 to the main railway station.

The Slovak national bus company is SAD (*Slovenská autobusová doprava*) (*www.sad.sk*). Two companies manage Coach Line Bratislava–Vienna: SkyEurope Airlines (*www.skyeurope.com*) and Eurolines (⟍ *02 5542 4870; www.eurolines.com*).

Slovaklines (*www.eurolines.sk*) buses also depart from stands in front of the main railway station for destinations within Slovakia. Eurolines (⟍ *02 5556 7349 & 02 5557 7485;* m *0900 211 222*) depart from the bus station for international destinations.

BY HYDROFOIL The Slovak passenger shipping company LOD sails down the Danube from Vienna, upstream from Budapest (*www.lod.sk*). From Budapest check out www.mahartpassnave.hu. International connections from Austria and Hungary are possible on the Danube which is also linked with the Rhine, the Black Sea and the Main. LOD's sales and ticket information: ⟍ 02 5293 2226

The docking area is near to the centre, five minutes' walk from Hviezdoslavovo námestie at Fajnorovo nábrežie 2. Walk past the Reduta towards the Danube then turn left and walk along the embankment. The Lod office at the dock is open Monday–Wednesday 08.30–17.00, Thursday and Sunday 08.30–17.30, Friday–Saturday 07.00–17.30.

Twin City Liner (*www.twincityliner.com*). Booking information in Vienna (☎ *+43 1 588 80 – DDSG Blue Danube*). Booking information in Slovakia (m *0903 610 716 – Flora Tour & Travel*). The Twin City Liner is a new high-speed catamaran which makes three daily trips from Vienna to Bratislava and back. The catamaran leaves Vienna at 08.30, 12.30 and 16.30. The departures from Bratislava are at 10.15, 14.15 and 18.15.

GETTING AROUND

PUBLIC TRANSPORT The transport system is impressively well organised with buses, trams and trolleys all linking up, they all run on time, are comfortable and clean and the prices are staggeringly low. Therefore, visitors should buy (and stamp) a ticket to give encouragement. There's a route planner at www.imhd.sk. The ticket machines offer 15 possibilities – some in English and German as well as Slovak. Bear in mind that it is difficult to find a shopkeeper or ticket seller who will change a large denomination note in order to get coins for the ticket machines. If you use an ATM, you may spend fruitless and frustrating hours wandering the streets trying to break a 1,000Sk note. Try to plan the initial journey or ticket-buying session for a time during banking hours.

Tickets

Basic ticket 10 minutes	14Sk
Basic ticket 30 minutes (45 minutes at weekends/holidays)	18Sk
Basic ticket 60 minutes	22Sk
Tourist 24 hours both zones	90Sk
Tourist 48 hours both zones	170Sk
Tourist 3 days both zones	210Sk
Tourist 7-day pass	310Sk

There are two zones in Bratislava based on concentric circles. I would suggest always buying the 30-minute ticket (45 minutes at weekends/holidays) costing less than 50p because you can get anywhere in the city within 30 minutes, with the exception of Zlaté Piesky which is in zone (*pasmo*) 2 and requires a second ticket. You may be able to get away with using the 30-minute ticket, but for peace of mind you can pay 4Sk more for an hour's ticket. Plain-clothed inspectors can impose a 1,400Sk (€38) fine payable on the spot.

Trams There are 13 tram routes running all around town, numbered 1–17 with a few missing numbers. Be aware that some trams (like route 14) run on one continuous line, around in a ring (not on two lanes going forward and back), so the route going home to the hotel may not follow the same streets, especially in town, as you came in on.

Buses There are 85 bus routes, numbered 20–198 with a few missing numbers and 18 night bus routes, numbered 501–518. Probably the bus route you will use the most is the 29 to Devín.

Night buses cover all parts of the city, however they run only three times a night.

Trolleybuses There are 12 trolleybus routes, numbered 201–212, running mostly in the hills and northern parts of town. Trolleys also can go around in a loop and come back on a different route from the way you went.

Wheelchairs and pedestrians See *Chapter 2, Getting around*, pages 32–3 and 37 for ideas.

Taxis Some say local taxi drivers are a brat pack who rip off foreigners at every possible occasion. This is a little outdated stereotype; almost all those I met were courteous, extremely friendly and helpful. Taxis around the city should cost 200–400Sk, while from the city to the airport is approximately 300–400Sk. From the city to Vienna Airport costs 2,500–2,800Sk. Some reputable firms are listed below.

- **ABC Taxis** ↘ 02 161 00
- **Airport Taxi Service** ↘ 02 4364 3033
- **Euro Taxi** ↘ 02 160 22
- **Milan Gálik** Profi Taxi; ↘ 02 162 22, non-stop m 0903 768 666 & 0905 768 666. Cost 200Sk within town.

- **Taxi Trend** ↘ 02 16 302; m 0905 716 302 & 0903 216 302; www.taxitrend.sk. Very good prices and efficient service for transfers to & from the airport. My charming chauffeur charged 175Sk (€ 4.70) for a journey from the city centre to the airport!

CAR RENTAL The rates of Slovak car-rental agencies are substantially cheaper than those of western firms, ranging from 690–1,500Sk per day and the process is marked by much less red tape. Slovak companies usually charge koruna (and cheaper) while the international companies charge euro. The international companies found at the airport are detailed on pages 74–5.

- **Ab-Wickam** Kopcianska 65; m 0905 653 551 (office hours), mobile hotline: 0903 655 390; e info@ab-wickam.sk; www.ab-wickam.sk. Operating long-term & short-term rent-a-car since 2001, with Škoda Fabias from 590Sk per day, Volkswagen Golfs from 1,240Sk per day. *Office opens specifically for*

clients, after phone call or email message.
- **Auto Rotos** Račianska 184/B; ↘ 02 4487 2666; e pozicovna@auto-rotos.sk; www.autorotos.sk. Good deals available with Škodas; the Fabia from 600Sk per day, the Octavia from 1,500Sk per day. *Open Mon–Fri 08.00–18.00, Sat 08.30–14.00.*

TOURIST INFORMATION

⛵ BKIS Bratislava Cultural & Information Centre Klobučnicka 2; ↘ 02 5441 5801; f 02 5441 5348; tourist information; ↘ 02 16 186; e bkis@ bkis.sk; www.bkis.sk. Renovated premises now features 3 computer terminals with tourist information. The Bratislava City Card is available here which gives many discounts on museums, public transport & other services. *Open Jun–Sep Mon–Fri 08.30–19.00, Sat–Sun 09.00–17.00; Oct–May Mon–Fri 08.30–18.00, Sat 09.00–15.00, Sun 10.00–15.00.*

⛵ BKIS Klobučnicka 2; ↘ 02 5443 3715. There is also a shop inside the BKIS office offering a range of maps, postcards, small folk crafts & books on Bratislava. BKIS offers help with: *Accommodation* in Bratislava; ↘ 02 5443 3715; *Guides* to walking, sightseeing (in 13 languages); e guides@bkis.sk; *Thematic walks* through the historic centre; *Sightseeing* in a historic street car (*Jun–Aug*); *Sightseeing* in town (reservations required); *Trips* to the surrounding countryside; ↘ 02 5443 4059; f 02 5443 2708; *Translation & interpreting* services; ↘ 02

5443 4059; f 02 5443 2708; *Trips & walks*; ↘ 02 5443 1707; f 02 5443 2708; *Adrenalin programmes*; ↘ 02 5443 1707; f 02 5443 2708.

⛵ Ticket office For cultural events in Slovakia or abroad; ↘ 02 5443 2708; *Organisation* of cultural & social events with technical services & catering; ↘ 02 5441 4048; fax 02 5441 5348.

BKIS at main railway station Hlavná stanica; ↘ 02 5249 5906. *Open Jun–Sep Mon–Fri 08.00–19.30, Sat–Sun 08.00–16.30; Oct–May Mon–Fri 08.30–17.00, Sat–Sun 09.00–14.00.*

⛵ BKIS at M R Štefánik Airport *Open Jun–Sep Mon–Fri 10.00–19.00, Sat–Sun 10.00–18.00; Oct–May Mon–Fri 09.00–19.00, Sat–Sun 10.00–18.00.*

⛵ BKIS at Passenger Port (Tourist information Centre of BKIS) Fajnorovo nábrežie 2. *Open May–Sep Mon–Sat 10.00–17.00, Sun 10.00–16.00.*

⛵ BTS (Bratislava Tourist Service) Ventúrska 9; ↘ 02 5464 1794; m 0900 211 221; www.bratislava-info.sk. This office is not connected to BKIS but provides similar services; hotel leaflets, guidebooks, postcards, T-shirts, coins, etc. Information is given in English, German & more. Guided tours daily at 14.00 (2hr tours) for 450Sk (€ 12) pp in English. Tours in German Fri–Sun at 14.00 also 450Sk (€ 12) pp. *Apr–Oct open daily 10.00–20.00; Nov–Mar open daily 10.00–16.00.*

LOCAL TOURS

Organised tours can take you around town on foot, by bicycle or even on a little bus/train contraption.

Boat trips Fajnorovo nábrežie 2; ☎ 02 5293 2226; e travel@lod.sk; www.lod.sk. For trips from Bratislava. From Devín you can take a boat across to Hainburg in Austria.
Bratislava guided pub crawl Explore the local pub & bar scene with a local guide. Cost from 399Sk (€ 10.50). Information at e info@bratislavaguide.com.
Guided Bicycle Tour m 0907 683 112; e info@bratislavasightseeing.com; www.bratislavasightseeing.com. Also trips to Devín Castle, the Small Carpathian Wine Route, cycle tours.
Prešporáčik-Old Timer m 0903 302 817; Jana Fabianova, e fabian@gti.sk; www.presporacik.sk.

Leaves from Hlavnénámestie for a 30min journey, costing 200Sk (€ 6) pp, in English, German & more. The train also leaves from the passenger dock (*osobný pristav*) on the Danube for a 1hr tour (400Sk/€ 11) travelling at a leisurely 5km/h. A new Castle Tour takes 1hr with guides in English & German & leaves from the Hotel Danube at 09.45 & 13.45 almost every day, or at any time for larger booked groups. *Operates daily from Apr to the end of Oct 09.00–17.00, Sat–Sun from 10.00.*
Wine tour The local travel agents (below) can organise trips along the Small Carpathian Wine Route. Also check at the BKIS office on Klobučnícka 2 for day trips.

LOCAL TRAVEL AGENTS

Local travel agents can help with trips out of town, accommodation, excursions and car rental. They also have endless supplies of pamphlets about Slovakia.

ITC Travel Štefánikova 29; ☎ 02 5249 4593; www.itctravel.sk & www.itc-traveller.com. Offers complete opera & weekend packages to Bratislava.
Omega Tours Panská 12; ☎ 02 5443 1367; f 02 5443 1541; e omegatours@omegatours.sk; www.omegatours.sk. Operating for 10 years, Omega offers tailor-made tours, Danube cruises, Discover Slovakia tours, day trips.
Oneworld Travel ulica 29 augusta 2; ☎ 02 5273

1202; f 02 5273 1205; e oneworld@ oneworldtravel.sk; www.oneworldtravel.sk. Can arrange accommodation in Bratislava & other Slovak cities, sports & cultural events, transfers, wine tastings.
SATUR (Slovak Tourist Office) Miletičova 1; ☎ 02 5542 2828; f 02 5556 1426; e info@acr.satur.sk; www.satur.sk. Organises guided tours around Bratislava & day trips to the Small Carpathian Wine Route, Červeny Kameň, or traditional dinner.

WHERE TO STAY

For a relatively small city, Bratislava has more than its fair share of hotels competing for tourists, business visitors and local travellers, making for a healthy atmosphere of each hotel, pension or hostel trying to outdo the other in terms of facilities, price and bathroom freebies. The hotels have been sorted into price range, beginning with the luxury trio and following on with the four star, three star, two star and one star establishments. The listing of hotels within each category is purely alphabetical. Many hotels add on a previously unmentioned city tax, but as this is never more than 30Sk (€0.80) a night, it's nothing to get upset about. Bratislava is not such a huge city so hotels, pensions, hostels, private apartments and campsites are not divided into district, and only the hotel section is separated into five price categories. Bus (B), tram (T), trolleybus (TB) and night bus (NB) numbers are also given.

HOTELS
Luxury

⌂ **Crowne Plaza Hotel Bratislava** (223 rooms) Hodžovo námestie 2; ☏ 02 5934 8111; e cp.bratislava@ichotelsgroup.com; www.cpbratislava.com. TB 203, 205, 206, 208. Good location just north of the Old Town, opposite the Presidential Grassalkovich Palace, where the busy Staromestská highway zooms across Hodžovo námestie. The former Forum was completely renovated & regenerated, reopening as the Crowne Plaza in June 2005. With its state-of-the-art technical equipment & excellent business services, a pool, fitness centre & 2 superb restaurants Magd a Lena & Fusion, the hotel attracts both business folk & those seeking a little extra pampering while on holiday. Six floors of luxurious, well-appointed rooms, business accommodation on the fifth floor with its own reception & executive meeting rooms, 14 conference rooms with more than 1,200m² meeting space. Cigar Lounge, flower shop, hairdresser, gift shop, limousine service, Fitness Plaza (*open daily 05.30–23.00*) with sauna, whirlpool, solarium, gym & massage. Regency Casino (*open daily 13.00–04.00*). Sgl $$$$, dbl $$$$$.

⌂ **Hotel Marrol's** (42 rooms) Tobrucká 4; ☏ 02 5778 4600; e rec@hotelmarrols.sk; www.hotelmarrols.sk. Hotel Marrol's is a gem of a hotel, hiding away in a modest terraced building on a back street, 5mins' walk from Hviezdoslavovo námestie. The Messina restaurant ($$$) already has a great reputation around town for its Italian dishes & quality wine list & the Jasmine spa offers a retreat from the hectic business of the day. Sgl, dbl $$$$$, b/fast not inc.

⌂ **Radisson SAS Carlton Hotel** (168 rooms, 8 suites) Hviezdoslavovo námestie 3; ☏ 02 5939 0000; f 02 5939 0010; e reservation.bratislava@radissonsas.com; www.radissonsas.com. For location alone, this vast imposing hotel overlooking Hviezdoslavovo námestie wins hands down. The present building dates from 1912, when hotelier Henry Pruger created a Carlton-Savoy complex on the site of the Three Green Trees inn. Only 1min from the Opera House & Reduta & 2mins from the Old Town. Plush, chintzy furnishings, original glass atrium ceilings. Bedrooms in 2 styles: warmer, traditional golden hues or the modern, cooler colours. The bar has a homely, albeit smoky, ambience & the Opera Brasserie restaurant has changing foodie concepts. Fabulous buffet b/fast. Well-appointed fitness centre. Sgl, dbl, suites $$$$$.

Four-star hotels

⌂ **Botel Marína** (27 rooms) Nábrežie arm. gen. Ľ. Svobodu; ☏ 02 5464 1804; e info@botelmarina.sk; www.botelmarina.sk. T 4, 12, 13, 17; NB 502. Conveniently situated, a 10min walk upstream from the Old Town. A botel is a hotel on a boat. Botel Marina opened in July 2004 with small, claustrophobic twin cabins. The minuscule 'wet-style' bathrooms might not be to everyone's taste. The restaurant ($) is better in the evenings with a top-quality menu, but the b/fasts are comprehensive with fresh croissants & scrambled eggs. Sgl $$, dbl $$$, b/fast inc.

⌂ **Holiday Inn** (164 rooms) Bajkalska 25/A; ☏ 02 4824 5111; e holidayinn@holidayinn.sk; www.holidayinn.sk. T 14 from Námestie Ľ. Štúra to Slovanet stop then 8mins' walk. Handy for the airport, but otherwise it's a bit of a hike getting into town. Situated in an unattractive district. Rooms are furnished & equipped to the traditional Holiday Inn standard, comfortable & spacious. Large choice of eating & drinking venues, 'Wintergarden' restaurant ($$) & a bright brasserie offering excellent buffet b/fasts. Fitness centre with sauna, pool & solarium. Tennis courts. Sgl, dbl $$$, apt $$$$$, b/fast inc.

⌂ **Hotel Danube** (276 rooms) Rybné námestie 1; ☏ 02 5934 0000; e danube@hoteldanube.com; www.hoteldanube.com. T 4, 12, 13, 17; NB 502. Ugly exterior & garish bedrooms. Romeo e Giulieta restaurant ($$). Good views of the river & castle. Rooms all have cable TV, broadband & WiFi access. Non-smoking, family & rooms for disabled visitors also available. Fitness centre with pool, solarium, sauna, massage tables, jacuzzi, aerobics classes. Good pastries at the Café Viennois. Sgl/dbl $$$$$, b/fast inc.

⌂ **Hotel Devín** (100 rooms) Riečna 4; ☏ 02 5998 5111; e recepcia@hoteldevin.sk; www.hoteldevin.sk. T 4, 12, 13, 17; NB 502. For many years, the only 4-star hotel in Bratislava. The buffet b/fast is superb with great local sausages & cheeses. Good-sized rooms with very beige marble bathrooms, a woody bar, top-notch restaurant (Francúzska reštaurácia), voted best in town by a *Michelin*-esque local guide. Centrum Relax fitness centre offers Thai massage, pool, gym, jacuzzi, massage tables, squash courts. Sgl, dbl $$$–$$$$$, b/fast inc.

⌂ **Hotel Perugia** (14 rooms) Zelená 5; ☏ 02 5443 1818; e info@perugia.sk; www.perugia.sk. Luxury hotel right in the heart of the Old Town,

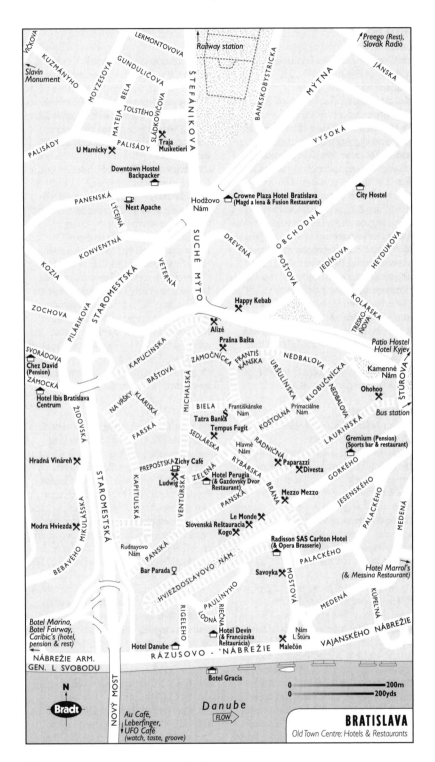

Railway station

Preego (Rest),
Slovak Radio

Slavín
Monument

U Mamicky ✗

Traja
Musketieri

Downtown Hostel
Backpacker

Next Apache

Hodžovo
Nám

Crowne Plaza Hotel Bratislava
(Magd a lena & Fusion Restaurants)

City Hostel

Happy Kebab ✗

Alizé ✗

Prašna Bašta ✗

Patio Hostel
Hotel Kyjev

Chez David
(Pension)

Kamenné
Nám

Hotel Ibis Bratislava
Centrum

Ohohoo ✗

Bus station

BIELA

Františkánske
Nám

Primaciálne
Nám

Tatra Banka

Tempus Fugit

Gremium (Pension)
(Sports bar & restaurant)

Hradná Vináreň ✗

Hlavné
Nám

Zichy Café

PREPOŠTSKÁ

Paparazzi ✗
✗ Divesta

Ludwig ✗

Hotel Perugia
(& Gazdovsky Dvor
Restaurant)

Mezzo Mezzo ✗

Modra Hviezda ✗

Le Monde ✗
Slovenská Reštauracia ✗
Kogo ✗

Radisson SAS Carlton Hotel
(& Opera Brasserie)

Rudnayovo
Nám

Bar Parada ♇

Savoyka ✗

Hotel Marrol's
(& Messina Restaurant)

Botel Marina,
Botel Fairway,
Caribic's (hotel,
pension & rest)

Hotel Devín
(& Francúzska
Reštaurácia)

Nám
L Štúra

Malečón ✗

NÁBREŽIE ARM.
GEN. L SVOBODU

Hotel Danube

RÁZUSOVO - NÁBREŽIE

N

Bradt

Botel Gracia

0   200m
0   200yds

Au Café,
Leberfinger,
UFO Café
(watch, taste, groove)

Danube
FLOW

BRATISLAVA
Old Town Centre: Hotels & Restaurants

reconstructed in 1993 by top Slovak architects Dušan Krep & Pavol Suchánek. Rooms are plush & pricey with period furniture & original artwork that

Three-star hotels

⌂ **Botel Fairway** (29 rooms) Nábrežie arm. gen. L. Svobodu; ☎ 02 5442 2090; e botel@fairway.sk; www.fairway.sk. T 1, 4, 5, 9, 12, 17; NB 502, 503, 504. Botel Fairway is a squared-off boat, moored further upstream from Botel Marina. Restaurant with a good selection of international dishes ($$). *Sgl, dbl $$, b/fast inc.*

⌂ **Botel Grácia** (30 rooms) Rázusovo nábrežie; ☎ 02 5443 2132; e hotel@botelgracia.sk; www.botelgracia.sk. T 11, 13, 14, B 88. Excellent location, moored nearer to the centre than the other 2 botels. Botel Grácia is on the Danube near Námestie Ľ Štúra & just upstream from the ferry dock. It was built as a boat & tugged to this location 14 years ago. Big cabins with more space than the other boats. In summer the restaurant ($) out on deck is very atmospheric. The huge suite sleeps 6, although you can squeeze in as many as you like, if the kids don't mind sleeping on the floor. Great buffet b/fast & charming dinner venue. The Cirkus Barok disco boat is moored next door & grooves away until 06.00, but the noise doesn't permeate. *Sgl $$, dbl $$$, suite $$$$$. B/fast inc. Negotiate on the suite for a longer stay.*

⌂ **City Hotel Bratislava** (254 rooms) Seberíniho 9; ☎ 02 4341 1592; e hotel@hotelbratislava.sk; www.hotelbratislava.sk. T 8, 9, 14 to Tomášikova stop, then a 5min walk. Situated in the Ružinov housing district of grey, high-rise *paneláky* buildings, out towards the airport, City Hotel is 3 star but with

can be purchased if it appeals. Restaurant Gazdovsky Dvor ($$). Situated in the pedestrian zone. *Sgl, dbl $$$$, apt $$$$$, b/fast inc.*

4-star aspirations. The 10-storey hotel splits in two regarding smoking & non-smoking rooms. The WiFi internet access in the bar is free, a bonus as most other hotels charge. It's handy for the airport & extremely popular with business travellers & coach tours. Fitness centre. Paradise Nightclub. *Sgl $$, dbl $$$, b/fast inc.*

⌂ **Hotel IBIS Bratislava Centrum** (120 rooms) Zámocká 38; ☎ 02 5929 2000; e h3566@accor-hotels.com; www.ibis-bratislava.sk. T 1, 5, 9; B 31, 39, 81, 83, 84, 93, 94, 131, 180; NB 503, 504, 506, 507, 508. Situated right next to the tram tunnel under Castle Hill, the Hotel Ibis has a convenient location & the tram noise is not too disturbing. Near to the Old Town & the castle, the rooms are simple & fairly featureless but good, smart bathrooms. Rather impersonal surroundings, run by the French Accor chain. Two rooms equipped for disabled visitors. Also has a business corner, restaurant & bar. *Dbl $$$, b/fast not inc.*

⌂ **Hotel Kyjev** Rajská 2; ☎ 02 5964 1111; e rezervacia@kyjev-hotel.sk, www.kyjev-hotel.sk. T 1, 4, 7, 11, 14, 17. Sky-rise 1960s' hotel located just behind the Tesco supermarket. One of the few cheaper hotels in such a central location. All rooms have en-suite bathroom & toilet & excellent views from rooms nearer the top of the 15 storeys. The restaurant is good but the lifts are not for the faint-hearted. Suitable for Soviet nostalgists & those on a tight budget. *Sgl, dbl $$, b/fast inc.*

Two-star hotels Hotels marked with two stars often offer both decent accommodation and good value for money but apart from Hotel Kyjev (rooms without a TV are 2-star), which is the best for location, the others are usually further out from the centre. Two-star hotels have en-suite rooms with bath and/or shower, television, radio and sometimes a fridge.

⌂ **Hotel Remy** (47 rooms) Stará Vajnorská cesta 37/a; ☎ 02 4445 5063; e info@remy.sk; www.remy.sk. T 2, 4 to Zlaté Piesky terminus; NB 514. A basic hotel, situated out by the Zlaté Piesky

lake resort. Simple, but clean rooms have en-suite facilities, satellite TV, radio & telephone. 1 dbl with facilities for disabled visitors. *Sgl, dbl $, b/fast € 1.25.*

Pensions

⌂ **Arcus** Moskovská 5; ☎ 02 5557 2522; e bratislava@hotelarcus.sk; www.hotelarcus.sk. T 3, 5, 7, 11, 17 from Kamenné námestie to Americké námestie. Intimate, friendly pension situated just northeast of the charming Medical Gardens (Medická

záhrada), within walking distance of the Old Town. Each room has unique character & bathrooms vary to suit taste. Long-term guests get separate kitchen & terrace. *Sgl $$, dbl $$$, b/fast inc.*

⌂ **Caribic's** (7 rooms) Žižkova 1/A; ☎ 02 5441

8334; e caribics@stonline.sk; www.caribics.sk. T 1, 4, 5, 9, 12, 17 NB 502, 503, 504. Situated in the old fishing quarter of town, out to the west of the centre, between the base of Castle Hill & the Danube. The pension has a superb fish restaurant (**$$$**) with maritime décor, brickwork & sea-shells. An excellent pension for honeymooners, as it is away from the bustle of the centre & very romantic. *Sgl $, dbl $$, b/fast inc.*

🏠 **Chez David** Zamocká 13; ☎ 02 5441 3824; e recepcia@chezdavid.sk; www.chezdavid.sk. Plush

kosher pension with excellent kosher restaurant (**$$**) attached, located on a hill leading north away from the Castle Quarter. The building's exterior is not very attractive, but the interior is tastefully furnished & all rooms are elegant with en-suite facilities. *Sgl $, dbl $$, suites $$$, b/fast inc.*

🏠 **Gremium** (5 rooms) Gorkého 10; ☎ 02 5413 1025; e cherrytour@mail.pvt.sk; www.gremium.sk. Situated above the Gremium pub. Clean with extremely basic en-suite bathrooms. Good for young people, sports fans, etc. *Sgl $, dbl $$, b/fast not inc.*

HOSTELS Quite a few hostels are open only in the summer as they are located in student dormitories. Ask at BKIS for a list of summer youth hostels (N Belojanisa, Nešporák, Domov Mládeže, Družba, Jura Hronica, Mlada Garda, Mladosť, Stu and Svoradov).

🏠 **City Hostel** (19 rooms) Obchodná 38; ☎ 02 5263 6041; e reservation@cityhostel.sk; www.cityhostel.sk. T 5, 7, 9, 13. The location, on Obchodná, Bratislava's 'Commercial Street' is very convenient & close to many pubs & restaurants, such as KGB & the 1st Slovak Pub. *Sgl $, dbl $$, trpls $$, suite $$, b/fast not inc.*

🏠 **Downtown Hostel Backpacker's** (44 beds) Panenská 31; ☎ 02 5464 1191; e info@ backpackers.sk; www.backpackers.sk. TB 203, 205, 206, 208, 212. Located near the Presidential Palace in

a historical building, Downtown provides clean, modern rooms & friendly staff. Kitchen & laundry available. Dormitories & a limited number of private rooms. *Dorms $, dbl $.*

🏠 **Patio Hostel** (57 beds) Špitálska 35; ☎ 02 5292 5797; e booking@patiohostel.com; www.patiohostel.com. T 1, 4, 7, 11, 14, 17; TB 202. Situated on the road leading from Tesco to the Medical Garden, Hostel Patio is a new hostel with accommodation in 2- to 8-bedded dorm rooms. *Dbl $, 8-bed dorms $.*

CAMPING

⛺ **Autocamp Zlaté Piesky** (40 chalets, 300 tent pitches) Senecká cesta 2; ☎ 02 4425 7373; e kempi@netax.sk; www.intercamp.sk. T 2, 4 to Zlaté Piesky terminus. Autocamp Zlaté Piesky (along with its sister Intercamp) is a good campsite at the 54ha lake resort. Zlaté Piesky is a large lake outside the centre where small cabins can be

rented. The bungalows have private shower, kitchen & small fridge. The apts sleep up to 4, with separate bedroom, family room & equipped kitchen area, also TV, private shower, own parking place & picnic area. *Chalets $, bungalow $, apt $$, Stamo (chalet for 10) $$.*

✗ WHERE TO EAT

Bratislava Old Town is wall-to-wall restaurant city with cafés, bars, cocktail venues, restaurants, self-service canteens, stand-up buffet stalls – you're totally spoilt. Slovak, international, Mediterranean, Mexican, Japanese; there's a great choice and it's doubtful that you'll need to book, apart from at the place of the month, because if your intended eatery is full, just totter two yards along the pavement and you'll find another option.

RESERVATIONS Major credit cards are usually accepted, but check first, before launching into the chateaubriand steak for two and champagne supper.

The sections on restaurants, cafés and pubs have all been divided into two main districts: Old Town and Castle District and Beyond the Old Town Gates, Centrum and further afield. Only occasionally will you have to take a taxi to your choice of chow venue, as the majority can be reached on foot.

RESTAURANTS
Old Town and Castle District

✘ **Divesta** Laurinská 8. In the land where pork is king, the longest lunch queues stretch right out of this veggie canteen & down Laurinská. Good choice of dishes, a lot of soya chunks, menu in English. $. *Open Mon–Fri 11.00–15.00.*

✘ **Due Amici** Ventúrska 7; ✆ 02 5464 8284; www.dueamici.sk. Classy Italian restaurant under low stencilled arches in Ludwig restaurant's former home. Lots of fish dishes, great antipasti and superb wine list. $$$. *Open daily 11.00–midnight.*

✘ **Gazdovsky Dvor** Zelená 5; ✆ 02 5443 1818; www.perugia.sk. Part of the Hotel Perugia & offering Hungarian-Slovak country cuisine in a rustic barn setting. $$. *Open Mon–Fri 07.00–23.00, Sat–Sun 08.00–23.00.*

✘ **Hradná vináreň** Námestie A Dubčeka 1; ✆ 02 5972 4256. Smart restaurant & wine bar located in the former royal stables in the castle grounds, with a smashing view of the Old Town & the Danube. Slovak specialities including game goulash. $$$. *Open daily 11.00–23.00. Day bar (denný bar) open daily 09.00–22.00.*

✘ **Mezzo Mezzo** Rybárska brána 9; ✆ 02 5443 4393; www.mezzo.sk. The subtler Mezzo Mezzo lurks just behind a brash Mcburger bar at Fisherman's Gate (Rybárska brána) & offers quality dishes in a snazzy setting. Well situated for a dinner before or after a performance at the National Theatre or the Reduta. $$–$$$. *Open Mon–Fri 08.00–01.00, Sat–Sun 09.00–01.00.*

✘ **Modra Hviezda** Beblavého 14; ✆ 02 5443 2747; www.modrahviezda.sk. The 'blue star' restaurant *en route* to the castle serving Slovak & Hungarian specialities in a stable setting. An 18th-century late-Baroque building with a history; allegedly the revolutionary Hungarian poet Sándor Petőfi used to come here for the delicious Bencze cabbage. $$. *Open daily 11.30–23.00.*

✘ **Ohohoo** Laurinská 19; ✆ 02 5464 7154. Italian restaurant with a huge salad bar & a good selection of seafood. Extended happy hour lasts 15.00–17.30 every day. English tourists might be bemused by the flag of St George displaying the words 'Bolognese' on the red cross. $. *Open Mon–Thu 08.00–23.00, Fri–Sat 08.00–midnight, Sun 12.00–23.00.*

✘ **Paparazzi** Laurinská 1; ✆ 02 5464 7971; www.paparazzi.sk. A 19th-century neoclassical building contains a chic Italian restaurant with pricey dishes, cocktails & a hip crowd amongst the sleek dark purple-&-black-tiled setting. Outside, a statue of a photographer sneaks a picture from around a corner. $$$. *Bar & cocktails open daily 11.00–01.00, restaurant open daily 11.00–23.00.*

✘ **Prašná Bašta** Zámočnícka 11; ✆ 02 5443 4957; www.prasnabasta.sk. Quiet courtyard & restful, cosy interior. Mediterranean salads & a good version of *bryndzové halušky*. Housed in the Powder Tower (Prašná Bašta), one of Bratislava's oldest buildings. Try Café Kút in the same courtyard. *Weekday lunch menu $. Mains $$. Open daily 10.00–01.00.*

✘ **Tempus Fugit** Sedlárska 5; ✆ 02 5441 4357; www.tempusfugit.sk. In a restored 15th-century Renaissance building. Intimate dining with an eclectic décor of grey pillars & minimalist seating, blending the old with the new. Speciality is whole roast suckling pig (3,000Sk or 5,900Sk for a minimum of 4 people, must be ordered 4hrs in advance). $$$. *Open daily 10.00–01.00.*

✘ **Zichy Café Restaurant** Ventúrska 9; ✆ 02 5441 8557. Elegant courtyard with a gargoyle spouting up out of flagstones. A lot of pork dishes done in trendy styles (189Sk) A tearoom underneath (*Čajovňa, open daily 14.00–23.00*) if you want to check out Zichy's cellar. $$. *Open daily 10.00–23.00.*

Beyond the Old Town gates, Centrum and further afield

✘ **Alizé** Hurbanovo námestie 6; ✆ 02 5930 6041; www.alize.sk. A smart, new favourite on the fourth floor of the former Baťa building. *Haute cuisine* fans will appreciate the interesting menu created by head chef Marián Harcinik featuring tuna salmon steak with a mosaic of seaweed & wasabi sauce; there's also hare & wild boar. Summer terrace with nice view. $$$$. *Open daily 11.30–midnight.*

✘ **Alžbetka** Mickiewiczova 1; ✆ 02 5292 3988; www.alzbetka.sk. Traditional restaurant in a nobleman's palace serves up Hungarian & Slovak portions. $$$. *Open daily 11.00–23.00.*

✘ **Au Café** Tyršovo nábrežie, Petržalka; ✆ 02 6252 0355; www.au-cafe.sk. Great setting on the Danube banks in the park. Au Café first opened in 1827. It offers Italian dishes in a very grey room & some of the close-cropped clientele are a little scary. $$$. *Open Sun–Thu 10.00–01.00, Fri–Sat 10.00–02.00.*

✘ **Bar Parada** Hviezdoslavovo námestie 14; ▥ 0904 332 523. Quiet, cavernous, Iberian-tinged bar & restaurant, refreshingly very light on the décor

3

& theme-bar tat. $$. *Open Mon–Thu 08.00–midnight, Fri 08.00–03.00, Sat 10.00–03.00, Sun 10.00–midnight.*

✕ **Caribic's** Žižkova 1/A; ☏ 02 5441 8334; www.caribics.sk. Specialising in seafood. Popular, reliably good but pricey fish restaurant on the ground floor of a former fisherman's house. $$$. *Open daily 11.00–midnight (pension open 24/7).*

✕ **Chez David** Zámocká 13; ☏ 02 5441 3824; www.chezdavid.sk. Kosher restaurant serving fresh, beautifully prepared Jewish cuisine. Closed on Sat. Daily lunch menu 107Sk, soups 57Sk. $$. *Open daily 11.30–22.00.*

✕ **Francúzska reštaurácia** (Hotel Devin) Riečna 4; ☏ 02 5998 5852; www.hoteldevin.sk. Usually quite a deserted restaurant, a mystery because the food is excellent. Don't let the brown furnishings put you off the delicious Gallic cuisine. Well-informed sommelier Štefan Valovič can advise on more than 200 Slovak wines. $$$. *Open daily 12.00–15.00 & 18.00–23.00.*

✕ **Fusion** Hodžovo námestie 2 (lower ground floor of Crowne Plaza Hotel); ☏ 02 5934 8080; f 02 5443 3265; www.ichotelsgroup.com. Innovative cuisine blending the tastes of the Orient with full-flavoured local produce. The first of its kind in central Europe: exotic & healthy cuisine based on head chef Saravanan Gurusamy's experience in Asia & Europe. Also sushi for 70Sk per piece. $$$$. *Open daily 18.00–02.00.*

✕ **Govinda** Obchodná 30; ☏ 02 5296 2366. Run by the Slovak Hare Krishna community, the entirely vegetarian Govinda has some very tasty Indian meals for a good price. It's popular as a lunch & dinner venue, but also contains a small tea house & shop with oriental goods. $. *Open Mon–Fri 11.00–20.30, Sat 11.30–19.30, closed Sun.*

✕ **Happy Kebab** (& Happy Pizza) Námestie SNP 7/8; ☏/f 02 5443 0383; www.happy-kebab.sk. The best kebab shop in town, not greasy but stylish, with beautiful blue Turkish tiles. $. *Open Mon–Thu 10.00–22.00, Fri 10.00–04.00, Sat 10.00–midnight, closed Sun.*

✕ **Kogo** Hviezdoslavovo námestie 21; ☏ 02 5464 5092; www.kogo.sk. Delicious Italian food in a swanky setting. Italian & Slovak fine wines. $$$. *Open daily 10.00–midnight.*

✕ **Leberfinger** Viedenská cesta 257; ☏ 02 6231 7590. Traditional Pressburg specialities in a historic building visited by Napoleon. A great venue for an afternoon meal on the summer terrace. Situated near Au Café on the other side of the river in Sad Janka Kráľa. $$. *Open daily 11.00–midnight.*

✕ **Le Monde** Hviezdoslavovo námestie 26; ☏ 02 5441 5411; www.lemonde.sk. Bratislava's swankiest restaurant now in its newer, larger setting of the reconstructed Kern House on Hviezdoslavovo námestie, Le Monde still offers great Mediterranean fare in a classy bistro setting. $$$. *Open daily 11.00–midnight.*

✕ **Magd a Lena** Hodžovo námestie 2 (ground floor of Crowne Plaza Hotel); ☏ 02 5934 8080; www.ichotelsgroup.com. Large, grand dining hall that can split into 2 venues. International cuisine & Mediterranean dishes. Choose from the à la carte menu or the international buffet. Popular Sun brunch. Soups $, fish dishes $$$, mains $$$. *Open daily 06.00–23.00.*

✕ **Malecón** Námestie Ľ Štúra 4; ☏ 02 5464 0167; www.malecon.sk. Situated in the pistachio-coloured Esterházy Palace, this roomy venue recreates the steamy ambience of Havana on a hot summer evening. Good mojitos (175Sk). Pricey but with live music each night from 21.00. $$$. *Open Sun–Wed 11.00–01.00, Thu–Sat 11.00–03.00.*

✕ **Messina** (Hotel Marrol's) Tobrucká 4; ☏ 02 5778 4600. Named after the 15th-century Italian Renaissance painter Antonello da Messina, this arty restaurant is really classy. The wood-panelled, chandeliered Messina serves Italian food: figs, prosciutto, shrimps & fried chocolate lasagne. $$$. *Open Mon–Fri 06.30–10.00 & 11.30–23.00, Sat–Sun 07.00–10.00 & 11.30–23.00.*

✕ **Opera Brasserie** (Radisson SAS Hotel Carlton) Hviezdoslavovo námestie 3; ☏ 02 5939 0400. Swiss executive chef Markus Niederhauser lets his imagination run riot in the old-time setting. International cuisine, Slovak dishes done in a lighter fashion. Locally adapted international food. $$$–$$$$. *Open Mon–Fri 06.30–22.30, Sat–Sun 07.00–10.30.*

✕ **Preego** Žilinská 4; m 0903 246 226; www.preego.sk. Scary entrance up a fire escape-style stairway behind the inverted pyramid of Slovak Radio conceals one of Bratislava's best-kept culinary secrets. If the stairs are like something from South Central LA, the interior is pure uptown Manhattan. Classy lounge with stylish lighting. $$$. *Café lounge open daily 10.00–midnight, restaurant open daily 11.00–22.00.*

✕ **Savoyka** Mostová 6; ☏ 02 5443 2002. Offering a fresh take on meaty standards; deer steak on rösti with sauce Bordelaise & fresh berries (888Sk) or loin of mouton on lavender with gratin potatoes & grilled vegetables (925Sk). Highly rated & located on the side of the Radisson SAS Carlton Hotel building, opposite the Reduta. $$$$. *Open Mon–Fri 11.30–14.30 & 18.30–23.30, Sat 18.00–23.00, Sun closed.*

✗ **Slovenská Reštaurácia** Hviezdoslavovo námestie 20; ↘ 02 5443 4883; www.slovrest.com. Rustic restaurant with Hansel & Gretel furniture, cartwheels dangling & an (unintentionally) amusing menu. 'Selections of our old mothers' is not very flattering. A good place to try Slovak Tokaj. $$. *Open daily 11.00–23.00.*

✗ **Traja Musketieri** Sládkovičova 7; ↘ 02 5443 0019; www.trajamusketieri.sk. A low-arched 17th-century cellar bar with bits of animal & frying pans dangling from the ceiling. Slovak & French wines. $$. *Open 11.00–23.00.*

✗ **UFO Watch Taste Groove** Nový most; ↘ 02 6252 0300; www.u-f-o.sk. To get there, walk across Nový most (New Bridge) on the walkway one level lower than the road. When you reach the far side, take the first set of steps down onto a lower level where you'll find the entrance to the lift. Locals are a bit fed up with this place as they can never get in to swan about the Phillipe Starck-inspired interior as it's always booked up by the Viennese for private parties. Expect a stratospheric bill for the progressive Mediterranean cuisine & overpriced wine list. Check out the 'loo with the view'. You'll find yourself flashing the residents of Petržalka far down below with only a swathe of frosted glass covering your modesty. The lift has a great live camera showing the lift shaft as you shoot up. Cover charge 150Sk. Membership from 5,000Sk. Tickets for lift & *Watch* observation deck (*open daily 10.00–23.00; 100Sk (€ 3)*). *Taste* (restaurant & bar) *open daily 11.00–23.00.* $$$$. *Groove* (exclusive nightclub) *open Sat midnight–04.00.*

✗ **U Mamičky** Palis`ády 40; ↘ 02 5443 4618; www.umamicky.sk. Up in the hilly, residential part of town *en route* to the Slavín Monument, you'll find a classy Balkan place, owned by a Macedonian gentleman & featuring a gorgeous garden. 'At Mummy's' features charcoal-grilled treats from the Adriatic every Tue & Thu. Top-quality Croatian & Macedonian wines. $$$. *Open daily 11.00–23.00.*

✗ **U Zlatého Vodnika** (At the Golden Waterman) Zlaté Piesky 15; ↘ 02 4425 9224. T 2, 4. Massive portions in the little hut on the lake. Sit on the terrace overlooking the water & be sure to try the grilled trout with garlic. They do doggy bags too. On the main road to Nitra & Žilina. $$. *Open daily 09.00–23.00.*

CAFÉS AND TEAROOMS Like its neighbours Vienna and Budapest, Bratislava has a long coffee-house tradition. Some traditional cafés still exist and many Slovaks love to while away an afternoon at the *cukráreň* (patisserie). On Sunday afternoons, they used to take the tram all the way to Vienna for a coffee, and the Viennese came to Pressburg (Bratislava) for their *kaffee und kuchen*. Do the traditional thing and order a *viedenská káva* (a heart-blasting coffee topped with whipped cream) and strudel (*štrúdľa*) with poppy seed and curd cheese (*makovotvarohová*). Most places also serve cappuccinos, lattes and variations on the java jive. As in Vienna, you'll get a tiny biscuit or bit of chocolate and often a glass of water with your brew. If you prefer tea, Bratislava has a growing collection of *čajovňa* or tearooms. Most are non-smoking and offer a variety of premium teas from all parts of the globe. Other favourite cake items include *krémeš* (huge cubes of solidified custard held in place with pastry), *bajgle* (glazed crescent-shaped rolls filled with walnuts or poppy seeds) and *šamrola* (pastries filled with cream and dusted with icing sugar).

Old Town and Castle District

🍵 **Café Kút** Zámočnícka 11; ↘ 02 5443 4957. A cosy café hidden in a courtyard next to the Prašna Bašta restaurant, endless cocktail variations, cool tunes, DJs, reggae. *Open Mon–Fri 08.00–23.00, Sat–Sun 16.00–23.00.*

🍵 **Čokoládovňa pod Michalom** Michalská 6; ↘ 02 5443 3945. The Austro-Hungarian nobility loved to go out for a hot choccie. Here they have 60 different kinds. *Open Mon–Fri 09.00–20.00, Sat–Sun 10.00–20.00.*

🍵 **Kaffé Mayer** Hlavné námestie 4; ↘ 02 5441 1741. Old-style Viennese *kaffee und kuchen*, one of 3 biggies on Hlavné námesti. Dark & reassuring with polished wood & great cakes. It even gets a mention in Patrick Leigh Fermor's *A Time of Gifts*. *Open Sun–Thu 09.30–22.00, Fri–Sat 09.30–midnight.*

🍵 **Kaviareň Radnička** Stará Radnička. One of the few non-smoking cafés in the city located under the arch of the Old Town Hall. It's a 'protected workshop' of the Kampino organisation, integrating people with learning difficulties into the community. *Open daily 09.30–21.00.*

3

London Café (British Council) Panská 17;
02 5443 1074. Smart white café, with restaurant
one side & café with 2 internet terminals the other.
Selection of daily papers from the UK. *Open Mon–Fri
09.00–20.00, Sat 09.00–15.00, closed Sun.*

Malewill Café Uršulínska 9; 02 5443 4440.
Malewill does 20 versions on the theme of coffee.
*Open Mon–Fri 10.00–midnight, Sat 12.00–midnight, Sun
12.00–22.00.*

Roland restaurant and café Hlavné námestie
5; 02 5443 1372. Located behind a gorgeous Art
Nouveau façade with a beautiful interior on the Main
Square & very proud of its *Churrascaria de Rodizo*
Brazilian barbecue. Features a model of the Amazing
Turk (see page 86). *Open daily 08.30–midnight.*

Schokocafé Maximilian Delikatesso
Hlavné námestie 3; 02 5443 5474. Two-level café
next to Roland. All-you-can-eat menu (500Sk).
Maximilian's huge shop window features a dripping,
oozing chocolate fountain, like something from
Willy Wonka's imagination. *Open daily
09.00–midnight.*

Beyond the Old Town gates, Centrum and further afield

Bagel and Coffee Story Štúrova 13; 02
5263 1655. Good bagels & coffees. Tofu salad &
mineral water (107Sk). *Open Mon–Fri 07.30–22.00,
Sat 08.30–22.00, Sun 10.00–21.00.*

Next Apache Panenská 28; m 0903 818 169;
www.nextapache.com. Fabulous café set in an old
Evangelical Lyceaum building with arched ceilings &
creaky wooden floors, there are rumours that Ľudovít
Štúr lived here. Created by Canadian Ben Pascoe, the
café & bar has a magnificent collection of secondhand
books. They serve 2 Fair Trade & 4 exotic coffees.
Open Mon–Fri 09.00–22.00, Sat–Sun 10.00–22.00.

Steam & Coffee Hviezdoslavovo námestie 3;
02 5920 4060. There are 5 Steam & Coffee outlets
situated around town, but this one, within the walls
of the stunning Carlton Hotel offers the best
location. It's a restaurant as well as a coffee shop,
with main dishes ($$), desserts, b/fasts in a setting
of maroon walls & polished wood. *Open Mon–Fri
08.00–midnight, Sat–Sun 11.00–midnight.*

Štefánka Café Palisády 59 (entrance on
Hodzovo námestie); 02 5262 0847;
www.stefanka.sk. Beautifully renovated traditional
Habsburg café with yellow walls, pine green
upholstery & polished wood. Run since 1904 by the
Hackenburger family & named after the much-loved
Princess Stephanie (1864–1945), daughter of Leopold
II of Belgium. She was married to Rudolf who
committed suicide at Mayerling (see page 114). *Open
Mon–Fri 09.00–22.00, Sat–Sun 10.00–22.00.*

THE AMAZING TURK

Wolfgang von Kempelen, the inventor of the Magic Turk chess-playing
automaton, was born in Bratislava in 1734 (died 1804) in the building to the left
of the University library.

In 1770, The Turk made its first appearance in front of the Viennese court. On
a signal from the Empress Maria Theresa, Baron Wolfgang von Kempelen slowly
wheeled his creation forward. The 1m-high wooden cabinet with a large
chessboard screwed to its top ran on four brass casters that not only allowed
it to move freely, but also raised it slightly off the floor so that the audience
could see that there was nothing hiding underneath. Behind the box sat a figure,
dressed in Oriental clothing and a bulky turban. Kempelen challenged audience
members to play the Turk at chess. Almost all were defeated. During its tours,
the Turk fascinated Napoleon, Benjamin Franklin, Edgar Allan Poe and computing
pioneer Charles Babbage. The chess player became the most famous automaton
in history. And along the way, Kempelen's work would unwittingly help to inspire
the development of the power loom, the telephone, the computer and the
detective story. In 1766, Kempelen was appointed director of the imperial salt
mines in Transylvania. He devised a system of pumps to drain the mines when
they became flooded with water. Following the success of this project, he was
asked to design the waterworks for Bratislava Castle. He devised a pump to
carry water up to the castle from the Danube, as before that all they had was
one well. See a model (not working) in Roland coffee house on Hlavné námestie.

Old Town and Castle District

Ⓨ **De Zwaan** Panská 7; ☎ 02 5441 9166;
www.dezwaan.sk. Belgian-owned pub with Leffe beer
on tap, 'The Swan' recalls an Amsterdam brown café:
cosy, dark, restful, very laid-back Low Countries.
Open daily 11.00–23.00.
Ⓨ **Dubliner Irish Pub** Sedlárska 6; ☎ 02 5441 0706;
www.irish-pub.sk. Packed with expats, stag parties &
bewildered locals. Football & ice hockey on massive
screens. *Open Mon–Sat 11.00–03.00, Sun 11.00–01.00.*
Ⓨ **Kristián Pub** Michalská 10; ☎ 02 5443 4038. The
best-kept draught Pilsner in Bratislava, & internet
access. *Open daily 14.00–midnight.*
Ⓨ **Verdict Bar** Panská 6; ㎡ 0910 930 143.
Nondescript venue, but a pleasant enough place to

sip a cold beer & watch the footie. *Open Mon–Thu
11.00–midnight, Fri–Sat 11.00–01.00, Sun
14.00–midnight.*
Ⓨ **Vináreň Velké Františkáni** Františkánske
námestie 10; ☎ 02 5443 3073. The most famous wine
cellar in town, in a late Renaissance building dating
from 1347. A selection of 130 Slovak wines on offer
within the bricked-up vaults. Live gypsy music every
night from 18.00 (see also Malí Františkáni at
Námestie SNP 24 in the following section). When
you totter out look up at the bedroom window
from where a Franciscan monk gesticulates gleefully.
Mains avg 200Sk. *Restaurant open daily 11.00–01.00,
wine cellar open daily 17.00–01.00.*

Beyond the Old Town gates, Centrum and further afield

Ⓨ **1. Slovenská krčma/1st Slovak Pub** Obchodná
62; ☎/f 02 5292 6367; www.slovakpub.sk. Pink
building on dusty Obchodná, this pub is made up of
11 separate rooms representing various periods in
Slovak history. *Open Mon–Thu 10.00–midnight, Fri–Sat
10.00–02.00, Sun 12.00–midnight.*
Ⓨ **17s Bar** Hviezdoslavovo námestie 17; ☎ 02 5443
5135. Great pizzas served until late, draught Czech
beer. Live music. *Open daily 12.00–midnight.*
Ⓨ **4 Izby** Heydukova 19. Just down the road from
the main synagogue, the 'Four Rooms' pub/club
offers Czech beer, a jukebox & table. Popular with
younger locals. *Open Mon–Fri 10.00–22.00, Sat–Sun
16.00–22.00.*
Ⓨ **Bistro Čajka** Nábrežie arm. gen. L. Svobodu (next
to Botel Marina). A delightful little stone hut, its walls
painted with seagulls (*čajka*) flying across a sky-blue
sky. Three tables by the gangplank down to the Botel
Marina. *Open daily 16.00–22.00.*
Ⓨ **Gremium** Gorkého 10; ☎ 02 5413 1025;
www.gremium.sk. Busy sports bar, with loud music, a
big screen & banks of TVs showing ice hockey &
football. Ticket office with betting (a bit like the pools)
on sports matches. $$. *Open daily 11.00–midnight.*
Ⓨ **KGB** Obchodná 52; ☎ 02 5273 1278. Clichéd
commie theme has busts & pictures of Lenin, Stalin,
& Gustáv Husák, Czechoslovakia's last communist
leader. *Open Mon–Thu 11.00–01.30, Fri 11.00–03.30,
Sat 15.30–01.00, Sun 15.30–23.00.*
Ⓨ **Korzo** Hviezdoslavovo námestie 11; ☎ 02 5443
4974. Windy terrace with tourist prices but a great
place to sip Zlatý Bažant (50Sk), soak up the sun &
stare at the cars whizzing over Nový most. $$.
Open daily 08.00–midnight.

Ⓨ **Kriváň museum boat and bar** Viedenská cesta
257; ☎ 02 6241 2227; www.leberfinger.sk/krivan.
Moored on the Danube on the park side, near Au
Café. Shipping museum & good place for a beer. *Open
daily 11.00–23.00.*
Ⓨ **Malí Františkáni** (Little Franciscans) Námestie
SNP 24; ☎ 02 5413 1236. A labyrinth of low-
ceilinged corridors leading to a medieval room with
some monk memorabilia. A cool venue on hot days.
Open daily 10.00–06.00.
Ⓨ **Mýtny Domček** Southern side of the Old Bridge
(Starý most); ㎡ 0911 433 763. A sweet pub in the
original tollhouse at the Petržalka side of the Old
(railway) Bridge. $. *Open daily 11.00–23.00.*
Ⓨ **Plzensky dvor** Cintorínska 26; ☎ 02 5292 6591.
Very popular with office workers at lunchtime
enjoying pub food, but canny visitors have also
discovered what great Czech beer they serve here.
$. *Open Mon–Sat 10.00–02.00, Sun 10.00–midnight.*
Ⓨ **Prazdroj** Mostová 8; ☎ 02 5441 1108.
Peppermint ice cream walls hide honest-to-goodness
Czech beer hall. *Open Mon–Sat 10.00–02.00, Sun
10.00–midnight.*
Ⓨ **Smíchovská Perla** Mariánska 11; ☎ 02 5296
4493. At the corner of Špitálska & Mariánska, this is a
huge Czech beer hall plus a sunny terrace. Live
music on Sat evenings. $. *Restaurant open Mon–Fri
09.00–22.00, Sat 10.00–22.00, closed Sun. Beer hall
open Mon–Thu 11.00–midnight, Fri 11.00–02.00, Sat
12.00–02.00, closed Sun.*
Ⓨ **Sparx** Cintorínska 32; ☎ 02 5296 8061;
www.sparx.sk. Formerly the Mamut (Mammoth) Pub
(*www.mamut.sk*) once the largest beer hall in central
Europe packing in 2,000 drinkers, now this vast

complex includes a. pub, cocktail bar, restaurant, disco, nightclub, strip joint, bingo hall, casino, internet café & self-service lunch canteen. $. *Open Mon–Wed 10.00–midnight, Thu–Fri 10.00–03.00, Sat 11.00–03.00, Sun 11.00–midnight.* ♀**Trafená Hus** Šafárikovo námestie 7; ☎ 02 5292 5473; www.trafenahus.sk. The name comes from the saying *Trafená hus zagága* (literally: 'the struck goose squeals') meaning a person with a guilty conscience who unwittingly lets the cat out of the bag. Lots of

Belgian brews. *Open Mon–Fri 07.00–midnight, Sat–Sun 10.00–midnight.* ♀**Umelka** Dostojevského 2; ☎ 02 5263 4754; www.umelka.sk. A 'pivný pub' opposite Komenského University, shady terrace marred by exhaust fumes from Old Bridge traffic. Woody interior designed by Devín organic woodcarver Peter Strassner (see *Chapter 000, Devín,* page 116). *Open Mon–Fri 10.00–23.00, Sat–Sun 11.00–23.00.*

ENTERTAINMENT, NIGHTLIFE AND RECREATION

In the spring and summer and even early autumn, Bratislava's Old Town comes alive in the late afternoon as the pavement cafés fill with people enjoying an aperitif or chilled beer in the sunshine before heading off to a restaurant, show or another bar.

The pretty, tree-lined Hviezdoslavovo námestie is crowded with people dressed up in their glad rags, gathering before a performance at the Slovak National Theatre or the Reduta. Even if your mission is to drink Bratislava dry, you should consider a night at the opera. You will never again have such a great opportunity to see world-class singers in a gorgeous setting for the price of a pint in London. Pick up a copy of *Kam do Mesta,* the pocket-sized monthly listings guide. It's in Slovak but fairly decipherable.

TICKET OFFICES

BKIS Klobučnícka 2; ☎ 02 5443 2708
Eventim Tickets online can be purchased at www.eventim.sk
Slovak National Theatre (opera) SND Ticket Office, Komenského námestie (behind the SND building); ☎/f 02 5443 3764. Standby tickets at the ticket office in the SND's historical building foyer (*Gorkého 4;* ☎ 02 5443 3890) 30mins before the performances. There are 2 prices as tickets go on sale 1 month before performances. In the unlikely event that there are still some tickets left, they can be purchased up to 10 days before the show for as little as €2 in the second balcony. As a guide to prices, tickets cost €15–30 (last-minute unsold tickets from

€3.50) for *Turandot,* €10–25 for *Aida* (last-minutes from €3). For some lesser-known operas, eg: *The Kiss,* regular tickets cost €2.50–10. *Ticket office open Mon–Fri 08.00–17.30, Sat 09.00–13.00.*
Slovak Philharmonic Slovensky filharmónie, Reduta building; Palackého 2; reservations; ☎ 02 5443 3351 or 02 5443 3352; f 02 5443 5956; e filharmonia@filharmonia.sk; www.filharmonia.sk. *Ticket office open Mon, Tue, Thu, Fri 13.00–19.00, Wed 08.00–14.00 & 1hr before performances.*
Ticket Portal ☎ 02 5293 3323. Tickets online at www.ticketportal.sk. Offices can be found in the shopping malls Aupark, Polus City Center & in the tourist offices of Satur & Hydrotour.

THEATRE Bratislava has a strong theatrical tradition, and while most performances will be in Slovak and out of reach for many visitors' ears, the Slovak National Theatre is a must for opera or ballet and venues such as the Puppet Theatre and the more alternative Stoka may have shows that appeal. Musicals, showing at the Nová scéna and sometimes at the beautiful Aréna, go down well in any language.

🎭 **Nová scéna SND** Kollárovo námestie 20; ☎ 02 5292 5741; e ns@nova-scena.sk. A popular venue for musicals such as *Hair & The Full Monty. Shows at 19.00.*
🎭 **Puppet Theatre** Dunajská 36; ☎ 02 529 23 668;

e bbdbrtis@stonline.sk; www.babkovedivadlo.sk. Performances for children. *Shows usually at 10.00 & 14.00.*
🎭 **Slovak National Theatre** (Opera & Ballet) Slovak National Opera House, Hviezdoslavovo námestie 1;

02 5443 3083; www.snd.sk. The beautifully restored Slovak National Theatre dates back to 1776 & offers drama, ballet & opera. Opera performances have subtitles in Slovak or German, so English speakers should familiarise themselves with the plot in advance. Performances usually start at 19.00. Find the schedule at the Slovak National Theatre at www.snd.sk. *Season runs Sep–Jun, summer break Jul–Aug.*

MUSIC
Music venues
♪ **Babylon Music Club** Karpatská 2; 02 5249 8005. Formerly a cinema, this boxy music hall with loads of neon hosts domestic & regional music acts almost daily. Ghymes (who are known for playing Slovak folk music in Hungary) perform here frequently.

♪ **Incheba** www.incheba.sk. Seal performed recently at one of the many huge pavilions.

♪ **Istropolis** Trnavské mýto 1; 02 5557 4939. Recent performances at this cavernous venue include the *Galileo* musical & a performance by Stomp!

♪ **PKO** Nábrežie arm. gen. L. Svobodu 3; 02 5441 6040. BKIS puts on concerts here like Omara Portuondo, a country music festival.

♪ **ŠH Pasienky** Trnavská cesta 29; 02 4437 2127. Huge stadium home to Inter Slovnaft Bratislava basketball team. Concerts by Demis Roussos & the like.

♪ **ST Arena** Near the Polus Center. Ice hockey arena used for spectaculars such as *Holiday on Ice.*

Classical music Given Bratislava's rich musical heritage – visitors have included such luminaries as Liszt, Mozart, Beethoven, Bartók, Dohnányi, Haydn as well as local boy Hummel – you'd be mad to miss a classical music production while in the presence of such greats.

The buildings of the Slovak National Theatre and the Reduta are beautiful historic monuments and the opera productions rival those in Budapest and Vienna for a much more reasonable price. Visit the elegant Mirbach and the Primate's Palace to hear chamber music concerts or piano recitals in an atmospheric setting. Many excellent choirs sing for free in churches such as the Lutheran church in the Old Town. The bizarre inverted pyramid building of Slovak Radio has amazing acoustics.

♪ **Bratislava Castle Concert Hall** 02 5441 4300

♪ **Klarisky Concert Hall** Farská 4; 02 5443 2942; www.mksba.sk. Concerts at the Church of the Sisters of the Order of St Clare.

♪ **Mirbach Palace** Františkánske námestie 11; 02 5443 1556. *Concerts every Sun at 11.30.*

♪ **Mirror Hall of the Primate's Palace** Primaciálne námestie; 02 5935 6111

♪ **Moyzes' Concert Hall** Vajanského nábrežie 12; 02 5443 3351

♪ **Music Centre Slovakia** Michalská 10; 02 5443 4003; www.hc.sk. Has a list of events: jazz, blues, classical.

♪ **Slovak Philharmonic, Reduta** Palackého 2; 02 5443 5242; f 02 5443 4581; www.filharm.sk & www.reduta.sk. On the same square is the Reduta Concert Hall, home of the Slovak Philharmonic, one of the best orchestras in central Europe. Daily classical concerts cost from £5. Operating for more than half a century, the Slovak National Philharmonic comprises 5 ensembles: the Slovak Philharmonic Orchestra, Slovak Philharmonic Choir, Bohdan Warchal Slovak Chamber Orchestra, Musica aeterna & the Moyzes Quartet.

♪ **Slovak Radio Concert Hall** (Slovenský rozhlas) Mýtna 1; 02 5727 3479

Folk music Many restaurants in Bratislava have folk music performances to accompany the food. Downstairs at the Korzo restaurant is particularly good. Large folk music performances can be seen at venues such as Istropolis. Bratislava's districts are dotted with culture houses where you can see performances or take part in a 'dance house' (*tanečný dom*), a combination of folk dance lesson and performance. The website www.tanecnydom.sk explains more and has details of upcoming events.

3

FRANZ LISZT Ventúrska No7 in Leopold di Pauli Palace (next to Zichy Palace). In 1820, Liszt (1811–86) gave a concert aged nine in the garden pavilion and started on his triumphal career. Liszt visited Bratislava 15 times. Also a bust of Liszt on Rudnayavo námestie.

BÉLA BARTÓK Klariská ulica. Hungarian Bartók (1881–1945) studied Slovak folk songs here from 1892–99. Bust of Bartók in pink stone, head emerging from stone at Špitálska 7. He lived and worked here from 1894–1908 – near the Sv Ladislav Church; monastery at number 5.

ERNÔ DOHNÁNYI (1877–1960) Hungarian composer/pianist studied at the Catholic School at the Convent of Clare Nuns on Klariská ulica.

WOLFGANG AMADEUS MOZART (1756–91) Ventúrska 10, Pálffy Palace. Mozart, aged six, gave a concert (accompanied by his father) for the local aristocracy in 1762; also his Requiem was performed in St Martin's Cathedral in 1834.

LUDWIG VAN BEETHOVEN Panská ulica 27. Beethoven (1770–1827) gave a concert at Earl Keglevich's Baroque palace here.

JOHANN NEPOMUK HUMMEL Klobučnícka 2. Hummel (1778–1837) was born here; now a museum to his life and work. Hummel succeeded Haydn as Prince Esterházy's concert master.

JOSEPH HAYDN Kapitulská 6. Haydn (1732–1809) conducted the première of his opera *La Canterina* here at the former Esterházy Palace, Kapitulská 6.

ANTON GRIGORIEVICH RUBINSTEIN Sedlárska 7. The great Russian pianist and composer Rubinstein (1829–94) was considered a rival to Liszt. In 1847, he lived and worked in the building that now hosts the French Institute. He is no relation to the 20th-century pianist Arthur Rubinstein.

♪ **Sluk** Balkánska 31, Rusovce; ☏ 02 6285 9125. A folk ensemble performs Slovak music & dance in and around Bratislava. Folk traditions from all over Slovakia are represented in unique arrangements.

Jazz and easy listening Bratislavans are mad about jazz and there are many places to hear live concerts in a funky setting, often with food and drink to accompany the cool tunes. The international jazz festival is one of the most popular events of its kind in central Europe. It takes place at the PKO cultural centre on the banks of the Danube.

♪ **Café Studio Club** Laurinská 13. A good place for live jazz music, with artists such as the local favourite saxophonist Peter Cardarelli.
♪ **Jazz Café** Ventúrska 5; ☏ 02 5443 4661. Cellar bar with live music, not just jazz, serving food too. Packed on Sat when there's usually Irish music. *Open daily 10.00–02.00.*
♪ **Metro Club** Suché mýto 6. Near the Crowne Plaza Hotel, plays jazz & nostalgic grooves until late. *Open Fri–Sat 20.00–04.00.*

♪ **Radosť** Obchodná 48; www.mojaradost.sk. A new chill-out bar attracting a hip young crowd. *Open Mon–Sat 17.00–04.30, Sun 17.30–midnight.*
♪ **Trafo music bar** Ventúrska 1; ☏ 02 2092 2744; f 02 2092 2755; e info@trafo.sk; www.trafo.sk. Connected to the trendy Camouflage restaurant, continue the evening here with house, techno, chillout, funky, pop, nu-jazz, hip hop, drum 'n' bass, special events every Sat night. *Open Tue–Sat 21.00–05.00.*

Contemporary Live music, particularly rock is still very popular and reggae goes down well too. Check out www.reggae.sk for more details.

♫ **Alligator** Laurinská 7. Blues & rock from rough 'n' ready young bands.

♫ **K-Bar** Bulharská, Trnávka district. Rock club a little way out of the centre with live music (Wed), karaoke (Thu) & discos at the weekend.

♫ **Nultý Priestor** Námestie SNP 12. The name means Zero Space, also connected to A4 club (*www.a4.sk*) providing a venue for non-commercial groups & individuals to put on shows of theatre, dance, music, cinema & any form of creative art.

♫ **Stoka** Pribinova 1; ☏ 02 5292 4470; www.stoka.sk. This alternative theatre offers live blues, world music & grunge/rock concerts 3 times a week. Beware, the name means 'sewer'. *Performances usually at 20.00.*

NIGHTCLUBS AND DISCOS When the lights go down, Bratislava becomes party central. There are many places where the beautiful people go to swing their pants.

☆ **Cirkus Barok** Rázusovo nábrezie; ☏ 02 5464 2091–3; www.cirkusbarok.sk. Disco boat near Námestie Ľ. Štúra. *Open Sun–Thu 11.00–04.00, Fri–Sat 11.00–06.00.*

☆ **Coyote Ugly** Rožňavská 1; ☏ 02 4463 8923; www.coyoteugly.sk. Recreating the film with blonde barmaids jiggling on the bar until late. *Open Mon–Thu 11.00–23.00, Fri–Sat 11.00–04.00, Sun closed.*

☆ **Duna** Radlinského 11; www.duna.sk. Dark, industrial club. *Open Tue–Wed 21.00–02.00, Thu 21.00–04.00, Fri–Sat 21.00–05.00, closed Sun–Mon.*

☆ **Flamenko Music Club** 14 Štefánikova; ☏ 0905 612 904. Dance until 05.00 at weekends to spirited Latino music with laid-back patrons interested in having fun. *Open Mon–Thu 11.00–02.00, Fri 11.00–05.00, Sat 14.00–05.00, closed Sun.*

☆ **Laverna 1224** Námestie SNP 25; ☏ 02 5443 3165; www.laverna.sk. A cellar disco with 2 bars, quieter table seating & a DJ-backed dancefloor. A favourite with celebrities & the in-crowd. *Oldies disco every Tue. Open daily 21.00–06.00.*

GAY BRATISLAVA The gay scene in Bratislava is quiet and discreet, yet there are some options for a big night out for gay men, less so for lesbians. Check out www.gay.sk.

☆ **4 Pink's** Župné námestie 3; e 4pinks@4pinks.sk; www.4pinks.sk. Newest gay club in town. *Open Sun–Thu 16.00–02.00, Fri–Sat 16.00–05.00.* ☆ **Apollon** Panenská 24; www.apollon-gay-club.sk. Bratislava's coolest gay club is tucked into a vaulted cellar with 2 bars & a friendly atmosphere. Their website has many useful links. Strippers on Wed. *Open daily 18.00–02.00.*

☆ **Café Antik** Rybárska brána 2; ☏ 02 5443 0262. Has a mixed, gay-friendly crowd.

☆ **Caffé Barbaros** Vysoká 20; m 0903 461 717; www.barbaros.sk. This café opened May 2004 & soon became one of the most popular gay meeting places. Lesbian day every Thu. *Open Mon–Thu 09.00–01.00, Fri 09.00–03.00, Sat 17.00–03.00, Sun 18.00–midnight.*

☆ **U Anjelov** Laurinská 19; ☏ 02 5443 2724; e anjeli@stonline.sk; www.anjeli.sk/start.aspx. A cosy café with a pink tinge, look for the winged cherubs outside the front. Desserts, cocktails, alcohol, little terrace in the summer. Also offers accommodation at Javorinská 9/a, up in the hills. The website has details. *Open Mon–Thu 09.00–midnight, Fri 09.00–01.30, Sat 13.00–01.30, Sun 13.00–midnight.*

CINEMA When looking for a film make sure it is *na tento týždeň* meaning 'showing this week'. Note the codes ST (with Slovak subtitles), ČT (with Czech subtitles) and be wary of films with SD (Slovak dubbing) or ČD (Czech dubbing). ČV means it's the Czech version.

Filmový Klub Ic.sk Špitálska 4; ☏ 02 5296 3396
Filmový Klub Múzeum Old Town Hall; ☏ 02 5443 4742
Filmový Klub Nostalgia Starohorská 2; ☏ 02 5296 1712; www.nostalgia.sk **Hviezda** Námestie 1 mája;

☏ 02 5296 7471
Mladosť Hviezdoslavovo námestie 14; ☏ 02 5443 5003
Orange IMAX Avion Shopping Park; Ivánska cesta 12; ☏ 02 4342 3033; e info@kinoimax.sk; www.kinoimax.sk

Palace Aupark (Multiplex) Einsteinova 18; ☎ 02
6820 2222; e aupark@palacecinemas.sk;
www.palacecinemas.sk
Ster Century Multikino Metropolis Vajnorská

100, Polus City Center; ☎ 02 4910 2222;
e info@multikinometropolis.sk;
www.multikinometropolis.sk
Tatra Námestie I mája 12; ☎ 02 592 72 151

FESTIVALS AND EVENTS

Bratislava celebrates a range of events throughout the year. Tickets and more information are available from the BKIS office at Klobučnícka 2; www.bkis.sk. The City Hall website (*www.bratislava.sk*) also has details of events.

Feb	**City Ball** Bratislava's high society puts on its finery at the Reduta. Carnivals also in February. See www.reduta.sk.
21–22 Apr	**Bratislava for Everybody** Bratislava local government arranges a series of open days when museums and galleries are open and free.
around 1–9 May	**Days of Europe Bratislava** An international festival of music, film, dance, fine art and fun.
8–17 Jun	**Beer Festival – Junifest** Beer flows freely for ten days at the Incheba exhibition and congress centre. See www.incheba.sk.
around 4 Jun	**International Festival of Water Sprites** A collection of attractions celebrating water.
17 Jun–1 Aug	**Cultural Summer 2006** A feast of music, dance, singing, crafts, amusements and gastronomic delights in Bratislava.
around Jun–Sep	**Castle Festivities of Bratislava** An international festival of arts and culture. For 13 weekends, the main courtyard of the castle is the scene of a series of concerts, classical and contemporary music. There are also Organ Music Days, a summer Shakespeare theatre and many other performances.
around 2–3 Sep	**Days of Masters of Úľúv** Úľuv is an organisation which specialises in folk art production, traditional crafts and specialist collaborations.
around 3 Sep	**Coronation Festivities** Bratislava is once again the town of coronations.
Sep–Oct	**Music Festival of Bratislava/Bratislavské Hudobné Slávnosti** The most prestigious festival of classical music in Slovakia, now running for more than 40 years. Look at the Bratislava City Hall website at www.bratislava.sk for details.
the whole of Oct, every even year	**Biennial of Illustrations Bratislava** The international competition is an exhibition of book illustrations for children and young people.
around 21–23 Oct	**Bratislava Jazz Days** The international jazz festival is one of the most popular events of its kind in central Europe. At PKO cultural centre. See www.bjd.sk for further details.
Nov	**Photography Month** Annual celebration of photography at venues around town.
around 2–10 Dec	**International Film Festival** Check out www.iffbratislava.sk.
6 Dec	**St Nicholas's Day and the Lighting of the Christmas Tree** An event to celebrate St Mikuláš with presents and lots of chocolate for the children.

Dec	**Christmas in the Castle** Full-day programmes devoted to Christmas events for children. More details on www.snm-hm.sk.
around 25 Nov–23 Dec	**Christmas Market** The Christmas Market fills the Main Square with stalls offering traditional arts and crafts.
31 Dec	**New Year's Eve Party in the City** Around 50,000 people gather in the tiny Old Town centre and are joined by several thousand tourists to enjoy live concerts, open-air discos and other cultural events. The climax is the midnight fireworks show over the Danube and the luminous animations on the river embankment.

SHOPPING

It's never going to compete with Paris or Milan, however Bratislava probably doesn't want to. It's quite happy with what it's got. There are swanky designer shops along Michalská and Ventúrska. Obchodná is the main shopping drag with teeny jeans shops and record stores. Aupark is within walking distance of the Old Town centre, a short hop across Nový most and hiding behind the greenery of Sad Janka Kráľa park, at the beginning of the Petržalka housing estate. Aupark also has a range of facilities, numerous restaurants and cafés, a multiplex cinema, rock-climbing wall and skateboard park. There are some fascinating speciality shops in Bratislava, from quality wine shops to rare books. Jewellery fans might pick up a bargain necklace here and there are some excellent outlets for fine art, glassware, ceramics and woodcrafts.

FOLK ART CENTRES AND SOUVENIRS There are many shops selling folk arts and crafts. The ÚĽuv centre for folk art production has a great selection of goods and gifts. ÚĽuv stands for *Ústredie ľudovej umeleckej výroby* (Centre for Folk Art Production) and has several outlets in Bratislava. Along Sedlárska (by the Dubliner pub) are several souvenir shops with all kinds of ideas to lessen the last-minute gift panic. Souvenirs include pottery, porcelain, woodcarvings, hand-embroidered clothing and food items. There is a number of excellent shops specialising in glass and crystal, while various associations of regional artists and artisans run their own retail outlets. Look out for folk ceramics from all regions of the Slovak Republic and woodcarvings from the eastern regions: Kyjatice (in the eastern part of Banská Bystrica region), Michalovce (Košice) and Spišská Belá (Prešov).

🏬 **BKIS** Klobučnícka 2; ☎ 02 5443 3715; e bkis@bkis.sk; www.bkis.sk. There is also a shop inside the BKIS office offering a range of maps, postcards, small folk crafts & books on Bratislava. *Open Mon–Fri 08.30–19.00, Sat–Sun 09.00–17.00.*
🏬 **Folk Folk** Rybárska brána 2; ☎ 02 5443 4874
🏬 **Karol Balogh Pressburg Souvenirs** Sedlárska 8. Wooden toys, nick nacks, ceramics. *Open daily 10.00–18.00 (in Jan 12.00–18.00).*
🏬 **Obchod na Korze** Sedlárska 10. Another souvenir shop. *Open daily 09.00–18.00.*
🏬 **Suveníry** Hurbanovo námestie 5. Glass tankards, shot glasses, badges, flags, baseball caps, crests, tie pins & 'I love Slovakia' stickers. *Open Mon–Fri*

10.00–12.00 & 13.00–18.00. Closed at weekends.
🏬 **Stará Tržnica gallery** Old Market Hall. Great T-shirts (350Sk) for presents with retro chic: Trabant, Aeroflot, CCCP, Che or humorous themes: 'Slovakia Drinking Team'. Also many football & ice hockey shirts. Ear & navel piercing from 150Sk. *Open Mon–Fri 10.00–19.00, Sat 10.00–15.00.*
🏬 **Ten Senses** Ventúrska 16; m 0903 388 864; www.tensenses.com. Quality gifts: handmade pottery, glassware, clothing, accessories & speciality foods. *Open Mon–Sat 10.00–22.00, Sun 14.00–22.00.*
🏬 **ÚĽuv** Michalská 4; ☎ 02 5443 2288; e craft@uluv.sk, www.uluv.sk

Bratislava is the third city making up the triangle of great Austro-Hungarian cities (Budapest–Vienna–Bratislava). All three have wonderfully atmospheric and traditional Christmas fairs but Bratislava is possibly the most inviting. Bratislava has a beautifully renovated Old Town centre which is totally pedestrianised and thus perfect for tottering around after one too many mulled wines (to keep out the cold, of course) without fear of being mown down by a Škoda careering across the icy roads.

The Bratislava Christmas Market takes place from 25 November to 23 December in the twin main squares of the Old Town: Františkánske námestie and Hlavné námestie right in front of the Municipal Museum and also on the graceful tree-lined square of Hviezdoslavovo námestie a few steps away. In December, the squares are packed with wooden booths offering Christmas gifts, ornaments and a wide variety of festive food and drink. Dishes to try include *lokše* (potato pancakes) available with a choice of fillings, grilled meats such as *ciganska pečienka* (gypsy cutlet), *langoše* (deep-fried doughnuts) or *chlieb mastou*, fresh bread smeared with lard and sprinkled with chopped onions, ideal for accompanying the mulled wine or the special Christmas punch drink. In 2006, the city commissioned the construction of new stalls inspired by the architecture of old Bratislava. Traders offer wooden toys, blown-glass ornaments, hand-painted pottery, Slovak folk art, beeswax candles and handmade gifts. Musical performances take place on a stage set up in front of the Municipal Museum and here you can also sample the special Slovak Christmas cabbage soup, *kapustnica*, a delicious, warming dish enhanced with homemade sausage, whipped cream and dried mushrooms.

FOOD AND DRINK

Billa In the Tatra Centrum, Hodžovo námestie 4. Excellent selection of Slovak wines & beers. *Open Mon–Fri 07.00–22.00, Sat–Sun 08.00–22.00.*
Čokoládovňa pod Michalom Michalská 6; ↘ 02 5443 3945. More than 60 versions of hot chocolate plus luxury choccies to take away. *Open Mon–Fri 09.00–20.00, Sat–Sun 10.00–20.00.*
Terno Aupark mall. Well-stocked supermarket for wines, beers, spirits & good bakery. *Open daily 09.00–22.00.*
Vinotéka Sv Urbana Klobučnícka 4; ↘ 02 5443 2537; www.vinotekasvurbana.sk. Quality wine shop with regular tasting sessions in the cellar & space for eating & drinking. A choice of 500 different wines: sparkling, international & Slovak. Cuban cigars. *Open Mon–Fri 10.00–18.00, Sat 10.00–14.00.*

NEWSPAPERS, BOOKS AND MAPS

Eurobooks Jesenského 5–9; ↘ 02 5441 7959; www.eurobooks.sk. *Open Mon–Fri 08.30–18.30, Sat 09.00–13.00, closed Sun.*
Reduta Palackého 1; ↘ 02 5443 0203. Gorgeous coffee-table books in a beautiful setting. *Open Mon–Sat 09.00–19.00, Sun 13.00–19.00.*
Slovensky Spisovatel Laurinská 2. Coffee-table books, maps, guides, literature. *Open Mon–Fri 09.00–18.00, Sat 09.00–13.00, closed Sun.*

For some unusual little gifts to take home go to the courtyard of the Old Town Hall (*stará radnica*) where there's an amazing elderly gentleman, Florián Takáč, selling metal Soviet badges, postcards, medals and military memorabilia from a tiny shop, *Solidus*. He's been there for ten years and loves meeting people as he can converse in English, German, French, Italian, Russian, Spanish, Polish, Hungarian and Slovak. Now he's learning Japanese, 'So I can provide a better service'.

Steiner Antikvariat Ventúrska 3 (in Academia Istropolitana courtyard) ☎ 02 5443 3778. Founded in 1847, ancient maps, ex-libris plates, secondhand books, etchings. Wonderful shop for browsing & fantasising about finding a treasure map. *Open Mon–Fri 10.00–18.00.*

SPORTS

PASSIVE SPORTS Bars in Bratislava show a lot of sports, particular during the colder months when guests sit indoors instead of sunning themselves on the pavement terrace. Ice hockey is extremely popular and Slovan Bratislava will take priority over Barcelona.

Football Pub Pri Starom Háji; ☎ 02 6280 4428. Behind Artmedia Bratislava football ground in Sad Janka Kráľa. Peppermint-coloured 1-storey building with huge terrace with wooden benches. *Open Sun–Thu 11.00–midnight, Fri–Sat 11.00–01.00.*

Senator (casino and pub) Panská 1; entrance on Rybárská brána opposite Mezzo Mezzo. Very popular with British football fans, packed out on Sun afternoons for live English Premiership games. $$. *Open daily 10.00–22.00.*

FOOTBALL Bratislava boasts three teams: Slovan Bratislava, FK Inter Bratislava and 2004–05 Slovak champions FC ArtMedia Bratislava. Slovan and Inter play near each other in the north of the city, whilst ArtMedia Bratislava are based at the park just south of the Danube.

FC Artmedia Bratislava Krasovského 1; ☎ 02 6225 0043; www.fcartmedia.sk
FK Inter Bratislava Vajnorská 100; ☎ 02 4437 1007; www.askinter.sk/futbal/index

ŠK Slovan Bratislava Tehelné Pole (National Stadium, capacity 30,000), Junácka 2; ☎ 02 5830 3521; www.skslovan.sk

HORSE RACING
Zavodisko Bratislava race track Staroháska 29; ☎ 02 6224 6289; f 02 6231 5221; www.zavodisko.sk

HORSERIDING
Ranch Podunajské Biskupice, Ulica Svornosti 11; ☎ 02 4552 3051. Equestrian school, horseback riding in the Slovak countryside. To get there, take bus 70 from Nový most.

ICE HOCKEY HC Slovan Bratislava are a world-beating team. The team won the 2005 Slovak league championship. The home ice is at the ST arena (*Odbojárov 9; ☎ 02 4437 2828; www.hcslovan.sk*). The stadium seats close to 9,000 people. Tickets to regular season games cost 100–200Sk. Open to the public also.

SWIMMING POOLS
Aulandia Aqua & Spa Paradise Einsteinova 18, Petržalka; ☎ 02 6820 1037; www.aulandia.sk In the Aupark shopping centre across the Danube River with heated pools, waterslides & hot tubs. *Open daily 10.00–22.00.*
Hotel Danube Has a good pool, open to the public. *Open Mon–Fri 10.00–12.00 & 14.00–22.00, Sat–Sun 14.00–18.00.*

Pasienky Pool Junácka 4; ☎ 02 4924 9351. Two pools: 50m adult pool & 25m children's pool. Cost: adult 65Sk, child 35Sk (*both open Mon 19.30–22.00, Tue–Fri 06.00–07.30 & 19.30–22.00, Sat–Sun 10.30–20.00*).
Zlaté Piesky Senecká cesta. Tram 2 or 4 to last stop. Swim outside in summer in the large, soft-water lake. *Open daily 09.00–18.00.*

TENNIS
National Tennis Centre Príkopova 6; ☎ 02 4920 9890; www.ntc.sk. Bratislava locals are very proud of their brand new sports hall. Voted Construction of the Year in 2003. Six tennis courts in a hall with a sliding roof.

HEALTH

Pharmacies For minor ailments, a visit to the nearest pharmacy (*lekáreň*) may suffice. There are many in Bratislava, some opening late and some offering a 24-hour emergency service.

✚ **Lekáreň Milosrdní bratia** Námestie SNP 11. Specialist pharmacy for diabetics. *Open Mon–Fri 07.00–18.00, Sat 08.00–12.00.*

✚ **Lekáreň Novafarm** Námestie SNP 20; ℡ 02 5443 2952. *Open Mon–Fri 08.00–19.00, Sat 08.00–17.00, Sun 09.00–17.00; also has 24-hour*

emergency service.

✚ **Lekáreň Pokrok** Račianska mýto 1/A; ℡ 02 4445 5291. *Open 24hr.*

✚ **Lekáreň 'U archanjela Gabriela'** Obchodná 12; ℡ 02 5443 2100. *Open Mon–Fri 07.30–18.30, Sat 08.00–13.00.*

Hospitals

✚ **Academy L Dérer Faculty Hospital** Emergency clinic, Kramáre, at Limbová ulica 3; ℡ 02 5954 1111

✚ **English-speaking Drienka** Drienova 16; ℡ 02 4333 5703

✚ **Faculty Hospital** Ružinovská ulica 10; ℡ 02 4433 2409

Dentists

✚ **Sydent** Björnsonova 13; ℡ 02 5245 3048; www.sydent.sk. English-speaking dentists Sylvia Deglovičová and Juraj Deglovič have a private clinic,

Sydent, just north of the Slovak Radio inverted pyramid building. *Surgery open Mon–Fri 08.00–16.00, at other times by appointment.*

BANKS AND MONEY Banking services are provided in Bratislava by both Slovak and foreign banks. Inside banks visitors can use the exchange offices during office hours (*Mon–Thu 08.00–17.00, Fri 08.00–15.00*) and ATMs outside or within a secure room accessed by swipe card. The most frequently accepted credit cards are MasterCard and Visa.

$ **ČSOB** (Československá obchodná banka) Michalská 18; ℡ 02 5966 5701; www.csob.sk. *Open Mon–Thu 08.00–17.00, Fri 08.00–16.00.*

$ **Tatra Banka** Františkánske námestie 3; ℡ 02

6866 1000; www.tatrabanka.sk. *Open Mon–Fri 10.00–18.00.*

$ **Tatra Banka** Dunajská 4; ℡ 02 5919 1000. *Open Mon–Fri 08.00–18.00, Sat 08.00–12.00.*

Exchanging currency There are many bureaux de change booths in the Old Town. Your can buy Slovak koruna in banks (see above). Hotels can also give somewhat higher rates outside banking hours. There are dozens of *zmenáreň* (currency-exchange offices) all over town. In Bratislava, there is an exchange office on Rybárska brána near Hviezdoslavovo námestie that is open until 20.00. More exchange offices can be found along Michalská/Ventúrska.

DISCOUNT CARD For getting the best out of the city, the **Bratislava City Card** (*www.bkis.sk*) is a great idea. Produced by BKIS (Bratislava Culture and Information Centre) and supported by the municipal government (*www.bratislava.sk*), it offers a free guided city tour, discounts on taxis, entry to Bratislava Zoo, the Municipal Museum, swimming pools and some restaurants as well as other guided tours and trips. Cards are valid for one (€5), two (€8) or three (€10) days and are available from all the BKIS offices: at the airport, ferry port, railway station and in Klobučnícka (Central Tourist Point) in the Old Town centre. Cards can also be found in some participating hotels. The card is validated when a member of the BKIS staff signs and dates it at one of their offices.

POST OFFICES Most post offices (*pošta*) open Monday–Friday 08.00–17.00. You can also buy stamps (*známky*) from some tobacconists (*tabák*) and street kiosks. Poste restante is available in major towns; write Pošta 1 (the main office), followed by the name of the town. The main post office at Námestie SNP 34–35 is open Monday–Friday 07.00–20.00, Saturday 07.00–18.00 and Sunday 09.00–14.00.

INTERNET Internet cafés have sprouted up all over Bratislava: expect to pay 60–120Sk per hour. Many hotels offer WiFi connections in rooms (for a fee) or some have free WiFi zones in their cafés and lobbies. Many hotels also offer fast broadband internet although if you are staying in an expensive hotel, the internet charge will be commensurately dearer and you'd be better off sitting in a café, accompanying your blogging with a cold beer.

@ **Internet centrum** Michalská 2. Has 5 machines. *Open daily 09.00–midnight.*

@ **Kristián Pub** Michalská 10; ☏ 02 5443 4038. With 5 fast machines. WiFi available. Cost 1Sk per min. *Open daily 14.00–midnight.*

@ **London Café** Panská 17. Two free machines in the British Council café. *Open Mon–Fri 09.00–20.00, Sat 09.00–15.00, closed Sun.*

@ **Mamutnet.sk at Sparx** Dozens of machines at Cintorínska 32, entrance at Ferienčíkova ulica; ☏ 5263 1011; www.mamutnet.sk. Printing, copying, burning & WiFi. Costs 60Sk per hr but about half that if you register. *Open daily 10.00–04.00.*

@ **Megainet** Klariská 4; ☏ 02 5443 5567; www.megainet.sk. With 6 machines, coffee, beer. Internet 1Sk per min (minimum 10min), Hotspot WiFi 2Sk per min, 40Sk per 15min, 120Sk per hr, 200Sk per 2hrs. *Open Mon–Fri 09.00–22.00, Sat–Sun 14.00–22.00.*

MUSEUMS

Bratislava is packed with museums and there is a great variety of themes, from wine to cars, from dungeons to clocks. Everyone will find something to entertain them on a rainy Wednesday afternoon. Museums in Bratislava are almost always open from 10.00 to 17.00 and always closed on Mondays.

UNMISSABLES

Arms and fortifications (and panoramic view) at St Michael's Gate/Tower; (*Michalská 24;* ☏ *02 5443 3044; open Tue–Sun 10.00–17.00; admission adult/child 60/20Sk*). Five floors of weapons and armour then a great view of the city from the top.

Chatam Sofer Memorial (*Nábrežie arm. Gen. Ľ. Svobodu; www.chatamsofer.com; open Mon–Fri 09.00–17.00; admission US$2 for tourists, Jews come to pray at no charge*). A Jewish cemetery was buried underground when the road level was raised in 1942. It contains 23 graves including that of Chatam Sofer, the great scholar and rabbi. The guide, Juraj Kohlmann, doesn't always stay at the memorial but you can call for an appointment on his mobile phone at ▥ 0903 221 842.

Clocks Museum Expozicia Historických Hodin (*Židovská 1; Dom 'U Dobrého Pastiera' – House of the Good Shepherd;* ☏ *02 5441 1940; open Oct–Apr Tue–Sun 09.30–16.00; May–Sep Tue–Fri 10.00–17.00, Sat–Sun 11.00–18.00; admission adult/child 40/20Sk, one ticket for two museums*). Clocks and watches made in Bratislava when it was Pressburg. Also combined with the Exhibition of Crafts just over the road on Beblavého ulica.

History of Bratislava and feudal justice in cellar at the Old Town Hall (*Primaciálne námestie; open Tue–Fri 10.00–17.00, Sat–Sun 11.00–18.00*). Under the Municipal

Museum (see below) and with the same entry ticket this is a great little museum. Children will love the gruesome dungeons and torture equipment.

Municipal museum Mestské múzeum (*Primaciálne námestie 1;* \ *02 5443 1473; www.muzeumbratislava.sk; open Tue–Sun 10.00–18.00; admission adult/concession 50/20Sk*). Massive museum with a series of seemingly endless rooms. The history of Bratislava is shown and some of the rooms have the original furnishings.

Museum of Jewish Culture (*Židovská 17;* \ *02 5441 8507; www.slovak-jewish-heritage.org/mblava.htm; open Sun–Fri 11.00–17.00; admission adult/child 200/20Sk*). The museum is housed in the late-Renaissance 17th-century Zsigray Mansion on the side of the castle hill by the tram tunnel. The moving exhibition features the history and culture of Jews living in the territory of Slovakia since the times of the Great Moravian Empire with a harrowing section on the Holocaust.

Farmaceutické Múzeum (*Michalská 26;* \ *02 5443 3596; open Tue–Sun 09.00–17.00; admission adult/child 20/20Sk*) The old *Lekáreň u Červeného raka* (Pharmacy at the Red Crayfish) reopened after renovation. Pharmacists were practising in Bratislava as early as the 14th century. Items gathered from 1890 in an 18th-century Baroque house.

Slovak National Museum - History museum at Bratislava Castle Historické Múzeum Bratislava Castle (*Mudroňova 1;* \ *02 5934 1626; www.snm-hm.sk; open Tue–Sun 09.00–17.00; admission adult/child 100/70Sk, separate ticket for the Treasury adult/child 20/10Sk*). A collection of exhibitions on three floors of the castle with silver treasures, antique furniture, arms and armour. Climb up three flights of grey marble steps to the cash desk, then even higher to the Crown Tower where you can go up a Hitchcockian stairway to the top of one of the four towers.

Slovak National Museum - Natural Science Museum Prírodovedné Múzeum (*Vajanského nábrežie; 2;* \ *02 5934 9122;* f *02 5296 6653; www.snm.sk; open Tue–Sun 09.00–18.00; admission adult/concession 100/50Sk*). On the top floor are two temporary exhibitions: maps and eagles; on the second floor is a permanent exhibit of the flora and fauna of Slovakia, with animals presented in naturalistic settings, on the first floor is Slovak culture, also very interesting. On the ground floor are temporary exhibitions.

Wine and viticulture Vinohradícke museum in the Apponyi Palace (*Radničná ulica 1;* ☏ *02 5920 5141*). The history of viticulture in Slovakia for over 2,000 years in a well-presented exhibition. This museum is closed for renovation of the palace until 2008.

OTHER MUSEUMS
Archaeological Museum (*Žižkova 12;* ☏ *02 5441 6034; open Tue–Sun 09.00–17.00; admission adult/concession 70/40Sk, combined ticket for this museum and neighbouring museums of Hungarian and German culture, see below*). In a 16th-century Renaissance building the museum features temporary exhibitions of artefacts from prehistoric times until the late Middle Ages.

Musical exhibition At the house of J N Hummel (*Klobučnícka 2;* ☏ *02 5443 3888; open Mon–Fri 10.00–18.00, Sat 10.00–14.00, Sun closed. Lunch break is 11.45–12.30 daily; admission adult/child 30/20Sk*). The museum is in the little peach-coloured cottage where pianist and composer Hummel was born. There is a shop selling CDs too.

Museum Arthur Fleischmann (*Biela 6;* ☏ *02 5443 4742; www.fleischmann.org.uk; open Tue–Fri 10.00–17.00, Sat–Sun 11.00–16.00, Oct–Apr Tue–Fri 09.30–16.30; admission adult/child 30/20Sk*). The family of pioneering sculptor Fleischmann (1896–1990) lived in this 16th-century Renaissance building in the Old Town. Fleischmann worked in ceramics, wood, wax, marble and bronze.

Museum of Culture of Carpathian Germans (*Žižkova 14;* ☏ *02 5441 5570;* f *02 5441 5570;* e *muzeumkkn@stonline.sk; open Tue–Sun 10.00–16.00; admission adult/concession 70/40Sk*). Showing the craftsmanship of ethnic Germans in Slovakia.

Museum of Hungarian Culture in Slovakia Múzeum Kultúry Maďarov na Slovensku (*Brämerova kúria, Žižkova 18;* ☏ *02 5441 2021;* f *02 5441 2023;* e *mkms@snm.sk; open Tue–Sun 10.00–17.00; admission adult/concession 70/40Sk*). Set in a 16th-century Renaissance building, and featuring details of Hungarian life.

Museum of Transport - Múzeum Dopravy (*Šancová ulica 1; tel 02 5244 4163;* f *02 5249 4021;* e *muzeumdophravy@slovanet.sk; www.muzeumdopravy.com; open Tue–Fri 10.00–16.00, Sat–Sun 10.00–17.00; admission adult/concession 40/20Sk*). More than 80 cars and 35 motorbikes make this a fun afternoon.

Milan Dobeš Museum (*Zámočnícka 13;* ☏ *02 5443 2305;* e *eks@stonline.sk; www.milandobes.sk; open Tue–Sun 10.00–18.00; admission adult/child 40/5Sk*). More of a gallery, really, showing constructivist and neoconstructivist contemporary art.

Slovak National Museum - Music museum at Bratislava Castle (*In the Bastion Luginsland;* ☏f *02 5441 3349;* e *musica@stonline.sk; open Tue–Sun 09.00–17.00, last entry at 16.15; admission is included in Bratislava Castle ticket*). With permanent and temporary exhibitions on the history of music and musical instruments.

GALLERIES

UNMISSABLES
Mirbach Palace (Mirbachov Palác) (*Františkánske námestie 11;* ☏ *02 5443 1556;* f *02 5443 2611; www.gmb.sk/en/mirbachov_palac; open Tue–Sun 11.00–18.00;*

Bratislava GALLERIES

3

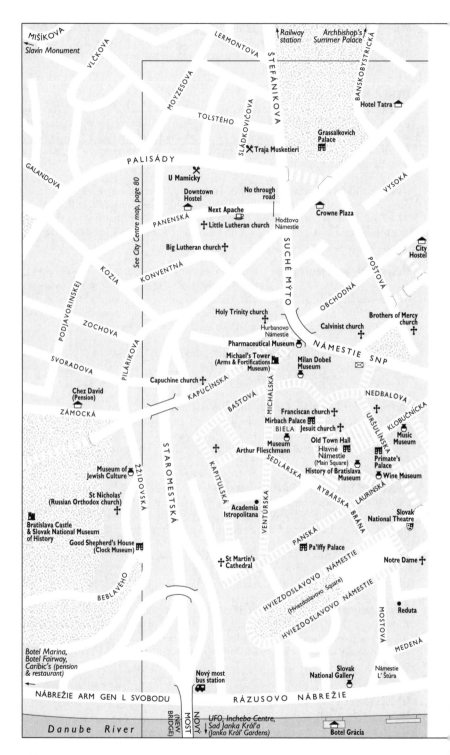

MIŠÍKOVA
Slavin Monument
VLČKOVA
LERMONTOVA
MOYZESOVA
ŠTEFÁNIKOVA
↑Railway station
Archbishop's Summer Palace
BANSKOBYSTRICKÁ
TOLSTÉHO
SLÁDKOVIČOVA
Hotel Tatra 🏨
Grassalkovich Palace 🏛
GALANDOVA
PALISÁDY
✗ Traja Musketieri
VYSOKÁ
See City Centre map, page 80
✗
U Mamicky
Downtown Hostel 🏠
No through road
PANENSKÁ
Next Apache
✝ Little Lutheran church
Hodžovo Námestie
Crowne Plaza 🏨
KOZIA
KONVENTNÁ
Big Lutheran church ✝
SUCHÉ MÝTO
City Hostel
POŠTOVÁ
PODJAVORINSKEJ
ZOCHOVA
PILÁRIKOVA
SVORADOVA
Holy Trinity church ✝
Hurbanovo Námestie
OBCHODNÁ
Calvinist church ✝
Brothers of Mercy church ✝
Pharmaceutical Museum 🏛
NÁMESTIE SNP
Capuchine church ✝
Michael's Tower (Arms & Fortifications Museum) 🏛
Milan Dobeš Museum ✉
Chez David (Pension)
ZÁMOCKÁ
KAPUCÍNSKA
BAŠTOVÁ
MICHALSKÁ
Franciscan church ✝
Mirbach Palace 🏛
BIELA   Jesuit church ✝
NEDBALOVA
URŠULÍNSKA
KLOBUČNÍCKA
Music Museum 🏛
STAROMESTSKÁ
Museum
Arthur Flieschmann
SEDLÁRSKA
Old Town Hall
Hlavné Námestie (Main Square) 🏛
History of Bratislava Museum
Primate's Palace 🏛
Wine Museum 🍷
Museum of Jewish Culture
ŽIDOVSKÁ
KAPITULSKÁ
Academia Istropolitana
VENTÚRSKA
RYBÁRSKA BRÁNA
LAURINSKÁ
Slovak National Theatre 🎭
St Nicholas' (Russian Orthodox church) ✝
Bratislava Castle & Slovak National Museum of History
Good Shepherd's House (Clock Museum) 🏛
PANSKÁ
Pa'lffy Palace 🏛
✝ St Martin's Cathedral
Notre Dame ✝
BEBLAVEHO
HVIEZDOSLAVOVO NÁMESTIE
(Hviezdoslavovo Square)
HVIEZDOSLAVOVO NÁMESTIE
MOSTOVÁ
Reduta
MEDENÁ
Botel Marina, Botel Fairway, Caribic's (pension & restaurant)
Nový most bus station 🚌
Slovak National Gallery
Námestie L' Štúra
NÁBREŽIE ARM GEN L SVOBODU
RÁZUSOVO NÁBREŽIE
Danube River
NOVÝ MOST (NEW BRIDGE)
UFO, Incheba Centre, Sad Janka Kráľa (Janko Kráľ' Gardens)
Botel Grácia

100

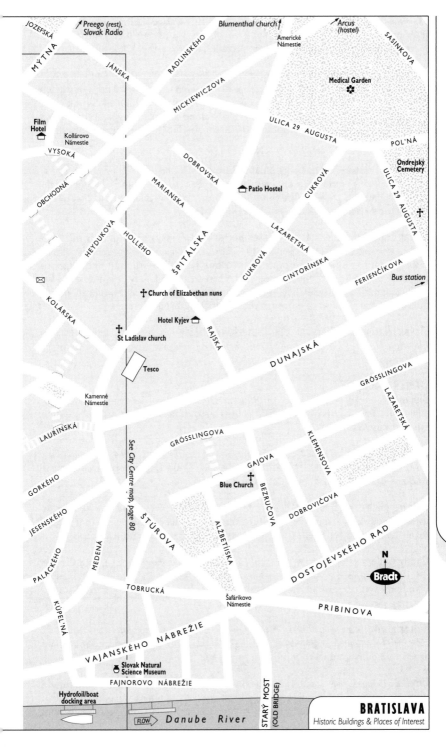

Preego (rest),
Slovak Radio

JOZEFSKÁ

MÝTNA

JÁNSKA

RADLINSKÉHO

Blumenthal church

Americké
Námestie

Arcus
(hostel)

SASINKOVA

Medical Garden

MICKIEWICZOVA

Film
Hotel

Kollárovo
Námestie

VYSOKÁ

ULICA 29 AUGUSTA

POL'NÁ

DOBROVSKÁ

OBCHODNÁ

MARIÁNSKA

HEYDUKOVA

HOLLÉHO

ŠPITÁLSKA

Patio Hostel

CUKROVÁ

Ondrejský
Cemetery

ULICA 29 AUGUSTA

LAZARETSKÁ

CUKROVÁ

CINTORÍNSKA

FERIENČIKOVA

Bus station

Church of Elizabethan nuns

KOLÁRSKA

Hotel Kyjev

St Ladislav church

RAJSKÁ

DUNAJSKÁ

Tesco

Kamenné
Námestie

GRÖSSLINGOVA

LAZARETSKÁ

LAURINSKÁ

GRÖSSLINGOVA

See City Centre map, page 80

GAJOVA

KLEMENSOVA

GORKÉHO

JESENSKÉHO

Blue Church

BEZRUČOVA

DOBROVIČOVA

ŠTÚROVA

ALŽBETÍISKA

DOSTOJEVSKÉHO RAD

PALACKÉHO

MEDENÁ

N

Bradt

KÚPEL'NÁ

TOBRUCKÁ

Šafárikovo
Námestie

PRIBINOVA

VAJANSKÉHO NÁBREŽIE

Slovak Natural
Science Museum

FAJNOROVO NÁBREŽIE

Hydrofoil/boat
docking area

FLOW Danube River

STARÝ MOST
(OLD BRIDGE)

BRATISLAVA
Historic Buildings & Places of Interest

admission adult/concession 60/30Sk). Like the Pálffy Palace (below), the Mirbach's interior is a match for the exhibits. Two of the rooms are lined with amazing wooden panels showing scenes of aristocratic life created in 1704–80.

Pálffy Palace (Pálffyho Palác) *(Panská 19; ☎ 02 5443 3627; www.gmb.sk/en/palffyho_palac.html; open Tue–Sun 11.00–18.00; admission adult/concession 60/30Sk).* Features an amazing permanent exhibit by Slovak artist Matej Krén called *Pasáž* where visitors walk along a visual gangplank through a seemingly endless library of bookshelves. Not for those with vertigo, unsettling yet fascinating.

Primate's Palace – Primaciálny palác *(Primaciálne námestie 1; ☎ 02 5935 6111; www.gmb.sk/en/primacialny_palac.html; open Tue–Sun 10.00–17.00; admission adults 40Sk, children and students (with card) free).* Pink wedding cake exterior, tapestries from Mortlake near London and the Hall of Mirrors.

Slovak National Gallery at the Water Barracks *(Rázusovo nábrežie 2; ☎ 02 5443 2082; www.sng.sk; open Tue–Sun 10.00–17.30; admission adult/concession 80/40Sk).* Exhibition of Gothic art, Baroque art in Slovakia, 19th-century art and religious art but the best exhibit is the 12 'character heads' by František Xaver Messerschmidt (1736–83). He was a talented woodcarver and you can play a guessing game as to what emotion each grimacing head expresses.

Slovak National Gallery at the Eszterházy Palace *(Námestie Ľ Štúra 4; open Tue–Sun 10.00–17.30; admission on the same ticket as above).* A venue for temporary exhibitions.

OTHER GALLERIES

Bibiana *(Panská 41; ☎ 02 5443 1388; www.bibiana.sk; open Tue–Sun 10.00–18.00; admission 10Sk for everyone over 3yrs old).* International house of art for children with all kinds of events.

Galleria 'Medium' *(Hviezdoslavovo námestie 18; ☎ 02 5443 5334; open Tue–Sun 10.00–17.00, Thu 12.00–17.00; voluntary donations).* Exhibition space for the students of the Academy of Fine Art and Design.

Galéria Michalský Dvor *(Michalská 3; ☎ 02 5441 1079; e jkrasula@gallery.sk; www.gallery.sk; open Tue–Sun 13.00–18.00).* The gallery was opened in 1995 by Jozef Krasula and Juraj Ulický. It features a gallery, art shop and tea house.

Gandy Gallery *(Panenská 30; ☎ 02 5441 0801; www.gandy-gallery.com; open Tue–Fri 13.30–18.30, Sat 11.00–16.00; admission free).* After 13 years in Prague, Nadine Gandy moved her exhibition space to Bratislava. She calls it a 'laboratory' as it's a meeting point.

Kulturfabrik *(Near Zlaté Piesky tram terminus 2 & 4, contact Laura Meskova; ☎ 02 5245 0046; e laura@kulturfabrik.sk; www.kulturfabrik.sk).* A new centre for arts and artists in a converted factory building.

Umelka *(Dostojevského rad 2; open Tue–Sun 11.00–17.00; admission free).* Exhibition space of the Slovak Union of Visual Arts (Slovenská výtvarná únia). An excellent place for exhibiting, one bright roomy hall with adventurous works and installations. Next to the Umelka pub.

Bratislava is a very green city. There are 809ha of parks and forests and 34 protected reservations. Most of this is formed by the Bratislava Forest Park (*Bratislavský lesopark*) to the north of the city. The hills above the city make an excellent cool getaway from the heat of the summer city. The hills are crisscrossed with hiking trails and cycle paths. Here are a few places to get some oxygen.

BOTANICAL GARDEN (*Botanická Záhrada* (*Botanická 3;* ꜱ *02 6542 5440; www.uniba.sk/bzuk/e_index.htm. T 1, 4, 5, 9, 12 to Botanická Záhrada stop; open 1 Apr–31 Oct daily 09.00–18.00, greenhouses open 09.00–15.00; 1 Nov–31 Mar Mon–Fri 09.00–15.00; admission adult/child 40/20Sk, annual season ticket 200Sk*). The 5ha Botanical Garden contains more than 5,000 species of exotic and domestic plants and 650 woodland species.

BRATISLAVA ZOO (*Mlynská dolina 1;* ꜱ *02 6542 2848;* f *02 6542 1868;* e *zoo@zoobratislava.sk; www.zoobratislava.sk. B 30, 31, 32, 37, 39, 92; open daily 10.00–15.00 winter; 09.00–18.00 summer; admission adult 60/99Sk (winter/summer), children & concessions 40/59Sk*). A modest zoo park set up in the hills to the west of town. Hippos, bears, monkeys, lemurs all in a hilly park. Children will also enjoy DinoPark with 22 lifesize dinosaur models lurking in the forest.

GRASSALKOVICH GARDENS (GRASSALKOVICHOVA ZÁHRADA) (*Open daily 09.00–19.00; 17.00 in winter*). Situated right behind the President's Palace this is a rather formal garden with little shade. Along the side are trees planted by visiting dignitaries and royalty.

HORSKÝ PARK Situated to the northwest of town, the 20ha Horský Park is a woody area with a network of paths. There is a gamekeeper's lodge in the middle which is a popular destination and also a 'Lourdes cave' with a Kalvária pilgrimage site founded in 1694 by the Jesuits, the City Council and the archbishop who decided to build it in the same place as where the Turkish guards had stood in the time of their raids.

JEWISH CEMETERY Žižkova ulica to the west of town, beyond PKO and the Chatam Sofer. An enjoyable walk following the Danube's eastern bank upstream. The walls of the cemetery along Žižkova are a popular free rock-climbing venue and always filled with lithe-limbed youngsters and spiderslovaks clambering all over them. Two entrances.

KAMZÍK (HILL) - KOLIBA (HILLY, GREEN SUBURB) The best-known part of Bratislava Forest Park (*Bratislavský lesopark*) is north of the city underneath the TV tower. Kamzík Hill (439m) offers cool woods and a range of trails to follow at the southernmost tip of the Small Carpathian mountain range. (See *Chapter 4, Bratislava region*, pages 117–18.)

MEDICAL GARDEN (MEDICKÁ ZÁHRADA) (*Open daily 09.00–19.00; 17.00 in winter*). A pleasant park to the northeast of the city where people take their lunch break, walk the dog or play frisbee. There's a children's playground at one side and a statue to the Slovak writer Martin Kukučin by the Croatian sculptor Ivan Meštrovic.

NÁMESTIE SLOBODY PARK On one side it claimed to feature the largest post office in the world, although these days the imposing building is occupied by the Ministry of Transportation, Post & Telecommunications, while one resident, the giant statue of former communist president, Klement Gottwald, has been removed. A space-age statue of a giant metal crocus-like flower rises up in the centre, its petals parting to reveal what could be a bosom with a particularly pert nipple.

ONDREJSKÝ CINTORÍN (*Ulica 29. augusta,* ↘ *07 5292 1628; open Nov–Feb 07.00–17.00, Mar & Oct 07.00–18.00, Apr & Sep 07.00–19.00, May–Aug 07.00–20.00; between 25 Oct & 8 Nov open 07.00–21.00 for the remembrance services & tending of the graves to coincide with All Saints' Day (1 Nov) & The Day of the Dead (2 Nov)).* Situated towards the east of the town centre and just south of the Medical Garden (*Medická Záhrada*), St Andrew's Cemetery is a tree-filled space with great atmosphere. A shaded spot in the height of summer. Many grave inscriptions in Slovak, German and Hungarian, revealing the city's trilingual heritage.

SAD JANKA KRÁĽA South of the Danube, this park seems like the first choice for those seeking a patch of green. The park was created in the time of Maria Theresa. Janko Kráľ was a revolutionary poet who used to walk there. There are several features of interest in the park and several restaurants. A 14th-century Franciscan church tower which used to stand in the Old Town was removed from the church and brought to the park in 1897. For mall rats, it's a pleasant stroll across the Nový most (New Bridge) and through this park to reach Aupark shopping mall.

SLAVÍN MONUMENT Situated up a well-to-do residential part of town to the northwest, Slavín Hill is crowned with a memorial to the 6,850 Soviet soldiers who lost their lives in the battle for Bratislava. The graves lie in a quiet garden and there are some interesting heroic statues by Tibor Bartfay. A 37m column also by Bartfay has a soldier raising a flag and a gold star on the top. Around the base of the monument are the names of the Slovak towns and the dates they were 'liberated' by the Red Army. At one side there is a peace garden instigated by Alexander Dubček.

ZLATÉ PIESKY Tram 2 or 4. In the heat of the summer, Bratislava residents head off on the tram to 'Golden Sands', *Zlaté Piesky*, a 32ha artificial lake surrounded by campsites and stalls offering snacks. Even the roar of the main road and occasional whiffs from a chemical plant nearby can't deter families from having fun, splashing about in the soft, clear waters of the lake. It also has an excellent and very popular restaurant. It has a little of a socialist-era children's camp about it and a main road whizzes past but it's worth a trip to go to U Zlatého Vodnika (see *Where to eat*, page 85). For camping, see Autocamp Zlaté Piesky in *Where to stay*, page 82.

THE MAJOR SIGHTS

CASTLES AND PALACES

Bratislava Castle (Bratislavský hrad) In *A Time of Gifts*, Patrick Leigh Fermor wrote that 'the symmetry of the huge gaunt castle and the height of its corner-towers gave it the look of an upside-down table'. Also called somewhat cruelly an 'upturned bedstead', Bratislava Castle as we recognise it today was created in 1430

NAPOLEONIC ARMY SOLDIER (Hlavné námestie) Leaning on a bench, leaning over and posing for photos behind those who sit down for a rest, watch out for the rabbit ears!

TOWN GUARDHOUSE (Hlavné námestie) A new statue of a guardsman standing in his sentry box arrived in April 2006. From the 17th century, a wooden sentry box stood in the south of the square until the 18th century when it burnt down. In 1767, a new brick guardhouse was built by M Walch, but removed in 1860.

ČUMIL (corner of Panská and Rybárska Brána) A man peering out of a manhole cover 'looking up skirts' by Viktor Hulík.

HANS CHRISTIAN ANDERSEN (Hviezdoslavovo námestie) The Danish fairytale teller visited Bratislava in 1841 and the statue shows a tall, skinny poet looking a bit bashful, a huge snail gazing up at him in awe of his imagination.

PHOTOGRAPHER (Laurinská 1) Peering around a corner by the Paparazzi restaurant. Fits in well with the restaurant theme.

POSMIEVAČIK - THE MOCKER (Panská 29) A grotesque gargoyle from a late Gothic façade. Horrible dwarf squatting with genitals sticking out. Various theories about his significance. Some say he is looking towards Vidrica, the red light district, and that's why he is aroused. Others say he represents a very nosey resident of the building who likes to spy on passers-by from a tiny bay window.

SCHÖNE NÁCI (Opposite the Antik Café at Rybárska brána 2) A real dandy, Ignác Lamár, he was nicknamed Schone Náci meaning 'Handsome Ignatius'. The statue depicts a real person who was famous for strolling the Korzo (a promenade stretching from Michalská brána to Hviezdoslavovo námestie). He appears quite friendly and jolly, but he was actually somewhat disturbed because of a trauma he experienced. Schöne Nazi had a fiancée before German troops came in World War II, but she was deported to a Nazi concentration camp where she died. He never recovered psychologically from this trauma and never married. He wandered the Korzo, smiling at everyone, then died completely forgotten.

SKATEBOARDER GIRLS (Poštová and Obchodná) One sitting on a fence, one below on a skateboard looking up.

Bratislava THE MAJOR SIGHTS

3

by King Sigismund of Luxembourg. There had been previous fortifications on the site, Celts and Romans had occupied the hill, then in the 9th century the Slavs built a fort on the hill which rises 85m above the Danube. The conquering Magyars also built fortifications on the hill and there was extensive construction work in the 13th century. King Sigismund reconstructed the castle and added outer defence walls, some 11m thick. The Habsburgs used the castle as protection when the Turks attacked Vienna. It received its trademark four corner towers between 1635 and 1649 when the Hungarian Viceroy, Pál Pálffy, called in Giovanni Battista Carlone to help. Maria Theresa called it 'her castle' and the Hungarian Crown Jewels were kept there when the capital of Hungary was moved to Bratislava and she converted it in to a grand palace in 1761. The interior was redesigned in a lavish Rococo style and a number of annexes were added on outside. Maria Theresa's successors did not share her love for the castle and it fell into disrepair. It was used for a while as a priests' seminary and a barracks. In 1811, it burnt down in a devastating fire and remained in ruin for 140 years until restoration work began in 1953. Today it houses exhibitions for the Slovak National Museum as well as state rooms of the Slovak National Council.

Archibishop's Summer Palace (*Námestie slobody 1*). Built in the second half of the 18th century. A magnificent Baroque palace designed by F A Hillebrandt, the royal architect in Vienna. The palace and its beautiful garden served as a summer residence for the Archbishop of Esztergom. In the outbuildings of the palace was a workshop of the famous sculptor G R Donner (1692–1741), a Baroque sculptor of Austrian origin.

Grassalkovich Palace (Grassalkovičov palác) Built in 1760–65 as a summer residence for Count Anton Grassalkovich, the president of the Hungarian Royal Chamber, this Baroque palace stands in an open space north of the Old Town and behind there is a French-style garden. The architect of the project was Mayerhoffer. Grassalkovich was an influential man and later became advisor to Empress Maria Theresa. The palace today serves as the residence for the President of Slovakia.

Mirbach Palace – Mirbachov palác A Rococo palace that was built by a rich brewer, Martin Spech, during 1768–70. Its last owner, Emil Mirbach, donated the palace to the town, provided that a gallery was established there.

Pálffy Palace – Páffyho Palác The palace was built in the middle of the 19th century in the place of older houses. During the last reconstruction, archaeologists uncovered the remains of a 13th-century Gothic house with a 14th-century tower.

Primate's Palace – Primaciálny palác The powder-pink neoclassical palace was built between 1777 and 1781 by Melchior Hefele for Cardinal Józef Batthyány, Archbishop of Esztergom and Primate of Hungary who used it as his winter palace. The tympanum on the roof features a mosaic based on a fresco by Franz Anton Maulpertsch and right on the top is a 150kg cast-iron black cardinal's hat. The palace has a collection of tapestries from Mortlake, London. The Hall of Mirrors was the scene of the signing of the 'Peace of Pressburg' treaty between Napoleon and Emperor Francis I on 26 December 1805 after the Battle of Austerlitz.

BRIDGES

Nový most – New Bridge, and UFO Pedestrians walk over the bridge on a level just below that of the traffic. The bridge was completed in 1972 as the finishing touch to a communist highway barging straight through the centre of the city. The project required the destruction of 226 buildings, two-thirds of Bratislava's Old Town.

Starý most – Old (railway) Bridge The tram to Vienna used to rattle across this bridge. Pedestrians can still walk across although it is a little nerve-wracking as the railway sleeper-style wooden boards are not all present and not where you expect them to be. Called many names throughout its history: Emperor Franz Joseph Bridge, Štefánik Bridge, Red Army Bridge and now Old Bridge.

Apollo most Opened 5 September 2005, *most Apollo* (literally 'bridge Apollo'), a very beautiful, curved white structure, was named after the oil refinery 'Apollo' situated on the left riverbank in this area before World War II, whose modern successor is the Slovnaft company. The Apollo Bridge became the only European project named as one of five finalists for the 2006 Outstanding Civil Engineering Achievement Award (OPAL Award) by the American Society of Civil Engineers. selected for its bold aesthetic statement.

Lafranconi most Another expressway bridge which is cycle-friendly and with a separated sidewall; runs about 1km west of the Old Town and into Austria.

CATHEDRALS AND CHURCHES
St Martin's Cathedral (Dóm Sv Martina) Building work on the three-aisled church lasted from the 13th century to the middle of the 15th. Between 1563 and 1830 it was the coronation church for the kings of Hungary and witnessed the crowning of 11 Hungarian kings and eight royal spouses. The tower is 85m tall and is topped with a 300kg gilded model of the crown of St Stephen, the first King of Hungary (in AD1000). The late-Gothic vaulting is by Hans Puchspaum under direct influence of master masons from Vienna. When in residence, the Archbishop of Esztergom invited a famous sculptor to the Austrian court, Georg Raphael Donner to Bratislava to establish a workshop and Donner stayed 11 years, creating many masterpieces. In 1734, he created a new high altar featuring an equestrian statue of *St Martin and the Beggar* which now stands in the southeast corner of the nave. In 1732–34 he built the Chapel of St John the Almsgiver in the north aisle with the kneeling figure of the donor, the Archbishop Esterházy. In 1884, Franz Liszt conducted his *Coronation Mass* here.

Brothers of Mercy Church - Kostol Milosrdnych Bratov (*Námestie SNP*) Originally built in 1683. In 1723–28 a Baroque complex was constructed on the site of an older church, with the façade reconstructed in 1884. The church has a dainty little Baroque interior, with paintings in the archways. Mass takes place Monday–Friday at 08.00 and 18.00, Saturday 08.00 and Sunday 09.30.

In front of the Brothers of Mercy Church and where today is the junction with Poštová ulica was Anča Korzo, the meeting point and promenade start point for labourers, maidservants and other working-class people. The Korzo for merchants and businessmen was at the junction of Michalská, Ventúrska and Sedlárska.

The Blue Church (Modrý kostolík) The full title is the Church of St Elizabeth. In 1907 it was the 700th anniversary of the birth of St Elizabeth (sv Alžbeta). Elizabeth, the daughter of Endre II of Hungary, was born in Bratislava and was the city's only well-known saint. The Hungarian architect and 'father of Hungarian Art Nouveau' Ödön Lechner was commissioned to design a church while Antal Durvay was in charge of the construction work. Lechner used concrete for the church and the unusual blue colour with little ceramic tiles.

Franciscan Church Next to Old Town Hall, Františkánske 2, constructed in a Gothic style in the 13th century with creamy arches and lots of Baroque ornamentation. There were Renaissance additions in the 16th–18th centuries, including a Baroque façade in 1760.

OTHER BUILDINGS AND AREAS OF INTEREST
Main Square - Hlavné námestie The square originated in the 13th century and from the beginning was at the centre of the town's social life. It was a place of

markets and festivities as well as public executions, which were very well-attended events. The square contains the Roland Fountain, many cafés and Art Nouveau buildings as well as the Old Town Hall.

Hviezdoslav Square - Hviezdoslavovo námestie The other great square for sitting, eating ice cream, checking out the girls, walking the dog, playing chess on a giant board, etc.

Ľudovít Štúr Square - Námestie Ľ Štúra The development of the present square started only after a branch of the Danube had been filled in during the 18th century. Bratislava sculptor Jan Fadrusz created a monument to Maria Theresa, which was unveiled on 16 May 1897 in the presence of Emperor Francis Joseph I. The monument was destroyed in 1921 during increased political tension following the attempted return of the former Hungarian King Charles. In 1938, a statue of M R Štefánik was raised on the site of Maria Theresa's monument. Štefánik was not a favourite of the communist regime. His statue was removed and the new statue of Ľudovít Štúr, one of the leaders of the Slovak National Movement in the 19th century, was raised.

Petržalka Petržalka (*Ligetfalu* in Hungarian, *Engerau* in German) is the largest city part of Bratislava. One-third of Bratislava's population lives in Petržalka, estimated at 130,000 inhabitants. Petržalka is the most densely populated place in Slovakia and also in central Europe. It is in most part a residential area with most people living in blocks of flats (*paneláky*) or panels, the pre-fab construction material.

Incheba Exhibition and congress centre offering 46,600m² of exhibition space. It is located on the right side of the river Danube in the 1960s' concrete housing district of Petržalka.

Good Shepherd's House - Dom u dobrého pastiera This burgher Rococo house of the second half of the 18th century was built for a merchant of Bratislava. After reconstruction in 1975, the Municipal Museum opened a unique exhibition of historical clocks here. The Good Shepherd's House is located by the New Bridge and is one of the houses that fortunately were not demolished during the 1960s.

St Michael's Gate - Michalská brána The last remaining gate tower from the four medieval gateways guarding the Old Town. Constructed initially in the 17th century in Gothic style it was given a Baroque renovation in the 17th century. Climb the tower for a spectacular view, admiring the military firearm museum on the way up. If you wonder why it's quiet, it's because of a local superstition which warns that students will fail their exams if they utter while passing under the tower.

Academia Istropolitana The oldest university in the territory of present-day Slovakia, founded by Hungarian King Mátyás Corvinus in 1465. After his death, the university ceased to exist in 1490. The Academy of Music and Drama has its seat in the building, which is today a national monument of cultural legacy. Academia Istropolitana building is located at Ventúrska 3.

Old Town Hall (Stará radnica) Right in the heart of Hlavné námestie (Main Square) is the Old Town Hall with its distinctive yellow tower and red roof. It was developed in the 14th century from a group of houses belonging to the mayors of the city to form the unusual conglomeration of styles and colours known as the 'House with the Tower'. The rib-vaulted late-Gothic passage leads to a beautiful courtyard with Renaissance arcades. Following a fire in 1733 the tower was restored in the Baroque style. The tower has a cannonball embedded in the wall from the time of the Napoleonic attacks.

Reduta The Reduta is a beautiful Baroque building and home to the Slovak Philharmonic Orchestra. It features a good bookshop on the ground floor.

Mostová 1-3 Designed by Budapest architects Dezső Jakab and Marcel Komoroa and built 1913–19 on the site of the former state granary.

Slovak National Bank - Národná Banka Slovenska The 111m-high construction on Mýtna ulica was a winning design of Martin Kusy and Pavol Panak, begun in November 1996 and opened in May 2002. The building is constructed from a concrete-steel skeleton with bearing poles.

Slovak National Theatre - Slovenské národné divadlo The Slovak National Theatre was constructed in place of the original theatre of estates during 1884–86 on the basis of designs by Viennese architects Fellner and Helmer. Since 1920 it has been the home of the Slovak National Theatre. In front is the Ganymede Fountain.

Slovak Radio building - Slovensky rozhlaš It's well worth the walk out towards the northeast of town to see this bizarre creation. A huge brown inverted pyramid balancing improbably on its pointed tip which looks like it has been rammed deep into the ground. It looks as though it is made of wood but actually it is brown metal. It was built during the years 1971–85 and broadcasting began from there in March 1985. You will pass this strange building on your left if you take the number 13 tram into town from the main railway station.

4

Bratislava Region

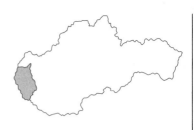

The Bratislava region is the only one of the eight Slovak regions that doesn't receive EU funds to help with its tourist promotion as its annual income exceeds the allowable limit. However, tourists and visitors will find it has much to offer; it just needs a bit of hunting down. The region stretches northeast from the capital along the Small Carpathian (Malý Karpaty) mountain range and a significant feature of this is the Small Carpathian Wine Route (Malá Karpatská Vinná Cesta) which ambles from Rača in the northern vineyard-rich suburbs of Bratislava along the eastern, sun-drenched slopes of the hills through oenologically enthusiastic villages such as Svätý Jur, Limbach, Pezinok, Vinosady, Modra, Dubová, Častá and Doľany. The map looks like a leafless tree as other villages on the route branch off to the east to places such as Slovenský Grob, famous for its goose feasts and the beautiful chateau of Budmerice. Close by the village of Častá is the impressive castle of Červený Kameň and there can be no better way of spending a Sunday afternoon than combining a castle tour with some wine tasting. You can even do it on a bike if you're feeling energetic. Walkers will also discover some romantic castle ruins such as Pajštún, hidden away in the woods. South of Bratislava, the region runs along the Danube River to Rusovce where Princess Stéphanie of Belgium lived in a castle with her second husband, Hungarian Count Lónyay. Rusovce also has the Roman town of Gerulata. Cyclists can follow the Danube cycle path which goes all the way to Štúrovo in the Nitra region, stopping off at Čunovo where the controversial Gabčíkovo Dam is located. There are many options for watersports such as rafting and canoeing on the Danube.

EVENTS IN BRATISLAVA REGION

February	**Pezinok** Ethnofestival
March	**Pezinok** Election of the Queen of Wine
April	**Pezinok** Wine markets, international competition, exhibition and wine tasting
	Devín National Run Devín–Bratislava
	Svätý Jur The 17th Annual Wine Exhibition
May	**Pezinok** *Ad Una Corda* international church choir festival, held every even year
	Červený Kameň The Turza Craftsmen Fair; see www.snm.sk/ck
	Červený Kameň Children's Day; a fun day out for all the family
27 May	**Pezinok** St Urban's Day; a celebration of the patron saint of wine-growing
June	**Pezinok** *Cibulák* theatre festival, vintage car competition; see www.cibulak.sk

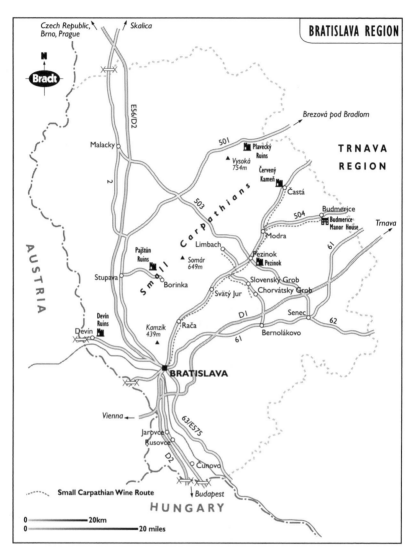

BRATISLAVA REGION

Czech Republic, Brno, Prague
Skalica
Brezová pod Bradlom
Malacky
Plavecký Ruins
Vysoká 754m
Červený Kameň
Častá
TRNAVA REGION
Budmerice
Budmerice Manor House
Trnava
Modra
Pajštún Ruins
Limbach
Somár 649m
Pezinok
Stupava
Borinka
Slovenský Grob
Chorvátsky Grob
Svätý Jur
AUSTRIA
Devín Ruins
Devín
Kamzík 439m
Rača
Senec
Bernolákovo
Small Carpathians
BRATISLAVA
Vienna
Jarovce
Rusovce
Čunovo
Small Carpathian Wine Route
Budapest
HUNGARY
0 ——— 20km
0 ——— 20 miles

	Pezinok The Opening of the Season of the Malokarpatská Wine Route
July	**Červený Kameň** Festival of Historic Fencing; see www.snm.sk/ck
	Pezinok Slovakia Matador, car race to the Baba Hill
July–August	**Pezinok** Promenade concerts every Sunday afternoon
August	**Pezinok** *Pezinský Permoník*; Small Carpathian exhibition and fair of minerals, fossils and precious stones connected with gold washing on Pezinok streets
	Červený Kameň Knightly Games
September	**Pezinok** *Pezinok Vinobranie* (harvest festival) wine celebration
	Rača *Vintage Festival in Rača*; a celebration of wine

October	**Pezinok** *Pezinský strapec* international ballroom dancing competition
11 November	**Pezinok** St Martin's blessing of the wine, tasting of young wines; 'Days of Open Cellars' regional promotion in private cellars
December	**Pezinok** 'Christmas Inspirations' festive market

HEADING SOUTH FROM BRATISLAVA ALONG THE DANUBE

JAROVCE Situated 4km south of Bratislava, on the southern bank of the Danube, the village of Jarovce was first mentioned in 1208 in a royal document, as being called 'villa Bán'. The first inhabitants were Slavonic. Like Chorvátsky Grob (see page 127), Jarovce was colonised by Croatians in the 16th century who fled north from the Turks army. It has preserved its Croatian character and became a suburb of Bratislava in 1972.

Getting there Off route 2/E75 heading south from Bratislava. Bus 91, 191 from Nový most.

RUSOVCE Rusovce has only been part of Slovakia since the 1947 Treaty of Paris. The white, crenellated manor house was built for the Zichy family in the second half of the 19th century in English Gothic style and later became a home for Princess Stéphanie of Belgium (see Štefánka café in *Chapter 3, Cafés and tearooms*, page 86). She lived out her days here with her second husband, Count Lónyay, after her first husband, Rudolf Habsburg committed suicide (see box, page 114). After Rudolf's death in 1889, Stephanie received no support from her father, Leopold II of Belgium. She married Elemér Lónyay, a Hungarian nobleman, and they lived at Rusovce until the end of World War I.

What to see
Múzeum Antická Gerulata (*Gerulatská ulica 69, Rusovce;* ⟍ *02 6285 9332; open May–Oct Tue–Sun 10.00–17.00; admission adult/child 30/20Sk*). Gerulata had been known about since the 16th century, but Slovak archaeologist Ján Dekan only discovered its exact location in 1965. He uncovered the foundations of a Roman military camp, part of the *Limes Romanus* defence system, dating from AD100–400. Traces of the Roman presence date from the years before Christ. Besides fortress architecture from that time, objects from burial grounds at the periphery of Gerulata are on display in the Lapidarium with votive altars and tombstones. To get there, take bus 91, 191 from Nový most for Čuňovo.

Rusovce Lake This former reservoir is a popular naturist swimming area during the summer. Swimming costumes are not necessary.

Getting there Bus No. 91 or 191 from the bus stop Nový most to Rusovce, bus stop MiÚ Rusovce. VKÚ tourist map No 127 Malé Karpaty–Bratislava.

ČUNOVO Located 5km further southeast of Rusovce is the tiny hamlet of Čunovo. The Ostrovné lúčky Nature Reserve contains rare orchids and another popular lake. It is possible to reach Čunovo on bicycle or rollerblade by a well-maintained cycle path. To find the footpath, cross to the southern bank of the Danube at Bratislava and look for the cycle route which is marked with a large 'C' in red, blue, green or yellow. The tarmac route leads south for 15–20km to Čunovo. You can cycle on both sides of the Danube as far as Gabčíkovo, then the cycle route continues along the northern bank only. The Danube cycle route on

4

The Mayerling mystery concerning the tragic death of Crown Prince Rudolf of Austria and his mistress, Baroness Marie Vetsera, has remained unsolved to this day. On 30 January 1889, the couple were discovered dead at the royal hunting lodge in Mayerling. First, it appeared to be a double suicide. Later, however, doubt was cast and people began to whisper about politically motivated murder. Crown Prince Rudolf was the only son of Emperor Franz Joseph I and Empress Elisabeth, the beloved 'Sissi' of the Slovaks, Hungarians and Italians. Rudolf married Princess Stephanie of Belgium in 1881. The marriage was arranged and the young couple had little in common. Stephanie was described as very formal and dull. Empress Elisabeth, who hated the court formalities, avoided Stephanie, referring to her as 'the plain bumpkin'. Soon after the marriage, the couple drifted apart and Rudolf searched for consolation with other women. He met Baroness Marie Vetsera in 1888 and they started a passionate affair. By 1889 the affair was known by many, including Franz Joseph and Stephanie. According to some, Marie was pregnant and the Emperor ordered Rudolf to end the affair immediately. Within a few days, the bodies of Rudolf and Marie were discovered at Mayerling. The most widely accepted theory is that there was a lover's pact: Rudolf shot Marie and then killed himself. Franz Joseph had wanted the lovers to separate but they could not bear life without each other. There is another theory that the couple were murdered and they were victims of a politically motivated conspiracy, cooked up by the French Prime Minister Clemenceau, who was conspiring to overthrow Franz Joseph and place the Germanophobe Rudolf on the throne. This way Austria could have loosened ties with Germany and signed an alliance with France. Rudolf refused to take part in the conspiracy and was killed to secure his silence. Certain facts point towards this theory. When Marie's remains were examined half a century later, an astonishing discovery was made. There was no sign of the use of firearms: instead there was a large trauma on her head. Allegedly, Rudolf's body showed signs of a violent confrontation before death. The tragic deaths shocked the Austro-Hungarian Empire and caused an immediate crisis of succession to the throne. The court did everything possible to cover up the scandalous incident (the official version was that Rudolf died of heart failure, with no mention of his lover), so it is likely the mystery will never be solved. The scandal isolated poor Stephanie even further from the Viennese court. She also had a bad relationship with her own father, Leopold II of Belgium, and had to fight him in court for her inheritance. Later she married Elemér Lónyay, a low-ranking Hungarian count and settled in Rusovce.

the northern bank begins just south of the Pristavný most, the bridge south of the new Apollo Bridge. Energetic cyclists may continue following the cycling route all the way to the Hungarian border at Štúrovo (160km).

What to see and do

Danubiana Meulensteen Art Museum (*Vodne dielo, Čunovo;* ↘ *02 6252 8501; www.danubiana.info; open May–Sep Tue–Sun 10.00–20.00; Oct–Apr Tue–Sun 10.00–18.00; admission adult/concession 60/30Sk*). An interesting and unusual modern art museum on the Danube bank. The blue-and-white building looks like a ship and it's the brainchild of Vincent Polakovič who decided to create the museum after an encounter with the ghost of his hero, Vincent Van Gogh. A Dutch millionaire, Gerard Meulensteen, put up US$1 million to fund the project. Čunovo is a centre for wild-water sports, slalom and rafting events.

Rafting

Action Land Na Hrádzi 174, Bratislava; ✎ 02 6252 8077; e info@actionland.sk; www.actionland.sk. Offers white-water rafting on the Belá, Danube, Hron & Váh rivers.

Čunovo Water Sports Resort m 0903 200553; www.rafting.sk. Phone to arrange a trip. Located 15km from Bratislava & a great destination for extreme sports enthusiasts. Unlike natural rivers, the channel surface is smooth & a team of lifeguards watches over. White-water rafting is made possible by the best manmade water channels in Europe, with a preparation channel & 6 levels of water difficulty, used as a training area for Olympic champions & top Slovak water slalom teams. The website www.mates.sk also has details of white water rafting at Čunovo. There is also rafting, hydrospeed & jet skiing.

Getting there From Bratislava, take bus 91 or 191 from under Nový most (New Bridge) to Čunovo. Then walk for about 3km following signs for the museum.

NORTH ALONG THE SMALL CARPATHIAN MOUNTAIN RIDGE

DEVÍN

Museum at Devín Castle (*Muránska ulica, Bratislava-Devín;* ✎ *02 6573 0105; open Tue–Sun 10.00–17.00; May–Sep Sat–Sun 10.00–19.00 also; admission to castle adult/concession 60/20Sk*). Devín is considered a vital part of Slovak history and it's an impressive sight when you arrive, probably by bus or boat, to see it rising up on a tall crag above the confluence of the Danube and Morava rivers. Dating from Roman times, the castle occupied an important strategic position on the cliff overlooking both the Moravia and the Danube and is one of the most important monuments of Slav and Slovak history. The first written reference to the castle dates from the year 864 when it was called Dowina. The hill was originally fortified during Roman times, and traces remain today. The Great Moravian Empire added to the fortifications in the 10th century, and from this vantage point, Moravian warriors won two major victories over their Frankish overlords. Hungarian nobles took it over in the 13th century, using it as a fort. A palace was added in the 15th century, and for a time it belonged to the notorious Báthory family (see box, page 168). In 1809, Napoleon's advancing troops blew up the fortress *en route* to a confrontation with Habsburg forces. It later became a central symbol for the Slovak National Revival, and Ľudovít Štúr organised a series of events to whip up national fervour before the failed revolution of 1848.

Getting there Bus 29 from Nový most to the terminus. There is a hiking route from the suburb of **Dúbravka** to Devín Castle. Take trams 1, 5 or 12 to the terminus and walk uphill along Pri kríži to Dúbravská hlavica Hill (356m). From there follow the yellow hiking trail to Devín. The trip through the Devínska Kobyla nature reserve lasts around 2¹/₂ hours.

🏠 Where to stay

🏠 **Hotel Hradná Brána** (12 rooms) Slovanské nábrežie 15, Devín; ✎ 02 6010 2511; f 02 6010 2512; e recepcia@hotelhb.sk; www.hotelhb.sk. B 29 from Nový most to terminus. Disabled access. The location, right on the car & coach park, is unfortunate but the general area is delightful, by the 2 rivers & under the towering Devín Castle ruins. It's a good base for Bratislava visitors who don't mind taking the 29 bus into town, & ideal for those who like hiking in the fresh air. The hotel is quite new & the interior was given a feng shui session, which may explain the pinky-custardy colours & gentle sloping ceilings. There's a jacuzzi in every bathroom. A 'relax centre' has a whirlpool, sauna, solarium, massages & recliner chairs. The congress hall 'Štúr' holds 150 businesspeople, & the restaurant 'Perún' offers international cuisine. $$. Sgl, dbl $$$$, apts, suite $$$$$.

A noblewoman of Devín Castle lay dying and presented her twin daughters each with an apple, to preserve as a good luck charm for happy lives in the future. The silly girls swapped apples. They did not know that they had both fallen in love with the same young hunter. The two young girls together bumped into the hunter and one, in a rage, threw her apple on the ground where it was crushed. Her sister died the next day, according to the mother's prophecy. Where the apple had smashed a tree grew. The other daughter that night was turned into a black goat. Sometimes, locals spot the ghost of a sad black goat nibbling at the leaves of an apple tree in Devín.

✗ Where to eat and drink

✗ **Pizzeria Istria** Slovanské nábrežie 48; m 0764 537 181; e ernestkovacs@istria.sk; Great outdoor grill restaurant with grilled fish, steaks flambéed in brandy. garlic & jars of pickled chilli peppers, 330g pizza avg 140Sk, grilled garlic sausage 39Sk a decagram, stuffed cabbage 90Sk, grilled mackerel 55Sk per 100g, trout 65Sk per 100g. $$. Open Mon–Thu 12.00–21.30, Fri 12.00–22.00, Sat–Sun 10.30–22.00.

✗ **U zlého námorníka** (At the Bad Sailor) Slovanské nábrežie 30; ✆ 02 6573 0332. Unusual furniture made by Devín resident Peter Strassner, with human or animal attributes: antlers, tongues, ears & phalluses (See also Umelka pub in *Chapter 3*, *Where to drink*, page 88). Fried cheese & chips 95Sk, soups 30Sk, grilled trout 8Sk per 10g, a litre of dry white wine 130Sk. $. Open Mon 12.30–21.30, Tue–Sun 10.30–21.30, closed on Thu.

What to see and do There is a hiking route from the Sandberg area close to the Devínska Nova Ves; total 4¹/₂ hours. There are cycling routes: from the Karlova Ves (8km), or along Morava, from Devínska Nová Ves (4.5km). There is also a special cycling route, which is a part of the informational pathway at the Morava River Floodplain. The tracks in Petržalka are linked to the cycle paths in Austria, leading along the embankment to the quaint town of Hainburg, which is at the crossroads of two interesting long-distance European hiking and cycling routes. In summer, you can also take a ferry across to Hainburg so don't forget your passport (adult €5, child €3).

Záhorská cyklomagistrála The 110km route passes through the most important sights in the Záhorie region. The route starts in Devín & it passes Veľké Leváre, Šaštín-Stráže, Holíč & Skalica & ends in Senica.

DEVÍNSKA KOBYLA NATURE RESERVE Devínska Kobyla lookout (514m) in the nature reserve offers gorgeous views of Devín Castle and the Danube River. The reserve has diverse flora with 234 mushroom varieties, rare orchids, Slovakia's biggest spiders, 1,100 different plants, 101 mosses and 110 types of lichen.

Getting there Trams 1, 5 or 12 from the centre, alight at the Saratov stop, walk uphill to Plachého ulica and follow the road towards the army base and skirt round to the right to reach the lookout.

DEVÍNSKA NOVÁ VES Occupied since prehistoric times and popular with the Celts and Romans, the village has the remains of two forts from the Great Moravian Empire period. Croats settled here after the Battle of Mohács in 1526 when fleeing the Turks. Volkswagen has a large car plant here.

It's right on the border with Austria and during the communist era it was watched over by dozens of guard towers.

Getting there Tram 1, 4, 5, 9 or 12 to Lafranconi most (bridge), then bus 92 to the terminus.

KOLIBA-KAMZÍK In Slovak, the chamois or small, goat-like mountain antelope is called Kamzík vrchovský (*Rupicapra rupicapra*) and the hilly area north of Bratislava also bears the name Kamzík. It's a very popular destination at weekends for Slovaks who want to escape into the beauty of nature without having to sit in the car for hours. Kamzík is delightful with little triangular wooden huts, resembling chunks of Toblerone, offering draught beer or *Kofola* (a Czech version of cola that locals mix with soda water) on tap, some scrummy hot dogs (*párky*) and other sustaining snacks. At the top is a huge meadow where locals can ski in winter. In summer, there's a bobsleigh run and a mountain-bike track. All year round you can sail downhill on a long chairlift. There are plenty of options for eating and drinking.

Getting there Trolleybus 203 from Hodžovo námestie to the terminus, then 20 minutes' walk uphill through woods, following the red-marked trail.

 Where to stay

Best Western Hotel West (100 beds) Koliba-Kamzík les; ℡ 02 5478 8692; f 02 5477 7781; e hotel@hotel-west.sk; www.hotel-west.sk. Beautiful location on top of wooded hills. Close enough to town for business folk but yet peaceful & separate from the city. A young, modern hotel surrounded by great hiking hills. Individually furnished apts for those staying a little longer with kitchen & direct phone lines. Restaurant offers Slovak & Mexican dishes (**$$**). During the summer, barbecues are held on the terrace. Conference rooms with capacity of 15 or 40 seats. Sauna, small pool, sunbathing studio. Hiking, mountain biking, tennis courts nearby. Nightclub for meetings or parties. Dbl **$$$**, suites **$$$$**, b/fast inc.

Where to eat and drink A selection of little huts by the bobsleigh run where you can find snacks: grilled sausage (*klobása*) costing 29Sk a decagram, frankfurters with bread and mustard (*párky, chlieb a horčica*) for 30Sk, coffee for 12Sk, draught Kofola 9Sk for 30cl, mulled wine 22Sk for 20cl and, of course, beer at 25Sk a half-litre.

Koliba-Expo Kamzíkov vrch; ℡ 02 5920 0610; e info@koliba-expo.sk; www.koliba-expo.sk. Now reopened after restoration. Look for the bright yellow, orange & brown building nestling in the forest just uphill from where the bobsleigh begins. The interior is rustic with red brick & carved wood. The restaurant's building was displayed at the 1967 World Expo in Montreal, which gave the place its name. When the exhibition ended, the massive wooden structure was taken apart & rebuilt in Bratislava. **$$**. *Open Mon–Sat 12.00–01.00, Sun 12.00–22.00.*

Veža restaurant Cesta na Kamzík 14; ℡ 02 4446 2774; www.restauraciaveza.sk. Built in 1975, the 200m tower reaches a height of 638m above sea level & gives a fantastic 360° panoramic view of Bratislava & all the surrounding countryside as it rotates gently. Watch where you put your handbag down as the outer & inner parts of the restaurant remain static & it may sail off. Seasickness may ensue in the sensitive. Décor is a creepy Habsburg/Soviet mélange. **$$**. *Open daily 11.00–midnight.*

Veža Café Cesta na Kamzík 14; ℡ 02 4446 2774; www.restauraciaveza.sk. Situated on the floor above the restaurant, the bar doesn't spin round, which perhaps is just as well as the clanking lift is enough to make you dizzy with nerves. The lift sounds like a wind tunnel & the café shakes in the breeze, you'll need a swift half (0.33l of Budvar for 38Sk) to calm your nerves. The café throbs slightly & feels like it's alive. There's another café on the ground floor for vertigo sufferers or those easily offended by the hideous 1970s' theme park with Maria Theresa-style décor. *Open daily 11.00–02.00.*

What to see and do
Summer bobsleigh run (Bobová dráha) (*Summer opening times Mon–Fri 14.00–18.00, weekends 10.00–18.00*). A popular destination is the bob track on Kamzík Hill. The track is 360m long, with ten bends, one jump and one crossing;

140m is in the woods before emerging into a beautiful meadow, Cvičná lúka, also used as a snowboarding area. Rides are speedy and descend 40m in altitude at a gradient of 19%. Drivers must weigh less than 110kg to ride.

Chair lift (Lanová dráha) (*Chair lift open Oct–Apr daily 10.00–16.00 on the hour every hour, May–Sep daily 10.00–18.00. Tickets are on sale at both end-stations at 60Sk (€ 1.50) one-way and 90Sk (€ 2.40) return*). Fifteen years after it fell into disuse, the chair lift connecting the Koliba-Kamzík Hill with the Železná Studnienka Valley and meadow reopened in September 2005. The lift descends and ascends for 186m in about 15 minutes and offers great views of the surrounding Bratislava hills, the foothills of the Small Carpathians.

Rohatka-Kaktus bike official downhill track Next to the chair lift down a steep hill with different levels of difficulty to Železná Studienka Valley, meadow and picnic area. In the summer of 1997, two enthusiasts known by their nicknames *roháč* (stag beetle) and *kačica* (duck) started to build a downhill track that was given the unofficial name of Rohatka, a composite of their two nicknames. The 1km track has jumps, berms or raised barriers, doubles, technical rock sections and there are levels of difficulty at different stages of the descent. Open all year, except during the ski season. Overall length of track is 1,920m. The start is at an elevation of 427m: it finishes at an elevation of 202m.

Železná Studnička (Iron Well) The water from the spring is rich in iron and a picnic and recreation area grew up around the well in a sun-trap valley. There are many small terraces and snack bars offering beer and hearty dishes.

Železná Studienka Valley The valley is found northeast of **Kamzík**, the hills just north of Bratislava. You can get there by the 43 bus from Patrónka, further out than Horský Park, and to get there you first have to take the 205 trolleybus from Hodžovo námestie. A much more pleasant route is by chair lift from Kamzík Hill. It's a 15-minute ride through the forest but a lovely way to relax and admire the leaves changing colour with the seasons. At www.ba-lesy.sk/index.php?7 you can find trail maps (in Slovak), including the *náučný chodník* (study trail).

☞ **POZOR!** You will see signs for both *Železná Studienka* and *Železná Studnička*. Don't worry, these names are interchangeable.

Malokarpatská Vínna Cesta (Wine Route) (*Štúrova 84, Modra;* ☎ *033 6474 302;* f *033 6400 484;* e *tik@post.sk; www.tik.sk & www.mvc.sk*). Day of Open Cellar Doors takes place mid November when dozens of wine cellars along the entire 40km route stretching from Rača to Trnava are accessible to the public between 13.00 and 21.00. For 800Sk (€ 22), visitors receive a map, a glass, a badge entitling entry to the cellars and bonus vouchers. Just don't forget who's the designated driver.

Malokarpatská cyklomagistrála This route goes through the bottom part of Malé Karpaty. It starts in Nové Mesto nad Váhom, at the northern end of the range and follows the eastern slopes through Vrbové, Trstín, Buková and Rohožník across the range to Vysoká pri Morave) on the Austrian border.

Štefánikova magistrála (hiking trail) Named after Milan Rastislav Štefánik (see *Chapter 6, Trenčín region, pages 170–1*). The trail begins near the Austrian border at Devín, and continues along the entire length of the Small Carpathians. Follow

SMALL CARPATHIAN WINE ROUTE

With some 7,300ha, the Small Carpathian Wine region is the largest in Slovakia. With Gothic churches and belfries, Baroque chateaux, walled towns, the aroma of roast goose and brass bands, it provides a great day out in the Slovak countryside. Two main towns located on the eastern slopes of the Small Carpathian Mountains, **Pezinok** and **Modra**, are known for wine. Viticulture was developed by Roman soldiers who worked in the vineyards when they weren't fighting. In the 16th century, German Protestants settled in the region, fleeing persecution in Germany and they brought many varieties of white grapes. The region produces 80% white, 20% red as the weaker sun conditions are better for whites such as Rizling vlašský (Weischriesling), Veltlínske zelené (Green Veltliner), Müller Thurgau, and Rulandské biele (Pinot Blanc) but the reds are good too. Maria Theresa particularly enjoyed the Frankovka modrá for its fertility-enhancing properties. Be careful, she had 16 children. Three major events highlight the year of wine growers: Wine Sampling in October, Blessing New Wine on St Martin's Day (11 November) and the spring Wine Market, although wine tasting is possible all year round. Modra's pottery works offers the chance to see how the famous ceramics have been produced for centuries. The two villages, **Slovenský** and **Chorvátsky Grob** are also well known for traditional ceramics, needle and lacework, houses painted with folklore ornaments and ancient wooden crosses in the local cemeteries. The main wine-producing villages and towns on the Small Carpathian Wine Route are Svätý Jur, Limbach, Pezinok, Slovenský Grob, Vinosady, Modra, Dubová, Častá and Doľany. Several more villages branch off to the left after Modra and wine can be sipped in Vištuk, Čataj Báhoň, Budmerice and Jablonec, on the border with Trnava region. The wine region stretches in a northeasterly direction for about 70km and can be covered by bike, or parts of it could be completed on foot. The altitudes in this mountain range vary from 132m above sea level near the Danube to as much as 768m at the peak of Záruby near Smolenice. The wine-growing region on the foothills of the Malé Karpaty (Small Carpathians) is just a stone's throw away from Bratislava. Rich vineyards stretch throughout the length of this area. Oak and yew trees prevail in the forests of the lowland whereas beech and ash are found in the higher regions. There is a large variety of plants, birds and small forest animals, but also herds of fallow, red deer, moufflon and wild boar. The region teems with cultural and historic monuments.

the red-signed trail to Biely kríž (White Cross) recreational area. From here, the yellow trail leads downhill for two hours into the town of Svätý Jur. The hilly ski resort of Pezinská baba is less than two hours further along the Štefánikova magistrála and the trail winds down into Pezinok after two more hours' tramp.

RAČA Rača is the first village on the Small Carpathian Wine Route and basically a leafy suburb of northern Bratislava. The first written references to the village in the 13th century called the village Okol. After attacks by the Tartar hordes, Germans were invited to settle and they named the area after a landlord, Rach. The Roman army under Marcus Aurelius brought the wine-growing tradition here in the 2nd century. Legend tells how Maria Theresa felt unwell before her coronation in Bratislava. She drank Frankovka modrá wine warm with sugar and immediately felt better. In 1767, the grateful empress granted Rača inhabitants the right to sell this wine to her imperial table. During the revolutions of 1848–49, the villagers enlisted in the Slovak Volunteer Corps. An ugly concrete housing estate brought the 20th century to Rača and only a few old village houses remain, found mostly on Alstrova ulica. These houses have rooms for pressing grapes and storing wine, and the owners open their cellars in the harvest season. Nowadays, Rača is one of the more prosperous districts and at weekends it makes a good starting point for hikes, cycling trips and setting off on the Small Carpathian Wine Route.

Getting there Trams 3 (from the railway station), 5 (from Námestie SNP), or 11 (from Námestie Ľ Štúra) in the centre of town.

Rača wineries

🍷 **Miloš Maťúš** Detvianska 33; m 0905 202 818; www.vinomatus.sk. *Open Mon–Fri 10.00–17.00.*
🍷 **Račianska viecha** (Rača wine tavern) Detvianska 17; ☎ 02 4488 6976. *Open Sat–Sun 09.00–01.00.*
🍷 **Villa Vino Rača** Pri Vinohradoch 2, Rača, Bratislava; ☎ 02 4920 2411; www.villavinoraca.sk. *Open Mon–Sat 10.00–18.00.*

SVÄTÝ JUR (SAINT GEORGE) The name translates as 'Saint George', and Svätý Jur is a picturesque 800-year-old town 16km northeast of Bratislava in the foothills of the Small Carpathians. The town's crest depicts St George killing a three-headed dragon with his lance. This is also the symbol of the three coldest months and St George kills winter on 23 April. In medieval times, local lords continued the sword-wielding behaviour and became the most feared in the Small Carpathians, their influence stretching as far as Bratislava. Svätý Jur is one of Slovakia's best-known wine villages. The most prominent building of the town is the early Gothic church with its wooden bell tower, situated in an upper part of the town called Neštich. Also found here are the ruins of Biely Kameň (White Stone) medieval castle (290m), which substituted the former Great Moravian fortification on the hill on the other side of the valley. The castle was probably built in 1270–95 by the counts of Svätý Jur. It was destroyed in 1663 by the Ottomans. Visitors can also see two partially preserved sides of the anti-Turkish fortification with two gates; the Renaissance Pálffy manor house from the early 17th century, which is now an educational institution, the Academia Istropolitana Nova; the Holy Trinity Church; the Black Plaque Column; the Piarist Monastery; the Zichy family's mansion and typical winemakers' town houses with original architecture. The first horse railway in the Hungarian Kingdom began running between Svätý Jur and Bratislava in 1840.

Getting there On the main Bratislava–Trnava railway line with trains every 20 minutes. On route 502 and buses every 15 minutes.

What to see and do

Literary and Homeland Museum (Literárne a vlastivedné múzeum) (*Prostredná 29; ☎ 02 4497 0476; www.muzeumpezinok.sk; open Tue–Fri 09.00–12.00 & 13.00–16.30, Sat 09.00–15.00, Sun (Apr–Oct) 13.00–17.00; admission adult/child 40/20Sk*). Showing the development of Svätý Jur from the Neolithic period to the present day.

Pivovar Codecon (*Prostredná 1; ☎ 02 4497 1911*). Founded in 1995, one of a few microbreweries in Slovakia (See Golem in Košice) operating in a 300-year-old monastery. Brewery boss František Šulka makes his Kláštorný ležiak 11.5ľ (Monastery light) following a long-established beer-making monkish tradition. It's hard to find this excellent beer in Bratislava so it is worth making the trip. Šulka plans a 14ľ dark beer, so build up a thirst on a long hike in the hills.

Sanct Georgen's Wein (*Hájniy 920;* ↘ *02 4497 1413; www.sgw.sk*)

Svätý Jur tour (↘ *02 4497 1132*) Phone to arrange a tour.

Vínne pivnice Svätý Jur (*Horné predmestie 16;* ↘ *02 4497 1442;* e *vinne.pivnice@ yahoo.co.uk; www.vinnepivnice.sk*). Private wine tastings for small and large groups in local cellars or they'll bring the wine to your own venue.

PEZINOK Pezinok's name comes from the Latin *terra Bozin,* referring to the gold mining that began in 1208. You can still find tiny bits of gold in the streams. The town evolved from a mining settlement into a wine-producing town when Germans colonised the area at the beginning of the 16th century. They have a saying here that the Pezinok men are the richest in the world as they have three types of gold: the precious metal, the wine and the beautiful local women. In the 18th century, Pezinok was indeed one of the richest towns in the Hungarian Kingdom and its fame and wealth was based on its superior wines. Every September, Pezinok, 20km northeast of Bratislava, plays host to Vinobranie, the west Slovak region's annual wine festival. Dozens of wine cellars, often little more than a family house with a barrel in the basement, throw open their doors to wine lovers and tourists. The castle on Mladoboleslavskáulica was built in 1300 as a water fortress in a Gothic style and was reconstructed in the 16th and 17th centuries. Currently the castle houses a typical wine tavern used for wine-tasting sessions. Pezinok is well known for its white wines: Rizling vlašský (Weischriesling), Veltlínske zelené (Green Veltliner), Müller Thurgau, and Rulandské biele (Pinot Blanc).

In September, Pezinok and Modra host the annual *burčiak* festival. The grape cider might taste like innocent juice but actually contains pretty potent alcohol. Burčiak is still fermenting when served and after a week, the white grape juice clouds up and starts bubbling. It should be consumed quickly, otherwise it becomes a drier cidery beverage.

PEZINOK WINE CELLARS

Ⓨ **LVS Pezinok** Šenkvická cesta 14/A; ↘ 033 6453 061. Offering Veltlínske zelené, Rizling Vlašský, Müller-Thurgau, Alibernet.

Ⓨ **Vinársky závod** Za dráhou 21; ↘ 033 6906 111; www.vitis.sk. Offering Veltlínske zelené, Rizling Vlašský, Frankovka modrá.

Ⓨ **Vinovin Peter Ščepán** Jesenského 2; ↘ 033 6413 252; www.vinovin.sk. Offering Frankovka modrá, Rizling Vlašský, Rulandské biele, Veltlínske zelené.

Ⓨ **Víno Matyšák** Holubyho 85; ↘ 033 6413 667. With excellent Müller-Thurgau.

Ⓨ **Vinohradníctvo Pavelka-Sobolič** Milan Pavelka & Milan Sobolič at Cajlanská 126; ↘ 033 6451 064; www.pavelkavino.sk. With 35ha of Rizling rýnsky, Rizling vlašsky, Müller-Thurgau, Rulanské biele, Frankovka modrá & the Neronet hybrid.

Ⓨ **Borik víno** Peter & Magdaléna Borik at Jilemnického 2A; m 0905 525 759; offering Chardonnay, Rizling rýnsky, Rulandské biele, Svätovavrinecké, Sauvignon, Frankovka modrá, Cabernet Sauvignon.

Ⓨ **Vínna pivnica Hacaj** Ján Hacaj at M R Štefánika 21; ↘ 033 6402 696; www.hacaj.sk. With Sauvignon, Müller-Thurgau, Svätovavrinecké & an excellent méthode Champagnoise sparkling wine,

Ⓨ **Víno Ludvik** Tehelná 11; ↘ 033 6413 443. Offering Rizling vlašský, Veltlínske zelené, Pesecká leánka.

Ⓨ **Vinkova** Tehelná 13; ↘ 033 6474 350; www.vinkova.sk. With Cabernet Sauvignon, Alibernet.

☞ **POZOR!** If you buy some *burčiak* to take away in an old fizzy pop bottle, don't screw the cap on too tightly.

Getting there Pezinok is on the main Bratislava–Trnava railway line with trains every 20 minutes. On route 502 and buses every 15 minutes.

Tourist information

ℹ **Pezinok information centre** 9 Radničné námestie, 902 01 Pezinok; ☎ 033 6901 107; f 033 6412 550; e informacne.centrum@msupezinok.sk; www.pezinok.sk. *Open Jun–Sep Mon–Fri 10.00–18.00, Sat 09.00–14.00; Oct–May Mon–Fri 10.00–18.00, Sat 09.00–12.00.*

ℹ **Pezinok tour** ☎ 033 6412 360
ℹ **BKIS** Klobučnicka 2, Bratislava. Organises a trip to Pezinok Museum (40Sk), the Modra Majolica factory & Červený Kameň (100Sk). The cost of the trip is 6,500Sk for 1–10 people, 7,500Sk for 11–40 people. Entrance fees & transport not included.

🏠 Where to stay, eat and drink

🏠 **Horský hotel Istota** (27 rooms) Kučišdorfská dolina 2559; ☎ 033 6402 937; e reservacie@ hotelistota.sk. Another mountain hotel, 7km from Pezinok off route 503, with pool, fitness, dry sauna, internet & rental of bikes, paintball & football. Hotel minibus available. *Sgl $$, dbl $$$, suites $$$$, b/fast inc.*

🏠 **Horský hotel Stupy** Pezinská cesta 5; ☎ 033 6402 156; e hotelstupy@pobox.sk. Situated 5km from Pezinok on route 503 to Pezinská Baba, FB in its own mountain restaurant, tennis courts, pool, sauna. *Sgl $, apts $$.*

🏠 **Hotel Lipa** (36 beds) Kollárova 20; ☎ 033 6412

402; e hotellipa@hotellipa.sk; www.hotellipa.sk. Hotel with its own excellent restaurant Preš in a 300-year-old stone cellar. *Dbl $$, apts $$.*

🏠 **Penzión 77** (7 dbl, 1 apt) Bernolakova 77; ☎ 033 6400 189; e penzion77@stonline.sk; www.penzion77.sk. A 3-star pension, all rooms have en-suite bathrooms, satellite TV, minibar & internet access. *Dbl $$, apts $$$.*

✗ **Zámocká vináreň** Mladoboleslavská 5; ☎ 033 6412 360. A wine cellar & restaurant in Pezinok Castle with a lovely summer terrace. Extensive menu with fish & game as well as Slovak classics. *$$. Open Mon–Sat 11.00–23.00, Sun 11.00–22.00.*

What to see and do

Malokarpatsky Múzeum (Small Carpathian museum) (*M R Štefánika 4; ☎ 033 6413 347; admission adult 40Sk*). Located in a Renaissance burgher winter house from 1739. Exhibitions on the history of Pezinok, feudal justice, handicrafts & guild trades. History of grape cultivation in the Small Carpathian region with a big collection of wine presses.

Mining educational walk A route leading around 14 interesting places in Pezinok, showing mining traditions & natural attributes. A leaflet & map (in Slovak, German & English) accompanies the walk. Details from the tourist centre.

Municipal Museum in Pezinok Stará radnica Old Town Hall (*M R Štefánika 1; ☎ 033 6412 306; e muzeumpk@pezinsko.sk; http://muzeumpk.pezinsko.sk; open Tue–Fri 10.00–18.00, Sat 10.00–16.00, Sun 13.00–17.00; admission adult/child 40/20Sk*).

Pezinok Gallery of Naïve Art (*Schaubmar mill, Cajlanská 255; ☎ 033 6404 035; open Tue–Sun 10.00–17.00; admission adult/child 30/10Sk*). The mill was built in 1767 & the reconstructed machinery from 1913 can be seen.

SKIING AT PEZINSKÁ BABA AND ZOCHOVA CHATA

Pezinská Baba is 12km from Pezinok and the most significant winter sport resort in the Malé Karpaty range (527m). There are three tracks for downhill skiing of 500m, 700m and 1,000m. Relief and grades are suitable for beginners as well as experienced skiers; there is one individual lift for children. Also a 9km track for cross-country skiing.

Lyžiarsky klub Baba Holubyho 18, 902 01 Pezinok; ☎ 033 6402 312; f 033 6451 136; e info@lkbaba.sk; www.lkbaba.sk. Ski pass per day: adult 350Sk, 250Sk.

Zochova chata ski centre 4km north; ☎ 033 6470 280; f 033 6470 223; e info@zochova-chata.com; http://zochova-chata.com. Ski pass per day: adult 450Sk, child 280Sk. You can stay here too. Sgl $, dbl $$, apts for 4 $$$.

LIMBACH The name Limbach possibly comes from the German word 'lindenbach' meaning a string of lime trees. The village coat of arms shows a tree and a curling rope. The tree should have been a linden but they made a mistake and drew a coniferous pine, a *limba* in Slovak, instead. Limbach puts its 116ha of vineyard to good use and produces the Limbašský Silvaner wine. Limbach is a good starting point for easy hikes to Tri kamenné kopce (Three rocky hills).

Getting there Head for Pezinok on route 502 and turn off to the left 2km before Pezinok. Buses run regularly from Bratislava main bus station.

KARPATSKÁ PERLA WINERY IN ŠENKVICE (6KM EAST OF PEZINOK)

Karpatská Perla winery is housed in a modern building on the outskirts of a village called Šenkvice, 6km east of Pezinok (*Nádražná 57, Šenkvice;* ☎/f *033 6497 0007; www.karpatskaperla.sk*). It's a business run by the Šebo and Záruba families, producing 500,000 litres of superb quality whites and reds a year. The name, Karpatská perla harks back to Pezinok in the 1850s when wine was sold under the name *Carpathian Pearl*. These excellent wines can now be found in restaurants all over Slovakia, from Poprad to Banská Bystrica and the Veltlínske zelené 2004 is a great introduction: light and crisp with almond hints.

Getting there Route 502 from Bratislava to Pezinok then signposted for Šenkvice.

MODRA Signs of settlement in the Modra area date back to 3000BC. A permanent settlement in the 9th century has been confirmed by well-preserved walls of the castle at Zamčisko. In 1361, Modra received servile Royal Town privileges from Hungarian monarch Lajos I. Between 1610 and 1646, Modra created its fortifications with three gateways. Some parts, including a gateway Horná Brána (upper gate) are preserved to this day. Sights include St Stephen's Church and the town tower. Modra is linked with Ľudovít Štúr, the famous Slovak patriot and father of the Slovak language. Štúr and his brother Karol are both buried in the churchyard of Jána Krstiteľa (John the Baptist) situated just south of the centre on Dolná, next to the ceramics factory. There is a statue of Štúr in the centre of Modra, erected in 1937, 81 years after Štúr died in Modra.

Modra is famous for its wine; you will see the signs 'Predaj vina' (wine for sale) all over town. However they have also made ceramics here since the 16th century. The old town gate of Modra became part of the pottery, first as a pattern then as a trademark. The style of fine china and ceramics called *habanská* from the Haban craftsman. The Habans, also known as Anabaptists, were a religious sect during the Reformation who rejected papal authority, the idea of private property and lived in communes. They fled religious persecution in Moravia and came to Modra in the early 1600s. Their religious character, favouring an elegant simplicity, influenced the style still seen today. The motifs use everyday images; flowers and patterns from hunting, dancing and wine pressing. The gentle curves and colours of yellow, blue, green and plum evoke the natural surroundings. The Habans also perfected the new majolica glazing technique and today the majolica factory, with five potters and 25 painters is one of the last makers of handcrafted pottery in Slovakia.

Getting there Route 502 from Bratislava, regular buses from Bratislava bus station.

What to see and do

Múzeum Ľudovíta (*Štúra Štúrova ulica 54;* ✆ *033 6472 765; www.snm.sk or www.muzeumlstura.host.sk; open Mon–Fri 08.00–16.00; admission adult/child 20/10S*). Housed in the neoclassicist former town hall, the museum opened in 1965 as a specialised literary museum, dedicated to Štúr's life and work. Also has information on ceramics in Modra.

Small Carpathian Information centre (*Modra Štúrova 84;* ✆ *033 6472 313;* e *infomodra@stonline.sk; www.tik.sk, www.modra.sk or www.modranet.sk*).

Slovenská Ľudová Majolika (Ceramics factory) (*Dolná 138, Modra;* ✆ *033 6472 941; www.majolika.sk; open Mon–Fri 08.00–11.00 & 13.00–15.00; admission adult/student 200/100Sk*). To arrange a factory visit call two days ahead.

Wine for sale (*Dolná 120, Modra;* ✆ *033 6472 430*).

Modra-Harmónia (✆ *033 647 3151;* f *033 647 3153; www.sazp.sk/rekreacia/modra*). Established in 1890 near Modra, the summer residence Harmónia evolved into a Malé Karpaty tourist resort.

ČERVENÝ KAMEŇ (*Častá;* ✆ *033 6495 132;* e *muzeumca.z@stonline.sk; www.snm.sk/ck; open May–Sep Mon–Fri 09.00–17.00, Sat–Sun 09.00–18.00; Mar–Apr & Sep–Oct Mon–Fri 09.00–16.00, Sat–Sun 09.00–17.00; Nov–Feb 09.30–15.30; guided tours last 90mins; admission adult/child 100/50Sk*). The name means 'red stone' and it's an impressive 13th-century castle that became the property of the Thurzó family in the early 16th century but from 1535 belonged to the powerful Fugger family who rebuilt the castle into a massive Renaissance fortress. The spectacular cellars (72m long and 9m high) are the largest in central Europe, a massive cavernous hall that held wine for the Fugger family and subsequent nobility like the Pálffys. The Fuggers were one of the richest families

---

MAGNA VIA

The Magna Via (Great Road) is a road of historical and cultural significance leading through five countries: Austria, Ukraine, Slovakia, Hungary and Romania. In Slovakia, the road crosses several countries, regions, micro-regions, towns and villages. Half of the overall length of 1,000km is located within Slovakia. The Magna Via arrives in Slovakia from Austria at Bratislava and heads northeast through Senec, Trnava, Topolčany, Prievidza to Martin then turns east to Liptovský Mikulas, Poprad, Spisske Podhradie to Prešov (where there is a superb restaurant called Magna Via) then heads due south to Košice then east to Michalovce and Sobrance before crossing into the Ukraine. The Magna Via was built in the 16th century and was initially travelled by horse-drawn carriages carrying passengers, letters and news. Gradually, more by-roads and connections were added; most of them were built during the 18th century. The Magna Via is the longest and oldest of all historic routes in Slovakia. The legacy of this historic post road relates directly to the present trend in tourism, that is travelling focused on the natural, historical and cultural heritage of the rural area. To date, 22 cultural roads are inscribed on the UNESCO World Heritage List. Magna Via hopes to become the 23rd.

in Europe who in the 16th century operated the largest copper-mining company of that time. The Fuggers made a fortune trading in copper, silver, gold and wine and were bankers to emperors and popes. The Červený Kameň castle originally was designed as the anti-Turkish fortress. The atmospheric dungeons have been used as a location for many films. After the Fuggers, the Pálffy family moved in and added beautiful Baroque interior decorations. Damaged during World War II, reconstruction started in 1947 and the castle is now an excellent museum displaying finely carved furniture and original weapons. The unusual *Salla Terrena* (winter garden), created in 1656, is the coldest room in the castle and features a manmade grotto guarded by chubby cherubs. An antiques market is held in the castle courtyard. Fairs, knightly displays, horseback riding and pony trekking take place in the surrounding meadows. There is a falconer's yard (*Astur*) in the castle area where raptor exhibitions are presented in summer (*booking of falcon shows:* m *0907 773 058; www.falconry.sk; open Tue–Sun 10.00–17.00*).

Getting there The castle is 30km from Bratislava and the best way to see it is on a tour (see *Local tours*, page 78). The Small Carpathian Wine Route trip usually combines a visit to the ceramics factory in Modra, and visits to wine-producing villages like Pezinok.

Alternatively, take a bus to the village of Častá then walk for 20 minutes uphill.

BUDMERICE CHATEAU The gorgeous, fairytale palace of Budmerice was built in 1889 in the Romantic style. The chateau, surrounded by an English park, is now used as The House of Slovak Writers. Ethnographic enthusiasts will enjoy the folk art room and its fascinating exhibition.

The chateau was another real estate possession of the massively wealthy and influential Pálffy family. Inspiration for the design of the manor came from Italian late Gothic, and French Renaissance (1848–1918), especially the Renaissance castles on the Loire.

Getting there Route 502 to Modra, then turn right onto route 504 to Trnava.

PLAVECKÝ CASTLE This defensive frontier castle was built in the second half of the 13th century. Along with the Korlátka and Ostrý Kameň castles, Plavecký defended the commercial Bohemian Route (*Česká cesta*) linking Bohemia and Budapest and was named after the Plavci tribe who guarded the Hungarian border rather than lost, land-locked swimmers (*plavecký* means 'for swimmers' in Slovak). In the late 16th century, the Fugger family and then the Balassa family took possession of the Gothic castle and converted it into an archetypal Renaissance fortress. At the end of the 16th century, one of Slovakia's first printing houses, belonging to Péter Bornemisza, a leading figure in the Reformation, was located here. During the Rákóczi uprising, the castle was occupied by rebels and in 1706 conquered by the imperial army, when it fell into ruin. The castle offers great views of the Záhorská lowland and Pohanská hill with an Iron-Age fortified settlement.

Getting there By car, take the D2/E65 motorway towards Brno, exit Lozorno and continue on route 501 to Plavecké Podhradie, the nearest village. The blue-signed tourist path leads to the castle; the walk takes 30 minutes.

HEADING NORTH TOWARDS MALACKY

STUPAVA Stupava, 14km north of Bratislava, on the western slopes of the Small Carpathians, celebrates the Záhorie region's most popular vegetable, the cabbage, at the beginning of October. At the *Dni zelá* (Cabbage Days), visitors receive bowls of sauerkraut and while munching they can examine displays of giant cabbages and impressive locally grown fruit and vegetables. Folk dance performances enliven the ambience and visitors can try *burčiak*, a half-fermented grape-cider drink and nibble on traditional cabbage dishes: Freshly cut cabbage and sauerkraut varieties, cabbage cake (*kapustník*) and cabbage soup (*kapustnica*) are on sale.

Getting there Route 2 heading north out of Bratislava towards Malacky.

BORINKA Now home to Bratislava's rich and famous, the beautiful village of Borinka nestles on the western slopes of the Small Carpathians. **Pajštún Castle** ruins is the main attraction. The castle is situated on a limestone cliff at 537m so walkers should be fairly fit to complete the 45-minute walk. Hikers are rewarded with a beautiful view of the southern Malé Karpaty and Záhorie lowland. In good weather you can spot the Alps in the other direction. Pajštún Castle was first mentioned in the 13th century. It was modernised in the 17th century. The steep, soaring walls of the castle are adorned by several sinister gargoyles leering down at walkers. I remember hiking here for a fantastic picnic in 1982. My hosts in Bratislava took a group of us for barbecued sausages and beer at the top. It was quite a tough hike through idyllic woods but well worth it.

The village of **Marianka** nearby is the oldest pilgrimage destination in the country. Visitors are drawn by a legend from 1330 that tells of a blind mendicant whose sight was restored when he washed in spring waters. The Pauline Monastery and Chapel of the Holy Well date from 1377. The Baroque sanctuary of Marianka Church hosts a magical statue of the Virgin Mary.

Getting there Hikers can reach Pajštún in about three hours from the town of Rača, at the start of the wine route, or approach from Stupava. By car, head for Brno on motorway D2/E65, take the Lamač exit and follow the road through Záhorská Bystrica to Borinka.

Buses leave Bratislava's main bus station for Borinka (45 minutes). From the middle of the village follow the red-marked trail. Buses to Marianka leave Bratislava every hour.

MALACKY Malacky was first mentioned in 1206. The name comes from Malaczka, meaning the 'settlement by the Malina stream' and also the Slovak word *mlaky* meaning puddles, although because the town's coat of arms features a wild boar, Hungarians believe the name comes from the word *malacka* (piglet). Malacky is the centre of the southern Záhorie region. The Church of the Ascension of Mary the Virgin has some creepy crypts, with the remains of many of the noble Pálffy family and in 1992 was used by Satanic cults for séances. Hungarian nobleman Ján Pálffy's heart is stored in a golden box in a special niche in the church wall.

HEADING EAST TOWARDS SENEC

GOLF AT BERNOLÁKOVO Teeing off since 1993, the nine-hole golf course at the Bratislava Golf & Country Club (*Bernolákovo;* ⚊ *02 5443 2008;* e *infos@golf.sk; www.golf.sk*) is 3,600m long and has a par 62. Golfers stroll through historical surroundings watched over by 200-year-old trees. The village of Bernolákovo is also graced by an 18th-century Baroque palace once owned by the Esterházy family.

Getting there Head northeast out of Bratislava on route 61 towards Senec. Bernolákovo is 16km east of Bratislava.

SENEC The Sunny Lakes (Slnečné jazerá), 25km east of Bratislava, is a popular resort with Bratislava families, attracted by the mild climate, warm water and 2,200 hours of 25°C sunshine a year. The sunny lakes are a collection of gravel pits, covering an area of 116ha and filled with clear, clean water. To the southeast of Senec toward the southeast there is a gravel pit called Guľáška, also known as Hlboké jazero (Deep Lake). It has the clearest water for windsurfing in Slovakia. The lake is mostly surrounded by fields, so nothing blocks the wind from any direction from rushing across the surface of the water. The resort has volleyball courts, minigolf, maxi-chess and toboggans as well as an open-air cinema during the summer. For children, there are also grassy beach areas, water bicycles, playgrounds, water chutes, merry-go-rounds and bouncy castles. Windsurfers use the eastern-most bay for entry into the water, where the water is clear, and the bank and entry to the water have fine gravel.

Aquathermal Park Senec (*Slnečné jazerá (Sunny Lakes – north);* ℡ *02 4564 8021;* e *info@aquathermal.sk; www.aquathermal.sk; 3hr ticket adult/child 300/200Sk, all-day ticket adult/child 450/350Sk, sauna world 100Sk, 45min full body massage 350Sk, 20min back massage 200Sk*). Aquathermal Park is a modern lido complex by the Sunny Lakes resort in Senec. Visitors leave their cash, clothes and other valuables in lockers and wear a chip wristband that tots up the bill during the stay and visitors settle up for the entry ticket, food, drinks, massages and extras when leaving. Four small and five large swimming pools are heated to 22–36°C by a thermal spring, gushing from a depth of 1,300m and a source temperature of 48°C. Senec's watery world attracts visitors with fun pools and entertaining attractions such as water rain, a waterfall, water jets, a sprinkle column and two water slides.

Getting there By car: Route 61/E571 heading northeast out of Bratislava. Dozens of buses leave Bratislava each day, journey time 35–50 minutes. From Bratislava's main railway station, trains leave in the direction of Galanta, Nové Zámky and Štúrovo. Journey time to Senec is 20 minutes.

GOOD GRUB IN THE GROBS

Between Pezinok and Senec, 10km southeast of the Small Carpathian foothills are two interesting villages which are excellent destinations while on the wine route, offering rib-sticking cuisine based on roasted goose meat.

CHORVÁTSKY GROB Chorvátsky Grob (Croatian Grob) is the heartland of Slovakia's tiny remaining ethnic Croat community. Folklore festivals take place in March, when women dress up in folk costume. In the 16th century, 200,000 Croats came to the Danube region, fleeing the Turks who were rampaging through the Balkans. They worked in agriculture and wine cultivation.

Getting there Bus 53 from Trnavské mýto in Bratislava to Čierna Voda. By car, take the D1/E75 motorway towards Senec and exit Senica.

 Where to stay

☗ **Hotel Kamila** (20 rooms, 4 suites) Čierna voda 611, Chorvátsky Grob; ℡ 02 4594 3611; f 02 4594 | 3631; e hotel@kamila.sk; www.kamila.sk. Situated 10km northeast of Bratislava, *en route* to Chorvátsky

✕ **Grobský dvor** Vladimír Minarovič at Vajnorská 3; ✆ 033 6478 889. A modern building with a covered summer terrace setting overlooking acres of vineyards. Light, thin potato pancakes, stuffed with minced beef. Baked goose is a seasonal speciality, available mainly in autumn, but a *husacie hody* (goose feast) for groups of 4 or more can be arranged at any time of year by calling in advance. $$$$. *Open daily 11.30–23.00.*

✕ **Grobská izba** Božena Piačková & Vladimír Piaček at Hlavná 193; ✆ 033 6478 582; e grobskaizba@slovensky-grob.sk. 70 places in a family setting, 1kg of roast goose for 725Sk, oiled *lokša* pancakes are 14Sk each. $$$$. *Open daily 11.00–22.00.*

✕ **Grobská reštaurácia** Adriana Jajcayová at Chorvátska 54; m 0907 243 507. 300 places in a huge white concrete box building. 1kg of roast meat 1,500Sk. $$$$$. *Open daily 11.00–23.00.*

✕ **Husacie Hody** (Goose Feast) Iveta Noskovičová at Pezinská 28; ✆ 033 6478 391. 60 places in a rustic farmhouse-style setting. $$$$. *Open daily 10.00–22.00.*

✕ **Husacina U Galika** (Goose at Galik's) Lipová 21, Slovenský Grob; ✆ 033 6478 550; m 0903 718 252; www.husacinaugalika.sk. Milan Galik's restaurant observes the traditional way of cooking its goose. Should you be incapable of any form of movement after the dinner, accommodation is offered, in one 4-bed room, two 2-bed rooms, or one 6-bed room. $$. *Open Mon–Fri 12.00–22.00, Sat 12.00–23.00, Sun 13.00–18.00*

✕ **Husacina u Gaštana** Adriana Cedulová at Záhumenná 22; ✆ 033 6478 402; e husacinaugastana@zoznam.sk; www.husacinaugastana.sk. With lovely open stone fireplaces. $$$$. *Open daily 11.00–22.00.*

✕ **Reštaurácia Husiarik** Marek Kostolanský at Družstevná 32; m 0903 754 863; e restauraciahusiarik@slovensky-grob.sk. $$$$. *Open Mon–Fri 11.00–22.00, Sat 12.00–23.00, Sun 12.00–17.00.*

✕ **Zelený Dvor** (Green Yard) Mária Pluhárová at Nová 49; ✆ 033 6478 349; e zelenydvor@zelenydvor.sk. Family restaurant, summer terrace. $$$$. *Open Mon 17.00–22.00, Tue–Sat 12.00–22.00, Sun 12.00–17.00.*

Grob, Hotel Kamila has great views of the Small Carpathian Mountains and is owned by Slovak actress Kamila Magálová who stays closely involved in day-to-day operations. Lots of activities and services: golf, tennis and horseriding, wine tasting, gourmet cuisine, folk music. Wellness centre with Finnish sauna, infrared cabin, vertical turbo solarium, cardio-fitness and an outdoor swimming pool. Also massage and aromatherapy. *Sgl, dbl* $$$, *suite* $$$$. *Buffet or à la carte b/fast inc.*

SLOVENSKÝ GROB Slovenský Grob (Slovakian Grob) is famous for its goose feasts which it has been staging for the last century. November is high season for roast goose in Slovakia.

Both villages are sweet but ordinary. The goose is the draw, especially when accompanied by some fiery *slivovica*, a white wine from the Small Carpathians or a rich Slovak Tokaj, the famous dessert wine. Visitors should also try *burčiak*, a young, still-fermenting wine.

Getting there The Sopravná agentúra DASK company (*Tehelná 25, Bratislava;* ✆f 02 4425 8106; m 0903 434 147; e info@da.sk; www.da.sk) offer microbuses, personal cars, airport (Bratislava, Vienna, Budapest, Brno, Ostrava, Prague and Košice) taxis, hotel taxis, bus transport, a freight service, a VIP service and special help with companies, weddings and groups who want to hold events in Slovenský Grob.

5

Trnava Region

Spas, wine and learning: these are the three attractions – two liquid, one erudite – that the chunky banana-shaped Trnava region offers. One of the smaller Slovak regions (71.53 km²), Trnava forms a semicircular belt around the Bratislava region, cutting it off from the rest of the country. Trnava shares borders with three countries: the Czech Republic (45km) and Austria (12km) to the north and Hungary (48km) to the south, creating plenty of opportunity for trans-border co-operation, trade and tourism.

The region is mainly flat, situated in the lush valley of the mighty Váh River, Slovakia's main waterway, between the Small Carpathians in the west and the Považský Inovec range to the east. The benign climate of mild winters and long warm, wet summers make it a great destination for tourists and business folk alike, as the economically dynamic region is filled with green fields criss-crossed with rivers and dotted with lakes, reservoirs and spa towns. The countryside; flat expanses of agricultural land dotted with little, one-street villages, is not as spectacular as in the northern mountainous regions but there are some beautiful castles and romantic ruins. The map shows more than 40 castles, palaces, mansions and ruins although only the most interesting half-dozen are detailed here.

The Trnava region is a fast-growing, exciting business region, well served by air, rail and the otherwise sparse Slovak motorway network. The region is part of the 'golden triangle' a development boom formed by Vienna, Bratislava and Györ in Hungary.

EVENTS IN TRNAVA REGION

1 January	**Trnava** *Trnavský novoročný beh* New Year's Run
March–May	**Trnava** *Music Spring* classical music concerts
April	**Trnava** *Lumen* gospel music festival; see www.festivallumen.sk
May	**Piešťany** 'Music Summer' promenade concerts
June	**Trnava** *Dobrofest* music festival; see www.dobrofest.sk (page 19)
June–August	**Piešťany** The 52nd classical music festival
August	**Piešťany airport** *Hodokvas* music festival
	Trnava *Trnavská brána* international folklore festival
	Smolenice *Below Smolenice Castle* concerts and fair
September	**Skalica** *Skalické dni* traditional crafts festival
November	**Galanta** *Galanta Music Days* opening concerts
December	**Piešťany** frost-hardy swimming in the Váh River

TRNAVA *Telephone code 033*

Lovers of sacral art, football fans and holidaying nuns will each find their own personal slice of heaven in Trnava where 11 significant churches are situated

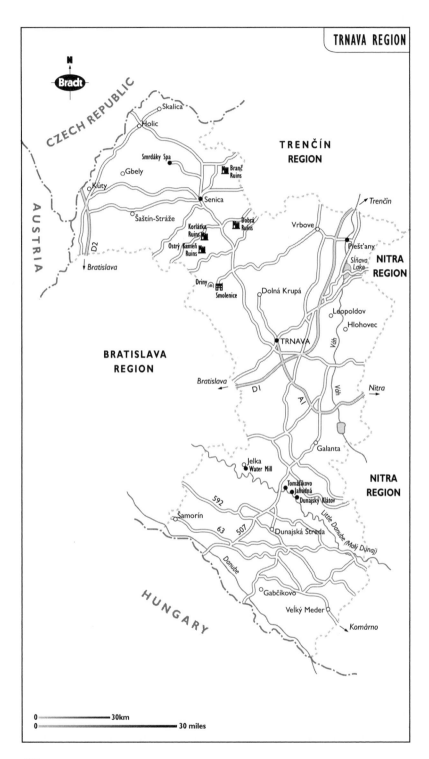

within the elegant city walls, a hop, skip or somersault away from the excellent range of hotels, pensions, restaurants, bars and cafés. It's a youthful university town and soccer mad with one of Slovakia's best teams (see box, *Slovak football*, page 55). It's also probably the wealthiest city in Slovakia after Bratislava with enthusiastic commercial investment.

An atomic power station is situated at Jaslovské Bohunice, just west of Leopoldov and in 2003, Peugeot built a colossal assembly plant on Trnava's outskirts. When the plant reaches full strength, it will produce 450,000 cars each year. By 2010, 60% of all Peugeot 207s will be made in Trnava. Along with Bratislava's Volkswagen and Žilina's Kia Hyundai plants, Peugeot will help make Slovakia in 2007 the world's largest per capita producer of automobiles. There are also many fine museums including the Galéria Jána Koniarka and the West Slovakia Museum. The main square has been restored but it is spoiled by some spectacularly ugly modern buildings right in the ancient heart, unlike Bratislava Old Town which at least pushes its *paneláky* (high-rise blocks built out of pre-fabricated panels) out over the Danube. Whereas Bratislava's Petržalka has a certain (mistaken) idealist retro charm especially when viewed in the context of the UFO café and Incheba, as if the town planners had a misguided space-age fantasy about modern, affordable housing for the masses, here Trnava's 1960s' architecture is just plain dowdy and depressing and all the more when contrasted with the beautiful clutch of churches in the centre of Slovakia's 'Little Rome'.

HISTORY Trnava (*Nagyszombat* in Hungarian, *Tyrnau* in German) is known as the 'Slovak Rome' because of its high concentration of churches and significant religious history. A huge statue of Pope John Paul II stands outside the university church (Katedrála sv. Jána Krstiteľa – John the Baptist), blessing the faithful. Rosaries dangle from his outstretched hands. The name of the town is derived from the Slovak word *trnie* meaning thorn bush, which are found along the riverbanks in the region. There were permanent settlements on the town's territory from the Neolithic period onwards. During the Middle Ages, an important market settlement arose here at the junction of two important routes: the Bohemia–Hungary and the Poland–Mediterranean route. In 1238, Hungarian King Béla IV made the settlement of Zumbothel a Free Royal Town and granted it the right to hold a market every Saturday, hence its Hungarian name Nagyszombat (Big Saturday). Originally a centre of agriculture, Trnava gradually developed into a destination for manufacturing, crafts and trade. The Roman Catholic Church and international trade have been Trnava's two main historical influences for over seven centuries. In the 13th century, the Hungarian rulers had invited Germans to settle in Trnava and settlements increased after the Tatar invasions in 1242. By the turn of the 14th century, part of Trnava was enclosed by a long wall, however the Slovak market and the Germans stayed behind this wall. The town, along with the rest of the territory of present-day Slovakia, gained importance when the Ottoman Empire conquered and occupied Hungary after the Battle of Mohács in 1526 and Trnava became the main religious centre of Hungary for more than 200 years. The Hungarian archbishopric was centred around the Cathedral of Saint John the Baptist and Saint Nicolas Church. Many ethnic Hungarians fleeing the Turks also moved to the town. In the 16th and especially the 17th century, Trnava was an important centre of the Counter-Reformation in the Kingdom of Hungary. Archbishop Mikuláš Oláh invited the Jesuits to Trnava in 1561 in order to develop the municipal school system. He opened a seminary in 1566 and in 1577 Trnava's priest Nicolas Telegdi founded a book-printing house in the town. Founded by Archbishop Péter Pázmány, the Jesuit Trnava University (1635–1777) was the only university of the Kingdom of

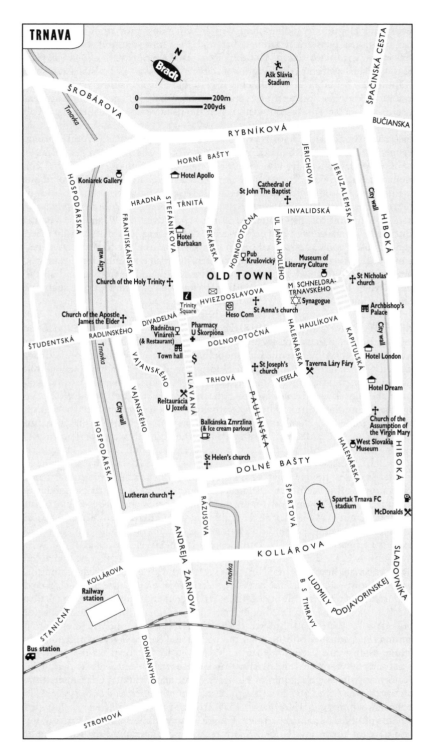

TRNAVA

ŠROBÁROVA

Trnavka

RYBNÍKOVÁ

ŠPAČINSKÁ CESTA

BUČIANSKA

Ašk Slávia Stadium

N
Bradt

0 ————— 200m
0 ————— 200yds

HORNÉ BAŠTY

Koniarek Gallery

HRADNA

ŠTEFÁNIKOVA

TRNITÁ

Hotel Apollo

JERICHOVA

Cathedral of St John The Baptist

INVALIDSKÁ

JERUZALEMSKÁ

City wall   HIBOKÁ

HOSPODÁRSKA

FRANTIŠKÁNSKA

City wall

PEKÁRSKA

Hotel Barbakan

HORNOPOTOČNA

UL JÁNA HOLLÉHO

UL JÁNA HOLLÉHO

Pub Krušovický

Museum of Literary Culture

M SCHNELDRA-TRNAVSKÉHO

St Nicholas' church

Church of the Holy Trinity

OLD TOWN

i Trinity Square

HVIEZDOSLAVOVA

Synagogue

Archbishop's Palace

Church of the Apostle James the Elder

DIVADELNÁ

RADLINSKÉHO

ŠTUDENTSKÁ

Trnavka

Heso Com   St Anna's church

Radničná Vináreň (& Restaurant)

Pharmacy U Škorpióna

DOLNOPOTOČNÁ

HAULÍKOVA

HALENÁRSKA

KAPITULSKÁ

City wall

Hotel London

Town hall

$

VAJANSKÉHO

HLAVANA

TRHOVÁ

St Joseph's church

VESELÁ

Taverna Láry Fáry

Hotel Dream

VAJANSKÉHO

Reštaurácia U Jozefa

PAULÍNSKA

Church of the Assumption of the Virgin Mary

HOSPODÁRSKA

City wall

Balkánska Zmrzlina (& Ice cream parlour)

St Helen's church

DOLNÉ BAŠTY

HALENÁRSKA

West Slovakia Museum

HIBOKÁ

Lutheran church

RÁZUSOVA

ŠPORTOVÁ

Spartak Trnava FC stadium

McDonalds

SLADOVNÍKA

ANDREJA ŽARNOVA

Trnavka

KOLLÁROVA

LUDMILY PODJAVORINSKEJ

B S TIMRAVY

KOLLÁROVA

Railway station

STANIČNÁ

Bus station

DOHNÁNYHO

STROMOVÁ

Hungary at that time. The importance of the town decreased in 1777, when the university was moved to Buda and in 1820, the archbishopric moved back to Esztergom. The 17th century was a difficult period in Slovak history, as there were many anti-Habsburg uprisings in the country. The revolts led by István Bocskai, Gábor Bethlén, György I Rákóczi and Imre Thököly had a negative effect on life in Trnava. However, from the late 18th century Trnava became a centre of the literary and artistic Slovak National Revival. The first standard codification of the Slovak language by the priest Anton Bernolák in 1787 was based on the Slovak dialect used in the region of Trnava. In 1844, Trnava was connected to Bratislava by the first railway line in the Kingdom of Hungary. It was pulled by horses as steam engines were used only after 1872. With the railway connection came a modernisation of the town, beginning with the construction of a large sugar factory, a malt-house and the Coburgh factory, later known as the Trnava Car Factory (*Trnavské automobilové závody*). Up until World War II, Trnava was also home to a significant Jewish minority. However, their freedom to move was restricted as early as in 1495 and also during 1539–1800. In 1870, 12 Jews were burned publicly in Trnava during a pogrom. In 1870, the Hungarian authorities banned the Slovak Foundation *Matica slovenská* during the time of harsh Magyarisation. In its place, the St Adalbert Association (Spolok sv. Vojtecha) was created to maintain the Slovak national conscience. Despite most of the town wall being demolished in the 19th century, during this and mainly in the early 20th century the town continued to grow behind this line of defence. After the creation of Czechoslovakia in 1918, the town became of the most industrialised towns of Slovakia. In 1978, after the decision of Pope Paul VI, Trnava became the see of a separate Slovak archbishopric. With the establishment of this archbishopric, Slovakia again became independent from Hungary in terms of Church administration for the first time in centuries. In 1993, the Slovak Republic was established and three years later, Trnava became the capital of the newly created Trnavský kraj (region). The French car manufacturer Peugeot began construction of a large automobile plant in Trnava in 2003. Trnava has 69,000 inhabitants comprising 98.5% Slovaks and a small number of Czechs and Hungarians.

GETTING THERE AND AWAY Trnava is situated 49km northeast of Bratislava and on the main rail route to Žilina and Košice. The train and bus station are situated conveniently right next to each other and ten minutes' walk south from the town centre. Trains run every two hours from Bratislava Hlavná stanica and take 35 minutes. By road it is easy to reach as one of the few stretches of Slovak motorway, the D1 and D61/E75 towards Žilina passes close by.

🚌 **Trnava bus station** (*autobusová stanica*) Kollárova 36; m 0900 211 911; www.sadtrnava.sk

🚆 **Trnava railway station** (*železničnástanica*) Kollařrova 36; ☎ 18 188; e info@slovakrail.sk; www.slovakrail.sk

TOURIST INFORMATION AND OTHER PRACTICALITIES

🔲 **Trnava Information Service** (TINS) Trojičné námestie 1; ☎ 033 5511 022; e tins@stonline.sk; www.trnava.sk. It's easy to spot the information centre as it's situated in the town hall tower which you'll spy as you walk up Hlavná from the railway & bus station. *Open May–Sep Mon–Sat 09.00–18.00, closed Sun; Oct–Apr Mon–Fri 09.00–17.00, closed w/ends.*

$ **Bank** ČSOB, Hlavná 14 ATM. *Open Mon–Thu 08.00–18.00, Fri 08.00–12.00.* TatraBanka, Hlavná 9. *Open Mon–Fri 08.00–18.00, Sat 08.00–12.00.*
✉ **Post office** Trojičné námestie 8 (at the corner of Trinity Square). *Open Mon–Fri 07.00–19.00, Sat 08.00–13.00.*
✚ **Pharmacy** Lekáreň U Škorpióna, Hlavná 5; ☎ 033 5511 510. *Open Mon–Fri 08.00–16.00.*

e Internet Heso Com Hviezdoslavova 13; ↘ 033 5516 669. 20 computers, friendly & filled with Trnava youth. *Open Mon–Fri 08.00–22.00, Sat–Sun* *15.00–22.00. Internet charges: from 10.00–18.00 0.80Sk per min, from 18.00–22.00 0.70Sk per min.*

🏠 **WHERE TO STAY** Trnava has a good range of hotels and pensions within the town walls.

🏠 **Hotel Apollo** (21 dbl, 3 apts) Štefánikova 23; ↘ 033 5511 939; e hotel.apollo@stonline.sk; www.hotelapollo.sk. On a busy shopping street & proud of its WiFi hot-spot status, popular with a younger crowd. Dated 1970s' interior décor, some unusual colour combinations. *Sgl, dbl $$, b/fast & city tax inc.*

🏠 **Hotel Barbakan** (17 dbl, 7 suites) Štefánikova 11; ↘ 033 5511 847; e hotel@barbakan-trnava.sk; www.barbakan-trnava.sk. Smart, modernised 3-star hotel with its own on-site brewery producing a lager which you can sample in its cellar pub. Smart rooms. Internet on 1 machine at reception, good restaurant.

Dbl $$$, suite $$$, big suite $$$, city tax 20Sk a night, b/fast inc.

🏠 **Hotel Dream** (15 dbl, 8 apts) Kapitulská 12; ↘ 033 5924 111; e hoteldream@hoteldream.sk; www.hoteldream.sk A friendly 3-star business hotel in a renovated building with new furnishings. *Dbl $$, small apts $$$, large apts $$$, city tax 20Sk.*

🏠 **Hotel London** (22 beds) Kapitulská 5; ↘ 033 5340 586; e recepcia@hotelondon.sk; www.hotellondon.sk. A modern business hotel & a good base for exploring the region. WiFi available. *Sgl, dbl $$, apts $$$.*

✘ **WHERE TO EAT AND DRINK**

🍴 **Balkánska zmrzlina** Hlavná 45. With a terrace where you can enjoy coffee, cakes & ice cream. $. *Open Mon–Sat 07.00–22.00, Sun 09.00–22.00.*

🍷 **Barbakan** Štefánikova 11; ↘ 033 55140 22. Good restaurant in the hotel. The pub is in a restored old grain cellar. $$$. *Restaurant open daily 10.30–midnight, café open daily 18.00–02.00, pub open daily 18.00–02.00.*

🍷 **Pub Krušovický** Hornopotočná 4. In a very sweet, pink 1-storey building with white icing. $. *Open Mon–Thu 10.00–02.00, Fri–Sat 10.00–04.00, Sun 12.00–midnight.*

🍷 **Radničná Vináreň** Hlavná 1. The bar is popular with students, the restaurant is more pricey & hence

emptier. $$. *Bar open daily 08.00–23.00, restaurant open daily 11.00–23.00.*

✘ **Reštaurácia U Jozefa** Hlavná 18; ↘ 033 5511 294; www.vinarenujozefa.host.sk. Atmospheric brick cellar on the main pedestrian street. $. *Wine cellar open Mon–Thu 10.00–23.00, Fri–Sat 10.00–midnight, Sun 12.00–22.00. Terrace open Mon–Sat 09.00–23.00, Sun 12.00–22.00.*

✘ **Taverna Láry Fáry**; Halenárska 15/1; ↘ 033 5533 050; www.laryfary.sk. In Hungarian, *láry fáry* means a lot of whinging & complaining, however the excellent selection of lighter Greek & Italian cuisine should not elicit any grouching. $$. *Open Sun–Thu 11.00–23.00, Fri–Sat 11.00–midnight.*

WHAT TO SEE AND DO Approaching from the railway and bus station, the first building of note you come across is the **Lutheran Church** at southern end of Hlavná ulica. Built in 1924, it has a reinforced concrete ceiling and a ground plan resembling an amphitheatre. At the corner of Hlavná and Dolné bašty, **St Helen's Church** is the oldest church in Trnava. It is a single-nave Gothic structure from the 14th century. A short walk northwards along Hlavná, the town's main pedestrian thoroughfare, leads past many shops, banks, pharmacies and restaurants. Just before the main square, you'll see the **town hall** (*radnica*) to your left. It stands on the plot of two medieval buildings and was rebuilt continually throughout the centuries, with a classical reconstruction with Baroque elements in the 18th century and an Art Nouveau façade added in the early 20th century. The classical **theatre** next door, built in 1831 was the first masonry theatre in the country. Just after the theatre, turn left and follow the road for two minutes to see the 18th-century **Church of the Apostle James the Elder** and also part of the original **town fortification**. Art lovers should make a short detour off to the right leading to **Koppel's Castle**, a beautiful mansion built in 1920 and now housing the gallery of J Koniarek. Return to the main **Trinity Square** (Trojičné námestie) and check out the **Church of the Holy Trinity** on your left at the beginning of Štefánikova. This street has several good hotels and restaurants and it's a good place to stop off for a coffee or a snack. At **Trojičné námestie**, you can't miss the **information centre** located in the eight-storey Renaissance **city tower**, dating from the year 1574. The staff are very friendly and helpful and can provide information about the city and surroundings. The **Holy Trinity statue** was created in 1695 by the sculptor Ján Krištof Khien and shows the Virgin Mary being crowned by the Holy Trinity. Over the square, the blot on the landscape is the department store **Obchodný Dom Jednota**, a nightmare of 1960s' design. From **Trojičné námestie**, head east along Hviezdoslavova, passing **St Anna's Church** on your right. It's a pretty, late-Baroque church built for the Order of St Ursula nuns who came to Trnava in 1724 after an invitation by Archbishop Imre Esterházi. Just after the church, turn right onto Halenárska passing on the corner the **Stephaneum** designed by famous Viennese architect J L Hildebrand. It's a Baroque structure dating from 1724 and part of the collection of university buildings dotted about town. Many of the buildings are covered in ugly graffiti and many are crumbling at the edges. On Halenárska, the **Orthodox Synagogue** dates from 1831 and although it was renovated in 1994 it still looks a little war-torn. The **memorial** to the Holocaust is by Slatinský and Szalatnay and was erected in 1947, and the synagogue hosts part of the Ján Koniarek Gallery. Another quick detour is needed now back westwards on the street opposite the synagogue, to see **St Joseph's Church** on Paulínska. It was built in Silesian Renaissance style and has a smart beige façade a little like a pyramid-shaped church organ. Back to Halenárska, and continue south to see the **Church of the Assumption of the Virgin Mary**, originally a Romanesque building from the 13th century, when the St Clare nuns settled in Trnava. The adjoining convent houses the **West Slovakia Museum** (see *Museums and galleries* below). Opposite is **Spartak Trnava** FC's stadium. Trnava is a soccer-mad city and the 'White Angels' are cheered on at their 18,000 capacity ground. Ice hockey is also popular and the winter stadium (*zimný stadion*) is nearby, over the main Hlboká highway past the ubiquitous McDonald's drive-in and petrol station. Passing the St Clares' Convent, walk along the beautiful tree-lined Kapitulská street, the most atmospheric in town, to the **Archbishop's Palace**, a lovely Renaissance mansion built for archbishop Mikuláš Oláh in 1562. In front of the palace, the **St Joseph sculpture** from 1731 commemorating a plague epidemic. The Gothic **Sv Mikuláš** (St Nicholas) Church with its twin towers is probably the most well-known landmark of Trnava. Opposite the main entrance, the 16th-century Renaissance **Oláh Seminary** now houses the **Museum of Literary Culture** (see *Museums and galleries* below). Behind St Nicolas Church you can see more of the fortified town walls and incongruously, a long concrete walkway leads from here to the Družba hospital and modern Trnava suburbs. Make your way back towards the main Trinity Square and take the first right to pass a group of grand university buildings along ulica Jána Hollého. The memorial plaque on the walls of the **Marianeum** is dedicated to Moyzes, who established the Foundation of Slovaka (NCM). The **Rubrorum** seminary next door has hosted a grammar school since 1853. The **Cathedral of St John the Baptist** contains a unique wooden altar, carved in 1640 and one of the largest in central Europe. In front of the cathedral, a statue of the late Pope John Paul II greeting visitors.

An interesting detour, if you have half an hour to spare while waiting for a train, is to visit the **smallest consecrated church in the world**; a miniature two-towered church situated in the garden of a family house on Tulipánová ulica.

To get there, from the train station turn right onto Dohnányho and follow the street under the railway line. Take the second right onto Tulipánová.

Museums and galleries
Galéria Jána Koniarka (*Zelený kríček 3;* ✎ *033 5511 659; www.gjk.sk; open Tue–Fri 09.00–17.00; Jul–Sep Tue–Fri 10.00–18.00, Sat–Sun 13.00–18.00; admission adult/child 40/20Sk*). A non-profit organisation showing 20th- and 21st-century art. Slovak and foreign artists shown in two exhibition spaces: the Koppel House and the Synagogue.

Galéria Jána Koniarka Synagogue (*Halenárska 2;* ✎ *033 5514 657; www.gjk.sk; open Tue–Fri 09.00–17.00; Jul–Sep Tue–Fri 10.00–18.00, Sat–Sun 13.00–18.00; synagogue closed 12.00–13.00; admission adult/child 40/20Sk*).

The West Slovakia Museum Západoslovenské múzeum (*Múzejné námestie 3;* ✎ *033 5512 913; open Tue–Fri 08.00–17.00, Sat–Sun 11.00–17.00; admission adult 40Sk*). Eight rooms of folk ceramics by local potter Štefan Parrák.

Museum of Literary Culture Múzeum knižnej kultúry (*Námestie sv. Mikuláša; open Tue–Fri 08.30–17.00, Sat–Sun 11.00–17.00; admission adult 50Sk*). Situated in the Renaissance building that was formerly the Oláh Seminar, built in 1561 as a high school. The museum shows works by Bernolák, Fandly and Bajza. Ask at the West Slovakia Museum.

PIEŠŤANY Telephone code 033

An atmosphere of genteel rest and recreation hangs over Piešťany. Spa guests, these days known as 'clients', those taking the water cure and those on a relaxing holiday all shuffle about the spa island like escapees from a Thomas Mann novella, occasionally making it across the Colonnade Bridge, past the famous statue of *The Crutch-Breaker* to the restaurants and cafés dotted about the parkland and Winterová, the pedestrianised main street. The town lies on the western bank of the Váh River, and the majority of visitors are accommodated on the Spa Island. In keeping with so-called 'health resorts' all over central Europe, most of the guests at Piešťany do their daily treatment but then spend the rest of the day shuffling about the park in slippers, smoking ciggies and drinking beer. They also like to whoop it up until late but still manage to be up and in the pool, thrashing up and down at 06.00 before enjoying a hearty breakfast of salami and sausage. It must be something in the water. Allegedly, Piešťany is one of the warmest and sunniest regions in Slovakia. The sun shines here for around 2,080 hours per year.

Spa hotels, like Piešťany, make a great holiday destination, if you don't mind being constantly shouted at in German. Piešťany makes a great base for exploring the surrounding Trnava and Trenčín regions and you can while away the evening in the pool which is open 06.00–21.00, where the healing thermal water will soothe your aching limbs. Those here for 'the cure' must do one treatment a day: medicinal mud packs, wallowing in the mirror pool or undergoing traction. 'Scottish spray' is one for the masochists: the lady with the high-power jets of hot and cold water has a wicked glint in her eye.

HISTORY First mentioned as having healing powers in 1549, Piešťany spas have long attracted visitors to their hot thermal springs and sulphurous mud. In 1778, Johann Erdödy built the first wooden bath house which the Erdödy family developed into the elegant buildings seen today. In 1889, local businessman

Ľudovít Winter leased the Piešťany Spa from Count Ferenc Erdödy for 100 years. In 1910–12, Winter built the gorgeous Art Nouveau Thermia Palace hotel and Irma Spa, imagining it as a luxury resort for those seeking a relaxing getaway or medical treatments for ailments ranging from arthritis, tendon and ligament ailments to nervous system complaints. Since the creation of the Thermia Palace complex, another five giant hotel-spa complexes have been added to the island, turning the idyllic space in the Váh River into a year-round leisure and wellness centre. There's even a nine-hole golf course to the north of the island and a network of cycle paths and pleasant gardens to stroll in.

GETTING THERE AND AWAY Piešťany is situated 82km northeast of Bratislava further along from Trnava on the main rail route to Žilina and Košice. The train and bus station are again right next to each other and 35 minutes' brisk walk west from the town centre, not to be attempted with luggage. A taxi costs 150–200Sk from the station to Spa Island/town centre.

There is a regular, direct bus service from Bratislava to Vienna (*www.eurolines.sk*).

From Piešťany to Nitra by local bus takes 85 minutes.

There are frequent train connections as Piešťany is on the main Bratislava–Košice line, the primary rail route across Slovakia. Trains run every two hours from Bratislava Hlavná stanica and take 75 minutes. A Bratislava–Piešťany train ticket costs 130Sk; a seat reservation costs 15Sk. From Piešťany to Trenčín by train takes 35 minutes, to Trnava by train takes 30 minutes.

By road it is easy to reach as one of the few Slovak motorways, the dual-carriageway D1 & D61/E75 from Bratislava towards Žilina passes close by Piešťany. A hire car (see pages 74–5 & 77) is also a good idea for exploring the region as local buses can be slow.

TOURIST INFORMATION AND OTHER PRACTICALITIES

🛈 Tourist information centre Pribinova 2; ☎ 033 7719 621–3; www.pic.piestany.sk. Sells Baedekers (the Slovak generic term for 'guidebooks'), internet services, information on Piešťany & details on accommodation. *Open May–Sep Mon–Fri 09.00–20.00, Sat 09.00–14.00, Sun 14.00–18.00; Oct–Apr Mon–Fri 09.00–18.00, Sat 09.00–14.00, Sun 14.00–18.00.*

🛈 Informačné stredisko Piešťany Nálepkova 2; ☎/f 033 7743 355; e incoming@ivco.sk; www.ivco.sk; www.ivco.sk. Sells Baedekers (the Slovak generic term for 'guidebooks'), internet services, information on Piešťany & details on accommodation. *Open May–Sep Mon–Fri 09.00–20.00, Sat 09.00–14.00, Sun 14.00–18.00; Oct–Apr Mon–Fri 09.00–18.00, Sat 09.00–14.00, Sun*

14.00–18.00.

🚂 Piešťany Express This is a little train which does a ring around the island, over the Colonnade Bridge & a bit of the town. *Open daily 09.00–21.00; 30Sk a ticket.*

$ Bank ČSOB, Námestie Slobody 17. 24hr ☎ 0850 111 777. *Open Mon–Fri 08.00–18.00.* VÚB, Námestie Slobody 11. *Open Mon–Fri 08.00–18.00.*

✉ Post office Poštova & Kukučinova corner. There is a second post office at Vážská 2. *Both open Mon, Thu & Fri 07.00–13.00 & 14.00–15.00, Tue 07.00–12.00, Wed 07.00–13.00 & 14.00–17.00.*

🖥 Internet Internet & herňa (saloon) Rázusova 11; ☎ 033 7735 116; e compnet@stonline.sk. *Open Mon–Fri 10.00–22.00, Sat–Sun 14.00–22.00.*

✚ Pharmacy Several on Námestie Slobody.

WHERE TO STAY

🏠 Hotel Magnólia (122 rooms) Nálepkova 1; ☎ 033 7626 251; f 033 7721 149; e magnolia@ profi.sk; www.hotelmagnolia.sk. Modern hotel overlooking the river Váh with a fitness centre, rowdy casino & guarded parking. *Sgl $$, dbl $$$, deluxe suite sgl $$$, deluxe suite dbl $$$$, extra*

bed € 20, city tax 30Sk (€ 1).

🏠 Hotel Patrícia (14 dbl, 2 sgl) Červená veža 4089; ☎ 033 7724 005; e info@hotelpatricia.sk, www.hotelpatricia.sk. A smart, 4-star family-run guesthouse on the other side of the river from town & situated up a hill in the woods. With its own

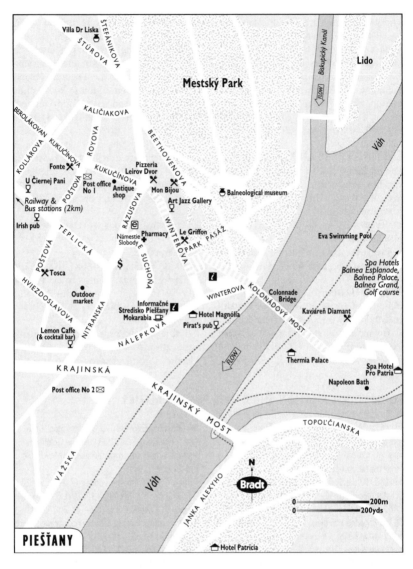

restaurant, café, wine bar, grill terrace, wellness centre, sauna & tennis court. *Sgl* $$, *dbl* $$$, *apt* $$$.

⌂ **Spa Hotel Balnea Esplanade** (243 rooms, 15 suites) Kúpeľný ostrov (Spa Island); ☏ 033 7755 7733; e reservations@spapiestany.sk; www.spapiestany.sk. A 4-star hotel situated right in the middle of Spa Island. The new water & sauna world is situated here. Indoor & outdoor pool offering massage jets, jacuzzis & deckchairs. The sauna world with infra sauna, sultry bath, Finnish sauna, solarium & relaxation zone is connected with water world. All manner of additional packages:

beauty, dental, 'slimline'. Superb restaurant & atmospheric coffee house with jazzy pianist. *Sgl* $$$. *Dbl* $$$ summer, $$ winter.

⌂ **Spa Hotel Balnea Grand** (140 rooms, 11 suites) Kúpeľný ostrov; ☏ 033 7754 117; e reservations@spapiestany.sk; www.spapiestany.sk. A 3-star hotel connected to the Hotel Splendid on one side, on the other to the Congress centre. 9-hole golf course. *Sgl* $$$, *dbl* $$.

⌂ **Spa Hotel Balnea Palace** (192 rooms, 6 suites) Kúpeľný ostrov; ☏ 033 7757 733; e reservations@spapiestany.sk; www.spapiestany.sk.

Spa hotel Balnea Palace, joined to the Balnea Esplanade (see above) & a slightly cheaper version of the two, at 3 & a bit stars. Connected to the balneo-rehabilitation centre, where the complex spa care is all included in the package. Guests can use the shopping passage, water & sauna world, coffee houses & night bar. *Sgl $$$. Dbl $$$ summer, $$ winter.*

⌂ **Spa Hotel Pro Patria** (101 rooms) Kúpeľný ostrov; ☏ 033 7756 262; e reservations@ spapiestany.sk; www.spapiestany.sk. A 2-star hotel & treatment centre situated in the southern part of Spa Island, close to mineral springs, near the thermal lakes. It has its own balneotherapy, where most of the treatments take place. *Sgl & dbl $$.*

⌂ **Thermia Palace** (111 rooms, inc. 15 suites) Kúpeľný ostrov (Spa Island); ☏ 033 7757 733; e reservations@spapiestany.sk; www.spapiestany.sk. Slovakia's first & only 5-star hotel, an Art Nouveau jewel with the gorgeous Irma Balneotherapy centre next door. After the first grand opening in 1912, the Thermia Palace became a world-famous centre for healing & relaxing. The hotel & the balneotherapy centre was designed by Budapest architects Ármin Hegedus & Henrich Böhm. The richly decorated interior of Thermia Palace hosts many remarkable architectural & artistic features, but the 2 most prominent elements are the staircase with stained-glass windows & the grand restaurant hall. Irma Health Spa is famous for its rare mud pool, a unique pool bath with a natural bottom, consisting of 10–30cm of unique Piešťany sulphuric mud & natural thermal mineral springs which rise directly into the pool. The Beauty Emporium with many treatments. Irma Health Spa has a department of special massage; 4-hands massage & Clarins Beauty parlour provides body & skin cosmetics. *Sgl $$$$. Dbl $$$$ high season, $$$ low season.*

✗ WHERE TO EAT

✗ **Čertova Pec** (Devil's Furnace) Three hiking trails go there, & the bus (sometimes!) in the woods. $$. *Open daily 09.00–22.00, disco bar Fri–Sun 20.00 to dawn.*
✗ **Fonte** Kukučinova 17. The daily lunch menu costs 99Sk for onion soup, Serbian steaks, rice & potatoes in a swanky interior. $$. *Open daily 11.00–22.00.*
✗ **Kaviareň Diamant** Kúpeľný ostrov (on Spa Island); ☏ 033 7756 351. Inside is all dark & woody but the covered terrace has a great view of the island. $. *Open daily 10.00–22.00.*
✗ **Le Griffon** Winterova 29; www.legriffon.sk. A mixture of Slovak peasant & Habsburg 'international kitchen' in this traditional restaurant established in1809. $. *Open daily 09.00–23.00.*

✗ **Mokarabia** Nálepkova 4; ☏ 033 7730 438. Plain, brown coffee bar. $. *Open daily 06.00–22.00.*
✗ **Mon Bijou** Beethovenova 16. Bright yellow corner building, brown striped wallpaper & Viennese café chairs. $. *Open daily 09.00–22.00.*
✗ **Pizzeria Leirov dvor** Winterova 1; ☏ 033 7729 309. A rustic, country-style restaurant with a few tables outside. Eat in or take-away, friendly service. $$. *Open Mon–Sat 09.00–22.00, Sun 10.00–22.00.*
✗ **Tosca** Moyzesova 3; ☏ 033 7625 468; e tosca.saradin@kios.sk. Located in a suburban 1-storey family house 5mins from the centre. $$. *Open daily 11.00–22.00.*

ENTERTAINMENT AND NIGHTLIFE

♀ **Art Jazz Gallery** Winterova 29; ☏ 033 7000 045. A popular venue for locals & visitors to take coffee or enjoy a light meal. *Open daily 10.00–23.00.*
♀ **Lemon caffe and cocktail bar** By roundabout Krajinská & Nitrianska; ☏ 033 7744 554. The interior is lemon & lime so that one's skin takes on a deathly citrus pallor. *Open Mon–Thu 08.00–midnight, Fri 08.00–03.00, Sat 10.00–03.00, Sun 10.00–22.00.*
♀ **Irish Pub** Teplická 41. Piešťany boasts 2 Irish pubs, this is the better one. *Open Mon–Thu 10.00–midnight, Fri 10.00–02.00, Sat 14.00–02.00, Sun 14.00–midnight.*

♀ **Pirat's Pub** Behind the Magnolia Hotel on the Váh riverbank; m 0905 236 219. Very good food in a friendly pub setting with a sea theme involving wheels, ropes, ceiling paintings, sky-blue walls & a view of the river. *Open daily 12.00–midnight.*
♀ **U Čiernej pani** (At the Black Lady) Teplická 44; m 0908 724 595. Quiz nights in English & Slovak held monthly in this typical beer hall. *Open Mon–Thu 10.00–02.00, Fri 10.00–04.00, Sat 14.00–04.00, Sun 14.00–02.00.*

WHAT TO SEE AND DO

The Colonnade Bridge This bridge over the Váh River connects Piešťany Town with Spa Island (Kúpeľný ostrov). The bridge was designed in 1930 by Emil Beluš, a renowned Slovak architect working during the period of Functionalism. The construction was carried out from 1931–33 by the construction company Pittel and Brausewetter. The bridge has a covered iron-concrete construction, consisting of seven bridge fields. It has three traffic lanes, one for driving (although it is closed to cars, the little train is allowed over) and two pedestrian walks. Small shops are located at either end. The inscription at the town end, next to the bronze *The Crutch-Breaker* statue (1933, Robert Kuhmayer) reads, '*Saluberrimae pistinienses thermae*', the title of a poem (1642) by Adam Trajan of Benešov celebrating the curative waters. There is a statue of Trajan in front of the Slovan Hotel, presently closed and awaiting renovation. At the island end of the bridge, the inscription urges, rather bossily, '*Surge et ambula*', that is, 'get up and walk'.

Kursalon Next to the Hotel Slovan designed by the Hungarian architect Ignác Alpár in 1894, houses a gigantic hall and the museum (below), restaurant and café.

Mestsky Park (sady A Kmeťa) With a cinema Fontána, art gallery and amphitheatre for musical and other performances.

Balneological Museum (*Beethovenova 5; \|f 033 772 2875; www.balneomuzeum.sk; open Apr–Sep Tue–Sun 09.00–12.00 & 13.00–17.00; Oct–Mar Tue–Sun 09.00–12.00 & 13.00–16.00*). A genuinely fascinating museum showing the history of spas, local history, and includes a beehive shaped like a man (the bees enter through his belt buckle!). The museum was founded in 1928 by the Piešťany Museum Society and the Winter family. The museum is located in the Kursalon (Spa Hall) built in 1894, with exhibitions of balneohistory, mineral waters in Slovakia, ethnography and archaeology.

Villa Dr Liska (*Štefánikova 1; \ 033 7722 508; open Mon–Fri 08.00–12.00 & 13.00 – 16.00 during the season also Sat–Sun 11.00–17.00*). 'History of the Slovak Spas' of existing and extinct Slovak spas. On the first floor, 'Sacral art from the collections of the Balneological Museum' and temporary exhibitions. Near the Lutheran Church.

Memorial room of poet Ivan Krasko (*Nábrežie Ivana Krasku 2; \ 033 7623 272; open Tue–Sat 11.00–15.00*). Part of the Balneological Museum, the Memorial Room of the important Slovak poet Ivan Krasko (1876–1958) who lived and worked in Piešťany from 1945–58. The exhibition is in his old lodgings and visitors can see original furniture, papers, books and photographs. Situated on the embankment of the river Váh.

SHOPPING

🕮 **Antique shop** Kukučínova 9; \|f 033 7729 135. Owned and run by Khosrov Ayrumyan & full of treasures. Open Mon–Fri 10.00–13.00 & 14.00–18.00, Sat 09.00–12.30.

🕮 **Colonnade Bridge** A chatty elderly gentleman sells souvenirs, postcards & stamps (but only for those buying a postcard), T-shirts & bags.

🕮 **Mestské trhovisko** Next to Nitrianska & Teplická. A huge outdoor market with Chinese clothing, sportswear, bags, some flowers, fruit & vegetables (radishes, spring onions).

ACTIVITIES AND EXCURSIONS

Spa Golf club Piešťany (*www.spagolf.sk*) In 1914, the first golf course in Slovakia opened on Spa Island and during the 1930s international tournaments took place with players from England, Germany, Scandinavia and the US. After 90 years, Piešťany spa restored the tradition and built a nine-hole course plus a clubhouse, golf shop, golf academy and driving range in the northern part of Spa Island

(Vrbinky). When playing two rounds of nine holes, the course has a par 66 and total length of 4,110m. Guests can try teeing off on the 'Full Swing' simulator. The spa hotel Balnea Grand is very near.

Napoleon Bath (Napoleonské kúpele) (*Open daily 08.00–20.00*). The three oldest buildings on Spa Island (1821) and open to the public. Here you can try the salt cave treatment for lungs, allergies and general well-being or a range of treatments from traction to psychology to water gymnastics. Guests can stay at the Pro Patria Hotel next door or one of the many Piešťany spa hotels and visit Napoleon during the day.

Termalné kúpalisko Eva Kupelný ostrov (Spa Island) (℡ *033 7752 350; open May Mon–Fri 14.00–17.00, Sat–Sun 13.00–18.00; Jun daily 10.00–18.00; Jul–Aug daily 09.00–18.00; Sep daily 11.00–17.00*). Outdoor swimming pool near the spa hotels where Olympic swimmer Moravcova used to train.

Boat cruise on the Váh River (*In summer season only; ℡ 033 7627 618; Mon–Fri 09.00, 10.00, 11.00, 12.00, 13.00 & 16.00; Sat–Sun afternoons only*).

Sľňava Lake (Sunny Lake) The most popular tourist resort in the area, downstream on the Váh from Piešťany. It's a great place for watersports; water skiing, canoeing, rowing, yachting and windsurfing as well as swimming in the river at a place the locals call 'The Currents'. Ratnovce village hosts various sports events during the summer. There is kayak racing and a water-ski championships at the end of August.

Watersports Ski-Bezovec, A Hlinku 59; ℡ 033 7737 189; m 0905 753 236; www.lyziari.sk. Rental of equipment (kneeboards, neoprene suit), beach volleyball, chess, bowling. *Open Jul–Aug daily 10.00–18.00.*

TRIPS AROUND PIEŠŤANY

Moravany nad Váhom A 16th-century castle to see the site where the *Venus* sculpture carved from a mammoth tooth was discovered by a farmer in 1939. It dates from 22000BC and can be seen in the history museum in the Bratislava Castle; 30 minutes by bus, or hike north.

Magnate's Castle Kostolec in Ducové An important archaeological locality, the great Moravian Magnate's Castle at Kostolec in Ducové, 7km north of Piešťany

Trnava Region PIEŠŤANY

5

is run by the Balneological Museum. The castle was built in the 9th century and demonstrates the rudiments of Slovak national history.

AROUND TRNAVA

Trnava is at the centre of a tall, thin region and heading north, there is a couple of interesting towns worth popping into if you are touring by car. **Hlohovec** has a Jewish cemetery where the mother of the German Romantic writer Heinrich Heine is buried. The local museum has the attractive setting of a late 15th-century Franciscan monastery, and offers the most extensive collection of beetles and butterflies among all the West Slovak museums. Travelling by train, you're sure to pass through **Leopoldov**, which along with Zvolen (in Banská Bystrica region) is one of the largest railway junctions in Slovakia. The only thing worth noting is the enthusiastic socialist realist murals on the station wall. At Leopoldov there is a preserved fort, built in 1665–69 to resist attacks by the Turks and also by rebels during the Thôkôly and Rákoczi uprisings against the Habsburgs. It has been used as a prison since the time of Kaiser Josef II, used by the communists and still in use now. It appears to be a beautiful 12-pointed star shape and although more modern aerial photos show a six-pointed star, it is still an interesting construction. Leopoldov also boasts one of the largest secondhand bookshops in Europe.

Situated 6km north of Trnava on a secondary road *en route* to Smolenice Chateau is Dolná Krupa. During the 18th century, the village was owned by the Bruinsvik family. Jozef Bruinsvik built a neoclassical manor house here from 1793–95 and surrounded it with an English park designed by the famous German landscape architect Heinrich Neblien. Beethoven visited Dolná Krupa several times between 1800 and 1810 at the invitation of the Bruinsvik family and he stayed in the pavilion in the elegant garden. It is now known as 'Beethoven's House'. Ludwig van Beethoven dedicated two of his works to Jozef Bruinsvik's granddaughters, Josephine and Theresa. The 'Hope' opus 32 to Josephine and the piano sonata in F-major opus 78 to Theresa. He composed the *Moonlight Sonata* opus 27 while staying at Dolná Krupa.

SMOLENICE CASTLE Smolenice Castle (*reception:* m *0805 92194; www.smolenice.com*) is located 60km northeast of Bratislava. It resembles a fairytale Bohemian palace with squared-off red roofing and one main fortified tower dominating the village of Smolenice below. It's an impressive sight for miles around but, unfortunately, visitors can't look around inside as the castle is now owned by the Slovak Academy of Sciences and hosts conferences. Surrounded by a beautiful park, the chateau looms over the village of Smolenice in the eastern foothills of Malé Karpaty (Little Carpathians). A watch castle built in the 14th century to guard the trading Bohemian Route (Česká cesta) was destroyed at the beginning of the 18th century during a revolt of the estates led by the Rákóczis, one of the wealthiest families in the Hungarian kingdom between the 16th and 18th centuries. Renovation of the castle in the Romantic style started in 1864 and was finished in 1955. The magnificent castle we see today was built by the Pálffy family (who also renovated Bojnice Castle, Trenčín region, see *Chapter 6*, page 164), another powerful Hungarian dynasty, whose name can be found all over Slovakia.

Smolenice Castle also marks the end of the Small Carpathian Wine Route (see *Chapter 4*, page 119) and the Small Carpathian Cycle Route follows the same wine route by bicycle … hic.

Getting there By train, there are two options from Bratislava: change trains at either Trnava or Kúty. The Trnava option is quicker by about 90 minutes. Through

Kúty, the trip will possibly be 60 minutes longer. For train departure times, check www.zsr.sk. There are about nine bus connections a day from Smolenice to Bratislava; see www.busy.sk.

DRINY CORROSIVE CAVE (JASKYŇA DRINY) (☏ 033 5586 200; e caves@ssj.sk; www.ssj.sk; guided tour lasts 35mins; open Tue–Sun 1 Apr–31 May 10.00, 12.00, 14.00, 15.00; 1–30 Jun 09.00–16.00 on the hour; 1 Jul–31 Aug 10.00–17.00 on the hour; 1 Sep–-31 Oct 10.00, 12.00, 14.00, 15.00; 1 Nov–31 Mar closed; admission adult/child 80/50Sk). In the 19th century, locals heard rumours of a mysterious hole in the Drinkový Mountains. The cave wasn't discovered until 1930 and it opened to the public in 1935. At present, a 410m section of the total 680m cave system is open to the public. The Driny cave has hanging curtain formations with snaggle-toothed edging, sinter waterfalls and snow-white lakes, lined at the bottom with little sinter balls, known as 'cave pearls'. The symbol of the cave is a stalactite formation resembling elephants' ears. Eleven species of bat live here too.

Getting there By car from Bratislava, take route 502 to Pezinok, Modra and Smolenice. Turn left just before the village of Smolenice. Signposted to the cave's parking area. Then walk for 15 minutes to reach the cave entrance.

OSTRÝ KAMEŇ (SHARP ROCK) CASTLE A 13th-century border castle, now in ruins, near the Záruby mountain peak (767m), the highest in the Malé Karpaty range. Like the fortress built where Smolenice Castle now stands, Ostrý Kameň was erected to protect the 'Bohemian Route' (Česká cesta). It was damaged during the Rákóczi uprising in the early 18th century and gradually fell into ruin, although parts of the walls, bastion and adjoining buildings are still visible. The castle ruins are hidden at the top of a hill (570m) between the Driny Cave and the Buková Reservoir.

Getting there There is a very minor road leading from Buková village; follow directions for Smolenice Castle then continue along route 502 and turn left for Buková just before the junction with the Trnava–Senice road (route 51). On foot, it's a 2km hike through the gorgeous Small Carpathian countryside from Buková village or reservoir.

From Plavecký Castle (in Bratislava region, see pages 124–5) it's a 10km hike on the red signposted trail (Štefánikova magistrála) heading northeast for about 45 minutes.

After the hike, visitors can cool down with a swim in the Buková Reservoir nearby.

KORLÁTKA CASTLE RUINS Situated 4km north of Ostrý Kamen, the ruins of a 13th-century Gothic castle, another victim of the destruction caused during the Rákóczi uprising, can be accessed best on foot. Head for the Buková Reservoir and continue north.

DOBRÁ VODA CASTLE RUINS The ruins of the Dobrá Voda ('good water') castle are found at the northern end of the Small Carpathian range. The castle was built in the 14th century to guard the way across the mountains, and was damaged during the Rákóczi uprising then burned down in the second half of the 18th century. In Dobrá Voda village, the great Slovak poet Ján Hollý (1785–1849) is buried in the graveyard of the Romanesque Catholic church.

Getting there By car, head for the village of Trstín via Malokarpatská vinná cesta (Small Carpathian Wine Route) from Bratislava, Rača, Pezinok, Modra, Casta and

Slovak swimmer Martina Moravcova was nicknamed the 'Slovak Fish' by the media during the the 2000 Summer Olympics in Sydney. Winning two silver medals, Moravcova became the country's first ever multi-medal winner at the Olympics. Although she trains for much of the year in Dallas, Texas, Moravcova's home town of Piešťany remains close to her heart. Moravcova is one of the most decorated female swimmers of all time. Her incredible collection of 66 medals includes two Olympic silvers, 22 World championship and 42 European championship medals. Moravcova also holds three world records, 16 European and 203 Slovak records. Her autobiography was published in 2003 just before she was voted 'Slovakia's sports person of the year' for an incredible sixth time in ten years. The book title *Martina s rodokmeňom Evy* ('Martina with the pedigree of Eva') refers to the Eva thermal swimming pool on Piešťany's Spa Island, where Moravcova trained as a child.

Smolenice (route 502). On the way there are three more castles to enjoy: the ruins of Biely Kameň (White Stone) near Svätý Jur, Červený Kameň Castle and Smolenice Castle.

Dobrá Voda Castle is 5km north of Trstín.

By bus from Trnava to Dobrá Voda. From the bus stop near the church take the red-stripe trail through the cemetery, walk through the wood near the Jewish cemetery; it then takes about 15 minutes to reach the castle.

SENICA *Telephone code 034*

Senica is the administrative and economic centre of the Záhorie region. First mentioned in 1217, the town acquired privileges and the right to hold fairs in 1396 and was the heart of the wool-making trade in the region. Amongst the buildings of note, a late-Baroque manor house, designed by FA Hillebrand in 1760 stands a little outside the centre of town. Restored in the1970s, it houses the Záhorská galéria. Senica's synagogue was built in 1866 in an Oriental style and now commemorates the pre-war Jewish community which has since disappeared. It's unlikely you would need to stay overnight in the area, but there is a good hotel in town should the occasion arise.

GETTING THERE Motorway D2/E65 towards Brno, exit Kúty and follow route 500 for 30km.

INFORMATION AND OTHER PRACTICALITIES
Infosen Námestie oslobodenia 17 (Dom kultúry – House of Culture) Senica; ☏ 034 6516 459; e infosen@stonline.sk; www.senica.sk or www.rsms.sk

WHERE TO STAY
Hotel Senica (19 rooms) Hviezdoslavova 62; ☏/f 034 6517 236; e hotelsenica@hotelsenica.sk; www.hotelsenica.sk. Modern hotel with clean facilities and restaurant ($$) offering Slovak and international cuisine. Sgl, dbl $$, apts $$$.

WHAT TO SEE AND DO
Branč castle ruins Situated 9km northeast of Senica, near the village of Podbranč, this medieval castle was built in the mid 13th century and protected the western frontier of the Kingdom of Hungary. There is a memorial to the Protestant priests

who were imprisoned in the castle jail in the period of counter-Reformation (1674). In the 18th century, it fell into ruins but you can still see the low outer barbican walls and a substantial amount of the inner keep, although the ruins are now low and modest. Branč Hill (475m), on which the castle perches is part of the Myjavská Pahorkatina range.

Getting there Along the trail marked with a blue stripe, 25 minutes from Podbranč, 2¹/₂ hours from Turá Lúka, 3¹/₂ hours from Myjava.

Smrdáky spa (*Prírodné liečebné kúpele Smrdáky;* \ *034 657 510;* f *034 657 5135;* e *reservations.smr@healthspa.sk; www.kupelesmrdaky.sk*). Just north of Senica is Smrdáky. The slogan is the rather unfortunate 'Do not let your skin suffer' and this is a very specific medicinal spa, treating many kinds of skin diseases with its soothing sulphurous water. Legend says that mineral springs were discovered a long time ago by a shepherd, who healed his painful feet while dangling them in the unusually pungent brackish water. Rumours about the spring's healing powers spread very quickly and people came from miles. At the time, the village near the spring was called Nová Ves (New Village). When the peasants and farmers gathered in the neighbouring towns for the annual fair those who came from Nová Ves were nicknamed *smrdáci* ('smelly ones') from the pungent water and that's how the town got its name. The hydrogen sulphide-rich mineral water and sulphurous mud water is excellent for skin diseases such as chronic eczema, psoriasis, dermatitis, acne, rosacea, prurigo, and skin conditions after burns.

Getting there By car from Bratislava, take the D2/E65 motorway north heading for Brno. Exit at Kúty and drive 30km east to Senica. From Senica, Smrdáky is 7km northwest on a minor, signposted road. Buses run frequently from Bratislava; change at Senica. From Trnava/Piešťany: from Trnava, route 51 leads to Senica then follow signs; from Piešťany, route 499 to Brezová pod Bradlom, then route 501 to Jablonica and route 51 to Senica.

 Where to stay There are three Danubius Group hotels situated in Smrdáky, all with the same reservation details: Prírodné Liečebné kúpele, 903 06 Smrdáky (\ *034 6575101;* f *034 6575 135;* e *reservations.smr@healthspa.sk; www.kupelesmrdaky.sk*).

🏠 **Centrál Hotel** (25 rooms, 4 suites) A 2-star modern building offering the same facilities as the Morava at a slightly lower rate. *Sgl, dbl* $$.

🏠 **Morava Hotel** (36 rooms, 4 suites) A 3-star hotel with comfortable rooms equipped with

bathroom, satellite TV and most rooms have a balcony. *Sgl, dbl* $$.

🏠 **Vietoris Hotel** (22 rooms, 3 suites) A 2-star concrete block offering the same facilities as the Morava and Centrál hotels. *Sgl, dbl* $$.

SKALICA *Telephone code 034*

The town of Skalica (population 15,000) is hardly known outside Slovakia, yet this charming town situated right on the border with the Czech Republic contains some fantastic and unusual architecture. Owing to its location, near both the Czech Republic and Austria, it was a meeting point throughout history and became a significant economic and cultural centre. The town's main activities were producing wine, the cloth industry and general trade. First mentioned in the 13th century, Skalica became a Free Royal Town in 1372. Buildings worth checking out include the Gothic **St Michael's Church** with its unusually shaped Renaissance belfry featuring a covered gallery. Beside it is the little 14th-century **St Anne's Chapel**. The Art Nouveau **House of Culture** (Dom Kultúry) designed in 1905 by Dušan Jurkovič features colourful mosaics created by the Czech painter Mikoláš Aleš on its façade. The town's information centre is found here. The small town was home to four monasteries, one of which was that of the Jesuits, whose church, monastery and 17th-century college can be seen. The 18th-century **Pauline Church** and monastery can also be found nearby as can the 16th-century **Franciscan Church** and monastery as well as the church and monastery of the Hospitaliers dating from the mid 18th century.

The old town is still laid out according to the original medieval urban plan, which included 2km of town fortification walls from the 15th century. Several sections of the 2m-thick walls are still standing. Skalica's most recognisable monument is the **St George's Rotunda** (*Rotunda Sv Juraja*), found on a hill just north of the city centre and offering the best view of Skalica. **The Pilárik Brothers Mill** from the beginning of the last century has wooden beams and is well preserved, although it has not been used for more than 40 years (*open 20 May–17 Sep Fri 14.00–18.00, Sat 10.00–14.00, Sun 14.00–18.00; admission free. It is also possible to arrange for a guided tour throughout the year*).

GETTING THERE Skalica is situated 90km north of Bratislava on the border with the Czech Republic. By car, take the D2/E65 motorway towards Prague from Bratislava and turn off at exit Kúty following route 2 to Skalica. To see more of the surrounding countryside, you could take route 2 all the way from Bratislava to Skalica; follow the signs for Malacky and Skalica.

By road from Trnava to Skalica, route 52 leads all the way in a northwesterly direction and you pass Smolenice Chateau, Dolná Krupa and Ostrý Kameň castle ruins and pass through Senica. By train from Bratislava to Kúty and then switch to a local train to Skalica; journey time 2–2¹/₂ hours. Direct buses take two hours from Bratislava. You may have to change buses in Senica.

TOURIST INFORMATION

🛈 **Skalica Tourist Information Office** Námestie Slobody 14, in the House of Culture; ☎ 034 6645 341; e tik@skalica.sk; www.skalica.sk

WHERE TO STAY

🏠 **Hotel Sv Michal** (9 rooms, 2 apts) Potočna 40; ☎ 034 6960 111; www.hotelsvatymichal.sk. Great venue for receptions, the wedding suite is furnished in Louis XIV style. Gourmet restaurant with superb wines from the Skalica region. Sgl $, dbl $$, apts $$. Restaurant ($$) open daily 11.00–22.00.

🏠 **Hotel Tatran** (22 rooms, 1 apt) Námestie Slobody 98; ☎ 034 6644 491; e recepcia@ hoteltatran.sk; www.hoteltatran.sk. A 1-star hotel located in the town centre with a restaurant & café. Sgl, dbl $, apts $, b/fast 120Sk.

✕ WHERE TO EAT AND DRINK

Skalica has long been a winemaking centre, and its most prestigious winery, Víno Masaryk can be visited right in the heart of town.

♀ **Víno Masaryk** Sasinkova 18A; ☎ 034 6646 960; e vino-masaryk@vino-masaryk.sk; www.vino-masaryk.sk. Alojz Masaryk has been making wine for 30 years. Since 2001, his vineyard has produced around 100,000 bottles of wine in 20 to 24 varieties.

From the vineyards surrounding Skalica comes the renowned Skalická frankovka a fruity red. A wine tasting (koštovka) can be arranged. Open Mon–Fri 07.00–16.00.

AROUND SKALICA

The region has several wine-producing villages but the most famous is **Borský Svätý Jur,** part of the **Záhorie Wine Route.** Pilgrims flock to **Šaštín Stráže** to see the statue of the Virgin Mary. In the 1970s, Pope Paul VI promoted the Church of the Virgin Mary of Seven Grievances to the status of basilica minor, the first in Slovakia. A good place to stay while exploring the Záhorie hill range and its vineyards is the **Gazarka resort** at Šaštín Stráže (*Gazárka, Alej 549, 908 41 Šaštín Stráže;* ✆ *034 6592 348;* e *info@gazarka.sk; www.gazarka.sk*) where there is both camping facilities and comfortable *chata* (hut). A four-bed *chata* for seven days costs 4,300Sk, a six-bed *chata* for seven days costs 8,600Sk, camping places are 100Sk a day, caravans 150Sk a day and the tennis court costs 100Sk an hour.

GETTING THERE Close to the D2/E65 Bratislava–Prague motorway, exit Kúty.

HEADING SOUTH FROM TRNAVA (CITY)

There is not so much to discover south of Trnava, although there are several good thermal pools, two watermills that the Slovaks are very proud of and cyclists can follow a route all along the north bank of the Danube. Environmentalists might like to visit the controversial dam at Gabčikovo, subject of decade-long arguments with neighbouring Hungary (see page 150).

GALANTA Galanta is a pleasant town on the Danube plain, 50km east of Bratislava. The history of the town is closely connected to the noble Hungarian Esterházy family, who left a rich cultural heritage in the area. The Renaissance castle has been open to the public since 1992, while the neogothic castle with its fun, chunky tower is under renovation. The town was made famous by Hungarian composer Zoltán Kodály's *Dances of Galant* (Galántai táncok). Kodály spent his childhood here and heard evocative melodies played by the Gypsy primás (lead violinist) János Mihók which he used as motifs to decorate many of his later works.

Getting there Regular buses leave Bratislava main bus station for Galanta; journey time is 80–95 minutes. Buses leave Trnava bus station every hour for Galanta; journey time is 50 minutes.

Where to stay and eat

🏠 **City Hotel** (85 beds) Vajanského 10; ✆ 031 7802 941. A non-stop hotel with basic facilities & bargain prices. *Sgl, dbl* $, *apts* $$.
🍴 **Cukráreň Tonka** Hlavna 24; ✆ 031 7803 749. Offers a range of cakes, ice cream, coffees & teas. $. *Open daily 10.00–19.00.*

✖ **Pizzeria Claudia** Hodská 50; ✆ 031 7801 511. Good pizzas. $. *Open daily 11.00–midnight.*
✖ **Reštaurácia Mladosť** Hlavná ulica; ✆ 031 7807 194. Typical Slovak dishes. $. *Open Mon–Fri 10.00–18.00.*

What to see and do
The Museum of National History and Geography in Galanta (*Vlastivedne múzeum v Galante, Hlavná ulica 8;* ✆ *033 7424 623;* e *vlast.muzeum.ga@stonline.sk; www.muzeum.sk/?obj=muzeum&ix=vmga; open Mon–Fri 09.00–16.00*). Cultural information on the region.

AROUND GALANTA Just east of Galanta is **Králová Lake** (*vodná nádrž Králová*), a huge reservoir with the **Kaskády resort** (*Únovce 504, Galanta;* ✆ *031 7883 333 (reception);* e *kaskady@kaskady.sk; www.kaskady.sk*), while west, by the town of Sládkovičovo is the **Vincov Les Thermal Lido** (*termálne kúpalisko;* m *0905 605 329;* e *vacko@nextra.sk; www.vincovles.sk; open Jul–Sep Mon 12.00–18.00, Tue–Sun 09.00–18.00*) with five pools. Stay here in 40 separate *chatky* (little huts) each with two rooms and suitable for four people. There is also a campsite and caravan

5

park. Part of the swimming pool's area is a 40,000m² lake where visitors can indulge in watersports and go fishing($$ *a week low season*, $$$ *a week high season*).

ŽITNÝ OSTROV REGION

Žitný ostrov (Rye Island) Žitný ostrov is the largest river island in Europe and is formed by the main stream of the Dunaj (Danube) and the Malý Dunaj (Little Danube). Several rivers flow across the island: the Váh, Slovakia's longest river, the Nitra, Hron, Ipeľ and the Žitava. Žitný ostrov stretches all the way from Bratislava to Komárno in the Nitra region along the north bank of the Danube and it forms the entire southern part of Trnava region. Visitors to Žitný ostrov will not even be aware they are on an island as it is so large and they will often cross the Little Danube without noticing.

Dunajská Streda (Dunaszerdahely in Hungarian) Dunajská Streda is the cultural and economic centre of the Žitný ostrov (Rye Island) region. The town has a majority Hungarian population and many signposts and shop signs are in Hungarian. The town once had a significant Jewish population and had two important synagogues, the **Oratory of Israelites** built at the end of the 1860s and the **Adasz Jiszrael Synagogue** built in 1927 in the Nemesszeg district. Though the latter was renovated after the war, the few Jews who returned from the war left the town later on and both synagogues fell into neglect and were demolished during 1950–53. Today only the memorial unveiled on 23 October 1991 commemorates the former Jewish quarter and the almost 3,000 Jews of the neighbourhood.

Getting there Dunajská Streda is situated 23km southeast of Bratislava on route 63 (E675) heading towards Komárno, Štúrovo and the river crossing to Hungary at Esztergom. Regular Bratislava–Komárno buses leave from Bratislava main bus station every 45–60 minutes; journey time is 55 minutes.

There are also regular buses from Trnava; journey time is 60–90 minutes. From Piešťany, you need to change at Trnava or Bratislava.

Tourist information
🖌 Turistická informačná kancelária Hlavná 50, Dunajská Streda; ☎ 031 5516 521

Where to stay and eat
🏠 **Hotel Bonbon** (70 rooms) Alžbetínske námestie 1; ☎ 031 5575 222; e bonbon@bonbon.sk; www.bonbon.sk. A 3-star hotel in the centre of town with a pool, solarium, sauna and tennis court. Typical Hungarian cuisine. Trips to Bratislava, the Small Carpathian Wine Route, Gabčíkovo. *Sgl, dbl* $$, *apts* $$$, *price includes b/fast and admission to the relax centre.*

What to see and do
Žitnoostrovské múzeum (Rye Island, *Csallókôz* in Hungarian) (*Žltý kaštieľ, Muzejná ulica 2;* ☎ *031 5522 402*). Established in 1964 with a permanent ethnographic exhibition and located in the Yellow Manor (*Žltý kaštieľ*) built in 1770 by Bishop Mikuláš Kondé, the Bishop of Varadín. It was rebuilt in the Classicist style at the beginning of the 19th century.

Thermal pool and lido (*Gabčíkovská cesta;* ☎ *031 5524 091*). With five pools and a temperature at the spring source of 56°C.

Topolniky (*Topolniky Termalne kupalisko and campsite ATC Topolniky;* ☎ *031 5582 358*). Just east of Dunajská Streda is this good thermal lido and campsite.

Veľký Meder (*Termál, Promenádna 20, Veľký Meder;* ☎ *031 5552 104*). A smart, new thermal pool and campsite south of Dunajská Streda with five pools situated in a forest. The water temperature at the spring source is a whopping 71°C.

Cycling Europe's longest cycling route passes through the Slovak Republic, stretching from Passau in Germany along the Danube, through Vienna, Bratislava and on to Štúrovo. Cyclists can then continue their journey by taking a ferry across the Danube into Hungary. You can cycle all the way from Bratislava to Štúrovo (on the other bank of the Danube is Esztergom, Hungary) in the Nitra region on the Danube Cycle Route (*Dunajská Cyklistická cesta*).

The VKÚ map (1:50,000) *Dunajská Cyklistická Cesta* divides the entire length of the Bratislava–Štúrovo route into 16 sections with details in English, Slovak, German and Hungarian (see page 54 for cycle route details).

GABČÍKOVO The Gabčíkovo hydro-electric power plant was created by damming up the Danube River. At Gabčíkovo there are 'beaches' and a lagoon caused by the dam. There are many opportunities for watersports and fishing. At Gabčíkovo, you can take a road heading southwest that crosses the Danube and goes onto a kind of watery enclave. The islands of Chko Dunajské Luhy, a long collection of islands and half-submerged wetland are a natural paradise that Hungarians say is threatened by the dam. The Hungarian side is called *Szigetkõzi tájvédelmi kórzet* (protected area of natural significance). It is possible to cycle or drive along this territory as far as Vojka nad Dunajom and Dobrohošť near Šamorín.

The town is named after the Slovak hero Jozef Gabčík. The town is famous for its English park with valuable oaks and exotic trees. In the park, there is the manor house built in the 17th century, rebuilt 100 years later in late-Baroque style. The district is renowned for its thermal spring and pool.

Gabčíkovo - village of the dam The Gabčíkovo dam system has been operating since the end of October 1992, diverting 80–90% of the Danube River water into

---

WATER MILLS OF THE LITTLE DANUBE

If you have the energy to canoe downstream on the entire length of the Little Danube (*Malý Dunaj*), you will sail past four historic water mills (*vodnýmlyn*) at Jelka, Tomášikovo, Jahodná and Dunajský Klátov. There is a fifth water mill at Kolárovo just over the border in the Nitra region presiding over where the Little Danube joins the mighty Váh River. First mentioned in 1894, the Jelka water pan mill was renovated in 1994. The Tomášikovo Land Water Wheel Mill, built in 1895, stands on piles and is connected to the riverbank by a wooden footbridge. The water sawmill at Jahodná is 7km downstream from Tomášikovo and tricky to spot as it is obscured by lush vegetation and picturesque small islands. Less than 2km from Jahodná is the village of Dunajský Klátov where a renovated brick water mill can be found. It was driven by waters of the Klatovské tributary of the Little Danube. The scene is particularly charming in summer when white water lilies grow abundantly. The mill was reconstructed in 1920 and was operating until 1941. Today it contains a permanent exhibition and forms part of the Museum of Žitný ostrov in Dunajská Streda.

More on these mills can also be seen at Galanta's Museum of National History and Geography (*Vlastivedne múzeum*). For rafting trips along the Malý Dunaj check out www.actionland.sk, a watersports company based at Čunovo.

Jozef Gabčík (8 April 1912–18 June 1942) was a Slovak paratrooper involved in Operation Anthropoid, the assassination of the 'Butcher of Prague' Reinhard Heydrich, chief of the Reich Security Main Office and architect of the Holocaust. Gabčík was trained in Britain for this special mission. At the end of 1941, Gabčík and his Czech colleague Ján Kubiš secretly parachuted into the Protectorate of Bohemia and Moravia to plan the assassination of Reinhard Heydrich, which they carried out on 27 May 1942. Gabčík shot Heydrich, needing two attempts and Heydrich died in hospital eight days later. Hitler ordered the SS and Gestapo to 'wade in blood' throughout Bohemia to find Heydrich's killers. More than 13,000 people were arrested. Nazi officials carried out an extensive search for the two men and discovered that they were hiding with other paratroopers in an Orthodox church in Prague. However, Gabčík, Kubiš and others all committed suicide before the Gestapo could get to them in the catacombs. In revenge, the Nazis carried out the complete destruction of the villages of Lidice and Ležáky. Winston Churchill, infuriated, suggested razing three German villages for every Czech village the Nazis had destroyed. Instead, the Allies stopped planning similar operations to assassinate top Nazis for fear of similar reprisals. Two years after Heydrich was killed, however, they attempted one more time, this time targeting Hitler in Operation Foxley which failed. Operation Anthropoid remained the only successful assassination of a top-ranking Nazi. A Czech legend states that if a person who is not a genuine member of Czech royalty puts the Czech royal crown on his head, he will die in one year and a day. Some claim that Heydrich, who had his office in Prague Castle, had tried on the royal crown exactly one year and one day before the fatal day.

the canal and reservoir. The remaining 10–20% of the water is allowed to pass through the Čunovo diversion weir and directly into the old river bed, the Hungarian branch system, and the Moson Danube. Some water from the Gabčíkovo Canal is diverted to recharge the Slovak branch system. The Gabčíkovo hydro dam complex is the largest engineering system built on the Danube. The construction of the dam, canals and reservoir system directly affected 3,900ha of fields and 3,400ha of floodplain forests in Slovakia and another 2,000ha in Hungary at the site of the original reservoir and Dunakiliti diversion weir, built before Hungary withdrew from the project. The Slovaks are proud of their dam and say the advantages of the water works are energy production, a revival of the inland Danube, the area called Žitný ostrov (Rye Island) between the Danube and the Little Danube (Malý Dunaj) and the development of the tourist industry. Hungarian environmentalists, on the other hand, say it caused untold damage to the Szigetköz region, the marshy land on the other, Magyar side of the river.

Watery wrangles The Gabčíkovo-Nagymaros hydro-electric dam, situated 40km downstream from Bratislava, has been an environmental disaster on all sides. The Gabčíkovo Dam Project was started in 1977 under the auspices of an international treaty between the then communist brother states Hungary and Czechoslovakia. The goal was to dam the Danube, all the way from Bratislava to Budapest, providing for a vital amount of clean hydro-electric energy. The idea was supported by the Austrians, who also looked for cheap energy sources at another country's environmental expense. The Czechoslovak government was desperate to find another source of energy to replace the brown coal, whose pollution destroyed most of the country's forests. The Hungarian government pulled out in 1989 after protests by the green lobby, and called for an international inquiry into the environmental effects of the dam on the Danube. They dismantled their dam at Nagymaros (east of Štúrovo and Esztergom, downstream from Gabčíkovo) The Czechoslovak government had already invested huge amounts of money and continued with a scaled-down version of the project, diverting part of the Danube in 1993. In 1997, the International Court at The Hague ruled in favour of Slovakia, but that Slovakia had acted illegally by diverting the river. The court ordered both sides to come up with a joint plan for the future of the project but the arguments wrangle on and the matter is no longer in the political limelight. Tragically, the environmental damage has already been done according to ecologists on both sides of the river.

Getting there Gabčíkovo is situated 24km southeast of Bratislava. Take route 63 (E675) towards Dunajská Streda and turn off at the village of Báč, just after Šamorín, onto the secondary route 506 signposted for Gabčíkovo.

Regular buses leave Bratislava main bus station for Šamorín, Gabčíkovo and other towns along the Danube; journey time to Gabčíkovo is 90 minutes.

Things to see and do
Gabčíkovo thermal pool (termálne kúpalisko) (*Pastuchovská ulica;* ↘ *031 5594 101; www.gabcikovo.sk*). There are three pools and a water temperature at source of 52°C.

6

Trenčín Region

Beautifully located at the foot of the Strážovské Vrchy Hills in the valley of the Váh River, the region of Trenčín, with its temperate climate, definitely deserves a visit. A rich history, a large number of historical monuments and numerous cultural events guarantee a visit full of leisure activities and discoveries. The region covers an area of 67.74km^2 and contains lush valleys and river basins gradually rising to hills and highlands. The sub-mountain areas around Veľká Javorina Mountain was earlier colonised by scattered hamlets and solitary hillside farms in places like Myjava and Lubina. The people bred cattle and sheep and produced butter and *bryndza* (sheep's cheese). In the winter, they would carve spoons and dishes, still found at craft fairs throughout the country. The region borders the Czech Republic to the north and includes the valleys of the Váh and Nitra rivers. Trenčín is a hilly, temperate region which is well known for its magnificent castles. The capital of the region, Trenčín City, dates back to Roman times when it was a military colony. Outside Trenčín Town, the White Carpathians have many mineral springs. Trenčín has several first-class spas located by healing mineral springs and the area also offers watersports, canoeing, rafting and sailing on the Váh and local reservoirs. The Váh is also lined with a chain of ruined castles and great hiking and cycling routes. Trenčín is an ideal starting point for short biking tours or longer trips. Owing to its close location to Považský Inovec, the White Carpathians, and Strážovské Hills, the Trenčín region is laced with a dense network of tourist marked trails at an altitude of 500–1,000m.

A predecessor of the Trenčín county existed already in the 9th century at the time of the Great Moravian Empire. During the 10th and 11th centuries, it was temporarily part of Bohemia and then Poland (*castellania Trecen*). The Trenčín county as a Hungarian *comitatus* appeared at the end of the 11th century, when virtually all of Slovakia was occupied by Hungary. When Slovakia became part of Czechoslovakia in 1918, the Trenčín county (*Trenčianska župa*) continued to exist until 1922, but it had completely different powers. The name 'Trenčín county' is sometimes used erroneously to designate the Trenčín region (*Trenčiansky kraj*) which was created in 1948.

EVENTS IN TRENČÍN REGION

April–May	**Bojnice** International Festival of Ghosts and Spirits
June	**Trenčianske Teplice** Annual Art Film Festival, founded in 1993
	Trenčín *Kukanova desina* Public beer crawl; see www.kukanovadesina.szm.sk
	Myjava International Folk Festival; music, dancing and singing
	Púchov Folk Festival; local colour and tradition

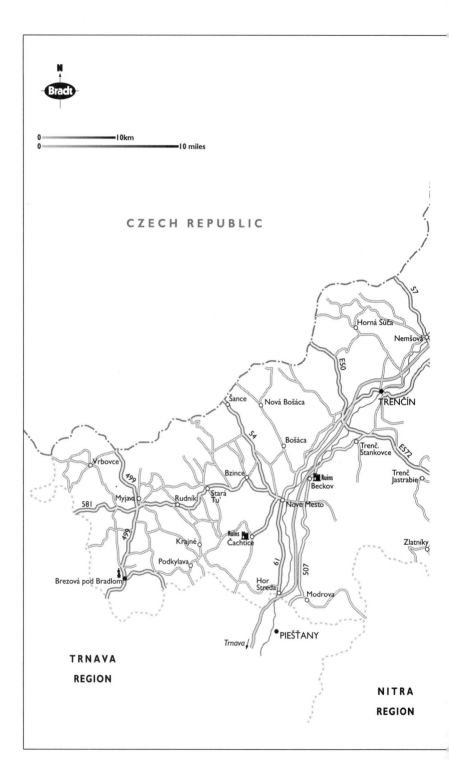

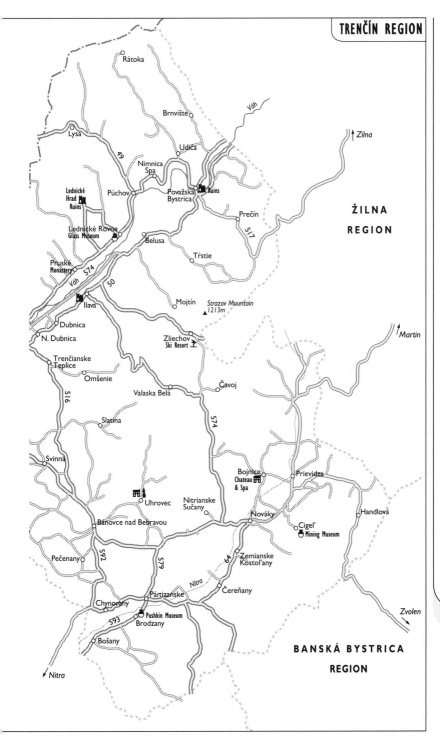

Rátoka

Brnvište

Udiča

Váh

↑ Zilna

Lysa

Nimnica
Spa

49

Púchov

Považska
Bystrica

Ruins

Prečín

517

Lednické
Hrad
Ruins

**ŽILNA
REGION**

Lednické Rovne
Glass Museum

Belusa

Pruské
Monastery

574

Tŕstie

Váh

50

Ilava

Mojtín

Strazov Mountain
▲ *1213m*

Dubnica

N. Dubnica

Zliechov
Ski Resort

↗ *Martin*

Trenčianske
Teplice

Omšenie

Valaska Belá

Čavoj

516

Slatína

574

Svinná

Bojnice
Chateau
& Spa

Prievidza

Uhrovec

Nitrianske
Sučany

Nováky

Handlová

Bánovce nad Bebravou

Cigel'
Mining Museum

Pečenany

592

579

64

Zemianske
Kostol'any

Nitra

Čereňany

Chynorany

Pártizanske

Zvolen

593

Pushkin Museum
Brodzany

Bošany

**BANSKÁ BYSTRICA
REGION**

↙ *Nitra*

| June–August | **Trenčianske Teplice** *Hudobné leto* Musical Summer Festival |
| July | **Trenčín airport** *Bažant Pohoda* Giant music festival; see www.pohodafestival.sk |

TRENČÍN Telephone code 032

Trenčín (*Trencsény* in Hungarian, *Trentschin* in German and *Laugaricio* in Latin) is one of the most immediately attractive cities in the country. Approaching the city by rail or road, you can't miss the imposing medieval castle looming above the city on a limestone cliff, looming high above the mighty Váh River. From the railway and bus stations, it's easy to find your way towards the castle and, after five minutes' walk, discover the charming Old Town centre nestling below the fortress. With good reason, Trenčín is known as the 'pearl of the Považie', the region along the Váh River. Like Trnava, Trenčín centre is a tense blend of charming old buildings and frumpy 1060s' creations painted in pastel shades of sky blue, pistachio, peppermint ice cream (a national colour favourite) and orangey-beige. The ancient Greek Ptolemy first mapped a settlement at the location that is now Trenčín, at a strategic juncture of a bluff outcropping of rock and the Váh River. Stop off first at the elegant Art Nouveau café of the Hotel Tatra for a restorative coffee or beer, then leave the main entrance and nip around to the right, following the façade around to where it meets solid rock. Here you can see the Roman inscription from AD179. The words were inscribed during the era of the Marcoman Wars. The town was then called *Laugaricio* and it was the most northerly place that Roman soldiers ventured in central Europe. These days, Trenčín is a lively town with a young, studenty feel. There are many pubs, cafés and restaurants in the centre and endless opportunities for relaxation, both sporty and sybaritic. Trenčín's population is 60,000.

GETTING THERE AND AWAY Trenčín railway and bus stations are five minutes' walk from the main square and old town centre. Timetables are available online at www.cp.sk.

Trenčín is situated 124km northeast of Bratislava on the main Bratislava–Košice rail line and the D1 & D61/E75 motorway from Bratislava to just south of Žilina.

Regular buses leave from most towns and villages in the surrounding regions.

☞ *POZOR!* The road system surrounding Trenčín is extremely chaotic and many signs are missing. It is possible to spend hours circling Trenčín, going in and out of the town centre before actually finding your destination. The Nitra traffic system is also tricky.

TOURIST INFORMATION AND OTHER PRACTICALITIES

⧉ Trenčin cultural and information centre Sládkovičova ulica; ☏ 032 161 86; f 032 7433 505; e kic@trencin.sk; www.trencin.sk. Provides assistance with tours, accommodation, balloon rides & night tours of the castle. *Open 15 Apr–15 Oct Mon–Fri 08.00–18.00, Sat 08.00–16.00, closed Sun; 16 Oct–14 Apr Mon–Fri 08.00–17.00, closed w/ends.*

✉ **Post office** Mierové námestie 21. *Open Mon–Fri 07.30–19.00, Sat 07.00–11.00.*

$ **Banks** Istrobank Mierové námestie 19. *Open Mon–Fri 08.00–17.00.* Ľudová Banka (Volksbank)

Šturovo náMestie 16. *Open Mon–Fri 08.00–16.00 (17.00 on Tue), Sat 09.00–12.30.*

⧉ **Internet** Mike Studio at back of Michalka vináreň, Mierové námestie 31; ☏ 032 7445 940. Only visit if you can overcome the aroma of wee. *Open Mon–Sat 09.00–22.00, Sun 13.00–22.00.*

Shop Bio Obchod Mierové námestie 29; www.bio-obchod.sk. Books & organic food.

🚕 **Taxi** Non-stop City Taxi Trenčín; ☏ 0907 118 651

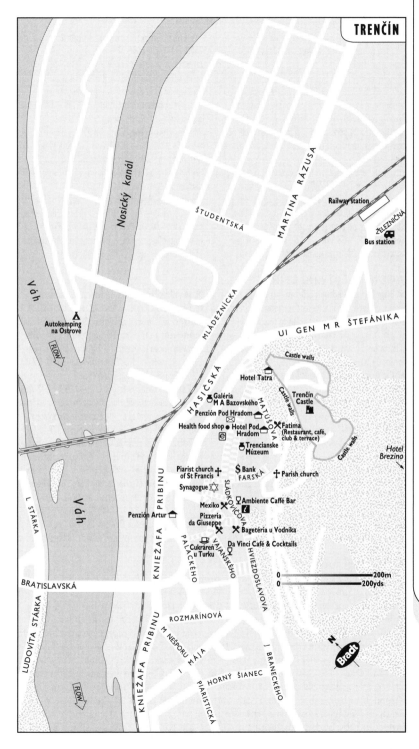

TRENČÍN

Nosický kanál

Váh

Váh

L STARKA

LUDOVITA STARKA

BRATISLAVSKÁ

KNIEŽAFA PRIBINU

KNIEŽAFA PRIBINU

M NEŠPORU

I MÁJA

PALÁCKEHO

ROZMARÍNOVÁ

HORNÝ ŠIANEC

PIARISTICKÁ

ŠTUDENTSKÁ

MARTINA RÁZUSA

MLÁDEŽNÍCKA

HASIČSKÁ

Autokemping
na Ostrove

FLOW

FLOW

Railway station

ŽELEZNIČNÁ

Bus station

Ul GEN M R ŠTEFÁNIKA

Castle walls

Hotel Tatra

Castle walls

Trenčín
Castle

Galéria
M A Bazovského

Penzión Pod Hradom

MATÚŠO...

Castle walls

Health food shop

Hotel Pod
Hradom

Fatima
(Restaurant, café,
club & terrace)

Trencianske
Múzeum

Hotel
Brezina

Piarist church
of St Francis

Bank

FARSKÁ

Parish church

Synagogue

SLADKOVIČOVA

Mexiko

Ambiente Caffé Bar

Penzión Artur

Pizzeria
da Giuseppe

Bagetéria u Vodníka

VAJANSKÉHO

Cukráren
u Turku

Da Vinci Café & Cocktails

HVIEZDOSLAVOVA

J BRANECKÉHO

0 ————————— 200m
0 ————————— 200yds

N

Bradt

⌂ WHERE TO STAY

⌂ **Autokemping na ostrove** ☎ 032 7434 013. In wooden chalets on the island (*ostrov*) in the Váh. *Open May–15 Sep.* $.

⌂ **Hotel Brezina** (20 rooms) Lesopark Brezina; ☎ 032 6528 171; f 032 6528 173; e recepcia@hotel-brezina.sk; www.hotel-brezina.sk. Situated in Brezina Park southeast of Trenčín Castle, with a restaurant ($$) popular with weddings, banquets & conferences. *Restaurant open daily 07.00–23.00. Dbl & suites* $$.

⌂ **Hotel Pod hradom** (12 rooms) Matúšova 12; ☎ 032 7481 701; f 032 7481 703; e asistent.tn@stonline.sk; www.podhradom.sk. A 3-star hotel on the winding street leading up to the castle, with a fabulous location & smart, modern facilities. *Restaurant ($–$$), café, terrace, sauna 100Sk per hr, whirlpool 100Sk per 20mins. Dbl* $$, *apts* $$.

⌂ **Hotel Tatra** (70 rooms) Štefánika 2; ☎ 032 6506 111; f 032 6506 213; e recepcia@hotel-tatra.sk; www.hotel-tatra.sk. Stylish Art Nouveau building below the castle & just off the main square. The top hotel in town with a good restaurant ($$$) & prices to match. *Sgl* $$$, *dbl* $$$$, *trpls & suites* $$$$$.

⌂ **Penzión Artur** Palackého 23; ☎ 032 7481 026; m 0904 339 654; e penzionartur@arturtn.sk; www.arturtn.sk. Pension with its own pizzeria & *vináreň* (wine cellar). Dbl have extra beds, separate bathrooms & whirlpools. *Dbl* $$.

⌂ **Penzión Pod hradom** (5 rooms) Matúšova 23; ☎/f 032 7442 507; m 0905 560 715; e phradom@tn.psg.sk; www.podhradom.sk. Connected to the hotel of the same name & offering the same service at lower prices. *Sgl, dbl* $$, *apts* $$.

✗ WHERE TO EAT AND DRINK

✗ **Bagetéria u vodníka** Štúrovo námestie 1. Strong coffee 20Sk, 30 different versions of baguette from plain ham 36/69Sk (small/large) to caviar 47/99Sk passing mushroom, cheese, tomato & chicken on the way. $. *Open Mon–Thu 09.00–21.00, Fri–Sat 09.00–03.00, Sun 11.00–21.00.*

✗ **Pizzeria da Giuseppe** Štúrovo námestie 5. Italian cuisine on the first floor, same alley. $. *Open Mon–Thu 10.00–23.00, Fri–Sat 10.00–01.00, Sun 13.00–23.00.*

⊏Ը **Cukráreň U Turku** Vajanského 1, a café with great cakes & 16 kinds of ice cream. *Open daily 10.00–18.00.*

♀ **Da Vinci café & cocktails** Vajanského 3. A smart café/bar with chic beige & brown décor & tulips on every table. $. *Open Mon–Thu 07.00–midnight, Fri 07.00–02.00, Sat 09.00–02.00, Sun 14.00–midnight.*

✗ **Mexiko** Sládkovičova 8. Mexican & Slovak specialities, lunch menu 99Sk. $. *Open Mon–Thu 10.30–22.00, Fri–Sat 10.30–midnight, Sun 12.00–22.00.*

♀ **Ambiente caffé bar** Sládkovičova 1. Upmarket bar with prices to match. Tall black stools, grey tiles, 1960s' style chairs. $$. *Open Mon–Thu 09.00–22.00, Fri–Sat 09.00–03.00, Sun 09.00–22.00.*

✗ **Fatima** Matúšova 6; ☎ 032 7440 083; f 032 7440 084. A restaurant, café, club & summer terrace. Great location for a meal after the castle. $. *Koliba open daily 18.00–05.00, café & canteen daily 10.00–22.00.*

✗ **Tatra Restaurant & Café Sissi** (Hotel Tatra), M R Štefánika 2; ☎ 032 6506 111. Top-notch restaurant & it's worth popping in for a coffee or snack to see the Art Nouveau interior, dating from 1901. There's also a traditional Slovak restaurant (*open Mon–Fri 10.30–02.00, Sat 18.00–02.00*) & a summer terrace Marcus Aurelius (*open Thu–Sat 17.00–21.00*). $$. *Restaurant open daily 11.30–14.30 & 18.00–22.00.*

WHAT TO SEE AND DO

Trenčín Castle (☎ 032 7434 431; *castle open May–Aug daily 09.00–16.30; Oct–Apr Sat–Sun 09.00–15.30; grounds open Tue–Sun 09.00–12.00 & 13.00–17.00; admission adult/concessions 80/40Sk*) is the third-largest castle in Slovakia, behind those in Spiš and Bratislava. It's one of the oldest and most significant castles in the country and was founded in 1111 as a royal castle. The oldest part of the castle is probably the Romanesque tower. Between 1302 and 1321, the castle was the seat of the powerful Hungarian magnate Matúš Čák (Csák Máté in Hungarian), 'Lord of the Váh River and the Tatra Mountains'. Čák had the castle remodelled and built a residential palace within the fortress walls. The medieval Matúš Tower named after him is the highest point in town and a symbol of Trenčín. After Čák's death in 1321, the castle returned to royal hands and reconstruction work was carried out by both Lajos (Louis) the Great and King Sigismund of Luxembourg.

The theme is inspired by the rich feudal history which took place in Slovak castles and palaces. The kingdom is named after the ruler Matúš Čák Trenčiansky, who because of his power and position was called the Lord over Váh and Tatras. Today, Matheus's kingdom (*Matušovo kráľovstvo;* ☏ *033 7743 133;* f *033 7740 548;* e *matusovo-kralovstvo@nextra.sk; www.matusovo-kralovstvo.sk*) lies in the western part of Slovakia and covers one-third of the country, including almost 1,100 towns and villages, where there are 53 picturesque castles, chateaux and manor houses. Some of the spooky haunted castles and romantic ruins are on hilltops and at the bottom of the hill you'll find a watch post giving information (in English also) about events in the kingdom; you can also buy souvenirs. Visitors can also call in at the Pilgrim Places of Matheus's kingdom, where there are food and drink facilities. If you buy a 'passport' for Matheus's kingdom, you can 'become its citizen, travel through its nine domains and acquire the stamps of passport controls of 53 castle demesnes and more than 100 Pilgrim Places'.

In 1475, Stefan Zápoľský obtained the castle with the domain for loyal service to the Hungarian King Mátyás Corvinus. Then the Thurzó family took over the castle and made fortifications against impending Turkish attacks. In 1560, Trenčín Castle and the domain were taken over by the Tyrolean Count Pirrhus dęArco.

From 1594 to 1835 the castle belonged to the Illesházy family who between 1704 and 1708 did the final building work. Like numerous others in Slovakia, Trenčín Castle burned down in 1790 and fell into ruin for 150 years, but eventually restoration work began in 1956. The castle tour of **Trenčianské Muzeum** (*Mierové námestie 46;* ☏ *032 7464 431;* f *032 7440 753;* e *office@ muzeumtn.sk; www.muzeumtn.sk/trencian1.htm; open daily May–Sep 09.00–17.00; Oct–Apr 09.00–16.00*) includes performances by fencers and falconers. English-speaking guides can be ordered at the museum telephone number given above. You can visit individually to see exhibitions of historical furniture and feudalism, although the guided tour of the 15th-century Illesházy family gallery of the **Zápoľsky Palace** (*Palác rodu zápoľských; tours start 09.15, then 09.45–16.45 last tour*) is usually in Slovak only. While the castle lay in ruin, the city grew into a prosperous industrial centre, known today for its clothing factories and for the Old Herold distillery producing one of Slovakia's best *slivovica* (plum brandy), *Bošácka*, made from yellow plums from Bošáca village, 20km west in the White Carpathians. Below the castle on the hillside is the old **Catholic parish church** (*Farský kostol*) of the Virgin Mary and a small upper square, reached by clambering up historic covered stairs (*kryté schody*) created in 1568 (renovated in 1708, 1886 and 1979; obviously high-maintenance steps) from wooden steps and square cobbles made of wood. The covered steps have a metal gate and padlock so it is not always possible to gain access this way. It is also possible to reach the imposing fortress by staggering up **Matúšova**, a steep winding side street starting from just behind Hotel Tatra. The compact Old Town contains a charming main square, **Mierové námestie** (Peace Square), lined with shops, banks and restaurants and adorned by a large **Piarist Church of St Francis** (1653–57) which is very Baroque and gilt inside. The **plague column** in the middle of the Old Town square was raised by Duke Mikuláš Illesházy in 1712 in memory of the victims of an epidemic which ravaged the city in 1710. Visitors can then pass behind the town walls through the **Lower Gate (Dolná brána)**, also known as the Turkish Gate, which features a 15th-century clock tower. Local superstition warns (or

THE WELL OF LOVE

According to legend, the well was dug by Omar, a Turkish soldier. Štefan Zápoľský, the cruel king of the castle had taken captive his true love, Fatima. 'I will give you silver, gold, jewellery, precious Persian carpets, anything you desire. Only set my Fatima free,' pleaded Omar. Scorning all offered riches, Zápoľský would only release her if Omar could provide the castle an internal source of water, thus enabling the fortress to withstand even the longest of sieges. For three years, Omar toiled and finally he struck water 79.2m down, saving his beloved fiancée Fatima. You can still see Omar's well of love, 500 years later, a potent tribute to the power of love. Couples come and throw coins into the well, paying homage to Omar and Fatima's love and hoping for similar fidelity and affection.

advises!) that if you speak when walking underneath the tower, you'll never marry. Once silently through the arch, turn right to find the grey concrete **Art Nouveau synagogue** (1912). Like so many in Slovakia, it was totally ransacked during World War II but is one of the few to be restored. It is used as venue for various art exhibitions. A statue appears on **Štúrovo námestie**. A water sprite wearing a top hat peers out of a well. From Štúrovo námestie, head north to Palackého, a street lined with elegant buildings, including the **Galéria MA Bazovského** (*Palackého 27; open Tue–Sun 09.00–17.00*), dedicated to Miloš Bazovský, a famous Slovak painter and sculptor who died here in 1968 and whose statues stand inside. Bazovský painted beguilingly simple depictions of peasant life from the 1930s. The guided walk, or prehliadka (*starts from the Town Tower;* ↘ *032 6504 317;* m *0915 475 020; tickets 1,000Sk, daily 10.00–20.00*) around Trenčín is in English, Slovak, German, Italian, Spanish, Russian, Dutch and other languages on request.

AROUND TRENČÍN

The hills and valleys around Trenčín make for pleasant outings by foot or bicycle. A few minutes away in a wooded dale is the spa town of Trenčianske Teplice, a famous spa built in the 14th century and famous for its hot mineral springs and mud.

The **pilgrimage site of Skalka,** just upstream from Trenčín, has two parts: Malá Skalka and Veľká Skalka. At Malá Skalka, Saint Benedict was thrown into the Váh, and there is a small Romanesque church with two towers dedicated to him, dating from 1208. A pilgrimage comes here on the first Sunday after 17 July, the anniversary of the canonisation of the saints Benedict and Andrew Svorad. Visitors can see the ruins of a monastery built in 1224.

SKALKA NAD VÁHOM GOLF DRIVING RANGE (*Contact Janka;* m *0904 524 293;* e *bosi@mail.t-com.sk; www.pgc.sk*). The First Golf Club (Prvý Golf) Trenčín was established at the end of 2001 with the aim of promoting golf in the Trenčín region. The First Golf Club Trenčín offers its services on a 100x250m driving range in Skalka nad Váhom (2km upstream along the Váh from Trenčín town centre) where golfers can tee off from 12 places, four of them under cover, so it is possible to exercise in the rain. There is one practice sand bunker.

POVAŽSKÝ INOVEC A hill range for nature lovers and hikers. The city of Trenčín can be used as a base for several hikes or walks in the wooded region. At the foot of the Inovec Mountain (1,042m) is Selec, a well-preserved traditional village.

STRÁŽOVSKÉ VRCHY Hikers can explore Ostrý vrch (768m), Omšenská Baba (669m) and Baske Mountain (955m) within this hill range.

TRENČIANSKE TEPLICE Trenčianske Teplice, 12km northeast of Trenčín, was built by sulphurous mud and hot springs. In the 14th century, it was considered one of the loveliest spa towns in the Hungarian Kingdom. Its healing waters, good for osteoporosis and motor neurone problems, still pull in the crowds today and it makes a great relaxation area as many hiking trails lead into the green hills surrounding the spa resort. The resort has 11 mineral springs and five hot sulphur springs. The big draw is the stripey *hammam*, a Turkish bath house built in 1871. Inside, visitors relax under Ottoman arches beside aquamarine tiles and mosaic-covered walls while marble fountains gush mineral-rich water. Unfortunately, the *hammam* still conforms to the ancient men-only rules. Women are allowed into the adjoining and newer Sina thermal swimming pool through a separate, plain white entrance that was used by servants in the last century.

☞ *POZOR!* The attendant sometimes lets female visitors peek inside the delightful Turkish wallowing hole. If the attendant is having a grumpy day, females can join the tour (*every Mon at 15.00*), organised by the tourist office opposite the *hammam*.

Getting there The most fun way is to take a train from Trenčín railway station for ten minutes along the eastern bank of the Váh to **Trenčianská Tepla** then continue on a lovely 5km forest railway. The narrow Bosnian Gauge track opened in 1909 and three electric tram cars operate along it. The original wooden waiting room was modernised in 1941 and is still used.

MATÚŠ ČÁK, THE LORD OF THE TATRAS

Trenčín Castle was the headquarters of Máté Csák (in Slovak Matúš Čák III Trenčiansky), a powerful Hungarian oligarch at the beginning of the 14th century. After Hungary's first royal dynasty, the House of Árpád had died out in 1301, the Kingdom of Hungary entered into a chaotic state. Numerous contesters aspired to the throne. Eventually, Charles Robert of Anjou, the pope's candidate, proved to be the strongest of them. Charles Robert finally drove his rivals out of the country and was crowned King of Hungary in 1310. However, during the turbulent times of the power struggle, some oligarchs gained significant power above parts of the Hungarian Kingdom. Máté Csák, the 'Lord of the Tatras and the Váh River', was one of them and controlled 13 counties and 50 castles. Together with another oligarch, Amadé Aba, they ruled almost the entire territory of what today constitutes Slovakia. Csák behaved like a real sovereign. He held court in Trenčín, he had his own army and his own currency. Csák and Aba united forces and fought Charles Robert at every possible opportunity.

However, in 1312, in the Battle of Rozhanovce (4km east of Košice), dubbed as 'the cruellest battle since the Mongol invasion of Europe' by the contemporary chronicle, Charles Robert mastered a great victory over Aba and Csák. The leaders of the Aba family perished in the battle and their rule over eastern Slovakia came to an end. Csák managed to retain control over his territories until his death in 1321. He became the oligarch who defied the king for the longest time, but his power started to decline after the Battle of Rozhanovce. Csák died in 1321 in Trenčín.

Tourist information and other practicalities

Z Tourist office Kúpeľňa 15; ☏ 032 6559 128.; *Open Mon–Fri 10.00–12.30 & 13.00–16.00.*

Where to stay, eat and drink

⌂ **Hotel Flora** (61 rooms) Ulica 17 novembra 14; ☏ 032 6554 555; f 032 6552 824; e hotelflora@ hotelflora.sk; www.hotelflora.sk. Modern, concrete hotel with some overwhelmingly orange rooms. *Sgl* $, *dbl* $$, *suites* $$$.

⌂ **Hotel Slovakia** (92 rooms) Masarykova 3; ☏ 032 6556 111; f 032 6553 504; e hotel@ hotelslovakia.sk; www.hotelslovakia.sk. Modern concrete block, 200m from the spas. Fitness centre, sauna and tennis court. Good restaurant. $$. *Sgl* $, *dbl & suites* $$.

⌂ **Parkhotel Na Baračke** Na Baračke 87; ☏ 032 6556 868; e parkhotel@polis.sk; www.polis.sk. A smart spa hotel and wellness centre at the end of the park. Delightful restaurant with top-notch dishes. $$. *Dbl* $$$.

⌂ **Penzión Baske** Ulica 17 novembra 23; ☏ 032 6553 428; e baske@stonline.sk; www.penzionbaske.sk. Named after the highest peak in the area, Baske (955m) in an elegant neorenaissance villa. Excellent restaurant. $$. *Dbl* $$–$$$.

What to see and do Trenčianske Teplice is a lovely green town; the **Teplička stream** passes elegant villas, many of which are also pensions. During the summer season, classical and traditional folk concerts, operas and theatre performances are staged at the *Kupelná Dvorana* cultural centre. An international **Art Film festival** is held here every year and visiting stars are honoured on the **Most slávy** (Bridge of Fame) in front of the **Miramare–Corfu** hotel complex. Celebrity visitors include Franco Nero, the first in 1995, Gina Lollobrigida (1996) and Catherine Deneuve (2000). The **Three Hearts (*Tri srdcia*) treatment house** was built in 1859 by Viennese Georg Sina, a benefactor of the Hungarian royal court. In 1835, Sina bought the entire resort from the Illesházy family, who had owned it for 250 years and turned it into a profitable spa centre. The **hydroelectric power station** (*budova vodnej elektrárne*) today used as an exhibition area. Visitors take the waters at various sanatoria. The **Krym Sanatorium** (*T G Masaryka;* ☏ *032 6554 111;* f *032 6552 960*) is a large concrete construction, while the **Sina sanatorium** is a more aesthetically pleasing 19th-century ochre mansion with a mirror bath. The Bauhaus **Machnáč Sanatorium** (*T G Masaryka;* ☏ *032 655 2401*) was built in 1932 by Czech architect Jaromír Krejcar. In the woods east of the centre and cut into the curve of the hillside is the **Zelená Žaba, or Green Frog** (*Ulica 17 novembra;* ☏ *032 6553 019;* f *032 6553 452*), a swimming pool complex built in 1937 by Brno-born Bohuslav Fuchs. Continue uphill to the **Na Baračke** restaurant, and head further up to Heinrich's Spring, then on to Krájovec (557m) for a splendid view over the Teplička Valley. The whole trek should take around two hours. Hikers reach a lake with a sports centre where visitors can play minigolf, tennis or rent a bike.

CASTLES ALONG THE VÁH RIVER

The mighty Váh cuts right across Trenčín region diagonally heading northeast especially between Trenčín and Považská Bystrica. The rich history of the Považie region can be seen in the countless castles and manor houses scattered across the Bielé Karpaty, Považský Inovec and Strážovské Vrchy mountain ranges. Many castles suffered during the Rákóczi uprising (1703–11) and fell into ruin but still make impressive sights by the river.

ILAVA & PRUSKÉ For travellers on the Bratislava–Košice train line, Ilava's castle looks impressive. It once dominated the Váh River but now the view is interrupted by the motorway and the railway line. Ilava Castle is a splendid

Gothic construction dating from the end of the 13th century. In the middle of the 16th century it was rebuilt into a fort. After 1856 the building complex with a double-spired Baroque church was further reconstructed into a prison. In 1938, it served as a concentration camp and its name evokes painful associations. Across the river from Ilava, Pruské boasts a 17th-century Franciscan monastery with works by the Slovak preacher and writer of Baroque poetry Hugolín Gavlovič (1712–87) and an elegant 16th-century manor house. In the local parsonage garden, there is a group of 700-year-old yew trees.

LEDNICKÉ ROVNE (*Schreiberova ulica, near the church;* ✆ *042 4693 824; open Mon–Fri 08.00–14.00; admission adult 10Sk*). An elegant 16th-century mansion situated in a large English-style park. Within the dark yellow walls is Sklárske múzeum, Slovakia's only glass-making museum.

Getting there Take the D1/E50 motorway to Ilava, exit Ilava on route 574 to Pruské then north on route 507 for 8km.

LEDNICKÝ HRAD CASTLE RUINS On a rocky crag, Kobulinka, near the Czech border lie the ruins of a 14th-century frontier outpost. Kobulinka rock is found near the northern end of Lednica village. After the Battle of Biela Hora in 1620, members of the Czech Brethren who had been persecuted in Bohemia found asylum in Lednica. The most famous part of the ruin is the atmospheric stairway carved right into the rock. To reach the top, visitors have to negotiate a slippery stone passage and up a rickety ladder which is a little unnerving but gives a great view of the lost-in-time village below.

Getting there Buses leave every three hours from Púchov or Dubnica nad Váhom. The local bus from Trenčín takes 90 minutes to do 30km.

By car, take route 507 heading towards Púchov and turn left at the village of Horovce.

PÚCHOV AND POVAŽSKÁ BYSTRICA *Telephone code 042*

These two towns are found at the most attractive part of the Váh where it wiggles and twists, followed in formation by the railway line, before arching towards Žilina. The river is so wide here it becomes more of a lake and the banks are dotted with holiday homes, mountain chalets and bungalows. Visitors arriving on the train from Bratislava will have the first feeling of being in mountain country as the Kysuce range rises up beyond the Váh. **Orlové manor house** (✆ *042 4323 724; open Tue–Fri 08.00–16.00, Sat–Sun 09.00–17.00; admission adult 40Sk*) is situated over the river from Považská Bystrica and contains a small museum of folk and shepherd traditions. At the end of the road, a yellow-marked trail leads to **Považský hrad** castle ruins; the castle was built in the 13th century, but burnt down in 1623. At **Považská Tepla,** visitors can take a trip through the narrow gorge at **Manínska Tiesňava**, which was created by the passage of water over the centuries. The green-signed trail leads to the village of **Kostolec**, bounding over the Veľký Manín peak (891m) like a mountain goat and descending to a small hamlet. Gourmets should visit **Hotel Wili** in **Púchov** to sample the delightful cuisine (**$$**) prepared by head chef Oto Hvizdák. The Považská Bystrica information centre (*Štúrova 9;* ✆ *042 4260 598;* f *042 4326 545;* e *tikpb@stonline.sk; www.tikpb.host.sk; open Mon–Fri 08.00–17.00; 1 Jun–30 Sep also Sat 09.00–13.00, closed Sun*) has friendly staff who can help with accommodation and trips.

NIMNICA SPA

Kúpele Nimnica (✆ *042 4632 912;* f *042 4632 654;* e *obchod@kupelenimnica.sk; www.kupelenimnica.sk*), situated just north of Púchov, Slovakia's newest spa was originally named after the Nosická dam nearby. The area was first mentioned in 1408 and belonged to the Lednica Castle domain and the Prílesok family. The first administration register of mineral water springs in the Austro-Hungarian Empire in 1763 contained a report of acid spring water in the area. The water was used for brewing beer, drinking and cooking. However, during most of the 20th century, the spa was forgotten. In 1953, while drilling a base hole for the **Priehrada mládeže (Youth Dam)**, a salty spring erupted below the level of the river Váh. The alkaline carbonic mineral water prompted the construction of Slovakia's youngest spa. The waters can treat digestive, respiratory and circulatory diseases. Accommodation is in 243 rooms in six hotels and also at **Hotel Neptún** (*Kúpele Nimnica;* ✆ *042 4632 901;* f *042 4632 900;* e *hotelneptun@hotelneptun.sk; www.hotelneptun.sk*), a 52-room modern complex (*dbl $$*).

Getting there By car, when the D1 motorway comes to an abrupt end just south of Púchov, continue on route 49 into Púchov centre, cross the Váh and take route 507 east towards Udiča. By train, the main Bratislava–Košice line stops in Púchov. From the railway station buses leave every 20 minutes for Nimnica.

SOUTHEAST FROM PÚCHOV

ZLIECHOV SKI RESORT AND STRÁŽOV MOUNTAIN (1,213m) near the folk village of Čičmany (in Žilina region) is found right on the border with Žilina region. Strážov Mountain is at the southernmost tip of the Malá Fatra range. Zliechov ski resort has easy trails and three tow lifts deliver skiers to the highest point of 880m. Recommended only for beginners. Also see the Strážov waterfalls in spring.

Getting there From Ilava, visitors need to drive east along a minor road heading for the little ski resort of Zliechov. One bus a day from Ilava takes 50 minutes.

PRIEVIDZA *Telephone code 046*

Prievidza (population 55,000) is one of those unsightly industrial towns that suddenly pop up amongst beautiful scenery. Rusting railway carriages lie around. The church is pretty, though, with the same 'stylish medieval' exterior look as Banská Bystrica's church. Prievidza is surrounded by lovely rolling countryside and half-a-dozen castle ruins. To get there follow route 64 from Partizánske.

TOURIST INFORMATION
🄸 **Tourist office Horná Nitra** Námestie slobody 4; ✆ 046 16 186; f 046 5423 135;   e tik@prievidza.sk; www.prievidza.sk

AROUND PRIEVIDZA

BOJNICE CHATEAU (✆ *046 5430 624,* e *marketing@bojnicecastle.sk; www.bojnicecastle.sk; open Oct–Apr Tue–Sun 10.00–15.00; May–Jun Tue–Sun 09.00–17.30; Jul–Aug daily 09.00–17.00; Sep Tue–Sun 09.00–17.00*). The turrets of Slovakia's most-visited chateau rise up out of the surrounding woods like a magical fairytale castle. Bojnice's original construction, a wooden fortress, was first mentioned in an 1113 document from Zobor Abbey near Nitra. During the 13th century it was rebuilt in stone. Towards the end of the 13th century, Bojnice was seized by the magnate Matúš Čák and he held sway until 1321.

For the next 200 years, the fortress changed hands between noble families: the Gileth, Leustach and Noffry. It is rumoured that Hungarian King Mátyás Corvinus liked to visit Bojnice and would hold meetings and banquets under the lime tree opposite the entrance, which was named after him. Look for the **700-year-old King Matej (Mátyás) lime tree** near the entrance, it's one of the oldest trees in Slovakia. Legend says that Matúš Čák planted the tree in 1301 when the last king of the Árpád dynasty, András III, died. In its prime, the lime had a 36m spread and was a favourite picnic spot. After Mátyás's death, Západský troops seized the castle and stayed until 1526. The following year, the castle was presented to Alexej Thurzó. The Thurzós transformed the Gothic fortress into a Renaissance seat. Pál Pálffy, a nobleman from one of the wealthiest families in the kingdom, bought the castle in 1637 from Emperor Ferdinand III for 200,000 gold pieces.

The Pálffys gave it a Baroque redesign in 1644. In 1852, Count Ján Pálffy (1829–1909), the last noble owner of the castle and the man responsible for its current image, inherited the castle. He was fascinated by the early Gothic royal architecture of France's Loire Valley and set about transforming the stately yet dowdy castle into a palace worthy of his vast art collection. He hired the famous Budapest architect József Hubert, who also did the redesign for another fairytale palace at **Smolenice** (see page 142), and began the remodelling project in 1890, painstakingly creating the late-Tyrolean Gothic look. He scoured Europe for period antiques and installed them in his dream palace. He erected a new pointed tower on the castle's west wing that gives such a unique skyline. He died in Vienna in 1909, his reconstruction project unfinished. In 1950, fire destroyed the castle towers but it was immediately restored. The interior is now a part of the Slovak National Museum. In 1970 the castle was declared as a National cultural monument. Check out the cave located 26m under the fourth courtyard; allegedly there's a secret passageway leading to beyond the castle walls. There are two lakes and also a moat, lake and mini-chateau folly on a peninsula.

Visit the fabulous interior with remaining collections of furniture, porcelain and paintings. Two tours are available: Grand tour (*veľký okruh*) 75 minutes; admission adult 130Sk, child (6–15) 70Sk, child (3–6) 10Sk. Little tour (*malý okruh*) 45 minutes; admission adult 80Sk, child (6–15) 50Sk, child (3–6) 10Sk.

The cash desk staff take their lunch break from 12.00–12.30. There is also a camera charge of 50Sk and a video charge of 150Sk. From May–September guides are available, in English, German and Slovak (minimum 10 people in group), cost 400Sk. Ask in advance for guides in Dutch, French, Italian, Polish, Russian or Hungarian.

Getting there Route 64 from Partizánske, turn left 5km before Prievidza. By bus from Bratislava; 3½ hours. Get off at the church in the town square, or just past the castle at Bojnice Kúpele (the spa). There are regular buses from Prievidza.

Tourist information
🆔 **AICES Bojnice** Hurbanovo námestie 41, Bojnice; ✆ 046 5403 251; e tik.bojnice@stonline.sk; www.bojnice.sk

🆔 **Bojnice Castle information** Sylvia Maliarikova; ✆ 046 5430 633; e marketing@bojnicecastle.sk; www.bojnicecastle.sk. Arranges English-language tours.

🏠 Where to stay and eat
🏠 **Hotel Lipa** (20 beds) Sládkovičova 20; ✆/f 046 5430 308; e recepcia@hotel-lipa-bojnice.sk; www.hotel-lipa-bojnice.sk. Clean & cheerful next to

St Martin's parish church in the centre. Friendly restaurant. $. Dbl $.

🏠 **Garni Hotel Mado** Jesenského 15; ✆ 046

5430 170; f 046 5426 781; www.mado.sk/hotel.
Friendly hotel run by Mado travel office. Sauna,
massage. *Dbl* $.
✗ **Penzión a reštaurácia Pod Zámkom**
Hurbanovo námestie 13; ☎ 046 5412 963;
e enuska@stonline.sk. Typical Slovak dishes, nice
terrace. $. *Open daily 10.00–22.00.*
⌂ **Penzión Družba** (20 rooms) Rekreačná 2;
☎ 046 5402 113; f 046 5402 115; e penzion@

druzba.sk; www.druzba.sk. Located 20mins' brisk
walk from the town centre, Družba has a great view
of Bojnice Chateau. Newly renovated with clean
rooms & FB. $. *Dbl* $.
⌂ **Rekreačné Stredisko** Bojnice-Hlboké; ☎ 046
5423 345; f 046 5426 781; e ck@mado.sk;
www.mado.sk/hlboke. A sports centre with basic but
cheap accommodation in little chalets in the hills
near town. *Dbl* $.

What to see and do
Knight's Days in Bojnice During the summer, crowds flock to see men in tights
creating historical reconstructions and performances.

Kúpalisko (thermal pool) Čajka (*www.sale.sk/cajka; open daily 09.00–19.00;
admission adult 80Sk*). One swimming pool (28°C), two children's pools (29°C).
Leisure facilities include water slides, children's playground, bouncy castles,
volleyball courts and swings.

Bojnice Zoo Zámok a okolie 6 (☎ *046 5402 975; www.zoobojnice.sk; open daily Mar
& Oct 07.00–17.00; Apr, May & Sep 07.00–18.00; Jun–Aug 07.00–19.00; Nov–Feb
07.00–15.00; admission adult/child 70/40Sk, camera 30Sk, video 40Sk student 45Sk*).
Established in 1955, Bojnice Zoo is the oldest in Slovakia. There are 280 species
on show including leopards, condors, orang-utans, antelopes and zebras.

Cycle routes In the Prievidza and Bojnice area there are more than 400km of
signed cycle-tourist routes in Hornonitrianská Kotlina. The routes are good for
road bikes as well as for mountain bikes. The most famous are the Bojnicky
Circle cycle road and nearby radials. The **Bojnicky Circle** along the Upper
Nitra leads under the Stražovské hills, Vtáčnik, the Žiarské hills and Mala Fatra
for 146km.

BOJNICE SPA In the hills, just above Bojnice Castle is a vast spa complex,
extremely popular with German-speaking visitors. The first thermal bath houses
were built at Bojnice in the 16th century. The natural, curative, hydrogen-carbon-
sulphate, calceo-magnesium thermal water gushing from nine springs has
temperatures of 28–52°C for treating diseases of the nervous system. The spa
offers balneotherapy, hydrotherapy, reflex treatment, rehabilitation, therapeutic
physical exercise, thermotherapy, electrotherapy and oxygen therapy in a restful
hilly park setting. I walked into the reception of Hotel Baník and saw an elderly
German lady whom I had spied two minutes earlier getting out of her car. She
already had a half-empty half-litre of lager resting on the desk as she checked in
– not wasting any time getting started on 'the cure'!

⌂ **Where to stay**
⌂ **Bojnice Spa** (510 beds) ☎ 046 5116 362; f 046
5430 026; e info@kupele-bojnice.sk; www.kupele-
bojnice.sk. Guests can choose from a variety of
hotels:

⌂ **Spa House Baník** Category 1A hotel. *Sgl, dbl*
$$.
⌂ **Spa House Mier** Category 1 hotel. *Sgl, dbl* $$.
⌂ **Dependance (hotel annex) Lux** *Sgl, dbl* $$.
⌂ **Dependance Slávia** *Sgl* $, *dbl* $$.

HANDLOVÁ Handlová has a charming centre and St Katarina's Church has a
gorgeous green and red church tower, 45m tall, topped off with a photogenic

onion dome. First mentioned in 1376, the Roman Catholic church was built in Gothic style. Renovated in 1603, it was given a partial Baroque makeover in 1710. In 1945, soldiers trashed the church and new reconstructions began in 1996. In contrast to the colourful tower, the interior is all plain white with an unusual neogothic altar. There is also a sweet white stone mini-church on route 50 leading north out of Handlová.

✘ Where to eat and drink

✘ **Slovenská reštaurácia** Námestie SNP 16. This restaurant comes highly recommended, and not just because they put an England World Cup football match on for us even though they were already watching a quiz show! It's a great venue for a summer evening meal. There are no walls and diners sit under a huge wooden roof around a giant stove. *Mains* $. *Open Sun–Thu 10.00–midnight, Fri–Sat 10.00–04.00.*

CIGEĽ MINING SKANZEN
Hornonitriansky Banský Skanzen (Mining Museum) (m *0903 042 525; admission adult/child 200/130Sk*). This is situated 10km southeast of Bojnice. Visitors can ride underground in a mine truck along a little railway. Tickets are available from Bojnice tourist office (*Hurbanovo námestie, 972 01 Bojnice;* \ *046 5430 303;* e *tik.bojnice@stonline.sk; www.bojnice.sk; tours Tue–Sun 08.30–12.30 & 14.30–17.30; arrange at least one day before*). Baňa Cigeľ (sometimes called just Cigeľ) is south of Prievidza (Trenčín region) next to Sebedražie.

PARTIZÁNSKE The industrial town of Partizánske used to be called Baťovany as it was a satellite of the rapidly expanding Czech shoe-making Baťa empire. The town grew up along the ideals of a garden city for the workers. The coat of arms shows a lady's high-heeled shoe. An older town emblem also showed a fire raging behind a blue hill. The fire was the sign for the SNP (Slovak National Uprising) which took place partly in the town. In recognition of the inhabitants' effort towards the SNP, the town was renamed Partizánske in 1949. There are many interesting castle ruins in the area.

Getting there Partizánske is 26km southwest of Bojnice and Prievidza on route 64.

BRODZANY
AS Pushkin Museum (*958 42 Brodzany;* \ *038 7487 263;* f *038 7487 272; www.snk.sk/brodzany/brodzany.html; open Mon–Fri 09.00–15.30, Sat 10.00–14.00*). Just south of Partizánske is a literary museum dedicated to the Russian romantic poet Alexander Sergeyevitch Pushkin, the only such museum outside Russia. The museum was set up in 1979 in a 17th-century Renaissance chateau where the great poet Pushkin often stayed.

Getting there Brodzany is 4km south of Partizánske off route 593.

BÁNOVCE NAD BEBRAVOU Bánovce nad Bebravou, 13km northwest of Partizánske, has an attractive town centre, crammed with 15 cultural monuments. Visitors can see the beautiful 15th-century church of St Mikuláš and an impressive statue of Ľudovít Štúr (see box, pages 190–1) reminds visitors that the leader of the Slovak National Revival was born nearby in Uhrovec. Just 6km east, the sleepy village of **Uhrovec** hosts an amazing coincidence. Two of Slovakia's most famous historical figures were both born, 106 years apart, in the same little house. Ľudovít Štúr was born on 29 October 1815 and Alexander Dubček came into the world on 27 November 1921. Dubček is buried in Slávičie Údolie cemetery in Bratislava.

Štúr's and Dubček's House in Uhrovec (*956 41 Uhrovec;* \ *032 7694 247;* f *032 7400 753;* e *office@muzeumtn.sk; www.muzeumtn.sk; open May–Oct Tue–Sat 08.00–15.00; Nov–Apr Mon–Fri 08.00–15.00*). Shows photographs, writings and details about the two great men.

Beckov castle ruins (*Open Tue–Sun 09.00–18.00. Knights Errant Association of Beckov Castle; www.bludni.sk*). From the D1 motorway or Bratislava–Košice railway line look east after Nové Mesto nad Váhom. Beckov castle ruins loom up impressively on a 30m limestone crag and are more striking than the famous but inconspicuous Čachtice castle ruins nearby. Built in 1208, it was then known as 'castrum Blundix'. It guarded the border between the Czech and Hungarian kingdoms. At the beginning of the 15th century, Matúš Čák took possession of Beckov. After his death, the ruler Sigismund gave the castle to Stibor zo Stiboríc, a Polish magnate who gave Beckov a redesign and brought in Venetian masons and painters who reconstructed the castle in the Renaissance style, yet preserving many original Gothic elements. The castle passed through many powerful Hungarian families: the Bánffy, Esterházy, Kaniszai and Nádasdy. Some found it uncomfortable and preferred to build mansions near to towns. When the Turks invaded in 1599, Beckov stood firm. It was damaged, like many others, during the Rákóczi uprisings against the Habsburgs and a large fire that broke out in the

THE BLOODY COUNTESS AND THE BAD PR

Čachtice Castle was the home of Hungarian noblewoman Erzsébet Báthory (1560–1614) who was known as the 'Bloody Countess'. In Slovakia, she was called Alžbeta Bátoriová-Nádašdy, krvavá grófka. Báthory allegedly tortured and killed more than 600 girls and then bathed in their blood in order to preserve her beautiful, youthful complexion. According to the legend, one day a servant girl accidentally pulled the countess's hair while arranging it, and Báthory slapped her so hard that her nose bled. She believed that the girl's blood had made her skin young and fresh again, and this is how she came up with the idea of bathing in blood. Erzsébet Báthory was married to Ferenc Nádasdy, a chief commander of Hungarian troops in their war against the Turks. Nádasdy's wedding gift to Elizabeth was Čachtice Castle, then in Upper Hungary (Felvidék). It is alleged that Báthory started to kill young women between the years 1585 and 1610. While her husband lived, she apparently kept her activities to a moderate level, but upon his death any restraints he may have imposed were completely removed.

Her possible victims were mostly local peasant girls, many of whom were lured to Čachtice by offers of well-paid work. When the girls arrived, they were tortured and killed. According to rumours, Báthory had an intense lesbian relationship with her maid Anna Darvulia who encouraged her sadistic tendencies. Darvulia taught her many new torturing techniques and was also involved in black magic and satanic ritual. It was Darvulia that made sure that the victims were only peasants and that no noble girls were taken. After her beloved Darvulia's death, Báthory became more reckless and started picking girls from the surrounding lower nobility. After the parish priest of Čachtice had lodged several complaints with the court in Vienna about the disappearance of girls, Habsburg King Matthias II assigned György Thurzó, the Palatine of Hungary, to investigate these complaints. Báthory and four collaborators were charged with sadistic torture, as well as mass murder. The collaborators charged were her maids, Dorota Sentéšová, Helena Jo and Katarína Benická as well as the dwarf manservant Ján Ujvári, nicknamed Fickó ('chap').

village in 1709 proved deadly. Strong winds blew sparks towards Beckov, setting the wooden structures on fire. Beckov has remained in ruins ever since. Historical and archaeological research was carried out in the 1970s. After the reconstruction in 1996 the ruins were strengthened and opened to the public.

Beckov museum (✆ *032 7777 217; www.obec-beckov.sk; open Tue–Sun 09.00–16.30; admission adult 30Sk, child (6–15) 20Sk, under 6 free)*. Beckov history.

Getting there By car from Bratislava, follow the D61/E75 motorway past Piešťany and exit at Nové Mesto nad Váhom. Head for Kálnica and turn left in town signposted for Beckov. Regular buses from Bratislava to Piešťany, Trenčín or Nové Mesto nad Váhom and change there.

ČACHTICKÝ HRAD CASTLE RUINS Čachtice's story is more interesting than the actual physical remains and is world famous for its association with Erzsébet Báthory, the bloody countess (see box, pages 168–9). The dolomite hill above Višňové village was inhabited in prehistoric times.

The castle is first mentioned in 1276, when it was a royal border fort. Like Beckov, it belonged to Matúš Čák at one time and also Stibor zo Stiboríc owned the castle until 1434. In 1602, a Hungarian commander Ferenc Nádašdy paid

According to the testimonies she applied ruthless methods of torture on her victims: red-hot pokers applied to the face and nose of her victims, opening the mouth and shoving the glowing iron inside. According to the allegations, endless ways of torture dreamed up: sticking pins under the maids' fingernails, covering young women in honey and leaving them to be stung to death by bees, or dousing naked victims in cold water during the harshest winter months until they froze to death. Despite the testimonies against her, Báthory herself was not brought to trial. Instead, she was walled up in a room in her castle, with only a slit to put food and water through. The Bloody Countess lived sealed in the tomb for three-and-a-half years. Her collaborators were all executed in 1611, except for Benická whose guilt could not be proved. She was more likely bullied by the other two maids. The two maids' fingers were ripped off with a pincer and then they were thrown alive into a burning pit. The dwarf, who was found to be less guilty, received a more 'lenient' punishment. He was beheaded first, then was thrown into the pit.

The story of Elizabeth Báthory is one of the bloodiest in history. However, according to many historians, Báthory was innocent. Báthory could have been a victim of a show trial and the case against her was politically motivated. Elizabeth Báthory was a member of the powerful Báthory family who gave a ruler, Gábor Báthory, to Transylvania. Also, after the death of her husband, Báthory inherited a huge wealth and many feared the rising power of the Báthory family in Hungary. The tabloid-style campaign against Elizabeth Báthory served one purpose: to discredit the Báthory family before the Hungarian nobility. According to historians, György Thurzó was behind the campaign, trying everything to blame Báthory for the deaths of the peasant girls who probably died in an epidemic. Báthory was never proved guilty and most of the evidence against her was hearsay. The statements of her accomplices were taken under torture so the veracity of such evidence is questionable. However, historical facts cannot ruin a good story. Báthory has been subject of numerous literary works, music and sensationalist films, teasing audiences with the unimaginable cruelty of the 'Bloody Countess' or 'Lady Dracula'.

36,000 gold coins for Čachtice and gave it to his wife as a wedding present. He died in 1602 and his widow, Erzsébet Báthory inherited the castle. It is alleged she used the castle as a venue for her bloodthirsty deeds between 1585 and 1610. When her crimes were discovered, she was immured in the castle for nearly four years and died there. Legends say that her ghost wanders about the ruins hoping to lure visitors to a snake with a golden key that will lead to hidden treasure. It's worth climbing the steep hill just for the chance of spotting Lady Dracula's spirit. In 1670, the imperial army plundered and set fire to the castle and also Čachtice manor house nearby. In 1708, Rákóczi rebels took over the castle around the time of the Battle of Trenčín and it fell into ruin. There are no roads up to the ruins; visitors have to follow some scraggy paths from Višňové.

Báthory's bloody tale has been the subject of endless books, websites, films and even operas. (See *Further Information*, page 310). A descendant of the Báthory family, Dennis Báthory-Kitsz is working on an opera and his website is http://bathory.org. The website at www.bathory.sk/bat_info/index.htm calls Báthory 'wonderful and cruel'.

RENAISSANCE MANOR HOUSE Malinovského ulica, Čachtice village. (*Open Tue–Sat 09.00–16.30; admission adult 10Sk*)

Getting there Čachtice Castle is situated 95km northeast of Bratislava, 25km from Trenčín. By car, take motorway D61/E75 and exit Piešťany heading for Vrbové. At Krakovany, take route 504 for Nové Mesto nad Váhom. In Čachtice village follow signs to Višňové and the castle. From Trenčín, follow motorway to Nové

Council, the government, of Czecho-Slovak resistance abroad which would lead to the creation of Czechoslovakia in 1918. In 1916, Štefánik and the Czecho-Slovak resistance gathered Czechoslovak troops to fight against Austria-Hungary and Germany. Due to Štefánik's personal diplomatic skills, the Allies recognised the Czechoslovak National Council as a de facto government and the Czechoslovak troops as allied forces in 1918. In January 1919, when the war ended, Štefánik went from Russia to France and Italy, where he organised the retreat of Czechoslovak troops from Siberia. His diplomatic skills were also required to solve arguments between the French and Italian missions in Czechoslovakia. In April, he went to Rome to negotiate at the Italian Ministry of War, where he also met his fiancée Juliana Benzoni for the last time. During this time there were serious arguments between Štefánik and Beneš and also Masaryk, concerning the position of Slovakia within Czechoslovakia. In April, Beneš wrote to a Slovak county head: 'I had a conflict with Štefánik...Everything is over between us. I mean absolutely (over). But keep it totally secret.' In May 1919, Štefánik wanted to return to Slovakia to see his family. He decided to fly from Italy and used an Italian military plane. On 4 May 1919, his plane tried to land in Bratislava, which was then under threat by communist Hungarian troops led by Béla Kun, but crashed near Ivánka pri Dunaji. Štefánik died along with two Italian officers. The reason for the plane crash is disputed to this day. The official explanation at that time was that the plane was shot down 'accidentally', because its Italian tricolour was mistaken for the similar Hungarian flag. Štefánik's sudden death combined with his recent quarrels with Beneš contributed to suspicion amongst Slovaks towards the Czechs during the First Republic of Czechoslovakia. Štefánik's personal motto was: *To Believe, To Love and To Work.*

Mesto nad Váhom and follow signs for Čachtice village. It is possible to walk or cycle from Čachtice main square to the castle, 5km away.

STARÁ TURÁ
Stará Turá Municipal Museum (*Ulica M R Štefánika 4;* ↘ *032 7763 123; open Mar–Sep Mon 13.00–16.00, Wed & Fri 09.00–12.00; Oct–Feb Wed & Fri 09.00–12.00; admission adult/child 40/20Sk*). The museum opened in 1976 in a former Roman Catholic school. In 1989, it became the Municipal Museum. The museum presents a history of the town. A significant part is devoted to a voluntary expedition and a battle from the 1848–49 revolutions near Stará Turá.

Tourist information
🛈 **Infotur Tourist Office** Husitská 3 (Hotel Lipa); ↘/f 032 7763 893; e infotur@stonline.sk; www.staratura.sk; *open Mon–Wed 08.00–16.00, Thu 08.00–15.00, Fri 08.00–17.00; Jul–Aug Sat 09.00–13.00 also.*

BREZOVÁ POD BRADLOM Situated 3km north of the town of Brezová pod Bradlom is Bradlo Hill (543m) and the tomb (Štefánikova mohyla) of Milan Rastislav Štefánik, the great Slovak hero who along with Czechs Tomáš Garyk Masaryk and Edvard Beneš, carved the first Czechoslovakia out of the Austro-Hungarian Empire after World War I. The tomb is a grand white stone mausoleum offering great views of the surrounding countryside. The tomb was designed by the National Artist Dušan Jurkovič. Štefánik was born in **Košariská**, 3km away and the modest one-storey house opened in 1990 as a museum (*906

15 Kosariska; ☎ 034 6242 626; e info@stefanik.info; www.bradlo.sk; open May–Oct daily 08.30–16.30; Nov–Apr Mon–Fri 08.00–16.00, Sat–Sun 10.00–17.00) with photos, letters from Masaryk and uniforms.

Getting there Regular bus connections from Brezová pod Bradlom to Piešťany, Trnava, Bratislava and Trenčín (change in Piešťany or Myjava).

7

Nitra Region

The Nitra region (6,343m²) stretches over the southwestern part of Slovakia where the northern edge of the Pannonian Plain meets the southwestern Carpathian foothills. Around 710,000 inhabitants live in this region, the third-most populated in Slovakia. Nitra has a flattened-off bottom as the Danube flows east, separating Slovakia from Hungary. The northern edge is outlined by the Považský Inovec and Tribeč mountain ranges. The northeastern part is marked by the foothills of the Považský Inovec and Štiavnické mountains. The region is rich in natural resources, including coal and clay, used in brick production. The topography of the region mostly comprises lowland and upland plains. Nitra is one of the warmest regions of Slovakia. The water from the region's Váh, Nitra, Hron and Ipeľ rivers flows into the Danube. Nitra has the most thermal springs in Slovakia, found in the areas of Podunajsko, Ponitrie and Dolné Považie. The majority of the region comprises high-quality flat farmland and it is one of the most productive agricultural areas in the country and known as the nation's breadbasket. Nitra has three protected areas: Ponitrie, the Dunajské wetlands and the Štiavnické Mountains. The region's capital, Nitra, is known as the 'mother of Slovak cities' and is situated on the banks of the Nitra River under the majestic peak of Zobor.

EVENTS IN NITRA REGION

May	**Nitra** *Musica Sacra* International Festival of Sacred Music
June	**Nitra** Pedigree Dog Festival
July	**Topoľčianky** National Stud Farm Championship
August	**Komárno** 'Danube Cup' International swimming competition
September	**Vráble** Vintage Wine Festival
	Nitra *Divadelná Nitra* International Theatre Festival (*www.nitrafest.sk*)
October	**Topoľčany** The famous Great Fair

NITRA *Telephone code 037*

Nitra (Nyitra in Hungarian, Neutra in German) is a spacious, green city with a young, student population, a good football team and a collection of wide-open spaces to relax in. Like Trenčín, Nitra has a beautiful location and, like Rome, it was founded on seven hills. Nitra combines a variety of restaurants, pubs and cafés with a wealth of history and architecture. Sitting on a summer terrace, you can admire the majestic Zobor Mountain rising up in the distance beyond the Nitra River and several expansive parks. Nitra and Bratislava are Slovakia's oldest cities, yet Nitra has a modern, buzzing ambience.

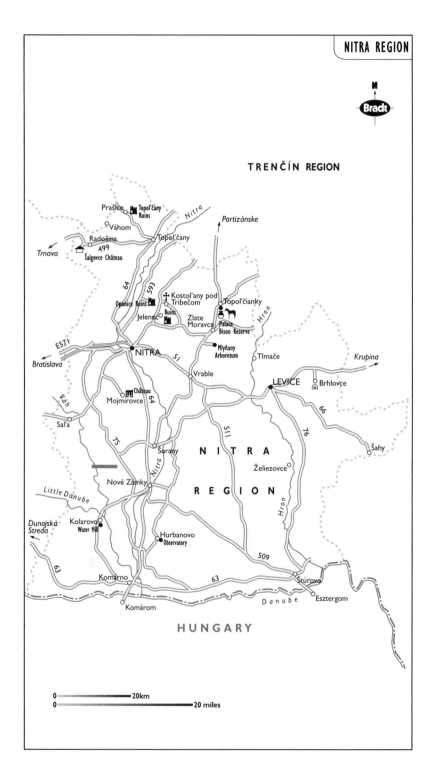

NITRA REGION

TRENČÍN REGION

174

Nitra Castle is the most popular attraction. It's located in the Upper Town which is a harmonious collection of well-preserved historical buildings. The cultural life in Nitra is very rich and a classical guitar festival is organised every year. Nitra's business life revolves around agriculture with the Agrokomplex Convention Centre drawing some 1.5 million participants a year. The Corgoň brewery, now owned by Heineken, produces one of Slovakia's favourite local beers. The areas around Nitra offer all manner of activities. It's rewarding to hike to Zobor Peak (586m) at the southern tip of the Tribeč range, from where there is a lovely view of this lush, wine-growing region. The national natural reserves at Zobor and Lupka are home to numerous species of animals and plants. The forest of chestnut trees in Jelenska Gastanica is particularly interesting to discover.

HISTORY Nitra was the first Slovak city. Small Slavic tribes first settled in the 7th century, although there may have been Quadi tribe settlements here in the 4th century. The colony thrived and eventually grew into the greater Nitra principality, which by the 9th century covered much of what is now west Slovakia.

In 828, Pribina, the first Slavic ruler on Slovak territory, ruled from Nitra. You can see Pribina on the 20Sk banknote. Although a confirmed pagan, he built

CHARACTERS IN NITRA'S HISTORY

SVÄTOPLUK'S TWIGS The well-known legend of Svätopluk's twigs appeared in a 10th-century fairy tale by the enlightened Byzantine Emperor Constantine Porphyrogenet. The Great Moravian King Svätopluk lay dying and asked his sons to go to him. He gave each son a twig and asked them to break it, which they could all do easily. Then he asked them to tie the three twigs together and then snap them. This task was more difficult. The king wanted to demonstrate the importance of unity. In spite of the warning, the Great Moravia was divided among the three brothers in 894. The country was weakened by wars and in 906 it collapsed.

SVORAD was a student of Saints Cyril and Methodius and lived in a cave on Zobor Hill to avoid the temptations of town life, instead spending his days fasting and meditating. However, this wasn't enough and to empathise with Jesus's pain, Svorad tightly wound a chain around his waist. It was so tight that skin grew over it.

VAZUL IN THE TOWER The tower in the east part of the castle area is called *Vazulova veža*. The tower is named after Vazul who was prince of the Nitra domain in the early 11th century. The first Hungarian King István I hated Vazul so much that he imprisoned him in Nitra Castle. In 1031, István's only son, Imre died suddenly while out hunting. Stephan chose his nephew, Péter Orseolo, as his heir. However, cousin Vazul had a legitimate claim to the throne. To thwart this, István sent an executioner to Nitra to blind Prince Vazul and pour hot lead into his ears. This was a brutal act by a king who was later canonised as a saint. Historians tried to defend his cruel act saying it was protecting Christianity against the heathen prince Vazul. In another legend, the monk Fulgentius made a prophesy that Vazul's eyes were like two suns and when he was blinded there were two days of darkness in Nitra. According to reports, this really happened but it coincided with a plague of grasshoppers which destroyed the harvest.

7

Slovakia's first church in Nitra. It was probably a clever political move because the Nitra principality was part of the greater Frankish Kingdom and the Franks used Christianity as a method of increasing their power over the Slavs. Some historians give a more romantic reason; that Pribina built the church as a gift for his Christian wife who came from Germany. In 833, Nitra was conquered by the Moravian Slavs and incorporated into the Great Moravian Empire, which lasted for 74 years before falling to the Magyars who then held sway on and off for the best part of a millennium.

Cyril and Methodius, creators of the Glagolitic (Old Church Slavonic) alphabet, an early precursor of the modern Cyrillic alphabet, participated actively in the formation of the Church and the first bishopric in Nitra. Today, the remains of a basilica discovered under Nitra Castle is believed to have been the first Christian church of western and eastern Slavs. Nitra enjoyed its golden era during the reign of King Svätopluk . One of the most valuable written documents in Slovak history is a letter from Pope John VIII to Svätopluk in 880 in which the Pope addressed Svätopluk as king and informed him of the appointment of Viching as Bishop of Nitra, which by then resembled a town consisting of five fortified settlements and 20 communities where skilled craftsmen worked and traded. The Benedictine monastery of St Hyppolite on the slope of Zobor Hill was the first in Slovakia. In 1248, King Béla IV, in appreciation for protection from the Tartars, promoted Nitra to the status of Free Royal Town with privileges similar to those of Székesfehérvár in Hungary. Medieval Nitra was divided into the Upper Town and Lower Town, each of which was then divided into several districts, each with its own alderman and local seals. There were several attacks by the Ottomans, but by the 18th century, Nitra enjoyed a peaceful existence and as the Upper Town and castle were well protected, they could start construction of many elegant buildings which visitors can see today.

GETTING THERE Nitra is 92km east of Bratislava and its only drawback is access as it's not on the Bratislava–Košice railway line, Slovakia's main train artery. Getting to Nitra by train is not recommended, though. Travellers have to change in Nové Zámky and the entire journey from Bratislava could take as long as three hours.

By car, a swift highway 51/E571 leads off from the Bratislava–Žilina motorway D61/E75 but the junction at the Trnava exit is atrociously signposted and you can end up circling Trnava for days in search of directions for Nitra. Local buses in the Nitra region can also be frustratingly slow, but frequent buses connect Nitra with Bratislava (90 minutes) and other main cities. Nitra bus station information office (✆ 037 7720 566; open Mon–Fri 07.00–17.00).

The main railway and bus stations are situated 1.3km south of the town centre. On leaving the station, walk along Družstevná opposite the entrances, turn left (you'll see the Corgoň Heineken brewery opposite) and follow Štefánikova trieda for 900m until the road forks with the right-hand turning into a pleasant, pedestrian street lined with shops and restaurants before opening out into the vast expanse of Svätoplukovo námestie.

TOURIST INFORMATION AND OTHER PRACTICALITIES

🛈 **Nitra information centre** Štefánikova I; ✆ 037 16 186; 037 7410 906; e info@nitra.sk; www.nitra.sk. Lots of books & postcards for sale, help with accommodation & trips. Open Sep–Jun Mon–Fri 08.00–18.00, Sat 08.00–12.00; Jul–Aug Mon–Fri 08.00–18.00, Sat 09.00–18.00, Sun 14.00–18.00.

$ **Bank** ČSOB, Štefánikova trieda 45, with an ATM. Open Mon–Thu 08.00–18.00, Fri 08.00–17.00. ✉ **Post office** Sládkovičova 2. You'll spy a huge 'Posta' on the roof in white letters by Svätoplukova námestie's vast expanse. Also includes Western Union for changing & sending money. Open Mon–Fri

07.00–19.00, Sat 07.00–12.00.

✚ **Pharmacy Lekáreň U Sv** Rafaela Štefánikova trieda 34. A list on the door gives addresses & opening times of other pharmacies. *Open Mon–Fri*

🏠 WHERE TO STAY

🏠 **Best Western Hotel Koruna** (16 rooms) Svätoplukova 2; ☏ 037 6512 317; f 037 6512 318; e recepcia@hotelkoruna.sk; www.hotelkoruna.sk. Welcoming hotel with a sauna & pool across the river from the centre. *Dbl $$$*

🏠 **Hotel Alexander's** (13 rooms) Mostná 68; ☏ 037 7920 401; e hotel@alexanders.sk; www.alexanders.sk. Great location in the centre with a view of the castle. Concrete box exterior conceals luxurious, Egyptian-themed rooms. *Dbl $$–$$$.*

🏠 **Hotel Capital** (22 rooms, 2 apts) Farská 16; ☏ 037 6925 201; f 037 6925 203; e hotelcapital@hotelcapital.sk; www.hotelcapital.sk. Well situated, smart & friendly with the enthusiastic Symfónia restaurant ($$), pool, sauna & massage. *Dbl $$*

🏠 **Hotel kastiel Mojmirovce** (41 rooms, 3 apts) Mojmirovce 1; ☏ 037 7798 201; f 037 7798 200; www.duv.sk. Gorgeous, renovated Baroque-Classicist chateau (1721) 15mins from Nitra off route 64 to Šurany, turn right at Ivanka pri Nitre. By the hotel is

08.00–17.00.

🛍 **Souvenirs** Lacnoška at Samova 5; m 0903 490 931. *Open Mon–Fri 09.00–12.00 & 13.00–18.00, Sat–Sun 12.00–18.00.*

an English park & a stud, part of Count Hunyady's 18th-century estate. The large stud was the pride of the Hunyady dynasty breeding Arabic, Spanish & Italic horses. In 1814, the first horse races in Austro-Hungary were held here. *Dbl $$.*

🏠 **Hotel Olympia Nitra** (94 rooms) Trieda A Hlinku 57; ☏ 037 6536 727; e olympia@hotelolympia.sk; www.hotelolympia.sk. A cheaper alternative, good for sporty types who can use the fitness centre next door. Restaurant offers healthy cuisine. *Sgl, dbl, trpls $.*

🏠 **Hotel Zlatý Kľúčik** (23 rooms, 4 apts) Svätourbanská 27; ☏ 037 6550 289; e info@zlatyklucik.sk; www.zlaty-klucik.sk. Swanky modern hotel at the foot of mount Zobor. *Dbl $$$.*

🏠 **Hotel Zobor** (60 rooms) Štefánikova trieda 5; ☏ 037 6525 381; www.hotelzobor.sk. Sauna, massage, fitness, Mexico restaurant. *Sgl $, dbl $$.*

✗ WHERE TO EAT AND DRINK

✗ **Boccaccio** Farská 36; ☏ 037 6522 713; www.boccaccio.sk. Great Italian restaurant with a huge wine list & classic dishes prepared by Bolognese chef Oreste Calzolari. Live music from 17.00. *$$. Open Mon–Sat 11.00–midnight, Sun 12.00–midnight.*

🍵 **Bonsaj a Čaj** Pri synagóge 3; ☏ 037 6522 582; www.bonsajacaj.sk. Teahouse, craft shop & Bonsai magazine editorial combined. *Shop open Mon–Fri 09.00–19.30, Sat 08.00–19.30, teahouse open Mon–Sat 10.00–19.30.*

✗ **Hotel Alexander's** Mostná 68; ☏ 037 7920 401; www.alexanders.sk. Imaginative dishes with fresh, local produce. *$$. Open daily 10.00–22.00.*

✗ **Hotel Atrium** Štefánikova trieda 8; ☏ 037 6523 790; www.hotelatriumnitra.sk. Good location, Slovak dishes. *$. Open Mon–Thu 09.00–23.00, Fri–Sat 09.00–midnight, Sun 11.30–23.00.*

🍷 **Irish Times Pub** Kupecká 12; ☏ 037 6575 106; www.irishtimespub.sk. I counted more than 20 Irish themed pubs in Slovakia. Live music & Irish stout.

Open Mon–Thu 08.00–01.00, Fri–Sat 08.00–03.00, Sun 11.00–midnight.

✗ **Mexico** Štefánikova 5; ☏ 037 6525 381; www.hotelzobor.sk. Popular pub restaurant with summer terrace, not-so-spicy dishes & pizzas. *$. Open Mon–Sat 10.00–midnight, Sun 12.00–midnight.*

🍷 **Nitrianska kráľovská vínna cesta (Nitra Royal Wine Road)** www.nkvc.sk. The largest & longest wine route in Slovakia. The four branches (Hornonitrianska, starting at the source of the Nitra River, Tekovská from Topoľčiany & Pukanec, Južnoslovenská from the Danube & Považská from Vrbove & Sered) all meet in Nitra.

🍷 **Pohostinstvo Pod Agátmi** Župné námestie 842, next to Župný dom. Friendly terrace pub just under the Upper Town. *$. Open daily 10.00–22.00.*

✗ **Zlatý Kľúčik** Svätourbanská 27; ☏ 037 6550 289; www.zlatyklucik.sk. Top Nitra restaurant with great presentation, dishes & service. *$$. Open daily 11.00–midnight.*

WHAT TO SEE AND DO The **Sv Emeram Cathedral** (*Katedrálny biskupský chrám svätého Emerama; open Tue–Sun 09.00–12.00 & 13.00–16.00; English-speaking guides at 300Sk per hr should be ordered 3 days in advance from the information*

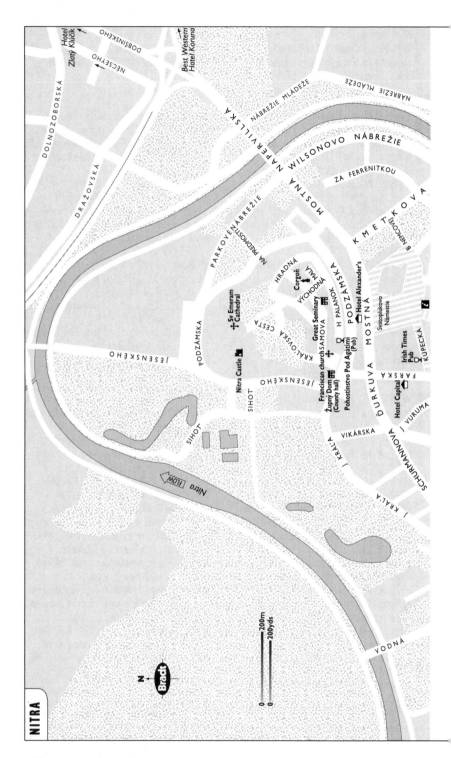

NITRA

Hotel
Zlatý Kľúčik
DOBŠINSKÉHO
NECSEYHO
Best Western
Hotel Koruna
NÁBREŽIE MLADEŽE
NÁBREŽIE MLADEŽE
WILSONOVO NÁBREŽIE
ZA FERRENITKOU
MOSTNÁ
K M E T K O V A
B NECSEYHO
DOLNOZOBORSKÁ
DRAŽOVSKÁ
NAPERVILLSKA
PARKOVÉ NÁBREŽIE
NA PREDMOSTI
HRADNÁ
MALA
Corgoň
VÝCHODNÁ
Sv Emeram
Cathedral
KRÁĽOVSKÁ CESTA
SAMOVA
Great Seminary
H PALÁNOK
PODZÁMSKA
Hotel Alexander's
Svätoplukovo
Námestie
PODZÁMSKA
Nitra Castle
SIHOT
JESENSKÉHO
JESENSKÉHO
Franciscan church
Župný Dom
(County hall)
Pohostinstvo Pod Agátmi
(Pub)
Ď U R K U V A
M O S T N Á
F A R S K A
Hotel Capital
Irish Times
Pub
KUPECKÁ
J VURUMA
SIHOT
SIHOT
VIKÁRSKA
J KRÁĽA
SCHURMANNOVA
J KRÁĽA
VODNÁ
Nitra FLOW
200m
200yds
N
Bradt
0
0

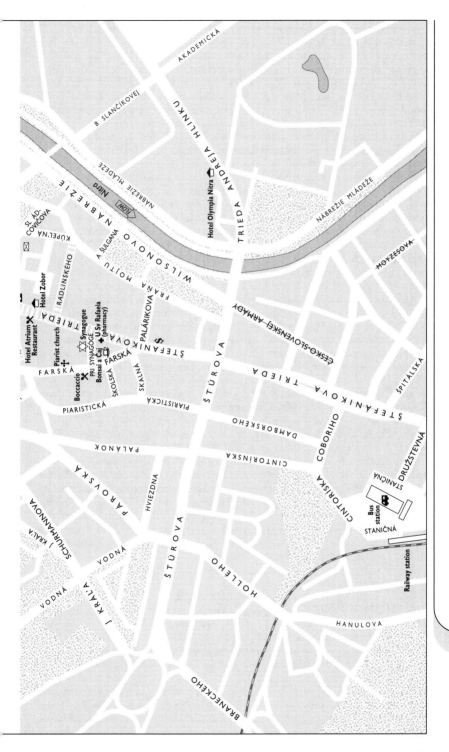

centre) in the heart of the **Upper Town** (*Horné mesto*) is a Gothic structure (1335) and the seat of an Roman Catholic bishopric, founded in 880 as the first bishopric of the western and eastern Slavs. It has a stunning interior and together with the **Bishop's Palace** (*Biskupsky palác*), forms a collection of three religious castle buildings. The **Upper Church** (*Horný kostol*, 1355) is an explosion of red marble and yellow-orange frescoes. An earlier version of **Nitra Castle** (*hrad*) stood here in Samo's 7th-century kingdom. The **Lower Church** (*Dolný Kostol*, 1642) is down some steps and the altar has a splendid 18th-century marble relief of Christ being taken down from the cross, created by the sculptor Pernegger. Down a gentle slope, the Rococo **Marian column** made by Austrian sculptor Martin Vogerl in 1750 commemorates two cholera epidemics in 1710 and 1739. **Pribinovo námestie** is presided over by a statue of Prince **Pribina** holding his sword and contemplating the ugly concrete benches surrounding him. The grand pink building opposite is the **Great Seminary** (*Veľký seminár*) containing a library with 60,000 ancient tomes, facing a **Little Seminary** (*Malý seminár*) on the western side. Next to the pink splendour, *Corgoň* the mythical Atlas figure that Nitra's beer is named after, tirelessly holds up a corner of the **House of Bishop Kluch** at the corner of Vychodná. Slovak sculptor Vavrinec Dunajský from Lubietová created the *Corgoň* in 1820 and you'll see every passer-by rub his worn feet for good luck. Legend tells how Corgoň was a blacksmith in Nitra's Upper Town. He had enormous strength and everyone admired his biceps. When he hit the anvil with his hammer, the whole Upper Town quivered. Head along Východná to Horný Palánok, from where there is a great view over the expanse of **Svátoplukovo námestie** and the houses of the older part of town. Back on Pribinovo námestie, it's a short walk down through narrow cobbled streets, passing the twin-towered 18th-century **Franciscan church** (*Františkánsky kostol Petra a Pavla*). Go under the arch and leave the Upper Town. The custard façade of the **Župný dom** (County Hall) dominates Župné námestie and the **Lower Town** (*Dolné mesto*). The **Nitra museum** (*Ponitrianské Múzeum Štefánikova 1; ☏ 037 7419 771; open Tue–Fri 08.00–17.00 Sat–Sun 10.00–17.00; admission adult/child 50/25Sk*) shows the history of the region and archaeological finds. Follow Mostná ulica north from Svátoplukovo náestie to the river Nitra and loop around to the left passing the football ground and the lovely town park with willows, a lake and woodpigeons cooing hypnotically. The 18th-century **Piarist church** on Farská ulica has two towers and looks beautiful when illuminated. The grand synagogue, a neo-Moorish building created in 1911 by Leopold Baumhorn testifies to the significant pre-War Jewish community. The **Memorial of the Holocaust** (Pri synagóge 3) commemorates more than 5,000 Jews from Nitra who perished in German concentration camps. In 1113, the Jewish community of Nitra was first mentioned in the *Zobor Deed*.

AROUND NITRA

THE SLOVAK MUSEUM OF AGRICULTURE (*Slovenské Polnohospodarske Muzeum, Dlhá 92, 950 50 Nitra; ☏ 037 6523 359; open 1 May–31 Oct Tue–Sun 09.00–17.00; 1 Nov–30 Apr Tue–Fri 09.00–17.00, Sat–Sun for groups with reservations only*). An open-air museum with grain threshing, oil pressing, bread baking and alcohol distilling. To get there, take the bus to Agrokomplex.

LUPKA (249m) is a nature reserve located to the southeast in Dražovce. A typical forest-steppe, it contains irises, wood anemones and meadow pulsatilla on the southern limestone slope. There are wild plum trees and grasses providing a home for rare insects.

ZOBOR HILL (586m) by chair lift (*lanovka*). A great hiking area in the Tribeč hills with a superb view of Nitra and the wine-growing region. There are several taverns in the area and some castle ruins to explore.

JELENEC Situated 12km northeast of Nitra just off route E571 is the village of Jelenec (Gímes in Hungarian). Throughout the Middle Ages it was owned by the same family. The Forgách family were lords of Jelenec for 600 years. From Jelenec, hikers can walk to Gýmeš Castle and reach the castle in 30 minutes on the yellow-marked path from the reservoir past the Remitáž recreation centre. The path leads along a ridge where there once stood *Studený hrad* (Cold Castle).

Where to stay

Autokemping Jelenec ❍ 037 6313 232; e rekreacia.jelenec@stonline.sk; www.jelenec.sk; *open 15 May–30 Sep.* Comprising 20 little chalets set in forested parkland. Watersports, fishing, hiking. $

GÝMEŠ CASTLE RUINS From Jelenec, you can walk up into the Tribeč hills and visit Gýmeš Castle. It was built in 1226 and is one of the wildest set of ruins in Slovakia. Gýmeš fell into ruins in the early 19th century and now nature is steadily taking over; vegetation grows over most of the crumbling stone, hiding much of the ruin and giving the impression from the village of Jelenec below that there are only a few crumbling walls. In fact Gýmeš is one of the larger ruins in Slovakia, with several caverns, intact archways, long tunnels leading from one side to the other, and breathtaking views of the green Nitra Valley below.

KOSTOĽANY POD TRIBEČOM Situated 16km northeast of Nitra in the Tribeč range, just beyond Gýmeš castle ruins, Kostoľany pod Tribečom is a little hamlet with Slovakia's oldest-surviving Christian Church of Sv Juraj (St George) which was built allegedly in the 10th century. It's pre-Romanesque in style and murals depict scenes from the Bible. Follow the red-marked trail for 30 minutes to find Jelenská Gastanica, the oldest chestnut tree plantation in Slovakia, established in 1241 by Count Forgách. Some of the beautiful trees in the 4ha forest are 350 years old.

Getting there From Nitra, take a left off the E571 when you see the sign for Jelenec. Once in the village, take another left at the sign for Gýmeš, and follow the road till you see a board with the castle's history printed in Slovak, German, Hungarian and English. Hike up the yellow trail for about 40 minutes till you reach a fork, then take the green-marked trail for another 10 minutes.

ŠURANY Driving to Nové Zámky on route 64, travellers pass through a succession of uninspiring one-street villages on a flat plain. The countryside towns in the Nitra region resemble those in Hungary with bland bungalows. However, in summer, the fields of red poppies are quite spectacular and look straight out of a Rippl-Rónai painting. The unprepossessing town of Šurany appeared briefly on the BBC, when actor and raconteur Stephen Fry presented an episode of the genealogy programme *Who Do You Think You Are?* Fry discovered that his grandfather, Martin Neumann, a Hungarian Jew, left Šurany in 1927 and emigrated to Bury St Edmunds. In Šurany, Neumann had worked as an agricultural advisor in the largest sugar beet factory in Europe, and was hired to teach the British about the cultivation of sugar beet. Emigrating to the UK, the Neumanns escaped the fate of more than 600 Šurany Jews, who were sent to Auschwitz. Šurany was first mentioned in 1138 as 'Villa Suran' in one of Hungarian king Béla II's documents. During 1663–84 the village was under

Turkish occupation and in 1725 most of it was demolished. In 1832, Emperor František I proclaimed Šurany as a royal town with market rights. In 1835, the first roller mill was built and in 1854 a sugar beet factory, the oldest in Europe. Production of sugar ceased in 2000.

NOVÉ ZÁMKY The first reference to the town writes of a wooden defence fortress against the Turks built on the west bank of the river Nitra in 1545. In 1571, a new fortress was erected on the other side of the river and that's where the name 'New Castles' (Nové Zámky) comes from. In those days it was called Castrum Novum and the fortress had a six-pointed star-shaped ground plan. The layout design can still be seen in the coat of arms. Following liberation after 22 years of Turkish control, the settlement was promoted to the status of town by György Szécseny, the Archbishop of Esztergom. In 1725, the bastions were demolished by Emperor Karol III. Anton Bernolák, a priest and a famous linguist, worked and lived here from 1793 till his death in 1813. His tombstone and his above life-size statue placed in a park that bears his name commemorate his significance for the Slovak nation. Sadly, there are few historical buildings in Nové Zámky as it suffered three heavy aerial bombardments in 1944–45. The Orthodox Jewish Synagogue has a memorial plaque to the victims of the Holocaust. Despite its surrounding natural beauty, Nové Zámky is today known more for its industrial zones with developed electrotechnical, foodstuff and machine industries.

Getting there Route 64 from Nitra. Regular trains and buses from Bratislava.

Where to stay

🏠 **Grand Hotel** (21 rooms) Pribinova 19; | 035 6400 475; e recepcia@hotelgrandnz.sk; www.hotelgrandnz.sk Smart hotel in the centre of town. Sgl & dbl $$.

🏠 **Korzo Hotel** (77 rooms) F Rákócziho ulica 12; ➐ 035 6400 432; e recepcia@hotelkorzonz.sk; www.hotelkorzonz.sk. Modern block hotel with a gym, sauna, pool tables & minigolf. Sgl $, dbl $$.

What to see and do
Thermal spa štrand (lido) (Štrand E Tatárika, Bezručova 21; ➐ 035 6424 252; open Jun–Sep). A well-designed park, ideal for summer relaxation. Three children's pools, one wallowing thermal pool and a 100m water chute.

Vlastivedné Múzeum (Pribinova 6; ➐ 035 6400 032; e muzeum@stonline.sk; open Tue–Sun 10.00–17.00). The museum of local history was established in 1935 and contains more than 20,000 exhibits.

THE FLOATING WATER MILL NEAR KOLÁROVO Mill Museum (➐ 035 7772 045; open May–Sep 10.00–19.00; admission adult/concession 20/10Sk). The only floating water mill in Slovakia can be found at Kolárovo at a meander in the Little Danube River in the southwest part of the Žitný ostrov (Rye Island, see page 148). It's a replica as the original was shipped off to the Slovak village museum in Martin in 1965. A romantic covered wooden bridge leads to the mill. It is the longest bridge with a complete wooden construction in Europe (86m long, 2.25m wide). Nearby are the remains of an earth castle built by Ľudovít the Great in 1349. It was first called the Castle of Peace then renamed Frog Castle. (See page 149 for details of the four other water mills).

Getting there From Nitra, take route 64 for Nové Zámky then head west on route 564, signposted for Kolárovo.

HURBANOVO Between Nové Zámky and Komárno is Hurbanovo, the site of the Hurbanovo Observatory (*Komárňanská 134;* ℡ *035 7602 484;* e *suh@suh.sk; www.suh.sk; open Mon–Fri 07.00–15.30*), built in 1870 and still in operation. Founded by Dr Miklós Konkoly-Thege from Budapest, it is one of the oldest observatories in central Europe. Hurbanovo is also famous throughout Slovakia as the home of the Zlatý Bažant brewery. The signs here are all bilingual: Slovak names in white, Hungarian in blue.

Getting there Route 64 from Nitra, 14km south of Nové Zámky.

✘ **Where to eat**

✘ **Kaštieľ restaurant** Komárňanská 112; ℡ 035 7602 219. One of Slovakia's classiest restaurants situated in the Hurbanovo manor house. $$. Open daily 11.00–22.00.

KOMÁRNO *Telephone code 035*

Komárno is one of the oldest towns in Slovakia. It has been settled continuously since the early Bronze Age. The less interesting half, Komárom, is over the river Danube in Hungary. 'Komár' is Slovak for mosquito, which buzz around irritatingly on summer nights. Komárno grew up around the confluence of the Váh and the Danube.

In 1848, the Hungarian General György Klapka led a rebellion against the Habsburgs and he is remembered in statues, cafés and street names all over town. When the borders were redrawn in the 1920 Trianon Treaty, Komárno was split in two along the Danube and the Magyar Komárom was left without a proper centre.

Komárno (population 40,000) is one of a handful of cities in southern Slovakia dominated by Slovakia's Hungarian majority (locals say the ratio is 70% Hungarian, 30% Slovak). Signs are in both Slovak and Hungarian, restaurants serve spicy Hungarian dishes, the language of choice may be Hungarian, but people addressed in Slovak switch over immediately without obvious irritation. In public places, visitors are greeted with the bilingual '*Dobrý deň–Jó napot*' (good day). Locals appear to get along together well, despite inflammatory comments from politicians like Žilina Mayor Ján Slota.

HISTORY The Romans built a military camp here in the 2nd century, but were pushed out by nomadic Avar tribes in the 4th century. Hungarian tribes took over in the 10th century and built the town's first fortress. King Béla (Belo) IV gave Komárno municipal rights in 1265. The fortress became the focus of the Hungarian Kingdom's anti-Turk defence system. Constructed between 1546 and 1557 and renovated over the centuries, the remains of the Komárno defence system are today the largest bastion fortification in central Europe. You can visit the new fortress (Nová pevnosť) by walking east along Hradná from the centre of town. You can also tour the 11 bastions: it takes an hour to walk around. The fortress defended the city well. The Turks never conquered the city, although they did manage to burn it to the ground in 1529. For 300 years, the town held out against the Turks who besieged it, set it on fire and conquered surrounding lands but never took Komárno.

Komárno was granted the status of a Free Royal Borough by Empress Maria Theresa in 1745. At the time, Komárno was the fifth-largest city in the Hungarian Kingdom with 10,000 inhabitants. The economy was based on trade and crafts, shipbuilding and boats were pulled upstream by teams of horses on the riverbank. Komárno supplied the Royal Court with fish from the 16th

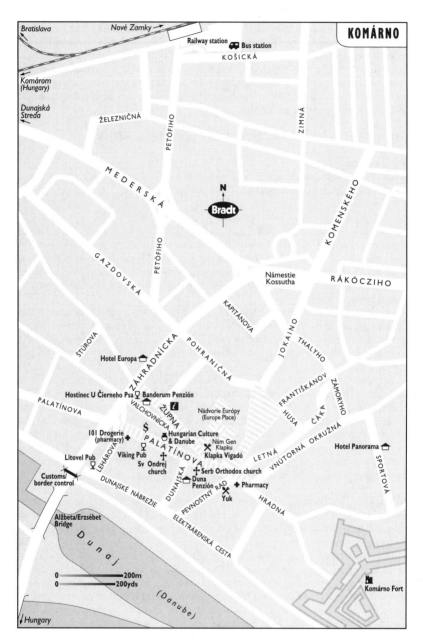

Map labels:

Bratislava · Nové Zamky →
Railway station · Bus station
KOŠICKÁ
Komárom (Hungary)
Dunajská Streda ←
ŽELEZNIČNÁ
PETŐFIHO
ZIMNÁ
MEDERSKÁ
N Bradt
KOMENSKÉHO
PETŐFIHO
GAZDOVSKÁ
Námestie Kossutha
RÁKÓCZIHO
KAPITÁNOVA
ŠTÚROVA
Hotel Europa
POHRANIČNÁ
JOKAINO
THALYHO
ZÁHRADNÍCKA
Hostinec U Čierneho Psa · Banderum Penzión
PALATÍNOVA
VALCHOVNÍCKA
ŽUPNA
Nádvorie Európy (Europe Place)
FRANTIŠKÁNOV
HUSA
ZAMORYHO
ČÁKA
101 Drogerie (pharmacy)
Hungarian Culture & Danube
PALATÍNOVA
Nám Gen Klapku
LEHÁROVA
Litovel Pub · Viking Pub
Sv Ondrej church
Klapka Vigadó
LETNÁ
Hotel Panorama
VNÚTORNÁ OKRUŽNÁ
SPORTOVÁ
Customs/ border control
DUNAJSKÉ NÁBREŽIE
DUNAJSKÁ
Serb Orthodox church
Duna Penzión
PEVNOSTNÝ RAD
Yuk
Pharmacy
HRADNÁ
Alžbeta/Erzsébet Bridge
Dunaj
ELEKTRÁRENSKÁ CESTA
0 — 200m
0 — 200yds
(Danube)
Komárno Fort
Hungary

century. Natural disasters were frequent. Earthquakes damaged the largest structures in 1763–83: a fire in 1848 destroyed two-thirds of the town. Komárno became part of Czechoslovakia in 1920 when the Treaty of Trianon divided the city in half at the Danube. On the Hungarian side of the river is the town of Komárom. Some 40,000 people live in Komárno today; in Komárom there are half that number. Komárno sits at the confluence of the Danube and the Váh, and the economy has been based around shipbuilder Slovenské Lodenice

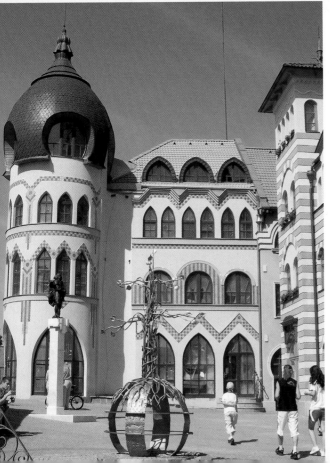

above **Banská Bystrica main square, with the Church of St Francis Xavier and the leaning Clock Tower** (LM) page 233

left **The unique Europe Place features typical architecture from every country in Europe, Komárno** (LM) page 186

left **Man playing the *fujara*, a traditional Slovak woodwind instrument** (STB) page 20
right **The indoor market in Bratislava's Old Town** (SLS/PCL) page 93

above Traditional Slovak dancers
performing in Košice
Slovakia (EJB/Alamy) page 17

right Girl and boy in traditional
Slovakian costume
(PTI/Alamy) page 14

above   **Train in High Tatras** (IIS/Alamy) page 260

below   **Donovaly Ski Resort, Nízke Tatry National Park** (IIS/Alamy) page 238

opposite page   **Rafting on the river Dunajec** (STB) page 267

next page   **The Valley of Five Spišský Tarns, High Tatras** (LG/Alamy) page 260

Komárno (Slovak Shipyards Komárno). In the late 1990s, the firm cut its workforce from 5,500 to 800. The effects were felt all around town: Unemployment is at about 25%, and in Europe Place shopping complex only half of the retail space is occupied.

GETTING THERE Komárno is located approximately 100km southeast of Bratislava.

By train: from Bratislava you have to take a slow local train into Komárno. It takes more than two hours. A quicker, but more expensive method would be to take the international Bratislava–Budapest train (but check it stops in Komárom), get off at Komárom in Hungary and walk across the bridge to Komárno. From Nitra, change at Nove Zámky; the 65km trip takes more than two hours.

Bus is better but the roads are slow. Direct buses from Bratislava take two hours 20 minutes. The train and bus station is situated north of the centre, ten minutes' walk away.

By car from Bratislava take route 63/E575 leading southeast through Šamorín, Dunajská Streda and Veľký Meder.

TOURIST INFORMATION AND OTHER PRACTICALITIES

ℹ Information centre Župná 5; ☏ 035 7730 036; e tik@komarno.sk; www.komarno.sk. Maps & advice. Open Mon–Fri 07.30–15.30.

$ Bank Slovenská Sporiteľňa; Palatínová 33, with an ATM & a bureau de change. Open Mon–Fri 07.30–17.00.

✉ Post office Corner of Záhradnicka & Biskupa Kiralya. Open Mon–Fri 08.00–17.00, Sat 08.00–12.00.

✚ Lekáreň-Gyógyszertár Pharmacy, Hradná 1. Open Mon–Fri 07.30–16.00, closed w/ends.

✚ 101 Drogerie Palatínová 20. A good place to stock up on bargain-priced cosmetics, suntan lotion & mosquito repellent. Open Mon–Fri 08.00–18.00, Sat 08.00–12.00.

🚕 Jasper Taxi m 0905 219 619 or 0903 219 619
🚕 AB Taxi m 0915 222 500

🏠 WHERE TO STAY

🏠 Banderium Penzión Námestie M R Štefánika 11; ☏ 035 7730 156; e info@banderium.sk; www.banderium.sk. Guesthouse in the centre with famous restaurant Banderium. Sgl, dbl $$.

🏠 Duna Penzión Dunajská 2; ☏ 035 7732 273; e penzionduna@stonline.sk; www.penzionduna.sk. Good pension in the centre, with its own salt

inhalation cave. Dbl $.

🏠 Hotel Európa M R Štefánika 1; ☏ 035 7731 349. Dbl $.

🏠 Hotel Panorama (24 rooms, 1 apt) Športová 1; ☏ 035 7713 152; e hotelpanorama@zoznam.sk; www.komarnohotel.sk. Dbl $, apts $$$.

✗ WHERE TO EAT AND DRINK

✗ Ali Baba Okružná 7 (between bastions V & VI); ☏ 035 7710 026; www.alibabakn.szm.sk. Classy restaurant within ancient walls. $$. Open Mon–Fri 10.00–23.00, Sat 10.00–03.00, Sun 11.00–22.00.

✗ Klapka Vigadó Námestie gen Klapku; ☏ 035 7730 053. Historic restaurant, local specialities. $. Open daily 09.00–23.00.

✗ YUK restaurant Pevnostný rad 1–3; ☏ 035 7713 057; www.yuk.sk. Unintentionally classic name. Hungarian cuisine. $$. Open Mon–Thu 10.00–22.00, Fri–Sat 10.00–midnight, Sun 11.00–21.00.

♀ Litovel Pub Dunajské nábrežie 10; ☏ 035 7731 419. Friendly pub with food on the Danube bank. $. Open daily 10.00–23.00.

♀ Hostinec u Čierneho psa Námestie M R Štefánika 14; ☏ 035 7730 701. Good bean soup at the Black Dog pub. $. Open Mon–Thu 10.00–23.00, Fri–Sat 10.00–midnight, Sun 11.00–22.00.

♀ Viking Pub Palatínová 14; m 0905 623 488. Courtyard beer garden. $. Open Mon–Thu 11.00–midnight, Fri–Sat 13.00–02.00, Sun 15.00–midnight.

WHAT TO SEE AND DO Tour the **11 bastions** (bašty) which defendeded against attacks by the Turks and Napoleon. Visitors can tour around all of them in about an hour. The fortresses form an arch over the town of Komárom with the Danube

River providing a flat southern border for the town. Fortresses had been built at the strategic position on the Danube and Váh since Roman times. The defence system proved effective against both the Tatars and Turks and were strengthened again to defend against Napoleon. There are three more forts on the Hungarian side: Monostor (*www.fort-monostor.hu*), the Danube bridgehead and Fort Igmánd.

The squat, stone bastions (*bašta*) were built into mounds ringing the city when Napoleon was tearing through Europe in the early 19th century; they were later used in 1848 by locals revolting against the Habsburgs. The revolution was led by György Klapka, whose statue in the city centre is honoured by Hungarians with flowers every 15 March (commemorating the 1848–49 revolution). At **Komárno Fort** (*Nová pevnosť;* \ *035 7731 476; open Tue–Sat 09.00–17.00*), east of the centre, right on the confluence of the two mighty rivers, you can see the constructions built on Roman foundations. Bašta VI, northeast of the train station, is a good place to begin or end a circle tour (1½ hours by foot) of the city's fortifications. With a **lapidárium** (*Okružná cesta;* \ *035 7731 476; open May–Oct Tue–Sun 10.00–17.00*), and a restaurant, Bašta, it's the best of the bunch.

The **Alžbeta/Erzsébet Bridge** across the Danube connects Komárno, Slovakia to Komárom, Hungary. During the day, it's a constant traffic jam as cars, lorries, pedestrians and cyclists make their way backwards and forwards. If you want to pop into the Tesco superstore, as if you needed another superstore after the overdose in Slovakia, you'll need your passport. Many Slovaks and many of the Hungarian majority living in Komárno cross the bridge daily to work or to buy a Hungarian lottery ticket or groceries. A new bridge replacing the existing 110-year-old Elizabeth Bridge is planned for construction during 2007–10. From the bridge, on Palatínová (Nádor utca in Hungarian), the twin-towered Baroque **Sv Ondrej Church** (1723–34) was radically rebuilt in 1748–56; there was then damage during an earthquake (1769–71), then a fire (1850–60), then the tower was rebuilt in 1896. Opposite the church is the **Múzeum maďarskey kultúry a Podunajská** (*Museum of Hungarian Culture & Danube, Palatínova 13 & Námestie gen Klapku 9; open Tue–Sat 09.00–17.00; admission adult/concession 40/20Sk*), guarded by a statue to Hungarian writer Mór Jókai (born in Komárno in 1825). The **Serb Orthodox Church** (Palatínova 32) has an exhibition of sacral monuments.

Námestie gen Klapku is named after general György Klapka who led the 1848–49 revolt against the Habsburgs. His statue dominates the square and is decorated with flowers every 15 March, the anniversary of the revolution. A figure emerges from a building every day at 10.00 and 16.00 to a Hungarian march melody. Walk through an alley to reach the bizarre **Europe Place** (*Nádvorie Európy*). It's worth visiting Komárno for this alone. Situated in the heart of Komárno, it's a 6,500m² courtyard that resembles a cross between a modern shopping village and a purpose-built Portmeirion, possibly designed to freak out visitors with its other-worldy ambience. Europe Place opened in December 2000 and consists of buildings designed in architectural styles from all European countries and beyond. Transylvanian turrets rise up opposite Iceland's representative, Spain's house features Gaudi-esque orange mosaics, while the Vatican City and Slovenia jostle for elbow room down a side alley. It's all a bit too new and clean but it's fun to wander around and to attempt to guess which architectural style represents which nation. There are several places to sit down and have a swift half if it all gives you a funny turn. **Art Café** (*Open Sun–Thu 10.00–23.00, Fri–Sat 10.00–midnight*) occupies the music pavilion in the centre. This round building with a terrace is an original construction transplanted from an English park where a military band played, and where the composer **Ferenc Lehár** conducted. Lehár, composer of the famous operetta *The Merry Widow*, was

The Beneš decrees refer to a series of laws enacted by the Czechoslovak exile government during World War II and immediately after the war by the first post-war government. The decrees were issued by President Edvard Beneš and were later ratified by the Czechoslovak Provisional National Assembly. The Beneš decrees cover various subjects such as the creation of the Czechoslovak exile government (decrees dated in 1940) and later, the organisation of the post-war Czechoslovak government. However, today, the Beneš decrees refer to the situation of the Germans and Hungarians in post-war Czechoslovakia. The decrees are based on the principle that Germans and Hungarians are collectively responsible for the crimes committed by the Nazis during World War II. The decrees ordered the confiscation of the property of Germans and Hungarians, without compensation. They also ordered the removal of citizenship for people of German and Hungarian ethnic origin. The decrees did not apply to Germans and Hungarians who could prove that they were loyal to Czechoslovakia during the Nazi occupation and were anti-fascist, however, the criteria to qualify as 'anti-fascist' remained vague.

The decrees provided legal basis for the expulsion of ethnic Germans, known as the 'Sudeten Germans', from Czechoslovakia. Sudeten Germans lived in Sudetenland, in the northern part of today's Czech Republic. The decrees themselves do not directly refer to the expulsion. At the Potsdam conference in 1945, the Allied powers agreed to the expulsion of some 11 million ethnic Germans from eastern Germany, Poland, Czechoslovakia and Hungary. After the decrees, some 2.4 million Germans were expelled from Czechoslovakia (around 90% of the ethnic German population). Czech historians say that approximately 19,000 died in the process; Sudeten German groups claim the number is far higher. Some 250,000 Germans, some anti-fascists, and also people required for the post-war reconstruction of the country remained in Czechoslovakia. Hungarians suffered a different fate from the Germans, because the western Allies did not approve the expulsion of ethnic Hungarians from Czechoslovakia, despite the efforts of President Beneš. However, many Hungarians left 'voluntarily' because they were stripped of their citizenship and property. Stripping Hungarians of citizenship meant depriving them of basic civil rights and making life unbearable for them in Czechoslovakia. Hungarian schools were closed down; Hungarian civil servants were fired en masse. In 1946, the Czechoslovak and the Hungarian governments signed a 'population exchange' agreement. Based on this, some 70,000 Hungarians were moved to Hungary in exchange for ethnic Slovaks living in Hungary.

To this day, the Beneš decrees remain a part of the legal order in Slovakia and the Czech Republic. Before the two countries' accession to the European Union in 2004, German politicians tried to make the abolition of the decrees a condition for the Czech Republic's entry. However, according to EU opinion, the decrees were not relevant for the accession and they were never discussed during the accession negotiations. The Czech and the Slovak governments are not willing to abolish the Beneš decrees because this would open the floodgates of property claims from Germans and Hungarians. So far European and international courts have refused to rule on cases concerning the decrees as most international treaties on human rights took effect after 1945/46. The decrees are still a living political issue in Germany, Austria and Hungary.

born in Komárno in 1870. There's a statue to Lehár in the little park next to the bridge, in the place where Lehár's family house once stood. The square and little park were created in 1980 on the 110th anniversary of his birth.

AROUND KOMÁRNO

Boat trips on the Danube (*Kom-Travel; Župná 6;* \ *035 7733 440;* e *info@komtravel.sk*). Organises boat trips in summer to Bratislava, Devín, Hainburg (Austria), Gabčíkovo, Patince, Štúrovo & Visegrád castle knights' festival in Hungary.

Fort Monostor (*www.fort-monostor.hu*). Fort on the Hungarian side of the river.

Danube Cycle Route A section passes through Komárno. It passes through the island of Ostrov Červenej, which is more of a leaf-shaped peninsula, and goes a few hundred metres into the town before continuing along the Danube's northern bank.

Thermal spa Komárno (*Termálne kúpalisko*) (*Vnútorná okružná;* \ *035 7713 014*). A spa with four pools and a water temperature at source of 45°C.

Thermal spa Patince (*Patince-Komárno;* \ *035 7787 754*). Water temperature of 26°C.

HEADING EAST

IŽA About 6km east of Komárno on route 63 to Štúrovo is the little village of Iža with Dievčí hrad (castle), the ruins of the Roman fortification, built at the turn of AD200 as a part of *Limes Romanus*, the fortified border of the Roman Empire. The site is a national cultural monument and will be turned into an open-air museum.

Getting there Route 63 from Komárno.

ŠTÚROVO Patrick Leigh Fermor's novel *A Time of Gifts* ends on the bridge between Štúrovo and Esztergom in Hungary. Štúrovo (Párkány in Hungarian) is named after the greatest Slovak hero Ľudovít Štúr, a writer, teacher, politician and revolutionary who rallied the Slovaks in the 19th century in their struggle for self-determination. When I lived in Budapest, Štúrovo, just over the river from Esztergom was the annual destination for long-term residents having to renew passport stamps for visas, this being the closest border to Budapest. It involved a quick ferry ride over the river and a trip to one of Štúrovo's mini-markets to buy a few bottles of the vastly superior Slovak and Czech beer and then back again. There wasn't a lot to do in Štúrovo and the Budapest city slickers were rather disparaging about Štúrovo's charms. Personally, I always enjoyed the day trip, especially the antiquated ferry and the *Closely Observed Trains* ambience. The ferry was replaced by the 500m **Mária Valéria Bridge** which reopened in October 2001. Originally built in 1895, it was destroyed in 1920 and rebuilt seven years later. Blown up in 1944 by retreating German troops, the bridge waited 57 years for its resurrection as the two constantly bickering nations could never agree on whether they wanted such a convenient, close link. Finally, Slovakia and Hungary each contributed €5 million to go with a €10 million grant from the EU. Whereas locals and visitors beforehand had to rely on a ferry to cross the water or take a 108km detour through Komárno, they can now stroll five minutes into Hungary. **Mária Valéria** was the daughter of Habsburg Emperor Franz Josef I

(1830–1916) and Sisi, sister of Rudolf who committed suicide at Mayerling (see page 114). Štúrovo is the most significant town in the historic Ostrihom region.

Getting there By train, Štúrovo is on the Bratislava–Budapest main line. The trip from Bratislava takes 90 minutes. Bus routes from Bratislava pass through Nové Zámky or Nitra, taking two–four hours.

☞ *POZOR!* The railway station is a 30-minute walk from the town centre. Taxis can be ordered on mobiles 0905 357 280 or 0907 188 655.

 Where to stay and eat

⌂ **Afrodita** (8 rooms) Komenského 119; ☎ 036 7522 413; e afrodita.st@szm.sk; www.afrodita.st.szm.sk. Basic rooms with balconies $.

⌂ **Hotel Atrium** (18 rooms) Hlavná 51; ☎ 036 7512 507; e atrium@hotelatrium.sk; www.hotelatrium.sk. Grand, pink building with a courtyard & nice restaurant. *Dbl* $.

⌂ **Hotel Thermal** (47 rooms) Pri Vadaši 2; ☎ 036 7560 111; hotel@vadas.sk; www.vadas.sk. You can't miss the dark pink building. Friendly & accommodating. *Sgl, dbl* $$.

What to see and do
Thermal pool Vadaš (*Hlavná 34;* ☎ *036 7511 410; www.vadas.sk*). One of Slovakia's biggest thermal pools with a territory of 4,052m² and 5 pools. Temperature at source is 39.7°C. *Open daily 09.00–19.00.*

Esztergom basilica (*Szent István tér 1, Esztergom, Hungary;* ☎ *+36 33 411 895;* e *bazilika.esztergom@muzeum.hu; open Apr–Oct daily 07.00–18.00, rest of year Mon–Fri 07.00–16.00, Sat–Sun 07.00–17.00; admission free*). Take your passport if you want to pop across the river and visit the vast basilica, built by József Hild in 1869.

NORTH FROM ŠTÚROVO

KAMENÍN WINE TRAIL The area north of Štúrovo has one of Slovakia's most important wine-growing areas. The first vineyards were cultivated by the Celts. The ancient tradition, sunny weather and good conditions on the southern slopes of the Farícka uplands produce a rich crop of grapes and delicious white wines. Since its founding in 1999, the membership of the Kamenín Wine Trail grew from six to 16 communities, where wine similar to Tokaj can be sampled in villages such as Búč, Bíňa and Kamenín. The village of Bíňa has large 11th-century ramparts and the wine-growing area at Kamenín on the slopes of the Belianské Hills. The entire Dolné Pohronie (lower stretch by the Hron river) region is part of the wine trail, which is interconnected with the international Danube Cycle Route by the Hron which flows into the Danube near Štúrovo.

LEVICE Levice, a town of 36,000 on the Hron River, is dominated by a 13th-century Gothic castle built on a rocky spur above the marshes to protect the route to the mining towns and the monastery fortress in Hronský Beňadik. In the 16th century, the castle was rebuilt into a Renaissance fortress, when it was incorporated into the kingdom's anti-Turkish defence system. However, the Turks destroyed the castle in the 18th century. It was partially rebuilt in the 20th century, but today remains in ruins. **Dobóovský kaštiel** Renaissance manor house and **Kapitánska budova** in the castle house the **Tekov Museum** (*Sv Michala 40;* ☎ *036 6312 112;* e *tmlevice@nextra.sk; open Jun–Sep Mon–Fri 09.00–18.00, Sat–Sun 10.00–18.00; Nov–Mar Mon–Fri 09.00–16.00, Sun*

Ľudovít Štúr, known then as Ludevít Velislav Štúr, (29 October 1815–12 January 1856) was the leader of the Slovak national revival in the 19th century, the author of the Slovak language standard eventually leading to the contemporary Slovak literary language, an organiser of the Slovak volunteer campaigns during the 1848 revolution in the Kingdom of Hungary, a member of the Diet of the Kingdom of Hungary, politician, Slovak poet, journalist, publisher, teacher, philosopher and linguist.

Štúr was born in Zay-Uhrovec (today's Uhrovec) coincidentally in the same house, where Alexander Dubček was born 106 years later (see pages 167–8), the second child of Samuel and Anna Štúr. He studied in Gyôr (now in Hungary), and excelled at languages: Hungarian, German and Greek. Aged 14, he switched to a school in Bratislava and became a member of the Czech-Slav Society which nurtured his interest in Slavic matters. Aged 16, Štúr composed his first poems. In 1835, Štúr was made co-editor of *Plody* (Fruits), a compilation of works by members of the Czech-Slav Society. A year later, he wrote a letter to the Czech historian František Palacký stating that the Czech language used by Protestants in Slovakia has become incomprehensible for the ordinary Slovaks and proposed the creation of a unified Czechoslovak language, as long as the Czechs would be willing to incorporate some Slovak words. When the Czechs wouldn't agree, Štúr and his friends decided to introduce a completely new Slovak language standard instead. In 1836, Štúr made his famous trip to Devín Castle to hold a meeting of the Slovak national movement where they decided to travel around Slovakia and drum up support for their ideas on national awareness. In 1841, he climbed Kriváň Mountain, an important national symbol for Slovaks. In 1842, Štúr petitioned the Viennese royal court asking the government to stop Hungarians persecuting the locals in Slovakia. A year later, Štúr and friends decided to codify the Slovak language standard, based on central Slovak dialects, into a common language that would unite all Slovaks. Later that year, Štúr was investigated by a special committee and accused of 'treason against the Hungarian

10.00–16.00; Apr–May & Oct Mon–Fri 09.00–16.00, Sat–Sun 10.00–16.00; admission adult/child 40/20Sk) and a concert hall.

Getting there Situated 38km east of Nitra on route 51. Regular buses from Nitra.

Tourist information

🛈 **AICES** office Ulica Sv Michala 2; ➘/f 036 6317 898; e dekampo@stonline.sk

🛈 **Levice info** ➘ 036 6350 263; f 036 6306 901; e pr@levice.sk & manager@levice.sk; http://eng.levice.sk

BRHLOVCE CAVE DWELLINGS Situated 14km east of Levice is a strange village with houses carved into the rocky cliff. The village is mentioned in 1275 when it was called Burfeu. It is thought that the villages carved dwellings into the rocky walls behind their houses to provide shelter from the marauding Turks in the 16th century. In the past similar dwellings could be found at other villages, but in Brhlovce they are still lived in and well preserved. Properties usually consist of a stone house with an enclosed courtyard and individual rooms carved into the south-facing rock. In 1983, the Slovak government declared the homes a Reservation of Folk Architecture, part of the Tekov Museum (Levice). The **cave house at Šurda 142** (*Marta Bozalková;* ➘ *036 6312 112; e tmlevice@nextra.sk; open Nov–Mar by appointment; Apr–Oct Mon, Thu, Sat, Sun 09.00–16.00; admission adults/concessions 20/10Sk*).

homeland'. Štúr lost his job but continued to lecture and publish his work privately. Slovak authors started to use the new Slovak language. In 1847, Štúr became a deputy for Zvolen in the Hungarian Diet in Bratislava. He gave speeches in which he demanded the abolition of serfdom in Hungary, the introduction of civil rights and the use of the Slovak language for teaching in elementary schools. During the 1848–49 revolution against the Habsburgs, Štúr went to Prague to get support for the new Slovak language. On 12 May 1848, the Hungarian government issued a warrant for the leaders of the Slovak movement: Štúr, Hurban and Hodža. Štúr fled to Prague and Zagreb then went to Vienna to participate in the preparations for an armed Slovak uprising. On 19 September 1848, in Myjava, the Slovak National Council declared independence from the Hungarian government and called on the Slovak nation to start an armed uprising. A year later, the Slovak volunteer corps was officially dissolved in Bratislava and the disappointed Štúr retreated to his parents in Uhrovec.

Štúr's brother Karol died in 1851, and Štúr moved into his house in Modra to care for Karol's seven children. He lived there under police supervision. In 1851, Štúr participated in Bratislava meetings concerning the reform of the codified Slovak language standard. In 1852, Štúr wrote his important philosophical work *Das Slawenthum und die Welt der Zukunft* (The Slavdom and the World of the Future), written in German, published in Russian in 1867 and 1909, in German in 1931 and in Slovak only in 1993. In it, he went over the events that brought the Slovaks to their disconsolate situation and suggested as a solution co-operation with Russia, moving from his Slovak national idea to pan-Slavism. In 1852, both his platonic love, Adela Ostrolúcka, died in Vienna and his mother died in Trenčín. Later that year, the only compilation of Štúr's poetry 'Spevy a piesne' (Singing and songs) was published in Bratislava. In December 1855, Štúr inadvertently shot and wounded himself during a deer hunt near Modra. He died 21 days later and a national funeral took place in Modra. Štúr is buried in Modra churchyard (see page 123).

Getting there From Levice, take route 51 for 16km to Zemberovce, turn right in the village and head south to Brhlovce. In Brhlovce, signs reading 'rock dwellings' point the way.

MLYŇANY ARBORETUM NEAR ZLATÉ MORAVCE

The Arboretum Mlyňany (*Vieska nad Žitavou 178, Slepčany;* ↘ *037 6334 571;* f *037 6426 931;* e *arboretum_mlynany@nextra.sk; www.arboretum.sav.sk; open daily 08.00–18.00; admission adult/child 50/20Sk*), situated 20km east of Nitra on the northern edge of the Podunajská lowlands was founded in 1892 by the Hungarian nobleman Dr István Ambrózy-Migazzi and his gardener Józef Mišák. The garden was created with the aim of proving that evergreen woody plants could thrive in Slovakia. Mlyňany contains 2,000 plant species from all over the world as well as 1,133 species of butterfly and 80 species of bird. Ambrozy-Migazzi's garden was inspired by his journeys to Italy and its rich vegetation. The 67ha park has the biggest collection of species of trees in Slovakia. The best time to visit is at the beginning of May when the rhododendrons are in blossom. There are also several lakes with many fish. Visitors can buy a guidebook at the entrance showing routes, all of which are lined with plaques labelling the plants in English.

Getting there From Nitra, take route E571 east towards Zlaté Moravce until you reach Tesárske nad Žitavou. Turn right and look for signs to Vieska nad Žitavou.

TOPOĽČIANKY The village of Topoľčianky, 30km northeast of Nitra, hosts a beautiful, elegant Renaissance palace. There is also a bison reserve and several stud farms. Chateau Topoľčianky, built in the 19th century in the Classical style operates as a hotel and museum.

Getting there From Nitra take route 65/E571 east towards Zlaté Moravce and there head north on route 511 for 6km.

Where to stay

Hotel Zámok Topoľčianky Parková 1; ❯ 037 6301 111; f 037 6301 863; e zamok@jf.sk. The chateau has an impressive façade (1840) with 4 Classical columns forming an arcade balcony. The gorgeous Renaissance courtyard has been sensitively restored. Zámocký Park, the castle grounds (31ha) are a lovely setting for a stroll. The grand building was used by the Habsburgs as a holiday home & also Tomáš Masaryk, first president of the Czechoslovak Republic, made it a presidential retreat. Sauna & massage. Dbl $, presidential suite $$.

What to see and do

Topoľčianky Museum (*Parková 1, Topoľčianky;* ❯ *037 6301 111; www.topolcianky.sk; open May–Aug Tue–Fri 09.00–15.00, Sat–Sun 12.00–16.00; Sep–Apr Tue–Fri 10.00–15.00, Sat–Sun 12.00–16.00; admission adult/concessions 70/50Sk*). Gorgeous furniture and weapons within historic walls.

Winery at Topoľčianky (*Vinárske závody, Cintorínska 31;* ❯ *037 6301 131; e info@vinotop.sk; www.vinotop.sk; free admission, tastings arranged by request, price varies*) Private wine cellars since 1993 producing excellent Chateau Topoľčianky. Regular wine tasting sessions.

National Stud Farm (*Národný žrebčín*) (*Parková 13;* ❯ *037 6301 613; www.nztopolcianky.sk*). Founded in 1921, breeds Arabian and other horses. Horse and carriage rides can also be arranged through the above telephone number.

Hrušov castle ruins The 13th-century ruins of Hrušovský hrad (castle) are found on Skalka Hill. The Gothic castle was built in 1293 and destroyed in 1708. The hike from Topoľčianky, following the green trail takes about three hours and offers beautiful views of the surrounding countryside.

European Bison Reserve (*Zubria obora*) near Zlatno (m *0903 634 369*). The European bison (*zubor*), 2.7m long and 1.9m tall, is the largest European mammal. The best time to see the bison is during feeding from 09.00–10.00.

Getting there From Topoľčianky, head through Žikava to the hamlet of Lovce. The reserve is signposted from the church and leads to the car park 500m from the reserve.

Topoľčany castle ruins Situated on the eastern slopes of the Považský Inovec mountain range, 38km northwest of Topoľčianky, Topoľčiansky hrad is the ruins of a 13th-century Gothic castle, abandoned in the 18th century.

Getting there Topoľčany Castle is near the village of Podhradie. From Nitra, head north on route 64 to Topoľčany and there turn off left. If the first village you come to is Jacovce, you're heading in the right direction. Continue on this minor road for 15km to Podhradie. The blue-marked trail leads from Podhradie to the protected archaeological site at Hole brehy and also Uhrad Hill (684m) with ancient fort foundations.

OPONICE CASTLE RUINS The village of Oponice is located between Nitra and Topoľčany just off route 593. The ruins, situated on a woody hill in the Tríbeč Mountains, are visible from the road. Follow the green-marked trail from Oponice manor house for about an hour. Legend says that Svätopluk, the Great Moravian ruler (see page 175) used to rest here and hid valuable treasure in the area. It will be found when Slovakia needs it most. The castle dates back to the 13th century when it belonged to Matúš Čák. It burnt down in 1645 and fell into ruin. In Oponice there are two palaces, one is a museum, the other, larger building lies in ruins. **Apponyi Museum** (m *0905 117 148; open Mon–Fri 13.00–17.00; admission adult/child 100/50Sk for guided tours in English and German).*

It was once the Apponyi library, at one time the biggest library in the upper lands of the Hungarian Kingdom. Hungarian nobleman Henrich Apponyi raised his niece, Geraldina, in Oponice. In 1938, Geraldina married the Albanian King Zog I and became the last Albanian queen. She died in Tirana in 2002.

Getting there Route 593 from Nitra heading north.

ŠALGOVCE 'THE CHÂTEAU' Hungarian nobleman Baron Šalgo built this Baroque château in 1767. Located between Topoľčany and Piešťany (in Trnava), 'The Château' as the hotel styles itself, is surrounded by rolling countryside and fertile vineyards. It's is run by British couple, Ann and David, and featured on the Channel 4 TV programme *A Place in Slovakia*. The hotel is luxury itself with French and Habsburg period furniture, Venetian crystal chandeliers, antique mirrors and silks from the east. Many of the rooms have original vaulted ceilings. The historic chapel, with its domed ceiling and 18th-century frescoes, is a unique setting for the Altar restaurant, offering a fusion of Slovak and French cuisine plus excellent local wines. The beauty salon offers a range of treatments from the Dead Sea, as well as the Château's unique therapies, using grapes from the Château's own vineyard.

Getting there Šalgovce is situated just off the Piešťany–Topoľčany route 499; turn right in the village of Radošina.

🏠 **Where to stay**

🏠 **Kaštieľ Šalgovce** (12 rooms) Šalgovce 28; \ 038 5395 155; e info@thechateau.sk; www.thechateau.sk. Luxurious, well-appointed rooms and excellent restaurant. $$$. Dbl $$–$$$$.

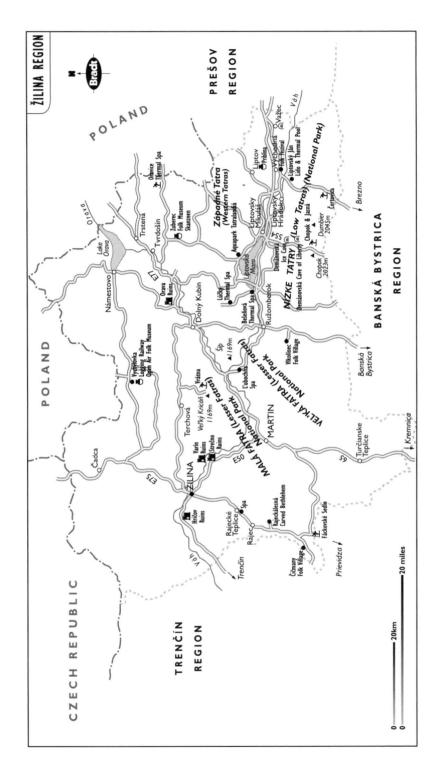

POLAND

PREŠOV
REGION

BANSKÁ BYSTRICA
REGION

TRENČÍN
REGION

CZECH REPUBLIC

POLAND

Čadca

Orava

Lake
Orava

Námestovo

Trstená

Tvrdošín

Oravice
Thermal Spa

Zuberec
Folk Museum
Skanzeen

Západné Tatra
(Western Tatras)

Vysoké Tatra
Tatralandia

Aquapark Tatralandia

Liptovský
Mikuláš

Liptov
Prihlina

Brezno

Váh

Vlažec

Východná
Folk Festival

Liptovský Ján
Lido & Thermal Pool

Liptovský
Hrádocko

Čertovica

NÍZKE TATRY (Low Tatras) (National Park)

Chopok & Jasná

Dumbier
2045m

Chopok
2023m

Demänovská
Ice Cave

Demänovská Cave of Liberty

Liptovská
Mara

Lúčky
Thermal Spa

Bešeňová
Thermal Spa

Ružomberok

Vlkolinec
Folk Village

Banská
Bystrica

Orava
Ruins

Dolný Kubin

E77

Šíp
1169m

Vyšný Kubín

Vychylovka
Logging Railway
Open Air Folk Museum

Terchová

Velký Kriváň
1169m

Vrátna

Ľubochňa
Spa

VEĽKÁ FATRA (Lesser Fatras) National Park

MARTIN

Turčianske
Teplice

Kremnica

65

MALÁ FATRA (Lesser Fatras) National Park

Várin
Ruins

Strečno
Ruins

E50

ŽILINA

E75

Hričov
Ruins

Rajecké
Teplice

Rajec

Rajecká
Spa

Rajecká Lesná
Carved Bethlehem

Fačkovské Sedlo

Prievidza

Trenčín

Čičmany
Folk Village

Váh

0 ___ 20km
0 ___ 20 miles

194

8

Žilina Region

One thing's for certain: you'll never be short of something to do in the Žilina region. This fascinating region borders Poland to the north and the Czech Republic to the west, with 60% of the land covered by forest. The region is made up of valleys surrounded by mountain ranges: the Western Tatras, the Low Tatras, the Great and Little Fatra mountains. In the flatter, lowland regions of Trnava and Nitra, the towns are usually more photogenic and interesting than the surrounding countryside. It's the opposite in the mountainous Žilina region; the delights are mostly rural and natural and the towns often an ugly 1960s' socialist blot on the landscape. On numerous occasions, I have ridden on a bus or train through the most glorious, breathtaking scenery imaginable, only to round a mountainside or emerge from a bend in the road and be faced with a view of unspeakable horror: grim *paneláky* (housing estates) sprouting up amongst the rolling hills like malevolent fungi after an autumn shower. Then there are the factories: ancient, rusting monuments to yet another unsuccessful five-year plan and strangely, yet sadly, always situated in a location of natural beauty. Dolný Kubín's (Lower Kubín) gleaming white concrete housing estates jar with the heart-stoppingly lovely Veľká Fatra landscape, however Vyšný Kubín (Upper Kubín, ironically situated south of Dolný Kubín) is very scenic with amazing houses with wooden onion domes. On the way from Dolný Kubín to Ružomberok, look west and you'll get a fantastic view of the Fatra Mountains across the green plain, a vast expanse of stunning valley. Ružomberok has a legendary odour from the paper factory but is surrounded by superb ski locations. Four national parks fall in the region, including the greatly underestimated Malá Fatra (Little Fatras), Veľká Fatra (Great Fatra), parts of the High Tatras (Vysoké Tatry) and Low Tatras (Nízke Tatry). There are also three protected areas (Kysuce, Horná Orava and the Strážovské Mountains), 62 national nature reserves, 39 natural monuments, around 2,500 cultural monuments, 3 *skanzens* (open-air folk museums), 19 listed monument zones, dozens of ski resorts and thermal spas. The historic Liptov region is known for the Liptovská Mara Reservoir and Mount Kriváň, a peak in the High Tatras that has a special place in Slovak hearts.

EVENTS IN ŽILINA REGION

April	**Čadca** *Pláriková Raková* National amateur theatre festival
June	**Orava Castle** A night-guided tour
July	**Východná** The largest celebration of traditional folklore
August	**Nizna** Rafting days on the Orava River
	Terchová Janošík Days Festival of Folklore
September	**Čadca** *Magnificat* Sacred music festival

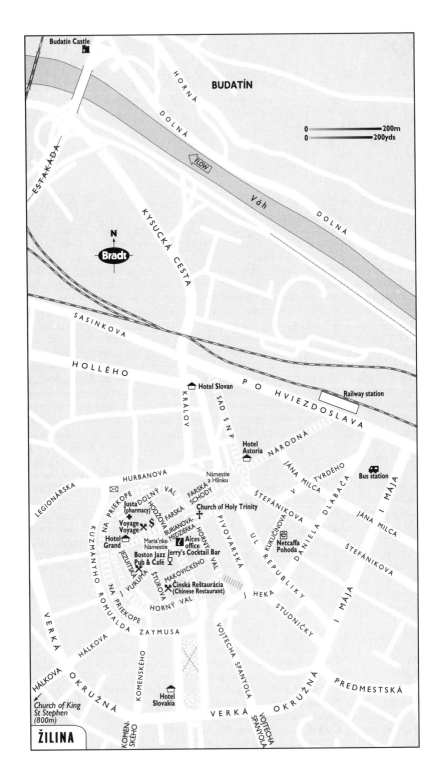

Budatín Castle

HORNÁ

BUDATÍN

DOLNÁ

0 ————— 200m
0 ————— 200yds

ESTAKÁDA

FLOW

Váh

DOLNÁ

KYSUCKÁ CESTA

N

Bradt

SASINKOVA

HOLLÉHO

Hotel Slovan

PO HVIEZDOSLAVA

Railway station

KRÁĽOV

SAD SNP

Hotel
Astoria

NÁRODNÁ

JÁNA MILCA

TVRDÉHO

Bus station

HURBANOVA

Námestie
a Hlinku

ŠTEFÁNIKOVA

DANIELA DLABAČA

I MÁJA

JÁNA MILCA

LEGIONÁRSKA

NA PRIEKOPE

DOLNÝ VAL

Justa
(pharmacy)

HODŽOVA

FARSKÁ

FARSKÁ
SCHODY

Church of Holy Trinity

V

KUKUČÍNOVA

ŠTEFÁNIKOVA

Voyage
Voyage

BURIANOVA

PIVOVARSKÁ

Netcaffa
Pohoda

KUZMÁNYHO

Hotel
Grand

Maria'nke
Námestie

MEDZIERKA

Aices
office

HORNÝ VAL

UL REPUBLIKY

Boston Jazz
Pub & Café

JEZUITSKÁ

J VURUMA

ŠTÚROVA

Jerry's Cocktail Bar

MAKOVICKÉHO

J HEKA

STUDNIČKY

NA PRIEKOPE

Čínska Reštaurácia
(Chinese Restaurant)

HORNÝ VAL

I MÁJA

ROMUALDA ZAYMUSA

VOJTECHA SPANYOLA

OKRUŽNÁ

PREDMESTSKÁ

VERKÁ

HÁLKOVA

HÁLKOVA OKRUŽNÁ

KOMENSKÉHO

Hotel
Slovakia

VERKÁ OKRUŽNÁ

VOJTECHA
SPANYOLA

Church of King
St Stephen
(800m)

KOMEN-
SKÉHO

ŽILINA

Žilina (Sillein in German, Zsolna in Hungarian and Zylina in Polish), situated 198km northeast of Bratislava, is the third most important city in Slovakia (population 86,000). It's located at the confluence of the Váh and Kysuce rivers. The Žilina region contains some of the most important tourist regions with top ski resorts, castles, spas, *skanzens* and glorious mountain countryside right on the doorstep. Despite the fabulous location, nestling in the Žilina Basin surrounded by five mountain ranges: Malá Fatra, Strážovské vrchy, Súľovské vrchy, Javorníky and Kysucká vrchovina and beside the mighty Váh River, the mostly modern, industrial town of Žilina is not one of Slovakia's most attractive cities. Žilina is, however, not without charm and its industrious past and present make it a vibrant business destination and the city centre has a good selection of restaurants and bars, however I would choose another town as a base. The road network of flyovers and unders surrounding Žilina are pretty chaotic and getting in and out of the city, certainly by car, is something of a nightmare.

HISTORY Žilina's territory was settled in the final Ice Age, 20000BC. There were settlements in the part of town now called Závodie. The town was inhabited in the Bronze Age, Iron Age and the Roman era. Slavic tribes settled in Žilina in the 5th century. During the reign of King Béla IV many Germans moved to the town, then called Sillein.

The name 'Žilina' first appeared in 1297 in documents. King Charles Robert I of Anjou during his royal visit in 1321 granted privileges of a Free Royal Town to Žilina which then were confirmed also by Sigismund I of Luxembourg (1397) and by Vladislaw II Jagello (1497). The oldest-surviving manuscript in the Slovak language, the *Žilinská kniha/ Silleiner Buch* (1370), a statement of rights for a free town, was discovered in Žilina. The town was occupied by the Hussites in 1429–35 and devastated by fire in 1521. Despite setbacks, Žilina prospered until the end of the 17th century when guilds of furriers, tailors, butchers, blacksmiths and drapers, etc worked here. At the end of the 17th century there were 16 guilds in Žilina and 200 manufacturers, 150 of them being drapers. During the Thirty Years War (1618–48), Žilina was repeatedly plundered and pillaged and went into a decline and only emerged from the slump at the end of the 19th century with the construction of the railway line. The Košice–Bohumín Railway was completed in 1872 and the Považská Railway to Bratislava in 1883. Žilina became an important railway hub for the Czechoslovak territories and a centre of forestry, chemical and engineering industries. The Battles of Budatín in 1848–49 saw important victories for Slovak rights when they overcame the Hungarian guards. After the battle on 4 January 1849, Ľudovit Štúr and Jozef Miloslav Hurban delivered rousing speeches calling on the people of Žilina to fight for national interests at what is now the Square of the Virigin Mary. A plaque on the wall at number 7 commemorates the event. Žilina has long been a hotbed of political life in Slovakia. In October 1938, seven political parties held talks and proclaimed the sovereignty of Slovakia, announced from the balcony of the Catholic House by Jozef Tiso. In 1938, controversial Catholic priest Andrej Hlinka (see page 199) organised a coalition meeting in Žilina to sign a formal demand for Slovak autonomy. He is remembered with a large statue (Otec národa – Father of the Nation) in front of the Tesco superstore on Námestie A Hlinku. Žilina's former mayor and nationalist politician Ján Slota (see page 11) continues the tradition of controversial leaders by making inflammatory statements about Hungarian and Roma minorities. Žilina and Trnava are the two most successful regions in terms of foreign investment. Korean giant Kia Hyundai is building its first European production base, a €1.1 billion investment, in Žilina.

Production of 300,000 cars a year should start in 2007. Under Slota, the city has installed an 800-million-koruna ecologically sound trolleybus system that has cut harmful emissions by 35%.

GETTING THERE There are frequent train connections along the main Bratislava–Košice line ($2^{1}/_{2}$ hours). Žilina is also well connected by bus to Bratislava and other cities. By car, take route E75 north from Bratislava to Žilina (198km; $2^{1}/_{2}$ hours).

TOURIST INFORMATION AND OTHER PRACTICALITIES

⊞ AICES office Burianova medzierka 4; ☎ 041 5620 789; e selinan@selinan.sk; www.selinan.sk. Tourist advice in a travel agents. *Open Sep–Jun Mon–Fri 10.00–17.00; Jul–Aug Mon–Fri 08.30–18.00, Sat 08.00–12.00, Sun closed.*

$ TatraBanka Mariánske námestie & Hodžova corner. ATM. *Open Mon–Fri 08.00–18.00, Sat 08.00–12.00.*

✉ Post office Na priekope; ☎ 041 5620 360. *Open Mon–Fri 08.00–16.00.*

✚ Pharmacy Lekáreň Justa, Sladkovičova 10. *Open Mon–Fri 08.00–17.00.*

🖳 Internet Netcaffa Pohoda Kukučínova 8; ☎ 041 5640 099. A proper café with orange walls & a nice, calm space; 8 machines, 39Sk per hr. *Open Mon–Thu 09.00–22.00, Fri 09.00–midnight, Sat 14.00–22.00, Sun closed.*

⌂ WHERE TO STAY If you have your own transport, the best place to stay in the Žilina region is Rajecké Teplice (11km south, see page 200), a lovely, relaxing spa town set in idyllic countryside. If you want to stay right in Žilina, here are some ideas.

⌂ Hotel Astoria (24 rooms) Národná 1; ☎ 041 5624 714; e manager@astoria-zilina.sk; www.astoria-zilina.sk. Modern hotel by Námestie A Hlinku. *Dbl $$.*

⌂ Hotel Grand (28 rooms) Sladkovičova 1; ☎ 041 5643 265; f 041 5643 266; e recepcia@hotelgrand.sk; www.hotelgrand.sk. Near the main square, comfortable rooms. *Sgl $$, dbl $$$.*

⌂ Hotel Slovakia (140 rooms) Námestie Ľ Štúra 2; ☎ 041 5124 111; e hotelslovakiamanager@ bb.telecom.sk; www.telecom.sk/hotelslovakia. Massive hotel with solarium, pool, massage & sauna. *Sgl, dbl $$.*

⌂ Hotel Slovan A Kmeťa 2; ☎ 041 5620 134; e hotel_slovan@stonline.sk; www.slovan-hotel.sk A modest 1960s-style hotel near the station. *Sgl $, dbl $$.*

✗ WHERE TO EAT AND DRINK Marianské námestie is completely surrounded by restaurants, cafés and bars which spread out onto the square in warmer seasons.

✗ Boston Jazz Pub and Café Mariánske námestie 24; m 0905 481 219. Good pizzas & grilled meats. *$. Open Mon–Thu 10.00–midnight, Fri 10.00–02.00, Sat 15.00–02.00, Sun 15.00–midnight.*

✗ Čínska reštaurácia Štúrova 5; ☎ 041 5626 674. Friendly Chinese restaurant just off the main square. *$. Open daily 08.00–23.00.*

♀ Jerry's Cocktail bar Mariánske námestie 21;

www.jerrys-bar.sk. A chic, plum and vanilla-coloured bar. *Open Mon–Thu 09.00–01.00, Fri 09.00–02.00, Sat 12.00–02.00, Sun 12.00–01.00.*

✗ Voyage Voyage Mariánske námestie 191; ☎ 041 5640 230; www.voyagevoyage.sk. Possibly the longest menu in central Europe. *$. Open Mon–Thu 08.00–midnight, Fri 08.00–02.00, Sat 09.00–02.00, Sun 10.00–23.00.*

WHAT TO SEE AND DO The most important and oldest architectural relic in Žilina is the **Church of King St Stephen (1200–50)**. A statue of controversial priest Andrej Hlinka is found on **Námestie A Hlinku** near a heart-shaped fountain beneath the **Church of the Holy Trinity** (1400) next to a Renaissance belfry, the **Burian Tower** (1530), dominating the Old Town.

The **Farské schody** (parsonage stairway) with 106 steps leads to **Mariánske námestie** (Square of the Virgin Mary), which is surrounded by arcaded 16th–17th-century burgher houses. Marianske námestie is a colourful

Andrej Hlinka (1864–1938) was a Catholic priest, whose name is inseparable from the Slovak independence movement of the 20th century. Before World War I, Hlinka regularly stood up to the Hungarian authorities, defending the rights of Slovaks. Under Hungarian rule, Slovaks were subjected to brutal Magyarisation, the forced assimilation into Hungarian culture. Slovaks had no right to use their mother tongue and the compulsory education was in Hungarian. Hlinka was arrested several times for incitement by the Hungarian authorities and sent to prison. In 1905, Hlinka became priest of his hometown, Ružomberok. The same year, Hlinka co-founded the Slovak People's Party, the first ever Slovak party, whose goal was to gain rights for Slovaks. Hlinka supported the idea that Slovakia should split from the Kingdom of Hungary. He also signed the Martin Declaration in 1918, expressing the Slovak politicians' urge to unite with their Slav brothers, the Czechs.

In the first Czechoslovak elections, Hlinka's Slovak People's Party won the biggest share of the Slovak vote. Later, the party's representatives started to pursue their demands for autonomy. This aim was achieved in March 1939, just before the beginning of World War II. However, the newly created Slovakia, led by Hlinka's successor, Catholic priest Josef Tiso, was little more than a Nazi puppet state. Although Andrej Hlinka died before the creation of an independent Slovak state, he was adopted as one of the symbols of the pro-Nazi republic. The infamous Slovak Nazi police troops, the Hlinka Guards, were named after him. Hlinka is a controversial figure in Slovak history. During the communist era, he was labelled as a 'clerofascist'. However, since the Velvet Revolution, Hlinka was re-evaluated. Many Slovaks honour him as the 'Father of the Slovak nation', streets are named after him and he is portrayed on the Slovak 1,000Sk banknote.

One of the most peculiar mysteries in Slovak history is the disappearance of Hlinka's body. His embalmed body lay in the Hlinka mausoleum in Ružomberok between 1941 and 1945. Later, when the Russian front was approaching, the body was removed to the safety of a crypt of St Martin's Cathedral in Bratislava. The body was last seen there in the 1960s and what happened to it thereafter is a mystery. There are various theories: some say the communists hid it, others that Hlinka's admirers took the body. During the 1968 Prague Spring soviet troops stormed St Martin's Cathedral crypt and fired shots at the empty glass coffin, supporting the theory that the communists were out there to destroy Hlinka's memory. Someone claimed that the body was located in Malacky, then others claimed it was in Ružomberok. There is also a popular legend that sounds like something from the *Da Vinci Code*. Three people took the body to protect it. When one of them dies, the remaining two confide in another person so there are always three people who know the location of the body, and they are waiting for an appropriate moment to reveal it. According to a more credible theory, the body is still somewhere in St Martin's Cathedral crypt. In 1990, there was an official investigation exhuming and examining five of the 100 tombs sealed into the crypt's walls. However, Hlinka's body was not in any of them. There is an ongoing debate whether a new investigation should be launched. Some people would like to carry on the examination of the remaining tombs; others prefer to let the dead rest in peace.

cobblestoned space lined with dozens of cafés, a pyramid fountain, a bronze statue of an angel plus a fairytale Jesuit St Paul's church with twin pointed towers. Visitors can dine at Chinese, Korean and Italian restaurants, but the most typical dish of the region is *bryndzové halušky* and dairy products made with sheep's cheese such as *korbáčiky, parenica* and *oštiepok*. From the northern part of town, visitors can spy **Dubník peak** (608m). Every year on 17 July, the declaration of the Slovak Republic is celebrated with a Bonfire of Sovereignty. On the top of the **Straník Hill** (769m) are two ski lifts, and it has the best conditions for paragliding in Slovakia with frequent competitions held here. The **Považská galéria umenia** (*Štefánikova; open Tue–Fri 09.00–17.00, Sat–Sun 10.00–17.00*) houses temporary contemporary art exhibitions, while nearby, the **Museum of Jewish Culture** (*Múzeum Židovskej Kultuřry*) (*Ulica Daniela Dlabača;* m *0908 694 333; open Fri 15.30–17.00, Sun 14.30–17.00*) documents Žilina's pre-war Jewish community of about 3,500. **Budatín Castle** (Budatínsky zámok) (*Topoľová 1;* ℄ *041 5001 511;* f *041 5620 033;* e *muzeum@pmza.sk; www.pmza.sk; open Sep–May Tue–Sun 08.00–15.30; Jun–Aug Mon 08.00–15.00, Tue–Sun 08.00–16.30; admission adult/concessions 40/20Sk*) was built during the refortification of the country after the Tatar invasion in the middle of the 13th century. It was a water castle, protected by the Váh and Kysuca rivers and a moat. The castle became involved in the revolutionary events of 1848–49 and on 10 January 1849 it was burned nearly to the ground and left to rot for decades. Today it houses exhibitions by the **Považie Museum in Žilina**. Among archaeological and historical exhibitions is the **Tinker Trade** display, which claims to be the only one of its kind in the world. June 2007 sees the 4th International Tinker Festival.

AROUND ŽILINA

HRIČOV CASTLE RUINS Situated 8km west of Žilina, the ruins of Hričov Castle looms over Hričovské Podhradie village. This Gothic castle was built in 1265 and fell into ruins in the 17th century. Built on a steep rocky hill south of the river Váh, it is a small yet attractive ruin in the central Povazie area. The first mention of a settlement at Hričovské Podhradie dates back to Mátyás Corvinus's reign. At the end of the 17th century, the castle was damaged by lightning and fell into decline. Some walls inside still have the original plasterwork. There is a small cave on the hill's western side where archaeologists found ceramics from the Greater Moravian Empire period.

Getting there Route 61 heading west out of Žilina, turn left at Hričovské Podhradie.

RAJECKÉ TEPLICE Rajecké Teplice, 11km south from Žilina, is an idyllic spa town, nestling in the bosom of the Malá Fatra Mountains and basking in excellent sunny weather for most of the year. A cluster of spa buildings and hotels are situated around a park and lake, the jewel of these being the luxurious Aphrodite. The Strážovské vrchy cliffs tower above and visitors can potter about the park, go for a swim, take a water cure or play tennis.

Getting there and away From Žilina take the local train or bus to Rajecké Teplice, 11km south. The local train takes 30 minutes; frequent buses take 20–30 minutes. Buses continually leave Rajecké Teplice bus station, in front of the Veľká Fatra Hotel for all destinations in the region.

Tourist information and other practicalities
⛵ **Rajecká Pohoda** Tourist information centre, Osloboditeľov 90; ℄ 041 5494 368; m 0908 935 321; e infocentrum@rajeckapohoda.sk; www.rajeckapohoda.sk. Open May–Sep daily

09.00–21.00; Oct–Apr Wed–Sun 09.00–18.00.
✉ **Post office** Školská 25. Open Mon, Tue, Thu, Fri 08.30–16.00, Wed 08.30–17.00.

⌂ Where to stay

⌂ **Hotel Aphrodite** (Slovenské liečebné kúpele) (47 rooms, 8 suites) Rajecké Teplice; ⟍ 041 5494 256; f 041 5493 674; e spa@spa.sk; www.spa.sk. A 4-star luxury health resort situated in the halcyon spa town of Rajecké Teplice & surrounded on all sides by the stunning Malá Fatra Mountains. From the stained-glass cupola, gold filigree & Roman columns of the reception areas to the pristine, stainless-steel Water World, it's all top of the range for quality & comfort. Sauna world contains a huge range of different style saunas decorated with gorgeous Ottoman mosaics. Good restaurant & café. Come for a cure or just relax: a range of packages available. Great advice on day trips. *Sgl* $$, *dbl* $$–$$$.

⌂ **Hotel Veľká Fatra** (46 rooms, 4 suites) Rajecké Teplice; ⟍ 041 5494 256; f 041 5493 674; e spa@spa.sk; www.spa.sk. Connected to Hotel Aphrodite by a covered bridge so you can stay in less glamorous surroundings but still enjoy the facilities & walk around in your cossie. Good bar & restaurant. *Sgl* $, *dbl* $$.

⌂ **Medical House (MH) Laura** (20 rooms) Rajecké Teplice; ⟍ 041 5494 256; f 041 5493 674; e spa@spa.sk; www.spa.sk. Right next to the huge outdoor pool (free use), a short walk from the other spa hotels. *Sgl, dbl* $.

⌂ **Skalka** (124 rooms) Rajecké Teplice; ⟍ 041 5494 256; f 041 5493 674; e spa@spa.sk; www.spa.sk. The recently renovated Baník Therapeutic House reopened as the Skalka with 3-star accommodation & gorgeous park surroundings. Situated 500m from the Hotel Aphrodite. Excellent rates. *Sgl, dbl* $.

⌂ **Villa Flóra** (5 rooms, 3 suites) Rajecké Teplice; ⟍ 041 5494 256; f 041 5493 674; e spa@spa.sk; www.spa.sk. Accommodation in a villa by the beautiful lake. Guests use the restaurant & facilities of Veľká Fatra Hotel. *Sgl* $, *dbl* $$.

⌂ **Villa Margaréta** (8 rooms) Rajecké Teplice; ⟍ 041 5494 256; f 041 5493 674; e spa@spa.sk; www.spa.sk. Luxurious accommodation in a modern villa with a lovely garden. Guests use the restaurant & facilities of of Veľká Fatra Hotel. *Dbl* $$.

✗ Where to eat and drink

✗ **Encián Restaurant & Marco Pizzeria** Osloboditeľov 90; ⟍ 041 5493 093. A friendly place with 26 good-value pizzas, meat, fish & poultry dishes. $. *Open Sun–Thu 09.00–22.00, Fri–Sat 09.00–23.00.*

✗ **Rybárska Bašta** (Fisherman's Bastion) On a little island in the lake & belonging to the Aphrodite, it's a lovely, romantic restaurant on balmy summer evenings when the lake has magical illuminations. Fish is the speciality here & they do it very well. Great wine list. *Open Mon–Thu 11.00–23.00, Fri–Sat 10.00–midnight, Sun 10.00–23.00.*

What to see and do

Thermal Pool Laura (*Open daily 09.00–19.00; admission adult/child 80/50Sk before 16.00, 50/40Sk after 16.00*). Large outdoor pool with free entry for guests at Hotel Laura. Mini-golf 50Sk.

Soľná Jaskyňa (*Osloboditeľov 83; ⟍ 041 5493 528; open daily 10.00–22.00; prices start from 200Sk*) A salt cave opposite the Aphrodite with blocks of salt from Pakistan and Poland. Breathing this for 45 minutes is good for the skin and nerves.

Kunerad mansion Walk for 6km through the most glorious countryside to this elegant yet crumbling chateau, awaiting reconstruction. Built in 1916, the chateau was the HQ for the 2nd partisan brigade during the Slovak National Uprising (Slovenské národné povstanie, or SNP).

Hiking in the region Nearby, up a steep hill is the **Budzogáň**, a rock shaped like a medieval mace. **Súľovské skaly** to **Slnečné Skaly** and several ruined castles are popular destinations.

Bicycle hire (⟍ *0915 837 480; open 08.00–20.00*). Charges: 100Sk for 1hr, 200Sk for 2hrs, 300Sk for 4hrs, 400Sk all day.

LIETAVA CASTLE RUINS Situated on Cibuľník Hill (633m) is the ruins of Lietavský hrad (castle) dating from the 13th century, and reconstructed frequently in the 15th and 16th centuries. It's a lovely hiking destination with great views.

Getting there From Žilina by bus to Lietava or Lietavská Svinná. From the Lietava bus stop hike along the blue trail up Cibuľník Mountain (395m). From Lietavská Svinná village centre, follow the blue trail up Cibuľník.

SÚĽOV CASTLE RUINS Súľovský hrad (castle) was built in 1470 in the natural reservation of Súľovské skaly at an altitude of 550m. The now-ruined castle is overlooked by Brada Mountain (816m).

Getting there The town of Bytča is a stop on the Bratislava–Žilina main railway line. From there, take a bus to Súľov then follow the red trail.

HEADING SOUTH FROM ŽILINA

RAJEC The hilly surroundings are famous for woodcarvers, tanners and furriers. See the craft traditions at the **Mestské Múzeum** on Námestie SNP 15 (↘ *041 5422 198; open Mon–Fri 08.00–15.00*). **Thermal spa Veronika** (*www.veronika-rajec.sk; open May–Jun Mon–Fri 10.00–18.00, Sat–Sun 09.00–18.00; Jul–Sep Mon–Fri 09.30–18.00, Sat–Sun 09.00–19.00; admission adult/child 110/70Sk*) has seven swimming pools, a beach volleyball court, a mini-golf course, table tennis and a basketball ground.

Rajecká Lesná Slovenský Betlehem (Rajecká Lesná; ↘ 041 5488 134; www.rajeckalesna.sk; *open all year 09.00–12.00 & 13.00–18.00. Holy mass Mon–Sat 11.00 & 18.00, Sun 08.30, 10.30, 16.00*).A little village off the Žilina–Prievidza main road (route 64) conceals an amazing woodcarving tableau. Pictures and tour guide descriptions really don't do justice to this incredible feat of linden woodwork. Master Jozef Pekara from Rajecké Teplice worked on the carving for 15 years and it was blessed on 26 November 1994 by the Bishop of Nitra. The Bethlehem is located in a specially built building next to the church. The enormous tableau (8.5m x3m x2.5m) featuring scenes from Slovak rural life, important buildings and religious scenes is incredibly detailed and, what's more, it moves! Trains chug through mountain tunnels, blacksmiths hammer anvils and peasants trudge uphill. There is also a lot of humour incorporated in the scenes: groups of wine tasters, folk musicians and log rollers are all depicted with great care and affection. Children and adults alike are entranced. Upstairs there is a gift shop with religious items and postcards.

Getting there Around 10km south of Rajecké Teplice on route 64. Buses from Žilina main bus station take 45 minutes; change at Rajec.

ČIČMANY Declared a historical reservation in 1979, the village of Čičmany is a living folk architecture museum, situated in the Strážovské Vrchy Mountains. In the 15th century, Bulgarians who fled the Turks came to the region and started decorating their houses with Balkan-style folk motifs. The dark wooden walls were painted with white designs: abstract geometric shapes, crosses, hearts, squiggles and swirls. As well as being decorative, the embellishments are also useful. The white paint is a lime varnish applied to protect the wood from natural decay. The designs are inspired by patterns embroidered into local folk costume.

A few pensions in town offer simple, cheap accommodation in the unique homes. In the winter, skiers take to the village's slopes on Javorinka Hill (972m), just to the south, and at the nearby Javorina ski resort. In the summer, there is hiking in the surrounding Strážovské hills.

The **Považské Múzeum** (✆/f *041 5001 511;* e *email.muzeum@pmza.sk; www.pmza.sk; open Tue–Sun 08.00–18.00, Mon 10.00–16.00; admission 20Sk*) owns two buildings, the Radena House and house number 42.

Getting there By bus: from Žilina, buses take 50 minutes and stop at the road leading into the village, 7km away. From here take a local bus or hike.

By car from Žilina, take route 64 south towards Prievidza, then turn right when you see the signs for Čičmany; journey time 30 minutes.

Tourist information
🛈 **Anna Kotercová** m 0907 298 583; www.cicmany-info.sk

🏠 **Where to stay and eat**

🏠 **Hotel Kaštieľ** Čičmany; ✆ 041 5492 119; m 0907 296 814; www.kastiel.cicmany.szm.sk. Elegant white chateau with popular restaurant (*open daily 09.00–21.00*), pub (*open daily 09.00–midnight*) &

bargain accommodation. *Dbl* $
🏠 **Penzión Katka** Čičmany No 50; ✆ 041 5492 132; m 0907 172 973; e penzionkatka@stonline.sk. Stay in one of the painted log cabins. *Dbl* $.

FAČKOVSKÉ SEDLO Situated on the saddle (*sedlo*) of a range in the south of the Malá Fatra hills, this is a traditional starting point for many hikes. There are also several ski lodges, lifts and slopes and a great restaurant.

🏠 **Where to stay and eat**

🏠 **Chata Energetik** turistická ubytovňa, Fačkovské sedlo; ✆ 046 5445 146; f 046 5445 421; m 0915 961 723. Sauna, fitness, massage, tennis, restaurant, accommodation, fantastic view, lyžiareň (ski store). $. *Open daily 12.00–18.00*.

🏠 **Salaš Kľak** Fačkovské sedlo; m 0862 5445 219. Traditional dishes in tasteful log cabin. The friendly waitress speaks good English. Packed at weekend lunchtimes with walkers enjoying a day out, a brisk hike in the hills followed by a hearty meal. $–$$. *Open daily 10.00–20.00*.

What to do

Walks From Fačkovské sedlo (802m) the signed posts lead to Čičmany (3 hours 25 minutes) and Kľak Mountain (1 hour 55 minutes). These are also part of the Cesta Hrdinov SNP. From Fačkovské sedlo, hikers can walk along 15 minutes' worth of the E8 route to Staré cesty (835m), or downhill to Prameň Nitr (645m), the source of the Nitra River, the fourth-longest river in Slovakia. The Nitra River springs from the ground in the Malá Fatra and heads south for 197km before flowing into the Danube at Komárno.

Drivers will pass the source of the Nitra, marked at the side of route 64 from Žilina to Prievidza, just south of Fačkovské sedlo.

Skiing at Fačkovské Sedlo (*Open daily 09.00–16.00; half-day ticket adult/child 230/180Sk, 5-day ticket Mon–Fri adult 900Sk*). Five tow lifts serve the slopes that include trails for beginners and good skiers alike. The highest point of the resort is at 790 m. A maintained 15km cross-country track is also available. There are five ski lifts working in the area with a slope length of 250–790m, elevation difference 50–260m. There are illuminated slopes and ski runs. The terrain is convenient for downhill skiing and suitable for both beginners and intermediate skiers. For cross-country skiing there is a regularly maintained ski run, 15km long.

The nine national parks in Slovakia and countless areas of natural beauty and preservation are criss-crossed with dense networks of well-marked hiking trails. The trails are colour-coded according to the level of difficulty and feature a red, blue, green or yellow horizontal stripe on a white square.

RED A challenging trail up and down steep hills. The most famous red trail through Slovakia is the 762km Cesta Hrdinov SNP (Path of the Heroes of the SNP) which crosses many mountain ranges with glorious views on its way from Bratislava to the Dukla Pass in the far northeast. SNP partisans used it as a supply route during the uprising in 1944.

BLUE A long, less-challenging trail connecting two major tourist attractions like a reservoir and a castle ruin.

GREEN Connecting two other, larger trails and a way of linking tourist attractions.

YELLOW Short linking trails: only a path between the most important trails and not leading to a tourist destination.

Follow the colour for your chosen route. It will appear marked on trees along the way at intervals of 300m or so. If the horizontal colour changes to a diagonal, this means that there will be a sign featuring information on the area's flora and fauna. Sometimes the trail will split in two and one path is marked by a standard horizontal green stripe while the other is a green square minus a quarter in the top right. This path leads to a tourist attraction, eg: a castle or cave, about ten minutes' walk from the main trail.

Occasionally the coloured trail will feature an arrow in the trail's colour to indicate the correct direction at a fork in the route. A smaller coloured square within a white square means that the trail has reached its destination.

VKÚ (Vojenský kartografický ústav) military maps produce excellent hiking and cycling maps from their HQ in Harmanec, near Banská Bystrica. With a distinctive green cover and numbered according to region, they are available from bookshops and tourist offices all over Slovakia and are priced around 120Sk (www.vku.sk).

MOUNTAIN RESCUE See Chapter 2, Sport, page 54.

The E8 route The longest trail, the E8 European long-distance route, also passes through Fačkovské sedlo and travels from the Atlantic, along the Rhine, Danube, Carpathian Mountains, Rila, Rhodopes and ends at the Bosphorus. In Slovakia it passes through Bratislava, Záruby, Veľkájavorina, Inovec, Fačkovské sedlo, Krahule, Krácova studňa, Donovaly, Chopok, Krácova Hoľa, Skalisko, Osadník, Sedlo Čergov and Dukla Pass. The Cesta Hrdinov SNP (Route of the Heroes of the SNP) follows the same trail (see box above).

TURČIANSKE TEPLICE SPA Situated on the edge of the Veľká Fatra National Park, the spa was first mentioned in 1281 when King László IV donated the territory, rich in thermal springs, to Count Peter. The healing effects of the thermal mineral water were popular with monarchs and noblemen. In 1423, King Sigismund of Luxemburg and his entourage appreciated the regenerative effects of the springs. Many famous royals came here including Maria Secianska, known as the *Venus of Muran* for her stunning looks. Drinking cures are recommended for diseases of the kidney, gall bladder and urinary tract.

Getting there By road, the spa is 23km south of Martin on route 65 to Kremnica. There are regular trains from Martin.

 Where to stay

Spa Hotel Veľká fatra (410 adult beds, 54 children's) Ulica SNP 519; \ 043 4913 301; f 043 4922 943; e marketing@therme.sk; www.therme.sk.

Spa Hotel Veľká Fatra has doctors' practices, a thermal pool, a fitness centre, & therapy & rehabilitation rooms all under one roof. *Sgl, dbl* $$.

ZNIEV CASTLE RUINS The now-ruined Gothic Zniev Castle was built in 1243 and abandoned in the 18th century. Its altitude at 963m puts Zniev in second place after Liptov Castle (1,001m) as the highest Slovak castle. The church at Kláštor pod Znievom ('monastery under Zniev') was formerly a pilgrimage destination and, in 1867, the first Slovak school was founded in the town.

Getting there Head south for 8km from Martin on route 65. Turn right at the village of Príbovce and head for the village of Kláštor pod Znievom, and then a short hike to the castle.

MARTIN *Telephone code 043*

The city is named after Martin de Tours, a knight of mercy who cut his coat in half to give to a shivering pauper. Situated 225km east of Bratislava on the bank of the Turiec River, Martin (population 61,000) is an important city for accessing much of central Slovakia and is also a centre of folk culture. Martin also has an extremely important role in Slovak history. Founded in 1340 and for a long period called Turčiansky Svätý Martin, the city became an important cultural centre only in the 19th century. In June 1861, a group of clergy and intellectuals gathered under a linden tree by the Protestant Church and announced the **Martin Memorandum** which stated that the Slovaks were 'as much a nation as the Magyars'. Two years later, the **Matica slovenská,** a foundation devoted to education, culture, literature and the arts, was created. Unfortunately, the 1867 *Ausgleich* between the Austrians and Hungarians gave the Magyars free rein to once again oppress the Slovaks and close all their schools by 1875. Martin remained a significant venue for Slovak self-assertion and, in 1918, the **Martin Declaration** was signed in the town, the Slovaks siding with the Czechs and thus ruining the Magyar plans for a continuation of 'Greater Hungary'. The Slovak language was first codified in 1848 and based on the Martin dialect to the eternal pride of locals, who claim they speak the purest Slovak in the land.

GETTING THERE AND AWAY By train, Martin's northern suburb of Vrútky is a stop on the main Bratislava–Košice railway line. From there, take bus 10 or 12 south for 8km to Námestie SNP. By car from Bratislava, the best method is to take the D1 motorway towards Žilina, then at Považská Bytrica follow route 61/E50 through Žilina looping towards Martin.

TOURIST INFORMATION AND OTHER PRACTICALITIES

Martin Information Centre Divadelné námestie I; \ 043 4238 776; e tik@martin.sk;

www.tikmartin.sk. *Open Mon–Fri 09.00–17.00.* $ **Slovenská Sporiteľňa Banka** M R Štefánika 9.

Open Mon–Fri 08.00–18.00.
✉ **Post office** A Kmeťa 11; ☎ 043 4223 211. Open Mon–Fri 08.00–16.00.

✚ **Pharmacy Lekáreň Bella Donna** M R
Štefánika 40. Open Mon–Fri 07.30–17.00, Sat 08.00–12.00.

🏠 WHERE TO STAY

🏠 **Autocamping Turiec** Kolónia Hviezda 92; ☎ 043 4284 215; www.autocampingturiec.sk. Situated in Vrútky, sweet little triangular chalets. $.

🏠 **Hotel Piatrová** (76 beds) Vrútky 038 61; ☎ 043 4284 298; f 043 4284 389; e euro@hotelpiatrova.sk; www.hotelpiatrova.sk. Pyramid chalet in the woods, great location for hikers & mountain bikers. Close to Martinské Hole ski

resort. Dbl $.

🏠 **Hotel Turiec** Andreja Sokolíka 2; ☎ 043 4221 017; e hotel-turiec@hotel-turiec.sk; www.hotel-turiec.sk. In a huge modern building. Sgl $, dbl $$.

🏠 **Penzión Čierna Pani** (21 rooms) Kuzmányho 24; ☎ 043 4131 523; e recepcia@cierna-pani-sk; www.penzion-cierna-pani.sk. Comfortable rooms, sauna, gym. Dbl $.

✗ WHERE TO EAT AND DRINK

☕ **Café Gallery** Daxnerova and Námestie SNP corner. Red velvet chairs in an ancient building with low arches. Open Mon–Fri 09.00–21.30, Sat 10.00–21.30, Sun 15.00–21.30.

☕ **Delikateso Belgian chocolate and café** M R Štefánika 50. A charming café. Open Mon–Fri 08.00–18.00, Sat 08.00–13.00.

☕ **Millennium café** Divadelné námestie 1. In the same light perspex building as the tourist centre. Open Mon–Sat 08.00–22.00, Sun 12.00–20.00.

✗ **Pasáž restaurant and café** M R Štefánika 48. Great summer salads. $. Open Mon–Thu 10.00–23.00, Fri 10.00–midnight, Sat 10.00–23.00, Sun 11.00–21.00.

WHAT TO SEE AND DO Martin is filled with grand tree-lined avenues and has more of a grid system than most Slovak towns, although this is marred by a bizarre one-way system. The city also has its share of *paneláky* and is famous for its engineering works but it has a spacious feel and is surrounded by glorious countryside and mountains. Martin lines up neatly around the main square formed by two parallel pedestrian streets, Osloboditeľov and Ulica 29 augusta which continues into Divadelná.

From the railway station, perpendicular to the aforementioned street pair, the first significant building is the **Turiec Museum** (*Turčianské múzeum; Andrej Kmeťa 2; open Apr–Oct Tue–Sun 09.00–17.00; Nov–Mar Mon–Fri 09.00–17.00; admission adult/child 30/15Sk*) containing a wealth of information on geology, zoology and botany. Just north is the **Múzeum Martina Benka** (*Kuzmányho 34;* ☎ *043 4133 190; open May–Oct Tue–Fri 09.00–16.00, Sat–Sun 09.00–17.00; Nov–Apr Tue–Fri 09.00–16.00, Sat 09.00–17.00; admission adult/child 30/15Sk*) containing the archive of local painter Benko in the house where he lived from 1958 until his death in 1971. Just north of the main square, the 1865 neo-Baroque **Matica Slovenska** building now houses the **Slovak National Literary Museum** (*Osloboditeľov 11;* ☎ *043 4134 152; open Tue–Sun 08.00–16.00; admission adult/child 20/10Sk*) showing the first writings by Slavs in what is now Slovakia, dating back to AD800. Martin's **tourist information centre** is found in a strange see-through green perspex building that must be hell to work in during the summer. Near Námestie SNP, the **Turiec Gallery** (*Turčianská galéria, Daxnerova; www.turiecgallery.sk; open Tue–Sun 10.00–16.30; admission adult/child 40/20Sk*) shows works by Ľudovít Fulla, M A Bazovský, Mikuláš Galanda and local painter Martin Benko. To the east of Námestie SNP, the **Slovak National Museum** (*Slovenské národné múzeum; open Tue–Sun 09.00–17.30; admission adult/child 30/15Sk*) has a colourful display of traditional Slovak dress and a photographic exhibit of famous Slovak, MR Štefánik.

Leading south, past the amphitheatre, visitors come to the **Slovak National Cemetery**, where many important Slovaks are buried. From a map displayed

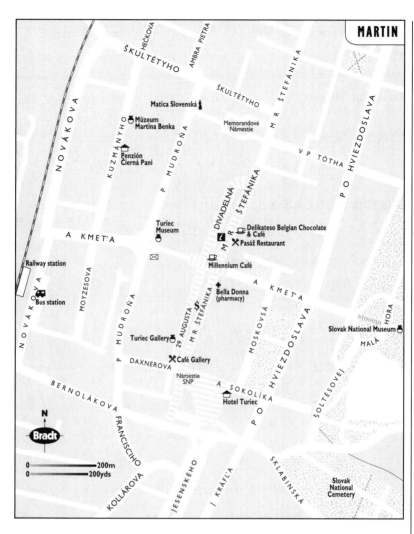

by the entrance you can find graves of Janko Kráľ, Andrej Kmeť, Martin Benko and Janko Jesenský amongst others. They're very proud of their **National Library** (*Slovenská národná knižnica*) *at Námestie J C Hronského 1* (✆ *043 4301 802;* e *snk@snk.sk; open Mon–Fri 09.00–18.00, Sat 08.00–13.00*).

AROUND MARTIN

MUSEUM OF THE SLOVAK VILLAGE IN MARTIN (*Jahodnícke háje, 036 01 Martin;* ✆ *043 4132 686;* e *snm-em@bb.telecom.sk; www.snm.sk/old/muzea/em/skanzen.htm; open 1 May–31 Aug Tue–Sun 09.00–18.00; 1 Sep–31 Oct 09.00–17.00; 1 Nov–31 Apr by appointment only; admission adult/child 30/15Sk*). The largest *skanzen* (openair folk museum) in Slovakia. Around 100 items of traditional folk architecture from the northwest of Slovakia have been collected in a 28ha park. Different regions are highlighted.

Getting there Just south of Martin, off route 65 to Turčianske Teplice. Local buses.

BLATNICA Situated near Martin, Blatnica is famous for its original houses of people who extracted oil from plants.

Karol Plicka Museum (✆ *043 4948 142; open Tue–Sun 09.00–17.00*) in an 18th-century mansion, has photos taken by the famous photographer.

Blatnica castle ruins Very wild, romantic castle ruins, the Gothic Blatnický hrad was built in 1252 and fell into ruin in 1744. Situated on the limestone Pliešovce Hill between the Gaderská dolina (valley) and Turčianska kotlina (basin) at an altitude of 685m.

SKLABIŇA CASTLE RUINS Built in 1309 on an older stronghold and ruined in the 18th century. On the small hill (626m) in the Veľká Fatra range above the Kantor Valley near the village of Sklabinský Podzámok, 9km east from Martin. Features on the Matheus's Kingdom Trail (*www.matusovo-kralovstvo.sk/panstva/hrad_sklabinsky.htm*).

☞ *POZOR!* Don't confuse Sklabiňa (castle ruins) with Sklabiná in Banská Bystrica (see page 244).

LÚČANSKÁ FATRA The western part of the Malá Fatra, not in the national park, is named after its highest peak Veľká Lúka (1,476m).

MARTINSKÉ HOLE (1,450m) Ski resort. A one-time great ski centre with lawn-covered slopes, Martinské Hole has been out of operation due to ownership debates. Access to the uphill resort is currently granted by one single chair lift that means long queues. There are, however, six tow lifts taking skiers up to easy, intermediate and difficult slopes. The highest point of the resort is at 1,450m, an ideal departure point for ski hikers who nevertheless need to be warned of the frequent mist above the crest.

ĽUBOCHŇA SPA
Situated between Ružomberok and Martin on the Váh River, this spa (*Obecný úrad Ľubochňa;* ✆ *044 4391 202;* f *044 4391 295*) was built at the end of the 19th century. Ľubochňa has been an independent spa since 1951, offering treatments for diseases of the stomach and nerve problems. The Kollárov Dom building was the venue for the foundation of the Slovak Communist Party on 16 January 1921.

SOUTHEAST FROM ŽILINA

STREČNO CASTLE AND STARÝ HRAD Situated on the cliff on the left bank of the river Váh (420m), Strečno was first mentioned in the reign of Matúš Čák. The ruins of Strečno Castle perch on a steep crag at the entrance to Strečno Gorge. Founded in 1321 and built on older foundations, it was an important position on the trade route leading through the Váh Valley. Reconstructed in Renaissance style in the 16th century and often in the hands of anti-royalists, the castle was burnt down in 1678. During the Slovak National Uprising (SNP), when outnumbered Slovak partisans battled Nazi troops during World War II, the first serious conflicts occurred in the hills around the village of Strečno. The castle was renovated in the early 1990s and turned into a museum inside showing the castle's development and housing an exhibition of the SNP. Near Strečno is a monument to French partisans who fought here in World War II.

Exhibitions in the castle museum (*Hrad Strečno;* ↘ *041 5697 400;* e *muzeum@ pmza.sk; www.pmza.sk/strecno.htm; open May–Sep daily 08.30–17.00; Oct daily 08.30–16.00; Nov–Apr closed; admission adult/concession 50/30Sk*) show the history of the castle and battles during the SNP. You can only pull into the car park for Strečno Castle if approaching from Žilina; approaching from Martin you'll dice with death attempting to cross the road. Route 18 from Žilina–Martin is a lethal highway, crammed with overtaking, speeding, tailgating silver BMWs and psychotic white vans.

Getting there Route 18/E50 Žilina to Martin.

Car ferry on the Váh (↘ *041 5697 430; open Apr–Sep 08.00–19.00; Oct–Mar 08.00–17.00*). Tickets cost 70Sk on the ancient hand-cranked ferry from Strečno to Nezbudská-Lúčka, from where a 30-minute hike leads you to the castle.

✘ **Where to eat** Beneath Strečno hrad is a nice pub, **Bufet pod Hradom**, below the cliff, although the road is incredibly busy and full of lorries thundering past.

What to do
Rafting on the Váh (*Plť na Váhu*) (*Strečno SNP;* m *0907 196 999;* e *prvapltnicka@ strecno.sk; www.strecno.sk; open 1 Apr–31 Oct*). Twelve-person rafts pass Strečno and Starý hrad and tackle the famous Margita and Besná rocks in the river.

Penzión Irenka (*Strečno 44;* ↘ *041 5697 673*). Operates a rafting service 10.00–15.00, transport to and from the rafting docks. Tickets 160–190Sk.

STARÝ HRAD-VARÍN downstream from Strečno at the next bend in the Váh is another impressive ruined castle on a crag. Also called Varínsky hrad, the castle was built before 1300 near a ford of the river to protect the trade route and collect tolls. The name Starý Hrad (Old Castle) was given after Strečno Castle was built 3km upstream and took over its functions. The Pongrácz family completed the complex with a late Gothic palace and rebuilt the fortifications in the second half of the 15th century. In the 18th century the castle lost its defensive function, was abandoned, and fell into disrepair. The castle offers a fine view of the Domašínsky meander, one of the natural highlights of the Malá Fatra National Park.

Getting there Take route 583 from Žilina to Varín or take a ferry across the Váh from Strečno. Varín is close to Nezbudská-Lúčka, the starting point for a 30-minute hike on the red trail to the castle.

VEĽKÁ FATRA NATIONAL PARK The gorgeous Greater Fatra National Park, running north–south between Martin and Ružomberok and bordered in the south by Turčianske Teplice, was established in 2002 and was a protected landscape area before that year. It's a vast 403.71km² area of unspoilt, undiscovered natural beauty, and you can walk all day in peace and solitude, feeling like the first explorer to set foot in a beautiful, flower-filled mountain meadow. Most of the area is covered by beech and fir forests, in some places by spruce and pines. The area around Harmanec is the richest yew tree region in Europe. The park is criss-crossed by hiking trails and has more cross-country skiing than downhill slopes. The highest peak is Ostredok (1,592m) in the south of the range. There are few roads in the Veľká Fatra and none running west to east, so a journey from Martin to Donovaly, involves a long detour. The website http://hiking.sk/hk/li/-velka_fatra_a_choc.html (in Slovak but decipherable) has details of all the *chata* in the region.

RUŽOMBEROK Telephone code 044

The name comes from 'rose' (*ruža*). Ružomberok, situated 261km from Bratislava in a valley to the east of the Veľká Fatra Mountains, came to the attention of football fans recently when its local team, MFK Ružomberok won the 2005/06 Slovak league. Its women's basketball team is also very strong. Ružomberok town centre spreads out mostly to the south of the mighty Váh River and the tree-lined avenues by the water are quite pleasant. It is not all greying concrete and ugly 1960s' tower blocks like some towns in the region, but many people speak of an aroma which hangs over the town from the paper factory. However, I sniffed hard and could not detect anything untoward. Signposts for the town's information centre have not been altered since the office moved and the directions will lead visitors in a confusing labyrinth which goes in a circle, good for working up a thirst for another *Zlatý Bažant*. The information centre can be found in the same block as the fabulous Hotel Kultúra, a retro gem of the Stalin–Baroque style with pink décor splashed around everywhere, both inside and out. In town, there are many bars, cafés and restaurants clustered around the central pedestrian zone of Námestie Slobody, Námestie S N Hýroša, Mostová, M Madačova, Dončova and K Salvu. Andrej Hlinka (1864–1938) was born near Ružomberok and was parish priest here. The marble Hlinka Mausoleum overlooks the square of the same name awaiting the return of the mysterious missing body.

GETTING THERE By train, Ružomberok is on the Bratislava–Košice line. Buses run every two hours from Bratislava. By car, on route 18/E50 between Martin and Liptovský Mikuláš.

TOURIST INFORMATION

🛈 **Information Centre** A Bernoláka 1; ✆ 044 4321 096; f 044 4313 611; e info@ruzomberok.sk; www.ruzomberok.sk. Very helpful. *Open 15 Jun–17 Sep Mon–Fri 08.00–18.00, Sat 08.00–12.00, Sun* 13.00–17.00; 18 Sep–15 Dec Mon–Fri 09.00–17.00, Sat 09.00–13.00; 16 Dec–31 Mar Mon–Fri 09.00–18.00, Sat 09.00–13.00, Sun 14.00–18.00; 1 Apr–14 Jun Mon–Fri 09.00–17.00, Sat 09.00–13.00.

🏠 WHERE TO STAY

🏠 **Chata Skalka** Hrabovo; m 0903 382 331; e mazuma@post.sk; www.liptov.sk/chataskalka. Just down the hill from the top of the cabin lift. *Dbl* $.

🏠 **Hotel Áčko** Hrabovska cesta 34; ✆ 044 4332 485; www.hotelacko.sk. This wacky building has multi-coloured stone blobs on the exterior walls & a shoulder-high Stonehenge in the front garden. Situated 1.5km west of town, near the cable car & Hrabovo ski resort. *Sgl, dbl* $.

🏠 **Hotel Kultúra** A Bernoláka 1; ✆ 044 4313 111; e recepcia@hotelkultura.sk; www.hotelkultura.sk. A large pink building with gym & restaurant. *Sgl, dbl* $$.

🏠 **Penzión Gejdák** Cesta na Vlkolinec; ✆/f 044 4320 297; e gejdak@gejdak.sk; www.gejdak.sk. Former sheep farm converted into a lovely chalet in the mountains. Learn about traditional sheep's cheese & sample it. *Dbl* $.

✖ WHERE TO EAT AND DRINK

✖ **Gato Borracho** Námestie A Hlinku 71; m 0908 959 694. The Drunken Cat does a good Margharita pizza. $. *Open Mon–Thu 10.00–23.00, Fri 10.00–midnight, Sat 12.00–midnight, Sun closed.*

♀ **Herňa Tenis Bar** Ulica Makovického 26 (by the football stadium). A *herňa* is a saloon or gaming house. The terrace out the back is good for a breather & a drink with a great view of the stadium & the mountains. *Open daily 10.00–23.00.*

🍷 **Hostinec u Fullov** Námestie slobody. A proper *krčma* (pub) in a 1-storey building with 12 tables & locals drinking draught Topvar. No food. *Open daily 09.00–22.00.*

✕ **Reštaurácia Koloseum** Hurbanova 5; m 0905 521 560; Mexican restaurant offering a wide choice of pizzas & Mexican specialities. $. *Open Mon–Thu 10.00–22.00, Fri–Sat 10.00–midnight, Sun 12.00–22.00.*

WHAT TO SEE AND DO

The Museum of Liptov (*Námestie Š N Hýroša;* ☎ *044 4322 468;* f *044 4322 469; open Sep–May Mon–Fri 08.00–16.00 Sat–Sun 09.00–13.00; Jun–Aug Mon–Fri 08.00–17.00, Sat–Sun 09.00–16.00; admission adult/child 40/20Sk*). Permanent exhibition focusing on the nature and civilisation of the Liptov region. Also an exhibition dedicated to Andrej Hlinka.

Gallery of Ľudovít Fulla (*Makovického l;* ☎ *044 4324 868; open Tue–Sun 10.00–17.00; admission adult/child 30/15Sk*). Shows paintings, graphics and illustrations by the Slovak artist Ľudovít Fulla.

MFK Ružomberok stadium (*www.futbalruza.sk*). Located about 1km west of the town centre.

Likavka castle ruins A 13th-century Gothic castle south of the Chočské vrchy hills, 2km north of Ružomberok on route 59/E77.

Skiing near Ružomberok
Hrabovo 1.5km west of town.

Sidorovo Mountain (1,099m) is a 3km hike from Ružomberok.

Malinné (1,209m) is a 5km hike from Ružomberok or take the cable car from Hotel Hrabovo. Great panoramic views over the Revúca and Váh valleys; look south towards Vlkolínec's (720m) beautiful valley.

Liptovské Revúce (22km south of Ružomberok) in the Veľká Fatra Mountains has got a very long slope. People say it's the longest in Slovakia. Located just off the Ružomberok–Banská Bystrica route 59/E77. Turn right at Liptovská Osada.

SOUTH OF RUŽOMBEROK

VLKOLÍNEC UNESCO WORLD HERITAGE SITE Allegedly named after the Slovak word for wolf (*vlk*), Vlkolínec nestles on the side of a mountain, surrounded by meadows and a landscape you expect Julie Andrews to come bounding through at any minute, bellowing out a tune. Vlkolínec is a fine enclave of old-style wooden longhouses dating from the 16th–19th centuries, a log bell tower and functioning covered well for potable water are all in use by the 30 or so remaining residents. Vlkolínec was turned into a *skanzen* in 1978, appearing on the UNESCO World Heritage Site list in 1993. It's one of five such sites in Slovakia (see page 20). During World War II, the area was a major site of the Slovak National Uprising. In retaliation for the involvement of several Vlkolínec residents, the Nazis burned down nearly a third of the village's houses. Log longhouses are set perpendicular to the steep main street; several are unfortunately spoiled by satellite dishes. Most houses have similar design with a living room followed by a back kitchen and a larder. The greatest architectural jewels are in the middle of the village, however; a wooden well and a belfry built in 1770.

House number 17 was converted to a peasant museum (*open Mon–Sat 08.00–17.00; tickets 40Sk*) filled with early 20th-century rustic furniture. One of the buildings near the top of the village has a shop offering beer, coffee, postcards and souvenirs. The shopkeeper plays the accordion (✆ *044 4325 834;* e *probilov@ post.sk*).

Tourist information
🛈 **Info centrum** ✆ 044 4321 023. *Open 15 Jun–15 Sep daily 09.00–17.00; 16 Sep–15 Oct & 15 Apr–14 Jun Tue–Fri 09.00–14.30, Sat–Sun 09.00–16.00; 15 Oct–14 Apr Tue–Fri 10.00–14.30, Sat–Sun*

10.00–16.00; admission adult/child 30/20Sk, 20Sk photo fee, 50Sk video fee; 150Sk guided tour, 300Sk with a language-translation handset.

Getting there By car on route 59/E77 6km south of Ružomberok on the road to Banská Bystrica. Look for a sign to the right leading 4km up a steep, narrow road to Vlkolínec.

HEADING EAST FROM RUŽOMBEROK

LIPTOV The historic Liptov region lies in a basin, surrounded by the Low Tatra Mountains. Some villages resemble a living museum of Slovak folk traditions. The mountain range provides excellent opportunities for mountain biking and hiking in the summer, skiing and snowboarding in the colder months. The territory of the Žilina region belonged to the Liptov, Orava and Turiec counties from the Middle Ages until 1923. The Liptov region is packed with recreational opportunites, with spas, skiing resorts and the large reservoir of Liptovsksá Mara. The website www.liptov.sk is really useful with tourist advice and last-minute fantastic accommodation bargains. Prices start at 200Sk (€5.50) per person per night.

LIPTOVSKÁ MARA Liptovská Mara is the largest lake (360 million m²) in Slovakia, formed by a dammed reservoir, constructed in 1969–75 and involving the flooding of 13 villages. The dam is 1,200m long. Precious houses were removed to the *skanzen* in Pribylina. The articular church in Palúdzka was relocated to the village of Lazisko. The most attractive features of a holiday in Liptovská Mara are folklore, typical architecture and regional dishes created from sheep's cheese.

Where to stay
🏠 **Liptovská Mara** ATC Liptovský Trnovec; ✆ 044 5598 459; f 044 5598 458; e info@ atctrnovec.sk; www.atctrnovec.sk.

Trnovec has good lido bungalow accommodation, mini-golf and a yacht port.

What to do
Maria boat trips (✆ *044 5593 100; open 1 Jul–31 Aug; tickets 40–60Sk. Sailing times at 10.00, 12.00, 14.00 & 16.00*). A one-hour trip from Liptovský Trnovec.

LIPTOVSKÝ MIKULÁŠ Telephone code 044

The town of Liptovský Mikuláš is situated at the eastern tip of Liptovská Mara Lake. It makes a good base for exploring the historic Liptov region and the Chočské vrchy and Western Tatras (Zapadné Tatry) to the north of town. The small pedestrianised town centre is clustered around the beautiful Sv Mikuláš Church and a stream flows through the completely renovated streets.

GETTING THERE By train, Liptovský Mikuláš is on the main Bratislava–Košice railway line. It takes four hours to Bratislava, two to Košice. By car, on the D1 motorway and route 18.

TOURIST INFORMATION AND OTHER PRACTICALITIES

▪ **AICES head office** Liptovský Mikuláš, Námestie mieru I; ☎ 044 5514 541; f 044 5514 448; e info@ infoslovak.sk; www.infoslovak.sk

▪ **Tourist information office** Námestie mieru I; ☎ 044 5522 418; f 044 5514 448; e infolm@ trynet.sk; www.lmikulas.sk. Very helpful. *Open 15 Jun–15 Sep Mon–Fri 08.00–18.00, Sat 08.00–12.00, Sun 11.00–16.00; 16 Sep–14 Dec & 1 Apr–14 Jun Mon–Fri 09.00–17.00, Sat 08.00–12.00, Sun closed;*

15 Dec–31 Mar Mon–Fri 09.00–18.00, Sat 08.00–12.00, Sun closed.

Slovak caves Administration Hodžova 11; ☎ 044 5536 411; f 044 5536 311; e caves@ssj.sk; www.ssj.sk. All caves in Slovakia.

$ **Slovenská Sporiteľňa bank** Štúrova I; www.slsp.sk. *Open Mon–Fri 08.00–17.00.*

✉ **Post office** M M Hodžu 9. *Open Mon–Fri 08.00–18.00, Sat 08.00–11.00.*

WHERE TO STAY

⌂ **Chata Aquapark** (100 beds) Ulica SNP I, Ondrášová; m 0905 842 094; e nemecp@pobox.sk; www.liptov.sk/aquapark. Smart chalet-style pension. *Dbl $.*

⌂ **Grand Hotel Permon** (286 beds) In Podbanské, 24km northeast near Pribylina Skanzen; Podbanské 18; ☎ 052 4710 111; f 052 4490 133; e hotelpermon@hotelpermon.sk; www.hotelpermon.sk. Huge, modern hotel up in the foothills of the western Tatras. Conference rooms, bowling alley, pool (water temperature 28–29°C), gym. *Sgl $$, dbl $$$, apts $$$$.*

⌂ **Hotel Klar** Ulica I, mája 117; ☎ 044 5522 911; e hotel@klar.sk; www.klar.sk. Not the world's most

attractive lodgings but nevertheless clean & good prices. *Dbl $.*

⌂ **Hotel Steve** (45 beds) Ulica I mája 699; ☎ 044 5528 999; m 0908 930 888; e hotel@steve.sk; www.hotelsteve.sk. Extremely friendly & welcoming hotel, often used by businessmen but also suitable for families & travellers. WiFi hotspot, gigantic bedrooms, restaurant & pub next door. *Sgl, dbl $$.*

⌂ **Penzión Ajda** (6 dbl, I apt) Požiarnicka 5; Dušan Rajniak; m 0903 504 233; ☎/f 044 5514 440; e info@ajda.sk; www.ajda.sk. Newly built guesthouse next to a stream, Jaloveianka, in the suburb of Ondrášová. *Dbl $–$$.*

WHERE TO EAT AND DRINK

✕ **Liptovská Izba** (Liptov Room) Námestie Osloboditeľov 21; ☎ 044 5514 853. Slovak cuisine specialities. *$. Open Mon–Sat 10.00–22.00, Sun 12.00–22.00.*

✕ **Gurman** Ulica I mája 17; ☎ 044 5520 252. Lots of steaks. *$. Open daily 07.00–20.30.*

⛾ **Route 66** Billa shopping centre; ☎ 044 5623 017; www.r66.sk. *Open Mon–Thu 09.00–midnight, Fri 09.00–02.00, Sat 10.00–02.00, Sun 11.00–midnight.*

WHAT TO SEE AND DO Námestie Osloboditeľov is dominated by the beautiful **Sv Mikuláš Church.** The square is famous as the venue for the execution of **Juraj Jánošík**, the 'Slovak Robin Hood' (see box, page 227). In **Palúdzka,** a suburb of Liptovský Mikuláš next to the lake, there is a *kaštieľ* (palace) (bus 2 or 7 from Štúrova for 1km west) where Jánošík was tortured in the dungeon before his gruesome execution. Local boy Janko Kráľ is honoured with the **Múzeum Janka Kráľa** (*Námestie Osloboditeľov 30; ☎ 044 5522 554; open Sep–Jun Tue–Fri 09.00–16.00, Sat 10.00–17.00; Jul–Aug Tue–Fri 09.00–16.00, Sat–Sun 10.00–17.00; admission adult/child 30/15Sk*), in a peach-coloured Baroque building showing details of the life of Slovakia's leading Romantic poet plus the added bonus of a reconstructed torture chamber where Jánošík was questioned. The **Gaľeria P M Bohúňa** (*Tranovského 3; ☎ 044 5522 758; open Tue–Sun 10.00–17.00; admission adult/child 50/30Sk*) has the second-largest art collection in Slovakia after Bratislava's National Gallery and illustrations and pictures by Ján Hála who worked in Važec for 40 years. On the same street, an exhibition **Tatrín and Petitions of the Slovak**

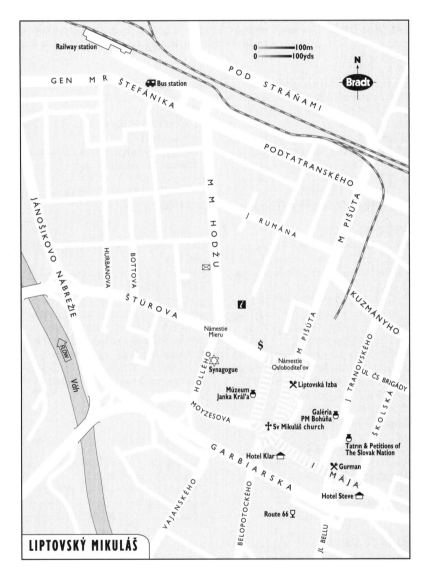

LIPTOVSKÝ MIKULÁŠ

Labels on map:
Railway station
Bus station
GEN M R ŠTEFÁNIKA
POD STRÁŇAMI
N
Bradt
0 ▬▬▬▬ 100m
0 ▬▬▬▬ 100yds
PODTATRANSKÉHO
JÁNOŠIKOVO NÁBREŽIE
HURBANOVA
BOTTOVA
ŠTÚROVA
M M HODŽU
J RUMÁNA
M PIŠÚTA
KUZMÁNYHO
FLOW
Váh
Námestie Mieru
HOLLÉHO
Synagogue
Múzeum Janka Kráľa
MOYZESOVA
$
M PIŠÚTA
Námestie Osloboditeľov
Liptovská Izba
J TRANOVSKÉHO
UL ČS BRIGÁDY
ŠKOLSKÁ
Galéria PM Bohúňa
Sv Mikuláš church
Tatrin & Petitions of The Slovak Nation
Gurman
Hotel Klar
GARBIARSKA
I MÁJA
Hotel Steve
VAJANSKÉHO
BELOPOTOCKÉHO
JI BELLU
Route 66

Nation (*Tranovského 8;* ☎ *044 5522 546; open Tue–Fri 08.00–14.00*) recalls 10 May 1848 when leading intellectuals from Liptovský Mikuláš published Slovak demands in response to the Hungarian uprising against the Habsburgs. Just west of the main square, a large Classical synagogue (1906) (*Hollého 14; open 15 Jun–15 Sep 10.00–17.00*) commemorates the significant pre-war Jewish community. There is a harrowing memorial plaque on the façade.

AROUND LIPTOVSKÝ MIKULÁŠ

HAVRANOK (☎ *044 4322 469; open daily 09.00–16.00; tickets 10Sk*). Archaeological open-air museum. By Úložisko Hill on the lake's western bank, with a reconstructed 100BC Celtic settlement.

SVÄTÝ KRÍŽ ARTICULATED WOODEN CHURCH OF EVANGELIC LUTHERANS

(↘ 044 5592 622; open daily 09.00–16.30). Slovakia's largest wooden church was constructed after Habsburg King Leopold I decreed in 1681 that Protestant churches could only be built outside towns, facing away from roads, and without hard building materials. An illiterate carpenter, Jozef Land, oversaw the construction of the church which took eight months and didn't use a single nail. The church can hold more than 6,000 people. To get there head southwest of Liptovský Mikuláš on route 18.

SKISERVIS NIŇAJ & ONDRUŠ (Závažná Poruba 451; ↘f 044 5547 349; m 0905 357 133; e skiservis@nextra.sk; www.skiservis.sk). Service, ski rentals, other equipment and bike rental.

BURTON SNOWBOARD SCHOOL (Ulica Bellova Centrum; ↘f 044 5621 594; m 0905 318 551; e burton@snowboard-school.sk; www.snowboardschool.sk). One of the first professional snowboard schools in Slovakia, with outlets in Demänovská Dolina/Jasná (Low Tatras), with 20 instructors and 70 snowboard sets for rent.

HORSERIDING (Liptovský Michal 2; ↘ 044 4392 594; m 0908 200 077; e peter.muzila@stonline.sk; www.liptov.sk/chalupkamuzila). Stay in well-appointed log cabins (250Sk per person per night) and go horseriding in beautiful Liptov countryside. Instructors available.

CASTLES BY THE LAKE LIPTOVSKÁ MARA

Liptov castle ruins at Liptovská Sielnica, north of the lake. Ruins of the highest castle in Slovakia built in the 13th century on the place of a Slavic stronghold. Destroyed in the 15th century.

Getting there There is a good 8km hike from Kalameny (near Lúčky Spa). Take the yellow-marked trail through the valley of Kalamenianka for 1km to a mineral spring. Also check out the Lučanský Waterfall (vodopád). The yellow trail forks here and the right trail rises to pass Sedlo pod Kráľovou (733m) where it meets the red trail from Bukovina and both trails lead to Liptov Castle.

Liptovský Hrádok Ruins of a Gothic lowland castle known as Nový hrad (new castle), built in 1341. Located on the bank of the river Belá.

Getting there Liptovský Hrádok is 10km east of Liptovský Mikuláš, just off the D1/E50 motorway, exit Liptovský Ján.

 Where to stay and eat

⌂ **Grand Castle hotel and restaurant** (15 rooms, 3 apts) Liptovský Hrádok; ↘ 044 5207 711; f 044 5225 284; e castle@grandcastle.sk; www.grandcastle.sk A restored and truly impressive 17th-century manor house with swanky rooms and a good restaurant (Magdaléna Zai. $$. Open daily 10.00–22.00) located in the former prison.

Sgl $$–$$$, dbl $$–$$$$$
⌂ **Shalom rekreačný dom** (5 rooms) Smrečany 45; ↘ 044 5586 357; m 0907 871 649; e shalom@lmx.sk; www.shalom.sk A good base for the Western Tatras. Large family house offers religious summer camps for children, sporting holidays and homely atmosphere. Wheelchair-friendly. Dbl $.

LIDOS BY LIPTOVSKÁ MARA

Aquapark Tatralandia (↘ 044 5477 811; f 044 5477 810; e info@tatralandia.sk; www.tatralandia.sk; open 18 Mar–2 June daily 10.00–21.00; 3 Jun–2 Sep daily

09.00–21.00; all-day ticket adult/concessions 490/390Sk, 'Western Pass' 590/480Sk). The largest of all the new aqua parks with 21 different water slides, nine pools (indoor and out) and thermal mountain water, this is a great place for families with young children. In the same resort, you can also visit the Šiklúv mlýn Wild West City (*www.western.sk*) with horseriding shows, country music dance courses, theatrical performances in historical costumes, and much more. A very safe but fun way to experience climbing is the Tarzania Trail, which has hanging ropes and different hurdles to overcome. Sauna centre with steam, Finnish, dry sauna, massage, relaxation zone, children's corner and karaoke.

Getting there Situated on route 584, 4km west of Liptovský Mikuláš, heading towards Liptovský Trnovec.

Liptovský Ján thermal pool (*Liptovský Ján;* \ *044 5263 477;* f *044 5208 903; open Jun–Sep Thu–Sun 09.00–19.00; Jul–Aug 09.00–21.00*). The water is good for skin diseases, gynaecological problems, joints and general relaxation. In the Sorea Máj Hotel.

Getting there Liptovský Ján is just off the D1/E50 motorway. The exit, 6km east of Liptovský Mikuláš is called Liptovský Ján.

 Where to stay

⌂ **Penzión Kúria Rudolf** (17 beds) Starojánska 70; \ 044 5263 404; e recepcia@urudolfa.sk; www.urudolfa.sk. 18th-century villa guesthouse. *Sgl, dbl* $.

⌂ **Penzión Maco** (26 beds) Liptovský Ján 335; \ 044 5263 300; e ladislavmassay@zoznam.sk; www.liptov.sk/penzionmaco. Friendly B&B close to all the attractions. *Dbl* $.

Thermal spa in Bešeňová (*Bešeňová 136;* \ *044 4307 700;* f *044 4392 852;* e *info@besenova.com; www.besenovacom.sk; open daily 10.00–21.00; admission adult/concessions 120/60Sk*). Based around hot, healing springs gushing from a depth of 1,987m. Depending on the season, the water in the pools ranges from 36–40°C. Thermal water in six pools is especially beneficial for health problems and is great for easing away stress. **Liptovská Štiavnica** nearby has a beautiful white manor house with an onion dome and conical turrets converted into a church in 1973. There is also the rare socialist realist mural *The Battle for Love and Truth.*

Getting there Bešeňová is halfway between Liptovský Mikuláš (12km west) and Ružomberok, at the western tip of the lake, next to the D1/E50 motorway (exit Ivachnová).

Lúčky Spa (*Liptovské liečebné kúpele, Lúčky;* \ *044 4392 828;* f *044 4392 370;* e *info@kupelelucky.sk; www.luckykupele.sk; accommodation in several bath houses combined with therapeutic or preventitive treatments; dbl* $$). Lúčky (pronounced 'looch-key') Spa is situated in the eastern part of the Choč Mountains, 621m above sea level. The spa specialises in treating gynaecological problems. The crucial factor is the healing, earthy 32°C mineral water containing natural carbonic acid gases. The healing process uses tub baths, peat wraps, steam baths and other water therapy procedures, along with massage, and complemented by rehabilitative calisthenics and physical therapy.

Getting there Lúčky is 3km northwest of Bešeňová at the western tip of the lake, next to the D1/E50 motorway (exit Ivachnová).

PRIBYLINA MUSEUM OF LIPTOV VILLAGE (*Pribylina;* ↘ *044 5293 163, part of the Museum of Ethnography Liptovský Hrádok, Hviezdoslavova 141;* ↘ *044 5444 485; www.liptovskemuzeum.sk; open all year 16 May–30 Jun daily 09.00–17.30; 1 Jul–15 Sep daily 09.00–18.30; 16 Sep–31 Oct daily 09.00–16.00; 1 Nov–15 May Mon–Fri 09.00–15.30, Sat–Sun by appointment only*). Folk architecture of the Liptov region is presented in the Museum of Liptov Village, which opened in 1991 after 20 years' preparation. Demonstrations of folk, artisan and craft techniques, concerts in the early Gothic church of the Virgin Mary at Liptovská Mara and in the Gothic-Renaissance manor house at Parížovce, the oldest preserved noble residence in Liptov, offering fencing duels, falcon training and traditional tastings of liqueurs and cheeses.

Getting there The museum is situated beyond the village of Pribylina in the direction of Podbanské. Situated 6km north of the D1/E50 motorway, exit Liptovský Peter.

NÍZKE TATRY NATIONAL PARK (LOW TATRAS) With a territory of almost 73.000ha, NAPANT (Národný park Nízke Tatry) is the largest national park in Slovakia. It's one of the most popular destinations for skiers and its charm has long been kept a secret by central Europeans. Despite the name, the Low Tatras have nothing to do with the High Tatras. They're separated from their higher namesake by the river Váh valley. Established in 1978, it is a large range oriented in the west–east direction, and almost 100km long. Its highest peak is **Ďumbier** (2,046m). The Demänovská cave system has a 23km labyrinth of corridors. Dense forests cover approximately 70% of the park's area. They range from mixed forests of lower elevations to mountain spruce and dwarf pines at higher elevations. The rocky part is inhabited by the mountain chamois of Tatra origin (*Rupicapra rupicapra tatrica*), and marmot (*Marmota marmota*) live in the mountain meadows. Travelling through the Low Tatras, visitors will find they constantly have to pull off the road to stop and gaze in gob-smacked wonder at the incredible views, a symphony in all the shades of green.

For more information on the Low Tatras, see *Chapter 9, Banská Bystrica Region*, page 240.

SKI AT CHOPOK AND JASNÁ Chopok offers some of the best alpine skiing opportunities in Slovakia. Skiing takes place on both sides of Chopok Mountain (2,024m): Chopok Juh (south) and Chopok Sever (north), known as Jasná. Jasná, is particularly recommended. Gossips mention local business battles as the reason for the lack of improvement on the southern side which preserves the communist-era style skiing facilities.

Jasná, located 15km due south of Liptovský Mikuláš, is the ski paradise of Slovakia, boasting longer and more varied tracks than all the High Tatras' slopes combined. A total of 28km of regularly maintained skiing tracks cover over 900m of altitude difference and there are many modern chair lifts, including a new high-speed, six-person lift. For expert skiers, the 2,000m-long racing trail with a drop of about 600m between Luková and Záhradky, and the 1,200m-long FIS slalom trail dropping 310m between Priehyba saddle and Záhradky are the best choices. The summit is not accessible from the north as the ski lift was dismantled. Free-riders looking for steeper, less trampled terrain on the southern slopes have to hike up 400m from the upper station on Mount Chopok to the summit, the second-highest peak in the Low Tatras (Ďumbier is the highest at 2,046m). They can drop down into the Chopok Juh Basin where Poma lifts serve the resort. Snowboarders also have a U-ramp at their disposal at the bottom station Jasná-

Lukova. Once you venture on the southern side make sure you get back on the right side in time as the ski lifts tend to close a good hour before sunset. In addition there is no easy transportation between the two sides of the mountain. During the day on Jasná, the best place to stay is the lowest station, Záhradky, where slope-side vendors in tents sell bargain beer, mulled wine and sausages. Several chair lifts depart from here, as well as a Poma lift that passes by a tough mogul ride, recommended only for experienced skiers. In the evenings, 1.6km of track including the FIS track is illuminated. There are also groomed cross-country skiing trails varying between 1km and 2.5km, ski schools, kid centres, ski service and rental. Numerous hotels at the base stations offer saunas, pools and gourmet cuisine. A one-day ticket for adults for both sides of the mountain costs 490Sk; a three-day pass is 1,350Sk. For more information, check www.chopok-jasna.sk.

Getting there From Bratislava follow the directions to Nitra on E571, then to Banská Bystrica. Drive on road 66 then turn left to road 72. Turn left at Bystrá to reach the southern slopes of the Chopok Mountains.

 Where to stay and eat

🏠 **Hotel Grand** (122 rooms) Demänovská dolina; ☏ 044 5591 441; f 044 5591 454; e hotelgrand@ jasna.sk; www.grandjasna.sk. 4-star mountain hotel in the centre of Jasná with gourmet restaurant. Fusion Asian-Italian cuisine ($$) created by star chef Palo Pavlík, superb wine list. *Sgl $$$, dbl $$$$*.

🏠 **Hotel Liptov** (234 beds) Demänovská dolina; www.tatry.net/sk/jasna/liptov/rezervacia/ (reservations through the website). 2-star hotel in the centre of Jasná, 200m from the ski resort Otupné, close to a mountain lake Vrbické pleso. Humno restaurant with fireplace. Skates & ice-hockey gear rental, night skating. *Sgl $, dbl $$*.

🏠 **Hotel Ski & bungalowy** (168 beds) 2-star mountain hotel is located in the ski & tourist resort Záhradky, 1km from Jasná. Next to the hotel is the

FIS downhill track chair lift starting point, that takes skiers almost to the top of Chopok peak. *Dbl $$$*.

🏠 **Hotel Tri studničky** (37 rooms) Demänovská dolina; ☏ 044 5478 000; f 044 5478 004; e hoteltristudnicky@jasna.sk; www.tristudnicky.sk. Smart 4-star mountain hotel 8km from Jasná centre, with a restaurant supervised by famous TV chef Vojtech Artz from Markíza TV's *Chuťovky* show. *Sgl $$$, dbl $$$$*.

🏠 **Kamenná Chata** pod Chopkom; ☏ 048 6170 039; www.kamennachata.sk. A modest mountain refuge by Chopok (2,024m) Mountain. Access only on foot. *$*.

✗ **Štefánikova Chata** pod Ďumbierom; ☏ 048 6195 120; www.chatamrs.sk. Mountain refuge by Ďumbier (2,045m). Access only on foot. Great food. *$*.

DEMÄNOVSKÁ DOLINA The dolomite Demänovská Valley (e caves@ssj.sk; www.ssj.sk) stretches for 44km² and is located on the northern slopes of the Low Tatras, south of Liptovský Mikuláš. It was created by the Demänovká River and its tributaries gushing under the main crest of the Low Tatras in the extent of Krupová hola (1,927m), Chopok (2,023m), Derese (2,003m), and Polana (1,889m). The Ďumbiersky ski-track is on the ridge from Chopok to Ďumbier (2,045m) and to Štefánikova chata (hut) into the saddle of Polana.

DEMÄNOVSKÁ JASKYŇA SLOBODY (Cave of Liberty) (*Demänovská Dolina;* ☏ *044 5591 673;* e *djslob@ssj.sk; www.ssj.sk. Traditional tour (admission adult/child 150/80Sk) Tue–Sun Jan–May entry at 09.30, 11.00, 12.30, 14.00; Jun–Aug 09.00–16.00 on the hour; Sep–Oct entry 09.30, 11.00, 12.30, 14.00; Nov–Dec closed. Long tour (admission adult/child 300/140Sk) has slightly more restrictive hours).* The cave is part of the Demänovské jaskyňe, the longest cave system in Slovakia. It is distinguished by the magnificent colours of the stalactites and stalagmites and the uniqueness of their shapes. White, yellow, orange, black and their various shades mingle in the rocky waterfalls. Veľký dóm (Great Dome) is very impressive and the largest accessible underground space in Slovakia. English interpreting possible.

Getting there Head south for 6km on route 584 from Liptovský Mikuláš to Brezno.

DEMÄNOVSKÁ ĽADOVÁ JASKYŇA (ICE CAVE) (✆ 044 5548 170; e demlad@ ssj.sk; www.ssj.sk; open Tue–Sun 15–31 May 09.30, 11.00, 12.30, 14.00; 1 Jun–31 Aug 09.00–16.00 on the hour; Sep 09.30, 11.00, 12.30, 14.00; 1 Oct–14 May closed; admission adult/child 150/80Sk). Like the Cave of Liberty, this ice cave is part of the Demänovská jaskyňa cave network. One of the oldest known caves in the world, first mentioned in 1299. It is very different in character with magnificent ice ornamentation. The ice in the interior is in the lower parts of the cave, especially in the Kmeťov dome. The bones of a cave bear were discovered in the cave and in the past were thought to be the bones of a dragon, earning the cave the original name of Dragon Cave. Seven bat species have been observed in the cave.

Getting there Head south for 10km on route 584 from Liptovský Mikuláš to Brezno.

SKI AT ČERTOVICA When travelling from one side of Mount Chopok to the other, the ski centre of Čertovica is about halfway on the winding mountain road, just at the mountain pass. For good skiers it is worth making a stop there to enjoy a few steep rides. The ski centre at Čertovica offers eight downhill tracks (two blue, four red and two black) with a total length of 12km from altitudes of 1,120m to 1,463m. There are five ski tows of which one takes skiers up to the top Čertova svadba (1,463m). From there a number of different tracks lead down to the pass. In turn the track with its top station in the pass is suitable for beginner skiers and snowboarders alike, but the resort is primarily for advanced skiers. Services include snow cannons, ski school, ski kindergarten, ski service, ski-equipment rental, several fast-food stalls and two restaurants. A day pass costs 240Sk.

Getting there From Liptovský hrádok follow route 72 south.

⌂ Where to stay

⌂ **Penzión Boca** (42 beds) Vyšná Boca; ✆ 044 5280 197; e penzionboca@bb.telecom.sk; www.penzionboca.sk. Sturdy hostel just north of Čertovica. Rustic restaurant ($), summer terrace. Sgl, dbl $.

VÝCHODNÁ AND VAŽEC Východná is the venue for the annual Slovak Folk Festival, held June–July and attracting folk groups from every region. There are no accommodation possibilities in the village but it's only 15km east of Liptovský Mikuláš and during the festival, a campsite is arranged in the area. Važec was once known as the most beautiful village in Slovakia. Tragically, the entire village was constructed from wood and burnt down in a catastrophic fire in 1931.

Važecká Jaskyňa (cave) (Contact Milan Orfánus; ✆ 044 5294 171; e vazecj@ssj.sk; www.ssj.sk; open Tue–Sun Feb–May & Sep–Nov 10.00, 12.00, 14.00, 15.00, Jun 09.00–16.00 on the hour; Jul–Aug 10.00–17.00 on the hour; Dec–Jan closed; admission adult/concession 60/50Sk). Located on the edge of Važec village, the cave was discovered in the 1920s. The cave is quite small but it is rich in stalactite and stalagmite decoration in delicate shapes and colours, including thin quills, on delightful sinter lakes and miniature dams. A significant part of the cave is filled with the sediments deposited by the former waters of the Bielý Váh (White Váh) River. The bones of a cave bear were discovered in the cave.

Pavol Országh (1849–1921) was born in Vyšný Kubín and worked as a lawyer, dramatist, translator and a member of the Czechoslovak parliament; however he is also considered one of the most important Slovak poets of all time. He worked as a court employee in Dolný Kubín and practised law between 1875 and 1899. In 1918, Országh became a member of the newly created Revolutionary National Assembly, the provisional governing body, in Prague. From 1919, he served as its representative.

In 1919, he was named leader of the re-established *Matica slovenská*. In 1954, the Literary Museum of P O Hviezdoslav was established in Dolný Kubín. A festival of amateur reciters named Hviezdoslav's Kubín has been held there since. From 1875 onwards, Országh wrote under the pseudonym 'Hviezdoslav' which means 'glory of the stars'. Previously, he had used the pseudonym Jozef Zbranský. His real surname, Országh, is quite common in Hungarian and means 'country'. Hviezdoslav died in neighbouring Dolný Kubín.

MALÁ FATRA NATIONAL PARK (LESSER FATRAS)

There is a fairytale quality to the beautiful Malá Fatra National Park whose 226km² territory was declared a national park in 1988. Craggy peaks in unusual shapes soar skywards, deep gorges lead to enchanted valleys and the wild, romantic scenery is filled with legends of robbers and highwaymen, magic and treachery. The name 'Malá' means 'lesser' but some peaks are higher than those in big sister Veľká Fatra (Greater Fatras National Park). The highest peak is the national symbol **Veľký Kriváň** (1,709m) south of Terchová. The Malá Fatra is basically one big lump of karst rock. The highest waterfall is found at Šútovo (38m), near the Vratná Valley. Interesting folk villages can be seen at Štefanová and Šípková near Terchová and visitors can explore the country of Juraj Jánošík, the Slovak Robin Hood. One of the highlights of the Malá Fatra is the **Vratná Valley**, a thickly forested region that many consider Slovakia's most beautiful valley. The Vratná Valley is one of the most accessible and satisfying mountain regions with spectacular scenery, hiking and skiing routes and plenty of accommodation options, especially around Terchová. It's packed with visitors in the summer and winter seasons but strangely deserted in spring and autumn.

DOLNÝ KUBÍN Slovakia's most famous poet, Pavol Országh Hviezdoslav, remembered in Bratislava's most beautiful square, was born in Vyšný Kubín. The mostly wooden building burned down and painter Ľudovít Fulla depicted what remained of it in 1921. Nowadays, only a modest memorial stands on the site, although a huge commemoration to the poet was planned during the 1960s. Hviezdoslav worked as a lawyer all his life but created complex rich poetry that is difficult to translate. Hviezdoslav is buried in Vyšný Kubín Cemetery.

Orava Gallery (*Dolný Kubín; Hviezdoslavovo námestie 11;* \ *043 5863 212;* f *043 5864 395;* e *ogaleria@nextra.sk; www.oravskagaleria.sk; open Tue–Sun 10.00–17.00*) is housed in the beautiful Caplovic Library building. Hviezdoslav's life and work is well documented and also archaeological, ethnographic and nature exhibits.

INTERESTING SIGHTS SOUTH OF ORAVA

ISTEBNÉ WOODEN CHURCH (*www.dolnykubin.sk*). Before 1985, the village of Istebné was blackened by soot from the alloy plant and quarry. The local population threatend to all move out and finally dust separators were fitted onto the factory chimneys. Istebné is worth a visit to see one of Slovakia's four surviving wooden Lutheran churches built in 1686 with support from the King of Sweden. A separate bell tower was added in 1731.

Getting there Istebné is 6km west of Dolný Kubín just off route 70 to Martin.

LEŠTINY A wooden Lutheran church built in the late 17th century. A simple barn structure from the outside, but the interior walls, staircase and ceiling are covered in 18th-century naïve folk painting.

Getting there Approx 1km south of Dolný Kubín turn off route 59/E77 towards Ružomberok and head down a very minor road signposted for Leštiny and Malatiná.

PODBIEĽ This village northeast of Dolný Kubín on route 59 is delightful, with rows of 64 smart wooden cottages typical for the area, five of which are renovated and can be rented. Podbieľ has a sweet church with a red spire and white walls.

FRANTIŠKOVA HUTA Just out of Podbieľ on route 584 is a ruined ironworks building. The remains of the building, known as 'hámor', is used as a festival site for folk and country music as well as a demonstration of 17th-century iron smelting, held annually at the end of August.

TVRDOŠÍN This village has a wooden church which looks a bit modern. A charming main street with one-storey houses in multi-coloured pastels around a green square. A large open-air market is set out in front of the church. From Tvrdošín to Oravský Podzámok is a fabulous road (route 59/E77); next to the village of Krivá the woody, triangular-shaped hills look gorgeous in the spring.

ORAVA CASTLE (*Museum; tel; 043 5816 119; www.oravamuzeum.sk; open May 08.30–16.00; Jun 08.30–17.00; Jul–Aug 08.30–17.30; Sep–Nov 08.30–16.00; Nov–Apr closed; castle admission adult/child 140/80Sk, chapel adult/child 60/30Sk*). Orava is possibly the most spectacular fortress castle in Slovakia. Where other castles on rocky crags loom over their respective towns, here Orava leaps into the sky, announcing itself. It's a fantastically romantic fortress, with cliffs and rugged ramparts; everything you want from a castle. The 13th century stronghold was extended in the 15th and 16th centuries; the final design is from the 17th century. There are many legends connected with the castle. One tells how the owner of the castle, a knight called Donca, was very cruel to his servants and subjects. His wife took the side of two maids and he threw a wobbly and killed her with his sword. He tried to ask for forgiveness but too late: her ghost then kept turning up to haunt him. She still appears in the castle twice a year on Palm Sunday and All Souls' Day (2 November). The castle is the venue for lots of Christmas events. One of the first horror films, *Nosferatu* (1922), was filmed here. The castle museum is fascinating and well put together.

Getting there By car, route 59/E77 from Dolný Kubín.

☞ *POZOR!* Don't look for a town called Orava. It's a historical region and mentioned in the names of the lake, towns and villages. For example, the town beneath Orava Castle (*Oravský hrad*) is called Oravský Podzámok, which is a bit confusing as first it's a *hrad* (castle), then a *zámok* (palace/mansion). Just keep looking out for 'Orav' at the beginning of names and you'll be in the right area.

Situated near the Polish border, the town of Námestovo sits by the shores of Orava Lake, a huge manmade reservoir and dam created in 1954 when five villages were flooded.

Námestovo has several good bars and restaurants with great terraces overlooking the lake. The tiny Baroque **Church of St Cross** (1769) on the little island of **Slanický ostrov** is all that remains of the lost Atlantis villages of Slanica, now submerged.

A sightseeing boat sails to Slanický ostrov (island). The Church of St Cross is situated on the island with a museum (m *0905 915 108; www.oravskagaleria.sk; open 15 May–15 Sep Tue–Sun 09.00–17.00*) of folk sculpture with pieces made by unknown stone carvers and cutters from past centuries. Slanícka osada and Prístav are two most important summer leisure and sport centres located to the south of the lake by route 520. Orava Lake has excellent conditions for windsurfing, yachting, diving and other watersports. Water bicycles, boats and motorboats are available for hire.

TOURIST INFORMATION AND OTHER PRACTICALITIES

Oravská priehrada-Slanická Osada (*Námestovo;* m *0905 915 108; www.slanica.sk*) has details of accommodation and entertainment in the area. Boat to the island from Slanická Osada or from a quay near the Goral Hotel, 15 Apr–15 Sep, first sailing 09.00, last sailing to island 16.00, last sailing back 17.00.

WHERE TO STAY

➤ **Hotel Studnička** (25 rooms) Oravská priehrada, 029 01 Námestovo; ☏ 043 5522 111; m 0911 511 111; e hotelstudnicka@ hotelstudnicka.sk; www.hotelstudnicka.sk. *Hotel open Fri, Sat, Sun 14.00–20.00, from June 2006 open daily; dbl* $.

WHAT TO SEE AND DO

Soľná Jaskyňa (m *0911 811 111; open daily 10.00–20.00*). Connected to the Hotel Studnička, this private sea salt cave is excellent for stress, allergies, skin problems and asthma.

Sightseeing cruise (m *0905 358 182; www.plty-orava.sk*). Down the Orava River under the rocky cliffs of Orava Castle on a wooden 'forefathers' raft' (*plt*). From here the Orava River flows south past the spectacular Orava Castle (see page 221).

ANTON BERNOLÁK

Anton Bernolák, the father of the Slovak literary language was born in 1762 in Slanica, the village now submerged beneath Orava Lake. Bernolák studied in Ružomberok, Bratislava, Trnava, and then studied theology in Vienna. He was highly educated, spoke several languages and had a broad knowledge of history, economics, medicine, nature studies, aesthetics, music and politics. In 1790, Bernolak published a textbook, *Grammatica Slavica* of the first Slovak grammar, based on the Western Slovak dialect, using a phonetic system 'write as you hear'. He also created a dictionary, known as the 'Slovar slovenski cesko-latinsko-nemecko-uherski', published after his death in 1813. This became the vocabulary manual for the Slovak literary language. Bernolak's Slovak was used until 1851, when it was replaced by a language developed by Ľudovít Štúr, based on the Central Slovak dialect.

ZUBEREC

Museum of the Oravian Village (Múzeum oravskey dediny Zuberec-Brestová) (*027 32 Zuberec;* ⟍ *043 5395 149; www.zuberec.sk; open Jun & Sep daily 08.00–17.00; Jul–Aug daily 08.00–18.00; Oct–May Tue–Sun 08.00–15.30; admission adult/concessions 60/50Sk, guide in English 300Sk with advance booking).* A superb *skanzen* in a 20ha site by the Studený potok (stream) showcasing 70–80 wooden homes dating back to the 16th century. All 75 structures were complete originals, taken apart piece by piece, catalogued, and then put back together in a year-long process in 1968. The *skanzen* is a real treasure and well worth hunting down in the beautiful deserted forests of the Skorušinské vrchy hills.

Getting there By car, southeast on route 584 from Podbiel. By bus from Liptovský Mikuláš, direction Trstená, in Zuberec head for Zverovka. By train from Kraľovany–Podbiel, then change to bus to Zuberec.

Thermal spa in Oravice (*Termálne kúpalisko Oravice, Technical authority in Tvrdošín;* ⟍f *043 5322 748; www.oravice.sk; admission adult/child 140/15Sk).* The thermal spa at Oravice is very popular with Polish bathers from over the border 15 minutes away. The two brownish outdoor pools have temperatures varying from 32–37°C. The spa is beneficial for those suffering problems of the locomotive system, urinary disorders and the kidneys and are also excellent for stress busting. There is a gorgeous view of the Roháč Peak (2,083m) in the Western Tatras and surrounded by countless buffets selling sausages and beer.

Meander Park (*Oravice 109;* m *0905 800 260;* ⟍f *043 5394 107;* e *info@ meanderpark.com; www.meanderpark.com; open 2 Apr–25 May 12.00–21.00; 26 May–30 Sep 09.00–22.00; 1 Oct–23 Dec 12.00–21.00; 24 Dec–1 Apr 11.00–22.00; admission adult/child 3hrs 330/200Sk (3hrs), full day 490/280Sk).* Nearby is a new yet empty expensive pool lido complex. Large pool at a temperature of 35–36°C, a small pool at 36–37°C with a 100m water chute into small pool.

Meander Ski Park (*During ski season open daily 09.00–16.00; charges adult/child 550/400Sk, 6-day 2,700/1,970Sk).* Opposite the lido: blue run 1,300m, black run 1,100m.

MALÁ FATRA NATIONAL PARK (LESSER FATRAS)

There is a fairytale quality to the beautiful Malá Fatra National Park whose 226km² territory was declared a national park in 1988. Craggy peaks in unusual shapes soar skywards, deep gorges lead to enchanted valleys and the wild, romantic scenery is filled with legends of robbers and highwaymen, magic and treachery. The name 'Malá' means 'lesser' but some peaks are higher than those in big sister Veľká Fatra (Greater Fatras National Park). The highest peak is the national symbol **Veľký Kriváň** (1,709m) south of Terchová. The Malá Fatra is basically one big lump of karst rock. The highest waterfall is found at Šútovo (38m), near the Vratná Valley. Interesting folk villages can be seen at Štefanová and Šípková near Terchová and visitors can explore the country of Juraj Jánošík, the Slovak Robin Hood. One of the highlights of the Malá Fatra is the **Vratná Valley**, a thickly forested region that many consider Slovakia's most beautiful valley. The Vratná Valley is one of the most accessible and satisfying mountain regions with spectacular scenery, hiking and skiing routes and plenty of

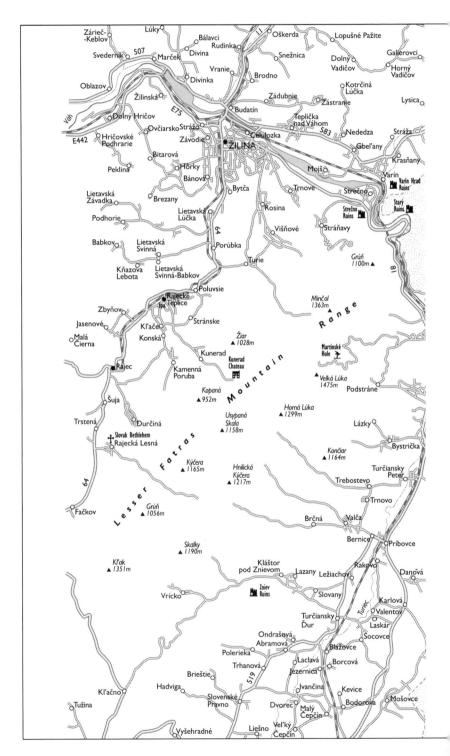

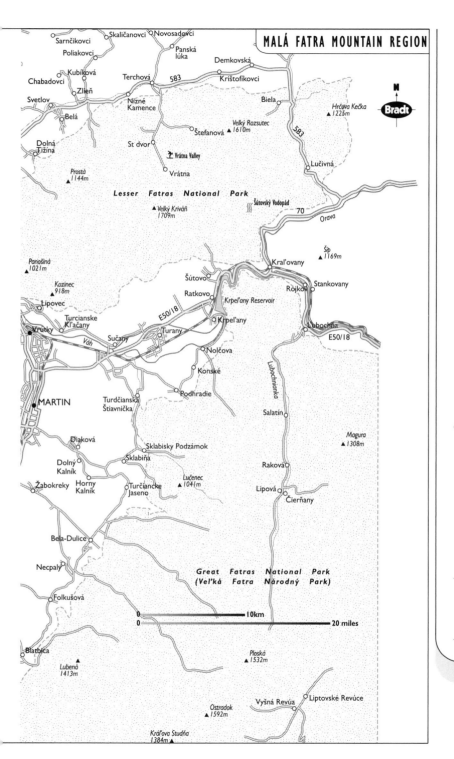

MALÁ FATRA MOUNTAIN REGION

accommodation options, especially around Terchová. It's packed with visitors in the summer and winter seasons but strangely deserted in spring and autumn.

TERCHOVÁ The quaint, attractive town of Terchová was the birthplace of Slovak national hero Juraj Jánošík, to whom the town pays homage with a statue and museum. In the winter, Terchová teems with international visitors drawn to the massive Vratná Dolina ski centre (which takes 9,050 people up the mountain every hour). Many people in Terchová offer rooms to strangers, and there are plenty of accommodation variations. The road leading south out of Terchová towards the Vrátna Valley (look for the Jánošík statue looking out over the town) gives the first inkling as to the beauty of the mountains, with its jagged rock formations soaring into the clouds. Drive through Tiesňavy (Narrow Passage) to reach a magical valley. The Jánošík statue, created by Ján Kulich in 1988 is an impressive 4m shiny metal creation placed on a crag above the town. **Jánošík Days** folklore festival in Terchová takes place over the first weekend in August.

Tourist information and other practicalities

⊞ Tourist office Ulica Sv Cyrila a Metoda 96; ☎ 041 5993 100; e ztt@terchova.sk, www.terchovaregion.sk
Mrs Gabriela Chrobáková ☎ 041 5002 307; e mks@terchova.sk

⊞ Co-op supermarket Vratňanská cesta; ☎ 041 5695 126. Good for hiking provisions. *Open Mon–Fri 06.00–19.00, Sat 06.00–14.00, Sun 08.00–12.00.*
✉ Post office Sv Martina 297. *Open Mon, Tue, Thu, Fri 08.15–12.00 & 13.00–16.00, Wed 08.15–11.30, 13.30–15.00 & 15.30–17.00, Sat–Sun closed.*

Getting there The local bus from Žilina takes one hour; 50Sk. By car take route 583 Žilina to Terchová, 26km east, look for the giant silver statue of Jánošík.

 Where to stay and eat Terchová is full of accommodation options in private pensions, operated by local families.

⌂ Hotel Diery Biely Potol; ☎ 041 5695 322. A big building to the east of the town.
⌂ Hotel Gold Next to the Co-op. A 3-star hotel with a terrace café (*open daily 10.00–20.00*). *Dbl* $$.
⌂ Penzión Lacek Školská 1273; ☎ 041 5695 500; m 0904 536 111. *Dbl* $.

⌂ Penzión Malá Fatra Jan Ďurko at Terchová 176; ☎ 041 5695 413; m 0903 522 389; e malafatra@nextra.sk; www.durko.sk. *Dbl* $.
⌂ Privát Mária Školská 144; ☎ 041 5695 501; m 0903 304 276. *Dbl* $.

VRÁTNA DOLINA The enchanted valley of Vrátna is another good bet both for run freaks and open-space riders. It is in fact five separate resorts (Paseky, Poludňový Grúň, Príslop, Tížinka, Chleb), unfortunately without connections to one another once you wish to remain on your skis. However from the 2005/06 season, shuttle buses connect the separate centres. Good skiers and snowboarders out for some virgin areas should head for Chleb (1,647m), the upper station where a new, high speed eight-person gondola was opened for the 2005/06 season to reach its terminus at 1,450m. From Chleb, expert skiers and snowboarders can storm down on 750m of groomed black slopes or drop into the free-rider space behind Chleb and hike along the ridge to find one's own line of descent. The long black slope is a candidate for the best run in the country so it is worth checking this resort if for nothing else. In all there are five areas, 14 surface lifts and two gondolas, a new eight-person gondola, 17 ski trails with a total length of 10.6km and cross-country trails. A one-day adult pass is 620Sk, three days 1,700Sk. Check www.vratna.sk. In warmer months, visitors can hike along many of the trails used by Jánošík and his band when they were hiding out from the authorities.

'Stop! Your soul belongs to God and your money belongs to me!' Juraj Jánošík uttered these words when he stopped carriages packed with nobles travelling around the Malá Fatra Mountains.

Juraj Jánošík (1688–1713) is a legendary folk hero who symbolises the oppression of the Slovak nation. At a very young age, Jánošík joined the *Kuruc* forces (anti-Habsburg rebels) and when the rebellion was over he served in the imperial army for a while. Later he became a bandit and started to fight social injustice in his own way. He robbed the rich and gave much of it to the poor. Some claim that he mainly robbed Hungarian nobility and helped the poor Slovaks. There are many legends about Jánošík. He allegedly possessed supernatural powers, making him resistant to bullets and arrows and enabling him to move from one place to another much faster than ordinary humans. According to a legend, his powers were given to him by three witches. The witches gave him an alpenstock, a belt and a shirt and from then on he always carried these items with him. However, his magic didn't work when he was eventually captured near Ružomberok. Allegedly, a girlfriend, driven by the huge bounty, betrayed him, destroying his magic things. He was tortured and then given a death sentence. His crimes were so severe that he received the harshest form of execution. He was hanged in Liptovský Mikuláš main square on a hook that pierced through one of his ribs. Jánošík is very much loved by Slovaks: the first ever Slovak film was made about him in 1935. He exists in Polish folk tales as well and Poles claim him as their own folk hero.

Getting there The local bus from Žilina takes one hour; 50Sk. By car, take route 583 Žilina to Terchová, 26km east, look for the giant silver statue of Jánošík.

 Where to stay

Chata Vrátna (50 beds, 44 dorm beds) \ 041 5695 739; e vratna@vratna.sk; www.vratna.sk. A giant chalet at the base of the chair lift. *Sgl, dbl* $, *apts* $$.

Hotel Boboty (139 beds) Štefanová; \ 041 5695 227; e hotel_boboty@vratna.sk. Large hotel right in the gorge, pool, gym & free ski bus to the resort. *Dbl* $$.

What to see and do
Symbolic cemetery Štefanová near Chleb chair lift. Tablets bear the names of victims of the mountains, a 'memory to the dead and warning to the alive'.

Rafting trips (m *0903 546 600, 0903 306 566*). A trip on the Orava River costs 400Sk per person.

Chair lift (*Runs 08.00–16.00 on the hour; admission adult/concession 250/170Sk*). The chair lift takes visitors up to Snilovské sedlo (1,520m).

Vychylovka Historical Logging Back Swath Railway (*Historická lesná úvraťová železnica – HLÚŽ; \ 041 4397 219; www.kysuckemuzeum.sk; operates for a minimum 10 people 7 May–29 Oct Mon–Fri 09.00–17.00 diesel locomotive, Sat–Sun 09.00–18.00 steam locomotive. Admission adult/child 80/40Sk. Train timetable 09.15, 10.30, 11.30, 13.00, 14.00, 15.00, 16.00, 17.00*). In the past, the Kysuce–Orava narrow-gauge logging railway from Oščadnica to Lokca was a vital link through the dense forests of northern Slovakia. The line was created by joining the Kysuce and Orava sections in 1926 and was used for timber transport until the beginning of the 1970s. In 1971, the line closed and was disassembled apart from an 8km stretch between Chmúra and Tanečnik. The line is administered by the Kysuce Museum and makes a delightful way to approach the *skanzen*.

The Museum of Kysuce Village Vychylovka (*Múzeum kysuckej dediny Vychylovka, 023 05 Nová Bystrica-Vychylovka;* ❧ *041 4397 350;* e *kysuckemuzeum@stonline.sk; www.kysuckemuzeum.sk; open Mon–Fri 09.00–17.00, Sat–Sun 09.00–18.00; admission adult/child 50/25Sk*). Open-air museum with 34 buildings bringing the life and culture of the Kysuce area into focus, with folklore groups, folk cuisine and singing. Buildings include an early 19th-century brick Virgin Mary chapel relocated from Zborov and a water-powered sawmill from Klubina.

THE KYSUCE REGION The mountainous Kysuce region, up by the Polish and Czech borders, has not been discovered by visitors, yet it is charming and full of interesting sights.

The *skanzen* is run by the **Kysuce Museum in Čadca** (*Moyzesova ulica 50;* ❧ *041 4321 386; open 1 Apr–31 Oct Tue–Fri 09.00–17.00, Sat–Sun 09.00–18.00; admission adult/concessions 20/10Sk*). The tiny ski resort at **Oravská Lesná** (❧ *043 5524 682*) has one long run on two possible routes. West of Žilina, in **Bytča**, there is a Renaissance manor house (1571–74) and Popper lager is also brewed in the village. The elegant **Radoľa** manor house is near Kysucké Nové Mesto.

9

Banská Bystrica Region

Banská Bystrica is one of Slovakia's largest regions with stunning countryside and fantastic tourist sites: the historic mining towns of Banská Bystrica, Banská Štiavnica, Kremnica, Špania Dolina, the ski resorts of the Low Tatras, thermal baths and hiking trails. The land of mountains, valleys, hollows and dales with a rich mining history is situated right in the centre of Slovakia. The highest altitude-peak is Ďumbier (2,046m) and the lowest point is at the Ipeľská kotlina (128m). The northern border is flanked by the Starohorské vrchy hills and the Nízke Tatry; the southern border by the Ipeľ River and the Cerová vrchovina Mountains, both bordering Hungary. The landscape contains three national parks: Nízke Tatry, Muránska planina and Veľká Fatra, and also the protected landscape areas of Ponitrie, Štiavnické vrchy, Cerová vrchovina and Poľana, which belongs to a biosphere reserve under the UNESCO programme 'Man and Biosphere'. The region is drained by three rivers: the Hron which springs up at Kráľová hoľa (peak), the Ipeľ which springs at the southern slopes of the Čierťaž in the Veporské vrchy, and the Rimava which starts at Fabová hoľa in the Stolické vrchy. The hilly relief of the hollows and highland relief of the mountains are typical for most parts of the region. The majority of the Banská Bystrica region is forested; only settlements are cleared of trees. The region is developing its infrastructure and transport connections to meet EU norms. The northern part of the region has great natural conditions for tourism, especially in the Low Tatras and Starohorské vrchy.

The Lower Tatras range has a large number of hotels and well-appointed slopes. The Donovaly Valley, 28km north of Banská Bystrica, is one of the biggest ski resorts in Slovakia. In the areas around Banská Bystrica are numerous protected natural sites, including the Low Tatras National Park (811km²), the largest National Park in Slovakia. The highest mountain in the Low Tatras is Mount Chopok (2,024m).

EVENTS IN BANSKÁ BYSTRICA REGION

June	**Banská Bystrica** 'Eurofolklore' international folklore festival
June–July	**Zvolen** Castle Drama and Opera Festival
August	**Kremnica** *Kremnica gagy* joke festival
September	**Svätý Anton** Days of St Hubert hunting feast at the museum
October	**Detva** Roma festival
December	**Banská Bystrica** Musical displays and Christmas customs

BANSKÁ BYSTRICA *Telephone code 048*

Banská Bystrica (Neusohl in German, Besztercebánya in Hungarian) is a buzzing, fun town with a huge student population. Situated right in the heart of Slovakia, 224km from the capital and surrounded by mountains (Nízke Tatry, Veľká Fatra and Kremnické vrchy), visitors can feel overwhelmed with so much to do and see.

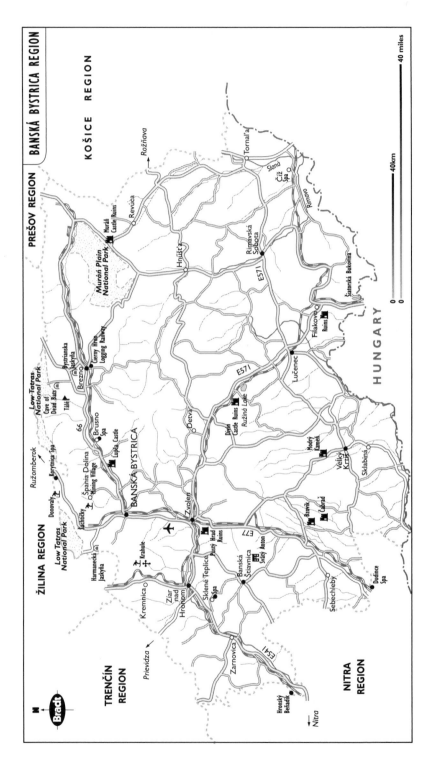

PREŠOV REGION

KOŠICE REGION

ŽILINA REGION

TRENČÍN REGION

NITRA REGION

HUNGARY

Bradt

N

0 ⊢─────────⊣ 40km

0 ⊢─────────⊣ 40 miles

Rožňava

Tornal'a

Slaná

Číž Spa

Rimavo

Revúca

Muráň Castle Ruins

Muráň Plain National Park

Hnúšťa

Rimavská Sobota

E571

Šiatorská Bukovina

Filakovo Castle Ruins

Lučenec

E571

Bystrianska jaskyňa

Čierny Hrad Logging Railway

Brezno

Low Tatras National Park

Cave of Dead Bats

Táľe

66

Brusno Spa

Lupča Castle

BANSKÁ BYSTRICA

Detva

Divín Castle Ruins

Ružiná Lake

Modrý Kameň

Veľký Krtíš

Sklabiná

Ružomberok

Korytnica Spa

Donovaly

Špania Dolina Mining Village

Low Tatras National Park

Harmanecká jaskyňa

Králiky

Ráčkov

Zvolen

E77

Pustý Hrad Ruins

Bzovík

Čabraď

Prievidza

Kremnica

Žiar nad Hronom

Sklené Teplice Spa

Banská Štiavnica

Svätý Anton

Sebechleby

Dudince Spa

Žarnovica

E41

Nitra

Hronský Beňadik

230

However, you won't feel claustrophobic in the friendly and open main square, Námestie SNP and the surrounding pedestrian streets and green spaces. It's easy to escape the town and head for the hills and the fresh air of the least populated Slovak region. A large network of hiking trails start from the town suburbs. In winter, Banská Bystrica attracts cross-country and downhill-skiing enthusiasts, as a number of ski resorts are near, including the Donovaly resort famous for dog-sledge racing. Banská Bystrica is not only geographically but culturally and historically at Slovakia's heart. The city is home to 90,000 citizens and some of the country's most significant cultural and historical icons. The town grew wealthy as a result of the medieval mining industry and many architectural gems date from then. During World War II, the town was a centre of anti-fascist resistance and the military and political base for the Slovak National Uprising (SNP) remembered in Slovakia's most striking and unusual museum. The town of Banská Bystrica is the administrative, economic and cultural centre of central Slovakia. Among the many monuments and buildings is the Clock Tower which leans like the Tower of Pisa. The city is home to several excellent art galleries, museums and one of Slovakia's top universities, named after scientist-linguist Matej Bel (1684–1749).

HISTORY Prehistoric man discovered Banská Bystrica's mineral riches however rapid growth only began in the Middle Ages with intensive copper and gold mining. The first report of the town dates from 1255 when Hungarian King Béla IV granted it royal privilege and Banská Bystrica soon attracted attention. German settlers, lured by the town's new status, helped make Banská Bystrica wealthy and famous with their advanced mining techniques for gold, silver and copper. The glory days of mining from the 14th–17th centuries left an architectural legacy of Gothic and Renaissance patrician mansions as well as churches in styles from Romanesque to Baroque. The historic Old Town is clustered around a sensitively restored medieval marketplace, now named SNP in honour of the struggle against fascism during World War II. In 1494, a mining entrepreneur from Krakow and a banker from Augsburg formed the Thurzó-Fugger Copper Company (1494–1546) to exploit the mineral riches and which by the 16th century had become the leading producer of copper in the world. In 1589, threatened by the approaching Ottoman army, the town fathers fortified the town with stone walls and built little onion-domed churches into the fortifications, the remains of which can be seen to this day. As a leading centre of the Protestant Reformation, Banská Bystrica fought off the Ottomans, Hungarians and Catholic Austrian Habsburgs. By the 17th century, the mines had given almost all they had to give and Banská Bystrica's industries turned to paper, timber and textiles. During World War II, the town was the centre of anti-Nazi opposition in Slovakia. The Slovak National Uprising, one of the largest movements of anti-fascist resistance in Europe, began in the surrounding hills on 29 August 1944. Slovakia's third-largest city is still best known for this heroic struggle when 30,000 locals died.

GETTING THERE AND AWAY From Bratislava, trains take three–four hours, and passengers are usually required to change in Zvolen.

Direct buses to and from Bratislava take 3–4¹/₂ hours. By car from Bratislava, take route E571 to Zvolen, then the E77 to Banská Bystrica.

TOURIST INFORMATION AND OTHER PRACTICALITIES

⚡ Slovak Tourist Board (SACR) head office Námestie Ľ Štúra 1, PO Box 35; ☏ 048 4136 146; f 048 4136 149; e sacr@sacr.sk; www.sacr.sk
⚡ KiS tourist office Námestie SNP 14; ☏ 048 16

186, 048 4155 085; f 048 4152 272; e kis@ pkobb.sk; www.banskabystrica.sk, www.kisbb@sk. *Open 15 May–15 Sep Mon–Fri 09.00–18.00, Sat 09.00–13.00; 16 Sep–14 May Mon–Fri 09.00–17.00.*

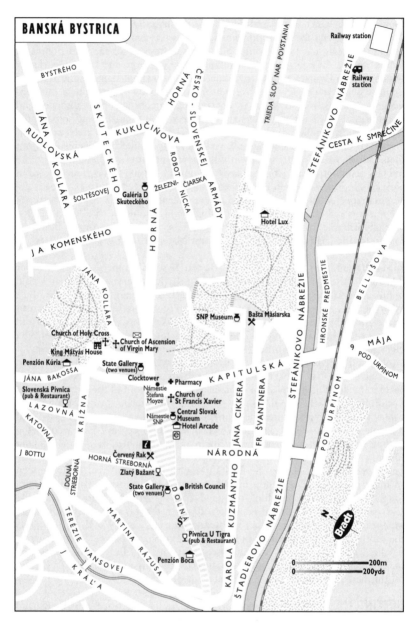

BANSKÁ BYSTRICA

Railway station

BYSTRÉHO

HORNÁ

ČESKO - SLOVENSKEJ

TRIEDA SLOV NAR POVSTANIA

ŠTEFÁNIKOVO NÁBREŽIE

Railway station

JÁNA

RUDLOVSKÁ

SKUTECKÉHO

KUKUČÍŇOVA

ROBOT NÍCKA

ŽELEZNI- ČIARSKA

ARMÁDY

CESTA K SMREČINE

KOLLÁRA

ŠOLTÉSOVEJ

Galéria D Skuteckého

HORNÁ

Hotel Lux

J A KOMENSKÉHO

HORNÁ

JÁNA KOLLÁRA

Church of Holy Cross
King Mátyás House

SNP Museum
Bašta Mäsiarska

Church of Ascension of Virgin Mary

HRONSKÉ PREDMESTIE

BELLUSOVA

MÁJA

Penzión Kúria

State Gallery (two venues)

KAPITULSKÁ

ŠTEFÁNIKOVO NÁBREŽIE

POD URPINOM

JÁNA BAKOSSA

Clocktower

Pharmacy

Slovenská Pivnica (pub & Restaurant)

LAZOVNÁ

KRÍŽNA

Námestie Štefana Moyze

Church of St Francis Xavier

JÁNA CIKKERA

FR ŠVANTNERA

POD URPINOM

KATOVNÁ

Námestie SNP

Central Slovak Museum
Hotel Arcade

J BOTTU

HORNÁ STREBORNÁ

Červený Rak

Zlatý Bažant

NÁRODNÁ

DOLNÁ STRIEBORNÁ

State Gallery (two venues)

British Council

DOLNÁ

KUZMÁNYHO

ŠTEFÁNIKOVO NÁBREŽIE

$ Bank

Pivnica U Tigra (pub & Restaurant)

MARTINA RÁZUSA

Penzión Boca

KAROLA ŠTÁDLEROVO NÁBREŽIE

TERÉZIE VANSOVEJ

J KRÁĽA

Bradt

0 ————— 200m
0 ————— 200yds

Banská Bystrica region information centre
Dolná 35, Banská Bystrica; ☎ 048 4153 591; f 048 412 5122; e sosbb@bb.psg.sk; www.slovanet.sk/sosbb

British Council Dolná 7; www.britishcouncil.sk. Open Tue 12.30–18.30, Wed 10.00–18.30, Thu 12.30–18.30, Fri 12.30–17.00, Sat 09.00–13.00.

$ Bank ČSOB, Dolná 12. Open Mon–Thu 08.00–18.00, Fri 08.00–17.00.

✉ **Post office** Námestie Štefana Moyzesa 1. With amazing Socialist worker murals. Open Mon–Fri 08.00–19.00, Sat 08.00–12.00.

✚ **Pharmacy** Lekáreň pri prameň Kapitulská 11. Open Mon–Fri 07.30–18.00.

e **Immedia Internet** Námestie SNP 3. 40 machines, 20Sk for 1hr.

WHERE TO STAY Those with transport will relish the secluded hunting/ski retreat at Šachtička (see page 236), north of Banská Bystrica, however there are also good choices in town.

⌂ **Hotel Arcade** Námestie SNP 5; ⤫ 048 4302 111; fax. 048 4123 126; e arcade@mail.viapvt.sk; www.arcade.sk. A 3-star hotel right in the centre, in a historic building dating from 1576. Good wine cellar restaurant. *Sgl, dbl* $$.
⌂ **Hotel Lux** (140 rooms) Námestie Slobody 2; ⤫ 048 4144 141; f 048 4143 853; e lux@ hotellux.sk; www.hotellux.sk. A 3-star business hotel in a tower block in the city park opposite the SNP Museum. B/fast not inc. *Sgl, dbl* $$.

⌂ **Penzión Boca** (23 beds) Dolná 52; ⤫ 048 4152 254; f 048 4152 253; e penzion.boca@stonline.sk; www.penzion-boca.sk. A pension, cocktail bar, pub & restaurant all in one on a major pedestrian street in the centre. *Dbl* $$.
⌂ **Penzión Kúria** (11 rooms) Bakossova 4; ⤫ 048 4123 255; f 048 4152 959; e kuria@kuria.sk; www.kuria.sk. Stylish pension built in 1759, rustic restaurant. *Dbl* $$.

✖ **WHERE TO EAT AND DRINK**

✖ **Bašta Mäsiarska** Kapitulská 23; ⤫ 048 4129 281. A snack bar on the ground floor, café on the first floor & restaurant ($) on the top floor. *Open daily 09.00–23.00.*
✖ **Červený rak** Námestie SNP 13; ⤫ 048 4153 882; e post@cervenyrak.sk; www.cervenyrak.sk. Famous restaurant 'Red Crayfish' with a smoky cellar bar, summer terrace, good food & massive portions; a good place to try the local speciality *haruľa* (potato pancakes). $$. *Open Mon–Sat 11.00–22.00.*

✖ **Pivnica U Tigra** Dolná 36; ⤫ 048 4124 919. Popular pub & restaurant with excellent dishes. $. *Pub open daily 09.00–22.00, restaurant daily 10.00–22.00.*
✖ **Slovenská Pivnica** Lazovná 18; ⤫ 048 4155 036. Wood décor in cellar, excellent traditional dishes. $. *Open Mon–Sat 11.00–22.00.*
♀ **Zlatý bažant** Námestie SNP 11; ⤫ 048 4124 500. Great pub in the cellar. *Open Tue–Sat 08.00–midnight, Sun–Mon 10.00–midnight.*

WHAT TO SEE AND DO Most historical monuments and interesting buildings are found on or around the picturesque main square, **Námestie SNP**, which in summer is filled with terrace cafés and flowers. The square has a Mediterranean ambience and in summer, the spacious squares and streets are bathed in a golden light, children buzz around the square on bikes and queue for ice cream, students drink beer on the many terraces – everyone seems to have time to enjoy life. The square is dominated by a leaning **clock tower** (*Hodinová veža*) built in 1552. Visitors can climb the spiral staircase (*open Apr–Oct 10.00–17.00; admission adult/child 20/10Sk*). Most buildings on the square and the surrounding streets are well-preserved Gothic, Renaissance, and Baroque burgher houses. The **Thurzó House** (*Thurzov dom*) at Námestie SNP 4 is an elegant white building with little squashed oval windows on the top floor and intricate paintwork. From 1492 to 1540, the building served as administrative offices for the Thurzó-Fugger Company. Today it houses the **Central Slovak Museum** (*Stredoslovenské Múzeum; www.stredoslovenske.muzeum.sk; open Mon–Fri 08.00–12.00 & 13.00–16.00, Sun 10.00–17.00; admission adult/child 40/20Sk*) Across the square at number 16, the **Benicky House** (*Benického dom*) resembles a doge's palace with Renaissance portals, and a second-floor arcaded loggia, decorated with stunning lunette vaults and ornaments. In front of this building is a black obelisk commemorating the Red Army's liberation of the city in 1945 and behind it a bulky, busy **Fountain of Stones** (*Kamenná fontaná*). At the top of the square, a plague column stands in front of the 17th-century **Church of St Francis Xavier** (*Katedrála Sv Františka Xaverského*) with its solid yellow façade and boxy twin towers.

The oldest part of town is the complex of castle buildings just to the north of Námestie SNP, clustered around a square guarded by a barbican and the 16th-century former Renaissance **town hall** (*radnica*), now housing the **State**

Gallery (*Dolná 8;* ↘ *048 4124 167; open Jul–Aug Tue–Sun 11.00–18.00; Sep–Jun Mon–Fri 10.00–17.00, Sat–Sun 10.00–16.00; admission adult/child 30/20Sk*) showing Slovak art from the 20th century on. The one-nave parish **Church of Ascension of the Virgin Mary** (*Farský kostol Nanebovzatia Panny Márie*) was built in 1255 by German settlers in Romanesque and Gothic styles. A side chapel dedicated to St Barbara, patron saint of miners, contains a precious Gothic carved wooden altar by Master Pavol of Levoča (see page 271). It is the oldest building in the city and sensitive restoration has brought out the beauty of its beige and pink walls. Behind glass is a preserved 15th-century three-dimensional tableau showing Christ on the Mount of Olives, based on a Durer etching and with Jerusalem depicted to resemble Banská Bystrica. In 1452, the Slovaks constructed the **Church of the Holy Cross** (*kostol Sv Kríža*) just behind, as a kind of reply to the 'German' Church of the Virgin. Damaged in a great fire of 1761, it contains a magnificent organ dating from 1779. **King Mátyás House** (1479) is a five-storey late-Gothic palace with a stone balcony built for the wife of Hungary's enlightened king. The gateway in the remaining castle wall leads to a peaceful cemetery (*open daily 07.00–18.00*). From Námestie Štefana Moyzesa, follow Kapitulská southeast to find the incredible **SNP Museum** (*Múzeum slovenského národného povstania; Kapitulská 23; www.muzeumsnp.sk; open May–Sep Tue–Sun 09.00–18.00; Oct–Apr 09.00–16.00; admission adult/concession 50/20Sk*), built by architect Dušan Kuzma and sculptor Jozef Jankovič in 1969. It is built in two segments, which wags joke resemble everything from a mushroom to a deep-pan pizza to a burger bun split down the middle, but is supposed to depict a Slovak folk hat like one Jánošík might have worn. The split represents the breakthrough that the SNP movement created in Slovak history, rather than, as some say, the split between the Slovak and Czech nations, which was not the point at the time. In between the two halves is a moving statue and an eternal flame. The museum is worth a visit; it is well arranged and contains fascinating details on the anti-fascist movement. Behind the SNP Museum is a spacious park. The little tower across the car park, dotted with tanks, anti-aircraft guns and planes, is the **Bašta Mäsiarska**, built in 1587 as part of the defensive walls and now a popular restaurant. North of the park the **Galéria D Skuteckého** (*Horná 55;* ↘ *048 4125 450; open Tue–Sun 10.00–16.00; admission adult/child 40/20Sk*), in a house designed by the artist, shows works by the Slovak Jewish painter Dominik Skutecký (1849–1921) who lived and worked in Banská Bystrica.

SOUTH OF BANSKÁ BYSTRICA

SLIAČ AIRPORT Sliač International Airport (↘ *045 5443 323;* e *handling@ airportsliac.sk; www.airportsliac.sk*) , historically also known as 'Three oaks' (*Tri duby*), is situated between Zvolen and Banská Bystrica. The airport dates back to before World War II although regular passenger flights started in 1947. Since July 2003, the airport connects the Banská Bystrica region with the rest of the world, as regular passenger flights were re-established. Czech Airlines fly to Sliač six times a week with the 45-seater ATR 42. Military aircraft use Sliač and in the summer, eight local travel agencies use charter airlines to fly holidaymakers from Sliač to Bourgas, a Bulgarian Black Sea resort.

SLIAČ SPA (↘ *045 5443 794;* f *045 5443 794;* e *sales@spa-sliac.sk; www.spa-sliac.sk*). The spa is situated between Banská Bystrica, and the district town of Zvolen, surrounded by extensive forests, parks and plains. First mentioned in 1244, during the reign of King Béla IV, Sliač spa began operation in the 16th

All over Slovakia there are bridges, squares and streets commemorating the SNP (Slovenské Národné Povstanie), the Slovak National Uprising which was one of the biggest anti-fascist insurrections during World War II. The uprising attempted to remove the pro-Nazi government of President Tiso. Josef Tiso, a Catholic priest, came into power on 14 March 1939 when Slovakia had ceded from Czechoslovakia and became independent under German protection. In December 1943, the underground Slovak National Council was formed with the signing of the so-called 'Christmas Treaty'. Backed by the exiled Czechoslovak government in London, the council was responsible for preparing the uprising. In March 1944, Slovak army lieutenant-colonel Ján Golian took charge of the preparations. Approximately 3,200 Slovak soldiers deserted and joined partisan groups or the Soviet Red Army. On 27 August 1944, a group of partisans in Martin killed 30 members of a German military mission. The next day Nazi troops arrived to put down the rebellion.

The Slovak National Uprising was launched officially on 29 August 1944 from Banská Bystrica. At the beginning, the rebel forces had an estimated 18,000 soldiers, a total which later increased to 60,000, plus 12,000 partisans. There were many foreign troops and people involved: in total, 32 nations participated in the uprising. The insurgents used biplanes and armoured trains to fight the German army. The last armoured train, called *Hurban*, and used in the Slovak national uprising, is exhibited in Zvolen.

The rebels hoped to get help from the Red Army which advanced towards Slovakia from Poland. However, the Soviets failed to penetrate quickly the Dukla Pass, the mountain pass in the Carpathian Mountains between Poland and Slovakia. The battle for Dukla Pass started on 8 September 1944 and lasted for two months, taking a tremendous toll: 85.000 Red Army soldiers lost their lives. By the time the Red Army entered Slovakia through the Dukla Pass, the organised resistance was crushed by the Germans. By the middle of September, there were 48,000 German troops under the command of General Hofle to suppress the uprising. By mid October, a further 35,000 troops were sent from Hungary. By the end of October 1944, the uprising was crushed by the German forces, although partisan warfare continued up to the end of the war. Following the uprising, the retaliation was ruthless. The Nazis razed 93 villages to the ground: their populations were shot or transported to concentration camps. The biggest massacre took place in Nemecká with around 900 killed and in Kremnička, with 747 killed. Altogether at least 5,300 died in these actions.

During the communist regime, the Slovak National Uprising was pictured as the most glorious chapter of Slovak history. Nowadays, the uprising is viewed as a more complex matter. The main military objectives were not achieved due to the fact the uprising was launched prematurely. The Slovak population paid heavily: at least 20,000 died during the uprising. However, the uprising and the following guerrilla struggle bound significant German forces. Although the uprising failed, some political legitimacy was achieved. In the autumn of 1944, the leaders of the Slovak National Council went to London to negotiate, eventually, the status of Slovakia in post-war Czechoslovakia. As a result of the uprising, Slovaks participated in the post-war arrangements on the winners' side, despite having a pro-Nazi government for six years.

century. In the past it was one of the Hungarian Kingdom's most popular spas. The present Sliač spa, with the dominant Spa Hotel Palace complex (*dbl* $$), dates back to the 1930s. The healing water contains sulphates, carbohydrates, magnesium and calcium, as well as a high level of carbon dioxide, with an isothermic temperature of 33.3°C. There are only three other similar spas in the world, in Argentina, Spain and Australia. The water benefits heart problems.

Sliač spa is located in the foothills of the Slovenské Rudohorie Mountains, surrounded by forest at a 373m altitude.

HEADING NORTH FROM BANSKÁ BYSTRICA

SKI AT ŠACHTIČKY-ŠPANIA DOLINA Šachtičky is a small resort in the Low Tatras 8km north of Banská Bystrica. It is used mainly by locals as their secret ace hidden from tourists who head for larger ski centres and miss this excellent little resort boasting tiring and difficult tracks and one of the steepest tow lifts in the country. This lift takes skiers up from 800m to 1,104m from where they can select from among a 500m long-slalom trail, an 860m giant slalom trail, and a number of practice trails. A cross-country trail takes sporty folk all the way to Donovaly, some 20km away, however check that the tracks have been maintained recently. A one-day pass for adults costs 520Sk, for a three-day pass expect to pay 1,430Sk. Après ski is excellent with several buffet stalls, two Koliba mountain restaurants, the bar and restaurant at Hotel Šachtička and also down in the Špania Dolina Valley are several top restaurants.

The skiing centre is situated behind **Pánsky diel** Hill (1,100m), which is criss-crossed with mountain-bike trails, hiking trails and cross-country ski routes. A marked path leads from Šachtičky through Špania Dolina to Donovaly and is suitable for hiking and cross-country skiing.

Getting there Take route 59/E77 north out of Banská Bystrica towards Ružomberok. After 2km turn right signposted for Sasová suburb and keep following the road uphill.

For Špania Dolina stay on route 59/E77 and turn right after 6km signposted for Špania Dolina.

Where to stay and eat

Horský hotel Šachtička (44 dbls, 3 apts) Šachtičky 34; ℡ 048 4141 911; f 048 4145 670; e reservation@sachticka.sk; www.sachticka.sk. One of the best hotels in central Slovakia, located at the top of a mountain 15mins' drive north of Banská Bystrica, 45min by foot from Špania Dolina. Something really special, particularly if you have your own wheels. Fitness centre, solarium, 3 kinds of sauna, jacuzzi, pool, massage, stables with 10 horses, ski slopes on the doorstep. A great base for cross-country skiing, biking & hiking. Two kolibas (mountain cottage restaurants), a wonderfully atmospheric restaurant ($$; open daily 07.30–21.00) with a

hunting lodge theme, blazing fires & stuffed trophies. Basic, comfortable rooms with balconies & gorgeous views. Price includes pool, fitness centre, spa, table tennis, parking. Dbl $$, apt $$$.

✕ Koliba Center Šachtičky 34; ℡ 048 4141 911; e reservation@sachticka.sk; www.sachticka.sk. Two typical Slovak cottage restaurants situated between the hotel & the ski slopes. Try Slovak & Hungarian specialities inside the cottage or outside in front of a roaring fireplace. Fine dining also available in the hotel's luxurious restaurant, superb wine list & charming service. $$. Open daily 07.30–21.00.

ŠPANIA DOLINA – A SLOVAK SHANGRI-LA Hidden away in the hills, accessible only by foot, bike or one minor winding road, Špania Dolina is like a secret paradise where time stands still. The village lies in a valley but also creeps up the sides of the hills: the lowest part is at 722m while the highest part is at 1,100m. The tiny hamlet (population 150) has seen hard times, the collapse of the iron-ore mining industry and with it the hamlet's economy and the SNP battles when 15 locals died fighting the Nazis, however Špania Dolina has a jovial ambience, maybe because village life is concentrated around two pubs on the main square (Klopačka and a more spit 'n' sawdust pub). Tools used by prehistoric miners date back to 2000–1700BC. Medieval mining at Špania Dolina, together with other villages in the area, contributed to the success and wealth of the region and Banská Bystrica was the copper metropolis of Europe. The mines and the whole surrounding area belonged to the Chamber of Mines. Most of the profits went to two companies controlled by the Fugger and Thurzó families. The well-known bankers exploited the miners, leading to numerous uprisings, the largest being in 1525–26. The House of Fugger funded a laboratory for the famous alchemist Paracelsus in Špania Dolina and the prominent French thinker Montesquieu also visited. Small miners' houses crept up the steep hillsides and the village grew with new technical buildings: workshops, storage houses, ore crushers, sample rooms and maps houses as well as private houses and workshops for blacksmiths and carpenters. In the 18th century, the copper ore deposits were almost exhausted. The mines closed down in 1888 and the economy of the village is now based on tourism. It is a lovely village to explore, climb hills, stagger up the steep covered 161-step stairway to the Roman Catholic church (1593) looming above the main square and wander past old miners' cottages. Many shafts, water channels and interesting features are described on boards in Slovak and English dotted about the village. With EU Phare (to develop new member states) funding, they have created a kind of living, working museum, teeming with fun and interest.

Getting there The local bus takes 30 minutes from Banská Bystrica (platform 8). By car: follow route 59/E77 north out of Banská Bystrica in the direction of Donovaly and Ružomberok. About ten minutes out of town is a turn-off, a single-lane road winding through the forest up to Špania Dolina.

Tourist information and other practicalities

Ⓘ Pod Panským dielom microregion information centre Námestie SNP 13, Slovenská Ľupča; ✆ 048 4723 216; f 048 4723 217; e tic@slovenskalupca.sk; www.panskydiel.sk

⚒ Jedivo a potrebné m 0905 319 454. Village shop next to the pub with some souvenirs. Open Tue–Fri 08.00–14.00, Sat 08.00–11.00.
🚕 Funtaxi ✆ 048 4148 484; m 0907 188 505; www.funtaxibb.com. Rates 13.50Sk per km.

Where to stay, eat and drink

🏠 Chalupa (7 beds) Špania Dolina 187; m 0905 218 665; e andyluco@andyluco.sk. Another lovely miner's house with 7 beds in various permutations. $.
🏠 ChalupaGrant (10 beds) Horná 48; ✆ 048 4123 808; e chalupagrant@chalupagrant.sk; www.chalupagrant.sk. Stay in a renovated 200-year-old miner's house. $.

🏠 Penzión Klopačka Špania Dolina 102; ✆ 048 4198 440; e klopacka@wesco.sk; www.klopacka.sk. Fab pension, restaurant and terrace on the main square. Sgl $, dbl $$. Restaurant ($) open Mon–Sat 10.00–22.00, Sun 10.00–20.00.
♀ Banícka krčma Typical local pub on the main square. Open Mon–Sat 10.00–20.00.

☞ **POZOR!** Špania Dolina makes a fabulous afternoon walk downhill (20 minutes) from Šachtička, admiring miners' cottages on the way. However, after a soup and several thirst-quenching beers, it's much more of a struggle going back up the steep, sometimes slippery, slope (45 minutes).

HARMANECKÁ JASKYŇA (CAVE) The cave (Dolný Harmanec; ✆ 048 4198 122; e harmanj@ssj.sk; www.ssj.sk; open Tue–Sun 15 May–31 May 10.00, 12.00, 14.00, 15.00; 1 Jun–30 Jun 10.00–16.00 on the hour; 1 Jul–31 Aug

10.00–17.00 on the hour; 1 Sep–31 Oct 10.00, 12.00, 14.00, 15.00; 1 Nov–14 May closed; admission adult/child 120/60Sk) lies northwest of Banská Bystrica on the boundary of Veľká Fatra and Kremnické vrchy, near the town of Harmanec. Thanks to its characteristic snowy coloration, it acquired the name White Cave. The largest accessible section is *Dom pagôd* (House of Pagodas), characterised by its massive architectural formations. The symbol of the cave is the bright white rock vase. Anyone who succeeds in tossing a coin into it will be rewarded with a wish.

Getting there Situated north of Harmanec on route E577. Take a bus leaving Banská Bystrica main bus station (platform 9) to Horný Harmanec. A train from Banská Bystrica to Turčianske Teplice–Diviaky goes through the valley and mountains, passing through 22 tunnels; the longest is 4.498m. Get off at the Harmanecká jaskyňa stop. Check the timetable at the railway station in Banská Bystrica, as the train does not run very often.

SKIING AT DONOVALY (*www.skidonovaly.sk/uk.html*) Donovaly is one of Slovakia's best-equipped ski resorts. Nestling in a deep valley some 30 minutes north of Banská Bystrica and 960m above sea level, Donovaly is not for experienced skiers. It is one of the best beginner terrains in the country and snowboarders can also feast upon the wide and relatively gentle slopes situated to the south (Záhradište) and southeast (Nová Hoľa) parts of the resort. In the 2005/06 season, Donovaly opened a Telemix 6/8, a hybrid facility featuring six-person chair lifts and eight-person gondolas on the same cableway. The lift, serving the longest run of 2km rises to the Nová Hoľa summit station (1,360m) and allow better access to the resort's extensive slopes and backcountry areas. Apart from this new lift, a further 15, mostly surface, lifts serve the Nová Hoľa location as well as the lower-lying Záhradište tracks. The Záhradište tracks are especially recommended to beginners as well as for children for whom a complete snow park was opened in December 2005. As the slopes are covered by grass a small amount of snow is enough already. Cross-country skiers can enjoy a total of 30km of routes through lovely snow-dusted forest land which is quite accommodating. The centre also boasts a professional ice rink and night skiing on the illuminated Záhradište slope until 21.00. Lifts also link individual localities in the area and people can catch ski buses at weekends. Customer service in Donovaly is up to western standards: there is a number of *chatas* (mountain huts) serving food and drinks, and snow-related entertainment includes husky dog sledges and competitions as an extra.

Donovaly ski centre holds dog-sledge competitions. For adults, a one-day pass is 640Sk, for three days expect to pay 1,170Sk.

Getting there From Banská Bystrica. Donovaly is 26km north on the road to Ružomberok.

Tourist information
🄸 **Info Donovaly** Námestie Sv Antona Paduánskeho 136; ✆ 048 4199 900; f 048 4199 909; e info@donovaly.sk; www.parksnow.sk. *Open Mon–Fri 08.30–12.30 & 13.00–16.00.*

Where to stay
🏠 **Hotel Žiar Donovaly** Donovaly 18; ✆ 048 4199 901; f 048 4199 717. Great hotel in Donovaly. *Dbl* $.

🏠 **Tatran & Magura Apartment Hotels** m 0902 365 555; e info@skidonovaly.com; www.liptov.sk/skidonovaly. Two apartment blocks only 10m from the chair lifts at Donovaly. *Apts* $-$$$.

KORYTNICA SPA (*Fatranské liečebné kúpele;* ☎ *048 4396 930;* f *048 4396 926;* e *korytnica_odbyt@bb.telecom.sk*) Korytnica is 4km east of Donovaly. The first spa buildings were built in 1824. After two great fires in 1911 and 1921, a large part of the spa was destroyed. Recently, the thermal complex was restored again. The Korytnica Spa is situated in the Low Tatra National Park under Prasiva Mountain (1,675m). Thanks to moderately mineralised and hipotonic mineral water, containing sulphates and carbonates, the water is efficacious in treating gastric problems. You can buy bottled Korytnica mineral water at all major supermarkets.

ĽUPČIANSKY HRAD AT SLOVENSKÁ ĽUPČA (☎ *048 4187 428; open Jul–Aug Tue–Sun 10.00–16.00*). An impressive fortress castle, founded in 1250 and originally used as a royal hunting residence. Reconstructed in the 17th century, when the noble Ľupča family added arcades to the courtyard and altered the arches. After a fire in 1860, the castle was used as an orphanage and during the last days of communism it was home to nuns. Continuous use has kept the castle in a good condition. The well has five underground passages leading from it and during Turkish raids it was used to smuggle people from the town into the castle. Tours visit the torture chamber in the dungeon and climb the castle tower. Slovakia's oldest tree, a massive 700-year-old lime, stands next to the castle gate. Legend says that King Mátyás Corvinus liked to sit under the tree, just like the lime tree at Bojnice Castle. It is 25m high with a trunk circumference of almost 7.5m.

Getting there Around 10km east from Banská Bystrica on route 66 to Brezno. On major bus and train routes also.

BRUSNO SPA (*Kúpele Brusno;* ☎ *048 4194 674;* f *048 4194 200;* e *marketing@ kupelebrusno.sk; www.kupelebrusno.sk*). Situated 12km further east along route 66 after Ľupča Castle, Brusno's significance as a spa town grew in the 19th century. The alkaline sulphur springs are good for treating digestive diseases, gall bladder, liver and pancreas problems and obesity. Therapy is based on water-drinking treatments, complemented by hydrotherapy, electrotherapy, rehabilitative exercise and massages. Spa guests have a great view of the peaks of the Low Tatras and Prašivá Hill.

Getting there On route 66 20km from Banská Bystrica.

BREZNO Brezno (269km from Bratislava) is an attractive town clustered around the Hron River. Inhabited since prehistoric times, the town arose from an old Slovak settlement. Immigrant German miners built a typical market square in the early 13th century. In 1265, the Hungarian King Béla IV issued a charter for the hunters from the Liptov area allowing them to use wood from the surrounding region known as *Berezuno*. The name is derived from the Slovak word *breza* or birch. In the 19th century, Brezno was one of the centres of the Slovak national movement. Since World War II, it has become much more industrialised.

Getting there On route 66 20km further east from Brusno.

Tourist information

ⓘ **Brezno tourist information office** Námestie M R Štefánika 3; ☎/f 048 6114 221; e tikbr@brezno.sk; www.brezno.sk

ⓘ **Microregion Horehronie** ☎ 048 6452 420; e webhotline@zelpo.sk

Banská Bystrica Region EAST OF BANSKÁ BYSTRICA

9

239

ČIERNY HRON LOGGING RAILWAY The *Čiernohronská lesná železnica* (forest railway) (*Hlavná 56;* \ *048 6191 500;* e *jazda.vlakom.chz@isternet.sk; www.chz.sk/mnu01a.html*) runs between Chvatimech (6km west of Brezno) and Čierny Balog. Built in 1908, transportation of timber began a year later. Volunteers have preserved a 17km stretch of the original 131km line. In 1992, little tourist trains began operating on a 12km line between Chvatimech and Čierny Balog is prolonged on weekends in July and August to include the Čierny Balog–Vydrovská dolina section with a steam locomotive. Sights passed on the way are Chvatimech, Valaská railway bridge over the Hron, Hronec station, Svátý Ján watch house, Šánske, Krám and Čierny Balog.

Getting there On route 66 6km west of Brezno.

BYSTRIANSKA JASKYŇA (CAVE) (\ *048 6195 133;* e *bystrj@ssj.sk; www.ssj.sk; open Tue–Sun Jun–Aug 09.00–16.00 on the hour; Jan–May & Sep–Oct 09.30, 11.00, 12.30, 14.00; Nov–Dec closed; admission adult/child 80/40Sk, a visit lasts 40min).* One section of the 2km-long cave under the Low Tatra Mountains is called 'Hell'. Winding corridors with beautiful curtain-shaped honeycomb-like decorations are open to the public. Visitors will find the cave at the southern edge of the town of Bystrá, near Tále golf course. The most beautiful part of the cave is called *klenotnica* (jewellery box) and other sections, such as *peklo* (hell), *katakomby* (catacombs) and *zrútený dóm* (collapsed dome) are also very striking. The cave also offers speleotherapy; therapeutic breathing exercise sessions in the cave.

Getting there Take route 66 back west to Chvatimech, turn right and head north on route 72 for 4km.

GRAY BEAR GOLF COURSE AT TÁLE (\ *048 6712 512;* f *048 6712 514; infotale@tale.sk; www.tale.sk, www.graybear.sk, www.golftale.sk).* Situated 8km north of Brezno, just off route 584 to Liptovský Mikuláš, the Gray Bear golf course is the first 18-hole course in Slovakia. It opened on 8 August 2002 with Tony Jacklin as a special guest. The 60ha, par-71 course, co-designed by Robert Walton, has a total length of 6,266m. There is a clubhouse and driving range as well as a pitch-and-putt course. Additional services include rental and sale of golf equipment, small golf academy, training hours and children's summer camps.

Getting there From Bystrianska jaskyňa turn left off route 72 onto route 584 and drive for 2km.

JASKYŇA MŘTVYCH NETOPIEROV (CAVE OF DEAD BATS) (*Book tours at* m *0905 135 535;* e *jmnroman@host.sk)* Located 2km north of Tále at Trangoška (route 584) is the Cave of Dead Bats (*Jaskyňa Mřtvych Netopierov*), so named because of all the bat bones found there. The cave is cold and windy and many hibernating bats don't make it through the winter. The cave is not open to the public, but the Speleo Club of Slovakia will take visitors on a 1km tour on a route that is illuminated and equipped with fixed iron ladders and bridges. Not suitable for children under six, elderly or unfit visitors.

NÍZKE TATRY NATIONAL PARK (LOW TATRAS) (*Internátna 2, Banská Bystrica;* \ *088 4130 888;* f *088 4130 820;* e *napant@sazp.sk; www.nizketatry.sk).* The Low Tatras National Park (Národný park Nízke Tatry, abbreviated as NAPANT) straddles the Banská Bystrica and Žilina (see page 217) regions. There are several important ski resorts in the Low Tatras: Jasná, Mýto pod Ďumbierom, and Tále. These are also hubs of hiking and cross-country skiing trails. The steep northern slopes of the range are popular among climbers. Other attractions include an 18-hole golf course near Tále and Korytnica spa. The national park is dotted with *chatas* (mountain refuges) where hikers can turn up unannounced and stay overnight with prices hovering around 300Sk per person per night. Type in 'chata' at www.nizketatry.sk for a complete list of venues, prices and services.

MURÁŇ PLAIN NATIONAL PARK (MURÁNSKA PLANINA) Situated to the southeast of the Low Tatras, beyond the Horehronské podolie range, is the undiscovered Muráň Plain (*Muránska planina*) National Park. It's a forested, karst upland, a 20,318ha plateau in the northeast of the Banská Bystrica region and one of the youngest national parks in Slovakia, opened in 1996 when Vladimír Mečiar held sway. East of Brezno, in a relatively unpopulated area, the Muráň Plain preserves its original character well. Deep valleys with a number of waterfalls have been formed in limestone and dolomite rocks. The abundance and great variety of karst forms of the territory are represented by 170 caves, often with dripstone decoration or glaciations, 14 chasms with Michňova (105m) the deepest, and 70 karst springs. There is a rich variety of flora and fauna including an abundance of molluscs, bugs, butterflies and newts. Eye-catching salamanders, rare golden eagle (*Aquila chrysaetos*) and the big and cuddly eagle owl (*Bubo bubo*) all live here. The caves are home to around 18 species of bats. The ruins of Muránsky Castle with its famous Cigánka cliff and also the castle at Predná Hora give a taste of history to this territory.

MURÁŇ CASTLE RUINS The village of Muráň, 24km east of Čierny Balog, is the starting point for the hike up to the castle. Follow the blue or red trail, Mária Széchy's Path, for 90 minutes.

The castle was built in 1271 on a limestone rock called *Cigánka* (gipsy girl). It defended the road from Gemer to Liptov and Zvolen. At an altitude of 938m it is the third-highest castle in Slovakia after Liptov Castle (1,001m) and Zniev (963m). Reconstructed and enlarged over the centuries, by the 1620s it covered the entire hill. In 1644, Ferenc Wesselényi took control of the castle with the aid of Mária Széchy who lived there with her sister and who later became his wife. Mária was known as the 'Muráň Venus' because of her beauty. Wesselényi was appointed Hungarian palatine (the king's representative in Hungary). In 1666, Wesselényi joined a conspiracy plotting to overthrow the Habsburg emperor Leopold but died the following year. Mária bravely defended the castle until 1670 when imperial soldiers conquered it. The castle burned down twice and was abandoned in the 18th century.

Getting there From Brezno, take route 530 to Tisovec, turn left onto route 531 and continue for 12km to the village of Muráň. Buses every hour from Brezno take one hour.

ČÍŽ The village of Číž (pronounced 'cheese') at the southern part of the Teška River valley was settled by the late Stone Age. The spa (*Prírodné jódové kúpele Číž* (Natural iodine spa) \ 047 5593 133; f 047 5591 121; e cizkupele@cizkupele.sk; www.kupeleciz.sk) was built after 1860 when locals drilling for a well found an iodine spring, later named Themis. The spa opened in 1889 with buildings modelled after a Swiss convalescent hospital. The spa has cold, hypotonic salty springs used to treat neurological disorders in children and adults, bowel problems, hypertension and post-operative conditions. The unusual healing effects of the iodine-bromine water make the natural iodine spa at Číž one of a kind.

Getting there From Fiľakovo take route 571 east for 40km. Trains from Fiľakovo to the Lenartovce stop, 2km east of Číž.

RIMAVSKÁ SOBOTA Rimavská Sobota is situated 289km from Bratislava in a very poor, neglected part of the country. The main square is attractive with some historic buildings and the elegant Church of St John the Baptist. It is possible to join the **Gothic Route** (*Gotická cesta*) trail at Rimavská Sobota, the most southerly attraction on a huge 276km route, looping up around the Košice, Prešov and Banská Bystrica regions and taking in 24 villages and nine towns, dominated by incredible Gothic churches. For more on the Gothic Route see page 271.

LUČENEC Lučenec was first mentioned in 1128 and, situated very close to the border with Hungary, the population is Slovak, Magyar and Roma and the atmosphere cosmopolitan and Wild West. During the 1848–49 uprising against the Habsburgs, the city was burned to the ground, but managed to resurrect itself within ten years. At the turn of the 19th century, Lučenec was a thriving commercial centre and larger than any other town in present-day Slovakia. However, today it's a somewhat scruffy border town with a clutch of interesting buildings. Sadly, the elegant Art Nouveau synagogue (corner of J A Komenského and Sokolská) is on its last legs. Designed in 1925 by Lipot Baumhorn, the creator of more synagogues than any other European architect, the building is now only a crumbling shell. In the 1930s, the Jewish population of Lučenec was 2,100 out of a total town population of 9,000. When the area was annexed to Hungary in November 1938, many Jews were sent to forced labour camps. In May 1944, when the Nazis took control, a ghetto was created in the town. Most Jews were deported from Lučenec to Auschwitz in June 1944.

Getting there There is a very fast highway, route 50/E571 from Zvolen, filled with lorries and silver Audis overtaking on bends. Regular buses from Zvolen take one hour (59km).

Tourist information
🔲 **Lučenec information centre** Masarykova 14; ➐ 047 4512 022; f 047 4331 513;
e info@lucenec.sk; www.lucenec.sk

 ### Where to stay and swim
🏠 **Best Western Hotel Reduta** Vajanského 2; ➐ 047 4331 237. A 3-star hotel in the centre in a beautiful 1820 building originally a casino. Dbl $$.
Thermal spa Dolná Strehová ➐ 047 4897 211; f 047 4897 210; e podniksluzieb@stonline.sk. Dolná Strehová, halfway between Lučenec and Veľký Krtíš,
is famous for its thermal springs and huge spa spreading over a 6ha area. Its thermal spring water is 36°C and there are 5 swimming pools (sports, relaxing, sitz bath and 2 for children). Open 15 May–21 Aug 08.00–19.00.

FIĽAKOVO Situated 14km southeast of Lučenec and almost on the Hungarian border, Fiľakovo (Fülek in Hungarian) is a mostly Hungarian-speaking, ramshackle town notable for its photogenic castle ruins (*open Tue–Sun 10.00–18.00; admission adult/child 50/20Sk*), perched on a volcanic crag about the small town. Legend tells how a shepherd named Filek was out walking with his dog, Füles ('long-eared'), and they found treasure which they used to build a castle. Built originally as a wooden structure in 1246, the structure was strengthened in 1551 to prepare for Turkish invasions. In 1554, 10,000 invading Turks captured the castle and stayed for 39 years. Explanatory boards in Slovak, Hungarian and English give detailed accounts of the castle's history.

Getting there Route 71 from Lučenec.

ŠOMOŠKA AND THE STONE WATERFALL
Located 10km south of Fiľakovo, Šomoška straddles the Slovak–Hungarian border. The castle ruins stand in Slovakia while the village beneath, Šomoškô is in Hungary.

The castle was built in 1323, occupied by the Turks in the 16th century and destroyed in 1703. The castle is still in good condition, with a main tower and (new) pointed roof dominating the little village below. The hike from the village of Šiatorská Bukovina passes an unusual rock formation, the stone waterfall (*kamenný vodopad*), created by basalt lava which four million years ago hardened into curved columns resembling liquid rock pouring into a stone sea. Such basalt columns are found only at seven places in the world: Slovakia, the Czech Republic, Hungary, Italy, Northern Ireland, Wyoming and California.

Getting there Take route 71 south out of Fiľakovo towards the Hungarian border.

DIVÍN CASTLE AND RUŽINÁ LAKE
Northwest of Lučenec on route 50/E571 are the ruins of a Gothic castle, built in the second half of the 13th century by Lučenec lords to protect routes to the central Slovak mining towns. A new anti-Ottoman defensive line was added in 1559 with a modern bastion and two corner bulwarks. It didn't work and the Turks took the castle in 1575 and stayed until 1593. In the 17th century, the last owner of Divín was Imre Balassa, a rich Hungarian noble who used the castle as a base for a life of robbing. A relative, János Balassa, was imprisoned twice for plotting against the Habsburgs. The imperial general Strasoldo demolished the castle in 1694 to drive out the bad Balassas. A 17th-century fortified Baroque church and a Renaissance manor house still stand and watch over the beautiful Ružina Reservoir, which is used in summer for swimming and windsurfing.

☞ *POZOR!* Don't confuse Ružina with another lake, Ružin, 18km northwest of Košice.

Getting there Follow route 50/E571 north out of Lučenec to Mýtna, turn left at the village's main intersection and follow the road to Divín. The ruins are in the village, the lake is nearby.

DETVA
On the second weekend in July, this small town hosts one of the best-known folk festivals in Slovakia, *Folklórne slávnosti pod Poľanou*, 'Folklore Festival under Poľana'. Poľana is a range of hills north of Detva, topped by Polianka Peak (1,457m). The 42nd season of this annual folklore festival features a folk handicrafts market at Detva's natural amphitheatre and Dom kultúry A Sládkoviča (✆ *045 5455 202; www.fspdetva.sk*). The village cemetery has carved wooden grave markers (*kopjafa*) resembling totem poles that are a feature of traditional rural Hungary. **Podpolianské Múzeum** (*open Mon–Fri 08.00–16.00*) has a large collection of handcrafted folk objects.

Getting there Detva is on the Lučenec–Zvolen highway 50/E571.

MODRÝ KAMEŇ CASTLE
Modrý Kameň (Blue Stone) Castle was built in 1137, as protection against the Tartars. In the 16th century, it was part of the Hungarian Empire's defence against the Turks. However, in 1575, the Turks conquered the castle and stayed for 18 years. While retreating in 1593, they blew up the castle and left it in ruins. It was finally demolished in 1683. In 1730, wild Magyar

nobleman Gábor Balassa built a Baroque mansion house over the original Gothic ruins, and the elegant manor house now houses the **Museum of Puppet Cultures and Toys** (↘ *047 4870 218;* e *hrad@procomp.sk; open May–Oct Tue–Sun 09.00–17.00; Nov–Apr Mon–Fri 08.00–15.00*) which also includes an exhibition on the history of dental technology.

Getting there Situated 32km southwest of Lučenev on route 75 to Veľký Krtíš. The Gothic ruins and Baroque manor are 5km north on route 527.

SKLABINÁ Literature-loving Hungarians make pilgrimages to Sklabiná (Szklabonya in Hungarian) the birthplace of one of the great figures of Magyar literature, Kálmán Mikszáth (1847–1910), author of *Tót atyafiak* (Slovak Kinsmen), *A jó palócok* (The Good Palots) and *Beszterce ostroma* (The Siege of Bystrica). The house where Mikszáth lived is opposite the cemetery (*Pamätný dom Kálmána Mikszátha, Sklabina 188;* ↘ *047 4886 113;* e *mkms@snm.sk; www.snm.sk; open May–Oct Tue–Sun 10.00–17.00; Nov–Apr by appointment; admission adult/child 40/20Sk*) houses a modest exhibition with photos and the writer's works.

THE HONT WINE TRAIL Since 2000, the *Hontianska vínná cesta* (Hont Wine Trail) has been based at Hokovce (in Nitra), 4km south of Dudince. An association of 34 wine-producing villages, mostly in the former historic Hont county, promotes rural tourism, including the regional wine-growing and viticultural traditions. There are gourmet evenings and wine tastings, and regional events such as the May celebration of St Urban, the patron saint of wine growers, and the wine-tasting competition of the Hont wine Trail Grand Prix. Hont takes its name from the lord who ruled the land during the foundation of the Hungarian Kingdom. The territory spreads from Nagymaros (in Hungary on the Danube) to Banská Štiavnica from the Danube to the north, from the river Hron to the east and from Banská Štiavnica to the south. Today the former seat is located in Hungary. Above Hont towers the legendary mountain of Sitno (1,000m), 4km south of Banská Štiavnica.

DUDINCE SPA The spa of Dudince (*www.kupeledudince.sk*) is situated in the southwestern corner of Banská Bystrica region on the border with Nitra. It is Slovakia's youngest spa town and one of the hottest places in the country. These springs are beneficial to the treatments of locomotive organs and therefore diseases of these organs, as well as neural disorders, are mainly treated in this spa. The water contains minerals beneficial for joints, muscles and bones. The thermal spa has a temperature of 28°C. **Medical House Diamant** (*Dudince;* ↘ *045 5502 111;* f *045 5583 418;* e *diamant@diamant.sk; www.diamant.sk*). There is also a large, modern hotel (*Sgl $$$, dbl $$*).

Getting there Route 66/E77 from Zvolen. Regular buses from Zvolen take 50 minutes.

STARÁ HORA IN SEBECHLEBY This folk architecture reserve displays a collection of remarkable vintners' houses and cellars built from stone, clay and wood in the 16th century during the period of battles with the Turks. The settlement and a small church are 3km north of the village of Sebechleby. Visitors can also sample local wines.

Stay in Mladá Hora nearby in little Toblerone-chunk chalets. Contact Dana Chebeňová, Tatranská 95 (↘ *048 4111 012;* e *info@sebechleby.sk*).

Getting there Route 66/E77 from Zvolen, turn right at Hontianske Nemce.

Tourist information
☑ **Tourist Information Office Dekampo** Sv
Michala 2, Levice; ☎ 036 6222 219; f 036 6317 898;
e dekampo@stonline.sk

BANSKÁ ŠTIAVNICA *Telephone code 045*

Known as Selmecbánya in Hungarian, Schemnitz in German, the town and environs were put on the UNESCO World Heritage list in 1993 and visitors will immediately see why.

Lying in an immense wooded basin caused by a collapsing volcano, the ancient mining town is chock full of beautiful buildings, elegant churches, a fascinating *skanzen*, and a historic mining and water-pumping system. A legend tells of a shepherd who spotted two lizards gleaming in gold and silver. He followed the lizards to their den and found big nuggets of gold. The town grew wealthy from the gold and silver mines.

HISTORY Celtic tribes were the first prospectors for gold and silver in the hills and the town grew up in the 11th century directly over the pits, clambering uncomfortably up the steep slopes of the Glazenberg and Paradayz hills. Hungarian King Béla IV granted the town its charter in 1238 and six years later it became a Free Royal Town. Banská Štiavnica was soon one of the most important mining centres in Europe, so strong that earthquakes and struggles for the Hungarian crown couldn't halt its economic progress. The early 16th century saw the first golden period for Banská Štiavnica. The Fugger family took a lease on the mines and used the money to build splendid houses, Renaissance palaces, churches and much of Holy Trinity Square. The town suffered after 1526 when the Turks defeated the Hungarians at Mohács, following which the Habsburgs built a massive fortification system. In 1627, the miners were the first in the world to use gunpowder to blow out the galleries and another first came in 1732 when the ingenious miners used steam-driven machines to pump out water. The water was pumped out into 40 lakes and left to evaporate. The 18th century saw a second golden age for the city, peaking in 1740 with a production of 60kg of gold and 23 tons of silver. With a population of 30,000, the city was the third largest in the Hungarian Kingdom behind Bratislava and Debrecen. In 1762, the Academy of Mining and Forestry was founded, considered to be the first polytechnic university in the world.

GETTING THERE From Bratislava, take a train to Zvolen and change for the Banská Štiavnica scenic route. By car, from Bratislava take route E571; turn right onto a minor road to Banská Štiavnica. There is a car park on Akademická next to an archaeological dig.

TOURIST INFORMATION AND OTHER PRACTICALITIES
☑ **Banská Štiavnica tourist information office**
Námestie sv Trojice 3; ☎/f 045 6949 653;
e tikbs@banskastiavnica.sk; www.banskastiavnica.sk.
Open 1 Oct–30 Apr Mon–Fri 08.00–16.00, Sun 10.00–15.00, Sat closed; 1 May–30 Sep Mon–Fri 08.00–16.00, Sat–Sun 10.00–18.00.
$ **VÚB Bank** Bratská 17. *Open Mon–Fri 09.00–17.00.*

✉ **Post office** Kammerhofská 30; ☎ 045 6912 292.
Open Mon–Fri 08.00–12.00 & 12.30–17.00, Sat 08.00–12.00.
✚ **Pharmacy Lekáreň U Spasiteľa** Andrej Kmeťa 13. *Open Mon–Fri 07.30–12.00 & 12.30–16.00, Sat–Sun 07.30–09.30 (odd weeks).*
🚕 **Taxi** ☎ 045 6921 900; m 0903 814 468, 0905 185 233

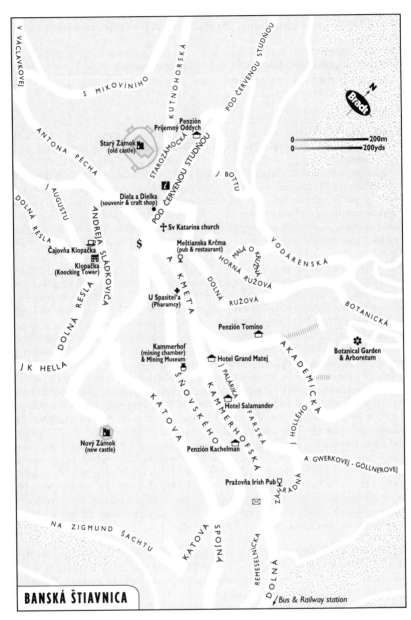

BANSKÁ ŠTIAVNICA

 WHERE TO STAY

🏠 **Hotel Grand Matej** (19 rooms)
Kammerhofská 5; ☏ 045 6921 231; e grandmatej@
grandmatej.sk; www.grandmatej.sk. A 3-star hotel in
the centre with an atmospheric restaurant. Sgl $, dbl
$$.

🏠 **Hotel Salamander** (25 rooms, 4 suites)
Palárikova 1; ☏ 045 6913 992; e salamander@

euroweb.sk; www.hotelsalamander.sk. A 3-star hotel
on the main square in an elegant grey 16th-century
building, stuffed with antiques. Café, ice cream
parlour, good restaurant. $. Sgl $, dbl $$.

🏠 **Penzión Príjemný Oddych** Starozámocká 3;
☏ 045 6921 301; e penzion@prijemnyoddych.sk;
www.prijemnyoddych.sk. A 3-star pension; the name

means 'pleasant rest'. Pub too. *Pub open daily 10.00–22.00.*

🏠 **Penzión Tomino** (17 beds) Akademicka 9; ☎ 045 6921 307. Slovak & foreigner price: 600Sk. In the city centre in a beautiful building. Enjoy a meal in the lovely courtyard restaurant. *Dbl* $, *apt* $$.

🏠 **Penzión Kachelman** (8 rooms) Kammerhofská18; ☎ 045 6922 319; e kachelman@kachelman.sk; www.kachelman.sk. Simple, stylish rooms. *Dbl* $.

🏠 **Autocamp** Počúvadlo lake; ☎ 045 6994 112. With pitching areas & little bungalows. *Open 15 Jun–15 Sep.*

✖ WHERE TO EAT AND DRINK

🍺 **Pražovňa Irish Pub** Kammerhofská 31; ☎ 045 6920 076; www.prazovna.sk. Popular Irish pub with lots of party nights. *Open Tue–Thu 12.00–01.00, Fri 12.00–04.00, Sat 15.00–04.00, Sun–Mon closed.*

✖ **Reštaurácia Matej** Akademická 4; ☎ 045 6912 051. In the Hotel Grand Matej, with an atmospheric terrace & excellent meaty grill. $$. *Open daily 12.00–22.00.*

✖ **Meštianska krčma** Andrej Kmeťa 2; ☎ 045 6920 202; great terrace above Akademická with draught Plzeňsky Prazdroj, delicious *pirohy* (ravioli stuffed with sheep's cheese & topped with bacon & onions). $. *Open Mon–Fri 09.00–23.00, Sat 10.00–23.00, Sun 14.00–23.00.*

☕ **Čajovňa Klopačka** A Sládkoviča 7; ☎ 045 6920 692. A tea house in the Klopačka building with 124 kinds of tea. *Open daily 11.10–23.20.*

SHOPPING

🛍 **Diela a dielka** (slovenských výtvarníkov), Námestie Sv Trojice 7; ☎ 045 6920 143; www.dieladielka.sk. A fabulous craft shop with jewellery, clothing, paintings, drawings, ceramics, candles & teapots in an elegant setting. *Open Mon–Sat 09.00–13.00 & 14.00–17.00, Sun 09.00–13.00 & 14.30–17.00.*

WHAT TO SEE AND DO Banská Štiavnica's Old Town contains over 360 protected buildings and other cultural monuments. The centre of the city is the **Námesite Sv Trojice (Holy Trinity Square)**, surrounded by beautiful late-Gothic and Renaissance houses and the classical **Lutheran Church**. In the middle of the square is imposing **Baroque plague column**, a work by Italian sculptor Stanetti. Just south of the square, the one-nave **Sv Katarína Church** has gorgeous late-Gothic vaulting and a beautiful interior with woodcarvings and stonework.

Looming above the square, the **Starý zámok** (Old Castle) (☎ *045 6911 541; open Oct–Apr Mon–Fri 08.00–15.00; May–Jun & Sep daily 08.00–16.00; Jul–Aug 08.00–17.00*) originally was built as a Romanesque basilica with three naves. In 1546–59 the basilica was converted to an anti-Turkish fortress. The lapidary in the building contains interesting Renaissance sculptures and headstones. From the old, continue uphill to the new.

The sweet, cuboid **Nový zámok** (New Castle) (☎ *045 6911 541; open Oct–Apr Mon–Fri 08.00–15.00; May–Jun & Sep daily 08.00–16.00; Jul–Aug daily 08.00–18.00*) was built as a watchtower and part of a warning system during the wars with the Turks. It contains the **Museum of the anti-Turkish wars**. The **Klopačka** (Knocking Tower) nearby was used to wake up the miners by pounding a mallet on a wooden board. The white Baroque tower is covered with wooden shingles and has a small spire on the top. The former **Kammerhof** (Mining Chamber) is the largest complex of buildings in the town. It houses the **Mining Museum** (*Banské Múzeum, Kammerhofská 2;* ☎ *045 6949 422; www.muzeumbs.sk; open May–Oct daily 09.00–17.00; Nov–Apr Mon–Fri 08.00–16.00*) with a rich collection of models of mining machines.

Check out also the Baroque town hall **(Radnica)** where the clock displays the time counter-clockwise. It's a lovely town to stroll around and explore. It's also possible to walk to **Calvary Hill**, home to an 18th-century triple-domed cathedral. A photogenic Baroque complex was constructed on the dormant volcano and is accessed by a tree-lined climb past 14 Stations of the Cross. To the north of town is the gorgeous **Arboretum Kysihýbel** (*Lesnícka 11;* ℄ *045 6911 145;* e *meno@fris.sk; www.fris.sk*) with species planted 1838–61. The garden is home to 250 non-native plant species, including Californian Giant Sequoias and Japanese Crytomeria. Situated 2km south of town on the road to Levice, the **Outdoor Mining Museum** (*Banské Múzeum v prírode, J K Hella 12; tel 045 6911 541; open 1 May–30 Sep Tue–Sun 09.00–16.00; 1 Oct–30 Apr Tue–Fri 08.00–15.00, w/ends by appointment*) has been a major tourist attraction for 30 years. Visitors descend 70m below the surface and explore a real 17th-century silver mine.

It is also possible to hike to **Sitno Peak** (1,009m), lying in a nature reserve area south of town. At the summit, visitors receive a certificate showing they have climbed the legendary mountain. The first observation tower was built here in 1727 on the order of Mikuláš Koháry. The tower contains a small exhibition. On the eastern slope of Sitno Mountain are the ruins of Sitno Castle, built in the second half of the 13th century, to defend the medieval mining towns against the Turks. From 1629 it belonged to the Kohár family. Ferenc Rákóczi's Kuruc army conquered the castle in 1703 and destroyed it in 1710. A campsite and lake Počúvadlo are found 2km west of Sitno.

Situated 6km south of Banská Štiavnica on route 525 is **Svätý Anton**, a gorgeous late-Baroque mansion built in 1744–50 on the site of an older 15th century castle. The last owner was Bulgarian Tsar Ferdinand Couburg and the interior holds some treasures. In the museum (℄ *045 6913 932;* e *manton3@*

GOLD, SILVER AND COPPER TOWNS

In the 14th and 15th centuries, the mining towns of Slovakia had a very important role in Europe's economy: 40 % of Europe's gold came from these mines. Silver and copper mining was also very significant. The mining towns started to gain importance during the reign of Hungarian King Charles Robert. Precious-metal mining has always been a royal monopoly in Hungary and the king could claim the ore of precious metal excavated on land owned by private landowners. Charles Robert introduced a very important reform: the king released one-third of the mining royalty to the landowner who therefore became directly interested in the excavation of the precious metal discovered on his own land. After the reform, precious-metal mining prospered and the revenues generated by mining became the main revenues for the treasury for 200 years. However, the Turkish occupation of part of Hungary caused economic depression which hit the mining towns as well. The discovery of the overseas precious metal ores marked an end of the economic importance of the mining towns in Slovakia.

Kremnica was traditionally the centre of gold mining and was one of the richest towns in the Kingdom of Hungary. Because of the high gold production in the 14th century, the town received the title 'golden' (Zlatá Kremnica). Mining activity started here in the 13th century with the settlement of German miners. The town was given royal privileges by the Hungarian King Charles Robert in 1328. In the same year a mint was founded here which shortly became one of the main mints of the kingdom. Coins were minted continually (golden ducats of Kremnica, the so-called 'florins') for seven centuries. During the 14th and 15th centuries, the ducats produced here were highly praised for their quality and beauty and they were a very favoured currency all over Europe. The Kremnica Mint is still operating today, producing currency coins for the Slovak Republic and for many other countries as well.

stonline.sk; www.muzeumsv-anton.sk; open May–Sep Tue–Sun 08.30–16.00; Oct–Apr Tue–Sat 08.00–15.00) there are art exhibitions and displays of hunting and falconry.

BZOVIK FORTRESS Located on the Krupina Plain (*Krupinská planina*), Bzovik Castle has one of the country's best-preserved fortification systems. The square fortress, built in the 12th century as a Benedictine monastery, was damaged in a 15th-century attack by the Hussites, and fortified again to fend off the Turks. The castle has four four-storey bastions, with 20m-tall walls surrounding a courtyard where the remains of the cathedral stand.

Getting there On route 66/E77, 30km south of Zvolen.

ČABRAĎ CASTLE RUINS This Gothic castle, now in ruins, was built in the 13th century like Divín to defend access to the mining towns in central Slovakia. The castle was destroyed after a fire in 1812. Situated in the middle of the Krupinská planina (plain) on a hill (305m) above the Litava river valley, Čabraď is located in the country's largest national protected area for snakes and other reptiles.

Getting there Near the village of Čabradský Vrbovok, Čabraď Castle is tricky to reach. Head south on route 66/E77 from Zvolen, through Krupina and turn right at Dolný Hostinec for Bzovik. From Bzovik, Čabradský Vrbovok is 6km south on a minor road.

Banská Štiavnica was the centre of **silver** mining. The area was first mentioned in a document from 1156 as *terra banensium* or the land of miners. Banská Štiavnica was granted the privileges of a Free Royal Town in 1238 and then began the 'golden era of the silver town'. After the discovery of precious metal ores outside Europe, Banská Štiavnica lost its economic importance. However, in the second half of the 18th century, the town enjoyed its 'second golden age' thanks to the technological innovations introduced here in mining. In 1763, Maria Theresa founded the Mining Academy here which was the first technical college in the world. The town became the centre of mining science and technology development in Europe. Banská Štiavnica was added to the UNESCO World Heritage list in 1993.

Banská Bystrica was the centre of copper mining. In 1255, the King of Hungary, Béla IV granted the city free royal privileges and invited German settlers who started to develop the precious-metal mining. The first international copper enterprise in Europe called *Ungarischer Handel* (Hungarian Commerce), owned by the Thurzó-Fugger family, originated here. The Thurzó family, who controlled almost every mine, and the German banker and merchant Fugger family started their business at the end of the 15th century which developed into one of the biggest early capitalistic enterprises in European mining and metallurgy. The company became the principal producer of copper in the world; roofs of churches all over Europe were made from copper produced in Baská Bystrica.

Nová Baňa was granted town privileges by the great King Louis I in 1345 and became one of the seven royal mining towns. Mainly gold was mined here. In 1772, a steam machine was used to pump water from the mine shafts, the first time in Europe that a steam machine had been used in this way. **Pukanec, Ľubietová** and **Banská Bela** also belonged to the association of the seven royal mining towns.

HRONSKÝ BEŇADIK (✆ *045 6893 193;* e *pallotti@gmx.net; www.kl-hron-benadik.host.sk/default_ang.htm; open 1 Jul–31 Aug Mon–Fri 09.30–17.00. Sep–Jun).* Situated on the Hron River is a former Benedictine monastery in the village of Hronský Beňadik. The abbey was first established in 1075 and is the second-oldest church and monastery in the country. Follow the yellow-marked trail from the village square to see the plague chapel on Háj Hill dating from 1713. Sv Egídius Parish Church and Krivín Hill with an Iron-Age fort are pleasant destinations for an afternoon stroll. The Hron River is popular with anglers. Monastery visits are by appointment only.

Getting there Located 30km southwest of Banská Štiavnica, just off route 65/E571 from Nová Baňa to Zlaté Moravce. At the junction with route 76 turn left to Hronský Beňadik.

SKLENÉ TEPLICE SPA (✆ *045 6771 061;* e *info@kupele-skleneteplice.sk; www.kupele-skleneteplice.sk).* The town lies at the foot of Štiavnické vrchy at an altitude of 400m. The climate is warm, moderately humid, with cold winters. As early as the 16th century, hot springs in Sklené Teplice were used for steam baths in caves, as well as for glass manufacturing. The first written record about the spa is from 1549 by Juraj Wernher. The thermal water has a temperature of 27–38°C. Visitors can stay at the spa and take a range of 'cures' from weight-loss programmes to special packages for OAPs. Accommodation is in four large hotels, two of which are elegant, historic buildings. A unique feature by Penzión Park is a cave steam bath, a *parenica* (capacity eight people) (*open Mon–Fri 14.00–19.00, Sat–Sun 10.00–19.00; admission adult/concession 145/170Sk*) where thermal springs gush directly into an underground cave and guests wallow in the warm-water basin in atmospheric surroundings. It is also open to the general public.

ZVOLEN At first sight Zvolen seems little more than an immense railway junction, but the castle and collection of colourful burgher houses opposite on Námestie SNP are impressive and worth a visit. The imposing, chunky Gothic Zvolen Castle (✆ *045 5321 903;* e *zvolen@sng.sk; www.sng.sk; open Tue–Fri 10.00–17.00, Sat 09.00–17.00, Sun 10.00–16.00; admission adult/child 50/30Sk*) was built in 1370–82 by the Hungarian King Louis (Lajos) I of Anjou as a hunting residence, influenced by the Italian town aristocratic houses. It was rebuilt and fortified after 1548. In 1805, the castle was purchased by the state who used it as a barracks, offices and schools. During the Slovak National Uprising in 1944, it served as a headquarters of the partisan army. Every summer the Zvolen Chateau Festivities are organised here. On the ground floor the visitors can find the exhibition of a Gothic art lapidary; on the first floor is an exhibition of 16th–18th-century European art including works by Rubens and Hogarth from the collections of the Slovak National Gallery in Bratislava.

Tourist information
🛈 **Zvolen Information Centre** Trhová 4; ✆ 045 5429 268; e infocentrum@zv.psg.sk; www.zvolen.sk.   *Open Tue–Sun 10.00–17.00.*

AROUND ZVOLEN The scenic railway line between Zvolen and Banská Štiavnica (change at Hronská Dúbrava) was built by communist youth brigades in the 1950s. The journey takes 45 minutes but the station in Banská Štiavnica is quite a hike from the Old Town.

Zvolen has a second castle in its domain. The ruins of **Pustý hrad** (Deserted Castle) stand 2km southeast of Zvolen on a hill overlooking the Hron River. The castle was built in the 13th century and was at one time one of the largest in Europe. It consists of an older upper castle and the younger lower castle. A centre of feudal power in Zvolen region, it fell into decay in the 16th century after a new castle in Zvolen was constructed. In a northern district of Zvolen is the lovely **Arboretum Borová Hora** (*Borovianska 66;* ✆ *045 5320 814;* e *arbbh@ vsld.tuzvo.sk; www.arboretum.sk; open open Mon–Fri 07.00–15.00; admission adult/child 30/20Sk*), famous for its collection of 800 varieties of rose and 600 cacti. Visitors can either walk from Zvolen or take buses 4, 5 or 6 from the centre. Situated 5km north of Zvolen is the **Kováčova thermal lido** located in the Hron Valley. The lido has three pools, a 90m helter-skelter, a large campsite and sports ground. Halfway between Zvolen and Banská Bystrica is the unusual wooden church of **Hronsek**. Built in 1725–26, the church has Scandinavian elements and can hold 1,100 worshippers. As with all wooden churches, no nails were used in the construction. To get there you need to take a slight detour off the E77 road at Rybáre, through Sliač and Veľká Lúka.

KREMNICA Telephone code 045

Kremnica has one of the most attractive town squares, Štefánikovo námestie, in Slovakia. It is unusual because it is covered in a lush lawn and lined with 50 elegant Renaissance houses, while other squares are usually paved over. Kremnica's fame stems from having the oldest continually operating gold mint in Europe using ore from the richest gold mines in medieval Europe. Founded in 1328 by Hungary's King Károly Róbert, the mint still produces commemorative coins and medals. A castle and thick walls were constructed to protect the mint and they are still standing to this day. The castle and Sv Katarína Church blend into one impressive building towering over the square and providing endless photo opportunities. Visitors usually arrive by the 15th-century Lower Gate (*Dolná brána*), the only remaining entrance from the protective walls (and home to the information centre) and are faced with a stunning view. Kremnica contains a collection of beautiful historic buildings and it makes a perfect afternoon to stroll around the town and climb up to the Gothic Sv Katarína Church and see the five gold altars and reassembled organ with 3,500 pipes. Katarína was the patron saint of miners. There's plenty of other sights to explore including a 15th-century town hall (*radnica*) on the north side of the square, an unusual Baroque plague column and also on the square, the museum of coins and medals (*Múzeum minci a medailí; Štefánikovo námestie;* ✆ *045 6742 696;* e *muzeum@nbs.sk; www.mint.sk; three exhibitions: Two Faces of Money, open Oct–May Tue–Sat 08.30–13.00 & 14.00–16.30, Jun–Sep Tue–Sun 08.30–13.00 & 14.00–17.00; Town Castle and its exhibitions, open Oct–May Tue–Sat 08.30–12.00 & 13.00–16.30, Jun–Sep Tue–Sun 08.30–12.00 & 13.00–17.00; Art gallery, open Oct–May Mon–Fri 08.00–12.00 & 13.00–16.00, Jun–Sep Mon–Fri 08.00–12.00 & 13.00, Sat–Sun 09.00–12.30 & 13.00–17.00; admission adult/child 70/30Sk*).

GETTING THERE Situated in the heart of the Kremnické vrchy (hills), the town is a little tricky to reach. You can drive directly through the hills from Banská Bystrica but have to make a long detour north via Dolná Štubňa or south via Zvolen. Trains from Bratislava take 3³/₄ hours; change at Hronská Dúbrava. The stretch near Kremnica is very scenic and Kremnica station is delightful. Eight buses a day leave from Bratislava; change at Žiar nad Hronom.

TOURIST INFORMATION
🄸 **Information centre** Štefánikovo námestie 44 (in tower above Dolná brána); ✆ 045 6742 856;

e infocentrum@kremnica.sk; www.kremnica.sk. The information centre is also a travel agents & on the floor above is an exhibition devoted to skiing & physical education in Slovakia. *Open Mon–Fri*

WHERE TO STAY

🏠 **Hotel Golfer** J Horvátha 50; ☎ 045 6743 767; e hotel@golfer.sk; www.golfer.sk. Large, comfortable mountain hotel, surrounded by a mini-golf course with a golf simulator and academy. Pool, sauna & gym. Good restaurant $$. *Sgl $$, dbl $4, suites $$$.*

08.00–17.00, Sat 09.00–14.00; Jul–Aug Sun also 09.00–14.00.

🏠 **Pizza Penzión Veža** Dolná 4; ☎ 045 6744 231; www.penzion-veza.sk. Just outside the city wall, combining a pizzeria and pension in a pink building. *Sgl, dbl & trpl $.*

AROUND KREMNICA

THERMAL SPA KATARÍNA Situated just south of Kremnica is a thermal lido and campsite with slightly radioactive, highly mineralised water that is excellent for joints and muscular problems. The water temperature at the spring 900m deep is 46°C and gushes forth at a 36°C temperature. There are five pools available, a tennis court, gym, athletics field and football pitch. Space for caravans, tents and there are also 16 sweet little Toblerone-shaped chalets.

KRAHULE – THE CENTRE OF EUROPE (STRED EURÓPY) Krahule is very proud of its status as the geographical heart of Europe. There is a rock with a special plaque commemorating the point at 48°45'N, 18°55'E, and a flag ground with three naked flag posts situated behind the dear little white Sv Ján (St John) Church, built in 1529. The geographical claim goes back to the 18th century when local legend says an angel intervened to persuade local astronomers to make the bold declaration.

SKIING In the hills above Kremnica is a little ski centre (930–1,060m) with skiing, snowboarding, sleigh rides, a ski school and ski slopes. If you have a car, don't miss this delightful detour through stunning countryside, fruit trees and fir trees and fabulous views. The mini–resort has four lifts and long runs.
  Stred Európa (Centre of Europe) (*www.skikrahule.sk; sgl & dbl $*).

10

Prešov Region

Prešov (8,998km²) is the second-largest region in Slovakia and the most populated (790,000), significant when you consider how far it is from the capital. The main city Prešov is the third largest in the country, after Bratislava and Košice. The region contains countless historic, cultural, untouched natural sights and more to occupy visitors than perhaps any other region. The jagged relief includes alpine mountains, highlands, hills, plains and peaks. There are five nationals parks: the High Tatras, Pieniny, Poloniny and parts of the Low Tatras and parts of the Slovak Paradise. The Východné Karpaty (eastern Carpathians) are also a protected area of natural beauty. The Prešov region abounds in natural beauty: thermal and mineral springs, historic cities, gorgeous churches, much of the Gothic route and the Free Royal Towns of Levoča, Kežmarok, Stará Ľubovňa and Bardejov. The historic Šariš region surrounding Prešov Town is home to many castles, churches and historic sites.

Many of the historic Spiš towns are in Prešov region and I have included Spiš Castle and Žehra Church in this region − although they officially belong to Košice − because the nearest town and access points, Spišské Podhradie and Spišská Kapitula, are both in Prešov. The region contains most of the High Tatras, one of the best-kept ski secrets in Europe, and also waterfalls, caverns and more than 100 mountain lakes. The Pieniny Mountains are not so big but the 35km range is one of the most beautiful in central Europe. The wooden churches of the Ruthenian minority in the villages beyond Svidník and Snina are cultural heritage sites: 26 of the 27 main churches are in the Prešov region. The oldest is the Catholic Church of St Francis of Assisi in Hervartov, near Bardejov, which was built around 1500.

EVENTS IN PREŠOV REGION

March	**Poprad** Poprad's musical spring
April	**Poprad** International Roma Day
	Štrbské Pleso Carnival
May	**Poprad** *Popradský dostavník* Folk and country group competition
June	**Kamienka** Festival of folklore of Ruthenians and Ukrainians
	Humenné regional folklore festival of Ruthenians and Ukrainians
July	**Stará Ľubovňa Castle** Castle days
	Bardejov *Rolandové hry* Rolando's games
	Kežmarok European folk craft exhibition
August	**High Tatras** Annual pilgrimage to Kriváň's summit
	Spiš Castle International historica fencing festival
September	**Snina** Slovak Romany *Ternipen* festival
November	**Prešov** *Jazz Prešov* international festival

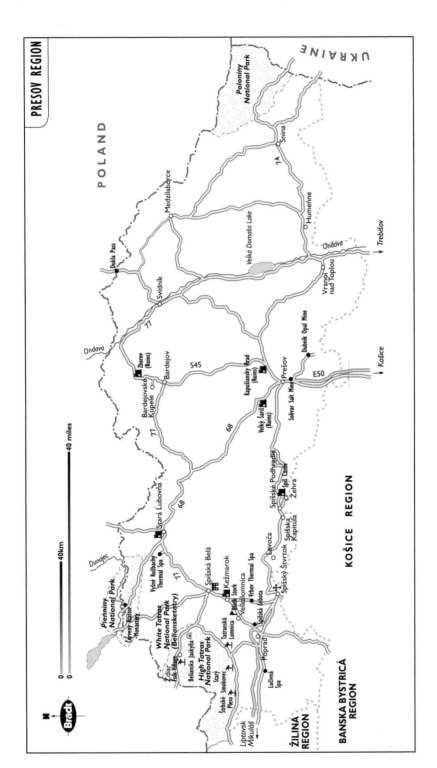

UKRAINE

POLAND

Poloniny
National Park

Snina

1A

Humenné

Medzilaborce

Veľká Domaša Lake

Trebišov

Dukla Pass

Ondava

Svidník

Vranov
nad Topľou

77

Ondava

Dubník Opal Mine

Košice

Zborov
(Ruins)

Bardejov

545

Kapušiansky Hrad
(Ruins)

Prešov

E50

Bardejovské
Kúpele

Solivar Salt Mine

Veľký Šariš
(Ruins)

68

77

Spišské Podhradie

Spiš Castle

Žehra

Stará Ľubovňa

68

KOŠICE   REGION

40km

40 miles

Dunajec

Pieniny
National Park

Červený Kláštor
Monastery

Vyšné Ružbachy
Thermal Spa

Spišská Belá

Kežmarok

77

Levoča

Spišská
Kapitula

Spišský Štvrtok

Ždiar
Folk Village

White Tatras
National Park
(Belianske tatry)

Belianska Jaskyňa

Starý
Smokovec

Tatranská
Lomnica

Black Stork

Veľká Lomnica

Vrbov Thermal Spa

Spišská Sobota

Strbské
Pleso

High Tatras
National Park

Poprad

Ľubovňa
Spa

Liptovský
Mikuláš

ŽILINA
REGION

BANSKÁ BYSTRICÁ
REGION

N

Bradt

254

Poprad was one of the original Spiš (Zips) towns, for centuries a collective of 24 towns which formed a semi-autonomous region within the Hungarian Kingdom. Poprad is one of Slovakia's most fun-packed destinations: a small, friendly city with a town centre crammed with shops, restaurants, cafés and bars and, for those seeking a quieter destination, a perfectly preserved medieval neighbourhood of Spišská Sobota just ten minutes' walk away. This charming picturesque village has a host of superb restaurants and pensions clustered around the peaceful Saxon square where it feels as if time has stopped and visitors can relax and enjoy the surroundings. Poprad is one of the best-situated cities in Slovakia. Nestling in the lush Poprad river valley beneath the spectacular High Tatra mountain range, this friendly city, the tenth largest in Slovakia, makes a superb base for exploring the stunning natural features of the region. The mountains rise up to an average 2,000m and provide a spectacular backdrop to the city's elegant heart with its pedestrian Old Town Square lined with colourfully painted buildings.

HISTORY In the 13th century Poprad became a significant trade route crossroads. It was one of the less important Spiš association members. Copper was mined in this area from the 16th–18th century. In the 18th century, the town gained the right to hold open-air markets. The majority of the population were farmers and simple craftsmen. In 1692, a paper-producing company was founded in Poprad and is the oldest company in the region. In 1871, Poprad was connected to the Košice–Bohumín Railway which boosted its development.

GETTING THERE AND AWAY By air from Poprad-Tatry Airport (TAT), 5km from town (*Na letisko 100;* ✆ *052 7763 875;* e *airport@pp.sknet.sk; www.airport-poprad.sk*). SkyEurope (*2km from highway E85; www.skyeurope.com or by phone at Bratislava call centre;* ✆ *02 4850 4850*) flies London Stansted to Poprad every Wednesday and Saturday. Ryanair is expected to join them. The airport is reached by bus 12 or taxis take ten minutes and cost 150–200Sk.

By train: Poprad is on the main Bratislava–Košice railway line, less than four hours by intercity train and five hours by regular *rýchlik* (fast) train. Train connections to other Tatra towns begin in Poprad (*www.zsr.sk, www.slovakrail.sk*).

For the High Tatras, take the *električka*, the little red electric train which travels regularly up to the mountains. Directions and information about the next stop are available in Slovak, German and English and also appear in red on an LED display attached to the ceiling of the train. A timetable is available for 15Sk from the AICES information centre. The journey from Poprad to Starý Smokovec (20Sk) takes 24 minutes and from there continue on the same train to Štrbské Pleso (20Sk) or change and head in the other direction for Tatranská Lomnica (20Sk). Trains run every hour.

TOURIST INFORMATION AND OTHER PRACTICALITIES

🛈 **AICES Information Centre Poprad**, Námestie sv. Egídia 15; ✆/f 052 7721 394; e infopp@msupoprad.sk; www.poprad.sk. *Open Sep–Jun Mon–Fri 09.00–12.30 & 13.15–17.00, Sat 09.00–12.00; Jul–Aug Mon–Fri 08.00–18.00, Sat 09.00–13.00, Sun 14.00–17.00.*

$ **Bank** ČSOB, Námestie Sv Egídia 83. *Open Mon–Thu 08.00–18.00, Fri 08.00–17.00.*

✉ **Post office** Mnoheľova 829/11. *Open Mon–Fri 07.00–18.00, Sat 08.00–12.00.*

🖥 **Internet EX-Café** Joliota Curiého 39. With 10 computers for 0.80Sk per min (minimum 10Sk).

✚ **Pharmacy** Námestie Sv Egídia 13. *Open Mon–Fri 07.15–17.30, Sat 08.00–12.00.*

🚖 **Rádio Taxi Plus** ✆ 052 7768 768; m 0903 181 108

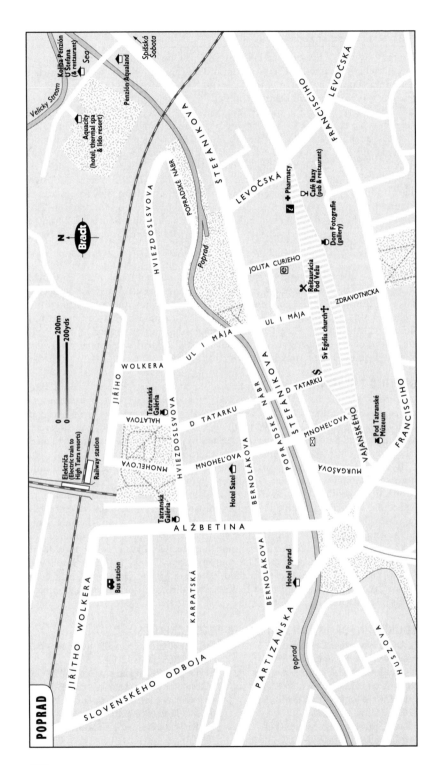

POPRAD

🚗 **Hertz car hire at Poprad Airport** Na letiško 100; mobile 0911 650 180
RTI Radio Tatras International www.rti.fm. On

1350AM & 94.2FM: gives weather reports, ski conditions & tourist information in English.
Mountain rescue ➘ 18 300 (non-stop); www.zhs.sk

 ## WHERE TO STAY

🏠 **AquaCity** (31 rooms) **Mountain View** (37 rooms) Športová 1; ➘ 052 7851 222 (direct UK booking on 01582 748840); e reservations@ aquacityresort.com; www.aquacity.sk. In the UK, book directly through specialists Czech Travel (see *Tour operators*, page 000). Delightful, fun-packed, environmentally friendly hotel with its own thermal water source that offers 4-star luxury at 3-star prices, plus a new 4-star Mountain View Hotel. The only hotel in the world with its own Olympic-length swimming pool. Vital World is a collection of saunas, whirlpools, solariums & a Snow Paradise with fresh snow daily. Vitalcentrum has relaxation & spa services with medical & rehabilitation services. The bedrooms are modern with interior design varying according to the seasons & moods. Eight restaurants, cafés & bars for guests & a superb buffet b/fast with a mountain view. Aquacity Mountain View *sgl* 💲💲💲💲, *dbl*
💲💲💲💲💲, Hotel Aquacity *sgl* 💲💲💲, *dbl* 💲💲💲💲.
🏠 **Hotel Poprad** (51 rooms) Partizánska 8; ➘ 052 7870 811; e Hotel-poprad@pp.pfg.sk, www.hotel-poprad.sk. A 3-star hotel with average-sized, rather dated rooms & bathrooms in good condition. The restaurant is bright & friendly. *Sgl* 💲, *dbl* 💲💲, *apts* 💲💲💲.
🏠 **Hotel Satel** (230 beds) Mnoheľova 825; ➘ 052 7161 111; e hotel.satel.poprad@satel-slovakia.sk; www.satel-slovakia.sk. Another 3 star, in a 1960s' block; dark, yet clean & functional with good restaurant. Very convenient for the railway station & town centre. *Dbl* 💲💲.
🏠 **Pension Aqualand** (9 rooms) Štefánikova 893; ➘ 052 7763 049; m 0911 302 922; e aqualand@aqualand.sk; www.aqualand.sk. Friendly family-run B&B, just across the Poprad River from Aquacity. *Dbl* 💲💲.

✗ WHERE TO EAT AND DRINK

✗ **High Tatras restaurant** Športová 1; ➘ 052 7851 111; e info@aquacity.sk; www.aquacity.sk. A stylish restaurant with minimalist furniture & a magnificent view of the Tatra Mountains through huge windows. The hotel also has a café, bar & several snack bars within the spa complex. 💲💲. *Open daily 07.00–22.00.*
✗ **Koliba Penzión u Štefana** Športová 1 (in Aquacity's car park); ➘ 052 7870 811. A 'koliba' is a rustic country restaurant serving traditional dishes. Meaty dishes & huge superb salads. 💲. *Open Sun–Thu 11.00–23.00, Fri–Sat 11.00–midnight.* You can also stay in the Koliba. *Dbl* 💲.

✗ **Café Razy** Námestie sv Egídia 58; m 0903 485 445. The name is written as C(afé)razy to show everyone its fun theme with a pub atmosphere, pizzas baked in a real fire & loud music. 💲. *Open daily 11.00–23.00.*
✗ **Reštaurácia pod Vežou** Námestie sv. Egídia 59; ➘ 052 7726 354. One of the most popular restaurants on Poprad's main square, this place has a hint of Bavaria in the carnivorous dishes. 💲. *Open Mon–Sat 09.00–22.00, Sun 10.00–22.00.*
✗ **City Bowling OZC MAX** ➘ 052 4664 247; www.maxcentrum.sk. With 10 lanes, a restaurant & bar in the Max shopping mall, near the airport. *Open Mon–Thu 10.00–02.00, Fri–Sun 10.00–03.00.*

WHAT TO SEE AND DO Námestie Sv Egídia (St Giles's Square) is five minutes' walk from the main Poprad-Tatry railway station and is a cluster of elegant religious buildings and a pedestrian street lined with brightly coloured buildings. In the centre, Sv Egídia Church dates from the 13th century, with 15th-century wall paintings. Next to the church building there is a separate Renaissance bell tower dating from 1658. The **Tatranská Galéria** (*Výstavná sieň, Alžbetina 30;* ➘ *052 7721 968; Elektráreň, Hviezdoslavova 12;* ➘ *052 7722 617; www.tatragaleria.sk; open Tue–Sun 10.00–17.00*) has two venues, one near the station showing 19th- and 20th-century paintings of the Spiš and Tatra regions and the other, in an old steam power station, focusing on the area's traditions of weaving. The **Dom Fotografie** (House of Photography) (*Námestie Sv Egídia 44;* ➘ *052 7723 818;* e *domfoto@domfoto.sk www.domfoto.sk; open Tue–Sun 10.00–17.00*) is the only specialised photographic institution in Slovakia, while the **Podtatranské múzeum** (Tatra Region Museum) (*Vajanského 4;* ✆ *052 7721 924; open Tue–Sun 09.00–16.00; admission adult/concession 40/20Sk*) traces the history of human settlements in the Tatra region from the Neanderthal period. Every visit to the Tatras should make time for a luxurious wallow in **Aquacity** (*Športová 1;* ✆ *052 7851 222; www.aquacity.sk; 1hr pool and sauna ticket adult/concession 50/35Sk; all-day 'super packet' ticket adult/concession 900/750Sk*), the world's most environmentally friendly holiday resort. Opened in 2005, the spa complex includes eight pools heated by water from an underground thermal lake, a suite of 17 sauna treatments, fun rides, relaxing whirlpools, a gym and an Olympic-sized swimming pool. New treatments include cryotherapy using very cold temperatures to help sportsmen and halt the aging process.

SPIŠSKÁ SOBOTA Calling it a 'suburb of Poprad' really doesn't do justice to this delightful lost-in-time village. It's like stepping back into another, more peaceful world. The deserted main square contains half-a-dozen excellent restaurants and pensions where you can stay and relax. The first documented reference to Spišská Sobota dates back to 1256, in a parchment of King Bela IV, where it was called *Forum sabathe* (Saturday market); the name translates as 'Spiš Saturday'. German settlers helped make Spišská Sobota one of the most important Spiš towns, competing with bigwigs like Kežmarok and Levoča. In the centre, **Sv Juraj (St George) Church** has an altar from the workshop of **Master Pavol of Levoča.** The separate Renaissance belfry (*zvonica*), a monumental rectangular block, is the largest of its kind in the Spiš region. At the southern

THINGS TO DO IN POPRAD WHEN YOU'RE DEAD

Leigh Banks

Jan Telenský is known as Mr Cool at his hotel of the living dead. However, Mr Cool has built his strange hotel in a very strange place indeed: Poprad, a city chilled all year round by icy breath from Satan's Peak (a Tatra mountain). There are rows of old tenement buildings decaying side by side, but recently things have changed. Mr Cool's landlocked hotel, Aquacity, has given this once-listless city a sense of purpose. It's also given it jobs, money and a burgeoning international reputation. Five years ago, if you wanted to visit Poprad, you had to fly to Bratislava and drive miles through mountains where grizzled bears survive like ancient armies. Now Poprad-Tatry Airport has a duty free and a café, and the city itself has the chance to become one of the world's most extraordinary holiday resorts. It's all because former Luton car worker Mr Telenský heard the future bubbling away, two miles underground and discovered that 'three little minutes of death' could change everybody's life.

The original part of AquaCity houses massage rooms, wet rooms, sweat rooms – all kinds of get-you-fit rooms, and bedrooms as big as the apartments that a few years ago you could buy in town for £5,000. There's even an Olympic-sized swimming pool. From the outside the original AquaCity is last year's colour: 1950s' Butlin's. No, worse than that, it's a tacky new-town leisure centre. Big and square. Yellow and brown. Tin and pine. Outdoor pools and crazy golf. The new part of AquaCity on the other hand is a masterpiece of stainless-steel balconies and smoked glass, a wonderful reflection of the mountains and the area's industrial history. The cryochamber takes pride of place at the entrance. Today's architects have created a minimalist ice palace for Mr Cool.

Jan Telenský said at the opening of phase two, 'I don't have to heat my hotel, the earth does it for me. It comes out of the ground too hot to handle, but I use the latest technology to cool it to around 35°C. The heat and the minerals in the end of the gorgeous square, the Evangelical church dates from 1777. The town museum (*Sobotské námestie 33;* ✆ *052 7721 323; open Tue–Sat 09.00–16.00; admission adult/concession 20/10Sk*) is a charming place showing furniture and religious items. Spišská Sobota, ten minutes' walk from Poprad centre makes a peaceful place to stay.

🏠 Where to stay

🏠 **Hotel Sobota** (12 rooms) Kežmarská ulica 15; ✆ 052 4663 121; e info@hotelsobota.sk; www.hotelsobota.sk. A new hotel with a superb restaurant ($$) with a wood & stone interior design that blends history with hedonism. *Dbl* $$.

🏠 **Sabato Pension & Restaurant** (6 rooms) Sobotské námestie 6; ✆ 052 7769 580; www.sabato.sk. Delightful 17th-century guesthouse with stylishly renovated rooms & a medieval-themed restaurant ($$). Kind waitresses in costume. *Dbl* $$–$$$.

LUČIVNÁ SPA Located 10km west of Poprad on route 18/E50, Lučivná was first mentioned in 1321 and belonged to the Cistercian monastery at Štiavnik. Earl Várady-Szakmáry created the park in 1866–72 and built a wooden hotel. The spa's first patients were drawn by the mountain climate and promises of a cure. The original spa, treating children and women with tuberculosis with hydrotherapy and moss baths, was changed into a medical house for children aged three–15, accompanied by their parents. The spa (*Kúpele Lučivná;* ✆ *052 775 4542;* e *kupelelu@sinet.sk*) has 250 beds for patients with non-tubercular respiratory diseases and circulatory diseases.

thermal waters improve health and lives. It makes me feel good to be able to give this to Slovakia and to the world.' It cost him £8m to build AquaCity One three years ago and he charged 'the people' £0.55 a day to use it. Then at the end of 2005, he ripped whole chunks down and began to rebuild it. The second phase brought him closer to £25m. 'When I first came here, my brother-in-law showed me a pipe coming up out of the ground. It had breath hot enough to melt your soul. So, I looked into the history of it and realised there was a natural miracle under my feet. An eternal source of power, warmth and health. It's been there for millions of years and it'll be there for millions more. I harnessed it.'

Cryogenics is a strange thing, something the Poles, a few miles across the border, made their own 25 years ago. Now it is moving out of the realms of mysterious medicine. It's accepted nowadays that a good icing transmutes your body and all of its fluids into a kind of mercurial soup healthier than *borsch*. It increases your rate of endorphins and eases pain. It heightens decision-making and relieves irritability. Rugby players are particularly fond of it. By 2008, the third phase of AquaCity, the Mountain View Hotel, should be complete at a total cost creeping towards £200m. This time Telenský is building a four-star hotel, an international shopping mall and glass-domed gardens to rival the UK's Eden Project in Cornwall. He has also discovered a second thermal lake which he intends to use to help heat the city's old tenement buildings. It's this vision which has won AquaCity the international Green Apple Award and a Green Globe 21 certificate for its eco-friendly achievements. Mr T has got the hotel, the geo-thermal lake and the Olympic-size swimming pool. He's got the cryochamber and finally, after a two-year wait, he's been granted his medical licence to chill. So, there really are things to do in Poprad when you're dead – and it could soon be one of the healthiest places on earth.

Travelling up to the High Tatra resorts on the *električka* from Poprad, visitors will be shocked to see a scene of devastation beside the railway tracks. Even now, nearly three years on, visitors are amazed and saddened by the devastation caused by a terrifying 100m/h storm which struck the region on the night of 19 November 2004. Huge swathes of the mountainside are now totally bare and ugly socialist-worker holiday homes are exposed, whereas before they were disguised by thick forest. Stumps and fallen branches of the sub-alpine forest still bear witness to the event. The most severe destruction occurred between Tatranská Lomnica and Tatranská Polianka, just under the Tatras' highest peak, Gerlachovský štít. During the night, 13,000ha (3,000,000m² of wood) of forest were knocked down, about one-third of the total forest area, leaving a swathe of devastation 60km long and 10m wide. Two people died and many villages in the High Tatras were cut off from the rest of the world. So much beauty and foliage lost is depressing, yet some people say the view is better.

VYSOKÉ TATRY NATIONAL PARK (HIGH TATRAS)

Covering a territory of 741km², the High Tatras (TANAP) are the most exhilarating mountain range in Europe. Yes, more exciting, more wild and more undiscovered than those staid old Alps. You'll feel like a real mountaineer, a true explorer of the wilds and you might not bump into another soul all day. The High Tatras (Vysoké Tatry) offer peace, solitude and fresh mountain air but also thrilling expeditions, stunning views and glorious weather. Wow the folks back home with photogenic masterpieces, soaring peaks, mountain meadows filled with flowers, serene mountain lakes, but beware of sudden blizzards. The High Tatras are the only truly alpine mountains in eastern Europe and one of the smallest high mountain ranges in the world. They are also the highest mountains in Slovakia. Narrow rocky crests soar above wide glacial valleys with precipitous walls while the lower slopes are covered by a dense coniferous forest of spruce, pine and some heavenly hidden mountain meadows blanketed with wild flowers. Twenty of the peaks are over 2,400m, while 30 valleys and almost 100 glacial lakes, including 30 large tarns, are scattered among them. Snow covers the mountains for 200–250 days a year making the Tatras an ideal ski destination. Around 1,300 species of plant decorate the slopes while animals include chamois, marmot, brown bear, lynx, eagle and wolf. July and August are the warmest months when the resorts can get very crowded, but it's always easy to find peace. Snow can fall as early as October and the higher hiking trails are closed from November to April. There are 600km of hiking trails of varying levels of difficulty to explore, a dozen or so resorts and many ski slopes, cable cars and lifts.

TAKING CARE IN THE MOUNTAINS The High Tatras are breathtaking and serene, yet the calm hides a deadly character. Every year, 15–20 people die in the Tatras. Visitors see that the Tatras cover a relatively small area compared with the Alps and are not as high, then imagine they can set off for a hike or long-distance ski without taking the same precautions. The weather is volatile at higher elevations and there can be glorious sunshine one minute, a blizzard the next, even in summer. Because there are no glaciers, visitors are lured into a false sense of security. Since 1990, 167 people have died in the mountains. Tatra tourism took off in the late 19th century and hiking and skiing deaths have epitomises Tatra turn-of-the-century luxury. Full of skiers & hikers in season. Ski rental in an adjacent building. Pool, good restaurant ($$). Sgl $$, dbl $$$.

⌂ **Hotel Hubert** (39 rooms) Gerlachov. A 4-star 'Vital Resort'; ✆ 052 4780 811; e hubert@hotel-hubert.sk; www.hotel-hubert.sk. Luxury hotel in a mountain meadow by a private lake. Huge range of facilities from horseriding to igloo room. Sgl $$, dbl $$$.

⌂ **Vila Mon Ami** (22 beds) Nový Smokovec; ✆ 052 4780 940; e monami@sinet.sk; www.monami.sk. A sweet half-timbered family house in neighbouring Nový Smokovec. Dbl with b/fast $$.

TATRANSKÁ LOMNICA (850m) Situated 4km along the *električka* line from Starý Smokovec, Tatranská Lomnica is the largest town as well as the most important ski resort of the eastern range of the High Tatra Mountains. It is famous for its four runs: two black, one red and one blue. Take the cable car up to Skalnaté Pleso (1,751m) from where a chair lift takes skiers further up to Lomnický štít (2,633m). From here you can enjoy one of the most amazing views; from the narrow, vertiginous saddle you can admire the lowlands of both Slovakia and Poland. Don't miss a drink in Kaviareň Dedo, the highest café in Slovakia. Once you become completely dizzy with the view, take one of the two black slopes. The one closer to the lift (No 3) qualifies as the most difficult run in the High Tatras. The red slope (No 2) leading from Skalnatá chata to 1,145m, as well as the blue descent to the bottom cable car station used to be highly scenic descents between the evergreens. Now, after the storm, there are only slopes to concentrate on, trying to avoid the grim torso of the formerly beautiful forest. Night skiing, served by one lift and a red slope, and ski jumping are possible in the Jamy area at the western end of town. The beauty of the cross-country routes has sadly been spoilt by the storm. The town has a lively après-ski scene with dancing and live music every night from 21.00–03.00 at the Hotel Grand Praha.

From the 2005/06 season, the ski centres at Hrebienok, Starý Smokovec and Tatranská Lomnica are operated by the same company called Tatra Cableways (*information line,* ✆ *052 4467 884; www.tld.sk*) and for the first time in history the same tickets can be used for everything at the resorts. An adult one-day ticket costs 1,220Sk, three-days costs 1,730Sk.

⌂ **Where to stay**

⌂ **Grandhotel Praha** (89 rooms, 9 apts) Tatranská Lomnica; ✆ 052 4467 941; e reservation@grandhotelpraha.sk; www.grandhotelpraha.sk. Like its sister, The Grand, Praha offers old-time luxury on an impressive scale. It looms over the town, a little like the hotel in *The Shining*, but inside there's nothing sinister about the chandeliers, piano music & charming service. Smart restaurant ($$). Dbl $$$–$$$$, apts $$$$$.

⌂ **Hotel Slovan** (165 beds) Tatranská Lomnica; ✆ 052 4467 851; e hotel-slovan@hotel-slovan.sk; www.bonbonshotels.sk. Functional 1960s' block in lovely surroundings. Dbl $–$$.

⌂ **Penzión Bélin** Tatranská Lomnica 50; ✆ 052 4467 778; e belin@tatry.sk; www.belin.sk. Large 19th-century inn near the station. Dbl & apts $.

⌂ **Penzión Erika**, Tatranská Lesna 1; ✆ 052 4422 397; e penzionerika@max.euroweb.sk; www.penzionerika.host.sk. Family-run pension with folk decorated restaurant ($). Dbl $.

Black Stork golf club and Hotel International Continuing the tradition of the first nine-hole golf course built in the Hungarian Kingdom in 1906, this new professional nine-hole course has fantastic scenery. There is also an indoor driving range, clubhouse and golf shop in the adjoining **Hotel International** (*Tatranská 754, Veľká Lomnica;* ✆ *052 4661 111; e international@golfinter.sk; www.blackstork.sk, www.international.sk*) with every conceivable amenity: sauna, gym, indoor & outdoor pool. Dbl $$.

The Belianske Tatry are found northeast of the High Tatras, and south of Ždiar. The famous **Green Lake** (*Zelené pleso*) valley is in Belianske Tatry. The brilliantly green lake is surrounded on three sides by a dramatic rock amphitheatre peaking at over 1,000m, offering views on the northern side of **Maly Kežmarský Štít** (Little Kežmarok Peak) and the unusual stone spire **Jastrabia veža** (Falcon Tower) which is located in **Malá Zmrzlá dolina** (Little Frozen Valley). The lesser-known peaks of Belianske Tatry are accessible enough to have been used for grazing sheep and cows. Records from as far back as 1310 show that shepherds from **Spišská Belá** grazed sheep here. Because this part of the Tatras lies close to Poland, shepherds from the Slovak Spiš region and Polish shepherds often quarrelled over the best slopes. Occasionally more serious conflicts broke out between smugglers moving herds of horses across the border via the Belianske Tatra valleys. The easy accessibility turned out to be the area's undoing. In order to extend pastures, shepherds burned out large pine forests and then later, swarms of tourists who wandered away from marked trails, finished off the destruction. Today, parts of the Belianske Tatras are closed to tourists, although you can hike to the Green Lake from Skalnaté Pleso above Tatranská Lomnica.

BELIANSKA JASKYŇA (CAVE) (*Tatranská Kotlina;* \ *052 4467 375;* e *belianj@ ssj.sk; www.ssj.sk; open Jan–May & Sep–15 Nov visits at 09.30, 11.00, 12.30, 14.00; Jun–Aug 09.00–16.00 on the hour; admission adult/child 150/80Sk*). Situated further along route 537 which strings the pearls of the High Tatra resort towns, from Štrbské Pleso to Tatranská Kotlina, the cave contains many large halls and domes, pagodas and lakes. Music concerts take place in August in the 'Music Hall' cave, although you'll share the acoustics with eight species of bat.

Tatranská Kotlina sanatorium (\ *052 4782 602;* e *marketing@santk.sk; www.santk.sk*) is a sanatorium for those with respiratory problems. Guests can do respiratory exercises in Belianska Cave. The **Pavilión Fontana hotel** is a three-star hotel in the hills (*dbl $$*).

ŽDIAR In the valley between the Belianske Tatras and the Spišská Magura mountain ranges is a folk village that also doubles up as a ski resort. A number of wooden buildings preserve and present the traditions of the **Goral** (Polish speaking) mountain people. The **Ždiarsky dom múzeum** (\ *052 4498 142; open May–Sep Mon–Fri 09.00–16.00, Sat–Sun 09.00–12.00; Oct–Apr Mon–Fri 09.00–15.00; admission adult/child 30/20Sk*) is a living example of the dress, daily life and feasts and ceremonies of the local inhabitants, most of whom in past centuries relied on shepherding for their livelihood. The wooden houses are characterised by painted ornamentation, especially around windows. Visitors can see folk costumes and crafts such as hand weaving, ride in horse-drawn coaches and listen to folk music and dancing groups. There are about a dozen houses in the village offering rooms. Continuing along route 67 to the Polish border, you'll find Ždiar's twin village, **Tatranská Javorina**, similarly decorated with folk architecture. Other villages such as Osturňa are also excellent places to find folk crafts such as delicate lacework.

Getting there Ždiar is 17km from Tatranská Lomnica. To find the village of Ždiar, leave Poprad and head northeast on route 67, go through Kežmarok and turn left at Spišská Belá continuing on route 67 towards the Polish border.

ŽDIAR SKI RESORT (860–1,160m) The spectacular backdrop for this unique village are the peaks and valleys of the Tatras region, perhaps best viewed from a

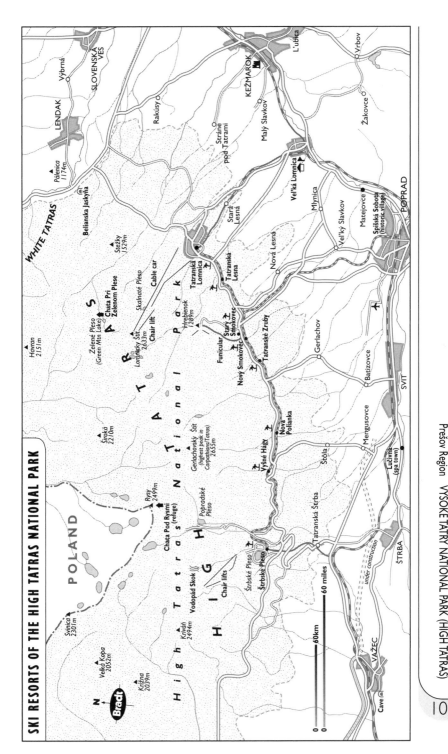

SKI RESORTS OF THE HIGH TATRAS NATIONAL PARK

POLAND

WHITE TATRAS

TATRAS National Park

High Tatras National Park

SLOVENSKÁ VES

Vybrná

LENDAK

Podspády 1174m

Belianska Jaskyňa

Hovran 2151m

Zelené Pleso (Green Mtn Lake)

Chata Pri Zelenom Plese

Skalnaté Pleso

Cable car

Stežky 1529m

Lomnický Štít 2633m

Chair lift

Strane pod Tatrami

Rakúsy

KEŽMAROK

Ľubica

Vrbov

Žakovce

Malý Slavkov

Veľká Lomnica

Mlynica

Veľký Slavkov

Matejovce

Spišská Sobota (historic village)

POPRAD

Tatranská Lomnica

Tatranská Lesná

Stará Lesná

Nová Lesná

Gerlachov

Batizovce

SVIT

Hrebienok 1289m

Starý Smokovec

Funicular

Nový Smokovec

Tatranské Zruby

Široká 2210m

Gerlachovský Štít (highest peak in Carpathians/Tatras) 2655m

Mengusovce

Lučivná (spa town)

ŠTRBA

Nová Polianka

Vyšné Hágy

Štôla

Rysy 2499m

Chata Pod Rysmi (refuge)

Popradské Pleso

Tatranská Štrba

Svinica 2301m

Veľká Kopa 2052m

Krížna 2039m

Kriváň 2494m

Vodopád Skok

Chair lifts

Štrbské Pleso

under construction

VAŽEC

Cave

N

Bradt

60km

60 miles

0

0

261

become so common that a **symbolic cemetery** (*simbolický cintorín*) has been established near **Popradské pleso** alpine lake to commemorate the lives of those who have died in the mountains. The first mass was held in 1936 and now the cemetery is home to dozens of wooden crosses and 250 plaques mounted on stone.

In an emergency, call the **Horská záchranná služba** (✆ *18 300 (non-stop); air rescue;* ✆ *18 155, 052 4422 820, 052 4422 855, or* m *0903 624 869).* All of the *chata* have telephones, and the rescuers are all trained in English and German.

 CHATA IN THE TATRA There is no better way to experience the Tatras than by staying in a high-altitude mountain refuge (*chata*). Sometimes they are a necessity and the manager will never turn anyone away. Camping is banned in the Tatra National Park (TANAP), so the cottages are the only way visitors can stay overnight (all rates per person per night).

🏠 **Chata Popradské pleso** (1,500m) m 0908 761 403; www.horskyhotel.sk. 90 beds. $.

🏠 **Chata Plesnivec** (1,290m) m 0905 256 722. 20 beds. $.

🏠 **Bílikova chata** (1,285m) ✆ 052 4422 439; www.tatry.sk. 27 beds. Located at the top of the funicular that runs from Starý Smokovec. $.

🏠 **Téryho chata** (2,015m) ✆ 052 4425 245. 25 beds. On the banks of a small alpine lake that in mid-June is still partially frozen. $.

🏠 **Chata pri Zelenom plese** (1,551m) m 0903 467 420. 50 beds. By a gorgeous green mountain lake. $.

🏠 **Zamkovského chata** (1,450m) m 0905 554 471. 25 beds. $.

🏠 **Chata pod Soliskom** (1,840m) m 0905 652 036; www.chatasolisko.sk. 13 beds. $.

🏠 **Horská chata Sliezsky dom** (1,670m) ✆ 052 442 5261; www.sliezskydom.sk. 130 beds. Silesian chalet. $.

🏠 **Zbojnícka chata** (1,960m) m 0903 619 000; Robbers' chalet at www.zbojnickachata.sk. 16 beds. $ b/fast inc.

🏠 **Skalnata chata** (1,740m) m 0903 247 656; www.tatry.sk. 8 beds. $. Small restaurant. $.

🏠 **Chata pod Rysmi** (2,250m) ✆ 052 442 2314. 14 beds. The highest *chata* in the Tatras, below the summit of Rysy (Lynx Peak). Owing to the lack of electricity, this *chata* is only open in summer & all supplies have to be carried up by Slovak-sherpas. $.

✗ **Rainerova chata** (1,290m) TANAP information centre for climbers; www.tatry.sk. No accommodation, just refreshments and information. $.

WHERE TO SKI IN THE HIGH TATRAS Most of the listed places are small, low-lying resorts with a couple of usually easy trails and some unsophisticated cross-country ski tracks.

There are three important ski resorts in the High Tatras. Going from west to east these are Štrbské Pleso, Starý Smokovec and Tatranská Lomnica. For daily snow reports, check www.tanap.sk/report.html.

Štrbské Pleso Outstanding cross-country skiing and excellent paths. One of the best ski resorts in Slovakia, with challenging slopes.

Solisko Above Štrbské Pleso. The most famous ski slope in Slovakia, and one of the highest, with lifts taking skiers to altitudes of nearly 2,000m.

Starý Smokovec With 3 separate ski centres, used by beginners and intermediates.

Tatranská Lomnica With two black runs, a red track and a blue slope.

Jezersko 31km from Kežmarok. This small ski resort has four tow lifts, the longest reaching 1,150m with a rise of 280m. There is another longish lift taking skiers

The start of tourism in the Tatras goes back to the 16th century. The first known explorer of the Tatras was Beáta Lasky, the lady of Kežmarok Castle. In 1565, Beáta decided to make a trip to the Tatras. The expedition took three days and she went as far as the Zelené Pleso (Green Lake). Unfortunately, the trip ended badly. This was an era when independent women with strong character were not appreciated. Beáta's husband, Albert Lasky was outraged by his wife's reckless behaviour and punished her in an inhumane manner. She was walled up in the highest tower of Kežmarok Castle with only two windows. One window served as a feeding hole, the other offered a view of Beáta's beloved Tatras. She was imprisoned for six years and only freed by the new owner of the castle, Johann Rueber. By this time, Beáta had gone mad and she died shortly after her release. According to the gossips, Beáta's trip was merely a convenient excuse for her husband to get rid of her because she was 20 years older than him. When she was out of the way, locked in the tower, Albert could enjoy his wife's vast wealth. Nowadays many trekkers follow Beáta's example, setting off from Kežmarok. Luckily, they do not have to face any consequences for such a trip.

up to 1,020m, while the remaining two lifts are short. On the long slope snow guns are installed. Night skiing, ski hiking & sledding are further options.

Podbanské 20km west of Štrbské Pleso. Podbanské is suitable for beginners and snowboarders as the slopes are gentle. The trails are at 950–1,100m. There are four tow lifts. Cross-country skiing, ski hiking, sledding, swimming, fitness, sauna, bowling.

Ždiar 26km from Kežmarok by the Polish border. Ždiar-Strednica is a spacious valley with a total of 5km of runs, seven tow lifts and only easy (blue) slopes for beginners and intermediate skiers. Snow conditions are particularly good; the season usually lasts from mid December until the end of March. Cross-country skiers can exercise on three loops of 1, 3 & 5km. Ski hiking and sledding is also possible, as is ski rental and a ski nursery.

ŠTRBSKÉ PLESO (1,355m) If you are not staying in the FIS Hotel just at the bottom of the ski lifts then be prepared for a 15-minute warm-up walk from the electric train or from your car to the slopes. The walk is worth the effort as the highest settlement in the High Tatras, Štrbské Pleso (1,335m) is one of the best ski resorts in Slovakia, with challenging slopes and an atmosphere familiar from ski trips to the Alps. Its facilities were built largely before the 1970 World Ski Championship, and the resort served a range of competitive European and world-class skiing events since then. Its pride is the Interski slope, just next to the ski jumps. This is an easy and relatively short run serviced by a chair lift and a Poma lift (with a platter to be placed between the legs). The resort has two ski jumps with heights of 90m and 120m, 26km of perfectly maintained cross country trails, two chair lifts and four T-bar lifts providing a capacity to lift 3,750 skiers every hour. Around 80% of the three main downhill trails are provided with a facility for high-pressure snowmaking. Facilities also include night skiing, paragliding, winter bungee jumping, an indoor swimming pool (25m), saunas and fitness halls. The longest run, serviced by a fast, four-person and 2 km-long chair lift is the **Predné Solisko** downhill trail. The 2,500m

10

intermediate track starts off at 1,850m, descending by 440m. The whole resort is equipped with snow cannons and ski rental. There are plenty of après-ski opportunities in Štrbské Pleso. A one-day ski pass for adults is 650Sk, a three-day pass costs 1,810Sk.

If you're interested in hiking to the summit of **Rysy,** set off from Štrbské Pleso and take your passport as the summit of Rysy is right on the Slovak–Polish border, just a snowball's throw from Zakopane.

Tourist information and other practicalities

Tourist information point Štrbské Pleso; m 0903 987 537, 0903 987 569

✉ **Post office** *Open Mon–Tue & Thu–Fri 08.00–13.00 & 14.00–16.00, Wed 14.00–17.00, Sat 08.00–10.00.*

Where to stay

Hotel Fis (170 beds) ✆ 052 4492 221; e hotelfis@hotelfis.sk; www.hotelfis.sk. Right next to the lake with a pool & sauna. *Sgl* $–$$, *dbl* $$–$$$.

Hotel Panorama (166 beds) ✆ 052 4492 111; e recepcia@hotelpanorama.sk;

www.hotelpanorama.sk. Fantastic gravity-defying hotel building; just make sure you're not in the overhang. *Sgl* $$, *dbl* $$$.

Solisko Hotel ✆ 052 4780 722; e solisko@sinet.vt.sk; www.solisko.sk. Next to the lake with superb spa facilities. *Sgl* $$, *dbl* $$$.

Where to eat

✗ **Hotel Fis** Štrbské Pleso. Offering Slovak specialities. $. *Open daily 11.00–23.00.*
✗ **Pizza Pino** Between hotels Panorama & Toliar; ✆ 052 7883 576. Good pasta. $.

Open daily 11.00–22.00.
✗ **Restaurant Koliba Patria** Next to the lake Štrbské Pleso, resembling a witch's hut. $$. *Open daily 11.00–23.00.*

STARÝ SMOKOVEC (1,018m) Six stations east on the *električka*, Starý Smokovec is the prototype of how a Tatra town used to look like in the time of the Austro-Hungarian monarchy. Lovely Art Nouveau wooden-framed houses are scattered about the town and the settlement makes sure that new constructions fit into the atmosphere. There are three runs above the town and they are quite long. In the oldest ski resort in the High Tatras, take the Italian-made train, which in a few years will probably end up in a museum, and go up to Hrebienok (1,285m), then go on a pull lift to do the black slope, or take the blue ride, ideal for snowboarders although it is not particularly wide, and get back to the point of departure. The resort is recommended to families with children learning to ski.

If the weather's reasonably good, the most rewarding climb is to follow the blue-marked path that leads from behind the Grand Hotel in Starý Smokovec to the summit of **Slavkovský štít** (2,452m), a nine-hour return journey. Look out for the strange church behind the hotel in the same custard and brown beam colours. Alternatively, take a narrow-gauge **funicular**, starting from behind the Grand Hotel (every 30 minutes), which climbs 250m to Hrebienok (45 minutes on foot), one of the lesser ski resorts on the edge of the pine forest. A one-day ski pass for adults is 650Sk; a three-day pass costs 1,810Sk.

Tourist information

Tatra Information Office Dom služieb 24, Starý Smokovec; ✆ 052 4423 440; e zcr@sinet.sk; www.tatry.sk. Organises mountain guides for tough

climbs. *Open Mon–Thu 08.00–17.00, Fri 09.00–13.00, Sat 08.00–13.00.*

Where to stay

Grand Hotel (79 rooms) Starý Smokovec; ✆ 052 4780 000; e reserve@grandhotel.sk;

www.grandhotel.sk. With its yellow walls, red roof & Tudor-esque half-timbered design, the Grand

Kežmarok (Käsmark, from the German for 'cheese market') is another lovely Spiš town. The castle doesn't loom dramatically from an imposing hill and it is quite plain, yet the town has plenty to offer visitors on a day trip from the Tatras. In 1385, the burghers of Kežmarok began a feud with their counterparts in Levoča which lasted for 200 years. The feud was over who could build the only warehouse in the Spiš region and Kežmarok was frequently attacked. The town was involved over the years in struggles between Poland and Hungary for control of the Spiš region and in Hungarian–Habsburg wrangles and always took the rebel side. In 1462, the castle was built by the noble Zápoľský family in a late-Gothic style. For many years the property of the noble Thököly family, it was confiscated by the Habsburgs as punishment for their support of the Kuruc rebels. The solid construction holds the **Múzeum Kežmarský hrad** (*Hradné námestie 55;* ☎ *052 4522 618; www.kezmarok.com; open Oct–Apr Mon–Fri 08.00–15.00; May–Sep Tue–Sun 09.00–16.00; admission adult/child 70/20Sk*). The main street and square leading south from the castle pass several interesting buildings. The 15th-century Catholic basilica of **Sv Kríž** with its separate **Renaissance belfry** are hidden down a back alley but worth the hunt. You can't miss the **New Evangelical Church** (*Nový evanjelický kostol; open May–Oct daily 09.00–12.00 & 14.00–17.00; Nov–Apr Tue & Fri 09.00–12.00 & 14.00–16.00*) at the other end of the centre from the castle. It's a garish, dark-orange creation which stands out against the snowy peaks. The Danish architect Theophil Hansen combined Byzantine, Moorish, Romanesque and Renaissance in a bizarre mélange. If you find it overwhelming, walk a few paces south to the calmer **wooden church** (*Drevený kostol*) erected during the period of Protestant persecution and behind it, a cemetery with a cosmopolitan mix.

GETTING THERE Buses and trains run every hour from Poprad; the journey takes 20–30 minutes.

TOURIST INFORMATION

🄸 **Kežmarok information centre** Hlavne namestie 46; ☎ 052 4524 047; e infokk@sinet.sk; www.kezmarok.sk. *Open Mon–Fri 08.30–12.00 & 13.00–17.00; Jun–Sep also Sat–Sun 09.00–14.00.*

WHERE TO STAY

🏠 **Max Pension** (10 rooms) Stary trh 9; ☎ 052 4526 324; email: duchon@stonline.sk. Situated in an old building in the centre. Sgl & dbl $.

🏠 **Privat No 1** (5 rooms) Michalska 1; ☎ 052 4524 600. In a family home with its own wine cellar. Sgl & dbl $.

WHERE TO EAT AND DRINK

✗ **Kežmarská reštaurácia** Hradné námestie 33; ☎ 052 4522 933; e gardos@sinet.sk. Atmospheric restaurant and terrace. $. *Open daily 10.00–22.00.*

✗ **U 3 Apoštolov** Hlavné námestie 9; ☎ 052 4525 725. Decorated with religious items. $. *Open Mon–Thu 09.00–22.00, Fri–Sat 09.00–midnight, Sun 10.00–midnight.*

WHAT TO SEE AND DO

Thermal spa in Vrbov Located 6km south of Kežmarok on route 536, Vrbov thermal lido (☎ *052 4523 479; open Jan–May 10.00–21.00; Jun–15 Sep 08.00–22.00; 16 Sep–31 Oct 10.00–21.00; Nov–Dec closed; admission adult/child 150/80Sk*) is said to have the most curative waters in central Europe because it not only has beneficial effects in treating rheumatism and other problems, but it is also potable.

SPIŠSKÝ ŠTVRTOK *En route* to Levoča from Poprad, don't miss this beautiful church, named 'Spiš Thursday'. The village was situated on an important crossroads of historic trade routes. The village dates from 1263 and the Zápoľský family founded a Minorite monastery here in 1672. The highlight is the 13th-century church which has a soaring pointed steeple that dominates the skyline for miles around.

Getting there On route 18/E50, 14km from Poprad to Levoča. Regular buses. depart from Poprad bus station every 10 minutes, journey time 24 minutes, ticket costs 22Sk.

SPIŠ TOWNS

There are 24 Spiš towns. The historic Spiš region stretched from the Prešov region in the northeast of the country, even slipping into south Poland for a few kilometres, south almost to the Hungarian border, to Rožnava in the Košice region. Pronounced 'spish', it is one of the most picturesque regions in the country. For many hundreds of years, Spiš flourished with a semi-autonomous status within the Hungarian Kingdom.

Spiš county could be compared to a Swiss canton. It has its own self-government and a peculiar culture. Every county developed independently from the others. It had its own dialect, folk-dress and verbal communication. Spiš has always been a melting pot of cultures and religions in a positive way. In the 12th century German settlers arrived, received royal privileges and traded successfully. Hungarians also appeared in the south of the Spiš region, where the Polish-speaking Gorals settled in the north. Rusyn and Ukrainian settlers settled in the more mountainous parts in the 14th century, bringing not only culture but a distinct religion and style of sacral architecture. There were also many Jews particularly around Huncovce and also Roma came in the 15th century, adding to the vibrant, creative cosmopolitan mix. The jewel in the Spiš crown was Levoča.

LEVOČA *Telephone code 053*

Levoča, with a main square lined with Renaissance palaces and burghers' houses, is the most impressive of the old walled towns. Levoča was the walled capital of the richest region in Slovakia, Spiš, from the Middle Ages until 1922. After Tatar raids had wiped out most of the inhabitants, the Hungarian rulers invited German settlers to repopulate the Spiš region in the 12th–13th centuries. The oldest document where Levoča is mentioned was issued by Hungarian King Béla IV in 1249; after a Saxon immigration wave, Levoča Town became the administrative capital of the Spiš region. In 1323, Levoča became a Free Royal Town. Between 1370 and 1410 the town was fortified with a wall. Thanks to its advantageous position on the crossroads of trade routes, the town grew rich and architecture blossomed. A fire in 1550 tragically wiped out almost every original Gothic masterpiece. Levoča stagnated in the 17th–18th centuries after the failed anti-Habsburg uprising, plagues and wars. Only the Breuer press kept up business. The final blow came in 1871 when the new Košice–Bohumín railway line bypassed Levoča and instead went south through Spišská Nová Ves, which flourished as the new regional capital.

In 1950, Levoča's historical centre was declared an Urban Preservation Area.

GETTING THERE By bus, take the regular Poprad–Prešov buses. Local trains from Spišská Nová Ves. By car, route 18/E50, 24km east of Poprad.

The entire 276km Gothic Route (*Gotická cesta*) snakes around towns and villages dominated by Gothic churches leading through the northwest area of the Prešov and Košice regions. Visitors can discover the cultural treasures of the historic Spiš and Gemer regions. It is the first thematic, cultural hiking path of its kind, leading through 24 villages and nine towns. The individual monuments are marked by brown and white informative signs with pictograms in the shape of a Gothic arch. Some of these gems include the castle complexes of Spiš, Krásna Hôrka and Murán castles, preserved historic town centres of Levoča, Kežmarok, Rožňava and Rimavská Sobota as well as museums, cathedrals and village churches with rare frescoes. The blossoming of Gothic art and architecture is connected to the arrival of German settlers during the 13th century. The Germans enjoyed privileges, which contributed to the prosperity of the towns. Thanks to the creative genius of the architects, woodcarvers, painters, masons and others, Gothic Spiš contributes to the wealth of European art.

TOURIST INFORMATION AND OTHER PRACTICALITIES

◪ AICES tourist office Námestie Majstra Pavla 58, 054 01; \ 053 16 188; \f 053 4513 763; e tiklevoc@nextra.sk; www.levoca.sk
✉ Post office Námestie Majstra Pavla 42. *Open Mon–Fri 08.00–12.00 & 13.00–17.00, Sat 08.00–10.00.*

✚ Pharmacy Lekáreň U Leva Námestie Majstra Pavla 24. *Open Mon–Fri 08.30–17.00, Sat 08.00–12.00.*
$ VÚB Bank Námestie Majstra Pavla 38. *Open Mon–Fri 08.00–12.15 & 13.00–16.00.*

🏠 WHERE TO STAY

🏠 Hotel Arkada (32 rooms) Námestie Majstra Pavla 26; \ 053 4512 255; e arkada@stonline.sk; www.arkada.sk. On the main square in a 13th-century building with a sauna & wine cellar. *Dbl $$.*
🏠 Hotel Satel (21 rooms) Námestie Majstra Pavla 55; \ 053 4512 943; www.satel-slovakia.sk.

Elegant 18th-century mansion with friendly staff. *Sgl, dbl $$.*
🏠 Penzión U Leva (18 rooms, 2 apts) Námestie Majstra Pavla 24; \ 053 4502 311; e penzion-uleva@stonline.sk; www.uleva.sk. Stylish modern pension on the main square. *Sgl $, dbl $$.*

✕ WHERE TO EAT AND DRINK

✕ Bagetka Námestie Majstra Pavla 43; m 0915 351 881. The popular baguette chain. *Open Mon–Fri 09.00–18.00, Sat 09.00–12.00.*

✕ Reštaurácia Slovenka Námestie Majstra Pavla 62; \ 053 4512 339; traditional Slovak dishes. *Open daily 10.00–22.00.*

WHAT TO SEE AND DO The town's best known attraction is **Sv Jakub Church** with its magnificent wooden winged altar carved by Master Pavol of Levoča, the country's most famous Gothic craftsman. The huge 18.6m altar is the tallest Gothic altar in the world and barely squeezes into the archway. The centre of the altar is occupied by three figures: the Madonna, St Jacob and St John. The lower part of the altar is taken by Pavol's vision of the Last Supper. Further south is the beautiful **Town Hall** (*radnica*) with frescoes and the **Spiš Museum** (*Námestie Majstra Pavla 40;* \ *053 4512 786;* e *muzeumle@isternet.sk; www.muzeum.sk; open May–Oct Tue–Sun 09.00–17.00; Nov–Apr Tue–Sun 08.00–16.00*) with icons, paintings and furniture. In 1615, the town hall was enlarged and the southern part, as well as the archways on the first and second floors, were added. The town hall building is attached to a **Renaissance tower**, which was built between 1656 and 1661 as a belfry. Outside, the **Cage of Shame** (*Klietka hanby*), is a 16th-century wrought-iron pillory built by Protestants to humiliate women accused of

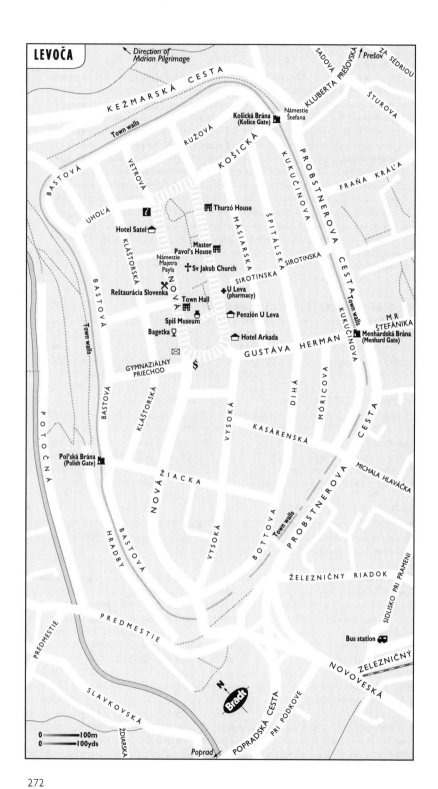

LEVOČA

Direction of
Marian Pilgrimage

KEŽMARSKÁ CESTA

ZA SÉDRIOU

SADOVA

KLUBERTA PREŠOVSKÁ

Prešov

ŠTUROVA

Town walls

Košická Brána
(Košice Gate)

Námestie
Štefana

RUŽOVA

KOŠICKÁ

PROBSTNEROVA

KUKUČINOVA

FRAŇA KRÁĽA

BASTOVÁ

VETROVA

UHOĽÁ

Thurzó House

MÄSIARSKA

ŠPITÁLSKA

Hotel Satel

Master
Pavol's House

SIROTINSKA

KLÁŠTORSKÁ

Námestie
Majstra
Pavla

Sv Jakub Church

SIROTINSKA

CESTA

Town walls

BASTOVÁ

Reštaurácia Slovenka

U Leva
(pharmacy)

KUKUČINOVA

M R
ŠTEFÁNIKA

Town walls

Town Hall

Penzión U Leva

Menhardská Brána
(Menhard Gate)

Spiš Museum

Bagetka

Hotel Arkada

GUSTÁVA HERMAN

POTOČNÁ

GYMNAZIÁLNY
PRIECHOD

Š

DIHÁ

MÓRICOVA

CESTA

BASTOVÁ

KLÁŠTORSKÁ

VYSOKÁ

KASÁRENSKÁ

Poľská Brána
(Polish Gate)

ŽIACKA

NOVÁ

VYSOKÁ

MICHALA HLAVÁČKA

HRADBY

BASTOVÁ

BOTTOVA

Town walls

PROBSTNEROVA

ŽELEZNIČNY RIADOK

SIDLISKO PRI PRAMENI

PREDMESTIE

PREDMESTIE

Bus station

ZELEZNIČNÝ

NOVOVESKÁ

SLAVKOVSKA

Bradt

POPRADSKÁ CESTA

PRI PODKOVE

ŽDIARSKA

0 ▬▬▬100m
0 ▬▬▬100yds

Poprad

According to the locals, the White lady of Levoča is still haunting the town, lurking around dark street corners at night. The White Lady is a real historic figure, called Julianna Korponay-Géczy (1680–1714) whose turncoat behaviour during the Rákóczi uprising led to her tragic end. During the uprising, Levoča was loyal to the rebels led by Ferenc Rákóczi II. The Habsburg forces tried to occupy Levoča but despite a very long siege they did not succeed. The help for the Habsburg forces arrived in the form of the beautiful Julianna who, in exchange for a huge sum of money, betrayed her town. During one night she stole the keys of the town gates and led the enemy into Levoča. Julianna had good contacts on both sides. Her father, Zsigmond Géczy was loyal to the rebels. For this reason, the rebels thought that they could trust her to send some letters containing strategically important information. Julianna, hoping to earn some more cash, informed the captain of the Habsburg forces about the existence of the letters. However, later when Julianna bothered to read the letters, she realised that they could put her father in serious danger. According to the letters, the rebels' meeting was supposed to take place at her father's residence. Julianna panicked and burned the letters. When the Habsburg captain asked about the letters, Julianna told him that she had burned them. However, at this point the Habsburg captain became suspicious and didn't believe Julianna's story. A process was launched against the woman, accusing her of smuggling rebel letters. Julianna was tortured and she was put in the Cage of Shame (which you can still see by the town hall) wearing a white dress. Finally, she was beheaded. The story upset the citizens of Levoča so much that after Julianna's execution, many people claimed that they saw her walking the town in a white dress and finally, the legend of the White Lady of Levoča was born. The Hungarian writer, Mór Jókai, wrote a novel entitled *The White Lady of Levoča* and numerous films also commemorate the story.

wrongdoing. Also on the square, at No 7, visitors can see the 15th-century **Thurzó House** (*Thurzov dom*), a burgher's home with lovely sgraffito decoration. Further along the square is **Master Pavol's old house** (*Dom Majstra Pavla; Námestie Majstra Pavla 20; ☏ 053 4513 496; open May–Oct Tue–Sun 09.00–17.00; Nov–Apr Tue–Sun 08.00–16.00*) displaying information on this little-known craftsman.

AROUND LEVOČA

MARIAN PILGRIMAGE On a hill overlooking Levoča is the neogothic Church of the Annunciation of the Blessed Virgin. Up to 250,000 people flock here for the annual Marianske Pilgrimage in the first weekend of July. In the 13th century, a small fort on the hill protected the townspeople from Tatar raids. To give thanks for being spared, they built a chapel, later a church, with a statue of the Virgin Mary. This statue is now the main symbol of the Marian Pilgrimage. During the Soviet era, it became a powerful form of protest against the communist regime. Pope John Paul II participated in the pilgrimage several times both before and after becoming Pope.

SPIŠ CASTLE AND SPIŠSKÁ KAPITULA Once seen, visitors will never erase the image of the Spiš castle ruins when thinking of Slovakia. It rises up majestically, almost organically from the limestone hill (634m) and dominates the surrounding countryside with its attitude and grandeur. It is the largest medieval ruin in central Europe and an irresistible photo opportunity with the snow-capped Tatra peaks framing the background. Spišský hrad (Zipser Burg) is the largest castle in Slovakia. The first official written record of the castle dates back to 1120, when it was used as a boundary fort on the northern frontier of an early feudal Hungarian state. The strong walls resisted Tatar raids in 1241 although it was damaged. Italian stonemasons strengthened the fortifications in the 13th century when working on the construction of Spišská Kapitula nearby. The castle burnt down in 1780 but is still spectacular and some of the 20 rooms are in good enough condition to host a **museum** (℩ 053 4541 336; open 1 May–31 Oct daily 08.30–19.00; admission adult/child 100/60Sk).

In 1993, the castle and its surroundings, including Spišské Podhradie, Spišská Kapitula and Žehra church were added to UNESCO's World Heritage List.

In **Spišské Podhradie,** there are a few shops, a bank, a post office (open Mon–Fri 08.00–12.00 & 13.00–16.00, Sat 08.00–10.00) and many helpful signposts: parking, WC, tourist information, first aid, etc.

From town, walk uphill to **Spišská Kapitula.** This one-street walled village has been the seat of the Spiš bishop and Holy See officials since the mid 13th century. Built during 1245–75, **St Martin's Cathedral** (open daily 10.00–17.00) is filled with beautiful frescoes and Gothic altars. Visitors can also see the Bishop's Palace, bell tower, canonical houses and the town walls at both the Upper and Lower Gates.

Getting there Regular buses run from Poprad to Spišské Podhradie, the small town under Spiš Castle. From the town it is 45 minutes' walk to the castle.

Tourist information
🄸 Tourist information centre Mariánské námestie 34. Open Mon–Fri 08.00–12.00, 12.30–16.00.

ŽEHRA Situated 4km southeast of Spiš Castle, Žehra village is remarkable for its little 14th-century **Church of the Holy Spirit** with its top-heavy onion dome, which looks out of proportion with the tiny church. The interior has priceless frescoes dating from the 13th–17th centuries. To reach the church, visitors climb 93 steps up the travertine hill.

Getting there Route 18/E50; just past Spiš Castle, turn right towards Hodkovce.

PREŠOV _Telephone code 051_

With nearly 100,000 residents, Prešov is the country's third-largest city and a seat of regional government in northeastern Slovakia. Despite its size, Prešov has a friendly, small-town ambience with the flavour of the surrounding Šariš county's villages. The region was inhabited as far back as the Paleolithic period. By the end of the 11th century the town had become part of the Kingdom of Hungary, and in the 13th century many German settlers moved to Prešov from the Spiš region. In 1299, Prešov received municipal privileges, and in 1374, was declared a Free Royal Town. In the 15th century Prešov joined the Pentapolitana, an alliance of five towns of eastern Slovakia (Bardejov, Košice, Levoča, Prešov and Sabinov). In 1572, salt mining started in neighbouring Solivar. In 1687, 24 prominent Prešov citizens and noblemen were executed for supporting the uprising of Imre Thököly in an event known as the Prešov Massacre. At the beginning of the 18th century, plague and fires decimated the population to a mere 2,000 inhabitants. However, within 50 years, the town had

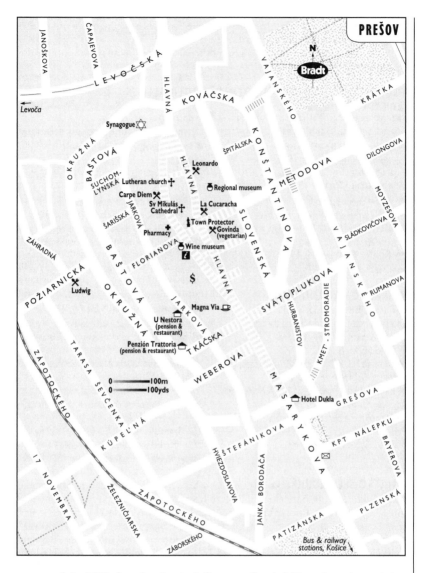

Bradt

← Levoča

Synagogue

KOVÁČSKA

ŠPITÁLSKA

Leonardo

Lutheran church

Carpe Diem

Regional museum

Sv Mikuláš Cathedral

La Cucaracha

Town Protector
Govinda (vegetarian)

Pharmacy

Wine museum

Ludwig

Magna Via

U Nestora
(pension & restaurant)

Penzión Trattoria
(pension & restaurant)

0 ▬▬▬100m
0 ▬▬▬100yds

WEBEROVA

Hotel Dukla GREŠOVA

KPT NÁLEPKU

Bus & railway
stations, Košice

recovered. In 1752, the salt mine in Solivar was flooded. Ever since then salt has been produced by boiling brine.

During World War II, Košice became part of Hungary and many institutions moved to Prešov, increasing its importance. During the communist regime, the town became an industrial centre.

GETTING THERE By train, from Bratislava, take the main Bratislava–Košice line to Kysak (15km south of Prešov), a journey of five hours 45 minutes, then transfer to a local train for Prešov (journey 20 minutes). Prešov is on a branch train line: to travel from Bratislava, nearby Košice and most of Slovakia it is necessary to change at the tiny village station at Kysak.

From Poprad, there are regular buses.

By car, there is an express highway to Košice and with the help of a tunnel also an easy trip to the Spiš and High Tatras areas.

Prešov bus and train stations are opposite each other about 1km south of the main square on Masarykova, which is served by trolleybus.

TOURIST INFORMATION AND OTHER PRACTICALITIES

AICES Prešov information service Hlavná 67; ☎ 051 16 186, 051 7731 113; f 051 7731 113; e mic@pis.sk; www.pis.sk A helpful centre with computers available for internet access. *Open Mon–Fri 09.00–18.00, Sat 09.00–13.00.*

✉ **Post office** Masarykova 2. *Open Mon–Fri 07.00–19.00, Sat 08.00–12.00.*
$ **VÚB Bank** Hlavná 61. *Open Mon–Fri 08.00–17.00.*
✚ **Pharmacy** Hlavná 77. *Open Mon–Fri 08.00–16.00.*

WHERE TO STAY

🏠 **Hotel Dukla** Námestie Legionárov 2; ☎ 051 7722 741; e recepcia@hotelduklapresov.sk; www.hotelduklapresov.sk. Modern block hotel opposite Tesco. *Sgl* $$, *dbl* $$$.
🏠 **Penzión Trattoria** Tkáčska 5; ☎ 051 7763 020; www.penziontrattoria.sk. A rustic pension in a huge

villa just outside the centre. *Sgl* $, *dbl* $$
🏠 **Penzión & reštaurácia U Nestora** Jarková 43; ☎ 051 7223 950. Based on a champion steeplechaser & filled with tackle. Good restaurant ($). *Dbl* $$.

WHERE TO EAT AND DRINK

✗ **Carpe Diem** Hlavná 95; ☎ 051 7723 051. Constantly voted one of the best in the country by Slovak gourmets. *Open Mon–Fri 08.00–23.00, Sat 09.00–23.00, Sun 10.00–23.00.*
✗ **Govinda** Hlavná 70; ☎ 051 7722 819. Vegetarian restaurant. *Open Mon–Fri 11.00–17.00.*
✗ **La Cucaracha** Hlavná 72; ☎ 051 7720 600. Latin American cuisine, this is the original cockroach establishment complete with pool table. *Open Mon–Thu 10.00–midnight, Fri 10.00–02.00, Sat 17.00–02.00, Sun 17.00–midnight.*

✗ **Leonardo** Hlavná 114; ☎ 051 7725 587. Opposite the newer Cucaracha. Italian & international cuisine, good steaks, pastas & tiramisu. *Open daily 10.00–22.00.*
✗ **Ludwig reštaurácia & penzión.** Požiarnická 2; ☎ 051 7481 958–60; m 0908 254 211. Very upmarket restaurant, with beautiful interior, chandeliers & Viennese coffee-house chairs. Terrace. *Open daily 11.00–23.00.*
☕ **Magna Via** Hlavná 27; ☎ 051 7720 435. Trendy café with great soups & salads. *Open Mon–Fri 09.00–midnight, Sat 10.00–midnight, Sun 15.00–22.00.*

WHAT TO SEE AND DO Like Košice, Prešov has a beautiful leaf-shaped main square, Hlavná ulica. All the interesting sights are based around this renovated square. The imposing **Neptune Fountain** was sculpted in 1840 by Markus Hollander, the first Jew allowed to live within the town walls. The 14th-century Catholic **Sv Mikuláš Cathedral** features modern stained-glass windows and a sumptuous Baroque altarpiece. The Crucifixion was carved by Master Pavol of Levoča. Behind Sv Mikuláš is the less ornate **Lutheran Church**, dating from the mid 17th century. Further north along the square, the **regional museum** (*Krajské Múzeum; Hlavná 86; ☎ 051 7598 220; open Tue–Fri 09.00–12.00 & 12.30–17.00, Sun 13.00–18.00; admission adult/child 40/20Sk*) gives an account of the Šariš region. On the corner of Hlavná and Floriánova, the **Wine Museum** (☎ 051 7733 108; e muzeumvin@stonline.sk; www.muzeumvin.sk; open Mon–Fri 08.00–18.00, Sat 08.00–12.00; admission adult/student 40/20Sk*) snakes through an ancient cellar system neighbouring the old prison on Jarková where 24 anti-Habsburg collaborators were held before execution in 1687. Prešov's ornate **synagogue** houses the oldest Jewish museum in Slovakia, the **Museum of Judaica** (*open Tue & Wed 11.00–16.00, Thu 15.00–18.00, Fri 10.00–13.00, Sun 13.00–17.00*) with an exhibition on the region's Jewish community, 6,000 of whom perished in the Holocaust. On Hlavná about 50m south of the cathedral is an unusual statue of the

Town's Protector with one arm holding a golden ball, one breast and one wing. Sculptor Dušan Pončák created the statue, which symbolises the connection between the past and the future.

AROUND PREŠOV

Situated 14km northwest of Prešov on route 68 towards Sabinov are two ski resorts, **Drienica** and **Lysá** (1,067m) are two larger tourist centres connected by a funicular railway. The large ski area is equipped with snow-making machines.

From Prešov centre, looking north, two medieval castle ruins can be seen on the distant hills. One is **Veľký Šariš**, ten minutes away on the Lipany train line. For centuries the mighty fortress was the centre of the Šariš region. The castle was never taken by force, a fact few castles on Slovak soil can claim. Unfortunately, in 1660 a gunpowder explosion seriously damaged the castle, a process of destruction completed by a fire in 1687. After that, the castle slowly fell into ruin. The second ruin **Kapušiansky hrad** is in the village of **Kapušany**, about 15 minutes heading out of town on the Humenné line. From the village the trail goes straight up the steep castle hill in a short but breathless 30-minute walk. Amalgamated into Prešov's southern suburbs is **Solivar salt mine** (✆ 051 7757 427; open Tue–Fri 09.00–17.00, Sat 10.00–16.00) where visitors can learn about rock salt mining which started in 1572. The **Dubník opal mines** (*Opálové bane Dubník, Červenica;* ▥ *0905 539 101. Information Centre, Opálové bane Dubník, Zimná 54, Spišská Nová Ves;* ✆ *053 4411 853;* e *opalovebane@stonline.sk; www.opalovebane.sk*), 18km southeast of Prešov in the Slanské vrchy hills, are a unique phenomenon. There is no other place in the world where opals were mined to such an extent and so long ago. Extraction of previous opals dates from 1597. The famous Dubník opals were known as Červenica opal after a nearby village. The height of their fame was at the 1873 World Fair in Vienna. The biggest Dubník opal was called the Vienna Imperial Opal and weighed in at 594g. In spite of the tremendous output from these mines, they were shut down in 1922. Shortly after the mine closed, opal thieves entered and destroyed what was left.

Located 9km west of Prešov is a wooden church at **Brežany.** The *tserkva* of St Luke was built in 1727 and renovated in the late 18th century. The three-part log building has an atypical external design remarkably influenced by Gothic Roman Catholic sacral architecture. The Baroque iconostasis dates from 1733. To get there, take route 546 heading for Gelnica and turn right at Rokycany.

BARDEJOV *Telephone code 054*

Bardejov is the economic and cultural heart of the Upper Šariš region, with more than 33,000 inhabitants. It is called 'the most Gothic town of Slovakia'. Bardejov was founded on an important trade route leading north into Poland and was first mentioned in writing in 1241 in the *Ipatyiev Monastery Chronicle*. Hungarian rulers in the Anjou dynasty devoted much attention economically to Bardejov and the city was granted numerous royal privileges. Saxon weavers arrived in the 12th century and the city prospered as a centre of the textile industry for the following 300 years. Bardejov built fortifications, held fairs and executed criminals. Bardejov became a Free Royal Town in 1376. Polish kings granted the city more rights in the 14th and 15th centuries. In the Middle Ages, the city took a firm stand against local bandits who were disturbing commerce in the region. Craftsmen and merchants worked to make Bardejov rich and the city had 64 professions and more than 50 guilds. To protect the city, a fortified wall was built. Construction lasted, on and off,

10

from the 14th to the 17th century, including additions, alterations and renovations. Today, visitors can still see seven original bastions from the Gothic fortification system and they form part of the UNESCO-listed World Heritage Site (2000).

GETTING THERE By car, from Prešov on route 545 (32km). From Poprad on route 67, then route 77.

Buses are much more convenient than trains, although the bus from Bratislava can take up to ten hours.

TOURIST INFORMATION AND OTHER PRACTICALITIES

☑ **Tourist information office** Radničné námestie 21; ☎ 054 4744 003; e spirit@spirit-travel.sk; www.tik-bardejov.sk. *Open Mon–Fri 09.00–12.00 &* *13.00–17.00, Sat 10.00–14.00, Sun closed.*

$ **ČSOB bank** Radničné námestie 7. *Open Mon–Fri 08.00–17.00.*

🏠 WHERE TO STAY

🏠 **Hotel Bellevue** (22 rooms) Mihalov; ☎ 054 4728 404; e hotel@bellevuebardejov.sk; www.bellevuehotel.sk. Lovely hotel southwest of town in the hills, great pool, good restaurant (**$$**). *Sgl $$, dbl $$–$$$.*

🏠 **Hotel Šariš** (19 rooms) Námestie SNP 1;

☎ 054 4724 373; e matt@po.psg.sk; www.hotelsaris-bj.sk. Not very attractive but convenient for the centre. *Sgl $, dbl $$.*

🏠 **Hotel Sport** (20 rooms) Kutuzovova 34; ☎ 054 4728 208. Modern block just north of the centre. *Dbl $.*

✖ WHERE TO EAT AND DRINK

✖ **Bar Bar Café** Radničné námestie 28. A friendly bar with narrow adobe walls. *Open Mon–Thu 10.00–23.00, Fri 10.00–02.00, Sat 12.00–02.00, Sun 13.00–23.00.*

✖ **La Bello** Radničné námestie 50. Slovak dishes. $. *Open Mon–Thu 07.30–23.00, Fri 07.30–01.00, Sat 10.00–01.00, Sun 10.00–22.00.*

✖ **Pirôžky** Rhodyho 1; m 0902 240 895. Delicious

pies. $. *Open Mon–Fri 08.00–16.00.*

✖ **Pizzeria la Fiesta** Radničné námestie 31; ☎ 054 4742 584. With 30 kinds of pizza. $. *Open Mon–Thu 10.00–23.00, Fri 10.00–01.00, Sat 10.00–midnight, Sun 10.00–22.00.*

🍵 **Roland Café** Radničné námestie 12. A lovely terrace on the square. $. *Open Mon–Thu 07.45–23.00, Fri 07.45–01.00, Sat 11.00–midnight, Sun 11.00–23.00.*

WHAT TO SEE AND DO Bardejov is packed with beautiful, historic buildings, the most precious being the monumental **Sv Egídius Cathedral**, built in the 14th century on the site of an older church. The 11 Gothic winged altars with panel paintings are priceless national treasures which have hardly any parallels in Europe. Check out the altar to St Apollonia, an aid in times of toothache in 1490–1510; she could save on dentist's bills. Tragically, the original main altar, the work of Master Pavol of Levoča, was destroyed in a fire; only two sculptures and one painting survive from that celebrated structure. Visitors can climb 184 steps to the **tower** (*admission adult/child 70/20Sk, photo permit 50Sk, video 100Sk*) to get a fantastic view of the main square and surroundings.

☞ *POZOR!* The stone spiral staircase is very steep and narrow. Coming down is hardest on the knee joints.

The rectangular square is flanked by attractive Gothic and Renaissance **burgher houses** and in the middle sits the sweet **Old Town Hall** (*Stará radnica*), completed in 1509 and now containing the **Šariš Museum** (☎ *054 4724 966; open 1 Oct–30 Apr Tue–Sun 08.30–16.00; 1 May–30 Sep daily 08.30–12.00 & 12.30–16.30; admission adult/child 40/20Sk*), established in 1903. Part of the museum, in a building (*Radničné námestie 27;* ☎ *054 4722 009; same opening hours*) at the opposite end of the square to Sv Egídius, contains the largest collection of icons in Slovakia. The Franciscan monastery and **Church of St John the Baptist**, at the southern corner of the main square, was built around 1380 by Augustinians. It is also possible to walk up the **Bardejov Calvary** on a hill just to the east of the town centre. Local priest Eduard Kacvinsky organised the construction in 1863–69. Jews were an important part of Bardejov's population from the 18th century and the complex of buildings contains an 18th-century synagogue, assembly hall ('Beth Hamidras'), ritual baths and administrative buildings, an urban rarity in eastern Slovakia.

BARDEJOVSKÉ KÚPELE The spa town outside Bardejov not only has healing thermal springs, but also a wonderful outdoor museum (part of the Šariš Museum). The first record of Bardejov Spa dates back to 1247 when Hungarian King Béla IV bequeathed the territory of the present-day spa together with its springs to the town of Bardejov. In 1505, small cabins were built and in 1777, a 12-room bath house was erected near the springs. The first scientific report on the Main Spring and the Spa Spring was written in 1795 by professor Pál Kitaibel from Budapest. Kitaibel considered the Bardejov waters to be among the most curative in Europe, suitable for treating epilepsy, hypochondria, gout and stomach problems. Kitaibel's report contributed to making Bardejov the most visited spa in the Hungarian Empire in the 18th century. There are four hotels: Astória, Ozón, František and Mier located near the spa.

Getting there Regular buses from Bardejov take ten minutes. By car, on route 545 from Prešov (50 minutes) then follow route 77 towards Zborov for 4km.

Tourist information
Tourist information centre **Herkules** Kino Žriedlo, 086 31 Bardejovské Kúpele; ✆ 054 4774
477; e info@herkules.sk; www.herkules.sk

Where to stay
Hotel **Astória** (51 rooms) Bardejovské kúpele; ✆ 054 4774 470; www.kupele-bj.sk. Built in 1898, the
Astória is only 2-star but nevertheless luxurious. *Sgl* $$, *dbl* $$–$$$.

What to see
The Exhibition of Folk Architecture in Bardejov Spa (*Muzeum Ludovej Architektury Vila Rákóczi, Bardejovské Kúpele;* ✆ *054 4722 072;* e *sarmus@nextra.sk; www.muzeumbardejov.sk; open 1 May–30 Sept daily 09.00–12.00 & 12.30–17.30; 1 Oct–30 Apr Tue–Sun 09.00–12.00 & 12.30–15.00*). A *skanzen* with wooden and thatch-roofed buildings built in the Rusyn folk tradition displayed in a 1.5ha park, housing 24 buildings, two wooden churches, granaries and stables brought from the surrounding Šariš region and dating back to the 18th century. The wooden church was built in Mikulášová in 1730 and was moved to Bardejov Spa in 1931.

AROUND BARDEJOV

ZBOROV CASTLE RUINS Hrad Zborov is located 8km northeast of Bardejov. The now-ruined Gothic castle also known as Makovica was built in the 13th century to protect the trade routes between Hungary and Poland. It became the property of King Mátyás (1470), Zápoľský (1536) and Gašpar Serédy (1548).

SVIDNÍK Svidník will appear to many visitors as the archetypal socialist city, filled with communist-era architecture and situated in the picturesque far eastern region of Slovakia and the gateway to the Rusyn region, filled with wooden churches. The town is situated at the confluence of the Ondava and Ladomírka rivers in the shade of the Ondavská vrchovina Mountains.

The oldest record of Svidník dates back to 1357. In the second half of the 14th century an important amber trade road led from the Danube and Tisza region through Svidník to Poland. Just 18km north is the Dukla Pass (*Dukelský priesmyk*), used throughout the centuries for trade and military purposes. The strategic significance led to the region being scarred by military action. In the 18th and 19th centuries, Dukla was frequently used by Russian military caravans heading for battles against the Hungarians. In World War I, the town was completely burnt down and more than 1.8 million people died in the eastern region, a third of the total population of modern Slovakia. During World War II, battles in the area occurred so often that a valley nearby was renamed the Valley of Death (*Dolina smrti*). The countryside between Svidník and the Dukla Pass is dotted with wooden churches and the Rusyn and Ukrainian culture is well documented at a museum and *skanzen* in Svidník. Visit the Slovak National Museum of Ukrainian-Ruthenian culture in Svidník (*Centrálna 258;* ✆ *054 7882 100; www.muk.sk*).

The Open-Air exhibition of the Museum of Ukrainian-Ruthenian culture in Svidník (*Nad Svidníckym amfiteátrom;* ✆ *054 7522 952; open May–Oct Mon–Fri 08.30–18.00, Sat–Sun 10.00–18.00; Nov–Apr by appointment*), which is filled with houses that have been relocated from surrounding villages.

Getting there By car, route 77 from Bardejov.

THE RUSYN MINORITY AND THE WOODEN CHURCHES

Slovakia has the highest density of wooden churches anywhere in Europe. On both sides of the Carpathian Mountains of the Slovak–Polish border region are located more than 100 wooden churches. The 27 wooden churches dating back to the 17th and 18th centuries in northeast Slovakia are of special significance. Below the Dukla, in a relatively small area, visitors can find 12 wooden churches. These churches (*cerkvy*) are in the characteristic architecture of the Rusyn (Ruthenian) minority. Quite often these churches are locked but there is a note on the door with the address of the person with the key. They are happy to show visitors around. Small donations are always appreciated.

GETTING THERE You really need a car to see these architectural gems dotted along minor roads which branch off the route E371 to Poland via the Dukla Pass.

DUKLA PASS One of the largest battles of World War II was fought at the Dukla Pass where Hitler placed troops to defend Nazi-occupied Slovakia. The Red Army approached in the autumn of 1944 and a devastating battle ensued. Two months later, 85,000 Red Army soldiers, and several thousand Czechoslovaks and Germans were dead.

Route E571 leads from Svidník to Dukla, a town in Poland. After 18km visitors will reach the border and see a statue of two hands handling a disc, in honour of mine disposal experts. Down the hill and across the street is the main monument to the Czechoslovak army, a 37m triangular stone edifice curving around a poignant statue of an elderly woman crying on the shoulder of a stony-faced soldier. In the memorial's shadow is a cemetery with six mass graves holding the unidentified bodies of 199 soldiers. A trail leads through the hills to the 52m lookout tower (*Open Apr–Oct Tue–Fri 08.30–17.00, Sat–un 09.30–18.00*) with its now-serene view of Slovak and Polish territory, the scene of the Dukla carnage.

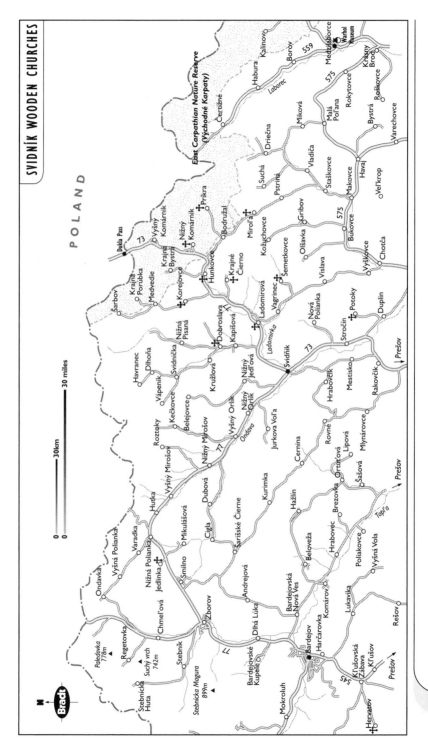

10

Jedlinka A bit on its own, Jedlinka is located back along route 77 to Bardejov. A three-tower Greek-Catholic Church of Protection of the Virgin Mary dating from 1763 and boasting a lavish Rococo iconostasis with a celebrated icon of the Virgin Mary.

Dobroslava In a small canyon 2km from the Valley of Death outside Svidník. Built in 1705, the Church of Saint Paraskieva was first repaired in 1880. The icon of the *Last Judgment* is remarkable for its gruesomeness.

Ladomirova The Church of Archangel Michael was built in 1742, one of the most architecturally interesting churches featuring towers, cupolas, onion domes and crosses.

Šemetkovce The little Church of Saint Michael the Archangel dating from 1752 is a typical three-part, log building. Next to the church is a newer wooden belfry with a pyramid-shaped roof.

Krajné Čierno Two churches in the village. One above the village is consecrated to Saint Basilius the Great, built in the first half of the 18th century. A new layer of lighter wood has been added to protect the original walls. The second has darker wood and a silver metal roof.

Hunkovce The wooden Church of the Demise of the Mother of God was constructed at the end of the 18th century. A distinctive three-tower church amongst trees on a hill above the road.

Korejovce Built in 1764, the Greek-Catholic Church of the Mother of God is a characteristic example of the three-section plan. Next to the church is a separate wooden belfry with three bells dated 1769, 1771 and 1835.

Nižný Komárnik One of the most beautiful wooden churches, based on a design by the Ukrainian architect Sičinsky, the Church of The Protection of The Mother of God was built in 1938.

MEDZILABORCE From Dukla, those with a car can cut through the countryside on well-maintained minor roads to Medzilaborce to pay homage to the Rusyn minority's most famous son.

Situated 531km from Bratislava and about as far as you can go in Slovakia, the town of Medzilaborce lies in the picturesque Laborec river valley; the name translates as 'between the Laborec'. As early as the 17th century, an important trade route went through Medzilaborce connecting Slovakia with Poland through the Lupkov Pass.

Modern Medzilaborce has more than 6,500 inhabitants, a considerable number of whom belong to the Ruthenian and Ukrainian minorities. Pop-art superstar Andy Warhol's mother, Júlia, came from Miková, a tiny hamlet 8km north of Medzilaborce and Warhol's parents emigrated from there to Pittsburgh. Medzilaborce remembers Warhol in the gigantic **Warhol Family Museum of Modern Art** (*Múzeum moderného umenia rodiny Warholovcov, ulica A Warhola 26;* \ *057 7480 072; http://art.box.sk/warhol/index2.html; open Tue–Fri 10.00–16.00, Sat–Sun 12.00–16.00*) which opened in 1991 and features two-dozen Warhol originals such as prints on cardboard, some hand-coloured, the oldest of which are the *Campbell's Soup I* and *Campbell's Soup II* pieces. The *Red Lenin* print and the *Queen Ntombi Twala of Swaziland* painted photo are two examples of Warhol's innovative use of colour. There are works by Andy's estranged older brother Paul who uses chicken feet to make imprints on canvas and Paul's son James who illustrates children's books. The collection includes Warhol family memorabilia and old photographs. Outside, a statue of Warhol under an umbrella looks at the

Bodružal The Greek-Catholic Church of Saint Nicholas was built in 1658 on the southern slope of the village. The church has a Baroque interior and incredible frescoes.

Príkra The Greek-Catholic Church of St Michael the Archangel was built in 1777 and is a three-section church on a small hill above the village. The bell in the highest tower dates from 1759.

Miroľa The Church to the Protection of the Mother of God dates from 1770 and is a good example of the Lemkov design, containing a detailed iconostasis.

Potoky This Greek-Catholic Church of Saint Paraskieva dating from 1773 is a newer belfry with a bell from 1839. The church has three onion-domed Baroque spires decorated with forged iron crosses.

THE SIX WOODEN CHURCHES DOTTED AROUND BARDEJOV

Kožany The church consecrated to the Meeting of the Lord with Simon was built in the second half of the 18th century. South of Bardejov off route E371.

Tročany The Church of St Luke from the 15th century is one of the oldest surviving tripartite wooden churches. Off route 545 leading from Prešov to Bardejov.

Hervartov The Roman Catholic St Francis of Assisi Church. Built around 1500, it is the oldest surviving wooden church in Slovakia. Around 8km southwest of Bardejov.

Krivé The church of St Luke built in 1826 contains a precious icon of the Virgin Hodegetria. Off route 77, Bardejov to Stará Ľubovňa.

Lukov-Venécia The Church of SS Cosmas and Damian dated 1708–09 has an unusual design. Near Krivé.

Hraničné The church of the Immaculate Conception of the Virgin Mary, dated 1785, has served both eastern and Catholic confessions. North of Stará Ľubovňa.

town he never visited while locals huddle from the wind in a bus shelter in the shape of a famous Campbell's soup can. Medzilaborce has a beautiful white church on a hill above the town but otherwise this unremarkable settlement has little going for it. Quite an appropriate home for Ondrej Varchola (his Slovak name) who so famously said, 'I come from nowhere'.

Getting there It's a fascinating day trip by hire car if you're staying in Poprad, Prešov or Košice. Otherwise, by train from Bratislava takes 9¹/₂ hours with changes in Košice and Humenné.

VEĽKÁ DOMAŠA LAKE The reservoir is known as the 'green pearl' of eastern Slovakia. The 1,510ha reservoir was created in 1962–67 by blocking the course of the Ondava River and flooding the surrounding countryside. There are five leisure centres with good campsites dotted around the lake, at Dobrá, Poľany, Holčíkovce, Nová Keľča and Valkov.

Tourist information
🛈 **AICES information centre** Stropkov; Hlavná 2; ✆ 054 7423 288; e tic@stropkov.sk; www.stropkov.sk

HUMENNÉ The otherwise unremarkable railway station at Humenné in the east of Prešov's long region has a statue of the Good Soldier Svejk, hero of Czech novelist Jaroslav Hašek's comic masterpiece. Humenné's other attraction is the *skanzen,* a **Museum of Folk Architecture and Living** (*Park Mieru;* ✆ 057 7755

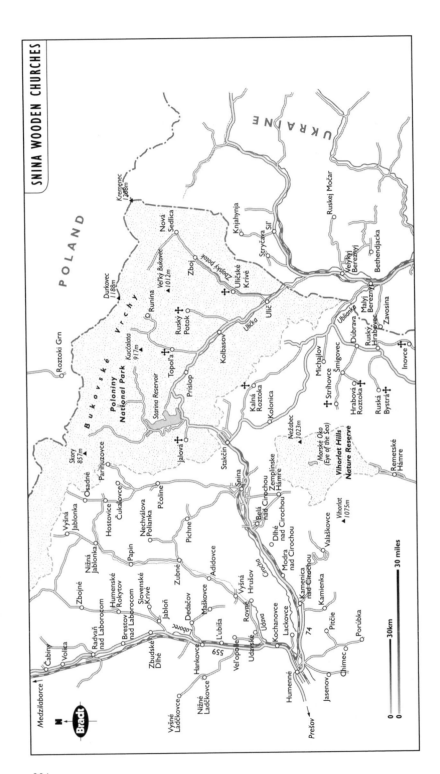

SNINA WOODEN CHURCHES

IN PREŠOV

Topoľa An unusual church dedicated to the Archangel Michael dating from 1700, one of the oldest wooden churches of the Byzantine rite.

Ruský Potok Church of the Archangel Michael dating from the 18th century with valuable 17th-century liturgical books written in the Cyrillic alphabet, printed in Ľvov.

Uličské Krivé Church dedicated to the Archangel Michael dating from the early 18th century has two impressive towers and a richly decorated Baroque interior.

Kalná Roztoka The 18th-century Church of St Basilius the Great is one of the few plastered wooden churches.

Hrabová Roztoka The 18th-century Church of St Basilius has a beautiful Baroque interior.

IN KOŠICE

Ruská Bystrá Church of St Nicholas the Bishop was built in the early 18th century. It has an original Baroque and Rococo interior.

Inovce Church of the Archangel Michael dating from 1836, with two towers and a central 'Imperial' door.

671; *www.skanzen.muzeumhumenne.sk; open May–Oct Tue–Fri 09.00–17.30, Sat 09.00–13.00, Sun 13.00–17.00*), with an impressively large collection of houses situated in a park in the centre of town. The wooden church has been brought here from Nova Sedlica, Slovakia's easternmost village.

The *skanzen* is part of the **Vihorlat Museum** (*Vihorlatské Múzeum, Námestie Slobody 1;* ✆ *057 7752 240; www.muzeumhumenne.sk*) situated in a huge four-wing Renaissance manor.

Getting there Regular trains from Košice (two hours) and buses from Prešov (two hours).

SNINA Snina is the gateway to another collection of wooden churches. Several of them lie in the Košice region, and I would also suggest visiting these churches while staying in Košice Town. However, because the majority of the churches are in the Prešov region they are all listed here.

Tourist information
🛈 **AICES information Centre** Strojárska 102,   e unitur@stonline.sk; www.snina.sk
Snina; ✆ 057 16 186, 057 7685 735;

POLONINY NATIONAL PARK This is the furthest east you can go in Slovakia. At Kremenec Peak (1,208m) a stone marks the spot where Slovakia, Poland and Ukraine all meet. The 10,973ha Poloniny National Park was established in 1997. The extremely well preserved natural character of the landscape was one reason for its inclusion on the UNESCO Man and Biosphere programme. The park is dominated by beech and fir forests, beautiful examples of virgin Carpathian forest and home to many deer, wolf, bison and moose.

Prešov Region   THE RUSYN MINORITY AND THE WOODEN CHURCHES

10

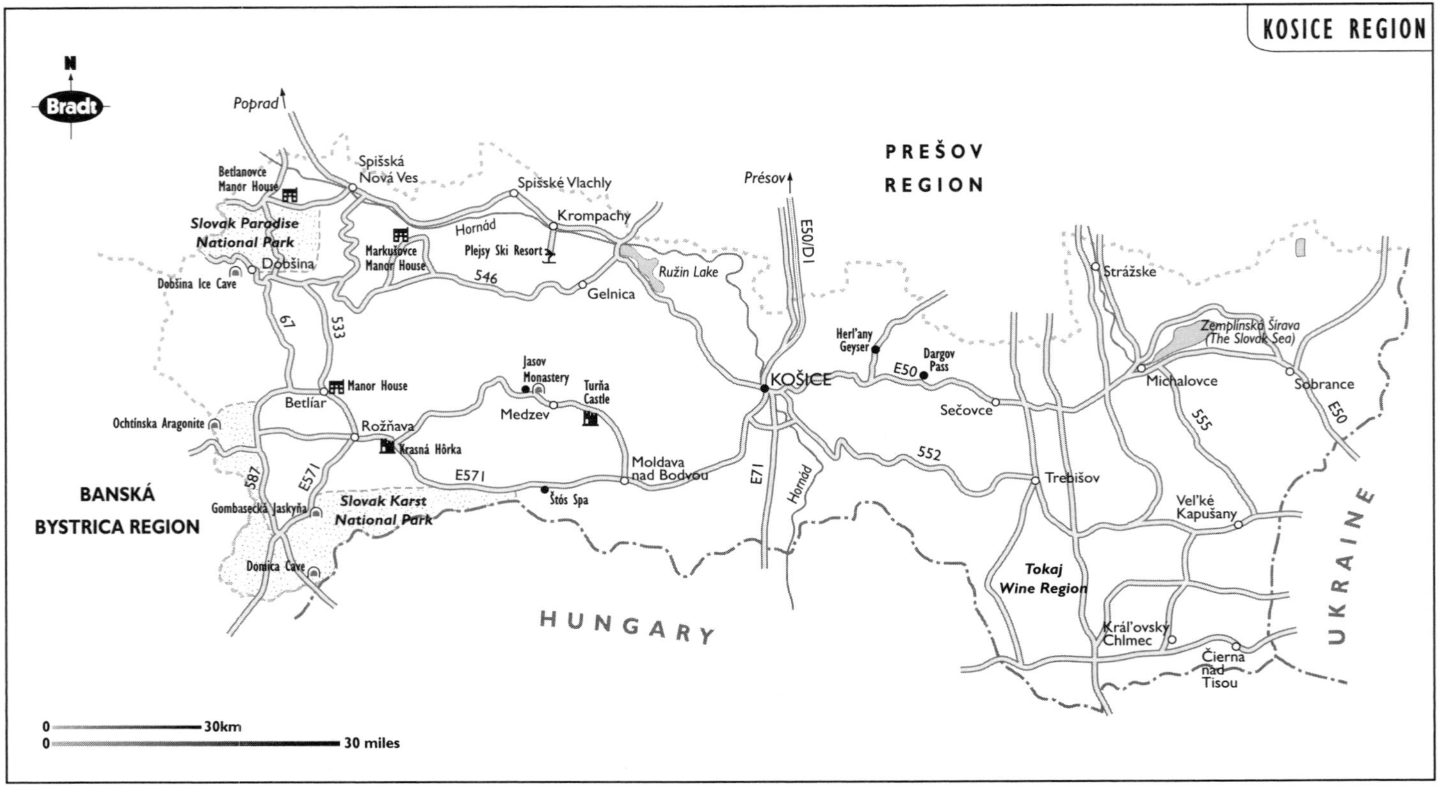

KOSICE REGION
PREŠOV REGION
UKRAINE
HUNGARY
BANSKÁ BYSTRICA REGION
KOŠICE
Présov
Poprad
E50/D1
E50
E71
E571
555
552
546
533
67
587
Hornád
Sobrance
Zemplínska Šírava (The Slovak Sea)
Michalovce
Strážske
Veľké Kapušany
Čierna nad Tisou
Kráľovský Chlmec
Trebišov
Tokaj Wine Region
Sečovce
Dargov Pass
Herľany Geyser
Ružin Lake
Gelnica
Krompachy
Spišské Vlachly
Plejsy Ski Resort
Spišská Nová Ves
Markušovce Manor House
Betlanovce Manor House
Slovak Paradise National Park
Dobšina
Dobšina Ice Cave
Ochtínska Aragonite
Betliar
Manor House
Rožňava
Krasná Hôrka
Slovak Karst National Park
Gombasecká Jaskyňa
Domica Cave
Medzev
Jasov Monastery
Turňa Castle
Moldava nad Bodvou
Štós Spa
0 30km
0 30 miles
N
Bradt

Košice Region

The Košice region is another long oblong of land in southeast Slovakia, situated south of the Prešov region. In the north, the region goes right up to Spišská Nová Ves and a little nobble pokes up into the Prešov region swallowing up Spiš Castle.

Spiš Castle details can be found in the Prešov chapter, along with its nearest village, Spišské Podhradie. Geographically, Košice is a very diverse region. The region contains several historic areas such as parts of Spiš and Gemer. The greatest mountain range running through the region is the Slovenské rudohorie (Slovak Ore Mountains). The heart of the region is the Košice Basin, flanked by the Slanské hory Mountains in the east, behind which spreads the eastern Slovakia plain. The Bodrog River gathers water from this lowland and leaves Slovakia, flowing into northern Hungary, the lowest elevation (94m) in the country. Four extensive natural protected areas lie in Košice, among them the jewel: Slovenský raj (Slovak Paradise), turned into a national park in 1988 in order to preserve its countless canyons, waterfalls and calcareous surface formations. The most beautiful pearls of nature are hidden underground in the southwestern part of the Košice region, in the depths of the Slovak karst (*Slovenský kraš*), the most extensive cave system is included in the UNESCO World Heritage list as a site of natural importance. Among the 12 caves open to the public in Slovakia, five are in Košice. The Dobšinská ice cave is the only European underground ice cave outside the alpine region. While Bratislava is one of the most prosperous regions in the new EU, the Košice region is the country's least-developed area and the second-poorest region in the EU, beaten only by Lubienskie region in Poland. There are many plans to improve infrastructure, especially the highways between the eastern region and the capital.

EVENTS IN THE KOŠICE REGION

June	**Košice** Cassovia folkfest; see www.folkfest.sk
September	**Malá Tŕňa** Days of Open Tokaj Cellars
October	**Košice** 13th international jazz festival; see http://jazzfest.ges.sk
	Košice Annual Peace Marathon; see www.kosicemarathon.com
November	**Košice** Košice folk days
	Košice Jazz for Sale

SPIŠSKÁ NOVÁ VES *Telephone code 053*

Situated 352km east of Bratislava, Spišská Nová Ves is the capital city of the Spiš region. This pleasant city of 40,000 makes an excellent base for visiting the many Spiš attractions and especially the Slovak Paradise. Along with Stará Ľubovňa (in Prešov), Spišská Nová Ves was one of the 13 Spiš towns pawned to the Poles in 1412, and when Poland was partitioned in 1772, the town fell to the Habsburgs

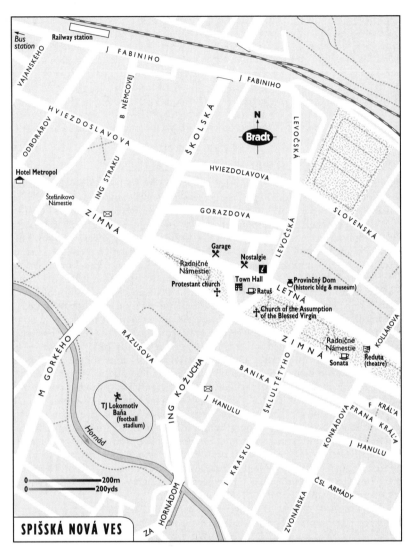

SPIŠSKÁ NOVÁ VES

who made it the capital of the Spiš region. In 1871, the new Košice–Bohumín railway line included the town which greatly helped its significance. The town centre is beautiful and green. Like Košice, it has a leaf-shaped main square and one side is called Summer Street (Letná ulica) and one side Winter Street (Zimná ulica) because of the way the sun shines. In between the two streets is a patch of green and some historic buildings. The 13th-century **Church of the Assumption of the Blessed Virgin** (*Kostol Nanebovzatia Panny Márie*) has Slovakia's tallest tower (87m), a Gothic spire added in the 16th century. Inside, there is a Gothic Crucifixion with two statues from Master Pavol's workshop in Levoča. Also in the central island, the Reduta (*Spišské Divadlo*) has a good restaurant within its elegant walls, as does the Classical **town hall** (*radnica*) nearby, dating from 1779. Next to the town hall is another **Classical Protestant Church** designed by Bartel and built in 1790–96 with a cross-shaped ground plan.

Letná is lined with elegant buildings including the handsome **Provinčný Dom**, housing the local museum (*Vlastivedné múzeum, Letná 50;* ☎ *053 4423 757; open Mon–Fri 08.00–12.00 & 12.30–16.30, Sat 09.00–13.00, Sun 13.00–17.00; admission adult/child 40/20sk*). There are also several excellent restaurants and some good hotels all adding to the town's considerable charm.

GETTING THERE By train, on the Bratislava–Košice line, there are regular connections from Bratislava; journey time five hours. By car, 8km south of Levoča on route 533, 24km east of Poprad on route 18, turn off onto route 536 at Spišský Štvrtok.

TOURIST INFORMATION AND OTHER PRACTICALITIES

✓ Tourist information centre Letná 49; ☎ 053 16 186, 053 4298 293; e brantnercc@stonline.sk; www.slovenskyraj.sk. *Open Jun–Sep Mon–Fri 08.00–17.00, Sat 09.30–13.00; Oct–May Mon–Fri 08.00–16.30.*

✉ Post office No 1 Štefánikovo námestie 7; ☎ 053 4421 000; *open Mon–Fri 07.00–19.00, Sat 07.00–11.30.*

✉ Post office No 3 J Hanulu 3; ☎ 053 4462 000; *open Mon–Tue & Thu–Fri 07.30–11.30 & 12.30–15.30, Wed 07.30–11.00 & 13.30–17.00.*

⌂ WHERE TO STAY

⌂ Hotel Čingov (20 rooms) Smižany-Hradisko; ☎ 053 4433 633; www.hotelcingov.sk. In the neighbouring village, good for Slovak Paradise. *Dbl* $.

⌂ Hotel Metropol (37 rooms) Stefanikovo nam 2; ☎ 053 4422 243; e hotel.metropol.snv@ ke.telecom.sk; www.hotel-metropol.sk. A modern block with a great restaurant ($$. *Open daily*

10.00–22.00), cocktail bar, lounge & patio. *Sgl, dbl* $$.

⌂ Park Hotel (20 rooms) Čingov-Hradisko; ☎ 053 4422 022; e parkhotel@vitex.sk; www.cingov.sk. A giant mountain chalet with basic yet smart, clean rooms. Restaurant ($), tennis court, sauna. *Sgl, dbl* $, *apt* $.

✗ WHERE TO EAT AND DRINK

✗ Garage Letná 35; ☎ 053 4414 344. Car accessories everywhere. $$. *Open Mon–Sat 10.00–22.00, Sun 12.00–22.00.*

✗ Nostalgie Letná 49; ☎ 053 4414 344. Top restaurant with relaxed style & great pasta, jacket potatoes, salads & soups. $$. *Open Mon–Sat*

10.00–22.00, Sun 12.00–22.00.

⌟ Ratuš Radničné námestie. A good café downstairs in the town hall. *Open Mon–Fri 09.00–23.00, Sat–Sun 12.00–23.00.*

⌟ Sonata Radničné námestie 4. Great café with blobby 1960s' lamps. *Open daily 10.00–22.00.*

SLOVAK PARADISE NATIONAL PARK

The Slovak Paradise (*Slovenský Raj*, pronounced 'rye') was made into a national park in 1988 in order to preserve its countless canyons, waterfalls and calcareous surface formations. The area received its name in 1921 when Gusto Nedobry, a teacher from Spišská Nová Ves, used the term 'Slovenský raj' in an article for a local tourist magazine. Covering a territory of 198km² and bisected by the river Hornád, the park has huge fir forests, limestone gorges, ravines, plateaux, waterfalls and pools. There are approximately 200 bat-infested caves and chasms here, but only one cave, the **Dobšinská Ice Cave**, discovered in 1870, is open to the public. The park features five educational trails helping nature discovery but the real draw is the 300km of hiking trails which have been specially designed to get the most from the natural surroundings. Trekkers clamber across canyons on ladders, vertiginous bridges, clinging onto metal rungs embedded in the rock wall and hanging from chains. Some of these require a level of fitness and expertise. The tallest ladder in Sokolina dolina reaches 100m and because of the hazards, the park created

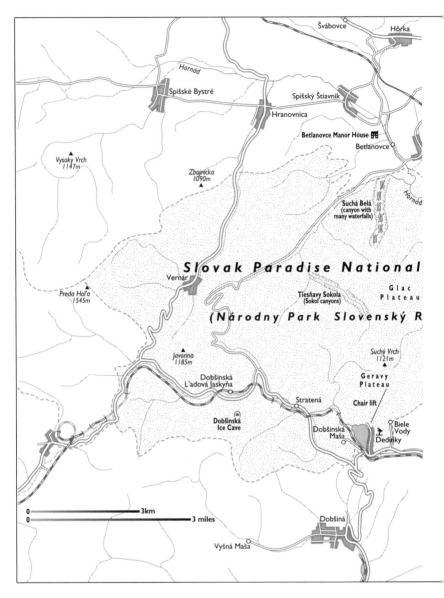

a year-round rescue service (*horská sluzba*) in 1954. For further safety, hikers are only allowed to go up some of the trails. Going down the ladders is too dangerous.

HS (Mountain rescue) Čingov; ☎ 053 4491 182   **HS** Dedinky; ☎ 058 7981 110

HIGHLIGHTS
Tomášovský výhľad (lookout) (667m) A rocky plateau on the southern slope of Ludmanka Hill with a spectacular view of the river Hornád and the Tatras. A two-hour hike is required from the village of Spišské Tomášovce.

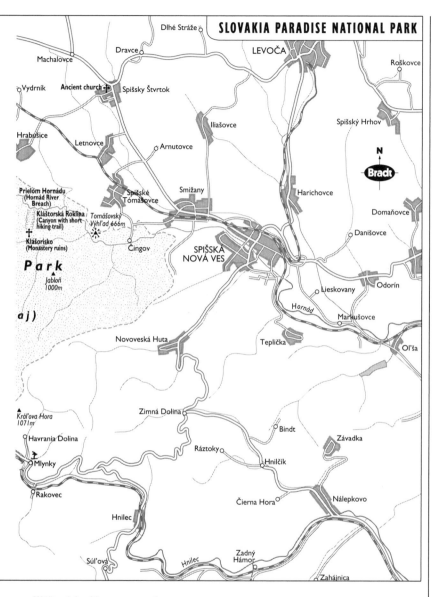

Kláštorisko Monastery ruins (770m) Restored Cartesian monastery, dating from 1307 with a little restaurant and *chata*, Chatová Osada. Situated in the north of the park, between the villages of Podlesok and Čingov.

Kláštorská Roklina (canyon) The shortest trail from the banks of the Hornád to Kláštorisko Monastery, with many waterfalls *en route* including Dúhový vodopád (Rainbow Waterfall).

Prielom Hornádu (Hornád Breach) A 16km canyon with steep, rocky sides. Tricky trail using chains, rungs and wooden bridges.

Suchá Belá One of the most romantic canyons with unusual 'window' waterfalls, rushing rapids and photogenic gorges.

Glac Plateau (1,061m) The most extensive plateau. Many trails lead here.

Tiesňavy Sokola (Sokol Canyons) A series of stunning canyons at the western edge of the Glac Plateau.

Geravy Plateau (1,032m) A wide plateau formed by a system of mountain meadows and copses. Five trails and many ski routes cross Geravy in varying directions.

Dedinky A tourist centre on the banks of the Palcmanská Maša Reservoir on the southern slopes of the Geravy Plateau, reached on a 2km stretch of funicular running along the southern edge of the Slovak Paradise.

Mlynky An important winter-sports centre with a system of lifts on the slopes of Kruhová and in the valley of Biele vody.

DOBŠINSKÁ ĽADOVÁ JASKYŇA (DOBŠINSKÁ ICE CAVE) (☎ *058 7881 470; entries 15 May–31 May & 1 Sep–30 Sep at 09.30, 11.00, 12.30, 14.00, 1 Jun–31 Aug 09.00–16.00 on the hour; admission adult/child 150/80Sk).*One of the most significant ice caves in the world and listed as a UNESCO World Heritage Site in 1995. In 1887, Dobšinská was the first cave in the world to receive electric illumination. The cave stretches for 2km (guided tour 515m) and in places the ice is 28m thick. The cave is essentially a vast underground lake, formed 9,000 years ago. The Kmeťov dome is spectacular and in the 18th century the bones of a cave bear were discovered and thought to belong to a dragon, leading to one cavern's name: *Dragon Cave*. It is possible to hike to the cave from Dedinky along a Slovak Paradise trail.

Getting there By car from Poprad, 20km south on route 67, turn left 4km south of Vernár signposted for Stratená. By train on the mountain railway, one a day from Gelnica (two hours) or Brezno (one hour).

BETLANOVCE The village is situated just north of the boundaries of the Slovak Paradise and was first mentioned in 1311. In 1725, it became the headquarters of the noble collective Ten Spiš Lancers. The village is very poor and the group of grand buildings, including a Gothic church (1309), a Renaissance manor (1568) and an 18th-century late-Baroque mansion, stand out incongruously.

Getting there By bus from Poprad, by car from Poprad on route 18/E50, turn right at Hôrka.

HEADING EAST FROM SPIŠSKÁ NOVÁ VES

MARKUŠOVCE MANOR Situated 4km southeast of Spišská Nová Ves on a minor road, this gorgeous Renaissance mansion dates from 1643 and was rebuilt later in the Rococo style. The custard-and-white building has a square ground plan and a round tower at each corner. Situated in a French garden, its summer house, Dardanelles (*Dardanely letohrádok*) contains a museum of period furniture (☎ *053 4498 421;* e *muzeum.spisa@post.sk; www.muzeumspisa.com; open May–Jun & Sep Tue–Sun 09.00–17.00; Oct–Apr Tue–Fri & Sun 08.00–16.00; admission adult/child 30/15Sk).*

SKIING AT PLEJSY Plejsy is a dynamically developing and increasingly popular ski centre at the northern slopes of the Krompašský vrch (1,025m) hills 45km northwest of Košice. If you're staying in the eastern part of Slovakia then this is definitely the resort to go to because of its superb slopes and conditions. The International Ski Federation approved its tracks as suitable for slalom, giant slalom, and super G races, so it is no wonder that Slovak racers picked Plejsy as their training grounds. The site is also the scene of the women's cross-country European Cup. There are nine downhill slopes totalling 8km and conditioned with artificial snow. Of the slopes the three longest ones (totalling 4.8km) are for advanced skiers; the rest are for beginners or snowboarders. The tracks are serviced by seven lifts of which one is a chair lift, which often prove to be insufficient in delivering the crowds – be prepared for some queuing, Although the resort is not located at a particularly high altitude (470–1,025m) it has a special microclimate that ensures good snow conditions even when other resorts have to shut down. A total of 15km of cross-country tracks are available for visitors. For a one-day adult pass pay 500Sk, a three-day ticket costs 1,320Sk.

Getting there By car, from Poprad turn right at Spišské Podhradie and follow the directions to Krompachy.

GELNICA Situated in the Hnilec river valley, Gelnica is one of the oldest centres of mining. In the 14–15th centuries, copper, silver, gold, mercury, lead and iron ore were all mined in Gelnica's surroundings. Highlights include a stone bridge over the Hnilec River, a ruined 13th-century castle and a mining museum (*Banícke Muzeum, Banícke námestie 1;* ℡ *053 4821 468; open Mon–Fri 08.00–16.00; admission adult/child 40/20Sk*) with items dating back to the Maria Theresa era.

RUŽIN LAKE (18KM NORTHWEST OF KOŠICE) From Gelnica to Košice, route 547 passes a large reservoir. Shaped like a fat letter 'v', the lake is 60m deep in some places. Boats, water bicycles and other sports equipment are available at a hire shop. Every year from 30 June–1 July, the campsite at Košická Belá holds a get-together for Slovak and foreign bikers.

HEADING SOUTH FROM SPIŠSKÁ NOVÁ VES

There are three groups of caves in the region.

OCHTÍNSKA ARAGONITOVÁ JASKYŇA (CAVE) (*Štítnik;* ℡ *058 4881 050; entries Apr–May & Sep–Oct 09.30, 11.00, 12.30, 14.00, Jun–Aug 09.00–16.00 on the hour; admission adult/child 120/60Sk*). The Ochtina Aragonite Cave is the most unusual cave in the country and the only cave in Europe embellished with white aragonite, a kind of calcite forming small bush- and nest-like decorations. There are only three aragonite caves in the world open to the public. The 300m cave was discovered in 1954 and the blue limestone walls are decorated with bursts of white aragonite resembling bunches of flowers. The Milky Way Hall is the main attraction and the white branches and clusters of aragonite shine like stars. Along with other caves of the Slovak karst National Park, the cave is on the UNESCO list of World Heritage Sites.

Getting there By car, from Rožňava, 10km west on route 526 to Štítnik. Regular buses from Rožňava take 20 minutes.

11

SLOVENSKÝ KRAS NATIONAL PARK The 34,611ha Slovenský Kras (Slovak Karst) National Park was established in 2002. Located in the southeastern part of the Slovenské rudohorie Mountains, it is the largest karst territory in Slovakia. The limestone mountain range, criss-crossed by rivers and streams has a collection of limestone and dolomite plateaux, canyons and subterranean karst phenomena: karst pits, caves and chasms. The most well-known caves open to the public are: Ochtinská Aragonitová, Gombasečká, Domica and Jasovská, all in the Košice region. The Slovak karst caves together with the Aggtelek Karst in Hungary were included in the UNESCO World Heritage list in 1995.

GOMBASEČKÁ JASKYŇA (CAVE) (*Slovenský kras, Plešivec;* ↘ *058 7882 020; entries Apr–May & Sep–Oct 10.00, 12.00, 14.00, 15.00; Jun 09.00–16.00 on the hour; Jul–Aug 10.00–17.00 on the hour; admission adult/child 70/40Sk*). Situated in the Slovak Karst National Park near the village of Gombasek, this is one of the most visually impressive caves. The Marble Hall (*Mramorová sieň*) has an amazing collection of ant-hill cone-shaped stalagmites and 3m-long glassy stalactites.

Getting there By car, from Rožňava 12km south on route 50/E571 heading to Plešivec.

DOMICA CAVE (*Dlhá Ves;* ↘ *058 7882 010; entries Feb–May & Sep–Dec 09.00, 11.00, 12.30, 14.00; Jun–Aug 09.00–16.00 on the hour, boat rides until 15.00; admission adult/child 120/60Sk, with boat ride 150/80Sk*). Situated right on the Hungarian border, the larger part of the cave is known as Baradla in Hungary. In theory, it could be an underground border crossing but spelunkers are not allowed through the connecting passageways. The cave was discovered in 1923 and visitors can ride in a little boat on the underground river Styx, admiring primitive wall paintings on a 140m trip. The cave is a UNESCO World Heritage Site.

Getting there By car, on route 50/E571 to Plešivec, turn left and head for the Domica–Aggtelek border crossing on route 587.

AROUND ROŽŇAVA

BETLIAR KAŠTIEĽ The beautiful Renaissance manor house (*Betliar grounds; open May–Oct daily 06.00–20.00; Nov–Apr daily 07.00–18.00; Betliar museum;* ↘ *058 7983 118; open May–Oct Tue–Sun 08.00–16.30; Nov–Apr Tue–Sun 09.00–14.00; admission adult/child 100/50Sk*) at Betliar displays its original interior and has received a Europa Nostra grant for restoration. The history of the chateau is connected to two noble Hungarian families: the Bebeks built the chateau in the 15th century and the Andrássys who took it over in the early 18th century. Its present appearance dates from the end of the 19th century when Emanuel Andrássy and his son Géza furnished it and collected many pieces of art and furniture. The historical library contains more than 15,000 volumes and there is a collection of guns, hunting trophies and exotic souvenirs from Asia and Africa. The chateau is surrounded by an 80ha park.

ROŽŇAVA Rožňava is the capital of the historic Gemer county and a former mining town. The name comes from a legend which tells of a man who took a nap in the local Rudohorie hills and dreamed of striking gold. When he woke he started digging and the dream came true. To mark the spot, he placed three red roses on the ground. The name 'Rožňava' comes from the Slovak word *ruža* (rose). Visitors can climb the 17th-century watchtower (*Strážna veža*) guarding the central Námestie baníkov (Miners' Square) and also see the local mining museum (*Bánicke múzeum, Šafárikova 43;* ↘ *058 7343 710; open Tue–Fri 08.00–16.00*).

Tourist information
🛈 **Information centre** Námestie baníkov 32;   www.roznava.sk. Open Tue–Sun 10.00–17.00.
↘ 058 7328 101; e tic.roznava@stonline.sk;

KRASNÁ HÔRKA AND ANDRÁSSY MAUSOLEUM (*Hrad Krasná Hôrka Krásnohorské Podhradie;* ↘ *058 7324 769; open May–Sep Tue–Sun 08.00–16.30; tours Apr & Oct at 09.30, 11.00, 12.30, 14.00, 15.30; Nov–Mar 09.30, 11.00, 12.30, 14.00; admission adult/concession 100/50Sk*).

Situated 6km east of Rožňava on route 50/E571 to Košice, the fortress at Krasná Hórka (Pretty Hill) is an impressive sight for miles around, perched on a cone-shaped hill. The 14th-century Gothic castle was rebuilt into a fort in Renaissance style and was inhabited until 1812. The last owner, Dionyz Andrássy turned the place into a family museum and since 1906 it has been open to public. The one-hour castle tour goes through 31 rooms, displaying weapons and in the Gothic palace, visitors can see a medieval torture chamber. In the chapel, visitors can see the mummified remains of Zofia Seredy lying in a glass sarcophagus. Spookily, Seredy's hand is raised and many legends surround the corpse. One says that Seredy died of humiliation when she discovered her husband's affair with the White Lady of Levoča (see *Chapter 10*, page 273). The official version claims that her hands were resting on a Bible when rigor mortis set in. In the village beneath the castle, Krásnohorské podhradie, check out the **Andrássy gallery** (*Obrazáreň Andrássyovcov, Krásnohorské podhradie;* ↘ *058 7324 258; open Jun–Aug Tue–Sat 09.00–12.00 & 13.00–16.30, Sun 09.00–14.00; Sep–May by appointment; admission adult/child 10/5Sk*) and 1km further east on the road to Košice, look left to see the splendid **Andrássy mausoleum** (*Mauzóleum Andrássyovcov;* ↘ *058 7322 034; open Tue–Sun May–Sep 08.30–17.30; Apr & Oct 09.30–16.30; Nov–Mar 09.30–14.30*) built by Dionyz Andrássy who married the Czech singer Františka Hablavcova against his family's wishes. When she died in 1903, Dionyz renovated Krásna Hôrka Castle as a homage to his beloved wife. The couple lie in the mausoleum which can be visited.

TURŇA CASTLE The ruins of Hrad (castle) Turňa, like Krasná Hôrka, sit on a conical hill (375m) on the left of route 50/E571 to Košice. The castle was built in the late 13th century and given as a present by King Béla IV to Count Tekus, for his support during the Tatar invasion. Tekus's descendants took the name Tornay, after whom the castle is now named. The castle had many owners, but in 1683 it was a possession of the Thököly family and the imperial general Schultz captured it and demolished it.

JASOV En route to Košice, an interesting detour takes place at Moldava nad Bodvou to see Jasov castle ruins, fortified monastery and more UNESCO-listed caves (*Jasovská jaskyňa Jasov;* ↘ *055 4664 165;* e *jasovj@ssj.sk; entries Apr–May & Sep–Oct 10.00, 12.00, 14.00, 15.00; Jun 09.00–16.00 on the hour; Jul–Aug 10.00–17.00 on the hour; admission adult/child 80/40Sk*). The Gothic castle was built in 1318 and destroyed in the 15th century, while the Premonstratensian monastery was built in the 12–13th century and 200 years later, rebuilt into a fort. The monastery has the only Baroque garden in Slovakia, populated with noisy peacocks.

Jasovská jaskyňa (cave) is worth visiting for the lovely sinter waterfalls and pagoda stalagmites. The cave is famous for graffiti scrawled on the walls in 1452

11

by Czech Hussites fleeing persecution by the Austrian Catholics. Premonstratensian monks discovered the caves in the 12th century and opened it to the public in 1846 as the first show cave. It is also used for treating allergic and asthmatic children.

Getting there By car, turn left off route 50/E571 at Moldava nad Bodvou onto route 550 and head north for Medzev, Jasov is 9km north on the banks of the Bodva river.

ŠTÓS Continuing on route 550 past Jasov and heading back towards Rožňava we come to Štoš, a mining settlement with a climate spa that helps ease respiratory and other illnesses. The clean air of the spa and surrounding forest has a therapeutic effect. The spa (*Kúpele Štós;* \ *055 4667 532;* e *marketing@kupele-stos.sk; www.kupele-stos.sk*) has 140 adult and 120 children's places.

KOŠICE *Telephone code 055*

Known as 'the Jewel of the East', Slovakia's second city Košice (Cassovia in Latin, Kaschau in German and Kassa in Hungarian) is home to the grandest Gothic church in central Europe excluding Prague. The city was first mentioned in 1230 as Villa Cassa. King Béla IV granted privileges to the Saxon settlers and the city thrived because of its location on the trade route between Austria and Constantinople and also because it had a monopoly in the supply of salt. On 7 May 1369 King Ľudovít the Great granted the city the first municipal coat of arms issued in Europe. Since 1994, they have celebrated this date as 'Košice Day'.

The city's historic sights, dating from various eras, are concentrated in the historic centre, an Urban Heritage Area. The reconstructed main street, like Prešov is a leaf shape and lined by Baroque and neoclassical burgher houses and palaces. Almost all Kosice's important buildings are squashed into the main street, Hlavná and its two squares at either end: **Hlavné Námestie** (Main Square) to the north of the cathedral and **Námestie Slobody** (Freedom Square) to the south. During the 1996 reconstruction, a large portion of city ruins was discovered. Two years of archaeological excavations unearthed artefacts revealing over 500 years of Košice city history. The most precious finds have been preserved and are now displayed in the **Archaeological Complex** (*Dolná brána – Podzemné Múzeum; open Tue–Sun 10.00–18.00; admission adult/child 25/15Sk*). The focal point is the soaring **Cathedral of St Elizabeth** (*Dóm Sv Alžbety*) (*open daily 05.30–19.00*). Construction began in 1378 and it was named after the daughter of Károly Róbert, the Anjou King with whom Košice had bitter wrangles over the salt market. The exterior with its gold spire and shimmering Zsolnay roof tiles is impressive, but inside, the Gothic vaulting is quite overwhelming. The Gothic **Chapel of St Michael**, situated at the south end of the cathedral was built in the 14th century. The structure served as a storehouse for weapons during the 16th century, when Turkish control of lower Hungary made Košice a key defensive position against Ottoman expansionism.

Hungarians make pilgrimages to Kassa to pay homage to Ferenc Rákóczi II and his wife Ilona Zrínyi, who are buried in the crypt on the left side of the nave. Rákóczi was a Transylvanian Hungarian rebel leader in the early 18th century who continued the family tradition of battling against the Habsburgs. He carried on until his defeat in 1717 when he was exiled to Turkey. In 1905, Rákóczi was pardoned and his remains returned to Kosice. On the north side of the cathedral, the **Urbanova veža** (*Urban Tower Wax Museum; open Tue–Sun 12.00–16.00*) dates from the 14th century and rests on its own set of arched mini-arcades. It has

Martina Hingis (born 30 September 1980 in Košice) is a former World No 1 Swiss tennis player. Not many people know she was born in Slovakia. Known as the 'Swiss Miss', she won five Grand Slam singles titles and nine Grand Slam women's doubles titles, before ligament injuries in both of her ankles cut short her professional tennis career at the age of 22. Martina is the daughter of two accomplished tennis players: a Czech mother, Melanie Molitorová, and a Slovak father, Karol Hingis. Her father is a tennis trainer in Košice. They named their daughter Martina (originally Martina Hingisová-Molitorová) after the great Czech tennis star Martina Navrátilová. Hingis's parents divorced when she was young and she moved with her mother to Moravia for a short period, then to Switzerland. Hingis entered her first tournament at age four and in 1993, the 12-year-old Hingis became the youngest player to win a Grand Slam junior title, the girls' singles at the French Open. In November 2005, after a long recuperation and many operations, Hingis announced that she would return to the WTA tour, starting her professional comeback at a tournament in Australia on January 2006.

recently been converted into 'the first and only wax museum in Slovakia' and Andy Warhol is one of the 'guests'. An outrageous collection of fountains, standing in a little park just to the north of the tower, is where the whole town appears to congregate on weekend afternoons. This is quite a surreal experience, as a loudspeaker blares out very loud pop music and the jets of water move in time. On the hour, pop songs are replaced by a performance from a 'bell tree'. This conglomeration of 22 bells attached to a tall wooden structure was a present to the city from a bank in 1997 and the quotation reads that the concept was to, 'Give happiness to the people of the town'. Beyond the fountain, if you can tear yourself away, is the grand **Austro-Hungarian theatre** (1899) and beyond that a knobbly plague column (1723) guarded by a dodgy-looking collection of gnomes and goblins. Off along a pedestrian side street is the romantic fairytale pseudo-Gothic **Jakab Palace** built in 1903. This was the first headquarters of Czechoslovak President Edvard Beneš (1945–70), who lent his name to the 1945 decrees (see page 187). Up at the northern end of Hlavná, visitors will spot a wooden church sitting in the garden of the **East-Slovakian Museum** (*Východoslovenské múzeum; Námestie Maratóna mieru 2;* \ *055 6223 061;* e *vsmuz@ stonline.sk; www.casovia.sk; open Tue–Sat 09.00–17.00, Sun 09.00–13.00*), whose exhibits include the gold treasures of Košice.

GETTING THERE AND AWAY By road, there is no direct highway or railway leading from Bratislava to Košice, 419km to the east. Slovakia is now in the process of connecting its key cities by express motorways, but this project will not be complete for a few years. However, smaller roads are generally in good condition. You can get from Bratislava to Košice on virtually one straight line on a route which changes identity, from the E571 to Galanta, then route 75 as far as Lučenec, before turning into the E571 to Rimavská Sobota, Rožňava and on to Košice.

By train, the idiosyncratic Slovak rail system makes travellers go to Košice in a high loop over Žilina, right up in the north of the country.

By air, regularly scheduled flights come to the international airport at Košice from Prague, Vienna, Brno and Moscow and the connection with Bratislava links Košice to all major European cities.

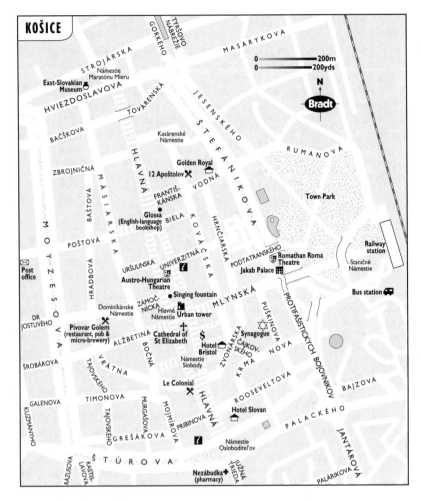

KOŠICE

East-Slovakian Museum

Golden Royal
12 Apoštolov

Glossa
(English-language bookshop)

Town Park

Railway station

Post office

Romathan Roma Theatre
Jakab Palace

Staničné Námestie

Bus station

Austro-Hungarian Theatre

Singing fountain

Urban tower

Pivovar Golem
(restaurant, pub & micro-brewery)

Cathedral of St Elizabeth

Synagogue

Hotel Bristol

Námestie Slobody

Le Colonial

Hotel Slovan

Námestie Osloboditel'ov

Nezábudka
(pharmacy)

✈ **Košice–Barca Airport (KSC)** 10km south of the centre; ☎ 055 6832 123; airport information; ☎ 055 6832 100; e dispecing@ssl-ksc.sk; www.airportkosice.sk

🚗 **Hertz car hire at Barca airport** ☎ 055 7896 041; f 055 7896 042. *Open daily 06.00–18.00.*

TOURIST INFORMATION AND OTHER PRACTICALITIES

🛈 **Information centre Košice** Hlavná 59; ☎ 055 6258 888. *Open Mon–Fri 09.00–18.00, Sat 09.00–13.00.*

🛈 **Mestské informačné centrum Košice (MiC Košice)** Hlavná 2 (inside Dargov department store); ☎ 055 6230 909; e info@miskosice.sk; www.mickosice.sk. *Open daily 09.00–19.00.*

$ **ČSOB bank** Hlavná 23. *Open Mon–Thu 08.00–18.00, Fri 08.00–17.00.*

✉ **Post office** Poštová 20. *Open Mon–Fri 07.00–19.00, Sat 08.00–12.00.*

✚ **Pharmacy** Lekáreň Nezábudka Štúrova 1. *Open Mon–Fri 09.00–17.00.*

Glossa (English-language bookshop) Hlavná 97; ☎ 055 6233 676. *Open Mon–Fri 09.00–18.00, Sat 10.00–13.00.*

🚗 **VIPTaxi** ☎ 16 500

🏠 WHERE TO STAY

🏠 **Golden Royal** (17 rooms) Vodná 8; ☎ 055 7201 011; e penzion@goldenroyal.sk;

www.goldenroyal.sk. Quality guest house in a side street. *Dbl $$.*

⌂ Hotel Bankov (16 rooms) Dolný Bankov; ☎ 055 6324 522; e hotel@bankov.sk; www.hotelbankov.sk. Boutique hotel, just outside town. *Sgl, dbl $$$.*

⌂ Hotel Bristol Orlia 3; ☎ 055 7290 077; e info@hotelbristol.sk; www.hotelbristol.sk. Smart hotel with its own Roman spa. *Sgl $$, dbl $$$.*

⌂ Hotel Slovan (171 rooms, 16 suites) Hlavná 1; ☎ 055 6227 378; e reserve@hotelslovan.sk; www.hotelslovan.sk. Košice's biggest & best hotel

located right in the heart of town. With 4-star facilities for businesspeople, conferences, professionals as well as families & travellers looking for a bit of luxury & comfort. The 10-storey building has comfortable beds, & good water pressure even on the top floor! Free WiFi internet & a fabulous buffet b/fast. Espace beauty & relax salon, night bar & casino. *Sgl $$$, dbl $$$-$$$$, apt $$$$$.*

✗ WHERE TO EAT AND DRINK

✗ Zlatá Praha restaurant (Hotel Slovan) Hlavná 1; ☎ 055 6227 378; f 055 6228 413; e reserve@hotelslovan.sk; www.hotelslovan.sk. Good choice of international, Slovak & Czech dishes with a top-notch wine list. *$$-$$$. Open daily 12.00-22.00.*

✗ Pivovar Golem Dominikánske námestie 15; ☎ 055 7289 101. Excellent restaurant & pub with its own microbrewery & 3 beers. *$$. Open Mon-Thu*

11.00-23.00, Fri 11.00-01.00, Sat 17.00-01.00, Sun 18.00-22.00.

✗ Le Colonial Hlavná 8; ☎ 055 7296 126. Elegant restaurant with an eclectic menu. *$$. Open daily 11.00-midnight.*

✗ 12 apoštolov Kováčska 51; ☎ 055 7295 104. The city's most famous restaurant, founded in 1910. *$$. Open Mon-Tue 10.30-23.00, Wed-Fri 10.30-midnight, Sat 11.30-midnight, Sun 11.30-23.00.*

THE GYPSY HEAT

It was said that a Roma's feet could set a street on fire. An incendiary dancer in Bohemian night – eyes burning like coals, sweat shooting like stars. Nowadays the Roma live in chicken sheds by the side of the road. Shacks made of wood and cardboard. They are travesties of their ancestral canvas-covered rolling barrels but the kids still sleep in stinking cupboards under the bed. Grey washing hangs stiffly from a dirty rope. A Tilley lamp and a cast-iron stove make shadows dance on the rotting walls. A TV screen spins and hisses. Campfires burn in the settlements at night. Drink, drugs and petty crime are the code of a road which has finally reached a dead end for half a million people. The welfare of the Roma has mattered so little for so long that a typical settlement was built on a toxic dump near Rudňany in eastern Slovakia. Nobody gave it a second thought. For centuries central Europe's gypsies have been condemned, the lowest of the low. Thousands died in German concentration camps. Then the state tried to control them by paying women to be sterilised. Today the Roma remain abandoned and impoverished. Most end up in the settlements on the outskirts of town, no running water, no sanitation and very little hope. Some get on the property ladder and trade up to the near-derelict tenement ghettos in places like Košice and Hermanovce, cities which are monuments to some terrible communist functional design. Others make their homes in the dank and dirty cellars of the inner cities. Post-communist governments have recognised that this tragic situation can only get worse. It has been estimated that in the next few years the Roma will make up one-fifth of Slovakia's population. However they will have hardly any education, be out of work and they will be chronically ill. This scenario is the true romance of the Bohemians. The Slovak government is co-operating with international agencies in a bid to end the plight. However, it will be decades before any real improvement is seen. Finally money at least is being thrown at the problem. In the past it has been simply abuse.

11

Tokaj is a historical wine region situated in northeast Hungary and Slovakia where wine has been produced since AD290. Tokaj is mostly associated with the Tokaji Aszú (or Tokajský výber in Slovak), an amber-coloured dessert wine which was appreciated by royalty and noblemen all over Europe since the 17th century. Famously, Ferenc Rákóczi II gave a few bottles of aszú from his Tokaj estate to King Louis XIV who, after tasting it, announced that it was 'the wine of kings; the king of wines'. Tokaji Aszú dates back to the mid 17th century. According to legend, the owner of the vineyard feared an attack from the Turks and the vintage was delayed by several weeks. By then the grapes left on the vine turned dry and very sweet. An unparalleled dessert wine was produced from this vintage and the special dessert wine was born. The sweetness of wine is measured by the number of *puttony* (or *putňa* in Slovak, a wooden container) of dried grapes added to the fermenting must. Traditionally only 3-, 4-, 5- and 6-*puttonyos* of Aszú is produced in Tokaj. Besides the famous Aszú, other varieties of white wine are also produced here, such as the Szamorodni, a light white which can be either dry or sweet. The Tokaji Hárslevelú, the Tokaji Muscat and the Tokaji Furmint are named after the grape varieties grown here.

Over 80% of the Tokaj region falls in Hungary, however a small part of the region is in Slovakia. There was a long-standing dispute between Hungary and Slovakia (then Czechoslovakia) over Slovakia's right to use the name Tokaj. During communist times, the Czechoslovak and Hungarian governments agreed that Czechoslovakia was not allowed to export wine under the name of Tokaj. In exchange Czechoslovakia received the right to export beer to Hungary. This deal shows that wine wasn't really appreciated during those days.

During the communist regime, the quality of the Tokaji wine deteriorated rapidly. The production was carried out in the collective farms system and more emphasis was put on the quantity than the quality. After World War II, the Russians took all the

WHAT TO SEE

Romathan Roma Theatre On a back street near the city park (Štefánikova 4) is the headquarters of Romathan, the only state-funded Romany theatre in Europe. Founded in 1992, after persistent lobbying by Roma political organisations, the company has grown to a staff of 46, including an ensemble of 34 musicians, singers, dancers and actors, led by first violinist and director Karol Adam. The goal of the theatre is to preserve and maintain Romany culture with traditional music from not only Slovakia but also Hungary, Poland, Russia and Romania. Music and theatre are used as weapons to fight racism that Roma people encounter on a daily basis. More information is available at www.romathan.sk.

Košice Zoo (*040 06 Košice–Kavečany;* ☎ *055 6338 103; www.kosice.sk/zoo; open daily 1 Apr–31 Oct 09.00–19.00; 1 Nov–31 Mar 09.00–15.00; admission adult/child 40/20Sk*). Created in 1979, the 292ha Košice Zoo is one of four zoos in Slovakia. It is situated in oak woods and the animals are mainly from Europe and Asia, although a new African yard is planned. Košice Zoo has successfully bred many animals; including camels, tigers, zebras and antelopes in captivity. The zoo also concentrates on cultural and educational activities for schools.

AROUND KOŠICE

To the north of Košice is **Hradova Hill** (466m). Archaeological digs between 1994 and 1997 discovered 14th-century towers and walls. The hill is a popular bottles of vintage Tokaji. They got a taste for it and demanded that Hungary sends an unworkably large quantity of Tokaji to Moscow. Cunning Magyar scientists on the collective farm made a version of Tokaji from lower-quality wines and sent that, to keep up with the demands. This had clearly a negative impact on the quality and reputation of Tokaji. However, after the change of regime wine production started to flourish and now the privately owned vineyards put great emphasis on quality.

According to an agreement on wine names between the European Community and Hungary signed in 1993, the geographical indication 'Tokaj' was reserved exclusively to the wines produced in Hungary. The agreement granted France and Italy a provisional permission to use the Tokaj name until 31 March 2007. The Italian authorities, questioning the legality of a prohibition, started a legal procedure, claiming that 'Tocai friulano' (a name used in Italy) was a grape variety and therefore the use of this name cannot be prohibited. However, in May 2005, the European Court of Justice delivered a favourable judgment for Hungary, confirming that the Italians have to stop using the 'Tocai friulano' name. According to certain newspaper rumours, the Italians started to broker a deal with Hungary and try to negotiate a further three-year period for the use of Tocai friuliano, offering to pay € 1,000 per day.

After many years of dispute, in June 2004 Slovakia and Hungary reached a deal concerning Tokaj. Under this agreement, wine produced on 5.65km² of land in Slovakia is able to use the Tokaj name. Many Hungarians voiced fears about the quality of the Slovak Tokaj. According to the agreement, Slovaks have to make Tokaji of at least three or more *puttonyos* /putňa. It remains to be seen how the quality will be monitored.

Many non-EU nations, notably the Ukraine, Australia and the US, produce liqueurs or dessert wines which they label 'Tokay'. However, these wines have nothing to do with the real thing.

destination for outings from Košice. **Bankov** (3km) offers pleasant opportunities for open-air barbecue parties and accommodation in the exclusive former meeting house of the city's political and business elite. The **Čermeľ Valley** has the largest woodland park in the Košice area. The **children's railway** (*http://147.232.145.11/info/kpz/timetb.htm has a timetable*) is an attraction taking children and adults alike up the valley to Alpinka leisure area, northwest of town. **Alpinka** (☏ *055 7293 601*) has a popular golf course. **Jahodná sport and relaxation centre** is 15km northwest of the centre where former PM Mečiar used to organise night-skiing events for his cronies.

FURTHER EAST FROM KOŠICE

HERĽANY GEYSER The only European geyser outside of Scandinavia, this geyser, 20km northeast of Košice, shoots 1,056 gallons of water 98ft into the air for 20 minutes once every 32–34 hours. Check with your hotel for the next gush.

Getting there By car, take route 50/E50 heading east in the direction of Sečovce and turn left at Bidovce. Head north for 8km to Herľany gejzír.

DARGOV PASS *En route* to Michalovce from Košice, the road passes through the Dargov Pass (*Dargovský priesmyk*) where 22,000 Soviet soldiers were killed liberating the region from the Nazis in 1945. In the hills above the village is a statue showing soldiers while in the village a war memorial and two tanks commemorate the event.

MICHALOVCE Michalovce (456km from Bratislava) is the easternmost large town before the Ukraine. With a population of 40,000, it is the cultural and economic centre of the lower Zemplín region. It is also the nearest town for visitors to the Slovak Sea (*Zemplínska Šírava*) but is a pretty depressing place, filled with high-rise *paneláky*. If you have transport, Košice, or one of the lake hotels, are much more pleasant places to stay.

Michalovce does have several interesting buildings, perhaps the best being the 1934 **Greek-Catholic Church of the Holy Spirit**, built in neo-Byzantine style, and the Baroque-neoclassical mansion belonging to the Sztáray family and now home to the **Zemplín Museum** (*Kostolné námestie 1;* \ *056 6441 093; www.michalovce.sk; open Tue–Fri 09.00–12.00 & 13.00–16.00; Apr–Sep also Sat 09.00–12.00, Sun 14.00–16.00*).

ZEMPLÍNSKA ŠÍRAVA (THE SLOVAK SEA) This artificial lake is 11km long and 3.5km wide with an average depth of 9.5m. There are seven recreational areas (Klokočov, Kemenec, Kaluža, Hôrka, Biela hora, Medvedia hora and Paľkov) dotted all around the 33km² lake, each equipped with boats, water scooters and water-ski hire shops. There are many places to windsurf or angle for a perch. Apparently, Zemplínska Šírava is the second-warmest area in Slovakia and the southern slopes are covered with vineyards where visitors can take part in the harvest.

The Vihorlat mountain range contains a tiny lake **Morské oko** (Eye of the Sea), 16km north of the Slovak Sea which makes a superb hiking destination. The website www.sirava.com gives links to all the resorts around the lake.

TREBIŠOV Situated 20km southwest of Michalovce, Trebišov is the gateway to the Slovak Tokaj wine-growing region. It's a small, industrial town with a few noteworthy sights including the ruins of Parič Castle built in 1786 using the stones from a 13th-century water castle, an attractive park and the neo-Gothic Andrássy Mausoleum, built in 1896. The mausoleum contains the sarcophagus of the last prime minister of Hungary, Count Gyula Andrássy.

THE TOKAJ REGION The hills of Zemplínske vrchy, south of Trebišov, are a continuation of the Zemplén range in Hungary. With the landscape comes the produce, and grapes to make the legendary dessert wine Tokaj are also grown here. Tokaj is known all over the world as a Hungarian speciality, but Slovak Tokaj should also be sampled. Slovaks cannot export Tokaj so this is the best opportunity to try some and buy some at the source.

The **Tokaj Wine Route** snakes around the villages of Bara, Čerhov, Malá Tŕňa and Veľká Tŕňa and in September there is a popular Days of Open Tokaj Cellars.

♀ **Family Macik Winery** Tokaj Vín, M R Štefánika 1941, Trebišov; \ 056 6726 850; e tokaj@ mail.viapvt.sk; www.tokaj-vino.sk
♀ **Chateau Viničky** Pražská 2, Košice; \ 055 6829

009; e vinol@vino-tokaj.sk; www.vino-tokaj.sk
♀ **J&J Ostrožovič** Nižná 233, Veľká Tŕňa; \ 056 6793 322; e odbyt@ostrozovic.sk; www.ostrozovic.sk

Appendix I

LANGUAGE

More than five million people speak Slovak in Slovakia and a few million more abroad, but it hasn't all been plain sailing, or speaking, for the Slovaks.

In AD863, Greek missionary brothers Cyril and Methodius came from Thessaloniki at the invitation of Great Moravian Prince Rastislav. They came to Great Moravia and from their native Macedonian Slavic dialect created the Old Church Slavonic alphabet, the origins of today's Cyrillic alphabet. They also translated liturgical books into Old Church Slavonic.

Pastor's son and national hero Ľudovít Štúr codified the Slovak literary language in 1843; before then, everything written down was in Czech.

Slovaks also had a hard time preserving their language as they were dominated for years by Hungarians and Austrians, both speaking and forcing Slovaks to speak languages with entirely different grammatical make-ups.

Slovak is a member of the Slavic group of languages, a large family including Russian, Ukrainian, Polish, Czech, Serbian, Croat and Slovenian, all of which have a devilish selection of possible endings, genders, declensions, conjugations and diacritical accents.

The Slovak vocabulary has about half that of English (approximately 220,000 words to English's 450,000).

Slovak is not as tricky to pronounce as Czech and less tiring for the tongue. It doesn't have the horrendous Czech 'ř' for a start. Having said that, neither is it a doddle.

However, a few choice phrases will not only endear you to the locals but also help decipher some of the tongue-twisting, vowel-free words that litter Bratislava's streets. Good luck! (*Mnoho šťastia!*)

PRONUNCIATION Once you learn the rules, pronunciation is not so difficult as, unlike English, there are no peculiar irregularities in how you say what you see. The vowels a, e, i, o, u are pure sounds, more like Spanish or Italian than English. Vowels can be either short (a, ä, e, i, o, u, y) or long (á, é, í, ó, ú, ý), basically pronounced with more emphasis, but keeping the same sound. Those consonants not included (b, d, f, g, l, m, n, s, v, z) can be pronounced as in English, with the exception of q and w which don't exist in Slovak except in some foreign words and names. The consonants k, p and t are as in English but not so aspirated.

a	as in **ah**
á	as in k**ar**ma
ä	as in c**a**t
c	like 'ts' in oa**ts**
č	like 'ch' in **ch**eeky
ď	like 'dy' as in **d**uty, *d* followed by *e* or *i* is also softened
dz	like 'ds' in hea**ds**
dž	like 'j' in **j**am

e	as in b**e**d				
é	as in th**ere**				
ě	like the 'ye' in **ye**s				
h	quite breathily				
ch	like 'ch' in Scottish 'lo**ch**'				
i/y	as in spaghett**i**				
í/ý	as in bel**ie**ve				
j	like 'y' in **ye**s				
ľ	pronounced 'ly' like the *l* in lurid				
í	a long, long 'l' emphasised				
ň	pronounced 'ny' like the n in **n**ewt, *n* followed by *e* or *i* is softened				
o	as in h**o**t				
ó	as in t**oe**				
ö	pronounced 'ur'				
ô	as in wh**oah**				
r	rolled, as in a Scottish accent				
ř	very rolled (but not followed by a ž in the scary Czech version)				
š	'sh' as in **sh**andy				
ť	pronounced 'ty' as in **t**una, *t* followed by *e* or *i* is also softened				
u	as in r**oo**t				
ú	as in sch**oo**l				
ů	pronounced more like a French 'u' with pouted lips				
w	only found in foreign words and pronounced as a 'v' (ie: WC is 'vay-tsay')				
ž	like the 's' in lei**s**ure				

WORDS AND PHRASES
Numbers

0	*nula*	5	*päť*	10	*desať*
1	*jeden*	6	*šesť*	20	*dvadsať*
2	*dva*	7	*sedem*	100	*sto*
3	*tri*	8	*osem*	1,000	*tisíc*
4	*štyri*	9	*deväť*	2007	*dvetisíc sedem*

Days of the week

pondelok	Monday	*piatok*	Friday
utorok	Tuesday	*sobota*	Saturday
streda	Wednesday	*nedeľa*	Sunday
štvrtok	Thursday	*víkend*	weekend

Months

január	January	*júl*	July
február	February	*august*	August
marec	March	*september*	September
apríl	April	*október*	Oktober
máj	May	*november*	November
jún	June	*december*	December

Time

včera/ dnes/ zajtra	yesterday/today/tomorrow
deň/ týždeň/ mesiac/ rok	day/week/month/year
teraz/ skoro/ neskoro	now/early/late
pred/ podľa	before/after
každý deň	every day

Basics

áno/ nie	yes/no
ahoj, čau, servus	hello (familiar)
čau, ahoj	goodbye (familiar)
ďakujem Vám (Ti)	thank you
dobré ráno	good morning
dobrú noc	good night
dobrý deň	good day
dovidenia	goodbye (polite)
nech sa páči	at your service (shops, restaurants)
niet za čo	not at all!
páči sa	if you please
prepáčte	excuse me (I'm sorry)
prosím	please
prosím?	excuse me (pardon?)
zbohom	goodbye – adieu

Meeting people

Ako sa máte? (máš)?	How are you?
Ako sa voláte?	What's your name?
Hovoríte po anglicky?	Do you speak English?
Hovorí niekto anglicky/ nemecky?	Does anyone speak English/German?
(Ne)rozumiem po slovensky	I (don't) understand Slovak
Pomoc!	Help!
Teší ma	Pleased to meet you
Vitajte!	Welcome!
Volám sa...	My name is...
Šťastnú cestú!	Bon voyage!
Všetko najlepšie	All the best

Questions

Ako ďaleko je do...?	How far is it to...?
Čo znamená...?	What does...mean?
Kde je.../ Kam?	Where is.../to where?
Čo?/ Prečo?/ Kto?	What?/Why?/Who?
Kedy je...?	When is...?
Koľko je hodín?	What is the time?
Koľko stojí lístok?	What is the fare?
Koľko to stojí?	How much is it?
Ktorý autobus ide do...?	Which bus goes to...?
Môžem Vám pomôct?	Can I help you?
Mohli by ste mi pomôct?	Could you help me?
Odkiaľ si/ ste?	Where are you from?

Transport/travel

autobusová stanica	bus station
bicykel	bicycle
cestovný poriadok	timetable
colnica	customs
električka	tram (also electric train in Tatras)
hlavná (vlaková) stanica	main (railway) station
hranicná kontrola	border check
letenky	plane tickets

305

letisko	airport
lístok (lístky)	ticket(s)
miestenka	seat reservation
naštupište/ kolaj/ smer	platform/line/direction
príchod/ odchod	arrivals/departure (train, bus)
prílet/ odlet	arrivals/departures (flights)
spiatočný lístok	return ticket
trolejbus	trolleybus
vlak	train
WC/ záchod	toilet
žena/ ženy-muž/ muži	lady/ladies–gent/gents (WC)
zastávka	bus stop
batožina	luggage

Places

baňa	mine
chata/ chalupa	hut, cottage, holiday chalet, mountain refuge
cintorín	cemetery
cerkev (cerkvi)	church(es) in Rusyn region
dedina	village
hora (hory)	mountain(s)
hrad	castle (fortress)
jaskyňa	cave
jazero	lake
kaštieľ	castle/palace
kláštor	monastery
kostol(ík)	church (little church)
most	bridge
námestie	square
ostrov	island
palác	château, palace
pleso	mountain lake
radnica	town hall
rieka	river
štít	peak
sad	park
ulica	street
veža	tower
vodopád	waterfall
zámok (zámky)	castle(s), manor house(s)

Hotel

Chcem dvojposteľovú izbu	I would like a double room
Chcem jednoposteľovúizbu	I would like a single room
Máte voľné izby?	Do you have any vacancies?
izba	room
kľúč	key
penzión	pension/B&B
poschodie	first floor
prízemie	ground floor
sprcha/ vaňa	shower/bath
ubytovanie	accommodation

In town

banka	bank
časopis	newspaper
divadlo	theatre
dospelí/ deti	adults/children
jarmok	market (outdoor)
kníhkupectvo	bookshop
konzulát	consulate
lekáreň	chemist
mestské trhovisko	town market
nemocnica/ lekárov	hospital/doctor
pamiatka	monument
pešia zóna	pedestrian zone
policia	police
tržnica/ trh	market
veľvyslanectvo	embassy
vstupné	entry (ticket)
výstava	exhibition
zmenáreň	bureau de change

Post

Anglicko, Veľká Británia	England, Great Britain
Austrália	Australia
Írsko	Ireland
Kanada	Canada
list	letter
Maďarsko	Hungary
Nový Zéland	New Zealand
pohľadnica	postcard
pošta	post office
Rakúsko	Austria
Spojené štáty americké	USA ('USA' will get there too)
trieda	airmail
známka	stamp

Eating and drinking

Ešte jedno pivo, prosím	Another beer, please
Dobrú chuť	Bon appetite
Na zdravie!	Cheers! /Your health
Prosím si, menu/jedálny lístok?	Could I see the menu?
Máte stôl pre jedného, dvoch, troch?	Do you have a table for 1, 2, 3?
Môžem platiť kreditnou kartou?	May I pay with a credit card?
Učet, prosím/ Zaplatím	The bill, please
Dvakrát pivo, prosím	Two beers, please
bezmäsité jedlá	vegetarian food ('meatless')
biele, červené, ružové	white, red, rosé (wine)
Borovička	local juniper spirit
bravčové	pork
cesnak	garlic
chlieb	bread
cukor	sugar
čaj s mliekom, s citrónom	tea (with milk, with lemon)

čapované / sudové pivo	draught beer
cestoviny	pasta
čerstvý	fresh
čistá voda	tap water
divina	game
džem	jam
grilovaný	grilled
hovädzie	beef
huby, šampiňóny	mushrooms
hydina	poultry
jablko	apple
jedálny lístok	menu
jeden pohár/ jedná fľaša	one glass/one bottle
káva	coffee
kačica	duck
kapor	carp
kapusta	cabbage
kaváreň, cukráreň	café
klobásy	sausages
kuracie	chicken
langoše	deep-fried giant flattened doughnut
lokša	potato pancake
losos	salmon
mäso	meat
maslo	butter
minerálna voda	mineral water
mlieko	milk
morčacie	turkey
morské jedlo	seafood
(ne) sýtená/ (ne)perlivá voda	(non) carbonated water
obed	lunch
opekaný	roasted
ovocie a zelenina	fruit and vegetables
párek (párky)	frankfurter sausage(s)
palacinky	pancakes
paprika	bell pepper/capsicum (also paprika powder)
paradajka, rajčina	tomato
piváreň	beer hall/pub
pivo	beer
plnený	stuffed
polievka	soup
pomaranč	orange
prílohy	side dishes (veg)
pstruh	trout
raňajky	breakfast
reštaurácia, jedáleň	restaurant, canteen
ryba	fish
ryža	rice
šalát	salad
šunka	ham
slanina	bacon
slivovica	plum brandy

soľ/ korenie	salt/pepper
suché, sladké	dry, sweet (wine)
svetlé/ tmavé pivo	light/dark beer
syr	cheese
vajíčka	eggs
varený	boiled
večera	dinner
vegetariánske jedlo	vegetarian dishes
vináreň	wine bar
vino	wine
vyprážaný	fried
vziať si so sebou	to take away
zapečená	baked
zemiaky/ hranolky	potatoes/chips
zrmzlina	ice cream

Useful

biely/ čierny/ modrý	white/black/blue
červeny/ žltý/ zelený	red/yellow/green
dobrý/ zlý	good/bad
fajčiť zakázané	no smoking
horúci/ studený	hot/cold
lacný/ drahý	cheap/expensive
veľký/ malý	big/small
naľavo/ napravo/ rovno	left/right/straight on
blízko/ ďaleko	near/far
otváracie hodiny	opening times
otvorený/ zatvorený	open/closed (shops)
pomoc, horí!	help, fire!
pozor!	watch out! beware!
sever/ juh	north/south
starý/ nový	old/new
tam or tlačiť/ sem or ťahať	push/pull (on doors)
vchod/ východ	entrance/exit
veľký/ malý	large/small
vstup zakázaný	no entry
východ/ západ	east/west
záchod/ WC (vay-tsay)	lavatory
Zavolajte políciu!/ lekára!/ sanitku!	Call the police!/a doctor!/an ambulance!

Appendix 2

FURTHER INFORMATION

BOOKS

History and culture

Axworthy, Mark W A *Axis Slovakia: Hitler's Slavic Wedge, 1938–1945* Europa, 2002

Brock, Peter *The Slovak National Awakening* Toronto UP, 1976

Chapman, Colin *August 21st. The Rape of Czechoslovakia* Cassell, 1968

Fonseca, Isabel *Bury Me Standing* Vintage, 1996

Henderson, Karen *Slovakia: The Escape from Invisibility* Routledge, 2002

Kirschbaum, Stanislav J *A History of Slovakia: The Struggle for Survival* Palgrave, 1996

Lackova, Ilona *A False Dawn: Volume 16: My Life as a Gypsy Woman in Slovakia* Hertfordshire UP, 2000

McNally, Raymond T *Dracula Was a Woman: In Search of the Blood Countess of Transylvani.* McGraw-Hill, 1983

Musil, Jirí (editor) *The End of Czechoslovakia* Central European UP, 1996

Petro, Peter *A History of Slovak Literature* Liverpool UP, 1996

Shawcross, William *Dubček and Czechoslovakia* Touchstone Books, 1990

Thorne, Tony *Countess Dracula: The Life and Times of Elisabeth Báthory, the Blood Countess* Bloomsbury, 1997

Literature

Dobšinský, Pavol. *The Enchanted Castle, and Other Tales and Legends (1880–1883)* Adapted by Ann Macleod. Hamlyn, 1967

Fermor, Patrick Leigh *A Time of Gifts* John Murray, 2004

Hviezdoslav, Pavol Országh, translated by Jaroslav Vajda *Bloody Sonnets* Obrana Press, 1950

Jašík, Rudolf, translated by Karol Kornel *Dead Soldiers Don't Sing* Artia, 1963

Kráľ, Janko, translated by Jaroslav Vajda *Janko Kráľ 1822–1972* Tatran, 1972

Kramoris, Ivan J *Anthology of Slovak Poetry* Obrana Press, 1947

Mikszáth, Kálmán, translated by Dick Sturgess *The Siege of Beszterce (1894)* Corvina, 1982

Pynsent, Robert B (editor) *Modern Slovak Prose: Fiction since 1954* Macmillan, 1990

Šimečka, Martin M, translated by Peter Petro *The Year of the Frog (1985–90)* Louisiana State UP, 1993.

Šmatlák, Stanislav, translated by M Hunningenová *Hviezdoslav: a National and World Poet* Obzor-Tatrapress, 1969

Sommer-Lefkovits, Elizabeth *Are You Here in Hell Too?* Menard Press/Central Books, 1995

Travel guides

Di Duca, Marc *Czech Republic: The Bradt Travel Guide* Bradt Travel Guides, 2006

Ellis, Dr Matthew and Wilson-Howarth, Dr Jane *Your Child Abroad: A Travel Health Guide* Bradt Travel Guides, 2005

Mallows, Lucy *The Bradt City Guide to Bratislava* Bradt Travel Guides, 2005

Phillips, Adrian and Scotchmer, Jo *Hungary: The Bradt Travel Guide* Bradt Travel Guides, 2005
Saunders, Colin and Narozna, Renata *Walking in the High Tatras* Cicerone, 2006

Language

Bohmerova, Ada *Slovak for You* Perfekt, 1996
Lorinc, Sylvia and John M *Slovak–English–Slovak Dictionary and Phrasebook* Hippocrene Books, 1999
Naughton, James *Colloquial Slovak* Routledge, 2003

MAPS

Slovensko autoatlas (1: 200,000) Mapa Slovakia, 2005
Slovenská Republika zempisný atlas, Mapa Slovakia, 2005
Slovakia map. International Travel Maps (ITMB Publishing), 2006
Nine cycling maps, 60+ tourist maps VKÚ military cartographers, Slovakia 2005

WEBSITES

www.aices.sk Association of Slovak information centres
www.bkis.sk Useful information at the BKIS Bratislava Cultural and Information Centre
www.bratislava.sk Bratislava Town Hall's site is an excellent introduction to the city
www.busy.sk Portal with links to train, bus and plane timetables
www.castles.sk Huge database of castles in Slovakia
www.cp.sk Unofficial but good train and bus connection search
www.dpb.sk Bratislava public transport site
www.enjoyslovakia.com Hotels, city breaks, tourist information
www.gay.sk Latest information on the Slovak gay scene
www.heartofeurope.co.uk Good introduction to Slovakia
www.holidayinfo.sk For the latest information on the snow, slopes, etc
www.hzs.sk Slovak mountain rescue service (in Slovak)
www.iarelative.com/slovaki2.htm Good links for Slovak genealogy in the US
www.imhd.sk/ba/ Public transport in Bratislava explained clearly
www.mapa.sk Mapa Slovakia interactive maps
www.panorama.sk Slovakia document store
www.sacr.sk Website for the Slovak Tourist Board, thematically organised travel information
www.sazp.sk Slovak Environmental Agency
www.ski.sk Ski information and up-to-the-minute snow reports
www.slovakheritage.org In-depth cultural information
www.slovakinvestmentproperty.com The best source for property investors
www.slovaklinks.com Giant list of links to all things Slovak
www.slovakrail.sk Link to the ŽSR Slovak Railway Company
www.slovakspectator.sk Online edition of the *Slovak Spectator*
www.slovensko.com Good source for Slovak news, well presented, informative
www.spap.sk Slovak shipping and ports
www.tanap.sk Tatra National Park
www.tasr.sk Daily news wire
www.teos.sk Good English–Slovak–English dictionary
www.whatsonslovakia.com Online Business Journal's entertainment magazine
www.zbk.sk Database of ATM cash machines throughout Slovakia
www.zsr.sk Railways of Slovakia, timetables and information

WIN £100 CASH!

READER QUESTIONNAIRE

**Send in your completed questionnaire for the chance to win
£100 cash in our regular draw**

All respondents may order a Bradt guide at half the UK retail price – please
complete the order form overleaf.

(Entries may be posted or faxed to us, or scanned and emailed.)

We are interested in getting feedback from our readers to help us plan future Bradt
guides. Please answer ALL the questions below and return the form to us in order
to qualify for an entry in our regular draw.

Have you used any other Bradt guides? If so, which titles? . . . .
. . . .
What other publishers' travel guides do you use regularly? . . . .
. . . .
Where did you buy this guidebook? . . . .
What was the main purpose of your trip to Slovakia (or for what other reason did
you read our guide)? eg: holiday/business/charity etc.. . . . .
. . . .
What other destinations would you like to see covered by a Bradt guide?
. . . .
Would you like to receive our catalogue/newsletters?

YES / NO (If yes, please complete details on reverse)

If yes – by post or email? . . . .

Age (circle relevant category) 16–25   26–45   46–60   60+

Male/Female (delete as appropriate)

Home country . . . .

Please send us any comments about our guide to Slovakia or other Bradt Travel
Guides. . . . .
. . . .
. . . .
. . . .

Bradt Travel Guides
23 High Street, Chalfont St Peter, Bucks SL9 9QE, UK
✎ +44 (0)1753 893444 **f** +44 (0)1753 892333
e info@bradtguides.com
www.bradtguides.com

CLAIM YOUR HALF-PRICE BRADT GUIDE!

Order Form

To order your half-price copy of a Bradt guide, and to enter our prize draw to win £100 (see overleaf), please fill in the order form below, complete the questionnaire overleaf, and send it to Bradt Travel Guides by post, fax or email.

Please send me one copy of the following guide at half the UK retail price

Title	Retail price	Half price
... .	....	....

Please send the following additional guides at full UK retail price

No	Title	Retail price	Total
...	....	....	....
...	....	....	....
...	....	....	....

Sub total ....

Post & packing ....

(£1 per book UK; £2 per book Europe; £3 per book rest of world)

Total ....

Name . . . .

Address. . . . .

Tel . . . .   Email . . . .

☐ I enclose a cheque for £. . . . . made payable to Bradt Travel Guides Ltd

☐ I would like to pay by credit card. Number: . . . .

Expiry date: . . . / . . .   3-digit security code (on reverse of card) . . . . .

☐ Please add my name to your catalogue mailing list.

☐ I would be happy for you to use my name and comments in Bradt marketing material.

Send your order on this form, with the completed questionnaire, to:

Bradt Travel Guides SKIA/1
23 High Street, Chalfont St Peter, Bucks SL9 9QE
✆ +44 (0)1753 893444   f +44 (0)1753 892333
e info@bradtguides.com   www.bradtguides.com

Bradt Travel Guides

www.bradtguides.com

Africa

Africa Overland	£15.99
Benin	£14.99
Botswana: Okavango, Chobe, Northern Kalahari	£15.99
Burkina Faso	£14.99
Cape Verde Islands	£13.99
Canary Islands	£13.95
Cameroon	£13.95
Eritrea	£12.95
Ethiopia	£15.99
Gabon, São Tomé, Príncipe	£13.95
Gambia, The	£13.99
Ghana	£13.95
Johannesburg	£6.99
Kenya	£14.95
Madagascar	£14.95
Malawi	£13.99
Mali	£13.95
Mauritius, Rodrigues & Réunion	£13.99
Mozambique	£13.99
Namibia	£14.95
Niger	£14.99
Nigeria	£15.99
Rwanda	£14.99
Seychelles	£14.99
Sudan	£13.95
Tanzania, Northern	£13.99
Tanzania	£16.99
Uganda	£15.99
Zambia	£15.95
Zanzibar	£12.99

Britain and Europe

Albania	£13.99
Armenia, Nagorno Karabagh	£14.99
Azores	£12.99
Baltic Capitals: Tallinn, Riga, Vilnius, Kaliningrad	£12.99
Belgrade	£6.99
Bosnia & Herzegovina	£13.99
Bratislava	£6.99
Budapest	£7.95
Cork	£6.95
Croatia	£12.95
Cyprus see North Cyprus	
Czech Republic	£13.99
Dubrovnik	£6.95
Eccentric Britain	£13.99
Eccentric Cambridge	£6.99
Eccentric Edinburgh	£5.95
Eccentric France	£12.95
Eccentric London	£12.95
Eccentric Oxford	£5.95
Estonia	£13.99
Faroe Islands	£13.95
Helsinki	£7.99
Hungary	£14.99
Kiev	£7.95
Latvia	£13.99
Lille	£6.99
Lithuania	£13.99
Ljubljana	£6.99
Macedonia	£13.95
Montenegro	£13.99
North Cyprus	£12.99
Paris, Lille & Brussels	£11.95
Riga	£6.95
River Thames, In the Footsteps of the Famous	£10.95
Serbia	£13.99
Slovenia	£12.99
Spitsbergen	£14.99
Switzerland: Rail, Road, Lake	£13.99
Tallinn	£6.99
Ukraine	£14.99
Vilnius	£6.99

Middle East, Asia and Australasia

China: Yunnan Province	£13.99
Georgia	£13.95
Great Wall of China	£13.99
Iran	£14.99
Iraq	£14.95
Kabul	£9.95
Maldives	£13.99
Mongolia	£14.95
North Korea	£13.95
Oman	£13.99
Palestine, Jerusalem	£12.95
Sri Lanka	£13.99
Syria	£14.99
Tasmania	£12.95
Tibet	£13.99
Turkmenistan	£14.99

The Americas and the Caribbean

Amazon, The	£14.95
Argentina	£15.99
Bolivia	£14.99
Cayman Islands	£12.95
Costa Rica	£13.99
Chile	£16.95
Chile & Argentina: Trekking	£12.95
Eccentric America	£13.95
Eccentric California	£13.99
Falkland Islands	£13.95
Panama	£13.95
Peru & Bolivia: Backpacking and Trekking	£12.95
St Helena, Ascension, Tristan da Cunha	£14.95
USA by Rail	£13.99

Wildlife

Antarctica: Guide to the Wildlife	£14.95
Arctic: Guide to the Wildlife	£15.99
British Isles: Wildlife of Coastal Waters	£14.95
Galápagos Wildlife	£15.99
Madagascar Wildlife	£14.95
Peruvian Wildlife	£15.99
Southern African Wildlife	£18.95
SriLankan Wildlife	£15.99

Health

Your Child Abroad: A Travel Health Guide	£10.95

Index

Page numbers in bold indicate major entries; those in italics indicate maps or charts.